MORE PRAISE FOR
MARY'S MOSAIC

"**P**ETER JANNEY, WITH passion and historical accuracy, has compelled us to become aware of the extraordinary life of Mary Pinchot Meyer, and to confront the long hidden facts and dark official secrets which resulted in her political assassination in 1964. As a result of Mr. Janney's decades long work, I have no doubt that, in significance and purpose, this murder ranks alongside the other assassinations of the 1960s. She was not only the singular soul mate and lover of President John Kennedy, but the inspiration for his commitment to turn our Republic away from the Cold War and toward world peace. *Mary's Mosaic* is a fitting, long overdue tribute to this courageous woman who was determined to secure truth and justice concerning the assassination of the man she loved and the mission they shared."

—Dr. William F. Pepper, Esq.,
author of *Orders to Kill* and *An Act of State*

"A fascinating story. . . . Peter Janney's unsparing analysis moves us closer to a reckoning. The truth, when repressed, is disgusting. When given some light, as Peter Janney's book has done, the truth can heal. Why can't we ever deal with the Kennedy assassination as maturely as we deal with all our new and clever technology?"

—Oliver Stone

i

Mary's Mosaic

Mary's Mosaic

THE CIA CONSPIRACY TO MURDER JOHN F. KENNEDY, MARY PINCHOT MEYER, AND THEIR VISION FOR WORLD PEACE

Peter Janney

Skyhorse Publishing

Skyhorse Publishing books may be purchased in bulk at special discounts for sales promotion, corporate gifts, fund-raising, or educational purposes. Special editions can also be created to specifications. For details, contact the Special Sales Department, Skyhorse Publishing, 307 West 36th Street, 11th Floor, New York, NY 10018 or info@skyhorsepublishing.com.

Skyhorse® and Skyhorse Publishing® are registered trademarks of Skyhorse Publishing, Inc.®, a Delaware corporation.

Visit our website at www.skyhorsepublishing.com.

10 9 8 7 6 5 4 3 2 1

Library of Congress Cataloging-in-Publication Data is available on file.
ISBN: 978-1-62636-127-0

Printed in the United States of America

Contents

PREFACE TO SECOND EDITION

O F ALL THE research findings presented in the first edition of this book, none is as significant as the discoveries I made following its publication in April 2012. These findings, outlined in the Post Script to this new edition, enabled me to finally locate the individual who I allege was either Mary Meyer's assassin or part of the assassination team that brutally terminated her life in October 1964. His name is William Lockwood Mitchell. On August 27, 2012, I politely confronted Mr. Mitchell on his doorstep in northern California, but he angrily refused to talk with me. Following this encounter, I reengaged with my former chief researcher Roger Charles, a Peabody Award-winning journalist and author. Mr. Charles then invited twice-nominated Pulitzer Prize investigative journalist Don Devereux of Tempe, Arizona to assist in our attempt to understand more fully the true identity of William Lockwood Mitchell and his 1964 associations. Along with private investigator Robert Arthur of Global Investigations and Security Consulting in Scottsdale, Arizona, we spent the better part of eight months researching various aspects of Mitchell's life. The shocking results of our investigation are thoroughly presented in the Post Script. My profound gratitude and appreciation for my research colleagues' efforts in this undertaking can never be fully expressed; without their prodigious exploration, too many questions would have lingered. Their fine-tuned skills and expertise, however, have now made it possible to further correct the historical record for one of the high-profile political assassinations of the 1960s.

The full genesis and final completion of *Mary's Mosaic* was not without significant cost and sacrifice in my life. With the accidental death at age nine of my best friend Michael Meyer (the middle child in the Meyer family), I would enter the emotionally turbulent world of grief and loss in the late 1950s. My own parents were unfortunately not equipped to handle this event and its impact in my life. Suffering a prolonged grief reaction, I became increasingly agitated and troubled. Both of my parents flourished – at least superficially – in the "mad men" alcoholic cocktail-party culture so commonplace in that era. Moreover, having a father who conducted his secretive career at the highest levels of the Central Intelligence Agency further complicated my predicament throughout childhood, and into adulthood. Into that mix were the added ingredients of my father's pronounced dipsomania and arrogance, creating the kind of self-perpetuating narcissism that, by definition, never allowed for any real self-examination or accountability.

In marked contrast to my parents, Mary Pinchot Meyer was, amidst her own sorrow, able to extend herself to me in a way that was profoundly healing in the years following her son Michael's death. In a very real sense, she became the mother I didn't have, the one who could allow the full expression of my vulnerability and sadness, and hold me throughout the emotional turbulence that ensued. An oasis in a traumatic storm, she enabled me, through her beneficence, to integrate the loss of my best friend, and move on.

Returning home from boarding school the day before Thanksgiving in 1964, I was unaware that Mary Meyer had been murdered five weeks earlier. As I sat down to dinner with my family, her death was announced to me almost casually by my mother, as my silent father stared vacantly into space. However unconscious I was of it, the full impact of Mary Meyer's murder – *and the way in which she died* – would haunt me for the next fifty years. As the tempestuous era of the 1960s progressed, with the political assassinations of JFK, his brother Robert, the Rev. Martin Luther King, Jr., and Malcolm X, in addition to the escalation of the Vietnam War, my disillusionment with America deepened. My disenchantment also brought added conflict and turmoil into my family, particularly with my father and his CIA career. During the post-Watergate era, with the 1976 public revelation of Mary Meyer's affair with President Kennedy, I began to get a sense of the magnitude of her life and the extent of her influence. Indeed, the 1976 discovery would become a seminal moment, as I began to suspect that her murder was, in fact, not a 'random act of violence,' but something that had been orchestrated by an act of state.

In the years that followed, my training as a clinical psychologist, coupled with extensive periods of intensive personal psychotherapeutic exploration, opened my 'doors of perception' to the cost of having had a father whose

CIA career had involved him in a conspiracy to terminate the life of someone whom I had deeply cherished. Facing that abyss and the implications it engendered, I came to a crossroads where choices and decisions had to be made. With the painful dissolution of my second marriage, I recognized that if I attempted to unravel this despicable deed and tell the story, the path ahead would be fraught with danger. It was not, I finally decided, a journey to be taken with a family to nourish and support, nor even a marriage to cultivate. Endangering another's life, even potentially, wasn't an option. Ultimately, if a greater portion of the historical truth surrounding the murder of Mary Meyer were to be known, the journey had to be traveled alone. It has, therefore, become the crucible of my life.

Each of us, sooner or later, has a rendezvous with destiny. What we do at that moment largely defines who we are, and what we become. Despite the choices we make, the sacrifices we endure, our destiny informs the life we embrace, and what we finally take with us when we depart. Whatever legacy I leave, I would hope that the province of historical truth during a very turbulent era of our country's history will some day begin to restore peoples' faith in a "government of the people, by the people, and for the people."

Finally, I wish to acknowledge my publisher Tony Lyons of Skyhorse Publishing and the entire Skyhorse staff who unhesitatingly supported my efforts in bringing this second edition to fruition. In particular, Cory Allyn was an indispensable asset in this effort. My sincere, heartfelt thanks to all of you.

—Peter Janney

FOREWORD

by
Dick Russell

E ARLY IN 1976, about six months after I began probing into the Kennedy assassination for the *Village Voice*, an article caught my attention in—of all places—the *National Enquirer*. The weekly tabloid was not generally known for its investigative veracity, but this particular story was thoroughly documented. The subject was Mary Pinchot Meyer, a Washington socialite who'd been shot twice and murdered while walking near the Potomac River on October 12, 1964. Since the originally accused assailant had been acquitted, the identity of her killer remained unknown. Publicly, so did the identity of her lover, until the *Enquirer* story alleged that for almost two years before his assassination on November 22, 1963, Mary Meyer had been having an affair with President John F. Kennedy.

The *Enquirer* recounted—and this would soon be corroborated in other periodicals—that Mary had kept a diary. The weekend after her death, a small group of people were said to have gathered at her Georgetown home in search of it. Cord Meyer, her ex-husband and a high official in the CIA, was there. So was James Angleton, head of the CIA's counterintelligence division, and his wife, Cicely, a close friend of Mary's. Also present was Tony Bradlee, Mary's sister and the wife of *Washington Post* editor Ben Bradlee.

The story went that none of them could locate Mary's diary and that her sister had later found it inside a locked steel box containing dozens of letters, including some from the slain president Kennedy. Bradlee had then turned the box over to Angleton, who took the material to CIA headquarters. James Truitt, a journalist for *Newsweek* and another friend of the Meyers', said he'd

1

received a letter from Angleton saying, "As to the diary and related papers, I burned them."

For more than twenty years, Angleton had been a "spook's spook" who roamed the Agency corridors looking to ferret out penetrations by the Soviet Union. Then in 1974, a new CIA director, William Colby, leaked word to the media that Angleton had also been in charge of Operation Chaos, a domestic intelligence-gathering program that far exceeded the CIA's original charter. Angleton was forced to resign. Not long thereafter, he began meeting with journalists for the first time, obviously intent on getting his side of certain stories on the record.

I was one of those journalists, although I never really understood why Angleton chose to wine and dine me on three occasions at his customary meeting place, Washington's Army and Navy Club. After all, the *Village Voice* hardly seemed like his cup of tea. And I did not disguise the fact I was looking into a probable conspiracy in the death of President Kennedy. Indeed, the first time we met, late on a mid-December afternoon in 1975 in the plush club lounge, I gave him one of my *Voice* articles to leaf through. Angleton lit a cigarette, took a sip of his martini, and said, "The subject is a far more complex one than reflected in your article."

After the assassination, Angleton's counterintelligence branch had been assigned as the CIA's direct liaison to the Warren Commission, of which former CIA director Allen Dulles was a member. I wondered, why Angleton's office? "Because we had the research facilities, knew the mechanisms of the KGB and foreign intelligence," Angleton replied quickly. "We knew every assassination in history, knew more about the sophistication of the Cuban DGI, that type of thing." Pretty obviously, he was trying to steer my thoughts toward possible foreign involvement. Angleton dismissed the rumors that Lee Harvey Oswald might have been an American agent as "completely false" and continued: "Unless one knows the dossiers that are in Moscow and Cuba, there can be no ultimate determination." Several times over the course of our get-togethers, he would raise the specter of the KGB's Department 13, which specialized in what those in the trade called "wet affairs" (assassinations).

Angleton was one of the strangest men I ever met: tall, bespectacled, stoop-shouldered, with his appearance calling to mind the image of an ostrich whose head seemed, despite itself, to be peering out at the world after a lifetime buried in the sand. But what secrets was he willing now to unearth, and what was his motivation? Was he still, in fact, covering someone's tracks—even, perhaps, his own? In April 1976, we met for the second time, and one of the first things I asked him about was the *Enquirer*'s revelatory piece about Mary Meyer and her diary. Angleton gazed out the window for a long moment. Then he replied that he had been acting in a private capacity for the family, and in no way for the CIA, which he hastened to add had nothing to do with her death. He went on to relate a fascinating, even occult, story.

Angleton and his wife had planned to go out to dinner and a show with Mary Meyer that October evening in 1964. When news came over the radio that someone had been killed in a park not far from where she lived, Cicely Angleton had a premonition that it was Mary. So that night, they drove over to her house, but found it completely dark. A grim foreboding grew stronger in Angleton's wife. Angleton said he'd called Meyer's answering service, which at first simply said that she wasn't in. But when Angleton explained they had a date with her, and that his wife was hysterical in the car, he was told of Meyer's death.

The entire time Angleton was relating this, I noticed that he was digging his fingers deeper and deeper into the wooden arm of the comfortable chair in the Army and Navy Club.

I have puzzled over that moment for many years. Over the course of time, I read Timothy Leary's memoir, which only added to the mystery of Mary Meyer. He maintained that he'd turned her on to LSD, that she may even have taken a "trip" with President Kennedy, and that she'd called Leary the day after the assassination indicating that "he was changing too fast; they couldn't control him anymore." *They* clearly implied that JFK had been assassinated by elements within our own government.

Now, with Peter Janney's remarkable book *Mary's Mosaic*, the questions that long haunted me have been largely answered. Now I see how Angleton had been trying to bend the truth, and why. Not only about Mary Meyer, but about who killed Kennedy, which all but certainly involved the same element of individuals.

Those questions had long haunted Janney as well, and in a deeply personal way. For, as a child growing up in close proximity to the Meyer family home in McLean, Virginia, one of the Meyer boys had been his best friend. Peter was himself the son of a high-level CIA official, Wistar Janney. When that son set out on his many-year quest to ascertain who was behind the death of his best friend's mother—and how this may have been related to the assassination of President Kennedy—the journey was one with many surprising, and heart-wrenching, twists and turns. In some ways, this book reads like a murder mystery, but ultimately it is more like a Greek tragedy: one that does not spare the Homer of this saga, Peter Janney himself.

3

In painstaking detail, he sets down the sequence of events around Meyer's demise, a sequence that leaves no doubt that the "official version" was concocted and an innocent black man charged with the crime. This is a story that recalls the Zeitgeist of the 1960s, from the civil rights movement to consciousness-raising through psychedelics—and the change wrought in Kennedy's conscience and leadership following the near apocalypse of the Cuban Missile Crisis, and through the influence and vision of a beautiful, amazing woman.

Mary's Mosaic is also a story about intertwined destinies, about human strength and weakness, and finally about forces of good and evil. The book makes a reader consider those possibilities within each of us, even as what unfolds is on a Shakespearean stage. For those were, indeed, momentous times, and times that reverberate to this day across our national landscape. As we live in one of the most polarized junctures in American history, Peter Janney gets at the root of the origins, the "primary causes" of dysfunctionality and disunion that we need to understand. The author has given us a penetrating insight into the still-hidden history of an era that few other books have achieved. As the philosopher Santayana once said, "Those who do not learn from history are doomed to repeat it."

I don't want to steal the thunder from what also stands as a mesmerizing page-turner, but here are some broad brushstrokes: In *Mary's Mosaic*, you will learn not only how covert actions are orchestrated, but the many-layered duplicity it takes to conceal the truth about them. You will see how, to use a cliché, "love conquers all"—when a woman of integrity is able to help bring a transcendent vision to the most powerful man in the world. You will observe her courage in seeking to bring out the truth of what happened to him, even knowing full well the powers-that-be she was up against. And you will contemplate, too, the courage of author Janney in pursuing what became a terribly agonizing truth about the role of his own father.

I wish I could anticipate that *Mary's Mosaic* will be widely reviewed by the major media. But after finishing this book, you will know why this cannot be the case. The CIA set out to manipulate the free flow of information long ago, a blow to our democracy that now sees near-total control by fewer and fewer large corporate owners. The Rupert Murdochs of today would not have been possible without the Ben Bradlees of yesterday, no matter their seeming ideological differences. That is another sad legacy of what happened almost fifty years ago to JFK and Mary Meyer.

So be prepared to be surprised, even astonished, and ultimately outraged by what is set forth in these pages. Not all the answers to what bedevils our nation are here, but enough to make you take a deep breath and realize that if we do not fight for what we believe in, and from the personal depths of our being, then America is doomed to the fate that befalls all imperial powers. Denial will be our downfall, the illusion that things like this do not happen here. But not if Peter Janney has anything to say about it.

Dick Russell is the author of two acclaimed books on the Kennedy assassination, *The Man Who Knew Too Much* and *On the Trail of the JFK Assassins,* as well as two recent bestsellers with Jesse Ventura, *American Conspiracies* and *63 Documents the Government Doesn't Want You to Read.*

For

Quentin and Mark Meyer.

And in memory of their brother Michael,

and, of course, their mother . . .

"For the greatest enemy of the truth is very often not the lie—deliberate, contrived, and dishonest—but the myth—persistent, persuasive, and unrealistic."

—President John F. Kennedy
Yale University
June 11, 1962

PART ONE

"I'M THINKING OF writing a book about my family," said the new Roman Emperor Claudius to his trusted friend King Herod.

"What sort of book?" inquired Herod.

"To tell the truth," whispered Claudius, looking around to make sure no one else was listening.

"Will you tell everything?" asked Herod.

"Everything," said Claudius emphatically, "as a historian should. Well, not great tales of heroic exploits, like Titus Livius wrote, no. But the plain facts, the kitchen details, even the gossip."

"Why? Why should you want to write such a book? Why rake it all up?" inquired Herod.

"Because I owe it to the others to tell the truth, to Posthumous and Germanicus," said Claudius.

"Why?" Herod beseeched.

"Because they're dead," said Claudius solemnly. "And a man should keep faith with his friends, even though they're dead. You see, I've been so very fortunate in my life, when they who were born more deserving, have not. I've had only three real friends in my life. Posthumous and Germanicus were two – third one is you."

"Listen Claudius," admonished Herod. "Let me give you a piece of advice. One last piece and then I'm done. Trust no one, my friend, no one! Not your most grateful freedman. Not your most intimate friend. Not your dearest child. Not the wife of your bosom. *Trust no one!*"

"No one?" asked Claudius, looking into Herod's eyes. "Not even you ?"[1]

---

1   From the 1976 BBC Masterpiece Theatre production of *I, Claudius.* (Based on: *I, Claudius: from the autobiography of Tiberius Claudius born 10 B.C. murdered and deified A.D. 54.* and *Claudius The God,* both authored by Robert Graves. New York: Vintage International Edition, 1989, originally published by Random House, 1935.

PROLOGUE

He was perfect for the CIA. He never felt guilt about anything.
— St. John Hunt, reflecting on the life
of his father, E. Howard Hunt[1]

THANKSGIVING VACATION IN the fall of 1964 offered a welcome respite from the rigors of boarding school life in New Hampshire.[2] At seventeen, I was full of both testosterone and a lust for freedom that didn't find much outlet at a New England prep school. I was a "lifer," as we used to say. I had arrived in the ninth grade, or what was commonly known in the English boarding- school system as "the third form." I would stay until the end and graduate, but that fall, in my fifth-form junior year, I felt engaged in a Sisyphean struggle to break free: five days off—this year with a driver's license!—followed by another long slog up the hill. It was 1964. Just a year and half more of this, I kept telling myself, and I'd be out of what seemed like jail. Adolescence, with all of its possibilities, sometimes felt like prison. Dreams and a rich fantasy life were often the only escape.

As the plane began its final approach into Washington's National Airport, I picked out a number of familiar places stretched out below, including my old alma mater, Georgetown Day School (GDS), the sight of which stirred a flood of memories from my childhood. Something had been lost while I was a student there; and, nearly a decade later, emotional scar tissue still lingered. My best friend and classmate, Michael Pinchot Meyer, had been killed when we were both just nine years old. It had been my first experience with death— losing someone I had been deeply fond of. I didn't want to think about it.

I consoled myself instead with the promise of freedom that lay before me. It was the Wednesday before Thanksgiving. My father would still be at work when I got home, but my mother and my younger brother would likely be

9

around. I would have most of the afternoon to cruise about town with old friends—certainly enough time to sneak a beer or two and a few cigarettes.

M y family's home was a modern architectural marvel for its time. A long, split-level structure, spacious and light-filled, with large picture windows in most rooms, the house was nestled in one of the last enclaves of Washington's woods, sheltered from the cacophony of distant traffic. At dinner that evening, I looked out from the split-level dining room through the living room's floor-to-ceiling windows. Beyond the verdant lawn was the concrete swimming pool, half-drained and dotted with logs to prevent winter ice from cracking its walls. I took my usual place at the table facing my brother, Christopher, with my mother to my left and my father to my right. On the wall behind my mother, an original black-and-white Morris Rosenfeld photograph, *Spinnakers Flying*, announced the family passion—sailing. My parents had met during summers spent on Cape Cod, and they had imparted their love of navigating the open sea to my brother and me. By the age of seventeen, I had already spent long stretches offshore in the Atlantic racing to Bermuda, and from Annapolis to Newport, Rhode Island.

During dinner that evening, my father mentioned that it was not too early to think about racing our sailboat from Annapolis to Newport again in the coming year. Sailing was a rite of passage for me, and I looked forward to continuing to master its intricacies under my father's guidance. The previous summer had already extended my knowledge and experience with a small group trip down the Dalmatian coast from Venice to Athens on a seventy-seven-foot Rhodes ketch. Its colorful skipper, a gallant, distinguished former World War II Marine combat captain named Horace ("Hod") Fuller, had been a delightful legend to sail with. An accomplished sailor, he sometimes kindly took me aside for tutorials on some of the idiosyncrasies of sailing in the Adriatic Sea.

There were, however, a couple of instances during the trip that disturbed me. Late one night, I had awakened to the sound of Hod Fuller having what sounded like combat nightmares from his World War II experiences. No one else in our group wanted to acknowledge it. Years later, my father, a career CIA senior official, having had his usual "generous" intake of alcohol one evening, remarked that "Hod Fuller was one of the best damn assassins we ever had. . . ." A bit stunned, I curiously inquired as to how he went about his assignments. In at least one instance, my father said, Hod had taken his victim out in a rowboat and shot him in the back of the head and then dumped him overboard.

But on the evening before Thanksgiving, diving into a sumptuous meal of veal scaloppini, I was happily anticipating the short recess that lay before me, and dreaming about being on the ocean again, a place where my freedom flourished. It was comforting to be home, to have a reprieve from academic pressures and boarding-school life, and to be with my family. Amid the challenges and turbulence of adolescence, hearth and home was still a place I could count on. It wouldn't last much longer, I soon discovered. I wasn't at all prepared when the conversation took a sudden turn.

"Mary Meyer died earlier this fall," my mother said, looking at me. I reached for my water.

"What do you mean?" I asked. Her words bludgeoned me.

"She was murdered while walking on the canal towpath," my mother explained. "They caught the guy who did it. She was taking one of her usual walks during the day. It was a sexual assault."

Reeling, I tried to make sense of what she was saying. "How was she killed?" I asked, trying to orient myself over the eruption of pounding in my chest.

"She was shot. It's very sad for all of us."

I pressed her for more details but absorbed little. Numbness and shock were setting in. I remember my mother mentioning Mary's funeral, and then something about how my father and another man had gone to the airport to meet Cord Meyer, who had been away on the day of his ex-wife's murder. My mother was doing all the talking; my father didn't say anything. He just sat there, staring vacantly off into space. There was something almost eerie about his silence.

My stomach was in knots. Was it only confusion, or was it fear? After a while, I excused myself from the table, saying that I had plans to go out for the evening. In fact, my only impulse was to go to my room and curl up in my bed. That night, I was in and out of sleep. I wanted to cry, but couldn't. Memories crashed through my mind like a hurricane's pounding surf. Seeing Georgetown Day School from the plane earlier in the day had already stirred something in me, and now there was no escape.

I had known the Meyer family since 1952, when I was five years old. My mother, Mary Draper, and Mary Pinchot had been classmates in Vassar College's class of 1942. My father, Wistar Janney, had met Cord Meyer after World War II, and they now worked together at the CIA. Our families were socially entwined—we went camping together, played touch football, visited each other's homes frequently. The Meyers had three children: Quentin, Michael, and Mark. Michael and I had been born less than one month apart, and Quentin—or "Quenty," as we called him—was a year and a half older. Mark and my brother, Christopher, were the same age, about two years younger than Michael and I. By the time Michael and I were seven, we were best friends, and often inseparable. We shared a number of bonds, especially baseball and fishing. We had been in the same class at Georgetown Day School for three years, our desks side by side for two of them.

As I lay crawled up in a fetal position that night, the shock of Mary Meyer's murder brought back a flood of memories of being at Michael's house in McLean, Virginia, just a few miles from my own house. One sunny spring day, we had been hunting for copperheads in the backyard forest behind the Meyer house. Brandishing knives like the "young bucks" we thought we were, Michael pulled a long stick out of a hole we'd been investigating. Suddenly, a snapping snake came out right behind it, narrowly missing his face. We pulled back, both screaming, and ran as fast as we could. We finally stopped, both of us shaking with an adrenaline rush and laughing uncontrollably. Regaining a bit of composure, we realized that both of us, out of fear and excitement, had urinated in our pants. Humiliated, a bit defeated, but still giddy from the adventure, we returned to the house. Michael's mother, Mary, was painting in a small studio just off the patio.

"Mom, a copperhead almost bit me!" Michael announced.

Mary Pinchot Meyer looked up from her canvas. Even then, I distinctly remember feeling that there was something unique about Michael's mother, beyond her glistening, radiant beauty. She was so unlike any other adult in my world at that time. Calm and still, at peace with herself, she had a presence and demeanor that struck me. Less than a year before, Michael and I had been playing baseball in front of their house when Michael sent one of my pitches zooming off his bat and over the house. I ran around to the back in search of the ball and came upon Mary reading on a blanket. She lay completely naked, her backside to the sun. I was breathless. She hadn't heard me coming, and I stood there for what seemed to me a very long time, gawking. At the time, I had no words for the vision that I beheld, but I knew that beauty such as hers was something I longed to know better. When Mary finally looked up and saw me, she wasn't embarrassed or upset, or even startled. She just smiled, letting me know that it was okay; no sin had been committed. I found the ball, ran back to play with Mikey, and felt somehow irrevocably altered, even blessed. But it wasn't anything I could describe at the time.

I had a similar feeling about Mary the day of the copperhead hunt. Mary's outer beauty seemed to be a manifestation of her inner freedom and peace. Whatever it was, it made me feel safe, and free. I remember her smiling at us in a prideful way. Here we were—dirty, sweaty, and soaked in piss, to boot—and Mary responded by being tender. She had guessed what must have happened and, laughing, directed us to the laundry room. We slipped out of our soiled clothes, put them in the washing machine, and put on the clean underwear that Mary had given us, along with a pile of clean clothes to wear.

"You two look like little Indians," she said teasingly. "Where's your war paint?"

I remembered how Michael's eyes had lit up with excitement.

"Mom, paint an arrowhead on my face!" he blurted out.

"Go get the watercolors I gave you, and I will!" she said.

We stood in our underwear on the patio under a warm spring sun. Mary made intricate designs that we took to be tribal symbols on our faces and arms while we began emitting loud Indian war cries. While Mary was painting my face, Michael went in search of two Indian headdresses.

Almost immediately, our exuberance erupted. Michael and I made guttural noises, each trying to outdo the other. War paint in place, we danced as we had seen Indians do on television. Flapping our hands over our mouths like trumpeters with plunger mutes, we shrieked louder and louder, jerking our bodies in wild leaps across the room. We strapped our knife sheaths onto makeshift belts, donned the headdresses, and descended into a kind of primal expression of childhood glee and human joy, running barefoot in circles. It was as if Mary's brushstrokes of "war paint" had transported us into a primal place of wildness that demanded a surrender to the life force itself. In a sudden, simultaneous move that was pure, unbridled innocence, we stepped out of our underwear. Naked now, our playing became even more frenzied. We ran through the woods toward a small barn, chased each other around a riding circle, and back to the patio, waving our knives in flagrant violation of every childhood safety rule known to man. As our excitement subsided, we dropped to the floor, laughing and exhausted from the thrill of what we had just experienced. Peace and serenity returned, but eventually I became self-conscious. Where were my pants? Shouldn't I have something on? Once again, Mary's tender gaze delivered me from any embarrassment.

"Mom, do we have anything to eat? I'm hungry!" asked Michael. We were putting on the clothes that Mary had given us, while Mary directed us to cookies and lemonade in the fridge. It seemed like an eternity had passed. A bit disoriented, I was calm—yet also exhilarated by the sense of an unknown powerful life force that had just moved through me. Mary's quietly spirited presence had made it all possible. It was as if she had extended *her* freedom to me, giving me permission that day to explore and experience my own boyhood wildness like no other adult ever had.

Mary's persona contrasted sharply with that of Michael's father, Cord Meyer. Insensitive and dismissive, Cord was arrogantly patronizing and never fun to be around. One day Michael and I went fishing on the Potomac River with Cord and his CIA friend and colleague Jim Angleton, who was also godfather to the three Meyer boys. I always found myself completely inhibited around Cord. Michael and I took turns climbing out onto a set of rocks that jutted out from the shoreline. There, we snagged herring by casting into a huge school of passing fish with a three-pronged snag hook. Cord's demeanor that day had been as intimidating as it was uncomfortable. He and Angleton spent most of the time criticizing our techniques. Already self-conscious, I had to watch my every move lest I provoke one of Cord's or Angleton's withering stares. Truth be told, I never liked Cord. Michael feared his father, inasmuch as telling me so. His dread of his father was such a contrast to the connection he had with his mother.

Sleep, if it came at all that dreadful night before Thanksgiving, was fitful as I wrestled with Mary Meyer's death. Ominously, one horrid thought was the realization that Quenty and Mark would now have only Cord, their aloof father. In my agitation, I continually tossed and repositioned myself, hugging a second pillow for comfort. At one point I woke up; it was still dark outside. I was soaked in moisture, then realizing that in my sleep, I had been crying for my lost childhood friend Michael, and the memory of what had occurred on December 18, 1956.

Just before Christmas vacation began, our school's holiday festivities took place—a Nativity play, Christmas caroling in the Georgetown Day School assembly, and painting ornaments in the school's art studio where Mary Meyer and Ken Noland sometimes taught together. The Meyer family didn't have television in the mid-1950s—only because Mary was against it. Her prescience regarding the docile passivity that television engendered was remarkable. But it didn't keep the two older Meyer boys—Quenty and Michael—from stealing away to a friend's house to engage the technological marvel. The way home to the Meyer farmhouse required crossing a busy thoroughfare known as Route

123. Two years earlier, the family's beloved golden retriever had been hit by a car and killed crossing that roadway. The two boys were on their way home, rushing to be on time for dinner. In the waning winter solstice light of Tuesday's evening rush hour, some cars had not yet turned on their headlights. The agile Quenty made his way across first, dodging cars as he ran from one side to the other. His younger brother wasn't so lucky. Michael was struck by an oncoming car and killed.

The next day, after returning home early from work, my father and mother summoned me from my bedroom, where I had been playing. I joined them in the living room, taking a chair opposite the fireplace. My mother sat on the sofa and my father reclined into his favorite orange Eero Saarinen Womb chair, his legs stretched out on the ottoman before him. He was sipping his usual first martini of the evening. Our house was resplendent with FAO Schwarz Christmas pageantry—holly, mistletoe, a towering spruce pine that twinkled with lights and ornaments, with colorfully wrapped gifts everywhere. It was an idyllic scene, but I sat with the unease of one who hears his name called and wonders what he's done wrong. I was braced for some kind of reprimand, but not for what came next.

"We have something to tell you," my mother said, looking in my direction without making eye contact. "Mikey Meyer was hit by a car yesterday. He was killed."

Her words rocked me to the core. The disturbance was cellular. The hollow silence of loss opened into my world. I couldn't contain it.

"That's not true! Tell me it's not true!" I shouted, before collapsing into tears.

"It's true," she said, trying to remain calm. I turned toward my father as though he might have a different version of the story to offer.

"Daddy, tell me it's not true, *please* tell me it's not true!" Hysterical, I threatened to throw a heavy ashtray through the living-room picture window. "Tell me it's not true, or I'll break the window!" I screamed.

I don't remember what came next, but I eventually found myself in my father's arms with my head against his chest. Feeling the thumping of his heart against my head helped calm my sobs. I remembered looking up at his face. For the first time in my life, I saw my father cry.

Later that evening, I overheard my parents talking about going to visit Cord and Mary after I went to bed. I insisted—*demanded*—that they take me with them. I didn't know why it was so imperative that I accompany them. After some resistance, they relented. During the fifteen-minute drive to Michael's house, darkness enshrouded everything, overtaking me. There was no moon or stars in the sky that night. Everything and everywhere was dark.

We entered the front door and walked down an unlit hallway into the Meyers' living room, where their own postcard-perfect holiday scene—the tree, the wrapped presents—seemed out of place. As my mother embraced Mary, I felt this house, so familiar just days before, was now alien to me. In spite of—or, perhaps, because of—the joy I had once felt in that house, it was almost unbearable to be there now. No longer would it be Michael's house; nothing would ever be the same again. Mikey had left, and a part of me had gone with him. Emptiness now became my new companion.

I was facing Michael's mother, whose gaze was fixed on me. She looked into my eyes, as she had done so many times before, but this time it was her sadness, not her serenity, that moved me. I was overwhelmed by it and wanted to look away, but she drew me into her arms. In that moment, the child-adult distinction evaporated. We were equals in our grief, connected by the loss of someone we both had deeply loved and cherished. As she cried, I felt no need to recoil in any discomfort. Even as a young insecure boy, I gladly stood to embrace and hold her, as she had done for me so many times before. It was a moment of transcendence at a very tender age—an experience of connection unlike any I had known before. And it would be decades before I understood the deeper gift she had bestowed upon me.

Mary walked me up the stairs to Michael's bedroom. "I want you to have something of Michael's to take with you," she said. "Find something you want, anything. Michael would have wanted that, I know." She left me alone in his room to contemplate, to face yet another level of the reality of my best friend's departure. I would never again be in that room with the Michael I had known and loved. Unbearably, I had to begin to face the loss that night.

Michael's funeral was held several days later in Bethlehem Chapel inside the National Cathedral. I was still perhaps too numb to register details of the service, but I will never forget the sight of Ruth Pinchot, Michael's maternal grandmother, sobbing on the sidewalk as we left the church. There was something so pure and powerful about her explosion of grief, the kind of public display of emotion that was simply "not done" among her set. But in that moment, Ruth didn't care what anybody thought, or how she might be perceived. Her honesty and courage were so much like her daughter Mary's.

Michael's casket was taken to the Pinchot family's estate, Grey Towers, in Milford, Pennsylvania, and then laid to rest in the Pinchot family plot in the

Milford cemetery. He had always shared with me so much about Grey Towers—its bountiful trout streams, waterfalls, and forests—but it would take me nearly fifty years before I could bring myself to actually visit his grave.

The late 1950s were not an auspicious time to be a grieving nine-year-old. The "in-vogue" thinking at that time was that beyond a certain point, displays of sadness were unbecoming. I was encouraged to accept what had happened and move on. In my attempt to do so, I sometimes stayed overnight with Quenty and Mark at the Meyers' house, and would wake up crying in the middle of the night. On those occasions, it was always Mary who comforted me. Expressions of sadness were okay with her, even embraced.

Soon, however, everything changed. Quenty revealed that his parents were divorcing, and that everyone was moving to Georgetown. Meanwhile, at my home, my parents were ill-equipped to handle my grief. They sent me to a psychiatrist, who, in true Freudian fashion, kept making a lot of allusions to my penis. During the six years following Michael's death, I floundered. My self-confidence eroded. Increasingly, I was impulsive, delinquent, and unruly. Unmoored and untethered, I packed on weight as I turned to sugar in an effort to self-medicate. At fifteen, I left home for boarding school in New Hampshire.

The woman who had comforted me in sorrow and reassured me in so many other ways was now gone forever. Like a volcano, the reality of her death had erupted, and reawakened something awful and inescapable. Why had my parents waited until I was home to tell me, I wondered? As I lay in my bed at dawn that Thanksgiving morning in 1964, the apprehension of uneasiness, even dread, engulfed me. There was something foreboding, something terrible—something I couldn't possibly know or understand at the time. And that feeling would continue to haunt me for more than forty years.

My father knocked on my bedroom door; it was time to get ready to go hunting. As I dressed, I thought back to what a terrible year it had been for Washington—and the nation. President Kennedy had been assassinated the previous November. In my American history course at school that fall, we were discussing something called the Warren Commission and its final report. I remember that our teacher, Mr. Fauver, had said something to the effect of, "Gentlemen, this is a shining example of what makes our country so great, our democracy so vibrant, a government for the people, and by the people." Reminding us that America was a republic, not a totalitarian state, he urged us to reflect on how President Kennedy's assassination would have been handled in a country that didn't have a democratically elected government.

Two years later, in 1966, New Orleans district attorney Jim Garrison was challenging the entire veracity of the Warren Report as a massive cover-up, implicating the CIA in President Kennedy's assassination. When I brought this to my father's attention for discussion, he became apoplectic that I should ever consider such a thing.[3] Sadly, it was the beginning of a never-to-be resolved rupture in our relationship, and a dramatic separation from my family into adulthood. That fall I entered Princeton as an undergraduate. The Vietnam War was approaching its full escalation, and I made it my focus to begin to understand what was taking place. Further enraging both my parents, I became increasingly vociferous about America's incursion into Southeast Asia, as well as what the CIA, and my father, were actually doing in the world.

Ten years later, in 1976—twelve years after Mary Meyer's murder—the *National Enquirer* broke the story about her relationship with President Kennedy. Awakened, but not yet fully conscious, I began a journey that culminated in this book. Somewhere inside the recesses of my being, I instinctively suspected there was a connection between the assassination of our president, and the slaying—less than a year later—of the woman he had come to trust and love.

INTRODUCTION

History would be an excellent thing, if only it were true.

—Leo Tolstoy

It's all about witness, brother. Every person who bears witness has to have the depth of conviction of a martyr. *You have to be willing to die.* That's the statement allowing you to live.

—Professor Cornell West, Princeton University
(*Rolling Stone,* May 28, 2009)

S O IT WAS in 1964, just before 12:30 P.M. on a crisp, sunny mid-October day in Washington, D.C., that a beautiful, affluent middle-aged white woman was murdered on the Chesapeake and Ohio Canal towpath during her accustomed walk after a morning of painting at her nearby Georgetown art studio. For more than five hours, her identity remained unknown to police—but not, I would discover many years later, to an elite high-level group of operatives within the Central Intelligence Agency (CIA). She was eventually officially identified by her brother-in-law, Benjamin C. Bradlee, at the D.C. morgue shortly after 6:00 P.M. Mary Pinchot Meyer had been brutally put to death.

Nearly five decades have passed since I sat at my family's dinner table on the night before Thanksgiving in 1964 where I first learned that my best friend's mother had been murdered. In the intervening time span of nearly half a century, nothing has dimmed the memory of what took place that night, nor the seminal childhood event of losing my best friend, Michael, eight years earlier, in 1956. Sometimes tormented, even haunted, I came to realize the necessity of a deeper reckoning—and not just emotionally or psychologically, as my chosen profession dictated, but some final resolution of knowing a more complete, unvarnished piece of the truth, and the direction from which it lay.

"We either make ourselves miserable, or we make ourselves strong," wrote the author Carlos Castaneda. "The amount of work is the same." As I meticulously attempted to unveil the facts surrounding Mary Meyer's murder, I repeatedly took refuge in Castaneda's words as the aftershocks of this event reverberated throughout my life in unimaginable ways. My journey—a rigorous, thorough research endeavor informed by my education as a Princeton undergraduate and later by my training as a clinical psychologist—began in 1976. It ended exactly thirty years later in shocking fashion.

There was nothing pretty or easy about waking up early one morning in 2006 and finally realizing that my own father—Wistar Janney, a career high-level CIA officer—had been involved in the "termination" of Mary Pinchot Meyer, someone I had grown to love and care about. Yet there is another horror in the death of Mary Meyer, a horror that reaches far beyond the personal. It is the intimate and undeniable connection between her murder and that of her lover, President John F. Kennedy, on November 22, 1963 in Dallas, Texas. After more than twenty years of my own study, I share the belief—based on substantiated evidence and research by a host of dedicated researchers and historians—that President Kennedy was ambushed by elements of his own National Security apparatus in what amounted to a coup d'état. It is clear that a highly compartmentalized, elite segment of the CIA, the U.S. military, the U.S. Secret Service, the Federal Bureau of Investigation (FBI), certain well-known organized crime figures, and, finally, Vice President Lyndon B. Johnson all colluded to overthrow the elected government of the United States.

Certainly, no one individual, or group of disaffected anti-Castro Cubans, or even elements of the Mafia, could have undertaken such a conspiracy independently, as some authors over the years have wanted to maintain. The forces behind President Kennedy's assassination not only had the means and power to conduct such an operation, but the extraordinary mobility and reach to launch a *second* conspiracy of monumental proportions—a cover-up of enormous magnitude that included a secret autopsy to alter the forensic evidence of President Kennedy's wounds, while staging the illusion of an "official" autopsy that amounted to a well-planned fraud—all of which has now been fully documented.[1] No domestic or foreign entity, other than America's own National Security apparatus, had the leverage, flexibility, mobility, and authority to orchestrate such a massive enterprise, which included the manipulation of all major media outlets.

Today, the CIA continues its efforts to cover up its role in the Kennedy assassination. According to author Joan Mellen, a special committee of archivists and librarians at the National Archives was convened in 2000 to examine a set of sealed records relating to the Kennedy assassination in order to determine whether they should be released to the public. Before any determination could be made, however, the group was visited by a man identifying himself as a representative of the Agency.

"He warned them that under no circumstances must they ever reveal to anyone what they had viewed in those documents," said Mellen in her book *A Farewell to Justice* (2005). So chilling had the CIA man's threat been, "no one talked."[2]

Twenty-five years earlier, in 1975, Senator Richard Schweiker of Pennsylvania, half of a two-man subcommittee within the Senate Church Committee, authorized to investigate the Kennedy assassination, had reviewed yet-unseen classified documents at the National Archives and came to this conclusion: "We don't know what happened [in Dallas], but we do know Oswald had intelligence connections. Everywhere you look with him, there are the fingerprints of intelligence."[3] In 2007, referring to Oswald's 1959 phony "defection" to Russia, Schweiker made it clear to author David Talbot that the ex-Marine Oswald "was the product of a fake defector program run by the CIA."[4] Schweiker was never convinced the CIA at any time came clean with what it knew. "I certainly don't believe the CIA gave us the whole story," said the former senator.[5]

In 1979, the House Select Committee on Assassinations (HSCA) concluded its three-year investigation with a finding of "probable conspiracy" in the assassination of President Kennedy, thereby calling into question the entire veracity upon which the foundation of the 1964 Warren Report had been built. Despite the recommendation that the Department of Justice investigate further, nothing ever took place—except that the most sensitive, most revealing files uncovered by the House committee were "lawfully" locked away until the year 2029.

A "shadow government"—what Cold War intelligence historian L. Fletcher Prouty once called "the Secret Team," and what Winston Churchill once referred to as the "High Cabal" that ruled the United States[6]—has eviscerated America's fledgling experiment in democracy. "On top of this," wrote Prouty in 1992, "we have now begun to realize that one of the greatest causalities of the Cold War has been the truth. At no time in the history of mankind has the general public been so misled and so betrayed as it has been by the work of the propaganda merchants of this century and their 'historians.' "[7]

The tapestry of President Kennedy's killing is enormous; the tapestry of Mary Meyer's, much smaller. And yet they are connected, one to the other, in ways that became increasingly apparent to me as I dug ever more deeply into her relationship with Jack Kennedy and the circumstances surrounding her demise. To understand the complex weave of elements that led to her death is to understand, in a deeper way, one of the most abominable, despicable events of our country's history.

Therein lies the cancerous tumor upon the soul of America. The CIA's inception and entrance into the American landscape fundamentally altered not only the functioning of our government, but also the entire character of American life. The CIA's reign during the Cold War era has contaminated the pursuit of historical truth. While the dismantling of America's republic didn't begin in Dallas in 1963, that day surely marked an unprecedented acceleration of the erosion of constitutional democracy. America has never recovered. Today, in 2012, the ongoing disintegration of our country is ultimately about the corruption of our government, a government that has consistently and intentionally misrepresented and lied about what really took place in Dallas in 1963, as it did about the escalation of the Vietnam War that followed, and which it presently continues to do about so many things.

Once revered as a refuge from tyranny, America has become a sponsor and patron of tyrants. Like Rome before it, America is—in its own way—burning. Indeed, the Roman goddess Libertas, her embodiment the Statue of Liberty, still stands at the entrance of New York harbor to welcome all newcomers. Her iconic torch of freedom ablaze, her *tabula ansata* specifically memorializing the rule of law and the American Declaration of Independence, the chains of tyranny are broken at her feet. She wears "peace" sandals—not war boots. While her presence should be an inescapable reminder that we are all "immigrants," her torch reminds us that the core principles for which she stands require truth telling by each and every one of us. As long as any vestige of our democracy remains, each of us has a solemn duty to defend it, putting our personal and family loyalties aside. "Patriotism"—real patriotism—has a most important venue, and it's not always about putting on a uniform to fight some senseless, insane war in order to sustain the meaningless myths about "freedom" or "America's greatness." There is a higher loyalty that real patriotism demands and encompasses, and that loyalty is to the pursuit of truth, no matter how painful or uncomfortable the journey.

"Historical truth matters," said former Princeton historian Martin Duberman, now a Distinguished Professor of History Emeritus at CCNY. "As a nation, we care little for it, much preferring simplistic distortions that sustain our national myths about 'freedom,' 'opportunity,' and 'democracy.' You can't grow into adulthood when you're fed pabulum all your life. And that's why we remain a nation of adolescents, with a culture concerned far more with celebrityhood than with suffering."[8]

Before this book, there has been only one published volume about the life and death of Mary Pinchot Meyer: Nina Burleigh's *A Very Private Woman* (1998). Many people in Washington who had known Mary Meyer felt Burleigh's account left out important details that were either overlooked or not considered, thereby creating more questions than answers. Some, like me, having given Burleigh considerable input, were further disappointed by her conclusion that Mary had indeed been murdered by the downtrodden, helpless Raymond ("Ray") Crump Jr. This had not been the conclusion reached by two other attempts before the Burleigh volume was published.

Most outstanding was author Leo Damore's book project "Burden of Guilt," which had been scheduled for publication in 1993. Damore's research for this manuscript was groundbreaking. With his 1988 publication of *Senatorial Privilege: The Chappaquiddick Cover-Up*, an incriminating exposé of Senator Ted Kennedy's nightmare on Martha's Vineyard and the death of Mary Jo Kopechne, Leo Damore established a reputation as a thorough, prodigious researcher. *New York Times* editorial columnist David Brooks, then writing in the *Wall Street Journal*, spoke of Damore as "a disciplined and relentless writer who makes his case more devastating because he never steps back and editorializes."[9] *Senatorial Privilege* landed Damore on the *New York Times* best-seller list for a number of weeks. Two of Damore's previous books, *In His Garden: The Anatomy of a Murder* (1981) and *The Crime of Dorothy Sheridan* (1978), found renewed readership with the success of *Senatorial Privilege*.

Robertson Davies, one of Canada's foremost men of letters, once remarked that Damore's work spoke to "a strong moral backbone. He writes of the moral choices people must make in their lives and the consequences of these choices—made or not made."[10] A graduate of Kent State University's School of Journalism and a reporter for the *Cape Cod Times* from 1969 to 1974, Leo Damore first published *The Cape Cod Years of John Fitzgerald Kennedy* in 1967. Drawing on anecdotes from neighbors, employees, friends, and acquaintances, the book sought not to sensationalize or focus on Kennedy's politics, sex life, or even his presidency, but to focus on capturing the flavor of the area where the young John Kennedy and his family spent their summers. "Leo wrote his simple but eloquent biography in a scholarly fashion," noted fellow Cape Cod journalist Frances I. Broadhurst, "painstakingly drawing from all local sources available in print or through hundreds and hundreds of interviews."[11]

After the release of *Senatorial Privilege*, Damore returned to his research on Mary Pinchot Meyer, which had originally been sparked by President Kennedy's longtime friend and closest adviser Kenneth ("Kenny") P. O'Donnell. Kenny O'Donnell and Dave Powers were President Kennedy's two closest aides and confidantes, part of the "Irish Mafia" that served the political careers of both Jack and his brother Bobby. In 1966, Damore had the good fortune to be introduced to O'Donnell by attorney James ("Jimmy") H. Smith, Esq., of Falmouth, Massachusetts. Both would work for O'Donnell's unsuccessful Massachusetts gubernatorial campaign in 1970. Shortly before O'Donnell's death in 1977, Leo Damore did a favor for the ailing Kennedy insider, having located an estranged family member. In appreciation, O'Donnell agreed to allow Damore to interview him in depth about Mary Pinchot Meyer, her involvement in the Kennedy White House, and her love affair with the president. That interview would inspire Damore's fascination with what he termed "the Goddess behind the throne. . . ."

I first met Leo Damore in the winter of 1992. He had already been researching Mary Meyer's life for nearly three years. Our friendship grew quickly. For nearly two years, we spent hours talking on the phone, interspersed with my visits to his Connecticut residence. Knowing Mary Meyer's family and some of her community as I did, I was often able to assist in his understanding certain dynamics of some of the people in Washington. While Leo shared with me a good deal of what he had uncovered, it was by no means everything, as I discovered many years later.

In the spring of 1993, a groundbreaking event occurred in the course of Damore's research. It allowed him, he told me, to finally solve the murder of Mary Meyer and uncover why certain forces within our government had targeted her for "termination." However, later that same year, Leo began a mysterious downward spiral of paranoia and depression, the causes of which may never be fully known. Several of his closest friends reported he believed his phone had been wiretapped, and that he was being followed. He told one close friend that he was convinced he'd been poisoned. In October of 1995, Leo Damore shot himself in the presence of a nurse and a policeman. An autopsy later revealed an undiagnosed brain tumor, but this was not without suspicion. Damore never completed a final manuscript for "Burden of Guilt," but his research—most of which eventually came into my possession—became one of the cornerstones for my own sojourn, as did my friendship with him.

As news of Leo's death spread, two well-known authors and one newcomer would begin vying to pick up what Damore had started. The first was the prominent investigative journalist Seymour Hersh. In November of 1995, less than a month after Leo's death, Hersh wrote to Damore's principal research assistant, Mark O'Blazney, seeking Damore's materials, saying that he knew how "active and very diligent Damore had been in his research—some of those he sought to interview told me of his requests, not only for his book *Senatorial Privilege* but in his current pursuit about the story of Mary Meyer. I also know from his earlier work that few had come to understand the [Kennedy] family as he had, essentially from his earlier book on Ted [Kennedy]."[12] Hersh's courtship of O'Blazney, who closely guarded Leo's vault, was short-lived, however. O'Blazney rightly claimed that Damore had bequeathed his research to him, since the author had been unable to remunerate O'Blazney for the work he had done during the last year of his life. As members of the Damore family considered mounting a legal battle for ownership, Hersh decided it was too big a bother, though he always suspected the real story behind Mary Meyer and her death to be a giant bombshell.[13]

Within a year, two other journalists came upon the scene almost simultaneously. The first was John H. Davis, an author of six books, who was a well-known, respected Kennedy assassination researcher, himself a Kennedy insider and a first cousin to Jackie Kennedy. Davis had an inside track to the Kennedy family that gave him a unique perspective. As a relative who had ingratiated himself, he knew many of the confidential workings of the Kennedy clan, including some family members' real beliefs about the Kennedy assassination. Davis himself had absolutely no confidence whatsoever in the Warren Report. In particular, his book *Mafia Kingfish: Carlos Marcello and the Assassination of John F. Kennedy* (1988) has remained a highly respected work with regard to the role of organized crime in JFK's assassination. With the assistance of attorney Jimmy Smith, Davis acquired access to Leo Damore's research on Mary Meyer. In May 1996, editor Fred Jordan at Fromm Publishing International offered Davis a hefty book contract that included an immediate advance of $110,000. The book was to be titled *John F. Kennedy and Mary Pinchot Meyer: A Tale of Two Murdered Lovers*, and was scheduled to be completed by June 30, 1997. Davis took the same position in his attempt as his predecessor Leo Damore: namely, that Mary Meyer hadn't been wantonly murdered, but assassinated because "she knew too much."

While John Davis was at work on his Mary Meyer book, author Noel Twyman published *Bloody Treason: The Assassination of John F. Kennedy* in 1997. The book was exhaustive in its research, ultimately laying the blame for the president's assassination at the front (and back) door of the CIA. Davis was unequivocal: Twyman had "completely solved the crime of the century." Bolstered by Damore's research, Twyman's book further substantiated for Davis why the CIA had a keen interest in Mary Meyer after the Warren Report was made public.

But like Leo Damore, John Davis would never complete his book about Mary, despite his access to Damore's discoveries and what certain members of the Kennedy family had shared with him. There may be several explanations for this. Both John Davis and Leo Damore ultimately linked the murder of Mary Meyer to the assassination of President Kennedy, which Davis had firmly come to believe had been masterminded by the CIA. Was it just coincidence that the two attempts to demonstrate a CIA conspiracy in the demise of Mary Meyer would never be published during this period? I don't think so. John H. Davis was a cum laude graduate of Princeton and, like Leo Damore, a prolific author and respected researcher. It was possible that Davis's alcoholism, well known to his close friends, prevented the book's publication, and the fact that he eventually suffered a severe stroke, though that didn't occur until 2002. When I interviewed Davis in New York in 2004, his disorientation and confusion were apparent; intermittently, he was incoherent. But his friend Jimmy Smith, who had been Damore's attorney and close friend, recalled a chilling telephone conversation with Davis in early 1999.

"John," inquired Jimmy Smith, "what the hell is going on with the book on Mary Pinchot Meyer?"

"Oh, I'm not doing that," replied Davis. "I decided I wanted to live. . . ."[14]

When I queried Smith about this remark, he said he was sure Davis's life had been threatened, that an attempt would have been made on his life had he published *John F. Kennedy and Mary Pinchot Meyer: A Tale of Two Murdered Lovers*. Davis's previous books on the Kennedy assassination and the Mafia made him no stranger to the world of organized crime. He likely would have been able to discriminate between a serious threat and one that wasn't.

Journalist Nina Burleigh contacted me in 1996 to talk about Mary Meyer. Our initial interview lasted several hours. I was heartened at the time by some of her insights, and for the next two years or so continued to offer suggestions when asked. Though Nina would eventually acknowledge my assistance, as well as quote me throughout, I was very disappointed by her conclusions in *A Very Private Woman*. Despite some well-researched biographical information on Mary's early life, Burleigh's portrayals of Mary's relationship with Timothy Leary, the nature of her relationship with Jack Kennedy, and her final disposition toward Mary's alleged assailant, Ray Crump Jr., and his attorney, Dovey Roundtree, were not only shortsighted, but also ultimately inaccurate and misinformed.

Who then bears the "burden of guilt," as Leo Damore once coined it, for the murder of Mary Pinchot Meyer? And who among us would weep for the ruined life of the wrongfully prosecuted Raymond Crump Jr.—a defenseless, meek young African American man scapegoated for a crime he couldn't have possibly committed? Who would dare to step forward to undertake the journey for the deeper truth of what really occurred? Author Leo Damore may well have given his life for this story. It is his burden—and Mary Meyer's—that I have ultimately endeavored to shoulder.

Members of my immediate and extended family, as well as Wistar Janney's remaining friends and community, may find my conclusions all too outrageous and troublesome. Everyone is, of course, ultimately entitled to his own opinion—*but not to his own set of facts*. And the hidden history of this narrative—the true facts beneath the surface, much of which is revealed here for the very first time—strongly supports the conclusions that I have established.

Whatever remaining anguish—mine, as well as the blemish upon the soul of America—my faith dictates that eventually it will have a redemptive impact, only because truth, when it is confronted and finally understood, has the power to heal.

1

Fate's Engagement

There are very few human beings who receive the truth, complete and staggering, by instant illumination. Most of them acquire it fragment by fragment, on a small scale, by successive developments, cellularly, like a laborious mosaic.

—Anaïs Nin

A patriot must always be ready to defend his country against his government.

—Edward Abbey

In some far place, where all the lovely things
Of earth are born, the gods no longer weep.
She has returned to them. And what she brings
We lose, but always keep.

—Mary Pinchot (Meyer)
(From her poem "Requiem")[1]

A CHILLY OCTOBER wind sent leaves scudding across the cobblestones of Washington's elegant Georgetown streets as Mary Pinchot Meyer set out on her customary early morning walk to her art studio. She was lithe and feminine, radiant with a beauty that still turned heads. On that day, too, she was almost ageless with grace. Her svelte frame belied the strength within her, fed perhaps by a rare reservoir of spiritual intensity. It was Monday morning, October 12, 1964. Two days later would be her forty-fourth birthday, the first without the man she had come to love, and with whom she had shared her hope for a world in pursuit of peace.[2]

In spite of the raw autumn temperature just above freezing that signaled winter's approach, there was the promise of an impending sun's warmth. Still, the weather called for several layers of clothing in anticipation of the longer walk along the Chesapeake and Ohio Canal that had become her daily ritual each afternoon after she painted. The walk from her Thirty-Fourth Street home took less than ten minutes. Her artist's studio, a converted brick garage with two skylights in its tin roof, was located in the alleyway behind her sister Tony and brother-in-law Ben Bradlee's N Street house, itself a poignant reminder, only because its location was just seven doors away from where her lover, the president, had lived before moving into the White House in 1960. That morning, however, she may have pondered the recent estrangement from her sister and brother-in-law. Months earlier, a schism had developed, primarily involving Ben, whom she had come to distrust. "Since his first marriage was a failure," she told her friends Jim and Anne Truitt, "he's trying twice as hard with Tony. One and a half would be enough."[3]

The capital city was still reeling from the unfathomable trauma that had taken place eleven months earlier in Dallas. It had left a deep wound in the fabric of America's soul and identity, and in the meaning of civilization across the globe. Festering, the wound wasn't about to heal, or even recede. That would require, among other things, an elixir called truth, not its subversion in the form of the so-called Warren Report that had emerged three weeks earlier from Supreme Court justice Earl Warren's commission on the assassination of President John F. Kennedy. For Mary, the report may have been further evidence of the infection that had already taken hold, long before the nightmare in Dallas. Like a viral cancerous army, rogue elements within the highest levels of the American government had usurped the hope and vision she and Jack had shared and nurtured, ending America's dream for the president's new trajectory toward world peace. She wasn't about to let the Warren Commission lie go unchallenged. She had made her decision to stand up and be counted.[4]

Since Dallas, Mary had experienced a rough year of adjustments, with no real end in sight. For months, she had attempted to retreat into her discipline as an artist. She was by now an established painter in the Washington Color School. Her dream of recognition as a contemporary abstract painter had started to be realized just five days before the horror in Dallas had struck. Her first solo art opening at the Jefferson Place Gallery in Washington had been a solid success. Reviewing her paintings on November 24, *Washington Post* art critic Leslie Judd Ahlander heralded Mary's artistry, writing, "Her work has always shown a quality which made one want to see more. Now she is working very hard and the results are gratifying indeed." Describing Mary's tondo (circular canvas) approach using acrylic paint, Ahlander had praised her presentation as "luminous and carefully thought out. . . . a lyrical and emotional statement rather than a cooly [*sic*] calculated one. It is easy to see that the artist has brought a great deal of thought to bear on the adjustment of areas and colors."[5] The recognition was an affirmation of the creative path she had long desired.

Mary's painting had provided some respite in the wake of the president's assassination and eventually led to a second 1964 exhibit in May with the Pan American Union's *Nine Contemporary Painters: USA* exhibit in Washington. Three of her most recently completed works, *Fire Island II, Clearing,* and *Foxglove,* had been included in the show. Overall, the exhibit had been even more successful than her first. In November, it was due to be shipped to the Museum of Modern Art in Buenos Aires for an international opening, her first worldwide public exhibition—one she would not live to witness.

Tormented since Jack's death, Mary had refused to accept the lies being peddled to the public. At times despondent, she had asked her friend and fellow artist Bill Walton, a Kennedy insider who had escorted her many times to White House functions that included stolen moments with the president, "why Bobby wasn't doing more about what had really happened to Jack in Dallas." Bobby did have a plan, Walton told her, to attempt to retake the White House, but time would have to pass first. Best to keep throwing herself back into her work, Walton counseled, as Walton himself was doing.[6]

It wasn't enough. She would take matters into her own hands, she had finally decided.[7] Throughout the past year, she had made it her business to learn what had really taken place in Dallas that late-November day. Like most Americans, Mary grieved over the violent death of her president; for her, however, his departure had also been uniquely personal. She and Jack had not only been lovers, but had also grown into the deepest of allies—kindred spirits in the pursuit of peace for the world. It hadn't been Mary's first attempt at such a feat. Nearly fifteen years earlier, she had worked tirelessly with her then-husband, war hero Cord Meyer, to promote a world government structure that might maintain the hard-won, fragile peace of a postwar nuclear world. But Cord had ultimately chosen a different path and, in doing so, had foreclosed on their marriage. With Jack, Mary had finally prevailed. Everything, at least for a few moments, had looked so promising. And that was really what she wanted—to give peace a chance.

Her prior access to Jack and his White House coterie had allowed her to quietly interrogate the few who would talk about that day in Dallas. She had read and collected some of the various reports and articles that questioned the falsehoods that had been propagated and were now worming their way into the public mind. Those writings occupied a special place in the bookcase in her bedroom, next to her diary, the final repository of reflections and analysis of what she had come to understand.[8]

The past year had also been a grueling duel with despair. It had taken a huge toll. "What's the use?" Mary bemoaned to her dear friend Anne Truitt before she had left for Japan earlier that year. "Everything I love seems to die."[9] Melancholy had periodically opened the wounds of past losses in Mary's life: her half-sister Rosamund's suicide in 1938; the death of her father, Amos, in 1944. Neither, however, had prepared her for the unspeakable horror of losing her son Michael in 1956. That tragedy had propelled her into an emotional typhoon that she struggled long and hard to resolve. While scar tissue might stop the bleeding, the wound of such a loss (as every mother either imagines or knows firsthand) never really healed.

With her friends Anne and Jim Truitt having left for Tokyo in early 1964,[10] Mary had recently, perhaps mistakenly, spoken to another woman she knew only peripherally, not realizing the woman had been sent to find out what Mary had learned about the dastardly deed in Dallas and its orchestration. Mary wasn't going to sit by and let it happen all over again, she told the friend, who suggested that it might be better to leave well enough alone.[11] The cover-up had reached its final public crescendo with the release of the Warren Report on September 24, about three weeks earlier. Mary had bought the abridged paperback version and read it with her trained editor's eye, making numerous notes in the margins and turning down page corners for markers. Sensing it had been crafted as the final narcotic designed to deaden any serious inquiry or public scrutiny, she had furiously confronted her ex-husband, Cord Meyer, a CIA honcho who in turn had informed his close friend and colleague Jim Angleton, also the longtime godfather to her children.[12] Of course, it hadn't been the first time she'd openly spoken out against their beloved Agency. During the preceding years, Mary—unlike other CIA wives—had been outspoken at cocktail and dinner parties, "always making wisecracks," one Agency wife remembered, about what the CIA was doing in the world.[13]

The art studio was cold when she entered it. Her morning ritual included turning on the electric space heater, pouring coffee from her thermos, and lighting up a Salem, so as to begin. The transition into painting allowed her to quiet, if only for a while, the challenges she knew she would soon face.

The hour was approaching noon as she stepped back from her morning's meditation—a tondo focus of unprimed canvas containing "swaying velvety semicircles of color" so rich in vivid acrylic pigment.[14] Whether that morning's endeavor was further informed by her recent thematic, ongoing analysis of peace and harmony wasn't known, but Mary's former intimacy with artist Ken Noland in the late 1950s had given her a particular vantage point for her evolving exploration. Noland's "target" paintings had influenced her, as they had expressed a distinct commentary about war. She had taken this target circular device in her most recent painting, *Half Light*, and expressed the four elements—fire, wind, water, and earth—using color to underscore harmony with the earth, and the universe itself. Her "one-world" harmony in the past year may have been an homage to Jack and their shared vision for world peace. It was, after all, only a vision—perhaps her vision, or their vision—of where mankind should always be focused now and in the future. There was still purpose to be explored, and she would continue to fight, even without Jack. Seven years later, someone by the name of John Lennon would sing a song called "Imagine," capturing where Mary had been headed.[15]

While Mary's work that morning may have echoed her recent painting *Half Light*, something within *Half Light*'s conception of one-world harmony might have died in order to be reborn. Hope and despair in the end had been engaged in an epic battle, and not just in her life alone. Stepping back from her morning's work, she might have thought of naming the painting *Lost Light*, or just *No Light* at all. The title would eventually emerge—as it always seemed to—however private the artist's meaning for the world to see. Her mother's discipline, from which she had built her own, would ensure it.

The day beckoned her to be on her way. Her usual long walk after a morning's artistic focus was another workday ritual she always looked forward to. The paint was still damp on the circular canvas. Having positioned an electric fan toward the wet painting, she collected her Mark Cross leather gloves and her sunglasses and pulled on her blue cable-knit angora hooded sweater over a lighter sweater and white oxford cloth shirt.[16] There was no need to take her purse; she liked to walk freely with no encumbrance. Her paint-spattered PF

Flyer canvas sneakers likely squeaked across the wooden floor as she pivoted out the door.

The October breeze suggested the cooler days ahead, bringing welcome relief from Washington's oppressive humidity, which sometimes lingered well into September. Even so, by noontime the day had already warmed. Circling the block to N Street, Mary walked down the steep incline of Thirty-Fourth Street toward the C & O Canal towpath. Crossing the inevitable M Street traffic, she found herself face-to-face with an approaching limousine, the long, black, official kind with government license plates that at an earlier time could have been taking Jack to some official function or meeting.

"Good-bye, Mary," yelled Polly Wisner, one of Washington's more aristocratic women. The wife of Frank Wisner, one of the founding fathers of CIA covert operations, Polly was preparing to fly to London without Frank, whose descent into a labyrinth of depression, mania, and compulsive talking, or logorrhea, had finally ended his intelligence career in 1962. Mary would never know that a year later, in 1965, Wisner would be found dead, an apparent suicide, a small-gauge shotgun his final companion. His daughter would wonder whether her father had suffered some kind of delayed guilt reaction over the CIA's recruitment and shelter of a number of high-level Nazis after the war.[17] But the small-gauge shotgun somehow kept emerging as "the final companion of choice." Just a year earlier, in August 1963, Mary's friend, Philip L. Graham, owner-publisher of the *Washington Post*, had allegedly embraced such a firearm for himself. There would be others, too, all unbeknownst to Mary. In 1977, the CIA asset George de Mohrenschildt, once in charge of keeping Lee Harvey Oswald positioned in Dallas, would also appoint the small-bore shotgun as his final companion—immediately before he was to be interviewed by an investigator for the House Select Committee on Assassinations (HSCA). Mary would not survive to witness the self-destruction that would explode in the years to come. She passed Polly Wisner, undoubtedly waving in response to Polly's greeting, and moved onward toward the canal towpath. Polly would be the last acquaintance to see Mary alive.[18]

As she continued walking, Mary might have cheered herself with thoughts of Thanksgiving and the anticipation of being reunited with her two boys, Quenty and Mark, due home in a little more than a month from their respective boarding schools, Salisbury and Milton Academy. She had been to Salisbury the preceding academic year to visit Quenty, the handsome son she'd called "mouse" when he was younger. There were those in the extended family who privately felt Quenty had been scarred by his father, Cord, and, of course, by the death of his brother Mikey. Like his father, Quenty had been known to exhibit a cruel disposition that was often visited on those more vulnerable and defenseless in their immediate and extended family. The meanness was a phase that Mary hoped he would grow out of, as children sometimes did. At Salisbury, Quenty was coming into his own, his athleticism in basketball and tennis readily apparent. During Mary's visit, his schoolmates had gawked at her the entire time, later telling Quenty his mother was "incredibly beautiful."[19]

The towpath was nearly deserted that Monday as Mary proceeded westward from Georgetown out to Fletcher's Boat House, a distance of about two and a quarter miles. Still, there was one young couple up ahead walking in the same direction as Mary. Just as they disappeared around the first bend, a young man wearing red Bermuda shorts ran past her on his way west. He was probably a student at Georgetown University, whose Gothic Healy Clock Tower soared above the tree line on a bluff overlooking the canal.

Once doomed to be replaced by a freeway, the Chesapeake and Ohio Canal had been saved through the efforts of Supreme Court justice William O. Douglas. Douglas had led protest hikes the entire length of the canal in 1954, wanting the most perfectly preserved example of America's canal-building era to be designated a national historic park. He had personally undertaken the campaign in the spirit of his boyhood hero, Gifford Pinchot, Mary's uncle and a pioneering conservationist who had twice been elected governor of Pennsylvania. In 1905, Gifford Pinchot had been appointed the first head of the U.S. Forest Service by President Teddy Roosevelt, his close friend.

While the C & O Canal itself had been declared a national historical monument under President Eisenhower, efforts to make it a national park had failed until President Kennedy took office, only because, according to one source, Mary had lobbied hard for the proposal.[20] Jack was, according to one insider, amused by Mary's entreaties; he found them endearing. Eventually, however, he came to rely more on her, convinced that her counsel had critical value on even more important issues.[21]

After Dallas, Mary's towpath excursions had become a sacred refuge, even in inclement weather. Not a drinker like so many of the other women in her circle, and willing to face the fury within, she had made walking an antidote for her agitation. But about a month or so after Jack's assassination, she later told her friend Jim Truitt, she had set out on the towpath one day in wintry weather, determined to sustain her fragile equilibrium, only to confront further anguish instead of the solace she'd sought. A short but violent snow squall had materialized, making visibility difficult, if not impossible. Coming toward her through the blinding snow was a ghostlike chimera taking form as it neared. It wasn't until she was nearly face-to-face with the person, she said, that she recognized Jackie. The two fell into each other's arms, crying and consoling one another in embrace, as only women know how to do.[22] Mary's discretion was always paramount, her capacity to comfort someone else even amid her own deepest anguish somehow readily available when called for. Jackie was adrift. Her life—and all of history—dramatically, irrevocably shattered, she needed as many anchors as she could find.

"Jackie kept repeating how happy she and the President had been in the White House," Mary later disclosed to Truitt about that day.[23] She hadn't disputed Jackie, although she easily could have, in view of the life she'd enjoyed with Jack. Mary had understood his conflicted hunger as perhaps only a uniquely enlightened woman could, viewing his sexual "wanderlust" for what it was—a symptom of his patrician hatred of the rejection he had been forced to endure from an empty, cold, and distant mother.[24] She wasn't threatened by it. "In addition to art, Mary was an acute judge of masculine character," her friend Anne Truitt would remark years later.[25] Historian Herb Parmet, in a groundbreaking biography of Jack, had interviewed a close confidential source who knew the score. The source had observed that Jack enjoyed a very different, and very special, life with Mary. "He could talk in ways she understood and their trust was mutual," Parmet would write in 1983. "When he was with her, the rest of the world could go to hell. He could laugh with her at the absurdity of the things he saw all around his center of power."[26]

Mary continued walking in her customary westerly direction, as the October noonday sun warmed the morning chill. Throughout the past year, there had been several incidents of someone intruding into her home. The incidents started in January, only weeks after Dallas. Then, after being away for some time that summer, she was sure someone had been inside her house while she was gone. In another instance, she had found the heavy basement door, which was impossible for her to move even with the help of her two sons, ajar. But the finale had been seeing somebody leaving her house as she had walked in. She was sure of it.[27] What were they after?

As an artist, Mary's philosophical perspective had undergone a major transformation when she embarked on a journey of personal exploration of mind-expanding potions in the late 1950s. So profound had been her journey that it allowed her to see her world in a way she had never before envisioned or experienced.[28] It may have also allowed her some deeper resolution about her son Michael's death, though nothing would ever dishonor his spirit in her life. Nonetheless, despite Michael's departure, Mary's awareness had expanded into the recognition of the connectedness of all living things, the breathing atomic structure of everything physical, all coexisting peacefully in harmony with one another. Here, cosmic joy was real, a blessing given to all who were willing to surrender. And here, within a sublime expanded consciousness, such exploits as domination and war lust were seen as infantile—mere vestigial reminders of an arrested evolutionary history.[29]

What if world leaders—those political titular heads of state—could experience the sacred connection of life force in harmonious coexistence, just as many artists and poets had envisioned? The pace of human evolution itself might take a giant step forward, ending the rampant Cold War madness, she told Timothy Leary in 1962.[30] At first, it had only been a pipe dream, something she imagined mostly within. Yet fate somehow kept managing to place her across Jack's path—or was it Jack across hers? She had sought Leary's counsel, but her discretion once again erected the boundary. She would never name names, never reveal her real plan. He had kindly given her some tools, suggestions for how to guide others through the psychedelic Garden of Eden. She had shared her emerging experience with a small group of eight women who were willing to engage a few powerful men in Washington. Leary, unaware of what was really taking place, said he would continue to periodically make himself available to help her.[31]

Mary had decided she'd take it in steps, and so one hot summer night in July of 1962 she and Jack smoked marijuana together in the White House residence. She was curious as to how he might react. At first, he had become "hungry" for food—"soup and chocolate mousse"—before their amorous embrace that evening, where she might have held a more tender man. The connection may have frightened him initially, but her self-assured presence and trust likely conveyed that he was, however momentarily, safe—safe in her arms, safe in her love, even safe in his own realization that it might be possible for him to face the sordid, fragmented sexuality that kept him from his own redemption.[32] Like Mary's ex-husband Cord, Jack too, was broken; and unwilling, or too frightened, to confront his world of wounded vulnerability— ironically the gateway from which real intimacy often sprang.

Later on, she had admittedly made "a mistake in recruitment" in her small psychedelic group of eight women. "I was such a fool," she had anxiously told Timothy Leary in Millbrook, New York, in September 1963. "A wife snitched on us. I'm scared," she'd blurted out, then burst into tears.[33] Discreet as ever,

Mary never mentioned names to Leary, but she had feared the worst at the time. With her husband dead, Katharine Graham now wielded more power in Washington than ever before. Mary had considered Katharine's husband, Philip L. Graham, whose name she never mentioned to Leary, to be "a friend of mine," a friend whom she described as "losing the battle, a really bloody one. He got drunk and told a room full of reporters about me and my boyfriend."[34] Leary hadn't realized at the time that Mary's "boyfriend" was the president. But the worst part was that Phil Graham had just allegedly committed suicide, another detail she kept from Leary, who couldn't quite fathom why the usually bold, courageous Mary was so upset. That day with Leary at Millbrook, she had voiced her worst fear, that even her own life might be in danger, finally asking whether, if she showed up unexpectedly at some point, he would be able to hide her. Yes, he could, he reassured her. But nothing had happened. There had been no repercussions. Maybe Phil Graham did commit suicide after all, she may have thought as she kept walking, perhaps not realizing that her paranoia had in fact been a case of heightened awareness.

The Potomac River was to her left as the towpath also veered left, narrowing a bit as it paralleled the elevated Canal Road to her right. Mary approached the narrow, thirty-foot-long wooden footbridge that spanned the shallow spillway drainage. It was almost the halfway mark to Fletcher's Boat House, her usual destination before turning back. The path ahead was empty. She stepped into a dense arbor of mature black cherry trees, river birch, and box elders, its wildness protruding beyond the city's boundary. It was likely one of her favorite parts of this particular route because of its comforting solitude. Dappled by sparking sunlight, the Potomac could be seen through a scrim of branches down a steep embankment and beyond a thicket of fire-scarred trees. But for the intermittent drone of passing cars above and to her right, she was alone with her thoughts and all of nature.

Unaware that she had been under surveillance for the past several weeks, and oblivious that day to the fact that she was being stalked, Mary might well not have heard the footfalls gathering speed behind her.[35] She had no reason to be concerned. Park Service police regularly patrolled the area, though for some reason they weren't present that day. Other pedestrians, bicyclists, and the fishermen and boatmen who frequented the river almost guaranteed the towpath's security in daytime. Mary had never feared for her safety in this place, or any other for that matter, despite the concerns her friend Cicely Angleton would later express that day. "Besides being one of the prettiest girls in the world, Mary had great courage," recalled her Vassar classmate Scottie Fitzgerald Smith, the daughter of author F. Scott, remembering their days as apprentice journalists in New York. "I wouldn't go down into those subways at night, but Mary was never afraid. 'Oh nothing will happen,'" Scottie remembered Mary saying.[36]

The towpath was an unlikely venue for an assault in broad daylight, yet Mary was abruptly seized from behind. Her assailant wrapped her in a close, hard embrace, pinning her arms against her side. Immobilized, the vigorous, athletic woman came alive as she fought hard to escape the lock of an aggressor she probably couldn't see. Squirming, groaning, trying to break free, she realized the strength of her attacker, and instinctively yelled out, "Somebody help me!" Again and again, she called out beyond the three-foot retaining wall of the canal to the passing automobiles on Canal Road less than 150 feet away.[37] A muffled explosion sent a ringing, echoing roar through her ears. She must have smelled the stench of burning flesh and gunpowder as something hard and hot seared into the left side of her skull just in front of her ear. A gush of wet warmth poured down her face, soaking the collar of her blue angora sweater, turning it red.

With a desperate lunge, Mary broke away, stumbling across the towpath to the wooded embankment border. Seeking refuge somewhere at the border's edge, holding onto a nearby birch tree, she brought her gloved hand to her left temple, only to draw away great smears of blood that darkly stained the leather glove. Assaulted by waves of nausea and weakness, falling to her knees and fighting to retain consciousness, she braced herself from falling farther, clinging to the smooth birch tree trunk. Failing to kill her with his first shot, the assailant seized her again, even more roughly. This time, he dragged Mary from the embankment clear across the towpath, out of the shadows and into the sunlight toward the canal's edge, her paint-spattered PF Flyers vainly seeking traction against the pebbled dirt, leaving parallel tracks that would mark the last path of her earthly life. Still, she struggled. But she didn't scream again. As she lost strength, her voice may have been quieted by both pain and fear. Or perhaps she silently beseeched the passing cars above, before something hard was pressed against her body over her right shoulder blade.[38]

Mary likely didn't hear the second explosion. There was only the hot path of metal that tore through her chest, severing her aorta. As the last echo of gunfire faded, death forced her final surrender and she fell upon the grassy ledge at the water's edge.

2

Murder on the Towpath

Make the lie big, make it simple, keep saying it, and eventually they will believe it.

—Adolf Hitler

HENRY WIGGINS JR. thought he heard "a whole lot of hollerin'" coming from the canal.[1] An employee of University Esso Service Station at Pennsylvania Avenue and 21st Street in Georgetown, Wiggins had been dispatched to pick up Bill Branch, the mechanic at the employer's other Esso Service Station at the north end of Key Bridge. Together, they were to service a stalled Nash Rambler sedan abandoned somewhere in the 4300 block on the north side of Canal Road. They had just arrived and Wiggins was taking out his toolbox when he heard screams coming from the canal. At first, he explained to police, he didn't pay too much attention: " . . . you know, that area down there—it could have been some kids playing, or a bunch of winos fighting." But then, he said, both he and Branch had thought they heard a woman screaming. The screams lasted for twenty seconds or more, they estimated, with the woman pleading, "Help me! . . . Help me! . . . Somebody help me!"[2] A gunshot rang out from the same direction as the shouting.

Henry Wiggins was a heavy-set, twenty-four-year-old black man who had served in the Army in a Military Police unit in Korea, and he was still fast on his feet. On hearing the shot, he had dashed across Canal Road toward a stone wall at the edge of the embankment overlooking the canal. Seconds before he got there, he heard a second shot. When he peered over the wall and down across the canal, Wiggins saw a man, "a Negro male," standing over a woman who lay motionless and curled on her side. Minutes later, Wiggins would give the police a description of the man, recorded on the department's Police Form PD-251. The "Negro male" was listed as having a "medium build, 5 feet 8 inches to 5 feet 10 inches, 185 pounds."[3] Also listed were the clothes Wiggins said the man was wearing: a dark plaid golf cap; a light, beige-colored, waist-length zippered jacket; dark trousers; and dark shoes.[4] Police would later measure the distance from where Wiggins stood at the wall to the murder scene to be 128.6 feet. It was close enough to make out specific details, certainly close enough to see that the woman was white, that the man standing over her was black, and that he stood with his hands down at his sides. "He was facing toward me but his head was bent down. He was looking at the body lying on the ground. Then, he looked up toward the wall where I was standing. He saw me. I was looking right at him," Wiggins recalled.[5]

Wiggins ducked behind the wall, but when he peeked back over it, he saw that the man held some kind of a dark object in his right hand. From the considerable distance of 128.6 feet, he couldn't say with certainty what the object was, but given the gunshots he had just heard, he assumed that it was a gun. "He just shoved something in his jacket pocket, looked at me a couple of seconds . . . turned away from the victim and *walked* [author's emphasis] down over the embankment there," he said. Wiggins couldn't say which way the man went after he disappeared over the embankment.[6]

But nowhere in Wiggins's initial description to police, or in his testimony nine months later at the trial, did he ever mention seeing any stains, blood or anything else, on the fully zipped light-colored beige jacket the man had been wearing. Indeed, the "Negro male" and his clothes, which Wiggins had described, appeared to be neatly in place; nothing was disheveled.

Racing back across Canal Road to the tow truck, Wiggins yelled to his assistant, Bill Branch, "A guy just shot a lady over there!" He hopped into the truck, started the ignition, made a U-turn, and sped back to the Key Bridge Esso Station, six-tenths of a mile away. Once there, he told station manager Joe Cameron what he had just seen. "It wasn't any long conversation," Wiggins said. "I just told him what happened." Wiggins immediately phoned the Seventh Precinct of Washington's Metropolitan Police Department. Before he had finished talking with the dispatcher, a police cruiser, already responding to the radio alert about the incident, pulled into the Esso station, sirens wailing. The alert had been broadcast at 12:26 P.M.

Wiggins climbed into the back seat of the cruiser, which took off in the direction of the Foundry Underpass, a distance of about four-tenths of a mile, to access the C & O Canal towpath. Reaching the Foundry's arched stone tunnel, which was as narrow as its roadway was rutted, "we dismounted from the police car," Wiggins recalled. "We ran down the tracks, the railroad tracks, down towards the scene and up the embankment to the [murder] scene."[7] Together, police officers Robert Decker and James Scouloukas approached the fallen woman with Wiggins. Blood saturated her blonde hair and soaked her sweater and gloves. There was a bullet wound near her left eye, and blood covered her face. Her body would still have been warm. A pair of smashed sunglasses lay near her feet. The scuffed ground indicated that there had been a struggle, and parallel tracks in the dirt from the towpath to the embankment indicated that the woman had been dragged to the spot where she lay. Surmising that the killer might still be in the vicinity, police officer Scouloukas returned with Wiggins to the cruiser to broadcast the description of the man Wiggins had seen.[8]

Meanwhile, police officers Roderick Sylvis and Frank Bignotti, who were on patrol in Scout 72, had also responded to the broadcast alarm. They pulled up on Canal Road, directly across from the murder scene, and climbed out of their cruiser. At that point, Decker motioned to them to drive to Fletcher's Boat House, which was just over a mile and a half to the west, in order to block off one of the canal's four marked entrances. Arriving at the boathouse area, Sylvis and Bignotti drove through the tight underpass tunnel below the canal and parked facing the canal from the south. From that vantage point, they would be able to see anyone leaving the towpath to access Canal Road, and they would have a full view of the canal itself, particularly the point where visitors could use an old, leaky skiff attached to a rope and pulley to pull themselves across the seventy-foot canal.

"We sat in the cruiser about four or five minutes and observed no one walking out from the towpath," Sylvis recalled. The two officers then settled on a new strategy. "We decided that it would be best if my partner went through the woods and myself proceeding along the towpath."[9]

As the officers began to position themselves, they saw a young white couple, thirtyish, walking westward on the railroad tracks, just below and parallel to the towpath. The two officers approached the couple for questioning. "I asked if they had seen anyone going out of the area before I got there," Sylvis said. "But they hadn't seen anybody, or heard any gunshots, screams, or any disturbance." After several minutes, the two officers made their way east in the hope that they might yet encounter the assailant. Perhaps, acting in haste, they let the couple go without requesting identification or contact information. It was an oversight, a lapse of protocol that would remain a cloud over the case for decades to come.[10] At that point, Bignotti entered the woods adjacent to the railroad tracks and Sylvis took the towpath, walking east toward the murder scene.

Officer Sylvis continued on the towpath "for about a mile" in the direction of the murder scene, slowly and vigilantly scouring the area for other people. After a while, a man poked his head out of some woods to the right and ahead of where Sylvis was walking. "He was looking up toward me by the railroad tracks at the edge of the woods about 150 feet away," Sylvis recalled. "Just his head is all I saw for a second." Sylvis saw the man only long enough to discern that he was a "Negro male."[11] Slowly, and with caution, the young officer approached the area where he had seen the man. The tangle of underbrush, vines, tree roots, and rocks that covered the embankment made it difficult to penetrate. Sylvis saw no one. Nothing disturbed the stillness of the woods but the breeze that rustled the fallen leaves. Hoping that his partner, Bignotti, was in the woods to his right, Sylvis yelled for him a number of times. "I was thinking maybe he could get behind the individual I'd seen, but Bignotti was not answering my call," said Sylvis. Coming out of the underbrush on the tracks, he finally spotted Bignotti crossing the tracks and caught up with him. But Bignotti had seen no one during his search of the woods. He had seen no evidence of the "Negro male" that his partner had seen.[12]

In the meantime, Henry Wiggins was beginning to lose patience. More than a half hour had passed since he and Officer Scouloukas had called in the report. Police cruisers had converged on the scene. Sergeant Pasquale D'Ambrosio of the Seventh Precinct Criminal Investigations Division arrived to escort Wiggins back to the towpath and to secure the scene. It was Wiggins's opinion that D'Ambrosio was the only officer doing anything proactive, not just standing around the dead woman's body, talking.[13]

The Homicide Squad arrived a few minutes before 1:00 P.M., just after the arrival of Chief Detective Art Weber, a twenty-three-year veteran of the police force, and three men wearing trench raincoats. "The description I got was for a Negro male wearing a dark hat and a light-colored jacket," Weber recalled. "I remember from the lookout—one of my ways of doing this—I had a picture in my mind of a stocky individual." He later confirmed that based on the description of the man sought by the police, he expected the man to be between "five feet eight or ten inches" tall.[14]

Twenty-nine-year-old detective Bernie Crooke was the youngest member of the Homicide Squad and had been on the job for only eighteen months. Even so, he had already seen a number of murdered women, "but none who looked beautiful when dead," he recalled years later upon first seeing the dead Mary Meyer. "She even looked beautiful with a bullet in her head."[15] Crooke surveyed the scene and detected what appeared to be drag marks. He also found a blue button with two frayed threads in the grass by a birch tree at the edge of the embankment, twenty-two feet from the body. Blood on the tree suggested that the victim might have grasped it from a sitting or a kneeling position. Detective Crooke joined Detective Weber, who was questioning Henry Wiggins at a spot approximately thirty feet from the body.

Wiggins explained that he had arrived at the 4300 block of Canal Road at approximately 12:20 P.M. to service a stalled Nash Rambler sedan. Laying out the sequence of events—the woman's screams, the sound of one gunshot and then a second—Wiggins told Crooke and Weber that he had ducked behind the stone wall because he didn't want the man he'd seen standing over the victim to see him. As he later testified, "I thought that would frighten him and cause him to act more quickly. But he's not afraid. He doesn't appear worried he's been caught in the act. He saw me and I guess he was excited, but he wasn't hasty or anything. He went over the embankment down into the woods. He took his time, but he was moving."[16] Weber then ordered police officers to search both sides of the canal and to sweep the woods all the way to the Potomac River. But if the Wiggins time chronology was correct, approximately forty-five minutes had elapsed since the murder. The assailant would have had plenty of time to flee the scene.

In Police Cruiser 203, Detective John Warner and his partner Henry Schultheis of the Third Precinct were waiting at a red light at Twenty-First Street and K Streets when they heard the initial broadcast at 12:26 P.M. Warner recalled that the broadcast description was for a Negro male in his forties, approximately five feet ten inches tall, wearing a light jacket and a dark hat, and armed with a gun.[17] In response to the bulletin, Warner and Schultheis turned right onto K Street and drove down the Key Bridge underpass to the woods' edge, where the towpath began. From there, they could look down on the set of railroad tracks that ran parallel to both the canal and the towpath. They saw no one. They waited in their cruiser until approximately 12:40 P.M., whereupon Warner decided he would walk westward on the railroad bed toward

Fletcher's Boat House, while Schultheis would "cover the area to the left of the railroad tracks to the [Potomac] river bank."[18]

Taking intermittent detours to search the woods between the railroad tracks and the high embankment to the towpath, Henry Warner soon discovered that some of the underbrush was so thick he couldn't get through it. After walking approximately half a mile, he came upon a five-foot-tall concrete culvert, large enough to conceal a man inside. Peering into it, he saw only water. He continued to explore the nearby underbrush, and looked under the tunnel where the spillway flowed into the Potomac. He found no one.

But as Warner walked back to the railroad bed and continued westward, he saw a young black man walking on the tracks. He was short, and he was soaking wet. "That indicated to me he'd either worked up a lot of perspiration from running, or else he had just come out of the river," Warner recalled.[19] The man was wearing a yellow sweatshirt over a white T-shirt, navy-blue corduroy trousers that were torn six inches below the left pocket, and black wingtip shoes. The zipper fly on his pants was unzipped. He shivered as Detective Warner approached him to ask his name. "Ray Crump Jr." he said, wide-eyed and diffident. Water dripped from the wallet Crump took from his pocket before he handed over his driver's license. Warner looked at the name and photograph to confirm his identity. According to his driver's license, Crump was 5 feet 3½ inches tall and weighed 130 pounds. Warner had to have observed that he didn't fit the description given in the police broadcast alert. He asked Crump if he had heard gunshots. Crump said he hadn't.

"How did you get so wet?" Warner asked. Crump said he'd been fishing off some rocks upriver. He'd gone to sleep and fallen in the water.

"Where's your fishing equipment?" Warner asked.

"It went into the river, too." Crump said.

"Your rod and everything?"

"Yes, sir." said Crump.[20]

Crump had an abrasion over his right eye. A fresh scrape on his right hand was bleeding. He told Warner that he had cut his hand on a rock as he fell into the river, before attempting to climb out.

Warner then asked Crump to show him where he'd been fishing. "I would help him see if I could retrieve his fishing gear for him," Warner later said. Motioning in a westerly direction from where the two were presently standing, Crump indicated that he had been fishing "around a bend over there." He and Warner then walked a little more than a tenth of a mile along the railroad bed toward the area where Crump said he had been fishing earlier that day. Voices and commotion then drew Detective Warner's attention to the fifty-foot embankment to his right. Sergeant D'Ambrosio, standing at the edge of the towpath, descended the embankment to join Warner and Crump. D'Ambrosio viewed Crump's slight stature and wet, disheveled appearance, and noticed his open fly.

Detective Bernie Crooke and Henry Wiggins were standing at the top of the embankment adjacent to the towpath when they heard D'Ambrosio shouting, "We got him! We got him!" As Wiggins looked down the embankment, he told the young detective that Crump looked like the man he'd seen. That was a good-enough identification for Crooke to confront the suspect. He identified himself as a detective assigned to the Homicide Squad and placed an incredulous Ray Crump under arrest.

"What did I do?" Crump asked. Detective Crooke warned him that he didn't have to talk or make a statement, but that if he did, it could be used against him at a trial. Even so, Crump seemed eager to talk. He had left his house in Southeast Washington that morning, he told the detective, with a fishing rod and some chicken innards as bait, and he had taken the bus to Wisconsin Avenue and M Street. He'd walked down the towpath and through the woods to the river to go fishing. Crooke wanted to know what Crump was wearing when he left home—had he been wearing a jacket and a cap? Crump told the detective that he had been wearing what he had on, and nothing else.

Detective Crooke then asked Ray why his fly was unzipped. Crump hesitated, looked down at his trousers, and replied that Crooke had caused it to unzip when he grabbed his belt. Crooke took offense at Crump's reply. He was standing in front of the suspect and hadn't touched him. Crump appeared to Crooke to be disoriented as he patted him down, and Crooke thought he smelled alcohol on his breath. Handcuffed, Ray Crump was led up the embankment to the towpath and past Chief Detective Art Weber. Like Detective Warner, Chief Detective Weber would later admit, under cross-examination at trial, that the man they had taken into custody that day didn't match the description that had gone out on the police radio bulletin. In spite of this, Weber instructed Crooke to take Crump to Homicide and book him for murder.

Ray Crump was put under arrest at approximately 1:15 P.M., and he waited quietly in handcuffs at the murder scene for almost a full hour before being taken downtown to Homicide for booking. He still didn't appear to understand what was happening, or what was about to occur. With a suspect now in custody, Sergeant Pasquale D'Ambrosio walked down to the Potomac riverfront where Ray Crump said he had been fishing. There were no rocks or fishing gear in sight. Homicide Detective Ronald Banta, who was overseeing a search for a jacket, a cap, and a murder weapon, joined D'Ambrosio. Meanwhile, someone who was never identified had already radioed River Patrolman police officer Frederick Byers of the Harbor Precinct "at about one o'clock or a little after" to instruct him to look for a "light-colored" jacket in connection with the shooting on the C & O Canal.[21] In response, Byers slowly navigated his police patrol boat through the Georgetown channel of the Potomac River. Close to 45 minutes later, three hundred yards upstream from Three Sisters Island—an outcrop of rocks covered with sparse vegetation—Byers observed a jacket floating in the water two feet from the shoreline. He maneuvered his boat as close as he could to the jacket and used a boathook to fish it out of the river. Returning downstream, he handed the jacket over to Detective Banta, who delivered it to Detective Crooke at Homicide about an hour later.[22] Inspecting the jacket, Crooke removed a sodden pack of Pall Mall cigarettes from the right-hand pocket.

Deputy Coroner Dr. Linwood L. Rayford arrived at the murder scene by 2:00 P.M. and pronounced the unknown victim dead at 2:05.[23] Dr. Rayford observed that rigor mortis had not yet set in, which meant that she couldn't have been dead for more than two hours. He also noted that the dead woman had been shot twice—once in the left temple anterior to her ear and once in the back. A tear in her corduroy slacks revealed an abraded knee, suggesting that the woman had been dragged or had crawled through brush. There were superficial lacerations and abrasions on her forehead, left knee, and ankle, indicating that she had fought her assailant.[24] Dr. Rayford ordered the body removed to the morgue by a D.C. Fire Department ambulance that had been parked at the Foundry Underpass. Police informed the coroner that a suspect, identified by an eyewitness, was now in custody.

Before going downtown to police headquarters, Henry Wiggins returned with Detective Edwin Coppage and U.S. Park Police detective Charles Stebbins to the exact spot from which he had seen the man standing over the dead woman. Wiggins noticed something peculiar: The stalled Nash Rambler that he and Bill Branch had been called to fix that morning was gone. The work order to service "a broken down car" on Canal Road had originated at the Key Bridge Esso Station. A trip ticket should have existed, but station manager Joe Cameron wasn't able to produce any record of the service call for the Nash Rambler. There was no sales slip, no receipt of payment, no indication that repairs had even been attempted. The vehicle's owner and registration were unknown. "I don't know the disposition of the vehicle because I didn't finish servicing the vehicle," Wiggins later said. "It was a stalled vehicle, but I don't even know that." His partner, Bill Branch, hadn't repaired the car, either, he later said. In the swirl of commotion that surrounded the murder scene, the Nash Rambler had disappeared.[25]

Ray Crump Jr. was sticking to his story. During the drive to police headquarters, he kept asking Crooke, "What did I do?" Each time, Crooke replied, "You tell me what you did." Crump would say only that he had been drinking. He had been fishing from some rocks and had fallen into the river. He was still shivering in his wet clothes, and Crooke suggested that he might be more comfortable if he took off his wet sweatshirt. In a white T-shirt that clung to his narrow chest, Crump appeared frail and childlike, much younger than his twenty-five years. A press photographer was waiting for the arrival of the black man suspected of murdering a white woman on the towpath. Crump bowed his head to avert the glare of flashbulbs as the photographer captured his arrival at police homicide headquarters.

Detective Crooke led Crump to a windowless interrogation room. Just a few months earlier, on June 22, 1964, the Supreme Court under Chief Justice Earl Warren had ruled in a 5-4 decision that a suspect had the right to have an attorney present during questioning. The ruling emanated from *Escobedo v. Illinois* and became known as the Escobedo Rule. Crooke was well aware of the ruling but chose not to inform Crump of his right to an attorney. The *Miranda* decision, which would have required Crooke to notify Crump, prior to questioning, of his right to an attorney, would not be decided for another two years.

"I think he's the guilty person," Bernie Crooke would later explain by way of justification for ignoring Crump's rights. "Not for any piece of evidence against him, but because of that other sense you develop about witnesses and defendants. You sort of know."[26] Crooke may have had an additional motivation to prove his suspect's guilt. One year earlier, a judge ruled in a defendant's favor arguing that the confession that Crooke had extracted from him was no good. "The judge said [Crooke] practiced very sophisticated methods of psychological brutality," a colleague said of the case. "Bernie couldn't even spell the words he used. And here he was, just a poor cop, trying to make a living."[27] Crooke apparently didn't want to suffer the humiliation of losing again.

Detective Crooke ordered Crump to put on the jacket that had just been fished out of the Potomac. It was a perfect fit. "It looks like you got a stacked deck," Crump said, close to tears. Crooke patted him on the back, and Crump began to cry.[28] Crooke felt certain that he was on the verge of extracting a confession when a lieutenant burst into the room, in complete contravention of the prohibition against interrupting an investigation, and he demanded to know when Crooke was going to set up the lineup. The young detective became furious. He ordered the officer out of the room and followed him.

"You've got all these goddamn detectives here, why can't they set it up?" Crooke wanted to know.

By the time Crooke returned to the interrogation room, Crump appeared to have pulled himself together. He had stopped crying and was staring at his shoes. Crooke decided to leave him to set up the lineup. Part of the preparation would involve instructing Henry Wiggins, his only eyewitness, what to do.

"He told me to go right up to [Crump], put my hands on him, and say, 'This is the guy. That's him,' so there's no doubt in my mind, no 'ifs' or anything," Wiggins recalled years later.[29]

Ray Crump was easy to pick out in the lineup. "The lineup isn't that close as far as the other guys being Crump's type, so he really sticks out," Wiggins recalled. Crump didn't react when Wiggins identified him. "He didn't act concerned, like he isn't bothered about anything. He looks like he knows what to do: just keep your mouth shut and don't say anything," Wiggins later said.[30]

What Henry Wiggins didn't remember that day was that he and twenty-five-year-old Ray Crump Jr. had been classmates, first at Briggs Elementary in Washington, then in junior high school, from which they had graduated in 1954. Neither school at the time was integrated, but Wiggins had gone on to Western High School and had graduated. Crump had given up on school after junior high. A friend of Wiggins's had reminded him that he knew Crump after Wiggins had identified him.[31]

Wiggins gave a formal statement about what he had observed that day, and Crooke showed him the windbreaker that had been found near the shoreline of the Potomac. "That looks like the jacket," Wiggins said, referring to the one worn by the man he had seen standing over the dead woman on the towpath.

Henry Wiggins was "satisfied" that he'd made law enforcement's case against Ray Crump. Even so, he knew that rumors had already begun to cloud the facts. "One of the detectives was saying they found Crump knee-deep in water in a shallow part of the river in a little inlet," Wiggins said. According to this version of events, Crump had said that "he was trying to retrieve his fishing rod," said Wiggins. Another version had it that Crump was in the water to wash the victim's blood off, while still another held that Crump was apprehended while he hid behind some rocks in the woods that bordered the river.[32]

Most of the speculation, however, centered on the identity of the beautiful dead woman. Who was she? And what was she doing on the towpath? Some parts of the canal, such as the concrete abutment and first arch supports of Key Bridge, had acquired unsavory reputations as havens for vagrants, truants, and dealers who supplied the affluent of Georgetown with recreational drugs. Henry Wiggins overheard one officer speculate that the murdered woman might have flirted with her killer. Wiggins didn't buy it. "She wasn't any bum or some old drunk like you'd expect down there," he said. "This woman you could tell was a lady."[33]

Detective Crooke gave Wiggins his card and told him not to talk to the press or anybody else about the case. Wiggins, who had once fancied himself cop material, apparently enjoyed his status at the center of this murder investigation; in fact, he had hoped to become a police officer in Washington, D.C., after his discharge from the Army. He had done some coursework—"in psychology, search and seizure, all that stuff"—and had passed the written exam, even dieted to meet the weight requirements, but "they still wouldn't take me," he said. He suspected that the color of his skin had something to do with his rejection.[34] In those days, the D.C. Metropolitan Police force was largely white. In any event, even though he hadn't passed muster as a potential police officer, Wiggins—a black man pointing the finger at another black man—seemed to be the ideal witness.

That afternoon, Ray Crump had been fingerprinted, photographed, weighed, and measured, but he wasn't tested for gunpowder burns or residue, which would have indicated whether he had recently fired a handgun. "His hands had been in water," Chief Detective Art Weber explained later at Crump's trial. "That would have washed away any nitrates that were present. The paraffin test wasn't what it's supposed to be. The FBI doesn't think much of it either, so we don't use it."[35] Lacking forensic evidence that would have linked Crump to the crime, police resorted to using his height and weight to help make their case. According to the intake documents, at the time of his arrest, Crump stood 5 feet 5½ inches and weighed 145 pounds—two inches taller and 15 pounds heavier than his driver's license indicated.[36] It was never clarified whether Crump had on his shoes with their 2-inch platform heels when he was measured, or whether he had been wearing wet clothes when he was weighed. Still, he was significantly smaller than the original description of the wanted man listed on Police Form PD-251: 5 feet 8 inches to 5 feet 10 inches tall and 185 pounds.

The Legal Aid Society of the District of Columbia had been alerted to Ray Crump's arrival. Legal Aid public defenders typically represented indigent clients at preliminary criminal hearings, at coroner's inquests, and at mental health hearings. "We were right there on the fourth floor of the courthouse, room 4830," said George Peter Lamb, a former defense attorney. "Our offices would be notified if someone was being brought in. It wouldn't be too long after the arrest. D.C. had the most restrictive laws on preliminary hearings of any federal court in the United States. Police were required to bring an arrested person before a magistrate as soon as it was feasible. To dillydally and hold a suspect in jail and interrogate the hell out of him was one sure way to result in the suppression of all evidence."[37]

Lamb was one of five new lawyers brought into the office by Edward "Ted" O'Neill, the sharp-tongued, indefatigable public defender. Lamb had been working in the Public Defender's Office of the Legal Aid Society for just one month when he met Ray Crump. A graduate of American University's Washington College of Law, Lamb had accepted a cut in pay to take the job, with an annual salary of just $6,900. It wasn't much, he later joked, for "a dyslectic with ulcers, married with two kids."[38] But he was fired up about the work. "What made it an incredibly exciting time to be a criminal lawyer was that the Warren Court was in full swing," he recalled in 1990. "Decisions were coming down that were upsetting long-established procedures that had been used as evidence in American courts for centuries." Lamb considered himself part of the revolution that was taking place in criminal law to balance the inherently unequal contest between the individual and the state.

As a public defender, Lamb reserved particular admiration for Judge David Bazelon of the U.S. Court of Appeals. "He was the bane of the conservatives," Lamb recalled. "He'd invite all these young lawyers into his chambers and tell us how to be better, and he would talk about what the responsibility of a public defender was: Whatever could be done for the richest of the rich, it was our job to do for the poorest of the poor. We spared no effort in that respect, and that was pretty thrilling, and really very exciting."[39] That afternoon, Lamb had hurried to the basement stockade to interview the new prisoner and to discern whether he met the criteria for a court-appointed lawyer.

He did. At the time of his arrest, Ray Crump had only $1.50 in his pocket. He didn't have a bank account. He didn't own real estate, an automobile, or any other valuable property, nor did his wife, Helena, his parents, or any other person who might have been able to assist in paying the costs of his defense. Lamb conducted a background check on his new client and found that he was married with five children. He had been twice arrested for disorderly behavior and he had served sixty days for shoplifting.

Years later, Lamb recalled how scared Crump had been. "He had to know when he was arrested that he would be charged with first-degree murder. You can be sure that during the time he went through the booking procedure at Homicide, the police were beating him up trying to get a confession out of him—not physically, because that was pretty much a thing of the past in this town." Crump was crying, Lamb said. He repeatedly told Lamb that he didn't know what had gone on at the canal, that he hadn't killed anybody, and that the police had arrested the wrong man.[40]

Lamb explained to Crump the first step: In a first-floor hearing room, the police would try to establish before a magistrate that there was enough evidence to hold him for a grand jury. Crump would either be charged or released. What Lamb didn't tell his client was that with U.S. Commissioner Sam Wertleb presiding—a "curmudgeon," in Lamb's opinion—the chances were slim that Crump would be let go. "It wasn't possible to get a fair hearing from him," Lamb said. "Wertleb almost always accepted the word of a police officer against that of a defendant, especially a black defendant."[41] Wertleb did inform Crump, however, of his right to counsel and to a preliminary hearing, but he declined to schedule the hearing. "I don't know why I'm here," Crump blurted out. "I was down there fishing and lost my rod. I almost got shot myself."[42]

Crump was held without bail. "The way to get around granting bail was to say Crump was a danger to the community by reason of what he's been charged with," Lamb recalled. "So denial of bail was purely on the basis of the heinousness of the crime. When, in fact, the only evidence the government had at this point was whatever Detective Bernie Crooke said it was."

With bail denied, "you've got to move quick to try to prevent the government from bringing an original indictment," Lamb said. "We went straight to the Court of Appeals on the bail issue and denial of a preliminary hearing the next morning with Ted [O'Neill] and I leading the charge. Already there was some strong heat coming down on this case from somewhere—we didn't know where. That's why we were in court so damn fast, to try to set up a preliminary hearing. The reason you wanted a prelim, it was the only chance you had to cross-examine witnesses and find out what the police had for evidence. So you freeze the case in a timeline so that it never gets any better, unless the police find something new. And all they had was Crump being in the vicinity of the murder. He was just somebody who'd been identified as being there."[43]

Shackled and under heavy guard, Crump was taken by federal marshals to the D.C. jail and placed in isolation. Crump changed into prison denims but kept his shoes. The guard urged him to confess, saying that if he did, he would get the help he was entitled to, possibly even a deal with the prosecutor, but Crump remained confused. "What was going on down in that place?" he wanted to know. The officers who arrested him hadn't told him anything. When he had been escorted in handcuffs past the bloodied body of the dead woman on the towpath, Crump had asked Detective Crooke, "You think I did *that?*" Crooke hadn't answered.

Meanwhile, something weighed heavily on the freshly minted public defender, George Peter Lamb. Though new to his job, he was savvy enough to know that it was highly unusual for Assistant U.S. Attorney Donald Smith to be representing the government at Ray Crump's hearing. "That was unheard of to send a senior man to one of these things," Lamb said. "Usually, a very inexperienced criminal assistant would be there just to observe the proceedings. So right away, we knew there was some 'Mickey Mouse' stuff going on."[44]

Donald Smith's presence signaled that somewhere within the corridors of the U.S. Department of Justice an alarm had sounded. But why? Surely not because of Ray Crump, who wouldn't have merited such high-level attention. It had to be the murder itself—and the murder victim. Given the crime's location—right in the heart of Washington's elite Georgetown enclave—was it that the dead woman was one of *them,* a person of consequence in her Georgetown milieu? But the police had not yet determined her identity.

Detective Bernard Crooke, on arriving at the D.C. morgue, was immediately granted access to an autopsy room where Randolph M. Worrell, the morgue technician, had already logged in the body of a white female, name and address unknown. Worrell had taken a sample of blood that would be delivered for classification to the FBI the following day. He had prepared the body for examination by removing her clothes in the presence of Deputy Coroner Dr. Linwood L. Rayford.

The autopsy officially began at 3:45 P.M. For Dr. Rayford, a tall, light-skinned black man with a military bearing and a handsome face, medicine had been a second career choice. As a student at Marquette University during World War II, Rayford had tried to enlist. "I wanted to be the first black Marine in the history of the Corps," he recalled. "But they wouldn't take me. I got turned down on account of my color."[45] Now a surgeon, Rayford had performed more than four hundred autopsies on gunshot victims, but none had been as disturbing as this one. "Things were not at all like they were supposed to be," he would say years later. The woman was five feet six inches tall and weighed 127 pounds. She was a beautiful corpse. Dr. Rayford had lifted the woman's arms and rotated them across her torso to determine the degree of muscular rigor. The limbs were relatively supple. He touched her thigh, stomach, and chest; the pale, almost translucent skin was cool, which told him that she had been dead only a few hours. Her blue-green eyes bore an expression that revealed that death had come as a complete surprise.[46]

The woman had been shot twice: once in the head and once in the back. Both entry wounds were a quarter of an inch in diameter and bore dark halos typical of powder burns. "The gun was fired from close range," Rayford would later testify. "It wouldn't be possible to produce these smoke deposits on a person's skin at anything but contact or near contact firing."[47] The FBI later confirmed this.

The victim's head wound was located an "inch and a half anterior to the left ear." The first bullet had entered the left side of the skull, "traversed into the right temporal lobe, fractured it, and ricocheted back where the slug was found in the right side of the brain," where Rayford recovered it. The second entry wound "was located over the right shoulder blade, about six inches from the midline." The bullet had passed through the shoulder blade "into the chest cavity perforating the right lung and the aorta, the largest vessel from the heart." The trajectory "had been angled from right to left and slightly downward."[48]

The woman likely survived the first shot to her head, but Rayford said that such a wound's attendant hemorrhaging and brain lacerations would probably have rendered her unconscious. Blood from the head wound would likely have splattered the assailant. In contrast, the second wound would have produced more internal than external bleeding because of its position under the shoulder blade.[49]

The second gunshot had been fired with particular precision: The bullet pierced the right lung and severed the aorta. Death would have been instantaneous. That bothered Rayford. The degree of expertise suggested the work of a professional. He had seen some messy gangland-style slayings, but nothing like the neat accuracy of the wounds inflicted on this victim. "Whoever assaulted this woman," Rayford said years later, "intended to kill her."[50]

Crooke took possession of the two bullets and the victim's clothing. He would deliver them to the FBI Crime Lab for testing the next day, but first he inspected the clothes for some kind of mark that might identify the victim. He found one. On the silk lining next to the fraying Mark Cross label inside one of the blood-soaked gloves, the name "Meyer" had been written in blue ink.

By telephone from the morgue, Crooke instructed the desk officer at the Seventh Precinct at Volta Place in Georgetown to call all the Meyers in the Washington telephone directory. The dead woman could well be visiting from another city, he remembered thinking, but it was more likely that she was a local resident on an afternoon stroll not far from her home.[51]

Crooke left the morgue and drove to Southeast Washington to retrace the bus route that Ray Crump said he had taken that morning, supposedly to go fishing on the Potomac. Anacostia was another Washington, a world apart from Georgetown. It was a crime-ridden ghetto of dilapidated houses where the majority of residents were black. Crooke knocked on the door of 2109 Stanton Terrace, S.E., and was invited into a tidy, spare living room by Helena Crump, a slender young woman who held the youngest of her five children, a baby, in her arms. Her eyes instantly reflected fear and anger, and with good reason. To the black community, the police represented both a threat and indifference. Crime festered in poor neighborhoods like Anacostia, mainly because law enforcement officials allowed it to do so.

Helena Crump had learned about her husband's arrest from a neighbor who had heard it on the radio. Ray Crump had been working as a day laborer at the Brown Construction Company's building site at Southeast Hospital. Construction was the best-paid job that an unskilled worker could get. It was better than hustling trash or the other menial work available to uneducated black men. The work was seasonal, and strenuous: unloading heavy bags of cement, mixing mortar, and pushing loaded wheelbarrows. It was backbreaking work for someone as slight as Crump. He had recently told his coworker Robert Woolright that he didn't think he'd be able to keep it up.

Woolright had driven to Crump's house to give him a ride to work on the morning of the murder. "Most of the time off and on, I pick him up whenever we was on a job together," Woolright had recalled.[52] He parked in front of Crump's house at 7:25 A.M. and waited for him to come out. Instead, his wife came out. She had been arguing with her husband, who'd said he was too tired to go to work that day and was "tired of hearing all that shit" about money. Helena handed Woolright a set of keys to the work shed at the construction site and returned to the house. Woolright drove away. A half-hour later, Crump announced that he was going out. Helena didn't know where he was going, but, she told Detective Crooke, he wasn't going fishing. She opened a closet door to show Crooke a fishing rod and tackle box packed in the corner. She also identified the damp Windbreaker that Crooke had brought with him in an evidence bag. It had been a Father's Day present from her and the children the preceding June.[53]

Ray Crump also smoked Pall Mall cigarettes, "the same as I do," said Elsie Perkins, Crump's neighbor. "I open mine from the bottom; he opens his from the top. That's how we can tell the difference in our cigarettes," she told Crooke, who had knocked on her door after leaving Helena Crump. Good-humored and garrulous, Perkins told Crooke that she was close with the Crumps and that she and Helena Crump maintained an informal security system. "It's just habit. She watched who came in my house and who went out. And I would look out to see who was coming out or coming in her house." That's how she happened to see Ray Jr. leaving his house around eight in the morning. "I just wanted to see who was coming out of the house."[54]

Crump got as far as the tree at the end of the sidewalk, then turned around, Perkins said. "That's how I happened to see the front of him, when he walked back to the house for something." Crump had been wearing a yellow sweatshirt, a half-zipped beige jacket, dark trousers, and dark shoes, she said. "He had on a white T-shirt because you could see it from the neck of his sweat shirt. And he had on a kind of plaid cap with a bill over it." When the Crumps' door closed again, Perkins had looked out "to see whether or not that was him coming out or his wife." She had watched Ray Jr. until he got halfway down to the bend that led over to Stanton Road. Crump wasn't carrying any fishing gear, although on previous occasions she had seen him with a fishing pole, "and he'd carry a dark little box with his fishing tools."[55]

Might Crump have been carrying a gun with him when he left the house? Perkins didn't think so. "I didn't see his pockets bulge like he was carrying a weapon," she told Crooke. She had never seen Ray Jr. with a gun in his possession, or known him to have one. Nor had anyone else in Crump's family or the community.[56]

A motive for the murder was proving elusive. Had Ray Crump gone to Georgetown intending to commit a robbery? An emerging version of events went like this: Crump accosted a well-dressed white woman walking along on the C & O Canal towpath. When she resisted, he panicked and shot her in the head without killing her. Still conscious, she had broken free and made it to the other side of the towpath at the top of the embankment, where Crump grabbed her, dragged her some twenty-five feet back to the edge of the canal, and pressed a gun to her back, this time issuing a fatal shot.

But had it been Crump that Henry Wiggins had seen standing over the dead woman, or was it someone dressed like him? The police maintained that it was Crump, who, they alleged, had fled the murder scene by descending the embankment to the Potomac, where he disposed of the murder weapon, as well as the hat and the jacket on the basis of which Wiggins had identified him. Because of their quick response in getting to the scene and cutting off all of the park's exits, the police believed they had trapped the assailant—who they now believed was Crump. The police claimed that Crump had tried to swim away since the river had been the only means of escape, but that the river's dangerous current had stopped him. Several people had, indeed, drowned there over the years. So, the police speculated that Crump had taken to the woods, trying to avoid capture. Discovering the exit at Fletcher's Boat House blocked by police, then momentarily being spotted by police officer Roderick Sylvis, he had made his way back eastward toward Key Bridge, where he was finally encountered by Detective Warner.

Police suspicions were bolstered by the fact that Crump had lied about going fishing. And he had lied about what he was wearing on the morning of the murder. The circumstantial evidence, the police believe, was mounting against him. What they didn't know was that Ray Crump couldn't swim. In fact, he was terrified of being in water over his head.

But what wasn't clear was how a panicked mugger, in the wake of a botched holdup, could have killed a woman with the cool dispatch of a professional assassin. According to Henry Wiggins, it had been a quick kill: Two shots were fired, the second of which came about eight to ten seconds after the first. Yet Wiggins had not witnessed the murder; he had only heard the shots and observed a man standing over the victim in the aftermath. And he had watched that man walk calmly away from the scene. The viciousness of the attack and the calm of the assailant were hard to square with the demeanor of the frightened, meek Raymond Crump Jr. By the end of the day, the murder weapon had not been recovered; and in its absence, the police had only Henry Wiggins's inconclusive account to link Crump to the murder.

October 12, 1964, had finally unfolded into an Indian summer gem with a temperature that rose into the low sixties. By the time the late afternoon sun had begun to set, every Meyer in the Washington telephone directory, save one, had been contacted. The one remaining Meyer lived in a modest two-story house, 1523 Thirty-Fourth Street, N.W., in Georgetown. Homicide Detective Sergeant Sam Wallace located number 1523, wedged into a narrow lot amid a cluster of houses. There were no lights on when he pulled up out front at about 5:30 P.M. A locked car was parked in the driveway. A hand-lettered sign at the door advertised "Free Kittens. Ring bell or call."

Neighbors identified the house as belonging to Mary Pinchot Meyer. They also disclosed that Mary's sister, Tony, and her husband, Ben Bradlee, lived around the corner at 3321 N Street, N.W. The block was familiar territory to the Seventh Precinct police because they had assisted the Secret Service in protecting President-elect John F. Kennedy until he moved from the neighborhood into the White House in 1960. Ben Bradlee had been close to the senator from Massachusetts, who lived in a red brick, three-story townhouse several doors down from his own.

Detective Wallace knocked on Bradlee's door and identified himself. Increasingly certain by process of elimination that the victim was Bradlee's sister-in-law, Wallace asked him if he would come identify the woman murdered earlier that day on the C & O Canal towpath. "Sometime after six o'clock in the evening," according to Bradlee, he identified Mary Meyer "with a bullet hole in her head" at the D.C. morgue. He would repeat the process for Deputy Coroner Rayford the following morning in the presence of his friend and pharmacist, Harry Dalinsky.[57]

The *Evening Star* ran a front-page, one-column story that evening: "Woman Shot Dead on Canal Tow Path." The article identified neither Mary Meyer nor the lead murder suspect, Ray Crump Jr. The article did note, however, that "police found a white jacket, possibly worn by the slayer, on the bank of the canal some distance from the scene about an hour later."[58] In fact, the jacket had been found along the Potomac River shoreline, not the canal. The inaccuracy aside, it wasn't known how or from whom the press acquired the detail about the jacket. Its inclusion in the article, however, seemed to support the emerging narrative that had Crump ditching his jacket before trying to flee the scene by swimming away from it.

By the following morning, Tuesday, October 13, the national print and television media had latched onto the story. In Washington, both the *Evening Star* and the *Washington Post* ran front-page stories that featured photographs of Mary Pinchot Meyer and Ray Crump, the latter shown in handcuffs at police headquarters. Shock waves reverberated throughout the tiny Georgetown enclave in which Mary had been so vivid a presence. With Bradlee's confirmation of her identity, the newspapers informed their readers that Meyer was the niece of former two-term Pennsylvania governor Gifford Pinchot, as well as "a Georgetown artist with a hundred thousand friends."[59] Her ex-husband, Cord Meyer, was identified either as "an author and government employee" or "presently employed by the Federal Government."[60] Neither paper mentioned his real work as a high-level operative within the CIA's Directorate of Plans, though in Mary's obituary in the *New York Times* the following day, Cord was said to be employed in New York by the Central Intelligence Agency.[61]

With no murder weapon found, Chief Detective Art Weber returned to the towpath to direct a search that would become unprecedented in its scope and manpower. Weber led forty Metropolitan Police officers, assisted by members of the U.S. Park Police, on a foot-by-foot search of the towpath area. Park Service police also closed a canal lock upstream from the murder scene. As the waters receded, two U.S. Navy scuba divers entered the canal. Six more Navy divers entered the Potomac River adjacent to the shoreline where Crump's jacket had been found the day before. Harbor police probed the river with grappling hooks and dragged the bottom with magnets in an area near the site of Crump's capture. They found a brimmed golf cap at the water's edge in the area where Crump had said he'd been fishing. The FBI Crime Lab would later link a single hair found on the cap to Crump. Detective Weber was buoyed by the find and felt certain that Ray Crump must have also disposed of the gun in that vicinity.

The searches ended at dusk and resumed the following morning, "when we returned with more men," Weber recalled. "We had mine detectors sweep over and around the forest in the woods." But two days of intense searching still did not produce the .38-caliber pistol that had ended the life of Mary Meyer. Nevertheless, Weber remained confident: "If the gun's here, we'll find it."[62] In fact, the gun would never be found.

In the absence of a murder weapon and with the attempted robbery theory seeming less likely, the police next considered sexual assault as the motive. Hadn't Ray Crump's zipper been undone when he was apprehended? But forensic evidence didn't support this theory, either. Four days after the murder, on October 16, 1964, the FBI Crime Laboratory delivered its forensic report to Chief Robert V. Murray at the Metropolitan Police Department (see appendix 1). This report, illegally withheld from Crump's defense attorneys for nearly nine months, was finally produced for the defense at the time of the trial in July 1965. Had it been available subsequent to October 16, when it was first delivered to police, Ray Crump Jr. would likely have been released for lack of evidence.

The FBI Crime Lab report documented that (1) there was no evidence that any "recently discharged firearm had been placed into one of these [Crump's alleged jacket] pockets"; (2) "no semen was identified on the clothing of the victim [Mary Meyer] and suspect [Ray Crump]"; (3) "no fibers were found on the suspect's [Crump's] clothing that could be associated with victim's [Mary Meyer's] clothing"; (4) "no Negroid hairs were found in the debris removed from specimens Q5 through Q9 [clothes Mary Meyer was wearing]. No Caucasian hairs were found in the debris removed from specimens Q12, Q13, and Q14 [Crump's beige jacket recovered after the murder, his yellow sweatshirt, and his T-shirt]"; and, finally, (5) "the examination of specimens Q13 and Q14 [Crump's yellow sweat shirt, and T-shirt] disclosed no indication of the presence of blood on these specimens." There had been two small "faint red smears" on the back of Crump's alleged jacket, which the FBI Crime Lab report had analyzed as having "a wax like appearance when viewed microscopically" and therefore concluded they were not blood stains, but possible "lipstick smears."[63]

In fact, the police had no real evidence against Ray Crump at all, other than his being in the vicinity of the crime. There was no blood, hair, semen, saliva, urine, or fibers from Ray Crump's clothing—no forensic evidence whatsoever—that linked Crump to Mary Meyer or the murder scene. Given the quantity of blood found at the scene and on the victim, it seemed unlikely that Crump—had he administered the gunshots that killed her—would have escaped without a single drop of her blood on his skin or clothing. It also seemed unlikely that Ray Crump, shorter than Mary Meyer and weighing not much more than she, would have been able to drag her twenty-five feet across the towpath in the midst of an intense struggle.

If not robbery or sexual assault, what had been the motive behind the murder of Mary Meyer? Why, in possession of only limited circumstantial evidence against Crump, had D.C. law enforcement officials not looked for other suspects? To be sure, Crump had denied wearing the Windbreaker and golf cap, and he had lied about going fishing the morning of the murder—both of which had severely damaged his credibility. But without a murder weapon and any forensic evidence linking him to the crime, police lacked sufficient evidence to hold him. Nonetheless, despite this evidentiary void, it seemed as if Crump's fate was being quickly sealed.

The morning after the murder—October 13—the case against Ray Crump received an unexpected boost. While Detective Crooke was delivering evidence to the FBI Crime Lab, a U.S. Army lieutenant named William L. Mitchell arrived at police headquarters. Introducing himself to Captain

George R. Donahue of the Homicide Squad, Mitchell said that he had read about the woman's murder that morning and believed that he had passed her while running on the towpath the day before. Stationed nearby at the Pentagon, Mitchell explained, he ran on the towpath most days at lunchtime. According to police, Mitchell "described in detail the clothes worn by Mrs. Meyer." He said she was crossing the narrow wooden footbridge, walking west "away from Key Bridge," when he had come to a complete stop to allow her to cross before him. About two hundred yards later, he said, he passed "a Negro male" wearing a dark cap and a light-colored Windbreaker jacket with dark trousers and dark shoes. The clothing description was almost identical to that given by Henry Wiggins in his recollection of the man he had seen standing over the dead body at the murder scene, noted the *Evening Star* two days after the murder.[64]

"Today's surprise witness impressed homicide detectives with the detail of his description of both Mrs. Meyer's apparel and that of the man he saw following her," said a reporter for the *Washington Daily News*.[65] In the public mind, the gallows for Ray Crump was already being prepared.

Mitchell's account, however, left a few details unexplained, and the police didn't seem to want to consider them. If Mitchell's timing was correct, could he really have run the distance to Key Bridge without hearing gunshots? And if Ray Crump had been "two hundred yards" behind Mary only a few minutes before the crime was committed more than a tenth of a mile away, after Mitchell passed him, he would have had to run with the strongest of intention to subdue Mary by the time Henry Wiggins claimed to have seen him standing over the body.

However foreboding, Mitchell's intrusion into the landscape boded ill for the poor, black day laborer Ray Crump. His account was enough to convict Crump in the minds of police, the public, and the media. The archetypical racial subtext of a downtrodden black man sexually assaulting an aristocratic white woman had immediately ignited the subliminal racial bigotry of Washington's elite corridors of power. The Army lieutenant, Mitchell, presented himself as a model citizen: He was a military officer, serving his country at the Pentagon. He was also white, and like it or not, his statement—and credibility—carried more weight than that of a black tow truck driver named Henry Wiggins Jr., though it further legitimized Wiggins's account as well. With no other leads, and certainly no other suspects, Mitchell's and Wiggins's statements taken together were enough to support a murder charge against Ray Crump, regardless of the dearth of real evidence.

3

Conspiracy to Conceal

Nobody believes a rumor here in Washington until it's officially denied.
—Edward Cheyfitz

It's not the crime that gets you, it's the cover-up.
—President Richard Nixon

O N OCTOBER 14, 1964, just two days after the Georgetown murder of Mary Meyer, her mourners filed into Washington National Cathedral for the funeral. The day was also her forty-fourth birthday. The burial service took place at 2:00 P.M. in Bethlehem Chapel on the lower level of the church. It was the same place that Mary had chosen for the funeral of her nine-year-old son Michael in December 1956.

After the funeral, Mary Pinchot Meyer was laid to rest next to son Michael on a ridge at the Pinchot family burial plot in the Milford, Pennsylvania, cemetery, just a short distance from her family's estate, Grey Towers. The previous year, the Pinchot family had donated a portion of their estate to the U.S. Forest Service. Mary, along with her sister and other family members, had accompanied President Kennedy to Grey Towers for the dedication on September 24, 1963, of the Pinchot Institute for Conservation. Publicly, the event had celebrated the environmentally conscious pioneering work of Mary's uncle Gifford Pinchot, but privately, the furtive glances between Mary and Jack that day marked a turning point for the secret lovers and their mission together. For on that day, during the dedication at Grey Towers, President Kennedy learned that the Senate had ratified his Limited Nuclear Test Ban Treaty with the Soviets by a vote of 80-19. His intention of creating such a treaty had been revealed for the first time three months earlier during his commencement address at American University. The unprecedented speed with which the treaty had been negotiated during the summer of 1963 was due in large part to his Soviet counterpart, Nikita Khrushchev. Kennedy and Khrushchev had become secret partners in the pursuit of world peace; both wanted to bring the Cold War to an end. The significance of the treaty ratification that day was not lost on Mary. She had, according to Kenny O'Donnell's statements to Leo Damore, become a beacon for Jack as he explored a new trajectory after the near calamity of the Cuban Missile Crisis, which could have easily made the entire planet uninhabitable had it not been resolved. Though there was no possibility of a public declaration of love, the two secret lovers had exchanged smiles and small nods on hearing the news from Washington that day. It was a turning point in President Kennedy's newfound political direction.[1]

But at her funeral a year later, among the elite of Washington who filled the pews—their presence a testament to her social standing and appeal—very few knew how extensive Mary's influence had been. The mourners included historian and presidential insider Arthur Schlesinger Jr.; journalist Theodore White; former presidential assistant McGeorge Bundy; Richard Helms, the CIA's deputy director for plans; Katharine Graham, owner of the *Washington Post*; and Madame Hervé Alphand, wife of the popular French ambassador. Also present was journalist Charlie Bartlett, a Yale classmate of Cord Meyer's and a very close friend of President Kennedy's, and his wife, Martha. The Bartletts had introduced Jack to Jackie at a dinner party in 1951. But Jacqueline Kennedy, flaunted as "a close friend" of Mary Meyer's, did not attend. Several of Mary's Vassar College classmates were also in attendance, including Scottie Fitzgerald Lanahan, the daughter of F. Scott Fitzgerald; my mother, Mary Draper Janney, and my father, Wistar Janney; and journalist Anne Chamberlin, also a dear friend to Mary. Cicely d'Autremont Angleton, another close friend of Mary's, was present and sat between her husband, Jim Angleton, and Cord Meyer.[2] In addition, a score of Mary's fellow artists lined the pews. Even in death, the "Georgetown artist with a hundred thousand friends" seemed to draw them all to her farewell gathering.[3]

Two of the four pallbearers—William ("Bill") Walton and Kenneth Noland—were artists, like Mary herself. Bill Walton had formerly been a journalist and a war correspondent. He was a close, discreet confidante to both Jack and Bobby Kennedy, as well as to Jackie. Divorced, and reportedly more inclined to the same sex, Walton had functioned as Mary's escort to many

White House social functions where she and Jack often captured a few intimate, stolen moments together. Ken Noland had been a progenitor of the Washington Color School of art in the late 1950s. He and Mary had been intimately involved immediately after her separation and divorce from Cord. New York art dealer André Emmerich, who did not attend the funeral, recalled that Noland had told him that "the art world in Washington was buzzing with rumors that Mary's murder was in some way connected with her love affair with JFK." On that day, however, secrets for the most part were being kept.

Was it mere coincidence or irony that Mary's two other pallbearers were high-level CIA officials Jim Angleton and Wistar Janney, both longtime close friends of Mary's ex-husband, Cord Meyer, who was also a high-ranking Agency operative? Of course, the mercurial, almost emaciated and ghostlike presence of James Jesus Angleton wasn't at all surprising. A close friend of Cord's since Yale, their friendship had endured and deepened as CIA colleagues. Angleton's outward proclivities and hobbies—photography, poetry, orchid growing, and fly-fishing, including designing and crafting his own fishing lures—suggested a modern-day Renaissance man of considerable talent and interest. Early on, he had ingratiated himself with Mary. She appreciated what appeared to be a man of unusual complexity and knowledge—so much so, in fact, that Jim Angleton had been designated as the godfather to the three Meyer children.

But Mary's close friendship with Angleton's wife, Cicely, had long ago made her aware of the shadows that lurked beneath Jim's exterior, nurtured by the endless rivers of gin and bourbon that spawned a kind of paranoia that demanded control and domination. Nonetheless, in 1964 Angleton was at the top of his game, and had already become something of a legend. A former member of the elite Office of Strategic Services (OSS) during World War II, Jim Angleton had distinguished himself early in his career; and for some unknown reason, Allen Dulles had handpicked him in 1954, when Angleton was only thirty-seven, for the position that he would hold for the duration of his career: chief of the CIA's counterintelligence division in the Directorate of Plans. Angleton would head the Agency's most secretive department. Colleagues, including many who feared him, often called him by such names as "Mother," "the locksmith," even "the CIA's answer to the Delphic Oracle." Angleton's reputation within the world of intelligence would remain epic during his entire life, and would extend even after his death in 1987. No one at Mary's funeral, however—except Angleton's titular boss, Richard Helms, and possibly one or two other Agency honchos—was aware that with the recently released Warren Report, Jim Angleton and his former chief, Allen Dulles (a Warren

Commission member), had just masterminded possibly the greatest cover-up in American history.

Mary Meyer had come to disdain the work of the intelligence establishment. It was one of the reasons why she had finally initiated her divorce from Cord. In 1951, Cord had succumbed to the recruiting tactics of Allen Dulles, seeing no possibility for the fledgling United World Federalists to keep the tenuous peace in an emerging Cold War. Seduced into betraying the vision that had originally united Mary with him in 1945, Cord's entrance into the CIA would eventually foreshadow a rupture in their union that would never heal. The Dulles inner circle soon surrounded Mary's life, complete with its lordly Ivy League sense of entitlement. No law, and certainly no moral compass, would be allowed to stand in the way of American hegemony, she soon learned. Her fights and pleadings with the man to whom she had pledged her deepest trust were to no avail. Mary's eventual escape in 1957, followed by divorce a year later, had been final, or so she thought.

Yet now, even in death, she was once again encircled. Mary's fourth pall-bearer was my father, Wistar Janney. Like Cord Meyer and so many others who joined the CIA in its infancy, Wistar Janney was part of an idealistic group of World War II veterans that never again wanted to see the possibility of a world at war. A strong, centralized post–World War II intelligence apparatus seemed like an almost ideal solution, and a good career for a group of men who were already, by birth, financially well endowed and secure. In the aftermath of World War II, America had come out on top. They wanted to keep it that way.

The youngest of six children of a wealthy, prominent investment banker, my father was raised in Bryn Mawr on Philadelphia's Main Line. His given name at birth, resembling an almost royal title, was Frederick Wistar Morris Janney. To his close friends, immediate colleagues, and family, he was "Wistar," or "Wis." To his CIA subordinates, he was known as Fred Janney. Educated at Phillips Exeter Academy, Wistar Janney graduated from Princeton in 1941. About to be drafted, he enlisted in the Navy to become a naval aviator, allegedly after viewing the movie *Flight Command,* starring Robert Taylor—in addition to having had yet another fight with his aloof, investment banker father. Piloting a Grumman Avenger torpedo bomber off the deck of an aircraft carrier in the Pacific theater, Wistar was not expected to survive by anyone in his family, including his father.

"When I strapped a Grumman Avenger to my ass, it was do or die," he murmured late one night, not wanting to recall the death of his fellow pilot and close friend Eddie Larkin during the Battle of Leyte Gulf in October 1944. He had not had the chance to reconcile with his father, who died unexpectedly just a few days before the largest naval battle in history. The father-son duo had remained estranged, in spite of the fact that Wistar's father—Walter Coggeshall Janney—knew his time was near. At the end of the summer of 1944, "Lord of the Manor" Walter elected to return to Bryn Mawr from his summer estate on Cape Cod in the station wagon driven by his caretaker-gardener John Martin, not in his customary chauffeur-driven Packard. Midway across the Bourne Bridge, which connected Cape Cod to the mainland, he ordered Martin to stop the car, whereupon he got out and took one last gaze at the Cape Cod panorama where his family and beloved progeny had, since the late 1920s, thrived amid the bounty and fortune he had amassed. At that moment, he told Martin that he would not live through another winter. Asking Martin "to stay on and take care of the estate and Mrs. Janney," he resumed his journey to Bryn Mawr.[4] The father-son schism, however, remained—passing through invisible ethers into the next generation and beyond.

Wistar Janney made sure that Eddie Larkin would be awarded the Navy Cross posthumously. Finally emerging victorious from battle, Janney himself came home with his own, and a slew of other medals. Every workday, he proudly wore his Navy Cross pin on his suit jacket's left lapel, sometimes along with his naval aviator necktie. Awarded one of Yale's first master of arts in Russian area studies in 1948, my father was soon recruited into the CIA by Allen Dulles, also a Princeton graduate. Technically, he was for many years a Soviet analyst in the Agency's Office of Current Intelligence (OCI), but it wasn't ever clear what Wistar's job(s) actually entailed. There were periodic trips to Europe, and then Iran. "Your father was a company man," said disaffected former CIA staffer and author Victor Marchetti in an interview for this book in 2005. More time would pass before I finally began to understand what that might mean.

At Mary's funeral, Wistar's pallbearer assignment had been requested by Cord in his hour of need. Wistar himself was never fond of Mary, particularly after she jettisoned Cord, devastating him, by all accounts. Moreover, what infuriated Wistar even more was the fact that over the years Mary had become increasingly outspoken about her displeasure with what the CIA was doing in the world. No other CIA wife had ever dared such public bluntness, certainly not Wistar's. But that hadn't stopped Mary Meyer, even if my father's well-oiled temper might be the kind of assault any civilized person would want to avoid. His signature point of view was that if you didn't work for the Agency, you really didn't know anything; furthermore, "opinions were like assholes—everyone had one," he would say as one of his favored retorts. Any discussion would quickly turn into what one friend in the late 1960s once called a kind of unending "Tet Offensive" with Wistar inevitably asserting at some point that the CIA had the only key to a treasure called "the truth." They (he, the CIA) knew; you didn't. End of conversation. How dare you think otherwise.

Seated immediately adjacent to Mary's casket was her ex-husband and their two remaining sons: Quentin, eighteen, and Mark, fourteen. Cord, habitually imperious, sobbed uncharacteristically throughout the ceremony. He had been away in New York on Agency business when Mary was murdered. Comforted by his CIA colleagues, as well as by Mary's mother, Ruth Pickering Pinchot, Cord was the recipient of a magnanimous show of support that included Ben and Tony Bradlee, Mary's younger sister and only sibling. Cord's grief, however, appeared to be purely ceremonial and ephemeral. After the funeral, he would "advise" his two remaining sons that there were to be no more tears over the loss of their mother.

Bishop Paul Moore Jr., suffragan bishop of the Episcopal Diocese of Washington, conducted the burial service from the Book of Common Prayer. A close friend of both Ben Bradlee and Cord Meyer, the bishop, like Cord himself, had gone to St. Paul's School, in Concord, New Hampshire, and then Yale, graduating in the class of 1941, a year and a half ahead of Cord. "I was away at a convention when the murder happened," Moore told author Leo Damore in 1991. "Benny [Ben Bradlee] called me and I flew in for the funeral."[5] Moore didn't have a pastoral relationship with Mary. "I knew her much better earlier [in her life]. She and Cord and my first wife and I were very close friends when Cord came back from overseas the same time I did, around the time they were married. I didn't see much of Mary in later years, so I wasn't close to her," he recalled. Even so, Moore was glad to officiate. "Over the years I've done weddings and funerals for the family. They weren't members of my parish or anything. I was, in an informal way, their official pastor. Most of those folks don't have any clergy friends they're close to. It's just that we're old friends, so it was natural for them to turn to a priest or bishop when they needed somebody."[6]

In his eulogy, Moore referred to "Mary's honesty, her friendship, her rare sensitivity, that beauty which walked with her and which flowed from her into each of our lives." But he could not answer the question that no doubt plagued many of those in attendance, although not all of them. "We cannot know why and how such a terrible, ugly, irrational thing should have happened. We can only sense that it was, in some way, bound up in this sin and sickness of the entire world."[7]

Perhaps at the time publicly oblivious, the suffragan bishop wasn't about to speak to any "pattern," invisible or not, among those who thought it possible to play God for the purposes of a well-ordered world. While Moore, like most Americans, may have been initially seduced into believing that Lee Harvey Oswald had killed the president, a few years later his personal awakening would impel him to champion civil rights for African Americans, stridently oppose the Vietnam War, and ordain an openly gay woman as a priest in the Episcopal Church. But that afternoon, Moore only requested prayers "for that poor, demented soul who has brought about this essentialist tragedy."[8]

"I remember catching a little criticism for that," Moore recalled. "Some folks thought it was inappropriate to pray for the person who had killed Mary. They were a little uneasy about it. This didn't come from the family. In fact, they thought it was okay—even positive." Moore's highest priority, he said, was "my relationship with the Pinchot family, which goes back to my parents. I didn't want to do anything that would in any way offend them."[9]

But even in the elite, affluent neighborhoods of Georgetown, home to many of Washington's global power brokers, the rumbling of rumors had already begun. There was talk, too, of some kind of cover-up, links to the Kennedy White House, perhaps even some CIA involvement, and even possibly "Soviet complicity" in her murder—this last from CIA counterintelligence chief Jim Angleton himself.[10]

Bishop Moore had not intended to presume guilt on the part of Ray Crump Jr. "On the contrary," Moore said in 1991, "I'm fascinated, obviously, because it's always bothered me. I never felt the police really put this case to bed. There was a lot of paranoia surrounding Mary's murder. And you know, you still hear a lot of rumors about it."[11] Moore's uncertainty, however, even in 1991, nearly thirty years after the murder took place, was not unique. There were a number of facts—and stories—that didn't add up, and were even contradictory, with more to come, leaving loose ends that inevitably "bothered" a lot of people, including me.

In the wake of Mary Meyer's murder on that October 12 afternoon, who among her close friends and family first knew that she was dead? And how did they come by that knowledge? The answers to these questions, depending on whom you ask, are riddled with confusion and ambiguity that persist to this day. The truth—elusive though it has been—about when and how Mary's friends and family learned of her death is part of the key to unraveling the mystery of who killed her, and why.

To begin, the first public revelation that Mary Meyer had been romantically involved with President Kennedy came through a story in the *National Enquirer* in its March 2, 1976, edition.[12] The details of the story had been given to the *Enquirer* by James Truitt, a close friend of Mary's (along with his wife, Anne), who had been a vice president of the *Washington Post* before he was abruptly fired by Ben Bradlee in 1969. The *Enquirer* story was strangely, even remarkably, well-documented, because Mary Meyer had confided her affair with President Kennedy to her friends, the Truitts. Jim Truitt, a seasoned journalist himself, had kept a record of everything Mary had shared with him. The *Enquirer* exposé revealed the fact that Mary had been keeping a diary of her affair, as well as the fact that she and the president had smoked marijuana in the First Family's residence in the White House. It also disclosed, for the first time, the fact that following her death, Mary's diary was found by her sister, Tony, in Mary's studio, and that this diary—labeled by Mary's closest intimates as just an "artist's sketchbook"—along with "several love letters" from JFK and other "private papers" belonging to Mary, had been given to the CIA's counterintelligence chief Jim Angleton to be burned, which he never did. The *Enquirer* story became an overnight bombshell that rocked Washington, already roiling and swirling through post-Watergate congressional hearings on illegal CIA activities, as well as further investigation into the Kennedy assassination.

Rightly sensing that there might be more to this story, Yale-educated journalist Ron Rosenbaum and his colleague Phillip Nobile went to work interviewing a number of principals close to Mary Meyer, including Jim Angleton and Ben and Tony Bradlee, as well as continuing to draw upon the input of Jim Truitt. In July, several months after the *National Enquirer* article appeared, Nobile and Rosenbaum published "The Curious Aftermath of JFK's Best and Brightest Affair" in the investigative weekly magazine *New Times*. The article has remained a seminal account of what allegedly took place during the immediate aftermath of the murder. The two journalists spent considerable time researching and interviewing their article, finally conceding the story was "immensely complex," and incomplete, primarily because many of Mary's friends and relatives "understandably drew back from the public controversy. Many refused all comment, others misled and misspoke."[13]

In their account, based on information gleaned from Jim Angleton himself, Rosenbaum and Nobile contended that the first person to realize that Mary Meyer was dead was Angleton's wife, Cicely. At some point during the afternoon of October 12, Cicely Angleton allegedly heard a radio bulletin about a murder on the C & O canal towpath. It is not known what level of detail the bulletin included—perhaps only that the victim was a middle-aged white female—but the location of the murder seemed enough to supposedly cause Cicely to fear the worst for her friend, who she knew was in the habit of daily walks on the towpath. In response to the broadcast, Cicely reportedly called her husband, the forty-six-year-old counterintelligence chief at the CIA. Jim Angleton was in "a big conference at CIA headquarters" when his wife's urgent call reached him. He was said to have been irritated by the interruption and told her that he thought her fear was a "silly fantasy." Reminding her of their plans to attend a poetry reading with Mary Meyer that same evening, he dismissed her paranoia and hung up.[14]

More than three decades later, Cicely Angleton would be the only close woman friend of Mary Meyer willing to talk with author Nina Burleigh, whose book, *A Very Private Woman*, was published in 1998. In interviews with Burleigh, it appeared that Cicely never mentioned the alleged radio bulletin on the day of Mary's murder—nor her alleged panicked call to her husband at CIA headquarters.[1] Simply incomprehensible was that Ms. Angleton might have forgotten such a detail, and that Burleigh—who acknowledged Rosenbaum's groundbreaking work—would not have asked her about it. "News of the murdered woman on the towpath traveled fast in white Washington," Burleigh wrote in *A Very Private Woman*. "And some of Mary's friends suspected immediately the victim might be their friend."[15] Other than Cicely Angleton, the so-called friends that Burleigh referred to were never identified. In addition, it also appears that Cicely Angleton may have revealed another layer of her husband's deceit, which her three children would inadvertently make public after their mother's death in the fall of 2011.

Even more perplexing, and certainly no less disturbing, was Ben Bradlee's account of who first learned the tragic news about Mary Meyer. More than thirty years after her murder, and twenty years after being interviewed by Rosenbaum and Nobile (to whom he never revealed the following event), Bradlee finally offered his own answer to the question of who first learned about the murder. According to Bradlee, it was he.

In his 1995 memoir *A Good Life*, the former executive editor of the *Washington Post* wrote that "[i]t was just after lunch" on the day of the murder when he received a telephone call from "my friend," asking if he had been listening to the radio—a reference, presumably, to the broadcast bulletin that Cicely Angleton claimed had alarmed her. Bradlee hadn't heard it. The caller also

---

1   Cicely Angleton twice declined to be interviewed for this book. She died on September 23, 2011.

asked Bradlee if he knew where Mary Meyer was. He didn't. "Someone [has] been murdered on the towpath," Bradlee reported the caller saying. "From the description," said the caller, "it sounded like Mary."[16] At the time of this call—"just after lunch," wrote Bradlee—Mary had been dead for less than two hours, but the police still didn't know her identity. That would only be finally confirmed "sometime after" six that evening, when Bradlee himself identified her corpse at the D.C. morgue.[17]

Until he wrote about it in 1995, Bradlee had never publicly mentioned the phone call, nor was this call ever referenced in any police report, or elicited in Bradlee's testimony at Mary's murder trial in July 1965. Furthermore, while Bradlee revealed the identity of the caller in his 1995 memoir, a fact that will later be discussed in some detail, he neglected to mention, or omitted deliberately, that his caller "friend" was a career, high-ranking CIA official.

Bradlee has never said why he waited more than thirty years to reveal the mysterious phone call. According to Rosenbaum, Bradlee had considered divulging Mary Meyer's affair with the president in his 1975 book *Conversations with Kennedy* (published a year before the story first appeared in the *National Enquirer*), "until others pressured him against it."[18] It was never known who the "others" were. By the time Bradlee published *A Good Life* in 1995, his CIA friend—the man who had first alerted him on the day of Mary's murder—had died.

The question still lingered: How could Bradlee's CIA friend have known "just after lunch" that the murdered woman was Mary Meyer when the victim's identity was still unknown to police? Did the caller *wonder* if the woman was Mary, or did he *know* it, and if so, how? This distinction is critical, and it goes to the heart of the mystery surrounding Mary Meyer's murder.

So does the following detail. The CIA caller's suggestion that something might have happened to Mary Meyer was plausible enough to send Bradlee rushing home to prepare his family for the possibility that the dead woman might, in fact, be his wife's sister. But it would not be until that evening—sometime before six, in Bradlee's recollection—that the police would knock on his door to inform him that the dead woman might be Mary. It was only then, shortly before six, that Bradlee went to the morgue to identify Mary's body.[19] This raises another question: If Bradlee had been given information "just after lunch" that Mary Meyer might have been killed, why didn't he go to the D.C. morgue, or police, sooner?

According to the 1976 Rosenbaum and Nobile account, Jim and Cicely Angleton arrived at Mary Meyer's house the evening of her murder to pick her up on their way to a Reed Whittemore poetry reading. They noticed her car was in the driveway, but her house was dark. They got no answer when they rang the doorbell. It wasn't clear whether Mary's house was locked, or whether, and how, the Angletons gained entry at that time. According to Angleton, it was at his wife's urging that he called Mary's answering service—perhaps from inside Mary's house, perhaps from another location; it was never known. Either way, Rosenbaum and Nobile's article claims that it was from Mary Meyer's *answering service* that Jim Angleton first learned that she was dead. The Angletons then went straight from Mary's house to Ben and Tony Bradlee's house where, according to Rosenbaum, they gave their condolences and offered to help with funeral arrangements. How did Mary Meyer's *answering service* know that she had been killed? And if the answering service had that information, who informed the service? Furthermore, why would they dispense it so freely? The police had only confirmed Mary's identity when Bradlee identified her body "sometime after" 6:00 P.M.[20]

Ben Bradlee returned home that evening after identifying Mary's body at the D.C. morgue. As he recalled in 1995, the Bradlee house was filling up with friends, "the phones rang, the doorbell buzzed. Food and drink materialized out of nowhere." He was surprised to receive a call from Pierre Salinger, President Kennedy's former press secretary, who was in Paris, expressing "his particular sorrow and condolences." The Bradlees had not been aware that Mary Meyer had known Salinger, or in what context.[21]

Another overseas call, this one from Japan, wasn't a surprise. Sculptor Anne Truitt had been one of Mary Meyer's closest friends. She and her husband, *Newsweek* journalist James Truitt, had moved to Tokyo in early 1964. As already noted, Anne and her husband had been well aware of Mary's relationship with the president, because Mary had confided to both of them about the affair. A number of other people in Jack Kennedy's intimate circle knew about the relationship as well, but Ben Bradlee, once again, couldn't seem to get his story straight. In 1976, according to Rosenbaum, Bradlee even denied "that he was aware of the JFK–Mary Meyer affair before the [1976] *Enquirer* story," though he admitted to having read through the diary in 1964.[22] Another source further confided to Rosenbaum that Bradlee had considered exposing the affair himself in his 1975 book *Conversations with Kennedy*, "until others pressured him against it."[23]

Anne Truitt's reason for calling the Bradlees wasn't only to offer sympathy. According to Bradlee's 1995 account, the purpose of Truitt's call was to inform Ben and Tony of Mary's "private diary," and the fact that Mary had asked her—not Jim Angleton—"if anything ever happened to me," to take possession of her diary. Anne issued an urgent directive that evening: The diary needed to be retrieved as soon as possible. Yet, according to Rosenbaum, Anne Truitt was desperately trying to locate Jim Angleton and found him at the Bradlees, whereupon she informed him about the need to procure Mary's diary immediately. Mary Meyer "had entrusted to her friends James and Anne Truitt the fact of her affair with JFK and the existence of a diary recounting some of her evenings with the President," noted Rosenbaum. It appears, then, with the Truitts in Japan, a decision was made by persons unknown that the diary was to now be safeguarded by Jim Angleton: "The Truitts were still in Tokyo when they received word of the towpath murder, and the responsibility for the diary was communicated to their mutual friend James Angleton, through still uncertain channels."[24]

Presumably, the revelation of this detail came from Jim Truitt himself, since Anne did not make herself available to be interviewed for the 1976 Rosenbaum article. More important, however, there was never a record or any mention of Mary Meyer herself instructing the Truitts, before they left for Tokyo, to make sure Jim Angleton took charge of her diary, should unforeseen events in her life take place. As Rosenbaum insightfully noted: "Before the Truitts departed for Tokyo in 1963 [sic], where Jim [Truitt] was made *Newsweek* bureau chief, Mary discussed with them the disposition of her diary in the event of her death. She asked them to preserve it, and to show it to her son Quentin when he reached the age of 21."[25] Angleton's role as "the diary's protector" was likely invented immediately after the Truitts were informed of Mary's demise, which brings us to a still unanswered question: Who called the Truitts in Tokyo to inform them of Mary's death? What "channels" were employed to inform Angleton of his newfound responsibility for the diary? Both questions have remained "dangling in the wind," and for good reason.[26]

The actual search for and discovery of Mary Meyer's diary immediately following her murder, and the differing accounts given by the people involved, have taken on a mythology in Washington that to this day remains an impenetrable labyrinth of confusion and deceit. Like idiot Keystone Kops, none of Mary's closest friends and family members could even get their own stories straight. There are at least three separate existing accounts of the search and discovery of what was eventually called "Mary's diary." A possible fourth account was never divulged by the cagey, tight-lipped, former journalist Anne Chamberlin,[2] who, shortly after Mary's death, according to Leo Damore, allegedly fled Washington out of fear. And a fifth account, which emerged in December 2011, casts doubt on the veracity of almost every one of the principal actors in this drama.

The first account of the search for Mary's diary came from the July 1976 Rosenbaum and Nobile *New Times* magazine article, just four months after the *National Enquirer* exposé in March. In Rosenbaum's version, the search took place inside Mary's house on Saturday, October 17, five days after her murder. It involved the Angletons, Tony Bradlee, Cord Meyer, and Anne Chamberlin. Ben Bradlee was not present. Jim Angleton, sometimes known as "the locksmith," was said to have brought along his bag of tricks: "white gloves, drills," and other implements that one might expect the CIA's counterintelligence chief to possess. The search party tapped walls, and "looked in the fireplace and turned over bricks in the garden." During the event, "the whiskey flowed," as it often did in those days. Cord Meyer reportedly "lit a smoky fire," while "Angleton pitched in washing dishes." One of the party members reportedly stepped into the garden and issued a skyward plea, "Mary, where's your damn diary?"[27]

The search party found nothing. Later that the same day, Tony Bradlee was said to have discovered a "locked steel box" in Mary's studio. Inside it was one of Mary's artist sketchbooks, a number of personal papers, and "hundreds of letters" of a personal nature. Some of them were reportedly "love letters" from Jack Kennedy, though it has never been established whether they had been written before or after he became president.[28] Tony Bradlee later claimed that the presence of a few vague notes written in the sketchbook—allegedly including cryptic references to an affair with the president—persuaded her that she'd found her sister's missing diary. But Mary's artist sketchbook wasn't her real diary. It was just a ruse.

The second account of the search for Mary's diary came from Ben Bradlee's 1995 memoir *A Good Life*. There, he asked the reader to believe that an iconic journalist wouldn't have bothered reviewing the material already published in 1976 (in part, based on Rosenbaum's interview with Bradlee), or even have checked his own sworn testimony in 1965 at Mary Meyer's murder trial, before delivering to the public his final statement about one of

---

2   Anne Chamberlin died on December 31, 2011 in Sarasota, Florida.

his sister-in-law's most intimate possessions. According to Bradlee, he and his wife, Tony, first looked for the diary the morning *after* the murder—Tuesday, October 13. Bradlee said they first went to Mary's house that morning, where they were taken aback to find Jim Angleton already inside. Angleton was said to have "shuffled his feet" in apparent embarrassment when he was discovered. At that point, Bradlee claims, the three of them together looked for the diary but found nothing.

Later that same day (Tuesday, October 13), Bradlee wrote, he and Tony decided to search Mary's converted brick garage studio, located in the alley behind their N Street house. "We had no key [to Mary's studio]," wrote Bradlee, "but I got a few tools to remove the simple padlock, and we walked toward the studio, only to run into Jim Angleton again, this time actually in the process of picking the padlock."[29] According to Rosenbaum, Angleton was furious at Bradlee's claim, calling him a liar, and denying he had ever been at the studio.[30] Bradlee went on to say, "We missed the diary the first time, but Tony found it an hour later."

What's stunning and fascinating about this account was that it completely contradicted Bradlee's sworn testimony at Mary's murder trial in 1965. There, he testified he was *inside Mary's studio on the night of her murder*—with no mention of any trouble whatsoever gaining entrance. Presumably, this took place after Anne Truitt's phone call from Japan alerting both Angleton and Bradlee that Mary had kept a diary of her affair with Kennedy, though Angleton was undoubtedly already aware of Mary's diary long before her murder, as the reader will come to understand in a later chapter. At the trial in July 1965, prosecuting attorney Alfred Hantman asked Bradlee the following:

Hantman: Did you have access to it [Mary's studio]?

Bradlee: Yes.

Hantman: Subsequent to the death of Mary Pinchot Meyer, did you make any effort to gain entry to this studio that was occupied by Mrs. Meyer?

Bradlee: I did, yes.

Hantman: When was this, sir?

Bradlee: The night of October 12.

Hantman: Was this studio or the garage which was converted into a studio secured in any manner?

Bradlee: Yes, it had a padlock on it.

Hantman: And were you able to gain access to this studio at that time?

Bradlee:	I did.
Hantman:	Now, besides the usual articles of Mrs. Meyer's avocation, did you find there any other articles of her personal property?
Bradlee:	There was a pocketbook there.
Hantman:	What did the pocketbook contain, sir?
Bradlee:	It contained a wallet, some cosmetics and pencils, things like that.
Hantman:	And did the wallet contain any money, sir?
Bradlee:	I don't think so. It may have, I just don't remember.
Hantman:	Were there keys to her automobile?
Bradlee:	Yes, there was a key there.
Hantman:	I have no further questions of Mr. Bradlee, Your honor.[31]

Bradlee never revealed during this interchange (nor was he asked) whether he was in Mary's studio alone, or in the company of someone else—such as Jim Angleton. Furthermore, if he had no trouble gaining entrance on the night of the murder, why the need of "a few tools to remove the simple padlock" the following day? Had "the locksmith" Angleton facilitated Bradlee's entrance that night? If Mary's actual diary was in her studio that night, it was likely stolen by Bradlee and Angleton at that time—the night of the murder—and given to Angleton for safekeeping.

A third account of the diary search came from Cicely Angleton's and Anne Truitt's November 1995 letter to the *New York Times* in response to William Safire's review of the 1995 Bradlee memoir. The two women for some reason felt it particularly urgent "to correct what in our opinion is an error in Ben Bradlee's autobiography." They wrote:

This error occurs in Mr. Bradlee's account of the discovery and disposition of Mary Pinchot Meyer's personal diary. The fact is that Mary Meyer asked Anne Truitt to make sure that in the event of anything happening to Mary while Anne was in Japan, James Angleton take this diary into his safekeeping.

When she learned that Mary had been killed, Anne Truitt telephoned person-to-person from Tokyo for James Angleton. She found him at Mr. Bradlee's house, where Angleton and his wife, Cicely had been asked to come following the murder.

In the phone call, relaying Mary Meyer's specific instructions, Anne Truitt told Angleton *for the first time* [author's italics], that there was a diary; and, in accordance with Mary Meyer's explicit request, Anne Truitt asked Angleton to search for and to take charge of this diary.[32]

"This search was carried out," Mrs. Angleton affirms, "in Mary Meyer's house in the presence of her sister, Tony Bradlee, and the Angletons, and one other friend of Mary Meyer's." That unidentified friend was Anne Chamberlin, still not wanting her name brought into the fray even thirty years later. But the Angleton-Truitt letter never revealed the date of the search, though it did assert that neither Cord Meyer nor Ben Bradlee were present. The two Mary Meyer confidantes then concluded their letter with the following: "When Tony Bradlee found the diary and several papers bundled together in Mary Meyer's studio, she gave the entire package to Angleton and asked him to burn it. Angleton followed this instruction in part by burning the loose papers. He also followed Mary Meyer's instruction and safeguarded the diary. Some years later, he honored a request from Tony Bradlee that he deliver it to her. Subsequently, Tony Bradlee burned the diary in the presence of Anne Truitt."[33]

Anne Truitt and Cicely Angleton now wanted the public to believe that Jim Angleton had "safeguarded" the diary on instructions from Mary Meyer. But if Mary had truly wanted Angleton to take possession of her diary in the event of her death, why wouldn't she have told him so herself? According to journalist William Safire, "in the mid-1970's" (the time when both the *National Enquirer* exposé and the Rosenbaum article had been published), Angleton's spiel was that it was only his "loyal concern for the slain President's reputation [that] led him to search for and destroy Meyer's diary,"[34] yet he never once mentioned that Mary Meyer herself had requested him to take possession of her diary, or destroy any part of it. Jim Angleton was a consummate, pathological liar and a master of duplicity—not only to Safire, but to everyone else—except to his close friend and colleague Cord Meyer and possibly in this instance Ben Bradlee, as the reader will eventually discover.

Furthermore, Jim Angleton never destroyed anything.[35] And both Anne Truitt and Cicely Angleton in 1995, it appears, either intentionally left out another critically important piece of the fable, or chose not to reveal a new level of subterfuge that would finally be inadvertently divulged at the end of 2011 by the Angleton children. It was this: In the fall of 2011, Tony Bradlee died. Reviewing her life in her obituary, the *Washington Post* quoted Ben Bradlee's memoir *A Good Life*: "The Bradlees saw CIA counterintelligence chief James J. Angleton picking the padlock on [Mary] Meyer's Georgetown art studio in an attempt to retrieve her diary."[36] This so upset Angleton's three children that they wrote a letter to the *Post* editor on December 2, 2011, in an attempt to correct the account. In doing so, the Angleton children made public for the first time the following (see author's italics below):

Anne Truitt, a friend of Tony Bradlee and Bradlee's sister, Mary Meyer, was abroad when Meyer was killed in the District. Truitt called Bradlee and said that Meyer had asked her to request that Angleton retrieve and *burn certain pages of her diary if anything happened to her* [author's italics].

James and Cicely Angleton were with Ben and Tony Bradlee at the Bradlees' home when Tony Bradlee received the call. Cicely, our mother, told her daughter Guru Sangat Khalsa, "We all went to Mary's house together." She said there was no break-in because the Bradlees had a key. The diary was not found at that time.

Later, Tony Bradlee found it and gave it to James Angleton. *He burned the pages that Meyer had asked to be burned* [author's italics] and put the rest in a safe. Years later, he gave the rest of the diary to Bradlee at her request.[37]

Is it now to be believed not only that Mary Meyer entrusted the safekeeping of her diary to Jim Angleton, but that she had also specifically instructed him to "burn certain pages of her diary if anything happened to her"? Nothing could be further from the truth. The conspiracy to conceal, on one level, clearly involved all of the intimates of Mary Meyer: her sister, Tony, her closest women friends—Cicely Angleton, Anne Truitt, and Anne Chamberlin—and, of course, her ex-husband Cord, Ben Bradlee, and Jim Angleton. However, the men conspired to something even more sinister.

Therein the diary's "Rubik's Cube" becomes even more mysterious, only because there were two conspiracies taking place simultaneously, both masterminded by the "Master Angler" himself—James Jesus Angleton. It is not known (nor likely ever will be) how Angleton twisted the arm of Anne Truitt to declare that on the night of Mary's murder she should call the Bradlees and inform them that such a diary existed and that Mary had told her to make sure Angleton took charge of it, should anything happen to her. The answer to the question of who called the Truitts in Tokyo to inform them of Mary's demise now becomes more obvious: It was Angleton himself.

Angleton's ostensible concern was to protect the reputation of both President Kennedy and Mary Meyer, and the emerging myth of Camelot. This is likely how he first got the Truitts to participate. Mary's diary, and any other of her incriminating papers or possessions, had to be commandeered and contained as quickly as possible for the sake of 'a nation in mourning for its fallen leader.' The other women—Cicely Angleton, Tony Bradlee, and Anne Chamberlin—then fell in line, wanting to protect their dear friend Mary and the fallen president. They all conspired to conceal two important facts: that Mary and Jack had been having an affair, and that there had been some level of drug use in their relationship, both of which were eventually revealed in 1976 by the *National Enquirer*, thanks to Jim Truitt, who finally broke ranks. There, Truitt revealed to the *Enquirer* that Mary and Jack had, in fact, smoked marijuana in the White House residence in July 1962. Whether the two together went on to share a psychedelic journey with a hallucinogen such as LSD or psilocybin will be discussed in a later chapter.

None of the women in this caper, however, was ever aware of the fact that Jim Angleton had already absconded with Mary's real diary on the night of her murder, or what the diary actually contained. The only people who knew the diary's contents immediately following the murder were Jim Angleton and Cord Meyer, the two CIA honchos, though Ben Bradlee certainly knew of its existence if it was retrieved from Mary's studio on the night of the murder. Whether Bradlee actually read the real diary in its entirety isn't known. Later on, as will be discussed subsequently, it appears Angleton shared the diary's contents with at least one other CIA colleague and one other individual.

And so the charade for the search for Mary's diary became a camouflage and deflection for something more sinister. Subsequent to the March 1976 *National Enquirer* bombshell, Tony Bradlee played down the contents of her sister's sketchbook, purported to be her diary, as inconsequential. By all accounts, Mary's artist sketchbook had allegedly been discovered by Tony Bradlee, though it's not known exactly when—possibly on Tuesday, October 13, the day after Mary's murder, or possibly not until Saturday, October 17. It was described by Tony in 1976 as "a sketchbook with a nice paisley colored cover on it. . . . It was kind of a loose leaf book, nothing like Ben's book he was taking things down in, just a woman's notes about what she had been doing. I swear I don't remember what was in it. I went through it so quickly. And I remember there were some JFK's in it. There were some references to him. . . . It was very cryptic and difficult to understand. Not much there, but some references to JFK."[38]

Sometime before 2004, Tony Bradlee also told author Sally Bedell Smith that "everyone thought it [the sketchbook] was full of all kinds of gossip which it wasn't. I think I burned it because there was interest in the diary [sketch-book], and I didn't want the kids to get into it."[39] (God forbid "the kids," or anyone else, should know the truth.) If the sketchbook was so innocuous and inconsequential, why was it destroyed? And why was it done so quickly after the initial public revelation of Mary's affair with the president in 1976?[40] Further-more, nowhere does Tony Bradlee ever reveal or mention anything to do with Mary's alleged request to Jim Angleton to "burn certain pages of her diary if anything happened to her."

Even more ludicrous, the principals in this caper couldn't keep their sto-ries straight as to what the sketchbook actually contained. Ben Bradlee ad-mitted in 2007 in an interview for this book that his memory wasn't what it used to be, but he was adamant about what he had seen:

"I had that diary in my hands for twenty minutes and thumbed through it. It was just an artist's sketchbook. If the thing had sixty pages in it, that's a lot. Most of it was swatches, colors. Every now and then in a little unused corner of a page, there would be writings. To call them diary entries magnifies it out of proportion. I never saw Jack's name in it. He wasn't referred to as 'the president' or 'Jack Kennedy.' It was about an affair. She obviously had more than one affair, too."[41]

Yet in his 1995 memoir, Bradlee recounted the reading of the "sketchbook" with his wife as something that clearly informed both of them of Mary's affair with the president. Not wanting to shatter the emerging Kennedy myth of Ca-melot, he and Tony felt that it was up to them to "decide what to do with the diary." He wrote the following:

"[A]nd we both concluded that this was in no sense a public document, despite the braying of the knee jerks about some public right to know. I felt it was a family document, privately created by Mary, privately pro-tected by her thorough instructions to Anne Truitt, which should be followed."[42]

He also wrote: "To say we were stunned [about the affair] doesn't begin to describe our reactions. Tony, especially, felt betrayed, both by Kennedy and by Mary."[43] Years later, in 2007, Bradlee reiterated the fact that "Tony was *shocked*, and I mean *shocked* [Bradlee's emphases], when she found out Mary had been having an affair with Jack."[44] Yet Bradlee, too, never mentioned anything about

Mary's request that Angleton burn designated pages of the diary upon her death.

Anne Truitt's final reflections about "Mary's sketchbook" may have revealed some of her confusion about what had taken place. Having been in Japan when Mary was murdered, it appears she only saw the sketchbook right before it was burned by Tony Bradlee in 1976. In an interview with author Sally Bedell Smith shortly before Anne's death in 2004, she referred to the "sketchbook" (advertised to the public as Mary's diary) as the "little notebook with a pretty cover." She told Smith that it "consisted mostly of jottings about Mary's art, and paint swatches on otherwise blank pages. Only about ten pages were devoted to Kennedy, who was never mentioned by name." Even more revealing, Anne Truitt was "just floored," she said, about its lack of details. There was "nothing, nada, a series of scrawls and notes, not in order, no chronology, no real facts."[45] Truitt also confirmed in this interview that she and Tony Bradlee had allegedly burned the sketchbook in Tony's fireplace sometime shortly after the *National Enquirer* exposé in March 1976.[46] Tony herself had stated in 1976 that "the diary [sketchbook] was destroyed. I'll tell you that much is true,"[47] later on clarifying that the destruction took place "after James Truitt's interviews with the *National Enquirer*."[48] Her statement implied that sometime between March and July of 1976, someone—or possibly a group of people—decided that the updated story to be given to the public would now include Angleton returning the sketchbook to Tony, who would then burn it in her fireplace in Anne's presence. It appeared that Tony made the decision unilaterally, but there was never any confirmation as to how this decision was made, who exactly made it, or when it occurred. And, again, Anne Truitt never said anything about Mary's alleged specific request that Angleton burn particular diary pages.

Finally, for some reason it has appeared that Mary's close friend Anne Chamberlin couldn't stand the heat. She wouldn't actively participate in the conspiracy to conceal. It was as if something had scared her. She didn't want any part of it, and she didn't want her name mentioned in any subsequent account. Anne Chamberlin left Washington abruptly after Mary's murder and fled to Maine. Twenty-five years later, in the late 1980s, she spoke to author Leo Damore, then went completely silent after Damore's "suicide" in 1995. Chamberlin's public, long-standing "*omertà* pledge" of silence has always aroused suspicion. Whatever she knew, she took with her to her death on the last day of 2011, save for what she shared with author Leo Damore, which the reader will come to know in a future chapter.

So is it to be believed that a former professional journalist like Mary Meyer would have relegated her deepest, intimate thoughts and revelations, something that was to be sacredly preserved for her children in the event of her death, to a mere artist's sketchbook—most of it color swatches with "cryptic" scribbles "in little unused corner[s] of a page"? Is the public so gullible as to believe that this haphazard "little notebook with a pretty cover" contained everything that Mary was struggling with during the final year of her life as she tried to make sense of all the dimensions and implications of her relationship with Jack, as well as the conspiracy that had put an end to his life, and the even bigger conspiracy she found herself witnessing to "cover everything up," as she had told Timothy Leary?[49]

Mary Meyer was a pensive, complex individual who had a lifelong penchant for serious reflection in written form. Having been a professional journalist for several years right after college, and having kept an extensive diary at the time of her half-sister Rosamund's 1938 suicide as well as a chronicle of her father's grief and mental deterioration, she had long embraced the tool of journal writing and the outlet it provided, particularly during times of crisis and duress. This earlier diary is still, in fact, in existence today.[50] Moreover, during her marriage to Cord, she was well aware of her husband's diary, and sometimes even invaded it to write comments on what he had written when she was unable to reach him any other way. Obviously, Mary knew the value of keeping a separate, special notebook for the pursuit of deeper reflection. But her artist sketchbooks were just that—sketchbooks that were clearly devoted to the details of her pursuits as a painter with a few notes to herself that she probably intended to reflect upon in more depth at a later time. Furthermore, she had confided to both Anne and Jim Truitt in 1962 that she was having an affair with the president. Before the Truitts left for Japan, she had told them that she was keeping a diary and that she wanted that diary safeguarded in the event of her demise so that her eldest son, Quentin, could read it when he turned twenty-one.[51] Why would any of Mary's closest friends believe that one of her sketchbooks, filled mostly with swatches of colors and vague, off-the-cuff thoughts and notes of her painting, would even remotely resemble a serious diary of a previously established journalist?

Jim Truitt, in turn, kept a diary-journal of his own about everything that Mary had shared with him. Curiously, Truitt's journal and "his 30 years of carefully kept records," according to his widow Evelyn Patterson Truitt, were stolen right after his 1981 death, an apparent suicide. In a letter Evelyn Truitt wrote to author Anthony Summers in 1983, she alleged that "ex-CIA agent Herbert

Barrows," who lived nearby, had stolen all of her husband's "carefully kept records."[52] The missing papers, of course, included Jim Truitt's own documentation of Mary Meyer's affair with the president. The theft seemed once again to implicate Jim Angleton, who was fast becoming legendary for such so-called "cleanups." Angleton had earlier absconded with the personal papers of his colleague Winston Scott, the Mexican CIA station chief, two days after Scott's suspicious death in 1971. Significantly, Scott's papers included classified documents, tapes, photographs, and a manuscript, most of which not only contradicted the findings of the Warren Commission, but further revealed Lee Harvey Oswald's connections in Mexico—things that the CIA wanted nobody to know about.[53]

Mary's self-possession had always been a hallmark of her character. However overwhelmed she had felt by the vast implications of what had occurred in Dallas, not only for herself, but for the world at large, her temperament and moral rectitude demanded that at the very least she attempt to make sense of it all. What better way to cope with the enormity of that task than to set aside periods of time for reflection, aided by a valuable tool she had utilized effectively in the past? Neither a recluse nor one to be intimidated by authority, Mary wanted to understand what had occurred. The sheer magnitude of Jack's assassination had catapulted her through endless shock waves, eventually forcing her to recognize the enormity of what had occurred—not only the events in Dallas, but the subsequent cover-up taking place right before her eyes. This cover-up, in fact, is the subject of a later chapter of this book.

"They couldn't control him any more," she sobbed on the telephone with Timothy Leary sometime in early December 1963, just after the assassination. "He was changing too fast. They've covered everything up. I gotta come see you. I'm afraid. Be careful."[54] Determined to understand and unravel what was taking place, she confronted what amounted to a mysterious jigsaw mosaic. The pieces had to be placed where they belonged. That process would take time, reflection, and awareness. What better way to engage the conundrum than to reclaim the exercise of journaling?

What then happened to Mary's *real* diary? (Hereafter, the word "diary" refers only to Mary's real journal/diary and not to her artist sketchbook.) The "diary as MacGuffin" in this piece of history doesn't need any Hollywood embellishment; the story is stranger than fiction, only because it's real. Yet no one has managed to put together the factual sequence of events that would unravel the mystery that has enshrouded this caper for nearly fifty years.

One of the most significant details in the 1976 Rosenbaum and Nobile article may have even eluded its own authors. It was this: The authors let it be known that after Jim Angleton arrived at the Bradlee house on the evening of the murder, and after he had fielded Anne Truitt's telephone call from Japan, he later returned to Mary Meyer's house that evening and ostensibly "rescued three kittens from the empty house."[55] If the real diary wasn't in Mary's studio on the night of her murder, as Bradlee and Angleton had likely investigated (given Bradlee's testimony at the trial), Angleton knew where to look for the diary in Mary's house, only because Anne Truitt had probably told him where to look when she reached him earlier that evening. Mary was "accustomed to leaving her diary in the bookcase in her bedroom," Rosenbaum noted. "The diary wasn't there after her death."[56]

But why, then, was Jim Angleton again in Mary's house the following morning, when Ben and Tony Bradlee surprised him there? If he had the diary, why go back? Perhaps Angleton wanted to be seen searching for the diary so that no one would suspect that it was already in his possession. But more likely, as the reader will come to understand, Mary's actual diary was highly incriminating of Angleton himself and the CIA's role in orchestrating what had occurred in Dallas. Determined to erase as much as possible from the last years of Mary Meyer's life, Angleton wanted to take into his possession and eliminate any *other* documents, papers, letters, or personal effects that might further jeopardize the Warren Report and the public's acceptance of Lee Harvey Oswald's guilt.

In a situation such as this, the unwritten rule of any CIA undercover operation is that the fewer people in the know, the better; compartmentalization is an absolute necessity—as long as it's maintained, and the story is kept straight. The only people who really knew what was taking place were the mastermind himself, Jim Angleton, his colleague Cord Meyer, and to one extent or another Ben Bradlee. What incriminated Bradlee, as will be further detailed later, was that he never once revealed during the trial the telephone call from his "friend"—the career high-ranking CIA official—that came "just after lunch," less than two hours after Mary's unidentified corpse lay sprawled on the C & O Canal towpath. Instead, he allowed the court to believe that it was only when Sergeant Sam Wallace of the D.C. police arrived at his house shortly before six that evening that he first became aware of his sister-in-law's demise.

No one in this cesspool's morass could ever be trusted, but it appears some part of the deceit was passed down to some of participants' children. After Anne Truitt's death in 2004, I talked with her daughter Alexandra in the latter part of 2005. When I introduced myself and told her of my book project, Alexandra was momentarily (and cautiously) hopeful that I might be taking a different slant from author Nina Burleigh's. Intriguingly, she made it clear that subsequent to Mary Meyer's death she had been "coached" that the subject of Mary's murder was taboo.

"I've heard over the years that a lot of people have been threatened," Alexandra said, after I mentioned author John H. Davis's remark to Jimmy Smith in 1999. "That's always been everybody's feeling around the whole event [Mary's murder] I've grown up with. You don't talk about it because it's dangerous." Later during our conversation, she added, "I'm incredibly discreet. I never talk about this. I talked about it with my mom. I think I know everything she knew. But I don't talk about it because it's dangerous." Alexandra became eager to know what I had discovered, but I wouldn't divulge any information over the phone. I suggested instead we meet in New York so that we could talk privately in person. Ambivalent about that prospect, she changed the subject.

"I thought Nina Burleigh's book was terrible," she said. "I thought it was badly researched and embarrassingly inaccurate." I then attempted to defend some of Burleigh's early descriptions of the Pinchot estate, Grey Towers, and their life in Milford, Pennsylvania—if only to keep our conversation going. It was already clear Alexandra knew much more than she was letting on. "I think it's too dangerous to talk to you, I really do," she finally said. Our conversation ended amicably. I suggested the possibility of some follow-up through email a couple of weeks later, but was quickly rebuffed.[57]

What could still be "too dangerous" to talk about more than forty years after the fact? The clue, of course, was Alexandra's comment that she had talked with her mother at some length, concluding, "I think I know everything she knew." Anne Truitt had concealed something. Like Anne Chamberlin, I wondered, had Leo Damore's apparent "suicide" in October 1995 immediately after the publication of Ben Bradlee's memoir, A Good Life, frightened Alexandra from talking further?

In late 1990, author Leo Damore conducted a two-hour face-to-face recorded interview with Timothy Leary, which will be discussed in some detail in a later chapter. During the interview, he told Leary that Mary's real diary still existed and he had discovered its whereabouts. "Angleton offered the diary in 1980 to a person who I know," Damore told Leary. "I know where it is, and the man who I believe has it is maddeningly this week in Hawaii."[58] Damore had sometimes cryptically referred to Mary's diary as "the Hope Diamond" of the Kennedy assassination, but he guarded the fact that he had come into possession of it and only finally shared this bit of information with his attorney at the end of March in 1993.

Meanwhile, Cord Meyer would maintain that Jim Angleton was a "very close friend of ours, and he successfully dealt with a diary that might have been embarrassing, assured that it didn't come out. That was not done to protect state secrets or anything like that. It was done to protect a friend."[59] Again, Cord does not mention that Mary had specifically entrusted her diary to Angleton, or asked him to "burn certain pages of her diary if anything happened to her." And which "diary" was Cord referring to? Mary's sketchbook, or the real diary that Angleton and possibly Bradlee had stolen on the night of the murder?

Sixteen years after his ex-wife's murder in 1980, Cord would finally reveal in his book *Facing Reality* who had contacted him in New York on the afternoon of Mary's murder to tell him what had happened—again, *before* police had any idea of the victim's identity. It was the same "friend" that had called Ben Bradlee "just after lunch," a man who happened to be a close CIA colleague—a fact that Cord, too, failed to mention in his account.[60]

4

Deus Ex Machina

Nothing can now be believed which is seen in a newspaper. Truth itself becomes suspicious by being put into that polluted vehicle. The real extent of this state of misinformation is known only to those who are in situations to confront facts within their knowledge with the lies of the day.

—Thomas Jefferson[1]

Think of the press as a great keyboard on which the government can play.

—Joseph Goebbels
(Hitler's propaganda minister)

WHILE THE MOST intense grief attended Mary Pinchot Meyer's funeral at the National Cathedral on Wednesday, October 14, the Reverend Jesse A. Brown also consoled a member of his own congregation at the Second Baptist Church in Southwest Washington, D.C., only a few miles away in distance, yet worlds apart in social class and community. Martha Crump had been undone by Mary Meyer's murder, too. Her son, twenty-five-year-old Raymond Crump Jr., was in police custody, charged with committing the crime. Reverend Brown spoke to Martha Crump that day not only of matters spiritual, but of matters practical as well. Something had to be done to help "Mr. Ray," whom he believed had been wrongly accused.

Like most black churches in the 1960s, Second Baptist was a stronghold in its community, a spiritual refuge with a social conscience. Community outreach, drug and alcohol abuse counseling, care for the elderly, housing assistance—Second Baptist offered guidance that went beyond tending to the souls of the faithful. The church had a well-established record of fighting race-based discrimination and social injustice. As its founding pastor, Reverend Brown led the charge.

The civil rights movement of the 1960s owed much to churches like Second Baptist, where members gathered to stoke the causes of equal and fair treatment under the law. The black church functioned independent of white interference—that is, until the churches became centers of organized activism. When that occurred, they also became targets for those who would rather see the churches burn than have their congregations achieve equality. Across the American south, black churches were being firebombed, members of their faithful lynched. Violence was rampant. By 1964, there was a siege mentality in black churches.

Shortly after Ray Crump's arrest, Reverend Brown had been trying, through ministry channels, to reach attorney Dovey Johnson Roundtree, someone he often referred to as a "righteous lawyer" and something of a legend already in the black community. In addition to being a "righteous lawyer," Roundtree was also a highly regarded associate minister of the Allen Chapel African Methodist Episcopal Church, and a sought-after public speaker. She was an attractive, petite woman with delicate features, and a complexion that belied her fifty years. The only hints of her age were the strands of gray that streaked her hair.

Roundtree had been raised with a fierce understanding of—and belief in—justice. The only thing she believed in more absolutely was God. Behind her graceful appearance was a will of iron. "Her voice, like her demeanor, was kind, deliberate and thoughtful," recalled attorney George Peter Lamb in 1991. "But she's all business. She likes to look you square in the eye. There was something impossibly appealing about her. It's difficult not to like this woman."[2]

Dovey Roundtree had seen up close the failings and abuses of power in an American legal system rife with racism. Born Dovey Mae Johnson on April 17, 1914, in Charlotte, North Carolina, she never forgot the night her grandmother, Rachel Bryant Graham, pushed her, her mother, and her sisters under the kitchen table as members of the Ku Klux Klan approached. Grandma Rachel extinguished the kerosene lamp, closed all the shutters, and braced her daughter and crying grandchildren for the worst. Like an approaching freight train, howling men on horseback galloped past their house. Grandma Rachel clutched a broom in case she needed a weapon, and her husband, the Reverend Clyde L. Graham, kept vigil through the slats of a shuttered window.

After Dovey's father died during the influenza epidemic of 1919, Grandma Rachel brought her daughter's family to live with her and her husband in the parsonage attached to the African Methodist Episcopal Zion Church, where he pastored. To the white bankers in Charlotte, Rachel Graham was just the Negro woman who did their laundry and ironed their shirts. To her granddaughter, "she was a force of nature." Darkness didn't scare her. Neither did the weather. While Grandpa Clyde took cover from summer thunderstorms, Grandma Rachel went out to the front porch to shake her fist at the lightning. The way she saw it, it was Mother Nature who was scaring her family, and that just wouldn't do.[3]

Grandma Rachel's courage had left an indelible impression on the young Dovey Mae Johnson, perhaps never more so than the day the pair took a trolley to downtown Charlotte. The inquisitive little girl wanted to see how the driver steered the vehicle and punched the tickets, so she took the seat behind him. "Get that pickaninny out of here!" the white driver yelled. "You know she can't sit there." Grandma Rachel took her granddaughter by the hand, yanked the stop cord, and, once descended, walked with her the entire way into town and back again. She was very quiet until much later that evening, when, with her family gathered at the table, she announced, "Something bad happened to Dovey Mae today." They listened by the light of the kerosene lamp, the family Bible open in front of Grandpa Clyde. "The mean old conductor man on the trolley car called her a bad name," she said. "I want to tell you all something. Now hear me, and hear me good. My chillun is as good as anybody."[4] During the years of struggle that followed, Dovey never forgot her grandmother's words that night.

That day was a galvanizing moment for Dovey Mae. Many years earlier, her grandmother had had a galvanizing moment of her own. When she was still a girl, Rachel had been attacked by the white overseer of a Greensboro farm where her parents had been slaves. "He was meanin' to bother me," she told her granddaughter. "I ran and fought, and he stomped on my feet to keep me from runnin' for good, he said. But I kept runnin'. He wasn't going to have his way with me."[5]

The broken bones in Rachel's feet never set correctly, and every night after that, she had had to soak her feet and massage them with a homemade salve of mutton tallow and turpentine, just to be able to endure the discomfort of wearing shoes. When Dovey learned this about her grandmother a few years after the incident on the trolley, she better understood something her grandmother used to always say: "No matter what any sign said, what anyone whispered or shouted at you, if you walked tall, no one could bring you down."[6]

Grandma Rachel was Dovey Johnson's beacon. Dovey listened carefully to what her grandmother told her, and she heard loud and clear that the path forward was one of education. Rachel had regaled her grandchildren with stories of her friend, author and educator Mary McLeod Bethune, who had worked her way from the cotton fields of South Carolina to found a black women's college in Florida. She would go on, during the 1930s, to be appointed by President Franklin D. Roosevelt as special adviser for minority affairs and director of African American Affairs in the National Youth Administration.

When Dovey was in seventh grade, Mary McLeod Bethune came to speak at Charlotte's Emancipation Day celebration. Grandma Rachel took the entire family to the event. "Mary, I want you to meet my grandchildren," she said to her old friend. After the event, Grandma Rachel took her granddaughter Dovey aside. "She's somebody," Grandma Rachel told Dovey, referring to her friend Mary Bethune, "and you can be somebody too."[7]

Dovey Mae Johnson attended Spelman College, where she worked three jobs, juggled majors in English and biology to prepare her for the medical career she envisioned, and edited the school newspaper. While there, she met Bill Roundtree, a student at Morehouse College, Spelman's brother school. The approaching war and other circumstances would keep them from marriage until some years later.[8]

Dovey Johnson graduated from Spelman in 1938. In 1941, she became Mary McLeod Bethune's personal assistant in Washington, D.C. The job blew open the young woman's horizons, introducing her to the day's leaders, including First Lady Eleanor Roosevelt. With the onset of World War II, Bethune selected her young protégé as one of the forty black women to train in the first class of the Women's Army Auxiliary Corps (WAAC).[9]

"You are not doing this for yourself," Bethune told Dovey. "You are doing it for those who will come after you." Despite her initial ambivalence, Dovey distinguished herself in the fight for a racially integrated WAAC regiment. The experience set her on a path to pursuing a career in justice and legal protection for those who needed it most. Law would become her life's focus and passion—so much so, it overshadowed her short-lived marriage to Bill Roundtree, which ended in divorce in 1947.[10]

Studying law at Howard University was an awakening for Dovey Roundtree. As her biographer, Katie McCabe, wrote of Dovey's passion for the law, "There was a simplicity about it, and an intricacy, and a logic. Closely reasoned opinions, precedents, constitutional principles—these, woven together, made a kind of sense that imposed itself on the scattered reality of human existence."[11] In addition to her regular law courses, Dovey did legal research for the NAACP legal team, which was headed by future Supreme Court justice Thurgood Marshall.

She passed the D.C. bar exam in December 1950 and was sworn in a few months later, in April 1951. She immediately set about developing a private law practice. Many of her clients came from her church. She allowed the poorest among them to barter for her legal services. In the ten years during which Dovey practiced with her law partner, Julius Robertson, before his untimely death in 1961, the two established a thriving practice. After Robertson's death, Dovey, who had led the vanguard of women ordained to the ministry in African Methodist Episcopal Church that same year, went on to make a name for herself as a one-woman legal aid society and a force to be reckoned with. By the fall of 1964, Dovey Roundtree was a sought-after defense attorney.

So when Reverend Brown contacted her in October 1964 and asked if she could bring a member of his church to her office, attorney Dovey Roundtree had already formed an opinion about the "Towpath Murder" from the front-page newspaper accounts that she had read. "The case sounded cut and dried and all but decided, what with all these so-called eyewitnesses," she recalled in a 1990 interview by the late author Leo Damore. She had read the newspaper reports that a tow truck driver near the scene, Henry Wiggins, had identified Ray Crump as the man standing over the corpse. She had also read about the jogger, Lieutenant William L. Mitchell, who had come forward the next day and told police he'd seen a black man dressed like the man Wiggins had described, trailing Mary Meyer as she walked along the canal.

"I met Crump's mother and his wife," Roundtree told Damore. "They were all fearfully upset and very worried that something was going to happen to Ray Jr. His mother just worried me to death. She called me day and night. She was afraid there was going to be a killing in the D.C. jail—which eventually became one of my concerns. He was in the D.C. jail, and they had predominately white guards in those days. And those in charge, the captains of the supervisors, were all white men."[12]

On her very first trip to the D. C. jail to meet Ray Crump, Dovey found him to be a diminutive little man. "He was no taller than me—I'm five feet four inches—and maybe 140 pounds," she recalled in 1990. "I never saw anybody as frightened as this man was! Crump was crying; he was pitiful. And to me, he was in a stupor. He asked me that question many times: 'What was really going on?' He didn't know what happened. I had to tell him. He didn't know a woman had been murdered."[13] She asked him to try to remember everything he did on the day of the murder.

But Crump couldn't remember very much, and what he did remember he had a hard time expressing. Roundtree was patient. Eventually, a story emerged. Crump had had a fight with his wife, Helena, that morning and he had refused to go to work. Instead, he had met up with a girlfriend named Vivian, whose last name was never made public. Both Crump and his mother, Martha, had finally offered that last bit of information, but Ray hadn't wanted to reveal his paramour's identity for fear of repercussions with his wife and the woman's husband.[14]

Crump then told Roundtree that he had taken a bus from his house on Stanton Road to a point where he met Vivian in her car. The couple stopped to buy beer, a half pint of whiskey, a bag of potato chips, and some cigarettes. The $1.50 left over was hardly enough to rent a motel room.

"They were trying to figure out where it would be a good place to go," Roundtree told Leo Damore in 1990. "He'd been fishing on the river on occasion. So it was someplace he knew about."

"I was goofin' around," Crump eventually disclosed.

"And I fully understood what he meant," Roundtree explained in 1990. "He had sex—the usual thing. He was drinking and he fell asleep. And the girl left. The next thing he knew he was trying to get himself together and he slipped and fell into the water. That scared him. He almost drowned. He didn't know how to swim. He was really trying to find his way out of the dang place. He wasn't familiar with that area at all. And he sort of roamed around. And then he heard something like an explosion."[15]

"I tried to pin him down," Roundtree continued. "I asked him, 'Well, what did it sound like?' Crump said he heard something 'like the backfire of a car,' but he paid no attention to it. He said he was afraid."

"Well, what were you afraid of?" Roundtree had asked him.

"I don't know. I was trying to get out of there and I couldn't get myself together," she remembered him responding.

"Well, you were half drunk," Roundtree replied.

"I had to get home," Crump had told her. "And then, all hell broke loose. Police all around. I didn't know what was going on."

"Do you own a gun?" Roundtree wanted to know. Crump said no. He never owned a firearm. His brother Jimmy had a .22 rifle because Jimmy used to go hunting, but not Crump. He didn't like hunting. He had never owned a gun and wouldn't have one with five children in his house, Roundtree recalled.

"That made sense to me, so I didn't pursue it," said Roundtree. "He wasn't given to armed robbery. He didn't have a record like that. He had a job. He was hustling the best way he could. He wasn't going out to rob anybody."[16]

But Crump did have a misdemeanor record: two drunk and disorderly charges and a conviction for petit larceny. Convicted of shoplifting, he'd been sentenced to sixty days in jail, a substantial sentence for a first offense.

"But it was at the whim of the judge," Roundtree said in 1990. "We didn't have dialogues about sentencing like we do now. And it may well have been, according to what Ray told me, that he was drinking at the time. And that could have made the judge angry, that would have aggravated it."[17]

Toward the end of their first interview at the D.C. jail, the bewildered Ray Crump again asked Roundtree, "What was really going on down there?" And again, Roundtree tried to explain that a woman had been murdered and that he had been arrested for the crime. Crump was already withering under the stress of being in prison. He was withdrawing and was increasingly unable to help with his own defense. That vulnerability convinced Roundtree to take his case. "Instantly, I felt this man was being used as a scapegoat. The crime just didn't fit him at all," she recalled. Roundtree believed that Crump didn't have the temperament to be a killer. "He wouldn't have the nerve. He was of such meekness, I came to know him to be frightened half out of his wits in fear of his life. And I was afraid for him."[18] So afraid, in fact, that Roundtree did what she had never done for any client: She visited him in jail every day.

But Crump had lied to police about going fishing, and he had lied again about what he had been wearing the day that he was apprehended. Trying to conceal his affair with Vivian, he had put himself in jeopardy with police. For Roundtree, the immediate priority was to find Vivian, his only alibi. She did so with the assistance of her private investigator, Purcell Moore.

But Vivian made it clear from the outset she didn't appreciate Dovey Roundtree's out-of-the blue telephone call to her home. Vivian did, however, corroborate Ray Crump's story—right down to the details about the beer, potato chips, whiskey, and cigarettes. Her version of events lined up with Crump's. They had walked out the towpath to a spot adjacent to the Potomac River, she told Roundtree. They drank a little, had sex on some rocks, and Crump fell asleep. She left without waking him. The corroborating details offered Roundtree her first glimmer of hope. But unfortunately, like Crump, Vivian feared the repercussions of exposing her extramarital affair—she believed her husband might kill her if he learned of it. She refused to testify in court. Only after Roundtree explained that Crump would likely face the death penalty did Vivian agree to sign an affidavit verifying she'd been with Crump the entire morning of the day of the murder, and that he had carried no gun. But without an appearance at trial, the affidavit was all but worthless. Crump's fabrications to police would then form the only cornerstone of the government's case against him. The noose around his neck was tightening.[19]

When Ray Crump was moved to a cellblock with other prisoners, guards taunted him at night. "How you doing, Crump? You know, it would be a lot easier on you if you just come out and tell what you did." Dovey Roundtree believed the guards were trying to extract a confession from Crump. "And I made him promise me. No matter what goes on, you tell the guards: 'Get my lawyer here.' Don't say anything else. I don't want them beating you up or messing with you. You just say: 'You get Mrs. Roundtree here.' And you say it loud, so that somebody in the other cells can hear you. That's what you've got to do. You got to fight fire with fire."[20]

Convinced of Ray Crump's innocence, Roundtree contacted the two attorneys in the Public Defender's Office of the Legal Aid Society who had been representing him—George Peter Lamb and Ted O'Neill. Even before her formal court appearance on Crump's behalf on October 28, Roundtree had begun her own investigation.[21] She learned that her client-to-be was a high school dropout who had married at seventeen. A father of five, Crump had sustained injuries in a serious automobile accident a few years earlier, and then had been beaten up and robbed by a gang in 1962. During his convalescence from both events, he had become addicted to alcohol. He was dirt poor—he didn't have a bank account and didn't own stocks, bonds, real estate, a car, or other valuable property, nor did his wife, parents, or any other person who might be able to assist him in paying the costs of his defense. He was an easy scapegoat. His defense, Roundtree believed, would require a Herculean effort.

Roundtree decided to visit Georgetown, "to familiarize myself with that community," she explained years later. "I wanted to get a feeling for that place." The house that Mary Meyer had lived in was still sealed. "Police were still conducting their investigation. They were still around but I had no conversation with them, though I'm sure one of the police officers recognized me, knew who I was. I went out there at least twice within that vicinity, to see what

I could see or hear." While looking at Mary's studio, Roundtree felt "an unfriendliness there." A black postman making his rounds, she recalled, "wanted to know what I was doing in the area."[22]

Retracing Mary Meyer's route on the day of her murder, Roundtree approached the intersection of 34th and M Streets at the base of the steep hill, where she came upon Dixie Liquors, a small package store adjacent to Key Bridge, known at the time for selling alcohol to the underage well-to-do children of Northwest Washington. Had Crump and his girlfriend stopped there, she wondered, to buy their provisions before walking out on the towpath?

Turning west on Prospect Place, Roundtree approached the picturesque bridge over the C & O Canal to the towpath. She crossed the bridge and followed Mary Meyer's westerly route, tracing the path that, according to the press, had been Mary Meyer's daily routine. She passed under the aqueduct from the first column of Key Bridge, and from there she headed toward Fletcher's Boat House, a total distance of just over two miles. About a half a mile west, she would cross the wooden footbridge and continue to walk the 637.5 feet westward (just over a tenth of a mile) to the exact spot where Mary Meyer's life had ended.[23]

The C & O Canal fell under the jurisdiction of the U.S. Park Police, some of whom had taken part in searches for the murder weapon that had killed Mary Meyer. The towpath was usually well patrolled, with Park Police cruisers covering the area from Georgetown to Seneca, Maryland, a tour of twenty-two miles. Mounted police on horseback usually covered the four miles from Georgetown to Chain Bridge, patrolling the towpath and the woods between the canal and the Potomac River. Park Police officer Ray Pollan knew the area under the Key Bridge well. He had come to know the regulars who gathered there drinking cheap wine out of paper bags, but he had never seen Ray Crump among them. Pollan had been off-duty the day that Mary Meyer had been killed. Had he been on duty that day, he told Leo Damore, "[t]here probably wouldn't have been a murder, because I would've been there."[24] Had the killer chosen a day when the towpath was relatively unattended?

Even before she became Ray Crump's attorney, Roundtree was aware of the "heavy heat" coming down on Crump's case. The young, ardent public defender, George Peter Lamb, had been keeping her informed after she expressed interest in the case. At the time, Lamb was focused on preparing for the preliminary hearing to which Crump was entitled to, regardless of innocence or guilt. Typically, a "prelim," as public defenders referred to it, would establish the evidence that the police had to support their charge of first-degree murder. Most important for a defendant, the preliminary hearing would afford the accused an opportunity to learn in advance the basis of the charges against him, as well as to allow his attorney to argue a lack of probable cause for his continued incarceration. Without significant evidence, particularly forensic evidence linking a defendant to the crime, there would be no legal basis for further detention. The defendant would, therefore, have to be released.

But it wasn't an "accident" or "oversight" that the Public Defender's Office hadn't been made aware, as they legally should have been, of the FBI Crime Lab report (see appendix 1) that had been delivered to police chief Robert V. Murray on October 16, just four days after the murder. Had this occurred, there would have been no further grounds to detain Ray Crump. The report clearly documented the lack of any forensic evidence linking Crump to the murder scene or the victim.

Compounding that travesty of justice, not only was Ray Crump being denied a preliminary hearing, but the coroner's inquest was conducted with an unusual lack of protocol. In 1964 in Washington, the inquest was typically held in a room at the D.C. morgue. While the inquest carried no actual legal authority, its outcome might influence a judge on matters involving bail or extended incarceration. Most lawyers didn't even bother to attend a coroner's inquest, but attorneys in the Public Defender's office usually attended because it was an opportunity to find out what the government actually had in terms of evidence against their client. The entire proceedings were entered into the court record. "You could nail down to some extent what facts and evidence were known at the time," recalled George Peter Lamb. "This generally gave you a good opportunity for early discovery."[25]

But on the morning of October 19—before the scheduled eleven o'clock coroner's inquest into the murder of Mary Meyer—a grand jury had indicted Ray Crump for first-degree murder. This was a considerable departure from legal procedure: Grand juries were usually convened after completion of a coroner's inquest. It was, in the view of Crump's Legal Aid attorneys Jake Stein and George Peter Lamb, a deliberate attempt by the government to circumvent a preliminary hearing for Crump. At the inquest itself, Crump's attorneys asked for a continuance in order to subpoena additional witnesses. The coroner denied the request and proceeded with the inquest over their objections. Asserting that inquest protocol had been violated and that Crump deserved a preliminary hearing, both Stein and Lamb refused to participate in the hearing. "The conniving that went on around this case was astounding," remembered Lamb.[26]

In spite of the objections, the coroner's inquest found that there was sufficient evidence to bring Ray Crump Jr. to trial for the murder of Mary Meyer. With Crump's attorneys absent, only one witness was called: Detective Bernie Crooke. His testimony amounted to hearsay. He alleged that the government's eyewitness, tow truck driver Henry Wiggins, had seen Ray Crump standing over the body of Mary Meyer "from a distance of nearly three quarters of a mile."[27] This was not only a physical impossibility, it was factually incorrect. The distance—128.6 feet, to be exact—had already been measured by police the day after the murder.[28] The all-white six-man jury, many of who were retired government employees, never even questioned the discrepancies.

With the government's case fortified by both the grand jury's indictment and the outcome of the coroner's inquest, Commissioner Sam Wertleb not only denied the defense's request for a continuance, but also its motions to subpoena six witnesses. Wertleb argued that the grand jury indictment had dispensed with any need for a preliminary hearing. In a separate case (*Blue v. United States*, 342 F.2d 894 [D.C. Cir. 1964]), decided only six days later on October 29, the D.C. Court of Appeals upheld a defendant's right to a preliminary hearing, arguing: "The denial of an opportunity for a defendant to consider intelligently the value of a pretrial hearing cannot be swept under the rug of a Grand Jury indictment."[29]

Without a preliminary hearing, the government could continue to conceal the FBI Crime Lab report from Crump's defense (see Appendix 1). This appeared to be their strategy. Had Crump been given a preliminary hearing, as he should have been, the FBI Crime Lab report would legally have to have been produced, and it freely acknowledged the holes in the government's case. Ray Crump would have undoubtedly been released. For nine months, the report would be buried, until finally a frustrated Dovey Roundtree demanded it be delivered. This was clear-cut malfeasance on the part of the government to manipulate the case.

"Despite police spokesmen repeatedly giving out provocative and inflammatory information to the press, all tending to point to the defendant's guilt," George Peter Lamb recalled, "they had very little evidence to back it up. They did everything possible to prevent any of the real details of the case being made public. The standard device in hot cases like this was to avoid the discovery process in a preliminary hearing or a coroner's inquest, and they got away with it. They didn't want to leave their case against Crump dangling in the wind, and they would do whatever was necessary to keep the defense from being able to see what little real evidence they had."[30]

Lamb's representation of Ray Crump Jr. had left him with an indelible memory. "There was something in Ray Crump that made me from the very beginning believe he wasn't guilty," Lamb said more than forty-five years later. "My measure of him in the cellblock and in the courtroom was that he didn't do it, and it had to do with how Crump dealt with me, how he answered my questions, how he looked me in the eye. I was a believer in Crump's innocence and so was Ted O'Neill, who ran the Public Defender's Office."[31]

Dovey Roundtree filed her appearance in the defense of Ray Crump Jr. on October 28, 1964.[32] Crump appeared for his arraignment on his indictment for murder two days later, and entered a plea of not guilty. A trial date was set for January 11, 1965. Roundtree, who had been in contact with Crump's former defense team, was aware of the prosecution's strategy. Her first move was to request bond for her client so that he could return to his work and his family. Roundtree hoped that she might have a sympathetic ear in federal district court judge Burnita Sheldon Matthews—a Truman appointee who had been a supporter of the Equal Rights Amendment since its inception in 1923 and was active in the suffrage movement. But Judge Matthews had a record of siding with the prosecution. As far as George Peter Lamb was concerned, "Judge Matthews believed all blacks were guilty, and the reason they were guilty was because they were indicted, and therefore they should plead guilty. Anything that a defense lawyer did to slow the process was interfering with justice."[33] True to form, Judge Matthews denied Ray Crump's bond on the grounds that the government had determined that he was "dangerous" and a "danger to the community."

An innocent man was being railroaded, Roundtree believed. Sorrow over the death of her grandmother Rachel just five days into her representation of Ray Crump only intensified her commitment to justice for her downtrodden client. The day of Ray Crump's arraignment, Roundtree had already filed a writ of habeas corpus on his behalf. Rather than attack the validity of the indictment, Roundtree charged that police had beaten Crump following his arrest on October 12, and that there had been a number of irregularities in the legal proceedings, chief among them the denial of a preliminary hearing.

"If there had been an orderly preliminary hearing with some leeway for discovery, we could have raised quite a bit of doubt with respect to probable cause," Roundtree told Leo Damore in 1990. "The government would have proceeded to the grand jury anyway and come back with an indictment, but I believe we could have established a great deal of doubt."[34]

The D.C. district judge denied the writ of habeas corpus on November 9, 1964. Anticipating as much, Roundtree had already begun preparing an appeal for the U.S. Court of Appeals for the D.C. Circuit. It was a shrewd move: She knew that the appeal wouldn't be decided for months, and the delay would afford her legal team much-needed time to prepare for trial. She also hoped that the media scrutiny focused on her client would abate in the intervening months.

Dovey Roundtree had another, more immediate situation that needed remedy. Her client was coming undone. His already fragile mental state was unraveling.[35] Deteriorating mentally and emotionally, exhibiting signs of paranoia, chronic terror, and increasing despondency, Crump believed his food at the jail was being poisoned. During Roundtree's daily visits, he cried uncontrollably. "He was pitiful and completely scared, as an innocent man would be," recalled Roundtree. "He didn't have a murderer's temperament."[36] The Roundtree remedy was a flash of brilliance: She filed a motion on November 12, 1964, for a mental examination of Ray Crump. "It was more than just for delay," she explained years later. "I had difficulty communicating with Crump. He was so withdrawn I came to know that really he was scared half to death."[37] Wondering whether her client was fit to stand trial, Roundtree also feared that brutality and taunting by prison guards would undo Crump completely.

Later that November, Ray Crump underwent a sixty-day psychiatric evaluation at St. Elizabeth's Hospital. Having already established that Crump had been robbed and severely beaten in 1962, Roundtree underscored that Crump had endured a head trauma that had never been properly evaluated or diagnosed. He suffered from excruciating headaches and had been known to have blackouts from binge drinking. He had been drunk the day of his arrest.[38] In spite of this, in January 1965, Dr. Dale Cameron, superintendent of St. Elizabeth's, found Crump competent to stand trial, stating "that [Ray Crump] is not now, and was not, on or about October 12, 1964, suffering from a mental disease or defect."[39]

Having removed her client from the perils of the D.C. jail, if only briefly, Dovey Roundtree awaited word on her appeal of Crump's denial of a preliminary hearing. The appeal, handed down on June 15, 1965, was denied by a 2-1 decision. Dissenting D.C. circuit court judge George Thomas Washington sided with Roundtree, arguing "that a defendant is entitled to a preliminary hearing even after an indictment," and that "a coroner's inquest was no substitute for a preliminary hearing." Judge Washington also noted that only one witness, Detective Bernie Crooke, had been called, and that he "gave mostly hearsay testimony," and that he was not subjected to cross-examination. Washington also expressed his skepticism on the record regarding Crooke's claim that "the government's chief eyewitness [tow truck driver Henry Wiggins] saw the defendant standing over the body from a distance of nearly three quarters of a mile."[40] A dissenting opinion was better than a unanimous decision, but it would do little for Ray Crump's defense or mental equilibrium.

It was now inevitable that Ray Crump would stand trial for the murder of Mary Pinchot Meyer. Already, Dovey Roundtree had begun to acquaint herself with the neighborhoods where Mary Meyer had lived and painted. She had explored the C & O Canal towpath. As the trial date approached, Roundtree redoubled her efforts to retrace the dead woman's—and her client's—steps. "On most Saturday afternoons, or whenever we got the chance," recalled Roundtree's first cousin, Jerry Hunter, a student at Howard University's law school at the time, "we went out to Georgetown and the canal. There wasn't a blade of grass we didn't know about."[41] It was during this time that Roundtree became aware that there were many more entrances and exits than the four that the government maintained they had guarded on the day of the murder. On one exploration of the canal towpath, Roundtree and Hunter ran into Detective Bernie Crooke, who wanted to know why they were bothering to investigate the area. "You know he's guilty," Roundtree remembered Crooke saying. "Why are you doing this?"[42]

Someone else was also bothered by Roundtree's investigations of the towpath. Almost from the beginning, she received phone calls around midnight. "The caller never spoke," she wrote in her 2009 autobiography, *Justice Older Than the Law*, "yet he or she stayed on the line, breathing into the phone until I hung up. Days would pass, and then once again would come the dreaded ring." She continued:

> The calls, it became clear, were tied to my visits to the crime scene. I often had the sense, there, that I was being watched. The sun shone, the park and towpath echoed with the shouts and laughter of runners and picnickers and fishermen on the autumn afternoons when we visited, but I could not shake off the sense of something sinister. The more we visited the crime scene, the more persistent the calls became, but I kept returning to the towpath area with George and Jerry because I was so absolutely convinced that only by memorizing the area, every

tree and blade of grass, would I be fully prepared for anything the prosecution might bring up at trial.[43]

In December 1964, Detective Bernie Crooke suddenly informed Roundtree that police had recovered Crump's hair from the sweater that Mary Meyer had been wearing when she was murdered.[44] This was a complete fabrication; the police had recovered no such forensic evidence. But they launched a crusade to permit them to take a sample of Crump's hair. Eventually, and against his will, they did, and it yielded a match of hair found inside the brimmed golf cap that had been recovered on the day after the murder on the shore of the Potomac River—684 feet west of the murder scene. Given the eyewitness reports of Henry Wiggins and Lieutenant William Mitchell, both of whom claimed to have seen a "Negro male" wearing a dark-brimmed golf cap, the government, with nothing better to go on, would extol this alleged match as proof that Crump was the cold-blooded killer.

The witnesses' statements, however, proved only that Crump had lied about wearing the cap. That wasn't good, but it didn't amount to murder. In its zeal to pin Mary Meyer's killing on Crump, the prosecution ignored an entirely plausible scenario: that Crump had actually told the truth about falling into the river. After all, his cap and Windbreaker had been found in the area where Crump claimed to have slipped off some rocks. The jacket had been retrieved by police two-tenths of mile west of the murder scene and the cap 416 feet east of where the jacket had been found. At that juncture on the Potomac River shoreline, any attempt to swim the quarter mile across the dangerous river current and undertow would have been daunting even for an accomplished swimmer, let alone someone who was terrified of being in water over his head.[45]

Who was Mary Pinchot Meyer, Roundtree wanted to know? She was familiar with the newspaper accounts that identified the slain woman as an up-and-coming artist, the niece of former Pennsylvania governor Gifford Pinchot, and a friend of former First Lady Jacqueline Kennedy's. Roundtree knew also that Mary had been divorced, though she was not yet aware that she had only obtained the divorce after granting Cord control over her sons' education.

Roundtree was puzzled. Police had reported finding nothing of significance when they searched Mary Meyer's house. She concluded that someone must have gotten there before them and wiped the place clean. "There was nothing to see; they didn't even see pictures of her children," Roundtree remembered. "I would have certainly expected something connecting her with somebody or with something, because there was precious little found in her dwelling. Nothing could connect her to anybody." Unaware of Mary Meyer's affair with the late President Kennedy, her diary, or her relationship with psychedelic guru Timothy Leary, Roundtree's instinct told her that something suspicious had taken place, and that this was not some random murder. Less than two months into the case, she and her defense team had begun to wonder, "Could [Mary Meyer] have been murdered and taken [to the C & O Canal towpath] with everything staged to look different?" She was troubled by something else: What had happened to the stalled Nash Rambler that Henry Wiggins had been called to fix? She pressed her private investigator, Purcell Moore, to find a repair order for the car, or the car's owner, but he came up dry on both counts.[46] Justice was not color-blind, however, and that was one reason she believed that Ray Crump had the deck stacked against him—that, and the fact that the prosecution had no other suspect.

"I thought we had enough evidence to go to trial," recalled former U.S. attorney David Acheson in an interview for this book in 2008. Acheson had been the Justice Department's U.S. attorney at the time of Crump's arrest. In fact, Acheson, son of former secretary of state Dean Acheson, had the distinguished pedigree typical of Mary Meyer's Georgetown neighbors. He had personally known Mary well, and had attended Yale in the same class as her ex-husband. He was fully aware that Cord was not the generic "government clerk" that Washington newspapers had made him out to be.

"The prevailing wisdom in the office at the time was that Ray Crump was guilty," recalled Acheson, "and we had to prosecute somebody. In a murder case like this where you have a plausible suspect, and you don't have enough evidence to go against anybody else, you really have to go to trial. You've gotta show the public you didn't just kiss the case off."[47]

Without Dovey Roundtree's commitment to Ray Crump's defense, Mary Meyer's murder might well have been relegated into history as a random sexual assault gone awry, a twist of fate for a woman who had been so fortunate in so many respects up to that point. Yet Roundtree was committed not just to the defense of her client, of whose innocence she was convinced, but also to the heart and soul of justice itself—the principle of equal protection under the law. And so, before the end of 1964, Dovey Roundtree was prepared to stake her entire professional reputation—as well as her own financial resources—on one of the biggest trials ever to take place in Washington.

5

Trial by Fire

The only new thing in this world is the history you don't know.
                                            —President Harry Truman

O N JUNE 11, 1963, President Kennedy delivered legislation to Congress that would become, after his death, the Civil Rights Act of 1964. In a landmark address from the Oval Office that evening, one day after his historic American University commencement address advocating world peace, the president said, "We face a moral crisis as a country, and as a people. Those who do nothing are inviting shame as well as violence. Those who act boldly are recognizing right, as well as reality." The next day—June 12, 1963—Medgar Evers, a leader of the National Association for the Advancement of Colored People (NAACP), was shot and killed in front of his wife and three children in his Mississippi driveway. His killer, the white supremacist Byron De La Beckwith, evaded conviction twice with hung juries in 1964 and would not be finally convicted for the murder until 1994. Two months later, in August, Martin Luther King Jr., the civil rights movement's most eloquent and charismatic leader, had filled the nation's capital and captured the country's attention with his inspiring dreams of racial equality.

Nearly two years later, as Ray Crump's murder trial approached in the summer of 1965, civil rights advocates were still marching across the American South. On televisions throughout the country, Americans witnessed images of racial hatred and its casualties: African Americans tear-gassed, beaten by police, bitten by police K-9 dogs, and lynched by racist mobs. Hatred and fear of the black man pervaded America in the months leading up to Ray Crump's trial for the murder of a white woman. The surrounding political and racial climate was not lost on Dovey Roundtree.

For Dovey Roundtree and her legal team, the U.S. attorney's pursuit of Raymond Crump Jr. for the murder of Mary Meyer was further evidence of the lingering racism that permeated the corridors of the American judicial system. It represented all that was unfair and unjust when it came to the failure of equal protection under the law for anyone who wasn't white. Without any financial remuneration and with only her own resources, Dovey Roundtree would stake her professional life on defending a victimized, dirt-poor young black man. For Roundtree, it wasn't just the life and future of one man that was at stake. She believed Crump was being conveniently scapegoated. Justice itself was on trial; and if the cause of justice was to be served, then everything in its way had to be confronted and overcome.

The prosecution's "declaration of war" on Ray Crump would unleash a righteous power for justice. Roundtree was ready to "act boldly," perhaps more so than ever before. Ray Crump couldn't pay his legal fees, so Roundtree committed her own resources to his defense. It was a terrific gamble, but one that Roundtree and her team considered supremely worthwhile. She would employ every skill she possessed to confront and defeat the government's case against her client, of whose innocence she was categorically convinced. As her friend and fellow attorney George Peter Lamb once remarked, "Dovey Roundtree was the world's greatest cross-examiner." A courtroom full of people would soon understand why.

The government, however, was still stonewalling Ray Crump's defense. Four months after the murder itself, Roundtree still hadn't been able to get a clear statement from the government's lawyers, and therefore she wasn't sure whether a murder weapon had even been recovered. Assistant U.S. Attorney Charles Duncan, the young black prosecutor initially assigned to the case by senior U.S. attorney David Acheson, was normally an ebullient man and quite friendly with Dovey. But he wasn't being helpful or cooperative when she ran into him on the elevator in the courthouse one day before Christmas.

"I've called you a couple of times," she remembered saying to him. "I wanted to come and talk to you about this case. I'm uneasy about this. A million eyes are on this case, and we're the ones that don't know what's really going on." But Duncan had been evasive and put her off. "It's just a straight case," she recalled him saying. "They caught him. He was down there."

"So were a lot of other people down there [on the C & O Canal towpath] that day," Dovey recalled saying. Duncan had shrugged his shoulders, said something to the effect that he didn't know whether he was going to continue with the case, and proceeded to walk away. How odd was this, Dovey recalled in 1991.[1] In fact, Dovey didn't know Charles Duncan had been offered a job as general counsel to the newly formed Equal Employment Opportunity Commission (EEOC).[2]

Meanwhile, Dovey Roundtree and her legal team had lost the battle for a permanent injunction that would have restrained the government from forcing Ray Crump to give samples of his hair. In early February, Crump was taken to the police captain's office to give a hair sample. He refused, and was then forcibly held down by several officers while hair was cut from his head. This infuriated Dovey. In mid-March, she filed a motion to suppress evidence—not only her client's hair, but any chemical analysis from the hair, as well as his shoes, and the cap and jacket (alleged to have been Crump's), all of which she argued had been taken either against his will or without his consent, violating his Fourth Amendment right to protection from unreasonable searches and seizures.

Roundtree was being stonewalled from every direction. Determined to establish exactly what evidence the prosecution had in its possession, she filed a motion for a complete bill of particulars. The motion would compel the prosecution to list everything or be held in contempt. In addition, they would have to turn over all evidence collected in connection with the murder, including eyewitness accounts, the murder weapon, the FBI Crime Lab report, items taken from Crump's home, and everything that Crump had used or worn on the day of the crime.

Finally, in early March, five months after the murder itself, the prosecution was forced to cough up what it had. No murder weapon had been found, but the two .38-caliber lead bullets taken from Mary Meyer's corpse would be entered into evidence, as well as Ray Crump's hair, the clothing he had been wearing that day—the beige-tan zippered jacket, the dark-plaid golf cap, dark corduroy trousers, black shoes—and an open package of Pall Mall cigarettes. A complete list of all persons at the scene, interviewed, or connected with the crime would also be produced. It was straightforward enough. What struck Roundtree as ominous, however, was the signature on the statement of evidence. Assistant U.S. Attorney Charles Duncan had been replaced by one of the toughest prosecutors in the criminal justice department: Alfred ("Al") L. Hantman.

"Oh, brother!" Dovey remembered thinking. "What are they doing to me!" Her heart sank as she contemplated what was before her.[3] With Hantman on the case, she knew they were bringing in the heavy artillery. As Assistant Chief of the Criminal Division in the Justice Department, Hantman would have a full staff, as well as a small army of ancillary personnel.

Alfred L. Hantman was, indeed, a big gun. Seasoned, tough, savvy, he was a 1948 graduate of George Washington University Law School and had been an officer in the U.S. Army Air Corps during World War II. He was counted among the top three attorneys in the criminal division of the Justice Department, where his career would span twenty-three years. Hantman had already tried a range of felonies, including murders; observers described him as "a screamer and a bully" in the courtroom. Tall, prepossessing, an imposing figure with bristling eyebrows and an extraordinary legal mind capable of prodigious feats of memory, he conveyed a formidable authority; and defense attorneys were known to work into the wee hours of the morning preparing to face him in a courtroom. Respected for being "a worker in the vineyard," Al Hantman was not, however, part of the old-boy aristocratic Ivy League club to which his boss, U. S. Attorney David Acheson, belonged.

Dovey Roundtree was well aware of Hantman's reputation, and she was troubled by this turn of events. With Hantman's appearance for the prosecution, she recalled later, she believed that "they were out to kill this boy."[4] In the District of Columbia, first-degree murder carried the death penalty. What Roundtree didn't know at the time was that a confidential internal Justice Department memo, dated February 24, 1965—five months before the start of the trial—noted the following: "[Hantman's] case is very weak from an evidentiary standpoint, and he needs all the evidence that he possibly can get to support his case."[5] (See Appendix 2.)

Of course, Al Hantman was aware that his case against Crump was entirely circumstantial. For that reason, he would attempt every possible maneuver to gain advantage in the months leading up to trial, including dueling with the defense over pretrial motions, evidentiary hearings, and the admissibility of various pieces of evidence. The rulings were almost always in Hantman's favor, an advantage that he maximized, and sometimes embellished. In one pretrial conference, Hantman went so far as to allege that Ray Crump had cleaned Mary Meyer's house—a complete fabrication that nonetheless introduced the possibility of the defendant's prior association with the victim. In response, Dovey Roundtree produced every single payroll receipt that Crump had received from the Brown Construction Company. In doing so, she made it clear that she would countenance no further deceptions of that sort.[6]

Making matters worse for Roundtree, the judge assigned to the trial was an unknown quantity. The Honorable Howard F. Corcoran had just been appointed by President Johnson to be a U.S. District Court Judge for the District of Columbia. It was an appointment that surprised many. At his Senate Judiciary Committee confirmation hearing, when asked about his actual trial experience, the prospective federal judge replied, "Zero." In spite of the embarrassed silence that followed, his nomination was approved. One insider speculated it was nepotism. Judge Howard Corcoran was the brother of the legendary Tommy "the Cork" Corcoran, an influential lawyer and D.C. power broker who had drafted much of the New Deal legislation for Franklin D. Roosevelt. Judge Corcoran's pedigree and education—Phillips Exeter Academy, Princeton, and then Harvard Law—placed him in the social class of Mary and Cord Meyer, as well as that of U.S. Attorney David Acheson, signaling an easy access to power. Pedigree aside, many felt that Judge Corcoran was not ready for a case like this. Some even speculated that because of his lack of experience, he would rule according to the letter of the law to avoid being overturned on appeal. For Roundtree and her team, it was another bad break, something that might work against her.

Judge Corcoran's law clerk for the trial was a young, agile attorney fresh out of Harvard Law School's prestigious Master of Laws program. Twenty-five-year-old Brooklyn-born Robert Stephen Bennett had graduated from Georgetown Law in 1964. He salivated at the prospect of being part of the action, and no place would be hotter than Washington in the summer of 1965. Thirty years later, having become one of Washington's and the nation's eminent criminal defense attorneys, he would find himself standing at the podium in the marbled United States Supreme Court representing President Bill Clinton in a sexual harassment lawsuit.

In response to Roundtree's wish to enter into evidence the fact of Mary Meyer's divorce and two surviving sons, Corcoran refused. "I do not want this woman's reputation dragged through the mud," he said. It seemed an odd response to the request, since "lack of relevance" might have kept it out just as well. Could Corcoran have learned of the unconventionality of the dead woman's lifestyle? The judge sustained Hantman's objection, however, when Roundtree tried to establish for the jury that Ray Crump was the father of five children. "Anything you can do to humanize the defendant, you try to get in," Roundtree said years later. "But it was clear that Corcoran intended to maintain a tight rein on the kind of evidence he was going to allow. Whether it was because this was his first case, or he was nervous, I don't know, but he was very strict."[7]

Judge Corcoran also barred any testimony that referred to the Central Intelligence Agency. Could he have been privy to the rumors of a CIA conspiracy link that surrounded Mary Meyer's death? That was unknown, but it appeared likely that as a first-timer on the bench, Corcoran sought to avoid any controversy whatsoever, and in that regard, any mention of the CIA would seem especially off-limits. The Warren Report's lone gunman assertion was already beginning to be challenged. There were rumblings swirling all over Washington and elsewhere about CIA involvement in President Kennedy's assassination, and Corcoran likely sought to steer clear of any mention of the Agency altogether.

Prosecutor Hantman, for his part, knew he was involved in a high-profile case, but at the time of the trial, he was unaware how high profile the case might become. He didn't know that Mary Meyer had kept a diary and that in it, she had written about her lover, the slain president. Nor did he know that Mary's diary was now in the hands of CIA counterintelligence chief Jim Angleton, and that Angleton's wife would be in court every day, observing the trial.

On Monday, July 19, 1965, a three-hundred-person jury pool convened in Courtroom 8, where the laborious process of jury selection would take all day. Dovey Roundtree and her defense team scored a partial victory with a jury of eight blacks and four whites; seven of the twelve jurors were women. There were also four alternate jurors. Before retiring for the day, the jury selected their foreman: Edward O. Savwoir, a forty-four-year-old African American program specialist at the Job Corps in the Office of Economic Opportunity in Washington.

The following morning, on a sweltering July day, the trial convened in the newly air-conditioned fourth-floor courtroom of Washington's U. S. District Court Building. It was packed to capacity with onlookers. Many would return day after day for the duration of the trial. Also present every day was Martha Crump, Ray Crump's mother, always accompanied by members of her church community. The courtroom's racial mix and class disparities reflected the divide between the murdered woman and the accused defendant, all interspersed with a noticeable number of unsmiling white men in impeccably tailored suits, reminding Roundtree of the significance of this case. "So many men in gray suits showed up," she recalled in 1991. "They were government people. I knew that. But I could never understand why so many at the time."[8]

The news media was a significant presence in the courtroom. Sam Donaldson, a young broadcast news reporter for the CBS affiliate, WTOP-TV, in Washington, sat directly behind the defense team, as did two nuns. Roundtree had no idea who they were, but she recalled that at different times, both Donaldson and the nuns said something similar to her: "You'll pull it out . . ." Her response to all of them: "Well, you must know something I don't know."[9]

Indeed, Hantman's long, thundering opening statement seemed to spell doom for the defendant he said had "deliberately, willfully, and maliciously shot and killed Mary Pinchot Meyer."[10] In graphic terms, Hantman portrayed Crump in a violent struggle with the victim, insinuating, with no evidence to support his position, that the murder had been the result of a sexual assault gone awry. Nothing about the victim, Hantman told the jury, would have attracted the attention of a thief, given that she carried no wallet and wore no jewelry.[11] Crump had tried to take her by surprise from behind, Hantman maintained, but she had struggled so powerfully that he had been forced to resort to brutality—shooting her in the head to subdue her, then dragging her twenty-five feet while she continued to struggle, before fatally shooting her again. An effective storyteller, Hantman captured and held the jury's attention with his vivid portrayal of Mary Meyer on her knees, fighting for her life even with a bullet in her head, tearing the defendant's jacket and his trouser pocket.[12]

Hantman continued in morbid detail: "We will show you that the blood stains on the tree were only two, two-and-a-half feet from the ground. We will show you that Mary Pinchot Meyer got away from the defendant. She ran back across the towpath toward the canal itself, away from the embankment; that she fell on that side of the towpath closest to the canal; that this defendant Raymond Crump, seeing the deceased getting away from him and believing that she might be able to identify him later, shot Mary Pinchot Meyer again right over the right shoulder."[13] Designed for high-impact courtroom drama upon the jury, the Hantman delivery was intended to be as brutal as it was damaging.

Next, Hantman gave the police reconstruction of Ray Crump's alleged attempt to flee the murder scene after tow truck driver Henry Wiggins had spotted him standing over "the lifeless corpse." The government's prosecutor extolled the professionalism and alacrity of the police response in closing off all of the exits in the towpath area "within four minutes" of the broadcast bulletin about the murder. Documenting that Crump was apprehended several hundred feet from the murder scene, but only after he "ran over the embankment, ran west 684 feet where he got rid of his light tan zipper jacket," and then, "426 feet beyond that, further west, [he] got rid of his plaid cap with a bill on it," Hantman maintained that Crump had "continued to run in a westerly direction towards Fletcher's Landing for some 1,750 feet beyond this, at which point he saw Officer Roderick Sylvis." Crump had tried to escape, said Hantman, by swimming across the Potomac but realized he wouldn't be able to do so. Detective John Warner finally apprehended Crump, who then lied about having been fishing that morning, as well as about the clothes he had been wearing. The beige Windbreaker jacket and dark-plaid golf cap would be found not far from the murder scene.[14]

Concluding his statement, Hantman once again implied that Crump had acted out of a premeditated intent to commit a sexual assault, thus casting the murder of Mary Meyer not a spontaneous act, but a killing in cold blood, the result of an attempted rape that had been derailed by a particularly feisty victim. Hantman made certain the jury knew that when Crump was apprehended, the fly on his pants was open, that his pant's pocket was torn, that he was soaking wet, that he had blood on his right hand, which was cut, and that he had a small cut or abrasion over one eye. All this could have only happened, Hantman maintained, from his struggle with Mary Meyer.

To bolster his contention that Crump's injuries must have resulted from his struggle with Mary Meyer, Hantman concluded his presentation with Lieutenant William L. Mitchell's statement to police the day after the murder. Mitchell had jogged past Mary Meyer at approximately 12:20 P.M., he said, about four minutes before the first shot was fired. Two hundred yards after passing Meyer, Hantman read aloud, Mitchell had told police that he had ran past a "Negro male dressed in a light tan jacket and dark corduroy trousers and wearing a dark plaid cap with a brim on it," and who was not carrying any fishing equipment.[15]

The prosecutor's opening statement left Dovey Roundtree in a kind of legal and emotional quicksand. Not only had Hantman's recitation been convincing and thorough, he had promised the jury that his witnesses would dispel any doubt as to the defendant's innocence, in spite of the fact that no murder weapon had been recovered. Regardless of the fact that the prosecution's case was built entirely on circumstantial evidence, it would take a grueling, formidable effort on Dovey Roundtree's part to rescue her client.

"I was completely overwhelmed by what he promised the jury he was going to present," Roundtree recalled in 1992. "It sounded like a different case entirely. I was scared to death."[16]

If she had been staggered—even a bit undone—by Hantman's performance, Dovey Roundtree had not shown it. She decided to reserve her own opening statement, then implored Judge Corcoran to let the record show that Hantman's statement had been so inflammatory, so prejudicial, that it was grounds for a mistrial. The judge declined to do so. Roundtree then insisted on seeing "the bloodstained tree" that Hantman said he would be bringing into the courtroom. The judge agreed, saying he wanted to see it, too; but already the proceedings were spiraling out of control. In an effort to maintain decorum, Judge Corcoran ordered an immediate fifteen-minute recess.

The first witness to testify was Benjamin C. Bradlee, who was then the Washington, D.C., bureau chief for *Newsweek*. "Did there come a time when you saw Mary Pinchot Meyer in death?" Hantman asked. Bradlee recounted that he had gone to the D.C. morgue on the day of the murder "sometime after six o'clock in the evening,"[17] accompanied by Sergeant Sam Wallace of the D.C. Metropolitan Police Department, where he had identified the body of his sister-in-law, Mary Pinchot Meyer. The inference of Bradlee's testimony was that it wasn't until Sergeant Wallace arrived at Bradlee's home that evening, just before 6:00 P.M., that Bradlee had any knowledge of the murder. Strangely, Hantman never directly asked Bradlee when he had *first learned* of the event. Instead, he inquired whether Bradlee had, subsequent to Mary Meyer's death, made "any effort to gain entry to this studio that was occupied by Mrs. Meyer." Contrary to what he would document in his 1995 memoir, Bradlee told the court that he had, in fact, entered Mary's studio that night with no difficulty, presumably alone, never indicating whether anyone else was with him.[18]

At no time was Hantman aware that Mary Meyer had kept a diary, or that she had been romantically involved with President Kennedy. Ben Bradlee was well aware of both, but he wasn't about to reveal anything further. More than twenty-five years later, in 1991, Hantman would remark to author Leo Damore that had he known these two facts, "it could have changed everything," because he was "totally unaware of who Mary Meyer was or what her connections were."[19]

Appearing to tread lightly, Dovey Roundtree began her first cross-examination. "Mr. Bradlee, I have just one question," she said.

Bradlee:	Yes, ma'am.
Roundtree:	Do you have any personal, independent knowledge regarding the causes of the death of your sister-in-law? Do you know how she met her death? Do you know who caused it?
Bradlee:	Well, I saw a bullet hole in her head.
Roundtree:	Do you know who caused this to be?
Bradlee:	No, I don't.
Roundtree:	You have no other information regarding the occurrences leading up to her death?
Bradlee:	No, I do not.
Roundtree:	Thank you, sir.[20]

Unaware of its far-reaching implications, Roundtree had asked the most important question surrounding the death of Mary Pinchot Meyer: *"Do you have any personal, independent knowledge regarding the causes of the death of your sister-in-law?"*

Ben Bradlee had withheld the fact that a group of Mary Meyer's intimates, including Bradlee himself, had immediately conspired to commandeer Mary Meyer's diary, letters, and personal papers—and given the entire collection to CIA counterintelligence chief James Jesus Angleton. In addition, he omitted the single most important event surrounding the murder of his sister-in-law: the telephone call from his CIA friend "just after lunch"—about four hours *before* her identity to police had been established. The same caller, the reader will recall, had also informed Cord Meyer in New York of Mary's demise later that afternoon—again, before her identity was known to authorities.[21]

During the first morning of the trial, Deputy Coroner Linwood L. Rayford testified that he had pronounced the then-unknown victim dead at the murder scene at approximately 2:05 P.M. The victim had been shot twice, he said in his testimony: ". . . the first [shot] was located an inch and half anterior to the left ear. . . . The second [shot] was located over the right shoulder blade about six inches from the midline." Rayford went on to delineate the path of each bullet. The first shot to the head, just anterior to the left ear and surrounded by a dark halo, traversed the skull across the floor of the brain, angling slightly from the back to the front. "In other words, going foreword from left to right, [it] struck the right side of the skull, fractured it and ricocheted back where the slug was found in the right side of the brain," he explained. The second bullet wound, also surrounded by a dark halo, had been fired over the victim's right shoulder blade, traversing it and the chest cavity, perforating the right lung and severing the aorta. Hantman questioned the significance of the "two darkened halos" that surrounded each gunshot wound. "It is suggestive of powder burns," Rayford responded. "This means that the gun was fired from rather close proximity."[22]

Rayford went on to explain that the victim had "superficial lacerations to the forehead, abrasions to the forehead, to the left knee and the left ankle." Hantman wanted the jury to know that there had been a violent struggle before and after the first shot had been fired, that Mary Meyer had fought hard, and that she had been dragged "clear across the path," after she clung to a tree, leaving traces of her blood. Whoever the assassin was, Rayford's detailed account made clear, he had been able to overpower the 5 foot 6 inch victim, who weighed 127 pounds, from behind.[23] In the midst of the struggle, the first shot, Rayford testified, would have produced "a considerable amount of external bleeding." The coroner's description of the precise angles of each shot implied that the assassin was likely ambidextrous and had expertise in the surgical use of a handgun.

Dr. Rayford's testimony gave Dovey Roundtree an opportunity. In her cross-examination, she asked the coroner whether "a person firing a weapon at this range would be likely to have powder marks [actual powder burns and/or the presence of nitrates] on his hands or her hands?" Rayford's reply: "Likely, yes."[24] There had been no evidence that Ray Crump had traces of nitrates on his hands. The lack of powder burns didn't prove Ray Crump's innocence, however; it only proved police negligence. In their zeal to pin the murder on Crump, and in their certainty that he was the man they were looking for, the police hadn't bothered to test his hands for traces of nitrates.

Yet no one except Dovey Roundtree seemed to question how a diminutive man such as Ray Crump, whose driver's license at the time of his arrest listed him as "5 feet 3½ inches and 130 pounds,"[25] had been able to subdue a strong, athletic woman who was taller than he was and weighed about the same. Moreover, no one in Crump's family or community had ever seen him in possession of any firearm, much less use one with any skill or precision.

Crump, however, had in fact been weighed and measured at police headquarters on the day of the murder after his arrest. Police listed his height as 5 feet 5½ inches, weighing 145 pounds,[26] but it wasn't clear whether he was wearing his 2-inch platform heel shoes at the time, or his wet clothes. In any case, Crump's height and weight, as well as his age—according to both his driver's license and the police booking record—were at a considerable variance from the "stocky 5 feet 8 inches to 5 feet 10 inches, 185 pounds Negro in his 40s, with a weight of 185 pounds," listed on Police Form PD-251 and broadcast shortly after the murder, based on Henry Wiggins Jr.'s eyewitness account. The discrepancy would become the cornerstone for Crump's defense.

After the lunch recess, Alfred Hantman, despite Dovey Roundtree's objections, displayed a fifty-five-foot-wide topographical map of the canal towpath and murder scene on the wall opposite the jury box. It was just one of fifty exhibits that Hantman would present at trial, including the bloodstained tree limb that Mary Meyer had clung to moments before she died. Such flamboyant displays by Hantman would eventually backfire, as the prosecution increasingly failed to fill the void of any real forensic evidence.

Hantman then called the map's creator, Joseph Ronsisvalle of the National Park Service, to the witness stand. "How many exits are there from the towpath between Key Bridge and Chain Bridge?" Hantman asked him. Ronsisvalle identified four: "There are steps to Water Street at Key Bridge. There's an underpass at Foundry Branch. There is an underpass at Fletcher's Boat House; and there are steps at Chain Bridge."[27] Hantman asked about the distances between exits, and made a point of telling the court that within four minutes the police were guarding and closing off all four exits.

In her cross-examination of Joseph Ronsisvalle, Dovey Roundtree proved why her colleague had once called her "the world's greatest cross-examiner." The many hours that Roundtree had spent combing and familiarizing herself with the towpath area were about to pay off. She not only revealed a fifth exit that Ronsisvalle had failed to mention, but also established through his testimony that there were many other places "where a person walking on foot could leave the area of the towpath without using any of the fixed exits."[28]

Hantman became unsettled. Roundtree had raised doubts about Ronsisvalle's knowledge of the towpath area—in fact, openly challenging his expertise. "It would be possible, would it not, for a person to take a path which you have not indicated and which counsel, through his questions, has not asked about which you do not know; is that not true?"[29] Hantman objected to her question, and Roundtree addressed Judge Corcoran: "I think that is a fair and proper question, Your Honor." The judge agreed, overruling Hantman. According to Judge Corcoran, Roundtree was "asking about his [the witness's] knowledge of the area. If he doesn't know, he doesn't know," said Corcoran.[30]

The judge's ruling helped Roundtree build the momentum she needed. She now revealed not only Ronsisvalle's complete unfamiliarity with many of the area's hidden exits, but also the fact that he had never himself walked along or explored the towpath, or any of the areas in question. It was a stunning revelation that undermined the prosecution's case, in addition to Ronsisvalle's credibility as an expert witness. Reasonable doubt was alive and well.

Before the end of the first day, the prosecution called its star eyewitness: tow truck driver Henry Wiggins Jr., who, Hantman made a point of noting, had been "a specialist in the Military Police Corps" for over three years and had "specialized training in the careful observation of people."[31] Roundtree objected to Hantman adding that detail, but Judge Corcoran allowed it.

On the witness stand, Henry Wiggins recounted having been sent by his manager, Joe Cameron, to pick up Bill Branch at the Key Bridge Esso Station, from which he proceeded to the north side of the 4300 block of Canal Road to service a stalled Nash Rambler sedan. Wiggins estimated that it was approximately 12:20 P.M. when he and Branch reached the stalled vehicle and got out of their truck. Branch, said Wiggins, went to the Rambler's passenger side to unlock it, while Wiggins himself started to remove his tools from the truck in preparation for diagnosing and fixing the stalled vehicle.[32] As soon as Wiggins was out of the truck, however, he heard "some screams. . . . It sounded like a woman screaming." He said that the screams lasted "about twenty seconds . . . coming from the direction of the canal."[33]

When the screaming stopped, Wiggins testified, he "heard a shot," again coming from the direction of the canal. In response, he "ran diagonally across the road" toward the three-foot wall overlooking both the canal and the towpath on the southern side of the canal. In the midst of crossing Canal Road, Wiggins explained, he heard "another shot just as I was reaching the wall of the canal." Hantman asked "how much of a time interval" had elapsed between the first and second shot, and Wiggins testified that it was only "a few seconds."[34] (His partner, Bill Branch, would later testify he thought it was closer to ten seconds).

Peering over the wall, Wiggins testified that he observed "a man standing over a woman lying on the towpath. The man was standing behind the body, facing my direction. The man's head, was bent down a little; he wasn't crouched. He was standing." Hantman wanted to know how much time had elapsed between Wiggins hearing the second shot and his seeing the man. "Just a fraction of a second," Wiggins testified. Hantman then asked what time of day it was when he had seen the man. In his testimony, Wiggins couldn't say for certain. "It was around 12:20 P.M., somewhere around there; it may have been later," he said.[35]

Henry Wiggins was certain about one point in particular: he had had a clear, unobstructed view of the man standing over the dead woman at a distance of 128.6 feet.[36] He told the court that the man had "looked up towards the wall of the canal where I was standing."[37]

Hantman:	Were you looking directly at him at that point?
Wiggins:	I was looking at him.
Hantman:	Then what happened?
Wiggins:	I ducked down behind the wall at that time, not too long, and I came back up from behind the wall to see him turning around and shoving something in his pocket.
Hantman:	Where was he holding this something that you speak of?
Wiggins:	He was holding it in his right hand.
Hantman:	Could you tell what the object was?
Wiggins:	No, sir, I couldn't.
Hantman:	Could you tell us whether it was light or dark or what particular color it was?
Wiggins:	It was dark, I believe, some kind of hand object.
Hantman:	And he put this hand object where, sir?
Wiggins:	Into his right jacket pocket.
Hantman:	After this individual put this dark object into right jacket pocket, what did you see him do?
Wiggins:	[He] Just turned around and walked over straight away from the body, down over the hill.[38]

Next, Hantman asked Wiggins to describe what the man in question had been wearing. Wiggins recalled that the man wore a cap "that buttons onto the brim," with a light-colored jacket, dark trousers, and dark shoes, all of which the prosecution contended that Ray Crump had been wearing that day. Hantman introduced each article of clothing as government exhibits. The clothes did, in fact, belong to Ray Crump, who had been seen wearing them as he left his home the morning of the murder.

But according to Wiggins, he had only seen the man standing over the body for "around a minute," and he "didn't get a very good look at his face." He qualified this last detail by adding, "but I did get a glance at it." Hantman asked Wiggins to state the race of the man he had seen. "He was colored,"

Wiggins replied. "I think I would estimate his weight around 185 or 180. He was medium build."

"Were you able to determine how tall he was?" Hantman asked.

"Well, I couldn't make an exact estimate to that," Wiggins responded.[39]

Dovey Roundtree would soon seize upon Wiggins's uncertainty. Hadn't the prosecution vaunted Wiggins's training "in the careful observation of people"? The following morning, the prosecution's star witness would squander his credibility in less than an hour. Hantman needed Wiggins to identify the clothes Ray Crump was wearing on the day of the murder, and confirm the exhibited items. Roundtree knew where he was heading and objected. Judge Corcoran sustained her objection, saying, "I don't see how he [Wiggins] can say it was [Crump's actual clothing] unless he walked up to the defendant and took it off of him." His one concession to the prosecution was to "allow look-alike testimony" only.[40]

Hantman became irritated. "I don't see how the Court could strike it if that is the witness's testimony." Judge Corcoran's response was sharp and un-equivocal: "If that is his testimony, it is subject to challenge."[41] The irritation was mutual. That Hantman had been, for the second day, engaged in loud gum-chewing did not endear him to the judge. In fact, Judge Corcoran had taken his young clerk, Robert Bennett, into his chambers during one earlier recess and had admonished him "never to chew gum" when presenting in a courtroom.[42]

In spite of the fracas with the judge, Hantman pressed on with Wiggins, who appeared not to comprehend the significance of the exchange over the admissibility of his testimony about the clothing.

Hantman: All right. Now, when did you first see these articles of clothing?

Wiggins: I first saw these articles when they were being worn by the defendant when he was standing over the victim at the scene.

Hantman: According to your best recollection, Mr. Wiggins, are these the same ones or do they look like the articles you saw on the man bending over the body of Mary Pinchot Meyer?

Wiggins: They are the same articles which I saw.[43]

Again, the exchange was not lost on the defense. Wiggins had unintention-ally started to dig his own grave. Dovey Roundtree would merely gave him a bigger shovel to dig deeper.

Roundtree: Do you remember, Mr. Witness, that you also said you had only a glimpse of the person you saw at the scene?

Wiggins: I remember that.

Roundtree: This morning nevertheless, Mr. Witness, you are prepared to tell this court and this jury that these are the pants?

Wiggins: That's right.

Roundtree: Positively?

Wiggins: Positive.

Roundtree: You are prepared to say that this is the cap?

Wiggins: That is the cap.

Roundtree: And that these are the black shoes?

Wiggins: That is right.

Roundtree: And that this is the jacket?

Wiggins: That is right.[44]

Wiggins had already identified Ray Crump as the man he saw standing over the victim. Roundtree used this opportunity to highlight the discrepancy between what Wiggins had reported to the police and the actual size of the defendant.

Roundtree: Would that, then, be an accurate estimate of what you saw, the man you saw weighed 185 and was five feet eight?

Wiggins: That wouldn't be an accurate estimate, no, ma'am.

Roundtree turned to face the jury.

Roundtree: Well, now, are you telling us you gave them [the police] information which was not accurate?

Wiggins: Well, this information which I gave them at that time which I was looking across the canal down on the subject there, would not be very accurate but as close as I can give. I give it to them as close as I could remember.

Roundtree: And you gave them, though, what you thought you saw from across the canal?

Wiggins: I tried to do my best.

Roundtree: All right. A hundred and eighty-five pounds; five feet eight.

Wiggins: That's right.[45]

If Wiggins was beginning to squirm, the increasingly exasperated, gum-chewing Hantman had to have been agitated. His star eyewitness, and his case, were crumbling on the second day of the trial. During his redirect, Hantman asked Wiggins again whether his view of the murder scene had been obstructed in any way. Wiggins reiterated that nothing had blocked his view. Yet Wiggins had contradicted his own testimony. Hantman had opened a problematic door. Dovey Roundtree merely walked Wiggins through it. Seeking to bolster Wiggins's credibility regarding Crump's clothing, Hantman had attempted something similar with Wiggins's description of the suspect's height and weight—both of which in no way matched Crump's. Inadvertently, Hantman had damaged the credibility of his star eyewitness so badly that his case would never recover. The description Wiggins had given police just minutes after the murder took place—"five feet eight, medium build, 185 pounds"—would be reiterated by nearly every one of the twelve policemen and detectives called to testify at the trial, except for two who remembered the height as "five feet ten inches." This was the description, they all testified, of the man they were told to look for, and it didn't come close to describing the defendant. Ray Crump shared just one physical feature with the man described on the police radio broadcast on the day of the murder: He was black.

By midmorning of day two, the defense strategy of reasonable doubt had started a crusade. With nearly each of the prosecution's twenty-seven witnesses, Dovey Roundtree would become a heat-seeking missile: If there was a weakness or discrepancy to be exploited, she would find it and expose it to the jury.

Bill Branch, Henry Wiggins's tow truck assistant on the day of the murder, took the stand right after Wiggins. Branch had told police that after Wiggins left the murder scene to call police, he, Branch, was too afraid to keep watch over the wall that overlooked the canal towpath. Instead, he sat in the stalled Nash Rambler and waited. Yet on the witness stand, he testified that he had remained at the wall overlooking the murder scene until Wiggins returned with police. Roundtree confronted Branch with the report he had given to police: "I [Bill Branch] didn't see anyone around her [the murder victim] at that time, I went back to the car."[46] His tail now between his legs, Branch finally took refuge in a convenient loss of memory—"I don't remember."[47]

It now appeared that Hantman, who had painstakingly rehearsed and written out the testimony of each of his twenty-seven witnesses,[48] had coached Branch to alter his statement to police. Surely, Hantman was aware of Branch's written police statement—that he had stayed in the car, and not remained at the wall overlooking the towpath. In addition to exposing Branch's charade, Roundtree had also managed to reveal one very important fact: Between the time that Wiggins had left and returned with the police, no one had been monitoring the murder scene.

After the day two lunch recess, the trial proceeded with the testimony of two police officers, patrolman Roderick Sylvis and Detective John Warner. A puzzling question had now been pushed to the foreground: if the man Henry Wiggins had seen standing over the corpse of Mary Meyer wasn't Ray Crump, then who was it? Together, the testimony of Roderick Sylvis and John Warner would reveal one of the most important facts never before understood: Someone else was eluding capture by police.

Hearing the police radio broadcast at 12:26 P.M., police officer Roderick Sylvis and his partner, Frank Bignotti, sped to Fletcher's Boat House to close off the exit.[49] They arrived, Sylvis told Hantman, at "12:30 P.M. or 12:29 P.M.," having driven their patrol car through the narrow underpass beneath the canal itself. Now facing north, with the towpath and canal in full view and the shore of the Potomac River behind them, they waited for "about four or five minutes."[50] Anyone attempting to leave the entire C & O Canal towpath area would either have to walk through the narrow underpass or cross the canal in an old leaky rowboat that was attached to a rope and pulley on each side of the canal. In fact, that meant there were two exits at Fletcher's Landing—two entirely different ways to exit the area—that offered immediate access to Canal Road and beyond.[51]

After waiting "about four or five minutes," no longer content, the two officers hatched a plan: Sylvis would walk along the towpath toward the murder scene, while Bignotti would walk through the woods adjacent to the railroad tracks parallel to the towpath, both heading east toward the murder scene. Leaving the entire Fletcher's Boat House area unattended, they risked allowing the killer to walk out unnoticed. Yet even that oversight paled to what was about to unfold.

Sylvis and Bignotti exited their patrol car and spent about five minutes positioning themselves for their eastward trek toward the murder scene. As soon as they started out, "maybe 50 feet at the most" from Fletcher's Boat House, Sylvis testified, they spotted a young white couple walking westward on the railroad tracks. The two officers approached the couple, informing them "that there had been a shooting on the canal." Sylvis inquired as to whether they had seen anyone leaving the area. "They did not observe anyone," Sylvis recalled during his testimony.[52] How long had the interrogation of the couple taken? The question had not been asked during his testimony. However, reviewing his testimony in an interview for this book in 2008, Sylvis was adamant that he had asked the young white couple a number of questions, and it had taken "at least five minutes, probably more."[53] That meant the time had to be approaching 1:00 P.M. before the two policeman began bushwhacking their way eastward toward the murder scene, a measured distance of 1.6 miles away. "I remember I proceeded very cautiously," Sylvis recalled, adding that he had been "taking a lot of time to be observant."[54]

Walking slowly and vigilantly for "approximately a mile east on the towpath," Sylvis told the court, he observed "a head jut out of the woods momentarily, just for a second, and went back. A head of a man, somebody stuck their head out of the woods, and were looking up at me, and pulled back again." From a distance of "about 150 or 160 feet," Sylvis identified the head to be that of a "Negro male." He didn't remember the man wearing a cap of any kind.[55] Sylvis then "proceeded very slowly towards the spot," sure the man had seen him. He yelled to his partner Bignotti for assistance, but Bignotti didn't respond, so Sylvis tried to "wave down someone on Canal Road" to assist him. That meant that it took him even longer to arrive at the spot where the "Negro male" had peeked out from the woods.[56]

How long had it actually taken officer Sylvis to walk "approximately a mile" before he saw the head of a "Negro male" jut out of the woods? Conservatively, it had to have been at least fifteen minutes or more. During his testimony, Sylvis told Hantman that it took him "approximately 10 or 15 minutes" additionally to reconnect with his partner after he had seen the mystery "Negro male." Reunited, Sylvis and Bignotti spent even more time searching the area together. "We stayed there for a few more minutes and looked around the area where I had seen the head, and then proceeded on back toward Fletcher's [Boat House]," testified Sylvis.[57]

Hantman:	Approximately what time was it when you saw this unidentified person about a mile down the towpath?
Sylvis:	I'd say about ten or fifteen minutes. Let me see—it would be about, about 1:45 or 1:50 [P.M.].[58]

Officer Roderick Sylvis's answer to Hantman's inquiry was very likely accurate. The problem, however, was that he had blown the answer he had rehearsed with Hantman, and Hantman knew it. At this very moment, the government's case against Ray Crump was in peril, and about to be pushed off the edge of a cliff. Why? Because it had already been established during the trial that Ray Crump had been arrested at 1:15 P.M. In fact, Crump had been in the company of Detective John Warner at a location of one-tenth of a mile *east of the murder scene* for a period of at least ten to fifteen minutes—before he was arrested at 1:15 P.M. The significance of this detail was that the "head" of the "Negro male" seen by patrolman Roderick Sylvis could not have been Ray Crump's.

Hantman, apparently aware he was standing in quicksand, tried another tactic: He asked Sylvis another rehearsed question.

Hantman: All right, sir. How long, all told, do you recollect your scout car was in the vicinity of Fletcher's Boat House that day?

Sylvis: I'd say about forty-five minutes.[59]

Forty-five minutes. This was the answer that appeared to lift Hantman out of the jam. If Sylvis and Bignotti arrived at Fletcher's Boat House at approximately 12:30 P.M. and they returned to their patrol car by 1:15, they came back just in time to conveniently hear the police radio broadcast that a suspect had been arrested. But there was just one problem with this version of events: There were no police radios at the crime scene or adjacent to the site of Crump's arrest. Someone would have had to walk back to a police vehicle at the Foundry Underpass to make the call, but no such a call—if one ever took place—was ever mentioned in the trial transcript or any police report.

Dovey Roundtree seized on the discrepancy in patrolman's Roderick Sylvis's testimony in her cross-examination:

Roundtree: Mr. Witness, do you know what time the defendant, Ray Crump was arrested?

Sylvis: I know it was approximately 1:15 when it came over the air.

Roundtree: Now, then, thirty minutes after that time you saw a man stick his head out?

Sylvis: Pardon?

Roundtree: Thirty minutes after Ray Crump, Jr. has already been arrested, you saw an unidentified Negro male stick his head out of the woods?[60]

Hantman immediately objected, stating that what Roundtree had alleged had not been Sylvis's testimony, in spite of the fact that it had been. This may have been one of the few moments during the trial where Dovey Roundtree missed a significant opportunity. Why didn't she ask Judge Corcoran to have the stenographer read back Sylvis's testimony, confirming that Sylvis had just testified that it had been "1:45 or 1:50 [P.M.]" when he saw the mystery "Negro male"? Sylvis, for his part, must have realized that he had been "off message," because in the next instant he corrected his testimony and said that he first saw the head of the man poking out of the woods at "approximately 12:45 [P.M.]."[61]

That would have been physically impossible. Having already testified that he had arrived at Fletcher's Boathouse at "12:30 P.M. or 12:29 P.M.,"[62] then waited "about four or five minutes," before deciding on a plan with his partner, only to then spend "at least five minutes, probably more" interrogating the young white couple before beginning to vigilantly walk "a mile east on the tow path," Sylvis would have had to have been a world-class runner to spot the mystery "Negro male" man at 12:45 P.M. It was, in fact, accurate that about an hour later, "about 1:45 [P.M.] or 1:50 [P.M.],"—Sylvis's initial response to Hantman—that he spotted the head of the mystery "Negro male," who could not have possibly been Ray Crump.

When Roundtree confronted Sylvis with the discrepancy, he had to have realized that by first telling the court that it was 1:45 P.M. when he saw the "Negro male," he had risked sabotaging the prosecution's case against Crump. Sylvis now wanted the court to believe that it had occurred at 12:45. But his initial answer to Hantman's inquiry of "about 1:45 or 1:50 [P.M.]" was the correct answer, and he confirmed that with me in 2008.[63] Crump, it will be shown, was already in the custody of Detective John Warner east of the murder scene as early as 1:00, which could only mean there was a second "Negro male" on the towpath that day and that he had eluded capture—as well as the attention of the court proceedings.

Indeed, a cornerstone of the prosecution's case was that the man Sylvis had spotted was, in fact, the fleeing Ray Crump. Prosecutor Hantman hammered that point home repeatedly throughout the trial. Should that assertion be successfully challenged, the case against Crump would crumble. That was about to happen, although it would again elude the scrutiny of the defense and remain hidden in the trial transcript until now.

Detective John Warner, scheduled to testify after Sylvis, had not been in the courtroom during Sylvis's testimony. It was customary to keep witnesses from hearing other testimony in order to reduce the possibility of collusion and fabrication. Warner was therefore unaware of the various conflicting time stamps that had jeopardized the prosecution's case. Warner testified that he had arrived at the Key Bridge entrance of the canal towpath at 12:29 P.M. with his partner, Henry Schultheis. They waited there until 12:40, he said, at which point Warner decided he "was going to cover the area between the railroad tracks and the towpath in the wooded area," while his partner would cover "the area to the left of the railroad tracks to the [Potomac] river bank."[64] Warner proceeded to walk westward toward the murder scene through the woods adjacent to the railroad tracks for what he estimated had been "forty-five minutes" before discovering the wet, somewhat disoriented Ray Crump more than one-tenth of a mile east of the murder scene itself. [65] If Warner's recollection was accurate, he would have come across Crump at approximately 1:25, ten minutes later than the official time stamp of Crump's arrest at approximately 1:15.

Under direct examination by Hantman, Warner proceeded to alter his testimony, saying that it had been 1:15 P.M. when he first saw Crump at a location one-tenth of mile east of the murder scene. Hantman appeared to be irritated with Warner for not following the script, so Warner, under cross-examination by Roundtree, eventually changed his testimony again to 1:14 P.M. (In their testimony during the trial, several detectives and police officers had already established that Detective Bernie Crooke had arrested Ray Crump on the railroad bed directly below the murder scene at approximately 1:15 P.M.)

The government's case was slowly spiraling out of control, yet the Roundtree defense team appeared to be missing another critical moment. Detective John Warner's testimony was undermining the prosecution's case. Warner told Hantman that he stopped Crump on the railroad tracks and identified himself as a police officer, and Crump took out his sodden wallet and handed over his D.C. driver's license. Crump, Warner testified, hadn't been running when he discovered him; "he was walking."[66] Warner had looked at the name and photograph on the license to confirm Crump's identity. He hadn't needed to read the physical description—5 feet 3½ inches and 130 pounds—to realize that Crump wasn't a match for the general broadcast, which had put the height of the suspect, according to Warner, at 5 feet 10 inches, though he wanted to maintain during the trial that he hadn't noticed Crump's physical description on his license. In the unlikely event that that were true, why wouldn't he have arrested Crump immediately?

Hantman:	Did you at any time say anything to him or did he say anything to you?
Warner:	Yes, sir. I identified myself as a police officer. I asked him who he was, and he replied, "Ray Crump."

He took his wallet out, and when he took his wallet out, water dripped out of his wallet as he handed me his D.C. driver's license.

I asked him then if he had heard any pistol shots. He replied no.

I said, "How did you get so wet?" He says, "Well, I was fishing from a rock, and I fell into the river and went to sleep, fell off the rock, fell into the river."

I said, "Well, where is your fishing equipment?" He said it went into the river, too.

I said, "Your rod and everything?" He said yes.

I said, "Well, where are your fish?" He said they went into the river too.

I said, "Who were you fishing with?" He said, "No one."

I asked him then if he would point out the spot as to where he was fishing from, I would help him, see if I could retrieve his fishing gear for him. And he says, "Yes, sir."

And he led us back up in a westerly direction, up the railroad tracks.

Hantman:	About what time was this when you first saw the defendant standing 32 feet in front of you soaking wet?
Warner:	This was 1:15 P.M., sir.
Hantman:	1:15?
Warner:	P.M., sir.[67]

Warner was asking an entire courtroom to believe that in the space of *literally no time at all*, he had spotted Crump, who "was walking," at "1:15 P.M." and at a distance that would be measured to be 532 feet east of the murder scene,[68] whereupon he proceeded to ask Crump a series of seven questions, with Crump giving his answer to each question, before the two then began to walk along the railroad tracks in the westerly direction toward where Crump said he had been fishing—only to then find themselves one-tenth of a mile later (532 feet) immediately parallel and below the murder scene, where Crump was supposedly interrogated and arrested at 1:15 P.M. by Detective Bernie Crooke.

Warner's testimony was as ludicrous as it was dishonest. Under cross-examination, he changed the time when he first came upon Ray Crump; it was now "1:14 [P.M.],"[69] an obvious attempt to reconcile with what previous police testimony had officially established as Crump's time of arrest of 1:15 P.M. This incensed Dovey Roundtree, who discerned in Warner's conflicting testimony further evidence of prosecutorial shenanigans. Yet in spite of a second demand for a mistrial—a demand Judge Corcoran rejected—it wasn't clear whether Dovey Roundtree, or even the jury, had grasped the full implications of Detective John Warner's testimony, which was simply this: *Ray Crump was not the only black man in the towpath area on the day of the murder.*

Detective Warner had clearly first come upon the defendant well before 1:15 P.M. and at a distance of more than a tenth of a mile *east* of the murder scene. His methodical, seven-question interrogation of Crump, followed by their walk together, had to have taken at least ten, maybe even as long as fifteen, minutes before the two eventually found themselves parallel to, and beneath the murder scene, the place where Crump would be, by all accounts, officially arrested at approximately 1:15 P.M.

If Crump was in the physical presence of Detective Warner at a distance of a tenth of a mile *east* of the murder scene sometime around 1:00 P.M., he could not have possibly been the same "Negro male" that officer Roderick Sylvis spotted approximately six-tenths of a mile *west* of the murder scene well past 1:00 P.M. Detective Warner's testimony had, therefore, inadvertently corroborated the fact that a second, unidentified "Negro male" had eluded police capture.

More policemen were called to testify the following day. Collectively, their testimony offered nothing in the way of incriminating evidence against Crump and, instead, expanded the grounds for reasonable doubt. A neighbor of Crump's testified that she saw Ray leaving his house the morning of the murder wearing his light-colored beige jacket and golf cap. In fact, some facsimile of a light-beige Windbreaker jacket—seen by eyewitnesses Henry Wiggins and allegedly by Lieutenant William L. Mitchell on the "Negro male" each of them saw—was the most conspicuous evidence that, according to the prosecution, identified the killer. For Henry Wiggins in particular, it had been the distinguishing piece of clothing, and it was a jacket very similar to the prosecution's exhibit that lay before the court. So important was the jacket as evidence, its very existence—including its location and whereabouts—seemed to have a life of its own.

A nd so, before the end of day three of the trial, a fascinating element—its real significance never realized during the trial, or afterward—was revealed. It involved possibly the most critical piece of evidence: the light-colored beige windbreaker jacket, allegedly worn by the defendant.

Harbor Precinct policeman Frederick Byers was called to testify. Under direct and cross-examination, Byers was adamant: He had received a radio call at "about one o'clock or a little after" to search in his patrol boat for a "light-colored beige jacket," which he would eventually find at "about 1:46 P.M." at a distance of 1,110 feet southwest of the murder scene.[70] How did he know where to look? Moreover, neither the defense nor the prosecution questioned the time—"about one o'clock"—that Byers asserted he received the call, nor why he had been asked *only* to search for a jacket, and not a golf cap. (The cap, the reader will recall, was found the day after the murder on the Potomac River shoreline, 684 feet from the murder scene.)

If the prosecution wanted to maintain that Crump wasn't arrested, by all accounts, until 1:15 P.M., how did police know to start looking for a jacket at "approximately one o'clock"? That was very possibly before Crump had even been spotted by any police officer, much less apprehended, and *before* Henry Wiggins identified Crump, subsequent to his arrest at 1:15 P.M., as the man he had seen standing over the victim wearing a jacket and cap.

Detective Warner, by all accounts the first police officer to encounter Ray Crump, had likely done so in the vicinity of 1:00 P.M., but he had had no means of communication with any other police officer until Sergeant Pasquale D'Ambrosio spotted him with Crump right before 1:15 P.M. D'Ambrosio had first arrived at the murder scene at 12:35 P.M. The Chief Detective, Lieutenant Arthur Weber, also the ranking homicide officer, and detectives Crooke and Coppage arrived at the murder scene at approximately 1:00 P.M.[71] There were no portable police radios at the crime scene. If there had been, Henry Wiggins and patrolman James Scouloukas would not have had to return to the police cruiser parked at the Foundry Underpass to call in a radio broadcast description of the killer.

The implication of Byers's testimony is inescapable: Someone, other than police, was monitoring the murder scene and the events unfolding around it. And it appears that someone, other than police, who had access to police band radio frequencies radioed Byers and gave him instructions to start looking for the jacket, and told him where to look for it. Whoever the caller was, he had to have known that Crump was no longer wearing his jacket *before* he was first spotted by Warner (somewhere in the vicinity of 1:00 P.M.) and subsequently arrested by Detective Crooke at approximately 1:15 P.M.

When the trial recessed for a three-day weekend on Thursday, July 22, Dovey Roundtree was still holding her own; her strategy of establishing reasonable doubt at almost every juncture was bearing fruit. Before the recess, Roundtree again focused the jury's attention on the description Henry Wiggins had given police of the man he saw standing over the body: 5 feet 8 inches, weighing 185 pounds. In her cross-examination of Chief Detective Arthur Weber, a twenty-three-year veteran and the ranking officer of the D.C. Homicide Squad in charge of the investigation, attorney Roundtree further highlighted this discrepancy:

Weber: We were looking for—to the best of my recollection—a Negro who had on a light-colored jacket and a dark cap.

Roundtree: Did that lookout not also include the fact that he weighed 185 pounds?

Weber: From my recollection that I remember from the [PD-251] lookout, I had—one of my ways of doing this—I had a picture in my mind of a stocky individual.

Roundtree: Did that not include also the fact that the lookout indicated he was about five feet eight or ten inches?

Weber: In my mind, yes.[72]

The chief detective's admission underscored the defense's position that the man Wiggins had seen could not have been the defendant, Ray Crump. That this came from the most senior ranking police officer at the murder scene, the man in charge of the entire investigation, would not be lost on the jury. But there was still one eyewitness left to testify, and that individual was potentially lethal to the defense.

The lean, trim William L. Mitchell took the witness stand the afternoon of Monday, July 26. The reader will recall that Mitchell, an Army lieutenant stationed at the Pentagon in the fall of 1964, claimed to have been out for his daily lunchtime run on the towpath the day of the murder. He had come forward to police, he said, because he recognized the victim from newspaper accounts, and believed she was being followed by a "Negro male," who was wearing clothes identical to those Henry Wiggins had seen. At the trial, Mitchell identified himself no longer as a military man but as a mathematics instructor at Georgetown University. He gave the same address he had given to police nine months earlier: 1500 Arlington Boulevard, in Arlington, Virginia, an apartment complex known at the time as the Virginian.[73]

The presence of Lieutenant William L. Mitchell had troubled Dovey Roundtree from the very beginning. What else, Roundtree wondered, might Mitchell add to the information he'd already given? How might he elaborate on what he'd told police the day after the murder? Mitchell had refused to return her phone calls in the months before the trial; she had little to go on. But whatever he said, whatever claims he might make in his testimony, she feared the jury was certain to believe him, simply because he appeared to be the quintessence of credibility: educated, a retired military officer, a Georgetown University mathematics instructor. And he was white. At a murder trial where the innuendo of an attempted sexual assault by a black man upon a white woman had captivated the attention of an entire city, William L. Mitchell indeed presented a formidable threat. Might the jury even go so far as to overlook the discrepancy in Wiggins's height and weight testimony, given Mitchell's corroboration to police of the clothing description that was nearly identical to what Wiggins had seen? Potentially, this spelled doom for Ray Crump, Roundtree told Leo Damore years later, because Ray had lied on two important counts: his clothing, and his reason for being in the area on the day of the murder. Without testimony from Crump's girlfriend, Vivian, Roundtree still feared the possibility of ruination for her client.

As a witness for the prosecution, Mitchell was a cool customer. He didn't fall into the same traps that had tripped up Henry Wiggins. When asked by Hantman to identify the exhibits of Crump's and Mary Meyer's clothing, Mitchell made certain to say only that they were "similar to the clothes worn by the individual," not the exact clothes he had seen that day. He described the "Negro male" he had seen following Mary as "about my height, about five-feet eight [inches],"[74] and then added that he, Mitchell, weighed "about 145 pounds." The reader will recall that this was the precise weight that police recorded for Crump after his arrest on the day of the murder.[75]

Mitchell was careful to stop short of saying that Ray Crump was the man he had seen. Doing so would have invited a fierce cross-examination from Roundtree, which might have aroused suspicion and damaged Mitchell's testimony. Instead, Mitchell slyly and repeatedly implied that the man he'd seen was indeed Crump. The man he saw, he told the court, "had his hands in the pockets of his jacket when I passed him." He carried "no fishing rod."[76]

Hantman asked Mitchell if he had seen anyone else on the towpath the day. Mitchell testified that he had twice passed "a couple walking together," as well as a younger runner—"about twenty"—wearing Bermuda shorts.[77] The runner in Bermuda shorts was never identified, and he never came forward. Patrolman Sylvis had already testified about seeing the couple, a point that corroborated Mitchell's account, bolstering his credibility, but Sylvis had obtained no identification and the couple never came forward to police. Aside from his own claim, no one ever substantiated that Mitchell had been on the towpath that day, or any other day.

In spite of Mitchell's calm demeanor, Roundtree probed for weak spots in his testimony, in which Mitchell reported with military precision his time on the towpath, and approximately when and where he was located at each of several critical points on the line of the murder. Roundtree focused on another detail that would undermine Mitchell's well-rehearsed precision: Had he been wearing a watch? Mitchell was forced to concede that he hadn't; he couldn't be entirely certain that the times he gave were exact. He admitted that he had based his accounting of the time he returned to the Pentagon on the "clock in the barbershop of the [Pentagon] basement athletic center," which read "a quarter of one." It was a small but significant detail, again establishing a degree of reasonable doubt about Mitchell's account.

Yet Mitchell's assertion that the man he passed weighed "about 145 pounds" was troubling to the defense. It was too close for comfort, in spite of Mitchell's claim that the man he had seen was "about my height, about five-feet eight [inches]," clearly taller than Ray Crump. The weight match wouldn't be lost on Hantman, who would exploit it for all it was worth, along with one other detail, in his summation. At the end of his testimony, William Mitchell's sheen was still untarnished; he remained a model citizen, and he had delivered precise eyewitness testimony that corroborated the less-than-stellar witness Henry Wiggins, thereby indirectly and ironically resuscitating the Wiggins testimony. At that point in the proceedings, in the eyes of the jury, it may have still been anyone's case to win.

The following day, the prosecution called its final witnesses. Agent Warren Johnson, an FBI firearms expert, told Hantman there were no powder burns or nitrates on Crump's hands or clothing because he had been in the water that day. Roundtree, however, had already established that the police had never tested Ray Crump, or his clothing, for the presence of nitrates. Moreover, she confronted Johnson with the fact that the standard paraffin test for nitrates in gunpowder typically involves the suspect being asked to wash his hands repeatedly throughout the testing procedure. If a suspect had fired a gun recently, the presence of nitrates would still show up. Since there had been no nitrates discovered on Crump's clothing or on any part of his body, she argued, there wasn't any evidence he had fired a firearm that day.

Agent Johnson's testimony did confirm—and underscore—that whoever killed Mary Meyer had shot her from close range and was likely highly skilled, possibly ambidextrous, in the handling of a .38-caliber revolver. In describing the shots, Johnson had corroborated Deputy Coroner Rayford's testimony about which hand had fired which shot.[78]

Next, Special Agent Paul Stombaugh, of the FBI's crime lab, testified that in twenty-one out of twenty-two characteristics, Ray Crump's hair sample was a match for a single hair found inside the golf cap recovered the day after the murder. This forensic analysis, he maintained, linked both the jacket and cap to the defendant. The cap and jacket on exhibit did belong to Ray Crump, but the hair match wasn't evidence that he was guilty of murder.

In her cross-examination of Stombaugh, Roundtree called into question the entire field of hair and fiber analysis. In preparation for the cross-examination, she had read a number of textbooks, a dozen of which were stacked on the defense table. Stombaugh wasn't able to answer questions about the latest literature in the field, because he hadn't read it. He was also unfamiliar with a University of Pennsylvania study Roundtree cited, showing that hair and fiber analysis was far from an exact science. She then compelled Stombaugh to admit that he had never published anything in the field and that he was not, in fact, an expert. But the witness attempted to fight back. He explained that his FBI laboratory relied heavily upon something called neutron activation in analyzing hair and fiber samples. "There is a great controversy raging right now," Stombaugh testified, and "this field [neutron activation] hasn't been perfected yet to the point where we can positively identify a hair of some particular person through this method."[79] That admission inadvertently succeeded in making Roundtree's case for her.

In the end, Stombaugh's testimony dealt more than one blow to the prosecution. The FBI's state-of-the-art forensic laboratory in Washington, D.C., had failed to find any forensic evidence—hair, clothing fibers, blood, semen, skin, urine, or saliva—that linked Ray Crump to either the murder scene or the body and clothing of Mary Meyer. Similarly, there had been no traces of Mary Meyer's blood, hair, fibers, or saliva found on Ray Crump. If the first gunshot had produced a wound that, according to Dr. Rayford, very likely spurted blood, wouldn't Mary Meyer's assailant be covered in it? Even if the killer had jumped into the Potomac River in an attempt to flee, it was unlikely that all traces of the victim's hair, blood, saliva, or clothing fibers would have been completely washed out of his clothes or body. But absolutely nothing had been found on the body, or clothes, of Ray Crump.

In his description of the man he had seen standing over the dead woman's body, Henry Wiggins had made no mention of any stains, blood or anything else, on the man's light-colored jacket. Given the intensity of the skirmish and the fight that Mary Meyer had put up, as well as the amount of blood that likely squirted from her head wound, the assailant would probably have been covered with bloodstains easily visible on a light-colored, zipped-up beige jacket, even from a distance of 128.6 feet. Furthermore, the man's golf cap was in place, not askew, only seconds after the fatal second shot. In the immediate aftermath, the man Wiggins saw exhibited no signs of having been in a violent struggle.

After calling twenty-seven witnesses and introducing more than fifty exhibits, the prosecution rested its case at the end of the day on Tuesday, July 27. The next morning, Dovey Roundtree delivered her opening statement on behalf of her client. In five full days of testimony, she stated, the government hadn't produced a shred of forensic evidence linking Ray Crump to either the murder scene or the body of Mary Meyer. There was no proof that Crump had handled or fired a gun the day of the murder, and no firearm had been produced. Roundtree maintained that the testimony of Henry Wiggins was flawed: The man he saw, described as five feet eight inches tall and 185 pounds, could not have been the defendant, Ray Crump. The defense's strategy was simple and effective: Three character witnesses testified for the defendant, the last of whom was Crump's pastor at the Second Baptist Church in Southwest Washington. Each witness stated that he or she had known Ray in his church and community for more than fifteen years, and testified to his good character.

Over the preceding weekend, Dovey had discussed with her defense colleagues, George Knox and Alan Robeson, the possibility of putting Ray Crump on the stand. She thought that doing so would persuade the jury, once and for all, that the shy, meek, harmless man was incapable of such a crime. But Knox and Robinson were against it. Why jeopardize, they argued, the fact that the government had been unable to prove its case? Roundtree listened, unconvinced.

On Monday, she rode the elevator to the courtroom. The elevator operator, a black woman, took her aside and told her that earlier in the morning the men from the all-white prosecution team had been chortling in the elevator about looking forward to destroying Ray Crump on the witness stand.[80] The moment changed everything; Providence had given her a sign. The prospect of her helpless defendant being metaphorically lynched in open court was too big a risk.

As Crump's last character witness left the stand, Roundtree stunned the prosecution by announcing that the defense would rest its case. She would call no further witnesses. She then told Judge Corcoran that she wished to renew a number of motions, including an immediate judgment of acquittal. Barring that, she wished to renew her motion for a mistrial. It was a bold, deliberate move that caught everyone off guard.

Judge Corcoran denied each of Roundtree's motions, but he and the prosecution had been taken by surprise. Hantman in particular was caught flatfooted and unprepared. For days, he had eagerly awaited the opportunity to interrogate Ray Crump on the stand, believing he could lead Crump to obliterate any chance of an acquittal. Still, Hantman had one last trick up his sleeve. In his summation rebuttal, he held up the shoes that Ray Crump had worn when he was arrested. Hantman drew the jury's attention to the two-inch heels in an attempt to make the case that Crump would have been taller than the 5 feet 5½ inches that had been recorded at the time of his arrest.

"This is what gave Lieutenant Mitchell the appearance that this defendant Raymond Crump was his [Mitchell's] size, his weight, which he said was five foot eight and 145 pounds," a desperate Hantman pleaded, hoping that the jury would not remember that Crump's driver's license had, in effect, established a baseline for his height and weight of "5 feet 3½ inches and 130 pounds." His closing ploy, along with everything else he had presented, still amounted to little; his case was, at best, circumstantial, if he had any case at all.

Dovey Roundtree, in response, delivered her arguments for reasonable doubt regarding Crump's guilt. First, she underscored the discrepancy between the 5 foot 8 inch and 185-pound suspect that was wanted by police and the actual height and weight of the defendant. Next, she noted that officers Sylvis and Bignotti had left the rowboat and the exit at the Fletcher's Boat House underpass unattended; anyone could have left the area undetected during the time they went on their search. Roundtree also explained that had there been a struggle between the victim and the assailant, such as the prosecution had underscored throughout, fibers from Mary Meyer's blue angora sweater would have been found on the defendant; yet there were none. Similarly, blood from Crump's cut finger would have been found on the victim's clothing, but had not been. Roundtree also reminded the jury that mapmaker Joseph Ronsisvalle didn't know about a number of exits out of the towpath area, through which an assailant could have easily fled. Finally, Roundtree asked, with the vast resources that the government had at its disposal—helicopters, scuba divers, the state-of-the-art FBI Crime Laboratory, more than forty police officers and detectives assigned to the case, the draining of the canal, the repeated combing of the murder scene area for weeks—why hadn't the murder weapon been found? Because, she argued, the real killer had escaped from the towpath area with the gun.

"I leave this little man in your hands," attorney Dovey Roundtree concluded to the jury, "and I say to you fairly and truly, if you can find that he is five feet and eight inches tall, that he weights 185 pounds, irrespective of what he wore that day—if you can find—I cannot from this evidence—and I say you must have a substantial and a reasonable doubt in your minds, and until the Government proves its case beyond such doubt, then you must bring back a verdict of not guilty."[81]

As the jury deliberated, they sent word for all photos that had been submitted as evidence. And they wanted the answer to two questions: (1) Had the police ever actually gone to the rock from which Crump said he had been fishing before allegedly falling from the rock into the water? (2) Was the defendant Ray Crump left-handed or right-handed? Judge Corcoran gave the jury the photos, but he told them that with regard to their other two requests "your recollection of the evidence controls."

The following morning, Friday, July 30, 1965, the jury found Raymond Crump Jr. not guilty of the murder of Mary Pinchot Meyer. Dazed and nearly catatonic, Ray had been standing behind the table along with his defense team. Dovey Roundtree embraced him. His mother, Martha, began singing praises to the Lord and other church members shouted hallelujahs throughout the courtroom. Mary Meyer's longtime friend Cicely Angleton was reportedly sitting in the back of the courtroom and showed little emotion. As Dovey led the now-wobbly Ray Crump out of the courtroom, her adversary, Alfred Hantman, cast one final, embittered look toward her. He had just lost the most important case of his career, and he would never congratulate Roundtree or even acknowledge her victory.

Immediately after the trial, Hantman received a call from Ben Bradlee. "What went wrong? Why had Crump gotten off?" queried Bradlee.[82] Hantman would always maintain it had been a racial verdict, still convinced in 1991 that Dovey's "ministerial" approach had profoundly affected the majority-black jury. "They'd take her word on anything," Hantman said. Even in 1991, he was still confident that he had assembled enough evidence to get a conviction.[83] His view was upheld by the Justice Department, which would always maintain that Crump had been guilty. The case, though unsolved, would never be reopened. U.S. Attorney David Acheson complained that Henry Wiggins had been a huge disappointment.

That night, an exhausted Dovey Roundtree, still very concerned for Ray Crump's safety, put him on a bus for North Carolina, but only after his belongings were released to him. From the $1.50 that he had had in his possession at the time of his arrest, Crump handed his defense attorney, the woman who had saved his life, the dollar bill, thanking her in the only way he could. She told him she would "treasure it" forever as a keepsake.

In the wake of the trial, jury foreman Edward Savwoir resented the insinuation, widely reported in the media and shared by the police department as well as many of Mary Meyer's friends, that the jury's decision had been racially motivated and that Crump had gotten away with murder. Savwoir never wavered from what he told reporters after the trial: "There were many missing links. . . . we didn't get the man on the scene." Even twenty-five years after the trial, Savwoir was emphatic: "There was no gun. They [the prosecution] never proved he [Ray Crump] was at the murder scene, they never proved he had anything to do with it. If Crump had a gun, someone in his community—his wife—would have known it."[84]

The case catapulted Dovey Roundtree, awash in accolades in the wake of her victory, to citywide and national prominence. "She was an incredible force in any courtroom she appeared," said her former colleague George Peter Lamb after the trial, "and it wasn't just because she's also a minister in a black church. Dovey's soul was rooted in the law and the fair application of justice for everyone—white or black. Everyone was entitled to it. She not only believed it, she lived it, and lived it fully. She was such a star, and a class lady."[85]

One of the first people to call and congratulate her was former U.S. assistant attorney Charles Duncan, now general counsel for the EEOC, the prosecutor who was first assigned by the Justice Department to prosecute the case. He confessed that he never thought she could win the case. Roundtree had to restrain herself. She reminded him of how many times she had tried to reach him in the beginning. "I appreciate your call, Charlie," she remembered saying. "It's mighty nice of you to call. But I wish you had made this call six months ago. It would have saved a lot of people a lot of grief!"[86]

Unfortunately, Raymond Crump's grief—and troubles—were only beginning. Dovey Roundtree believed that Crump's nine months in jail had transformed him from a gentle man into a violent one. Convinced he had been taunted, beaten, abused, and possibly raped during his incarceration, Roundtree was heartsick. "He was not a remotely violent man when he was jailed for Mary Meyer's murder in 1964," she wrote in 2009, "but he became one afterward, both in the District of Columbia and in North Carolina, where he eventually moved with his second wife."[87] In fact, after the trial Ray Crump's alcoholism became acute. Within the next few years, he would be charged with arson, assault with a deadly weapon, and violently threatening two girlfriends. In one fit of rage, Crump reportedly set his home on fire with his wife and children inside. His family escaped unhurt, and Ray was given a stiff prison sentence in North Carolina. Upon his release, he maintained his downward trajectory, committing arson once again and serving more jail time.

The condition known as *Post-Traumatic Stress Disorder* (PTSD) wasn't formally recognized until 1980, though working models dealing with its cluster of symptoms were engendered in the early 1970s. Like the innocent, ill-prepared young men sent into harrowing and prolonged traumatic combat conditions in places like Vietnam, Iraq, Afghanistan, and elsewhere, Ray Crump had been psychologically and physically maimed by the violence and brutality he was subjected to during his nine-month incarceration. Continually threatened, terrified, and increasingly unable to cope, what little ego strength he possessed disintegrated over time. Like many returning combat soldiers, he became a broken, shattered man, capable of violence to others and to himself. Unfortunately, for many of Mary Meyer's community and family in Washington, as well as people in the Justice Department, including Alfred Hantman, Ray Crump's subsequent path of violence and crime merely served to bolster their belief that Mary Meyer's true killer had gotten away with murder.

Crump's post-trial criminal career also impressed high-profile criminal defense attorney Robert S. Bennett, who had closely observed the trial as Judge Corcoran's law clerk. In his book *In the Ring*, published in 2008, Bennett wrote that he would have convicted Crump "because of the overwhelming evidence." In his view, Hantman had failed to get "into the heart and soul of jurors," because he had overtried the case, most notably with Henry Wiggins. "It diluted the impact of his evidence," Bennett recalled in an interview for this book in 2009. "Hantman was primarily responsible for losing the case." Bennett had been convinced of Crump's guilt in part because he "gave the police an unbelievable explanation of why he was on the towpath—that he went fishing—especially since his fishing tackle was never located."[88]

Author Nina Burleigh reached a similar conclusion about Ray Crump's guilt. In spite of having been told in her one interview with Dovey Roundtree that Ray had been having a sexual tryst with a girlfriend adjacent to the canal towpath area on the Potomac,[89] Burleigh nevertheless posed the same old, timeworn questions: "If he wasn't fishing, what was he doing there?" "Why did he toss his hat and coat in the water?"[90] According to Burleigh, "Dovey Roundtree the advocate would always contend in public that Crump was innocent," insinuating that she might believe otherwise in private, and even going so far as to suggest that the attorney's religious belief in Christian forgiveness rendered the factual basis of her clients' earthly guilt or innocence irrelevant.[91] Did Nina Burleigh actually believe that Dovey Roundtree would have staked her entire professional career and reputation, not to mention considerable financial resources, on the defense of someone whose innocence she wasn't unequivocally convinced of? If so, that conclusion was entirely at odds with everything that Roundtree stated or wrote publicly about this case, including her private journey from initial doubt to absolute certainty about Crump's innocence, detailed in her 2009 autobiography.[92]

Of all that she accomplished in her victory in the case of *United States of America v. Ray Crump, Jr., Defendant,* Roundtree wrote that she had been particularly gratified that she might have helped to ensure a continued search for the true killer: "I believe, too, that in winning acquittal for Ray Crump, I made it impossible for the matter of Mary Pinchot Meyer's murder to be sealed off and forgotten, as the government so clearly wanted to do. There is much about the crime that bears the most serious and sustained investigation, and to the extent that my efforts in defending Raymond opened the path for researchers seeking to know more about the troubling circumstances surrounding her death, I am gratified."[93] Such "serious and sustained investigation" was long in coming. For twelve years, those who knew about Mary Meyer's diary and her relationship with President Kennedy chose to remain silent, until the *National Enquirer* finally broke the story in 1976.

Dovey Roundtree never abandoned her belief that Ray had been a scapegoat, a "patsy," who had been set up to take the fall. "So far as I am concerned," wrote Roundtree in 2009, "there is in the complex and tangled web of certain truth and unconfirmed rumor, of inference and speculation and intrigue that surrounds the life and death of Mary Pinchot Meyer a single critical fact: Raymond Crump's innocence in her murder."[94] Roundtree's initial suspicions about the murder itself were fueled by a number of perplexing events that have never been explained: the menacing phone calls she received after each of her many excursions to the towpath; the mysterious disappearance of the stalled Nash Rambler that had brought Henry Wiggins and Bill Branch to witness the murder scene; the fact that neither a record of a repair order nor the identity of the vehicle's owner was ever established. Dovey's radar had been on high alert from the very beginnings of the case in 1964, and the 1976 revelations of Mary's diary having been sequestered by the CIA all these years, and of Mary's affair with the assassinated president, further convinced her that something much more sinister had likely taken place—as did three years of interviews with the late author Leo Damore in the 1990s.[95]

Nearly fifty years after the murder, the most important questions are still unanswered: If Raymond Crump Jr. didn't murder Mary Pinchot Meyer, who did? And, more important, why? In the absence of such motives as robbery or sexual assault, had there been perhaps some disgruntled, demented jealous lover lurking in the woods waiting to take revenge? That was highly doubtful. In the nearly fifty years of research and reporting on the murder, nothing of the sort has ever been suggested. In her community of friends and acquaintances, Mary had always been highly regarded and respected. She had no known enemies. There was no rancor between friends. "She was best friends to many," recalled Jim Truitt, and revered as "a Georgetown artist with a hundred thousand friends."

Who, then, was the man that Henry Wiggins had seen standing over Mary's corpse less than fifteen seconds after the fatal second shot was fired? His pristine, unstained clothes appeared to closely match the clothes worn by Ray Crump that morning. Was it possible that the man Wiggins had seen was the same "Negro male" that had briefly peeked out from the woods, the one spotted by police officer Roderick Sylvis—well after the time Crump was discovered by Detective John Warner? If so, who was he? And was he even a "Negro male," or someone purposely disguised to look like one?

The final question still remains: What, then, was the motive behind the murder of Mary Pinchot Meyer? The intent was clearly to kill her, but why? Was there something Mary knew, or had discovered, that made her dangerous? If so, what—and to whom? And did that imply some concern about who Mary Meyer was, and what she might be capable of ?

PART TWO

"LOOK WHO'S CALLED to visit us!" said Lady Julia, daughter of Caesar Augustus, First Emperor of Rome. "Gnaeus Domitius."

"I was on my way to Formiae," said the Priest Domitius from the College of Augers. "I felt I must call upon you, Lady."

"Do you know my son, Lucius?" asked Lady Julia.

"An honor, sir." extending his hand toward Lucius. "I took the auspices for your brother Gaius before he left for Syria. They were most favorable. I've never seen the liver of a ewe so clear. One could almost see through it. His death is inexplicable to me."

"And to us all," added Lady Julia.

A screeching overhead is then heard, as an approaching group of children that includes Claudius and his sister Livilla grow louder with the awareness of eagles fighting above them.

"Mother, Mother, the eagles are fighting! Look out!" A small animal drops from the claws of one of the fighting eagles and lands in Claudius's lap.

"What is it, Claudius?" asked Livilla.

"It's a wolf cub!" said one of the other children.

"Mother, it dropped right from its claws," exclaimed Livilla excitedly. "Let me have him!"

"Leave it be! It fell to Claudius, leave it be!" said the stunned Antonia, mother of Claudius.

"Look at the blood! Ye Gods, what does it mean?" asked Lady Julia. "Domitius, tell us what it means."

"Lady, I . . . "

"You know what it means, I can see. Tell us, I beg you!" demanded Lady Julia. "Children, go into the house. . ."

"No! Let them stay!" Domitius sternly warned. "The sign was given to you all, and given now, perhaps, because I am here to read it. But they must be sworn to secrecy. Who are the gods that watch over this house?"

"Jupiter and Mars," Lady Julia answered.

"Then do you swear, all of you, by these your gods that no word of what you are about to hear shall ever pass your lips?"

(ALL) "Yes, we do."

"The wolf cub is Rome," began Domitius. "No doubt of it. Romulus was suckled by a wolf as her own cub, and Romulus was Rome. And look at it: All torn about the neck and shivering with fear. A wretched sight. Rome will be wretched one day." Then looking at Claudius holding the wolf cub in his lap, he pauses. "But he will protect it. He and no other," said Domitius solemnly.

"Claudius as protector of Rome! I hope I shall be dead by then," Livilla mockingly laughed out loud.

"Go to your room! You shall have nothing to eat all day!" snapped her mother Antonia angrily. "Children, come in. Come inside."

"May I k-k-keep the cub, please, mother?" pleaded the stuttering, head-twitching Claudius to his mother Antonia. "Please, may I ?"[1]

---

1   From the 1976 BBC Masterpiece Theatre production of *I, Claudius*. (Based on: *I, Claudius: from the autobiography of Tiberius Claudius born 10 B.C. murdered and deified A.D. 54.* and *Claudius The God*, both authored by Robert Graves. New York: Vintage International Edition, 1989, originally published by Random House, 1935.

6

"Prima Female Assoluta"

We plan our lives according to a dream that came to us in our childhood, and we find that life alters our plans. And yet, at the end, from a
rare height, we also see that our dream was our fate. It's just that providence had other ideas as to how we would get there.
Destiny plans a different route, or turns the dream around, as if it were
a riddle, and fulfills the dream in ways we couldn't have expected.

—Ben Okri

There is no such thing as chance; and what seems to us merest accident
springs from the deepest source of destiny.

—Friedrich von Schiller

THAT MARY MEYER'S murder would become "officially" regarded as an erratic, random act of savagery, simply another unsolvable crime, ignored
the flourishing multidimensional panorama of her life and the particular network of relationships it had engendered. Far from indiscriminate, her murder
was deliberate; and, as the reader will eventually come to understand, precisely
motivated. For Mary Pinchot Meyer was in no way ordinary—nor easily intimidated—particularly during the years just prior to her murder in the fall of
1964. That left an unsettling question: Who was she, and how was she unique?
What accounted for her perseverance, her courage? And, for that matter, what
made her dangerous, and to whom?

In order to arrive at some understanding of why, and how, Mary Meyer's
murder was orchestrated, certain details of her extraordinary life warrant

deeper exploration. For her life's mosaic—the events, the people, the choices she made amid life's vicissitudes and circumstances—only begins to reveal the complexity and uniqueness of a woman who ultimately came to thrive within the Cold War's hidden history, a defining moment of which was President Kennedy's assassination in 1963, followed by Mary Meyer's less than a year later. This remarkable odyssey not only reveals a glimpse of a strikingly rare and exceptional woman, but raises another perplexing question: Why was her demise considered necessary at the time, and by whom?

Achieving a new level of understanding requires one to look a number of heretofore unseen details—events, experiences, and people—that formed the tesserae of a rich, complex mosaic that would finally illuminate Mary's life and death.

In their seminal 1976 article "The Curious Aftermath of JFK's Best and Brightest Affair," Ron Rosenbaum and Phillip Nobile were the first to pay homage to the relatively obscure woman who had made more than a considerable impression in the life of John F. Kennedy. How influential her impact may have been was unknown; but the authors, at the conclusion of their investigation, refer to her as "the secret Lady Ottoline of Camelot."[1] They relied on an unidentified source who, the authors claimed, was "in a unique position to comment authoritatively [about Mary Meyer's relationship with JFK]" and who, until 1976, had "never before spoken to the press about it." The unidentified source had "agreed to entertain a limited number of questions about the affair."

> "How could a woman so admired for her integrity as Mary Meyer traduce her friendship with Jackie Kennedy?"
> "They weren't friends," he [the unidentified source] said curtly.
> "Did JFK actually *love* Mary Meyer?"
> "I think so."
> "Then why would he carry on an affair simultaneously with Judy Exner?"
> "My friend, there's a difference between sex and love."
> "But why Mary Meyer over all other women?"
> "He was an unusual man. He wanted the best."[2]

How and why Mary Meyer and Jack Kennedy became intimately involved during the last few years of their lives is only part of the focus of Mary's mosaic.

Both seem to have been deeply affected by their union, sometimes taking enormous risks, in part for the sake of a better, hopefully more peaceful world in the future. How their paths intriguingly—and repeatedly—crossed, suggests some mysterious force at work: perhaps a trail of destiny, a shared fate, or the engagement of the force of redemption entwined in love.

Was it encoded in Mary Meyer's DNA to be so independent, strong-willed, even courageous? Quite possibly yes. According to folklore, Mary's French great-grandfather, Cyrille Constantine Désiré Pinchot, as a nineteen-year-old captain in the French army, had set out to rescue his hero, Napoléon, from the island of St. Helena, where he had been exiled following his defeat at Waterloo. But the plan failed, and young Captain Pinchot escaped on a fishing boat to England.[3] From there, he and his father, Constantine, and his mother, Maria, made their way to the United States in 1816, hoping that the New World would be a safe haven. Captain Pinchot's father immediately reestablished his mercantile business in New York, enabling him to purchase four hundred acres of prime farmland outside Milford, Pennsylvania. Constantine and Cyrille, the father-son team, embarked on a series of entrepreneurial projects that over time brought them considerable wealth and standing, using the crossroads of Milford as their hub.

Mary's great-grandfather Cyrille Pinchot married and had five children. His second son, James Pinchot, migrated back to New York during the late 1840s and made a fortune in the wallpaper business. In addition to his business acumen, James Pinchot possessed a highly developed social conscience—he created no slums, fouled no rivers, and accepted no deals with corrupt politicians. He never wasted any valuable resources, nor did he enslave any workers. His philosophy and worldview embraced the utilitarian vision of John Stuart Mill, defining social good as "the greatest happiness for the greatest number of people." James Pinchot had such a deep love and respect for the natural world that he became one of its guardians, sponsoring the first real conservation movement in the United States and endowing the School of Forestry at Yale University. James's oldest son, Gifford, would later refer to him as the "Father of Forestry in America."[4]

Wealthy James had married Mary Jane Eno of New York in 1864, and after their son Gifford was born in 1865, they had a daughter, Antoinette, in 1868, and a second son, Amos (named after Mary's father) in 1873. Retiring at the age of forty-four, James began concentrating his wealth on philanthropy. The family transformed the town of Milford in the early 1870s "from a fading entrepôt to a booming tourist mecca."[5] The Pinchot money also built the family "a country estate." In the late 1880s, James Pinchot conceived Grey Towers, a Norman-Breton bluestone manor with a fortress-like exterior, "complete with three 60-foot turrets." The interior consisted of "a medievalized great hall, 23 fireplaces, and 44 rooms," each filled with luxurious furnishings that matched those "of the old baronial days." The manor's panorama captured the entire village of Milford and the Delaware River valley, stunning any onlooker with the sheer size and scale of the mansion. Referred to as a "summer castle," it "drew all eyes—tourist and local alike—upward. In lifting them up, James Pinchot acknowledged his own elevation."[6]

The sons of James Pinchot—Gifford and Amos—were both Yale educated and members of the secret society Skull and Bones. President Theodore Roosevelt eventually named Gifford Pinchot the first chief of the newly created U.S. Forest Service in 1905, in which post he served for five years. Gifford ran for the U.S. Senate in 1914 as a Progressive, vociferously campaigning for reforms considered radical at the time: a woman's right to vote; a graduated income tax to be determined by the ability to pay; workers' compensation for injuries on the job; recognition of labor unions for collective bargaining; and prohibition of the sale and use of alcoholic beverages.

Gifford would lose the senate race against Boies Penrose, but would subsequently become the governor of Pennsylvania in 1922 and again in 1930. In between campaigns, he managed to marry Cornelia Bryce, the daughter of a wealthy and prominent family from Newport, Rhode Island. Cornelia, affectionately known within her family and friends as "Lelia," was an outspoken woman who greatly influenced her niece Mary Pinchot as she grew up. During Gifford's campaigns, Cornelia had addressed hundreds of housewives, urging them to demand the right to vote. She also marched in picket lines and supported factory workers and miners seeking safety, decent wages, and job protection in their work.

Writing in the *Nation*, Cornelia Bryce Pinchot defined herself as a woman who essentially knew no boundaries: "My feminism tells me that a woman can bear children, charm her lovers, boss a business, swim the [English] Channel, stand at Armageddon and battle for the Lord—all in a day's work!"[7] Cornelia was yet another female role model for Mary and her sister, Tony.

Mary Pinchot Meyer's mother was the journalist Ruth Pickering. Born in New York in 1893, she attended Vassar College and Columbia University, before becoming a journalist in New York, and working mostly for left-wing publications. An ardent, self-styled feminist who wrote for the *Masses*, the *New*

Republic, and the *Nation,* she became the associate editor of *Arts and Decoration.* Ruth, too, came from a family of courageous liberal thinkers. Her paternal grandfather, whom she referred to as Grandfather Haynes, reportedly lost his life in an underground railway while freeing slaves.[8]

Ruth's commitment to feminism entailed a rejection of the traditional female culture of the day. She was the kind of rare woman who dared to define herself, resisting the prescribed roles that most women found themselves playing. She became very active in the women's suffrage movement, and for many years shared a house with political socialist activist Max Eastman, his sister, Crystal Eastman, and Eugen Boissevain, who later married poet Edna St.Vincent Millay.

In 1919, Ruth married Amos Pinchot. She was twenty-six; he was twenty years her senior. Amos was by then a wealthy lawyer who supported a number of liberal left-wing causes. It was Amos's second marriage; he had divorced his first wife of nineteen years, Gertrude Minturn, who was from a prominent New York family. Whatever the cost to him socially, Amos was apparently willing to bear it in order to be with Ruth. An ardent pacifist, Amos exerted considerable influence in reformist circles and did much to keep Progressive ideas alive in the 1920s. A member of Teddy Roosevelt's inner circle during the Bull Moose Party campaign of 1912, Amos sometimes exasperated the former president with his moralistic criticism and views on the role of big business in America. He believed that World War I had, in fact, been caused by American and European imperialists, many of whom were bankers.

As a leader of the Progressive wing of the Republican Party, Amos always worked toward industrial and labor reform. He would become one of the founders, along with Norman Thomas and Roger Baldwin, of the American Civil Liberties Union (ACLU) in 1920. Always outspoken, Amos was a champion of causes, no matter what it might cost him politically or socially. That year, he and Ruth welcomed their first child. Her full birth name was Mary Eno Pinchot; she was born in New York City on October 14, 1920.

The 1920s were a heightened, progressive era for feminism and a wide spectrum of progressive causes. With the ratification of the Nineteenth Amendment to the Constitution in August 1920, women were granted the right to vote in all United States elections. Ruth Pickering Pinchot and Cornelia Bryce Pinchot became the grand dames of the Pinchot clan they had married into, shaping their family's values and mores. In 1926, the *Nation* invited Ruth, Cornelia, and fifteen other women to explore and comment on the nature of their personal feminism. Cornelia considered herself a "public feminist," committed to women's issues from a political and civic perspective. Ruth called herself a "new-style" feminist of the 1920s, though she spoke out when she felt that it was warranted.[9]

Many of the *Nation* women, including Ruth and Cornelia, emphasized their privileged status by membership in an organization called the Heterodoxy Club of Greenwich Village, a New York feminist society organized in 1912 by the Unitarian minister Marie Jenny Howe. Virtually every prominent suffragist, activist, and woman professional in New York attended its meetings, including such notables as Agnes de Mille, Charlotte Perkins Gilman, Elizabeth Gurley Flynn, Emma Goldman, Eleanor Roosevelt, and Mary McLeod Bethune (mentor to Dovey Roundtree). The Heterodoxy Club's biweekly lunch meetings became a model for the Women's Liberation Movement of the late 1960s. At early meetings of Heterodoxy, members would openly risk revealing their deepest feelings about their experiences growing up. Personal sharing and mutual support prevailed, and the resulting gatherings set the standard for the women's movement's consciousness-raising sessions of the 1960s and 1970s.[10]

Mary's parents were therefore the kind of role models who would encourage her to become as politically and culturally engaged as they themselves were. The Pinchot home environment fostered personal exploration of all kinds. To be sure, wealth and privilege played their parts in this—there were no worries about day-to-day survival, and Mary enjoyed more opportunities to engage her developing self than she might have under more straitened circumstances. But privilege didn't deserve all the credit; there was something innate in Mary that made her extraordinary. Her mother, Ruth Pinchot, recognized it early on. When Mary was just a toddler playing on a Long Island beach, her mother noted the confidence and sense of self-worth that her daughter possessed. These characteristics would serve her well her entire life. In a letter that Ruth wrote to Amos, she joked that their self-possessed child "is a perfect little bully. She knows she can make Elizabeth cry easily and teases her all the time. She's an aggressor and the devil."[11]

The Pinchot family shuttled between New York City and Grey Towers, the family estate in Milford, Pennsylvania. Women in the Pinchot clan grew up surrounded by an extended "family" of some of the day's most prominent thinkers and newsmakers: people like Max Eastman, Reinhold Niebuhr, Wisconsin populist and presidential candidate Robert La Follette, and Teddy Roosevelt. Mary was shaped and molded by all of these influences, as well as by her suffragist aunt Cornelia and her mother.

At age twelve, Mary was enrolled in the Brearley School, a posh private school for the WASP aristocracy on the Upper East Side of New York, just blocks from her family's Park Avenue apartment. Brearley boasted rigorous academics for the daughters and granddaughters of many well-known figures, including Margaret Mead, Franklin Delano Roosevelt, Eugene O'Neill, and eventually John F. Kennedy. As a preparatory school for young women, it espoused well-roundedness. Self-expression and exploration were given top priority, complementing and supporting Mary's family life.

Even as an adolescent, Mary was physically stunning to behold—a blonde nymph from an ethereal dimension, strong and beautifully proportioned, at once athletic and graceful, yet uncompromisingly feminine. In her teen years, her social life was bookended by debutante balls and New York City's nightlife. At the Ritz-Carlton or the Waldorf-Astoria, Mary was the belle of the ball. Weekends were filled with parties at New England's elite prep schools—St. Paul's, Choate, and Groton among them.

At 15, Mary Pinchot was invited to the Choate School Winter Festivities Weekend in February 1936 by William ("Bill") Attwood, whom she had met during the previous Christmas in New York. Bill Attwood would one day become President Kennedy's ambassador to Guinea. He would also be at the heart of a Kennedy-sanctioned secret mission in the fall of 1963 to explore a rapprochement with Fidel Castro, behind the backs of the Pentagon and CIA. But in the winter of 1936, Attwood was the guy with the prettiest date at Choate.

Had destiny itself already taken the young and beautiful Mary Pinchot by the hand? Not having yet met Attwood, she had actually gone to the annual 1935 Christmas "Interscholastic Dance" in New York with one of his classmates, Geoffrey Monroe Bruère. There had been dozens of Choaties and ex-Choaties there, and Geoffrey and Bill Attwood, both fifth-formers at Choate, had competed for her attention all evening. Young Attwood's ardor, however, was impressive, as was his disposition. Geoffrey, it appeared, was too much bluster and peacock strut for Mary's taste. Bill Attwood, on the other hand, was respectful, though not sycophantic. He had called her the very next day. They realized they both lived on Park Avenue only several blocks apart. Boldness then inspired young Attwood on the telephone that day, for he wasted no time, and no opportunity. He asked Mary if she'd like to go dancing at the Persian Room that afternoon.

Beauty is its own light, and Mary was coming into hers. She recognized that afternoon with Bill as an invitation for exploration. She liked the way he affectionately started calling her "Pinchy." Before the end of Christmas vacation, the pair went out on several more excursions, the entire city of New York their playground. One outing included a meeting with Bill's parents who, Mary would learn later, "were satisfactorily impressed." After that, he asked her to be his date at Choate in February. Mary didn't mention the fact that Bill's nemesis—Geoffrey Monroe Bruère—had already requested her favor, but she hadn't accepted. "That bastard Bruère!" Bill confided to his diary. It had all worked out, though. Pinchy chose Bill, at least for the time being, and he awaited her arrival with excitement.[12]

By February of 1936, young Jack Kennedy, a 1935 graduate of Choate, was increasingly worried about the state of his health. He was undergoing tests for colitis and being kept for observation at the Peter Bent Brigham Hospital in Boston that winter. Having already confronted death during his battle with scarlet fever as a child, along with endless chronic infirmities throughout his adolescence, Jack was already facing the possibility of an early demise. Several of Kennedy's biographers believed this was one reason he became so obsessed, even manic, about giving himself as much sexual pleasure as possible during his adult life.

While he was recuperating in early 1936, Kennedy's letters to his former Choate roommate Lem Billings bragged of how he was, even in precarious health, "catting about" with nurses, as well as the teenage girls he was dating. "B.D. came to see me today in the hospital and I laid her in the bathtub," he told Billings in one letter. "The next time I take her out she is going to be presented with a great hunk of raw beef, if you know what I mean."[13] How much of this was just sheer bravado (or wishful thinking) was unknown. But when it came to women, Jack already had a role model in his father. As his sons grew into manhood, Joseph P. Kennedy Sr. made clear his views on the real value of female companionship: "A day without a lay is a day wasted," he told them. The Kennedy males were such a libidinous wolf pack on the prowl that the young wolf cubs, at father's behest, would deliver female "companions" to the patriarch himself. "He even tried to make some of their [his sons'] conquests his own," noted historian Ralph Martin.[14] Along with their wealth and fine Irish good looks, the Kennedy boys would inherit their father's penchant for philandering—in addition to the duplicity and chauvinism that went along with it. Womanizing would become a Kennedy trademark.

Despite Jack's health concerns, he would leave the hospital on weekends to socialize. One event he wanted to attend was his former alma mater's Winter Festivities Weekend, which Choate allowed to recent graduates.[15] Typically, the students would invite girls for the weekend. The girls might stay in Choate's Memorial House or even in their boyfriends' rooms, while their dates would sleep on cots in the gym. Often, the boys left secretive, lascivious notes in their beds, hoping their girls would find and read them. The social weekend was filled with athletic events, sit-down formal dinners, and afternoon teas, culminating in a formal Saturday night dance.[16]

But how far could a tomcat like the young Jack Kennedy navigate the confines of a heavily chaperoned New England prep school dance? And what would a college boy, a freshman at Princeton no less, want with a parochial school function anyway? What drove Jack back to Choate that weekend remains a mystery. But he returned unaccompanied, a stag. Perhaps he thought the homecoming on familiar territory would be good for his self-confidence, which had lagged since being forced to take a medical leave from his studies at Princeton, still in the Class of 1939. Whatever the force that drew him backward (or perhaps forward) isn't known, but something propelled him; for during the gala Winter Festivities Dance of 1936, he would encounter Mary Pinchot for the very first time, etching into his being an unforgettable moment.

The Saturday night Winter Festivities Dance could have served as backdrop for a Hollywood film portraying a bygone era: tuxedos and tails worn by the young gentlemen, couture dresses for the debutantes-to-be. It was a gala for young people who would grow up to be dubbed "the Greatest Generation" for their service during World War II. Yet in February 1936, life for this crowd was an endless party. A full orchestra played the latest swing hits. Everyone danced.

Anyone could see that Mary Pinchot's beauty was alluring, and it certainly wasn't lost on young Bill Attwood. "God, she's a smooth looking babe," Attwood scribbled in his diary. "I just hope her success doesn't go to her head."[17] As the dancing progressed, Attwood unfortunately discovered he had a rival for Mary's attention. Jack Kennedy tapped Bill's right shoulder and asked to cut in. It wasn't the only cut-in he had to contend with that night, but it had to have been one of the more daunting—and it happened repeatedly. The young Kennedy was entranced by Mary's beauty; he kept coming back. To compound matters, Attwood wasn't feeling well that weekend. "Frequent trips upstairs to flood my throat with Listerine,"[18] Attwood noted in his diary, meant leaving Mary unattended in a sea of potential suitors, and none more aggressive than Jack. Destiny, that evening, seemed to have made its first mark.

How did Mary first respond to meeting Jack? The diary that she kept during that period might offer some clues, but Mary's descendents have opted not to disclose it, although admitting it still exists. In his 1967 memoir, however, Bill Attwood recalled the 1936 Choate dance and the rival he had in the future president of the United States. Attwood recounted on June 10, 1963, that he was talking with Mary and the president, who earlier that day had delivered his historic American University commencement address on world peace.

> I ran into the President at Joe Alsop's [house]. He didn't know I was back and suggested I come in for a talk. I remember that we sat in the garden talking about the Profumo case and reminiscing about our school days. Mary Meyer, a Washington artist who'd been my date at a prom twenty-eight years [*sic*] before, was between us, and Kennedy happily recalled having cut in on her on the dance floor. It was hard, at times like that, to realize he was President of the United States. And it was impossible to imagine that, inside of a year, both of them would be murdered, he in Dallas and she in Georgetown.[19]

It appeared, however, that the younger Mary had not been immediately smitten with Jack, evidenced by the fact that her relationship with Attwood lasted well into their undergraduate years, his at Princeton and hers at Vassar. All through Attwood's diary from late 1935 to 1939, he made entries about "Pinchy's" (Mary's) impact. "Pinch is really a damn nice babe!" he noted during his freshman year at Princeton. "I like to walk along the street with her for that reason. Makes me feel proud as hell."[20]

Three years into her relationship with Attwood, Mary attended the infamous—and rambunctious—Princeton House Parties weekend in April 1939, but it wasn't clear how deeply their romantic relationship progressed, or whether it was consummated sexually. The following month, Bill received "a very fine letter from Mary today, the kind I expected knowing how outstanding she is." But the letter contained an update that bothered him. "She'll be going to Williams [College] this weekend," Bill wrote in his diary. "I hope it rains the whole time!"[21]

For a period, Attwood remained undeterred. His father had recently fallen ill, and his mother was afraid and upset. He noted in early June how "the Pinchots are good people and have been a great comfort to mother during this period of stress." He seemed to find Mary more attainable as a result of her family's kindness toward his mother. Later that month, Mary invited him to be her guest at Grey Towers. During his visit, he didn't write about any intimate connection with Mary. Instead, he was "watching Mary and sensing her presence, imagining her to share my own life—swell thoughts couldn't help intruding upon the present."[22]

When activity coalesced around the tennis court, Bill noted that his girlfriend had a particularly aggressive game. "Refreshed, we undertook some tennis after lunch—and I surprised myself by downing Mary," Attwood later recorded. "She was pretty peeved! Since she was playing far below her par, but I felt quite satisfied. I was at least returning a majority of her shots." The man who had passed that game down to his daughter was also at the court that day. "We were all criticized by Mr. P who watched from the sidelines." Attwood seemed to have come away from the weekend feeling embraced by the Pinchot clan, as he "felt so much a part of the family," adding, "They don't come any better than that family."[23]

After the weekend, Bill, Mary, and her mother drove back to New York together. There was little conversation. In his diary, Bill recalled his experience on the trip back. "I contented myself with looking at her [Mary] as she knitted and listened to her occasional remarks—each one of which enchanted me, for I recognized them as reflecting thoughts which were identical with mine." Attwood's insecurity about his sweetheart, however, reared itself in his private musings that day. "Her profile—serene, wholesome, mischievous all at once—left me happy yet impatient. To be able somehow and some day to express my love to her without fear of rebuff—will that ever be possible? Or shall I, like Eliot's Prufrock, continue to shuffle along, bewildered and dumb for fear of risking what little of her affection I possess?"[24] Even in the throes of love, Bill Attwood eventually understood that he and Mary were destined for separate futures. He finally allowed himself to let go romantically, recognizing that it was ever meant to be.

In 1938, Mary's older half-sister Rosamund committed suicide. Amos Pinchot was so undone by his daughter's death that he lapsed into a temporary bout of hysterical blindness. It would be the start of a downward spiral into depression from which he would never recover. Rosamund had been the firstborn in his marriage to Gertrude Minturn. Like Mary, she was an exquisite classic beauty. Sixteen years older than Mary, Rosamund was a model of glamour and sophistication, endowed with an uncommon grace. At four years of age, she had learned to ride horseback. By the age of eight, she was entering equestrian competitions at New York's Madison Square Garden. At thirteen, "she rode five jumpers in one class."[25] In her teens at Grey Towers, Rosamund was given to riding naked on horseback by moonlight. Mary had witnessed her, Godiva-like, late one night. She was in awe of her beautiful and adventurous older sister.

Rosamund was a prolific diary keeper, and by the time of her death she had filled some fifteen hundred pages with private thoughts and recollections that were eventually edited and published by Bibi Gaston, her granddaughter, in 2008. The book, *The Loveliest Woman in America*, took its title from a compliment lavished on the twenty-three-year-old Rosamund in 1927 by British actress and poet Iris Tree. Rosamund had also been an actress, but her fledgling acting career was largely a flop after only a few films, and the Pinchot girls didn't take well to failure. No doubt compounding her pain had been a failed marriage, followed by a stormy affair with Broadway theater producer and Hollywood director Jed Harris. When she took her life in January 1938, she was thirty-four years old and had two young sons. The event shattered Amos, and left a scarring impression on Mary and the entire family.

Unlike many in New York's aristocracy who were untouched by the economic hardships of the Depression of the 1930s, Amos Pinchot was not immune to the downturn. In fact, he feared for the future of his family, often secretly dulling his anxiety with copious amounts of alcohol. The effects of his drinking became known to Mary one evening when she was about to graduate from Brearley. She had returned to the Pinchot apartment with her date. Amos, drunk, became combative and criticized his daughter's social life. Mary retorted in her own defense, and Amos slapped her across the face. Her companion that evening must have been shocked and embarrassed by the spectacle, yet already the unflappable Mary was not one to back down. It was the beginning of a break with her father.[26]

Perhaps inspired by Rosamund's example, Mary became a committed diarist. Starting when she was seventeen—soon after her sister died—she would use the act of writing as a tool for self-realization and reflection, especially in times of emotional crisis, and rely on it throughout her life. As noted previously, most of her earlier diary is still in existence, but its contents are unknown outside the family. However, in 1940, on the second anniversary of her sister's suicide, the *New York Times* published Mary's poem "Requiem," a remarkable disclosure of verse that divulged a stirring dimension of Mary's own persona. According to Bibi Gaston, "Requiem" had first been written in Mary's diary.

Requiem

I saw her lying there so calm and still,
With one camellia placed beside her head.
She looked the same, and yet, her soul and will
Being gone she did not seem dead.

I thought if one so loved and beautiful
Should wish to leave, perhaps there was a voice
That called her back—and she was dutiful.
Somewhere the gods rejoice.

In some far place, where all the lovely things
Of earth are born, the gods no longer weep.
She has returned to them. And what she brings
We lose, but always keep. [27]

So began Mary's published authorship, in the *New York Times* no less, at the age of nineteen, during her sophomore year at Vassar. Around the same time, Amos published his own poignant tribute, "To Rosamund," in the *Herald Tribune.*[28]

While Mary's initial path led to journalism, she had arrived at Vassar considering a career in medicine. She was drawn to the idea of helping people, but she ultimately preferred the arts and the literary life. Unlike many of her classmates, she frequently chose solitude over the clamor of endless parties, gossip, and Ivy League college weekends. While her beauty ensured she never lacked for attention, she wasn't attention seeking. Mary had little desire to flaunt her good looks, or her good fortune. Ego gratification wasn't her objective; her affirmation seemed to come from within. "Mary wasn't very gregarious," her Vassar classmate Scottie Fitzgerald Smith told authors Ron Rosenbaum and Phillip Nobile in 1976. "She didn't mingle about. She was an independent soul. I always thought of her as a fawn running through the forest."[29]

Mary's independence was already a well-established hallmark of her character by the time she entered college. At one point during her undergraduate years, Vassar's administration abruptly forbade the student body to patronize the drugstore adjacent to campus. No explanation was offered. Mary, in flagrant violation of the new edict, recruited a reluctant classmate and went to the pharmacy—to learn its side of the story. According to the classmate, it appeared that someone at the store—a proprietor or an employee—might have made an unwanted advance toward a Vassar student. Mary's former classmate had lost the specific details, but her memory of the event remained clear many years later. "Mary was a real rebel," she recalled. "I was just a fake rebel." Then she added, "Mary was exceptionally independent, but not a loner. She didn't need to 'run with the crowd,' like the rest of us."[30]

Social life at Vassar was as active as Mary wanted it to be. In addition to maintaining a relationship with Bill Attwood at Princeton, she traveled to Yale and Williams for weekend visits with other male friends—none of them flames. It appears that Mary met her future husband, Cord Meyer, during one of her visits to Yale, even though they didn't date at the time. Cord himself wrote that he only knew Mary "slightly before the war"; in fact, he was a year behind her in college (Yale '43), but graduated in December 1942 due to an accelerated wartime academic schedule.[31] The two did, according to one account, have several dates before Cord went to war.[32] During that period, Mary also crossed paths again with Jack Kennedy, but no relationship ensued. It was a time when the patrician class stuck together. "Everybody knew everybody then," recalled Scottie Fitzgerald Smith, and "everybody" was anybody with a similar social pedigree.[33]

That did, in fact, include Jack Kennedy, who according to one account, dated several members of Mary's class at Vassar, though not Mary. However charming, Jack was decidedly a wealthy playboy and always on the make. Mary would have been bored with this kind of man. She thirsted for something deeper, a man with purpose, a partnership of allies. In one of his impromptu campus visits to Vassar, Jack in fact introduced himself to a gullible classmate of Mary's. The two went on a date, during which Jack, eager to carve another notch, concocted a story that he had recently been stricken with leukemia and had only weeks to live. His gullible date felt so sorry for him, she took pity, and slept with him that night, unaware of the duplicity young Kennedy had employed in taking her for a ride.[34] The Kennedy calling card was already in full swing.

One of the most revealing glimpses into Mary's psyche at Vassar was a short story she authored in the spring of 1941 for the *Vassar Review and Little Magazine*. Published six times during the college year, the magazine enjoyed an independent circulation beyond the college community. The two-column, three-page short story, "Futility," depicted a young woman named

Ruth Selwyn, attending her friend Beatrice Barclay's cocktail party in New York. Bored by idle chitchat, Ruth stands away from the crowd, casting a gaze around Beatrice's recently redecorated living room. She makes a mental note of how "cold and angular" everything is: ". . . the furniture all chromium and corners, the women chicly cadaverous, the conversation brittle and smart and insignificant." Ruth can't wait to leave the party. She is on her way to an operation that will change her life forever. She has pleaded with Dr. Morrison to perform the procedure for weeks. The surgery will connect Ruth's optical nerves to the hearing part of her brain and the auditory nerves to her visual cortex, "so that everything the patient hears she sees, and vice versa." Commenting to his nurse, Dr. Morrison irritatingly says, "She wants something new. You know the type: bored with life, looking for excitement at any price—as though life weren't complicated enough as it is."

The day after the operation, Ruth is amazed. As she passes the florist's window, she notices that the orchids have been replaced by a variety of other flowers, and that the display includes two framed paintings, one of which features sunflowers by Van Gogh. At the sight of it, Ruth hears Stravinsky's "Sacre du Printemps." The sight of baby's breath elicits the sound of a calm sea washing up on a beach at night. Roses evoke a slow waltz. And "when her eyes moved along past them to a clear white orchid, the waltz ended in the sharp tinkle of thin glass breaking."

One dimension of Mary's story describes what is commonly known as *synesthesia*. It is, to some degree, a medical condition whereby in certain people and animals, a stimulus in one sense modality involuntarily elicits a literal sensation/experience in another sense modality. For example, the taste of a lime would visually evoke the color blue. The elicited synesthetic experience doesn't replace the normal experience; it just enhances it. Many artists, for instance, strive to train themselves to become more synesthetic: seeing the colors of sound; hearing some visual perception they wish to communicate; or describing the "personality" of a bedroom's doorframe.

One irony of "Futility" was that it foreshadowed a significant event in Mary's later life. The fictional character Ruth Selwyn was having a classic hallucinogenic experience after her operation. The ultimate experience of synesthesia is easily induced under the influence of most hallucinogenic substances, including the psychedelic LSD (lysergic acid diethylamide). As an emerging artist in the late 1950s, Mary would embark on her own exploration of psychedelics, including LSD and psilocybin. This wasn't superficial thrill seeking on her part; it was more the result of being in the vanguard of a group of people, many of whom were already established artists in quest of greater self-expression. Equally fascinating in "Futility" was Mary's commentary on orchids: "They look as though they had been grown in damp underground caves by demons. They're evil sickly flowers with no life of their own, living on borrowed strength." How ironic that someone would later appear in her life who was obsessed and surrounded by orchids, someone who had presented himself as a friend, before his betrayal.

Yet at its core, "Futility" was an allegory for an issue that Mary would encounter most of her life: the divide between narrowly prescribed cultural roles for women, and her own aspirations. The "chicly cadaverous" women, who had succumbed to a life of wanting for nothing, horrified her; yet all around Mary and her contemporaries, social influence dictated the grooming for such a life. In "Futility," Mary took aim at what she saw as the vapid existence dominated by the superficial pursuit of elegant, novel redecorating, filled with "conversation brittle and smart and insignificant." In spite of her social and economic mobility—the plush confines of Grey Towers, a first-class education, the cultural cornucopia of New York City—without a deeper purpose, without some higher calling and sense of inspiration and passion, Mary still risked slipping into the banal, the empty, the insignificant and self-absorbed, making life itself hollow.

By 1940 all of Europe would be struggling against the warlord march of Germany and Adolf Hitler. But that spring, Mary's life at Vassar continued untouched. Having been selected as one of the twenty-four most beautiful women in the sophomore class to carry the chain of daisies and laurel at commencement, Mary Pinchot had worn the wreath known as the Vassar Daisy Chain, Vassar's most famous tradition. In September, Germany began the devastating bombing of London—seventy-six consecutive nights of air strikes known as the London Blitz. Life in America was changing. While Glen Miller and Tommy Dorsey pumped out music with time to dance, young men, many of Mary's contemporaries, were disappearing late at night to enlist. It was just a matter of time. America was going to war.

By the summer of 1942, World War II had enveloped the entire country. The sophomoric college days of endless parties and gaiety had abruptly come to a halt. With the attack on Pearl Harbor in December 1941, an era—almost overnight—had ended. Academic calendars were curtailed; graduation ceremonies took place in December instead of June, if they took place at all.

Everywhere, the preparations and demands of a world at war were becoming all consuming.

But not even war could stop love. Mary had returned to New York after her graduation from Vassar. She found a job as a feature writer for United Press International (UPI), established her own column, and enjoyed rapid success.[35] On her own and away from her parents, Mary's fierce independence and self-confidence bloomed. Even in wartime, New York was an exciting place for a young woman just starting out on her own. And it was about to become even more so.

Robert ("Bob") L. Schwartz was a young Naval officer and a journalist for *Yank* magazine. Hailing from a Midwestern Jewish background in Salem, Ohio, the handsome Schwartz was tall, lean, and intellectually articulate by any standard. One Friday night, sometime during the summer of 1942, Bob was at one of his favorite after-work watering holes, Tim Costello's Bar in New York. That night, he noticed a woman so alluring, he felt impelled to meet her. The problem was that every other man in the bar felt the same way. Tim Costello, the bar owner, was particularly protective of Mary and operated as a kind of "guardian at the gate," particularly if the men became obnoxious.[36]

Schwartz made a move on Mary that evening and Mary let Tim know it was okay. The chemistry between Bob and Mary was instantaneous and mutual. As they began talking, fireworks exploded for both of them. From the bar, they went out for dinner and stayed up into the early hours of the morning, talking about almost everything. From the start, Schwartz recalled, Mary defined herself in terms of her pacifism and hatred of all wars, including the one before them in 1942. Wars and violence were anathema to her, and she wanted Bob to know that at the outset. "Mary wanted to do right by the world and there was no place for war," said Schwartz. "She had impeccable standards, which for me made her demanding in the sense that I had to choose to meet her at those standards, because she wasn't interested in trivia, at any level or any sort. She was far more special than I was." Daunted, Bob still attempted to rise to Mary's challenge. Never had he laid eyes on such an astoundingly beautiful, complex woman.

Schwartz recalled with great fondness how he walked Mary home that night, how she talked about the nature of the humorous in life. Her sophistication impressed and excited him, and he wanted to share his own sense of humor with her. As they walked past a bookstore window, Bob pointed out a book by an author that he considered very funny. A look came over Mary's face, Schwartz remembered, and he read from it her aversion to his taste. He might have been projecting, but he began to feel that Mary was thinking she had made a colossal mistake by choosing to spend the evening with him.

After they said good-bye that Friday evening, Bob chastised himself for pointing out the book to such an extraordinary woman. "Almost in tears," he recalled, he returned, despondent, to his residence at the Sheldon Hotel, convinced that he would never see Mary again. "I spent the entire weekend wondering if I would ever hear from her again, wondering if she would even answer, even if I called her on the phone," said Schwartz, as though it were yesterday, some sixty-five years later. "Mary was so special, so very special. She was incredibly multidimensional. Of course she was beautiful beyond measure, but she also had a beautiful mind with a standard of interest that defied normal boundaries."[37]

That Sunday at his hotel, he received a hand-delivered package. He opened it, only to find the very book he had pointed out to Mary. Inside, the inscription read: "Enjoy !" It was signed: "Mary." Bob believed it to be a sign. Mary was telling him: "Don't be put off by my bullshit. I want this relationship as much as you do." He clasped the book to his heart, and broke down and cried.

Bob Schwartz and Mary Pinchot became nearly inseparable. Mary moved in with him at his residence at the Shelton Hotel. "It was pretty magical," reminisced Schwartz. "As romances go, it was almost flawless. There was never a day less pleasant than the day before. We had a commitment to each other from the very beginning." Mary's intensity was both contagious and alluring. By nature, she required him to show up, and engage. Their connection deepened Schwartz's sensitivity and prompted them both to explore life's biggest questions. "She was very committed to her own truths, and they were of a very high order that involved a level of morality beyond normal comprehension," Schwartz remembered. He and Mary would spend almost three years together.

In addition to revealing more about her pacifism, Mary allowed her spiritual sensibility and the seriousness with which she approached it to be known. "Why are we really here?" Mary once asked Bob. Unable to seize the enormity of what she was asking, he attempted a joke and said, "I don't know, I'm from Ohio." Mary didn't like that. She demanded that he connect on a deeper level, and in time, he learned to meet her there.[38]

The two shared a passion for sailing. During the war, it was easy to charter big sailboats—yawls and ketches—for sailing on Long Island Sound. Often taking weeklong cruises, both alone and with friends, sometimes exploring the

Connecticut River, they found an idyllic peace during wartime on those the trips. When they weren't sailing, they would spend time at Grey Towers, what Mary called "the country place" and what Bob called "a royal palace." The pair swam naked in the estate's waterfalls amid the property's verdant idyllic acres.

"When I saw that place," said the smiling Schwartz, "one had to be impressed. It was like meeting Mary. If you're true royalty, you don't have to flaunt it, and she never did. I mean, what else would Mary have, if not something like Grey Towers? She exuded royalty but never had to flaunt it." Some Fridays, the two would ride the Wabash Railroad from Newark to Pennsylvania and Grey Towers. Excited to be together for the weekend, always enjoying a fast repartee, they played with childlike spontaneity. On one trip, they started a raucous pillow fight, chasing each other up and down the aisles. Laughing, feathers flying everywhere, they managed to draw other passengers into the fray.

But it wasn't all pillow fights and laughter. Even as a young woman, Mary would challenge the status quo of their relationship if she perceived some inequality. Schwartz remembered one weekend at "the country place" when Mary challenged Bob on what he recalled as "a certain failure of citizenship" that bothered her. Alone one evening at Grey Towers, Mary brought up the fact that she was always left in the kitchen to do the dishes after they had dinner, while Bob would habitually retire to the living room to read the newspaper. It wasn't right, Mary protested. At first, the issue completely eluded Schwartz, oblivious to any problem at all. After all, this was part of the culture of how men lived. "In less than a minute of reflection, I understood," said Schwartz recalling the incident.

"Jesus, I never really thought about it," Bob remembered saying to her at the time. "You're absolutely right. It's terrible!"

"It isn't terrible," he remembered Mary had quipped. "But it's time you got past it."

"I'll get past it!" Schwartz quickly responded. The subject never came up again, because it didn't need to.

Mary's mother, Ruth, seemed to approve of Bob, though he often wondered whether Ruth felt that he was worthy of her daughter. Nonetheless, his relationship with Ruth, as Bob described it, was "arms-length but with affection." In fact, it seems that Bob might have underestimated the esteem in which Ruth held him. Mrs. Pinchot confided to Bob that her daughter's friendship with a young woman named Liz Wheeler worried her. Liz was the daughter of John ("Jack") Wheeler, the head of the North American Newspaper Alliance and a major force in the syndicate of independent journalism in New York City. At the time, Jack Wheeler's stable of writers was impressive; it included Ernest Hemingway, Sheilah Graham, and F. Scott Fitzgerald. Liz, along with several other women boarders, had lived for a time with the Pinchots on Park Avenue. She and Mary shared an exceptionally close, intense friendship. Too close, it seemed, and too intense, for Ruth's taste. She worried that her daughter was having a lesbian relationship. When she confided her concern to Bob, he was stunned. The thought had never occurred to him. He assured Ruth it wasn't possible; they were just very close friends. "There wasn't any room for anybody else," Schwartz remembered telling Ruth Pinchot. He let it be known that he and Mary had a "vigorous" and "fulfilling" attraction to one another. Ruth seemed reassured and the subject never came up again.[39]

What this anecdote may have demonstrated was that Mary was endowed with an unusual capacity for intimacy. As her life progressed, people often flocked toward her, desiring the possibility of connection she offered. As Bob Schwartz recalled, "Mary never did anything that didn't have a sense of totality about it. If she made a commitment, she was right in your face with it. Her major dimension was the aesthetics about everything. You'd look at her and you'd see: *this is a special woman.*" The quality only deepened as Mary got older. Her friend Jim Truitt, who knew her well through the 1950s right up until her death, would recall, "Many of Mary's women friends, including Cicely Angleton, regarded her as their best friend, as she was to so many."[40]

During a transcontinental train trip to California, where Bob and Mary both had journalism assignments, they stopped in Salem, Ohio, to visit Bob's mother. At one point during the visit, Bob asked his mother what she thought about Mary. Her reply was unabashed. She made it clear to her favorite son that it was obvious Mary wanted to marry him.

"Are you sure?" Bob remembered asking at the time.

"A mother knows," she said, reassuring him.

Bob looked at his mother and smiled. "You've made me the happiest man in the world."

But Bob Schwartz would never ask Mary to marry him. In fact, it was he who ended the relationship. "I was only an enlisted man in the Navy," said Schwartz in 2008, considering a decision he had made so many years earlier. "Everything pointed to the fact that I was not socially, or in any way, equal to Mary. I didn't feel comfortable with everyone always looking at her on the street, but not really noticing me. Mary was a complete head turner. I had credentials of my own, but they weren't Mary credentials."[41]

There was also the formidable shadow of Mary's mother. Schwartz didn't believe that he would ever really get Ruth's "benediction" to marry her daughter. "I began to hear her mother's voice, not Mary's voice," Schwartz recalled. "Ruth Pinchot never said anything affronting about me, but made it clear in other ways that 'a Cord Meyer would be a better choice,' though no Cord Meyer had shown up yet." All the while, however, Mary had been making it clear to Bob how much he meant to her. So had her sister, Tony.

Late one evening at Bob's Seventy-Ninth Street apartment in New York, Tony Pinchot showed up unannounced at his door. Obviously aware of the impending breakup, Tony had maintained a friendship with Bob throughout the time he had a relationship with her sister. Tony confided to Bob that for years she and the rest of the family had "wearily" watched the endless parade of men that Mary kept dragging home for her parents and family to meet. Tony then emphatically, and in no uncertain terms, told Bob that it was he who was the true standout—the only one she *and* her mother ever wanted in their family. Even with that benediction, whether Schwartz believed he "needed to be out of his sailor's suit and a full-fledged adult before he could get married," something kept telling him his time with Mary had run its course, in spite of the fact that Mary had been so clear about wanting to be with him.

Many years later, Schwartz found himself conferring with a psychoanalyst with regard to his relationship with one of his children. His relationship with Mary, and the memory he had forged of *her leaving him,* kept coming up. After a bit of work, the analyst confronted him, not believing that it was Mary who ended it, but him. "For some reason you didn't think it was going to work," Bob recalled the analyst telling him. Pointing out he had repeatedly "pulled the rug out from under his relationship with Mary," it became clear the only way to deal with the pain and grief of a breakup was for Bob himself to orchestrate the termination, in a sense saying "you're not going to hurt me, I'm going to hurt you first." The breakup was difficult, Schwartz said. "I mean, three years night and day and nobody else, and never being bored for a moment. It was astonishing, and very hard to let go of. It ended with a series of trial separations."

Yet that was only one part of it. Somewhere within, Schwartz was adamant about the nature of fate and the destiny that accompanied it: "For whatever reason, a Cord Meyer was due to appear. When he did, we both accepted it, but not before we shaped each other's future. She never could be with anyone who didn't have some of the things I had, and I could never be with another woman after Mary who couldn't understand what Mary had been for me. Mary set the standard. She raised the bar for all of my future relationships. It ended with many tears on both our parts."

Regarding Mary's murder, Schwartz was shocked by the event. Even in 2008, he remained unsure what to make of it, though he didn't want to entertain any conspiracy theories. He was adamant about one thing, however: "Her wrestling with her assailant was quintessential Mary. It would have outraged her sensibilities to go down without a fight."[42]

Now in his eighties, a connoisseur and lover of ballet, Bob Schwartz ultimately compared Mary Meyer to what he called a *prima ballerina assoluta*. The term was originally inspired by the Italian masters of the early Romantic ballet and was only bestowed on a ballerina who was considered exceptional, and above all others. The first recorded use of the title was by the renowned French ballet master Marius Petipa when he bestowed it on the Italian ballerina Pierina Legnani in 1894. In the Soviet Union, Galina Ulanova and Maya Plisetskaya were eventually honored as such. Others awarded the distinction included Alicia Alonso from Cuba, and Margot Fonteyn from England. To date, no American ballerina has ever held the rank, though Rudolf Nureyev considered Cynthia Gregory to be deserving of such a title.

"Mary was a prima *female* assoluta," lamented Schwartz as he contemplated her murder, a tear rolling down his cheek. "She was what women were meant to be."[43]

7

Cyclops

This young man has only one eye, but he sees more with one eye than most people see with two.

—President Rufus Jones
Haverford College
(introducing Cord Meyer in 1947)

Fathers, go back to your children, who are in need of you. Husbands, go back to your young wives, who cry in the night and count the anxious days. Farmers, return to your fields, where the grain rots and the house slides into ruin. The only certain fruit of this insanity will be the rotting bodies upon which the sun will impartially shine tomorrow. Let us throw down these guns that we hate. With the morning we shall go together and in charity and hope build a new life and a new world.

—Cord Meyer Jr.
"Waves of Darkness" (1946)

There is a huge difference between patriotism and nationalism. Patriotism at the expense of another nation is as wicked as racism at the expense of another race. Let us resolve to be patriots always, nationalists never. Let us love our country, but pledge allegiance to the earth and to the flora and fauna and human life that it supports—one planet indivisible, with clean air, soil and water; with liberty, justice and peace for all.

—William Sloane Coffin
Former Yale University chaplain
(Riverside Church, New York City, 2003)

I N AN ATTACK on a Japanese stronghold on the island of Guam during the morning of July 21, 1944, Lieutenant Cord Meyer Jr. climbed up the steep beaches leading a machine-gun platoon of forty-four men in the 22nd Marine Regiment. That evening, the thirty surviving Marines dug in for the night in their foxholes. For hours, bullets had been flying everywhere. One had sideswiped Cord and literally cut the tip off a cigar that had been in the breast pocket of his jacket. He lit the cigar later that day and "pretended a courage" he didn't feel. That night, a heavy barrage of American firepower from ships offshore answered repeated Japanese assaults.[1]

Cord Meyer lay alongside his sergeant in a foxhole that was barely a foot deep. The two had agreed that one should keep guard while the other rested. Every two hours, they switched roles. To combat his fear as the night sky darkened with rain clouds, Cord tried to conjure lust by summoning pornographic images in his mind. "It proved a poor substitute," he would write two years later. The power of terror was as overwhelming as it was debilitating. With each attack, the lieutenant and his sergeant fought back and then endured the deafening silences between rounds.

Cord wondered how he had arrived at the place he now found himself: every moment facing down his fear of death. In a state of mental detachment, he was able to see the entire spectacle of war that confronted him. On one side were his countrymen, "lying in their scooped out holes with their backs to the sea, each one shivering with fright yet determined to die bravely." On the other side, "the poor peasantry from which the enemy recruited his soldiers were being herded into a position like cattle, to be driven in a headlong charge against the guns." How could it be possible, Cord had wondered that night, that such a human tragedy as war was now taking place? After all, "adult human beings of the civilized world did not slaughter one another. There must be some mistake which could be corrected before it was too late." Two years later, in 1946, Cord was awarded the O. Henry Prize for his short story "Waves of Darkness," in which he articulated a passionate appeal for world peace that would, at least for a period of time, inform every aspect of his life and work:

> What if he should get out of his [fox] hole and explain the matter reasonably to both sides? "Fellow human beings," he would begin. "There are very few of us here who in private life would kill a man for any reason whatever. The fact that guns have been placed in our hands and some of us wear one uniform and some another is no excuse for the

mass murder we are about to commit. There are differences between us, I know, but none of them worth the death of one man. Most of us are not here by our own choice. We were taken from our peaceful lives and told to fight for reasons we cannot understand. Surely we have more in common than that which temporarily separates us. Fathers, go back to your children, who are in need of you. Husbands, go back to your young wives, who cry in the night and count the anxious days. Farmers, return to your fields, where the grain rots and the house slides into ruin. The only certain fruit of this insanity will be the rotting bodies upon which the sun will impartially shine tomorrow. Let us throw down these guns that we hate. With the morning we shall go together and in charity and hope build a new life and a new world."[2]

But during early the morning of July 22, Cord experienced anything but "charity and hope." At 0300 hours, a Japanese grenade rolled into his foxhole, exploding in his face and killing his sergeant. Cord lay mortally wounded, contemplating death, bleeding everywhere, pieces of his teeth like half-eaten peanuts awash in his mouth of blood. The blast had shattered one eye completely and left the other so badly damaged it was swollen shut. With horror, Cord realized he was blind. Still conscious, he searched with one hand for his .45-caliber pistol to end his misery. Reviewing his short life, he realized that he had "no hatred in his heart against anyone, but rather pity."[3] Why had he not followed his conscience and refused military service, he bemoaned as he lay there dying, cursing nation-state savagery and war.

Cord's father had feared the worst for his sensitive, artistic son. Meyer senior had reportedly looked his four boys over, having had his own combat experience in World War I. "Of all his sons, he decided Cord Jr. would be able to take it least of all," wrote journalist Croswell Bowen in 1948. "If any of them crack up under it," he told Bowen, "it will be Cord." Cord's mother was also convinced he would be killed.[4]

Found the next morning, Cord was immediately transported to a nearby hospital ship, where the doctor told those around him, "He's got about 20 minutes to live," and listed him as dead on the battalion roster, causing his parents terrible distress. Cord would, in fact, live—and thrive; but his mistaken death notice foreshadowed his twin brother Quentin's loss a year later.

Cord Meyer Jr. was born in Washington D.C. on November 10, 1920. His twin brother Quentin was named for his father's best friend, Quentin

Roosevelt, son of President Theodore Roosevelt. The twin brothers grew up in Bayside, Long Island, as well as New York City. Wealthy and socially prominent with strong political ties, the Meyer family was an influential one.

Like their father, the twins Cord and Quentin were educated at the elite St. Paul's School in Concord, New Hampshire. The school was a breeding ground for those who would one day assume positions of power in business and politics. While Quentin often stood out athletically, Cord was the academic star who also had intense feelings of social responsibility. Gerald Chittenden, a former teacher at St. Paul's, recalled in 1948 that "Cord was fundamentally a poet," yet he was imbued with a kind of temperament "that had a fixed habit of going off the deep end; he blew like a half gale. He may sometimes have been a little absurd in those days, but when he cooled down as he sometimes did, he amused himself as much as he did the rest of us. There was no vanity in him."[5]

Yet, as Chittenden further observed, "the cold and faded oyster of cynicism drove him [Cord] to absolute fury." In point of fact, Cord's emotional intensity was a double-edged sword, and would remain so for the rest of his life. Channeled constructively, it might have compelled an entire country to seek out something yet unimagined. For as Chittenden astutely observed: "On questions of morals and morale, he [Cord] was always right."[6] But unfocused and without discipline, that same "absolute fury" could turn destructive and, like a cyclone, destroy everything in its path.

After graduating second in his class at St. Paul's, Cord entered Yale in 1939, just after war had been declared in Europe. Despite the distant thunder of marching German armies, Cord immersed himself in the academic cornucopia that lay before him. He was dazzled by the brilliance of Yale's legendary faculty. "I had great respect for Cord," recalled his classmate and former journalist Charlie Bartlett. "He was always a dedicated student of anything he took on. He got the best marks in our class because he worked so damn hard."[7]

During late-night dormitory arguments at Yale's Davenport College, the war in Europe inevitably took center stage. For Cord, there were no merits to debate. His was the heart of a conscientious objector when it came to all things war. "Of one thing, he was certain: War was a violation of all the things, all the accumulated learning, all the teachings of the poets and philosophers who were increasingly commanding his respect."[8] Cord's fundamental dilemma was this: If murder was against the law within a sovereign state, why, then, was it "a glorious achievement to be rewarded with appropriate honors and acclaim when committed on a member of a neighboring state?" The contradiction caused Cord to view war as nothing less than internationally sanctioned anarchy, and it would later become the chief organizing principle of his work for world peace.

Yet however "fundamentally a poet," or philosophically a conscientious objector, Cord became bound by the conventions of his time. Circumstances being what they were, he ultimately took refuge in Plato: "A citizen could not accept the protection of the laws and the education provided by the state and then refuse to obey those laws when they required him to bear arms in the state's justifiable defense." With Japan's attack at Pearl Harbor in December 1941, "the only question left for debate was which branch of the service to join," Cord recalled in 1980.[9] Like almost everyone who went to war, Cord's life would be permanently altered by it.

Enlisting in the Marine Corps Officer Candidate School at Quantico, Virginia, Cord completed his Yale graduation requirements early. By the time he graduated in December 1942, he had been elected to Phi Beta Kappa, played goalie for the Yale hockey team, and had been a publishing editor of the *Yale Literary Magazine*. His crowning achievement was receiving Yale's highest honor at graduation, the Alpheus Henry Snow Prize for being "the senior adjudged by the faculty to have done most for Yale by inspiring his classmates." Yale president Charles Seymour bestowed the honor on Cord, his voice quivering with emotion. Years later, journalist Merle Miller would recall that moment when Cord, in full Marine regalia, received the honor. "Tall and fair and handsome in his dress blues," Miller wrote, Cord received "no doubt what was his first standing ovation," and the applause and cheering seemed never to end. President Seymour told the departing graduates that it was up to them to "save our nation, indeed the whole world." One acquaintance who was there that day recalled, "We all knew whom Seymour had in mind to lead that battle; the rest of us would willingly, you might say worshipfully, be Cord's lieutenants in the fight."[10]

The reality of war came soon enough. Like many soldiers in combat, Cord wrote letters home, chronicling his experiences and their effect on him. So eloquent and forthright were Cord's letters that Edward Weeks, editor of the *Atlantic Monthly*, when shown the letters by Cord's uncle, decided to publish them even before Cord returned from the Pacific. "His writing, I felt, had a timeless style," Weeks told author Croswell Bowen in 1947. "Like Conrad, his prose gets you—so much so that you can't read it aloud. There is a maturity and vividness about his phrasing. He seems to reach out and grab the exact word he needs." Readers responded to Cord's collection of missives, "On the

Beaches," with enormous enthusiasm, and the *Atlantic* received an unusually high number of requests for reprints.[11] So began the opening of doors upon Cord's return.

Cord spent the rest of the summer and fall of 1944 in convalescence. Returning to his family in New York in September, he made frequent trips to the Brooklyn Navy Yard Hospital for the delicate removal of coral sand out of his one remaining eye. One piece of shrapnel was considered too dangerous to move. He also had to be fitted for a glass eye. He emerged as a hero from his convalescence, having earned the Bronze Star and Purple Heart. Cord's journal entry in September 1944 revealed a new sense of calling as he contemplated his future: "The general notion of what I have to do is clear. I owe it to those who fell beside me, and to those many others who will die before it's done, the assurance that I will do all that is in my small power to make the future for which they died an improvement upon the past. The question is how? In what field or endeavor? Where to begin? Education? Politics? Writing? Continue my education or not?"[12]

That fall, Cord began "seeing a lot of Mary Pinchot." He described her as "intensely concerned about the catastrophe of war which had beset their generation."[13] The two had met before Cord went to war, but no sparks had ignited. Their connection this time, however, fueled a passion that was as intellectual and spiritual as it was physical. For Cord, Mary was a "roman candle" who not only demanded and supported his vision of a world without war, but also shared an emerging focus on how to convince the masses of its rightness. It was to be a partnership of equals as their crusade began to take place on the world stage. Throughout the fall and into the winter of 1945, Mary and Cord deepened their union while forging and exploring the possibilities for action.

Still uncertain of a path for his vision, Cord entered Yale Law School in February 1945, commuting back and forth from New York. Not interested in entering his family's well-established, highly profitable real estate business, he considered a legal career to be a sound stepping-stone to public life. But the drudgery of the law curriculum bored him; he longed to continue writing. In April 1945, Cord received word that former Minnesota governor Harold Stassen, soon to be a U.S. delegate to the San Francisco Conference that would establish the United Nations, had chosen him to be one of his aides for the conference. Cord leaped at the chance and immediately went to Washington to meet with Stassen. The following day, he returned to New York where he and Mary were quietly married at her mother's apartment. The two would attend the conference together. Mary would report the event for UPI.

Stassen had chosen Cord on recommendations from a number of American colleges. He would not be disappointed. After the conference, asked about the quality of Cord's work, Stassen said, "[H]e turned in the best reports of the day of the proceedings and got them to me twice as fast as anyone else." Stassen would later say of Cord, "That young man has the best mind of any young man in America."[14]

Increasingly persuasive and articulate about his emerging vision for the prospect of a world without war, Cord was critical of the first UN conference in San Francisco. Despite the extravagant press claims that the conference had been a major step forward in ensuring a peaceful future for the world, Cord already knew differently. The proposed UN Security Council veto power, as well as certain other provisions, made it virtually impossible for the new organization to protect against armed aggression. "This is a step in the right direction," Cord told John Crider of the *New York Times*, "but there will have to be amendments to make it work. I don't see how it can prevent war unless it grows into something more than seems to be contemplated here. It seems to be the only practical solution at the moment, but it remains to be seen if it is workable." Cord concluded, "[T]he only real solution is a genuine federation of the nations so they would not be free to make war, but would be subordinate to a higher law."[15]

Cord had just articulated twenty-three words that might open an entirely new era: ". . . a genuine federation of the nations so they would not be free to make war, but would be subordinate to a higher law." It was May 2, 1945, barely a week after the UN charter conference in San Francisco had begun. The mission he and Mary would share for the next three years was coming into focus, and his presence at the conference wasn't going unnoticed. "There was a lot of talk about Cord Meyer who was a young political hopeful at that time," said Betty Coxe Spaulding, who attended the conference with her husband, Chuck Spaulding. "He was married to Mary Pinchot at that time, so Cord and Mary, Chuck and I, and Jack [Kennedy] and his girlfriend would spend time together."[16]

As it happened, or perhaps as fate would have it, Jack Kennedy was covering the event as a newspaper correspondent for the Hearst newspaper *Chicago Herald-American*. Whatever social temptations beckoned, young Kennedy did manage to file seventeen three-hundred-word stories, mainly focusing on the emerging tensions between Russia and the West. His stories always included his picture, byline, and a short bio—"PT-boat hero of the South Pacific and son of former Ambassador, Joseph P. Kennedy"—as well his authorship of the best-selling *Why England Slept*. Yet Jack's astute grasp of the unfolding post–World War II power grab was steadily drawing attention. Like Cord, he was being courted by the *Atlantic Monthly*'s editor, Edward Weeks. "I haven't changed my views that disarmament is an essential part of any lasting peace," Jack wrote back to the editor during the conference. In one Hearst dispatch, Kennedy wrote that "diplomacy might be said to be the art of who gets what and how, as applied to international affairs."[17] And like Cord, he would leave the conference with a sense of some inevitable showdown among world powers that the UN would, in the end, be completely powerless to stop.[18]

During the San Francisco UN conference, Jack and Cord had a legendary confrontation.[19] Still dazzled by Mary's allure, Jack was willing to try almost anything to stay connected with her. Sensing the intrusion, Cord would have none of it. Testosterone sparks of territorial infringement quickly flared amid whatever social discourse was taking place. Realizing Cord's position as a principal liaison to U.S. delegate Harold Stassen, Jack wanted to interview him for one of his press filings, but Cord snubbed him, declining the invitation. Jack never forgot the dismissal; years later, when Cord wanted out of the CIA and solicited Kennedy for the ambassadorship to Guatemala, the president ignored him. Joseph W. Shimon, a close Kennedy White House aide who talked and walked with President Kennedy daily, noted in 1975 that the president never forgave anyone who crossed him. "Bobby would threaten you," said Shimon, "he'd holler, scream, kick you, anything. Jack was a strong, deep, silent guy, really more so than people realize. Jack wouldn't threaten you. Jack would do it to you. He'd just pull that string and you're through."[20]

Cord and Mary left the UN charter conference discouraged. Despite the many efforts to find some unifying supranational authority against "the death agony of nationalism" that forever propelled one nation against another, the United Nations was neutered even before its inception. Recalling one of his mentors at Yale, Cord mused: "[Professor Nicholas] Spykman showed us that the existence of sovereign states had always led to wars. He didn't think anything could be done about it; he was quite cynical about the chances of peace."[21] The press had made extravagant claims about the conference as a major step toward ensuring peace throughout the world, but Cord felt differently. The proposed United Nations Security Council veto power, for example, made it virtually impossible for the new organization to protect against armed aggression. The Soviets, keen to protect their independence, had opposed all attempts to give the UN real power. So had the U.S. Senate, which prohibited the American delegation from proposing anything that would limit America's hegemony.

Cord's frustration with bureaucratic roadblocks, however, paled next to the wrenching horror he experienced upon receiving an early morning phone call from his mother on May 31. His fraternal twin brother, Quentin, had been killed in action during an entrenched battle with the Japanese on Okinawa. One of his wiremen had been hit by sniper fire. Quentin had rushed to help him and was killed by fragments from a Japanese grenade. The war between nations had just become even more personal, taking from Cord someone whom he had loved deeply

Though comforted by Mary, Cord was shattered by the death of his brother, yet there was little show of grief. Without expression, "absolute fury" and the emotional pain that drove it would eventually extract the kind of toll that forever torments a soul. Those closest to Cord would repeatedly remark how big a blow the death of his twin brother had been. "Cord was always very closed off emotionally and protective of his private life," recalled his former Yale classmate, newspaperman Charlie Bartlett. "I don't think he ever got over the loss of his brother."[22]

The letter Cord wrote to his parents after brother Quentin's death was disciplined, stoic, and philosophical. He spoke of his brother's bravery, of his lack of guile, and his belief that Quentin would go on living in the hearts and minds of those who loved him. Later attempting to make sense of the loss, he recalled a memory of Quentin where he "saw him in the moonlight with his head raised in a gesture of farewell, and though we were twins still young in his unconquerable grace, that I should have to answer how I spent my days since we parted, and that it was necessary that I should be able to give a simple, honest answer." A month later, he recorded in his journal that he had "opened the front page of a book to meet an introductory quote that read: *Thy brother's blood cries from the ground.* If I could only understand clearly what it said, then it should be done no matter what the obstacles or the dangers. We who survive are the debtors until we also die."[23]

Jack Kennedy's close friend Chuck Spaulding had known Cord well enough to be "fascinated by the difference between Meyer and Jack," perhaps sensing that either one of them might rise to the greatest of political heights. "Cord Meyer did come back from the war with the loss of an eye and the loss of a

brother in a similar respect to Jack and was so affected by it," Spaulding reflected. "But Kennedy was never affected like that [regarding the war death of
his older brother, Joe]. He was never pushed off this hard, sensible center of
his being."[24] Such became the hardened character of these men, both of whom
had looked up "the asshole of death" and survived war's slaughter. But though
he was imbued with the sensibility of a poet, the province of genuine human
intimacy often challenged and eluded Cord. His deepest emotional expression
seemed confined to his journal writing, in which he demonstrated an unusually
complex understanding and vulnerability that he was rarely able to express in
life. Jack Kennedy appeared content to avoid any intimacy in human relationships entirely. Emotionally crippled in his relations with women, he detested
being embraced, and then compulsively showered, sometimes as often as five
times a day, only then to crave the most intimate merging of all, sexual union.[25]

The impact of World War II on the men who returned was poignantly expressed by Mary Meyer's dear friend Anne Truitt in 1982: "Confronted by
the probability of their own deaths, it seems to me that many of the most
percipient men of my generation killed off those parts of themselves that were
most vulnerable to pain, and thus lost forever a delicacy of feeling on which intimacy depends. To a less tragic extent we women also had to harden ourselves
and stood to lose with them the vulnerability that is one of the guardians of
the human spirit."[26] Cord's anesthetization to grief would eventually maim his
capacity for sustaining intimacy in relationship, and not just with Mary.

After leaving the UN San Francisco Conference, Cord and Mary traveled
by train to Montana to take a month-long honeymoon. Cord already had
his next writing assignment for the *Atlantic Monthly*, entitled "A Serviceman
Looks at the Peace." The cross-country train trip provided many hours for
the essential discussion and reflection between the husband-and-wife team.
Cord found it difficult to write about the illusion that the proposed structure
of the United Nations was going "to be all love and kisses among the nations
of the world."[27] Mary's editing attempts only provoked his ire, eventually exas-
perating her to tears. The finished article, nonetheless, was blunt. Pulling no
punches, Cord sternly warned that "for those of us who have fought not for
power but because we believe in the possibility of peace, the Charter is nothing
more than a series of harmless platitudes. Weak and inadequate as it stands
today, it is all that we shall have won from the war."[28]

The article was due for publication in September 1945, and Cord submitted it at the very beginning of August. But a few days later, on August 6,

and again on August 9, the entire world witnessed a global event of unprecedented magnitude: the detonation of the atomic bomb upon Hiroshima and Nagasaki. The Atomic Age had begun. For Cord, the path was now illuminated ever more profoundly. "I knew then that the question of world government was no longer a matter to be talked about for the future," he told journalist Croswell Bowen. "I knew then it must come about immediately or we will all be finished."[29]

Edward Weeks, the editor of the *Atlantic Monthly*, was so impressed with Cord's latest essay that he advised his acolyte to give up law and go to graduate school at Harvard, a door that Weeks would help open. Weeks considered Cord to be the brightest intellectual star, and he wanted him to be surrounded by the best minds. He facilitated Cord and Mary's transition to Cambridge that September by giving Mary a job on the *Atlantic*'s editorial staff. Cord began taking courses at Harvard. In less than one month, Harvard would prove to be his launching pad to the world stage.

In October 1945, Cord was invited to the Dublin Conference on World Peace in Dublin, New Hampshire. Presided over by Supreme Court justice Owen J. Roberts, the conference included such notables as New York lawyer Grenville Clark; former governor Thomas H. Mahony; UN conference consultant and future secretary of the Air Force Thomas K. Finletter; and Emery Reves, author of *The Anatomy of Peace* (1945). Reves's book articulated the world federalist belief that the nation-state system was no longer viable. Given economic interdependence and capitalism's need for a borderless world, the nation-state could no longer assure prosperity or stability, now that civilization had to contend with nuclear weapons. Only a supranational world government would create the possibility of protecting peace and promoting prosperity throughout the world, while hopefully promoting democracy as well.

Cord agreed with this assessment, and he was able to articulate the vision in a way that no one else could. At the Dublin Conference that fall, his star began to rise. Norman Cousins, then editor of the *Saturday Review*, recalled walking into a bedroom and finding Cord sitting quietly on the edge of the bed, ". . . holding at bay some of the best minds in the country. Cord spoke quietly and with great intellectual force," Cousins recalled in 1947. "He was modest but not objectionably so. You lost all consciousness of his youth and were only conscious of his reason and logic."[30]

The rising star was now shaping the policies of a number of post–World War II veterans groups, including the American Veterans Committee (AVC). Ideas for a new platform for world peace initiatives were gaining acceptance.

He was asked by the *Nation* to write a series of articles that would bring into sharper focus a new policy for shaping and keeping the peace in the nascent nuclear age. Cord published "Waves of Darkness" in the January 1946 *Atlantic Monthly*. It would prove to be his best writing and one of the most insightful, penetrating war stories ever produced. The O. Henry Prize story gave a lightly fictionalized account of Cord's foxhole trauma, and the force of will it took for him to go on living. That fall, Harvard bestowed yet another distinction on Cord, designating him a Lowell Fellow, one of the university's highest honors.

In February 1947, all of the U.S. organizations committed to the possibility of achieving world government convened in Asheville, North Carolina. Out of this conference, a new organization was formed: the United World Federalists (UWF). Cord's presence at the conference won him further attention. His clarity of focus, entwined with his acumen for understanding, impressed the leaders of the various organizations represented at the conference. In spite of his youth—he was only twenty-six at the time—Cord was put forward as the person with the potential to lead the new movement for world government. When some in attendance protested Cord's nomination on the grounds of his youth, New York attorney A. J. Priest stood up on Cord's behalf.

"Too young!" Priest said. "May I point out that Hamilton, Jefferson, and Madison did their best work before they reached their 30s. I know this young man well. Despite my age, I know that I and others here would all be honored to make Cord Meyer our leader and to follow him."[31]

For the next two years, with Mary by his side, already mothering two young boys born within twenty-two months of each other, the charismatic war veteran would lead the charge for world government as the best hope to ensure world peace. Within two years, the UWF's paid membership of seventeen thousand supporters swelled to forty thousand members. The UWF had fifteen state branches, several hundred local chapters, and a galvanized student movement. In addition, Cord's new book, *Peace or Anarchy*, sold more than fifty thousand copies. Cord tirelessly traveled the country, attending conferences and giving speeches, one of which would be read into the *Congressional Record* on May 14, 1947, by Representative Chat Holifield of California.

World Federalism became part of the American political landscape, attracting wide interest by such notables as atomic scientists Albert Einstein and Edward Teller, political figures Chester Bowles, General Douglas MacArthur, and finally President Truman himself. In 1949, Cord delivered an impassioned statement before the House Committee on Foreign Affairs. It was inserted into the appendix of the *Congressional Record* by Senator Hubert Humphrey, a staunch supporter of the effort.[32] As political scientist Frederick Schulman reflected in the early 1950s, "World government had become for this generation the central symbol of Man's will to survive, and of his moral abhorrence of collective murder and suicide."[33]

As his renown took center stage that first year, Cord appeared to be one of the young men in the Western world who would forge the post–World War II trajectory of geopolitics. Certainly he was well positioned, but what if he should falter? Who else was capable of climbing similar heights? The July 1947 issue of *Glamour* featured an article entitled "Wise American Leadership Is the Hope of World," by Vera Michaels Dean. Written and published in three languages (English, French, and Russian), it outlined six basic requirements for the preservation of world peace. Immediately following the article was a portrait gallery of ten men, entitled "Young Men Who Care," ranked in order of importance. The first two, ironically pictured side by side, were none other than Cord Meyer Jr. and John F. Kennedy.

The caption under Cord's picture read, "26 years old and a writer. He cares deeply about world government. Brilliantly articulate, he argues its case with lucid, patient logic. Ex-Yale and ex-Marine Corps, he gives back for the eye he lost in combat. His urgent vision of one world. . . . or none."

Under Jack's picture, the caption read, "at 29, a Congressman. He believes good government begins at home. In a democracy which needs the best of its young men, here's one son of an influential father who didn't settle for a soft life. A veteran, he represents the Boston wharf district."

The remaining eight were positioned with four on each page.[34]

In the end, Cord's heroic effort to bring world government to the national political stage would be stymied by international events, as well as by his organization's inability to connect with the average American. Soviet Russia entered the nuclear world stage, testing its first successful atomic bomb in 1949. Relations with the Russians were already rapidly deteriorating in the aftermath of the Czechoslovakian coup, the Berlin crisis, a Communist victory in China, and, most dramatically, the Korean War. Such fear-laden World Federalist slogans as "one world or none" lost their appeal as the Federalist cause became enmeshed in its own complexity, internal politics, and inability to be more easily understood by the general public.

A new kind of fear was emerging. The growing paranoia over "Communism," coupled with Russia's elevation to superpower status, engendered a new mind-set, the era known as the Cold War. No longer persuasive concerning the darkening storms from every direction, the World Federalist movement receded. "Our attempts to transform the United Nations had been overtaken by events that could no longer be ignored or explained away," Cord wrote years later in his memoir *Facing Reality*.[35]

That was only one aspect of Cord's own downfall, however. During the years he tirelessly devoted himself to finding a solution for world peace, Cord had a companion other than Mary. A dark melancholy had descended upon the World Federalist hero, intermingled with bouts of nervous exhaustion. Whether driven by his "absolute fury," or his unresolved grief over the loss of his brother Quentin, Cord turned inward, despairing that the new world order was headed for nuclear Armageddon. Increasingly despondent, Cord took refuge in alcohol and nonstop chain-smoking, often finishing the first of several daily packs by midmorning. The World Federalist movement had, for Cord, run its course and failed in its mission; he returned to Harvard to resume his Lowell Fellowship, and to reflect on his defeat: "Two years spent in exhorting, pleading, warning, until my own reserves of confidence and hope had been so heavily overdrawn that it is hard for me to urge others on to action, when I now doubt the efficacy of any kind of action. Who am I to put myself against the dark and titanic forces that now mass themselves on the horizon of this new half-century? "Slowly, sadly, irreversibly, the tall world turns toward death like a flower for the Sun."[36]

Rudderless and morose, unable to envision his next move, the strain was taking a huge toll, and not just on Cord. Mary was now eight months pregnant with their third child. Having traveled constantly for more than two years, Cord barely knew his first two sons: Quentin, born in 1946, and Michael, born in 1947. Not only had Mary been the stalwart figure behind Cord's career—bearing his children, keeping house, editing his speeches and articles, and most important, aligning herself in complete support of the mission he had undertaken—she had exhausted her own reserves in the process. Incessantly preoccupied, Cord wanted only to know what the future might hold for him as his fellowship came to an end. The marriage began to show signs of trouble. Mary's impatience became even more apparent. Saddled with mothering two young boys, and a third son born in February 1950, she carried all the family burdens and daily chores.

Taking refuge in his journal, Cord wrote of how tired he was of his own career dilemma, "wrestling with terms of personal decision and action" as to where he should focus. Unable to reach him directly, Mary pursued Cord in his journal, leaving comments for him to ponder. "You are a romantic!" She scribbled next to one entry. "We're all in the same bed, Honey—pooped!"[37] As Cord brooded over the Korean War ("This is in all probability the rehearsal for larger and more decisive battles"), he ultimately reflected: "I am without hope. And yet I live from day to day as before." Here, Mary wrote in the margin: "When you say you are without hope, you imply that you thought humans were not what they are—humans."[38]

Their banter soon reached a bitter crescendo. In June 1951, Cord wrote a four-stanza poem entitled "Proper Tribute." The verse appeared as a thinly disguised expression of his feelings about Mary, and he surely meant her to take it as such when she discovered it.

Proper Tribute

Beauty, she wears carelessly like a bright gown,
Lent for a night by some indulgent guest
And is dismissed to find that no man loves
Only herself in that brief garment dressed.

She lacks the arrogance that lovely women
Habitually show. In genuine surprise
She smiles at praise that would-be lovers bring
As proper tribute to her transient eyes.

And in a way she's right. She never earned
With work or special talent her tall grace,
Her full breasts or her abundant hair.
By luck with genes she won her dreaming face.

But now that beauty's hers by nature's gift,
She must its burden bear and growing learn
What damage in poor hearts her passing wrecks.
And how for her desire sleepless burns.

Mary took the bait. She added a closing stanza of mocking self-criticism that was also a warning to her husband: If he considered her passive or dormant, she would prove him wrong.

She bites her fingernails,
Fails to shave under her arms,
Has no sense of humor,
And is a totally mundane soul.
But silence fires the imagination of the spiritually timid.[39]

Cord's decision in 1951 to work for the CIA was not about following a calling or answering destiny. He had wanted to continue writing, and he had hoped that his tenure as a Lowell Fellow at Harvard might lead to an academic post. But postwar economics being what they were, academia was not recruiting. Not even his contacts at Yale or Columbia panned out. He consulted Secretary of State Dean Acheson for a job in the State Department, but there was none for him.

It is not known exactly when Cord's first contact with Allen Dulles took place. Possibly contacted by Cord's father, Dulles had already been apprised of Cord's "splendid qualifications" as early as February 1951. By March of that year, the two had met in Washington, and Cord obviously went away intrigued by what Dulles had offered him, which remained top secret and classified. On March 31 that year, Cord acknowledged in his journal that he was busy filling out the required paperwork to work for the CIA.[40]

Following his interview with Dulles, he met with another Dulles protégé already at the CIA, Gerald E. Miller. Writing to Miller and Dulles in late May, Cord made it clear that he was "very much interested in the job we discussed," but asked if he could "accept on the condition that I might be free to consider one other possibility that might materialize during the first two weeks of July." He added, "In the remote event that this other thing developed, you would then still have more than two months to find someone else." It isn't clear from Cord's personal papers and letters what the "other possibility" was, though it may have been an academic appointment. Clearly, Cord's sights at the time included something more appealing than the CIA, and he wasn't hesitant about stalling Allen Dulles until July before committing to an Agency job that would begin the following September (1951).[41]

"If I had more faith in my creative talent," he recorded in his journal in December 1945, "I should write." The O. Henry Prize winner and best-selling author was so brilliant and talented, he could have excelled at anything he attempted. But his real passion was writing. With a leap of faith, he might have become a major literary figure during his lifetime. Free of the financial obligation to work, what then held him back from taking a chance to pursue a literary life? The same journal entry revealed perhaps a deeper reason that the literary life alone might not satisfy him—his ambition: "My peculiar temptation is not money, but notoriety and fame. This must be put aside. If it comes in the end, well and good. But it cannot be sought directly, for it corrupts all that we do and takes the mind from the object."[42]

And so Cord Meyer allowed himself to be seduced by Allen Dulles, a man bent on filling the Agency's ranks with East Coast, patrician Ivy Leaguers, whose arrogance would become evident in their disdain for anything in their way, including the rule of law. In making this decision, Cord turned away from his soul call, and also from Mary, abandoning the prospect of world peace for the waging of a new kind of war. He joined what would later be called the Directorate of Plans, the CIA's most secretive division dedicated to the manipulation of world order. Cord easily established himself as a rising star whose acuity often surpassed that of his peers, his well-born brethren—people like Richard Bissell, Tracy Barnes, Desmond FitzGerald, Richard Helms, even Jim Angleton—many of whom had come out of the Office of Strategic Services (OSS) after the war. It was a cozy arrangement of socially connected men from prominent families.

Yet for Cord, putting his talents to work for the CIA must have been bittersweet. There would be no more "quiet work—the labor of the mind and the heart, pure in the sense that it is done for its own sake and not for some ulterior end of wealth or power," as he once wrote.[43] And whether he acknowledged it or not, the dream that he and Mary had shared for world peace gave way to the realities of Cold War manipulation and the fearsome prospect of mutually assured destruction. The Cold War was, in fact, not cold, but hot, and it promised anything but world peace.

Somewhere in the bowels of the Washington E Street offices of the newly formed CIA, Cord Meyer transformed all his poetic, insightful visionary wisdom into perfecting schemes and strategies for America's greater power and control, the often subtle but effective attempts at world domination—no matter what the cost. Cold Warrior by day, increasingly frustrated and intoxicated at night, like many of his colleagues, the man who one journalist had once believed was destined to be "the first president of the parliament of man" was now weathering in corrosion. Yet still brilliant and talented, he achieved success quickly and often. Nicknamed "Cyclops" by his colleagues, his ubiquitous cigarette dangling from the right side of his mouth, its smoke forever wafting up through the corridor of his glass eye, Cord became known for arrogantly chiding anyone who had overlooked some important detail that only he himself could have grasped. Easily, he outflanked his colleagues and bosses.

"Cord Meyer always pissed off Dick Helms," recalled Victor Marchetti, the disaffected former CIA insider and noted author who had worked for Cord's boss, Richard Helms. "Helms was a traditionalist. He believed we should be spying, not the crazy things Cord had concocted. While the FI [Foreign Intelligence] section—the spies—couldn't do diddly squat against prime targets like the Soviets and Communist China, Cord was running all these crazy things like Radio Free Europe and Operation Mockingbird and having great success. He was very, very good at it, and his operations lasted a long time. He became the Agency's glamour boy."[44] In fact, during the course of his CIA career, Cord would be awarded the Agency's highest distinction, the Distinguished Intelligence Medal, on three different occasions, a feat only achieved by one other person: Robert Gates.

During the summer of 1951, Cord and Mary moved their family to the Washington suburb of McLean, Virginia, in advance of Cord's September start at the CIA. For Mary, the move was a relief. The boys were still very young—Quentin was five, Michael was four, and Mark was almost two. Mary looked forward to establishing a new family routine. They bought a grand old southern-style house on nearly three acres of land, just a few miles from Chain Bridge on the Potomac River. Known as Langley Commons, the house was built before the Civil War. It had a spacious, window-lined living room, a library, and a dining room with French doors that opened onto a landscaped terrace. The kitchen had been completely remodeled and updated. Upstairs, there were six well-spaced bedrooms and two renovated full bathrooms. Outside, there were large oak trees, rolling hills, and gardens, as well as a white-fenced riding stable, complete with a small barn. Mary, for her part, would be reunited with her sister, Tony, now married to Washington attorney Steuart Pittman and living nearby. Many of Mary's former Vassar classmates were also raising families in the area. Coupled with family life, the gaiety of the Washington social scene—dinner and cocktail parties, dances at the Waltz Group, Sunday-morning touch football games at Palisades Park—now took command as the Cold Warriors and the rest of the "Greatest Generation" ascended in their careers.

But if indeed silence sometimes "fired the imagination of the spiritually timid," Mary wasn't content to sit still where the life and future of her children were concerned. The fact that she was no longer crusading for world peace didn't mean that the future peace and happiness of her progeny could be neglected. She wanted something different from what she had experienced as a young girl. A new era of progressive education was unfolding in the early 1950s as Mary embarked on the search for a school in which to enroll her children. She came upon an educational experiment that embodied something she thought important.

Georgetown Day School (GDS) had first opened its doors in 1945. It was the first private, coeducational, multicultural, and racially integrated school in Washington, a city that was still mostly segregated. The school had been founded by seven families who wanted to create not only a learning environment committed to academic excellence and educational innovation, but also an overall educational experience that emphasized children of all races learning together. The school's educational philosophy grew out of such bold educational experiments as Black Mountain College in North Carolina, Goddard College in Vermont, and the work of German philosopher Rudolf Steiner, father of Waldorf education. Many of the teachers in the first racially mixed schools of the 1950s had been educated at Goddard and Black Mountain.

Led by the adventurous headmistress Agnes ("Aggie") O'Neill, herself a dear friend of Eleanor Roosevelt's, and her assistant, Bernard Wanderman, the school was first located just off Ward Circle adjacent to American University in Northwest Washington, behind what was then the location of a television station. The racially mixed, multicultural children who attended GDS were not just from wealthy, progressive, well-educated families from the "good sections of town." Many students took public transportation when their parents had little means of transporting them. The pupils were grouped together mostly by age, ability, and social development, not necessarily by grade level. A great emphasis was placed on each child's unique learning style. with "slower learners" often tutored by more advanced students under supervision. With a solid emphasis on both the performing and fine arts, the school required its students to participate in artistic endeavors such as class plays, ceramics, and painting.

Mary thought the school was attempting something unique and highly necessary. Much to Cord's dismay, she enrolled both Quentin and Michael, who would be placed in different groups. Later, their youngest son, Mark would also attend GDS for a while. Cord felt the school "too soft," not rigorously academic enough. How, after all, would this kind of environment prepare his progeny for St. Paul's and Yale? For Mary, however, the children's academic journey with its emphasis on the arts paralleled her own five-year artistic turning inward. Now seriously focusing her attention on painting, having transformed a former garden shed into a studio adjacent to the bricked terrace of the McLean house, she found herself teaching part-time in the GDS art studio, as well as taking courses with emerging Washington Color School icon Kenneth Noland.

Settling into the social life of Washington, Mary had another daunting role to fill: CIA wife. In the 1950s, the wives of upper-echelon CIA men were appendages to their husbands, like virtually all wives in America during that era. CIA operatives, however, were not allowed to discuss their work with their spouses. For Mary, this meant that the days of being Cord's partner, his chief sounding board and literary editor, were behind them—a dispiriting shift and a demoralizing change for a woman who had, in times gone by, thrived in a partnership of equals. Mortified, she witnessed the transformation taking place in the once-promising poetic visionary, as Cord became one of the men he had always disparaged and warned about—men who were "like rabbits staring with fascination at the oncoming headlights of the car that will crush them."[45]

Mary fought against being relegated to a role characterized by subservience, deference, and compliance. She confronted and argued with Cord over the CIA's mission, and, in particular, his work for the Agency. She began to discern what lay ahead and wanted no part of it. Her disdain manifested itself at parties and social gatherings, where she was alone among CIA wives in her critical views. Mary was, in the recollection of one of them, "always making wisecracks" about what the Agency was really up to. Some considered Mary's wisecracking disrespectful. Others suspected that her joking was a sign she knew more than she would admit. One insider, who spoke on condition of anonymity, said that Mary was well acquainted with the CIA's drug program, MKULTRA, and that Cord, in trying to appease his wife, had told her much more than he should have about many CIA undertakings. That source added, "Mary absolutely detested Allen Dulles and everything he stood for. She compared him to Machiavelli, only worse."[46]

Cord, for his part, knew he was alienating Mary. Just a few years earlier, she had been his most steadfast, trusted partner in their mission for world peace. Now, he kept her at arm's length. Emotionally adrift, alone, drinking too much, traveling on CIA business in Lisbon, Portugal, in February 1953, Cord found himself contemplating the city's harbor "for a moment in the precious sunshine."

I haven't seen the ocean in a long time, and though I love it, it often brings with it for me a vague sadness. Perhaps because it's so old and unchanging, it makes me think that I'm not young anymore and that unlike the sea, I'm changing, not necessarily for the better. I stood there with the wind blowing keenly enough for me to turn up my jacket collar and I was aware then, perhaps more clearly than anyone else, of all my faults and past mistakes.

I counted the more than ten years since the war and could think of very few acts of spontaneous generosity toward individuals, of many once bright talents rusting in disuse. And most of all, I thought of how through rude indifference and selfish carelessness I had so alienated Mary and of how all my days would be as lonely and melancholy as this one if she left me.[47]

Cord's reflections in moments of solitude demonstrated the kind of awareness that could have been a precursor to change, had he the will and commitment to act on his insights. Six months later, another event soon took place that might have helped Cord right his course, had he again been willing to take the first step.

During the Senate McCarthy hearings in the early 1950s, Cold War tensions fueled the public's fear that "Communist subversives" had infiltrated various arenas of the American government. Senator Joseph McCarthy launched a campaign of reckless and widespread character assassinations, fueled by unsubstantiated accusations against his political opponents, or anyone he considered a threat, or a "Communist sympathizer." Over the course of three years, McCarthy's attacks on the patriotism and the integrity of anyone he deemed suspect destroyed many reputations and lives. Two years into Cord's work at the CIA, McCarthy came calling for him.

"At 4 pm August 31 [1953]," Cord recorded in his journal, "I was in my office discussing with a branch chief certain lines of action we planned to follow against the Communists in Japan, when the phone rang and I was requested to go to the office of Dick Helms." Cord was told that he had become a target of the McCarthy Hearings. Accused of collaborating with Communists during his dealings with the American Veterans Committee in 1946, he learned that his loyalty had been called into question. Authors Cass Canfield, Theodore White, and James Aldridge, along with poet Richard Wilbur, were also implicated. "Well, they've apparently found something in your past," Helms said to Cord. "It looks serious." Cord was relieved of duty and sent home.

It might have been his chance to leave the CIA for good—an opportunity for redemption—but he wouldn't seize the opportunity. Instead, he spent the next couple of months writing a 130-page defense for what he called his "political trial."[48] Mary, too, was under suspicion. The indictment against her alleged that she had registered as a member of the American Labor Party of New York in 1944.[49] During his suspension, Cord used his time off to complete a play that he felt particularly proud of. He sent it to playwright Robert Anderson, who he hoped might assist him with the rewriting of certain scenes. The time away from the Agency rekindled Cord's literary fire. It also proved beneficial—however fleetingly—to his marriage.

Nearly three months later, on Thanksgiving Day, Allen Dulles personally let Cord know that the charges had been dropped, that he had been cleared of any wrongdoing. But the time off had already whetted Cord's appetite for something else. In early January 1954, he and Mary went to New York on a brief trip, during which Cord talked to a number of people about a job in publishing. "But I quickly learned that my friends in the established firms are going to find it very difficult to give me the kind of job and responsibility I'd like," he noted in his journal several days later.[50] Again, ambition and a need for fame and notoriety would squelch his recent renewed stirring of inspiration and interest in writing.

Clearly, Cord wanted out of the CIA and all government service, but was too insecure to cut his ties and strike out on his own. While McCarthy's witch-hunt had offended him, it seems that it hadn't been enough to cause him to walk away. When Cord returned to work, Allen Dulles sensed his discontent and, to assuage him, promoted him to chief of the International Organizations Division. As one of the major operating divisions within the CIA's Directorate of Plans, the division would merge with the Covert Action Staff in 1962. By November 1954, Cord noted in his journal that his resolve "to leave the government has been delayed by a promotion that keeps me so busy that I am so weary at night, I fall into bed after a quick glance at the newspaper." Then, in a reference to Kenneth Fearing's poem "Dirge," Cord wrote, "Bam he lived as wow he died [as wow he lived]." His next sentence read: "It's no good really."[51]

For Mary, too, it was "no good really." Cord's brush with McCarthyism had distressed them both. It had also opened a door to the possibility—and to Mary's hope—that Cord might choose another path, but he hadn't. His unwillingness or inability to disentangle himself from the CIA, which Mary openly despised, caused her to move further away toward independence. Increasingly, the stakes became higher—not only the stability of her family, but the integrity of her soul. Beyond her roles as mother, CIA wife, and homemaker, Mary still identified with something deeper within and longed to experience a fulfillment more profound. A tragedy would yank her out of her reverie: the accidental death of the beloved family dog, a rambunctious golden retriever. Struck and killed by a car on busy Route 123, which ran adjacent to their house, the dog had been the special favorite of Mary and Cord's middle son, Michael. His death veiled a Cassandra-like warning. Two years later, an even bigger horror would occur at almost the exact spot.

With Cord's return and new promotion within the Agency, the year of 1954 would become a defining moment in the Meyer family. Mary's mother, Ruth Pinchot, worried that both her daughters were being stifled in their married lives. She gave them each a round-trip ticket to Europe and a thousand dollars spending money. That summer, Mary and Tony went on what the two later referred to as "a husband dumping trip" to Europe. The trip proved the sisters' emancipation. Tony Pittman met her second-husband-to-be, Ben Bradlee, in Paris. The two ended up "exploring hungers that weren't there just days ago and satisfying them with gentle passion, new to me," Bradlee would recall years later.[52] Upon her return, Tony separated from Steuart Pittman. She would marry Bradlee in Paris the following summer in 1955.

For her part, Mary met "an Italian noble," as Jim Truitt described him in 1979, when she and Tony were in Positano. "I recall the name Jean Pierre (hardly Italian), and that Mary saw him on a yacht and swam out to meet him," Truitt noted.[53] Mary and Jean Pierre reportedly sailed the Mediterranean for a few days, before she rejoined Tony in Paris. On returning home, Mary didn't mention a word of it to Cord. But during the following summer of 1955, after attending Tony and Ben's Paris wedding, she and Cord traveled, of all places, to Positano. Again, she spotted Jean Pierre on his sailboat, in the company of a young American woman college student. Mary introduced Cord to Jean Pierre and suggested that the four of them go cruising on Jean Pierre's boat. The foursome sailed the Tyrrhenian Sea to Capri and then to Naples. If Cord suspected, he didn't let on. He returned to work in Washington, while Mary stayed on in Paris, allegedly to assist Tony in her new life. Both Tony and Ben Bradlee knew, however, exactly what Mary was really up to. She secretly returned to Italy and to Jean Pierre, where the pair went on an extended cruise and made plans for a life together.

Upon her return from Europe the second time around, Mary told Cord the truth. An entry in Cord's journal from the fall of 1955 reads: "About Mary—I have heard just two nights ago much more of that Truth I was trying to understand. Am still trying to digest it, but it makes me sick. Will put it down later." In another journal entry from that period, Cord wrote, "Mary has finally explained the motive that was so obviously lacking in all that she had said before, since her return from Europe."[54]

The motive, as Mary finally explained, was love. While she told Cord that her first encounter with Jean Pierre had been "sexually satisfying, but involving no deep emotion," she made it clear that she was now "in love with him and he with her," and that Jean Pierre intended to "emigrate to Canada to be able to obtain a divorce, and that he and Mary were to be married and live on a ranch in the West." Cord recalled the nagging suspicion he felt when Mary returned from Europe the first time, in 1954: "I remember half suspecting this when she first came back, but put it out of my conscious mind. I remember also her showing me a short story she had written about a brief affair. It was sophomoric in emotion and badly written. I remember criticizing its undeniable faults, and the reason I did so with so little respect for her feelings was undoubtedly because I again suspected that it was autobiographical."[55]

The revelation of Mary's affair only compounded Cord's alcoholism. At dinner parties, Cord's strident, argumentative disposition tended to dominate, even disrupt, all discourse. Sadly for Cord, his poetic sensibility had given way to bullying when alcohol took over. (In fact, alcoholism claimed many in the top echelon at the CIA throughout the 1950s and 1960s.) Once, years after he and Mary had divorced, he became so irked by something Ben Bradlee said that he reportedly lunged across the dinner table for Bradlee's throat.[56] Former U.S. Attorney David Acheson, Cord's Yale classmate, recalled in 2008 that "Cord had threatened to [physically] fight somebody at a dinner party at my house. We had to tell him to calm down. Cord could be downright mean."[57]

His son Michael sometimes feared him. As a father, Cord had little patience for three exuberant boys and their attendant noise, commotion, and disobedience. Michael had once confided his terror of his father's temper. It was something we shared—I of my own father, and he of his. We both had witnessed the reckless and explosive alcohol-fueled wrath of our fathers; the shared fear had been one of the things that had cemented our boyhood friendship.

Looking toward the small riding stable from the Meyer's terrace, the next house over was the six-acre compound known as Hickory Hill. Years later it would become the legendary "Kennedy Compound," occupied by the family of Robert F. Kennedy. But in the spring of 1955, its new inhabitants, Jack and Jackie Kennedy, became next-door neighbors of the Meyer family.

That May, Jackie suffered a miscarriage; a year later, she gave birth to a still-born daughter, while Jack was cavorting about Europe with Senator George Smathers. By the end of 1956, both marriages, the Meyer's and the Kennedy's, had been in turmoil for some time. It appeared that some force was still at work, keeping Mary and Jack aware of one another. Jack and Jackie left Hickory Hill for Georgetown in the fall of 1956. Mary would follow them a year later, but not before a trauma of unimaginable proportion.

During the fall of 1956, on her thirty-sixth birthday in October, Mary told Cord their marriage was over. She wanted a divorce. They had become strangers under one roof. Whatever grief she may have felt, Mary embraced the prospect of independence and all that it might promise—exploration as a painter, and the possibility of rekindling the flame with Jean Pierre. Convention would not enslave her, just as the quiet life of the CIA wife and homemaker had not satisfied her. Her children would have to adjust. Perhaps in time, she might have thought, they would come to recognize and understand the courage it had taken to save her own life, though initially they might blame her for such a cataclysmic disruption to the family. Whatever her disposition, it was about to be horrifically tested. Life's vicissitudes would make an unscheduled appearance early one December evening, a week before Christmas.

As the winter solstice light waned fast into dusk, the two older Meyer boys, Quentin and Michael, hurried toward home across the well-trafficked Route 123, already having been chastised for previous dinnertime tardiness due to their hypnotic television attraction at a neighbor's house. Some of the fast-moving cars already had their headlights on; some didn't. The faster, more-agile Quenty raced to the other side without incident. Perhaps he assumed that his younger brother was right behind him. He wasn't. Michael couldn't keep up with his older brother, and in the dark of the busy thoroughfare, he likely relied on the headlights of oncoming cars to tell him when it was safe to dash. Just nine years old, Michael Pinchot Meyer would not see the car that would take his life. His death was nearly instantaneous, and it took place where another auto had claimed the life of his beloved golden retriever just two years earlier. If the dog's sacrifice had forewarned the danger, it had gone unheeded.

Mary heard the screech of tires and the screams of her oldest son. She raced down the hill toward the awful scene. The driver who had struck Michael had become hysterical. An ambulance arrived, but it was too late. Mary would, for the last time, hold and accompany Michael to the hospital, but not before she paused to comfort the driver who had struck her son, her rare compassion anchored in some deeper dimension. The ever-delicate young Mikey would leave those who loved him in an interminable river of grief.

Laid to rest just before Christmas on a sloping hill near his grandfather Amos Pinchot in the Milford cemetery, Michael rested just a stone's throw from Grey Towers, where he had loved to fish and roam. Quenty, who would be eleven in January, could not bring himself to attend the burial; it was a decision that would later haunt him. Cord recorded in his journal that his youngest son, Mark, who was just six years old at the time, couldn't believe that "his brother lay in that narrow hole in the ground and neither could I." [58] The loss burrowed deep into Mary's psyche. The future seemed impossible to fathom. Within a decade, her own grave would be dug next to Michael's. A month after their son's death, Cord confided in his journal his hope that shared grief might yield reconciliation with Mary. His wish was that "our shared sorrow would be a bridge to a better life between us."[59] It was not to be.

Shortly thereafter, Cord wrote two pages that he titled "Notes."[60] The entry followed a sobering, truth-telling—and hope-dashing—confrontation with Mary about the state of their marriage. The first heading, "Her worries about him," enumerated the concerns that Mary had voiced about him during this encounter: "That he [Cord] is incapable of any commitment of heart and trust, too self-reliant, disillusioned and experienced to gamble again on the hope of a shared happiness." Cord then quoted Mary as saying, "Don't become an old fuddy-duddy. I've found you out just in time—almost too late." The woman who had once gushed to her friend Anne Truitt that Cord "rose on his toes as he walked"—a characteristic that she considered the hallmark of an interesting man[61]—now voiced her criticism in direct and devastating language.

The second entry in Cord's "Notes" reads: "That he drinks too much and will drink more." Mary had told him, "Sometimes I've known what you were [going] to say but you can't because of the wine. That's sad and shouldn't be." Mary had already sensed where Cord was headed. She wanted no further part of it. She feared that Cord "might prove irrelevant because of his short temper and excessive emotionalism," and told him "they don't take you seriously with your outbursts." She added that she did not think that Cord was "polite enough to survive." Finally, Cord noted that Mary had made it clear she felt that "her children might be a burden that he might come to increasingly resent. I've thought there was no reason why you should take care of my children."[62]

Cord next noted Mary's expectation "that he [Cord] would be cruel and thoughtless in his treatment of her," followed by Mary's next statement to him: "You weren't cruel to M., were you? They say you were but I'll make up my own mind for myself." "M." was clearly a reference to their deceased son, Michael, and further confirmed Michael's own terror of his father.

Mary attacked Cord's fidelity, calling him "incurably promiscuous," and remarking on his good fortune not to have been a philandering husband at a time when he might have been challenged to a duel. "You'd have had to be pretty good to survive all the ones you have had to fight," she said. On this point, at least, Mary offered a mea culpa. She admitted to Cord that she had not always "acted her age," that she herself might be "incurably promiscuous." After all, she added, "there are so many beautiful men."[63] And she wondered whether Cord, as he grew older, "might cease to be able to satisfy her [sexually]."

Cord's "Notes" were a kind of last will and testament of what his life and marriage had become. No longer able to hide in his journal alone, he'd been offered, in this final confrontation with Mary, a mirror, albeit her mirror, of who he had become and why she was leaving. Gone was the committed, evolving conscientious objector who, in a moment of illumination as he lay dying on the beach-battlefield of Guam, realized he had betrayed his deepest conviction—that war was just "the finished product of universal ignorance, avarice, and brutality," and decided, if he were to live through the night, he would do something about it. In that moment, he understood that "a little out of adolescent vanity, but more because he had failed to become a conscientious objector, as he ought to have done," he now fully grasped "the consistent series of decisions that led inevitably to where he lay [dying]." His courage in that moment—to live and accept the fate of whatever mistaken path his life had wandered—had prevailed, and won the duel over the "final ignominious act" of taking his own life in self-pity.[64] Gone, too, was the man who some had thought was destined not only to become the president of the United States, but also "the first president of the parliament of man. And if he becomes a writer, he's sure to win the Nobel Prize. At least."[65]

In 1967, Mary's prescience—and fear—about where Cord had been headed would be revealed. Mercifully, she would not be alive to read the article in *Ramparts* magazine that would expose Cord as the director of the CIA's notorious Operation Mockingbird, as well as head of the Agency's secret incursion into the National Student Association. Having infiltrated more than twenty-five newspapers and wire agencies, Operation Mockingbird had successfully manipulated the American media to promote the CIA viewpoint. It had been designed by Dulles protégé Frank Wisner in the late 1940s. Through it, the CIA bought influence at major media outlets by putting reporters on the CIA payroll, and vice versa. During the 1950s, an estimated three thousand salaried and contract CIA employees were engaged in propaganda efforts. One of the biggest initial supporters was Philip L. Graham, publisher and owner of the *Washington Post*. Under Cord's tutelage, Mockingbird became a stunning success. Whenever the CIA wanted a news story slanted in a particular direction, it got it.[66] This amounted to a subversion of democracy's most precious cornerstone, the free press. Secretly controlling the media had proven to be one the CIA's most powerful tools. The Agency didn't take kindly to being found out.

Upon getting wind of their exposure in *Ramparts*, the CIA immediately went to work to undermine and destroy the magazine. CIA operative Edgar Applewhite was ordered to organize a campaign to smear the publication and then render it financially bankrupt.

"I had all sorts of dirty tricks to hurt their circulation and financing," Applewhite told author Evan Thomas. "The people running *Ramparts* were vulnerable to blackmail. We had awful things in mind, some of which we carried off." In violation of the CIA charter, as well as the U.S. Constitution, Applewhite and his colleagues, including Cord, nevertheless acted with unabashed impunity. "We were not the least inhibited," Applewhite continued, "by the fact that the CIA had no internal security role in the United States."[67]

By then, Cord's unique brand of narcissistic pomposity had already become legend in Washington—so much so that he was brilliantly caricatured by Scottie Fitzgerald Lanahan's[1] 1967 *Washington Post* column, "NEWS to Me. . . ." In a parody entitled "Are You Playing the Games by the Rules in Washington?," Scottie, always imbued with an effervescent, even hilarious perspective, brought to life the very quintessence of Cord's personality:

> The most artistic practitioner of this game is Cord Meyer, the walking library who was recently revealed to have been running student activities all these years for the CIA.
>
> Let us suppose that some innocent creature, coming upon Cord on a Georgetown terrace at the cocktail hour, remarks that the Manchester

---

1   In April 1967, Scottie Fitzgerald Lanahan, daughter of F. Scott Fitzgerald, was still married to Samuel J. ("Jack") Lanahan.

Guardian has been somewhat unflattering about the handling of the Flamingo Republic crisis by the CIA.

"My dear fellow," Cord will say with a significant puff on his pipe, "I assume you have seen Yevtuchenko's masterwork on this subject in the Trans-crimean Review. 'Phenomenism versus Pantheism.' Otherwise, there is no use addressing yourself to this topic, don't you agree?"

One stroke, and he's won. The victim admits defeat by inquiring how his children are, and whether he's played any tennis lately.[68]

In January 1968, the Vietcong's Tet Offensive revealed just how tenuous (and misguided) America's incursion into Southeast Asia had become; the Vietnam War raged on amid increasing controversy. Throughout the world, student uprisings flared on university campuses as well as in the streets, from the United States to Mexico and France. Back home, Martin Luther King Jr. was assassinated in April 1968, Robert F. Kennedy in June. Antiwar protestors picketed the Democratic Party's national convention in Chicago in August; television would broadcast the brutal police response for nearly twenty minutes. Meanwhile, the Black Power salutes of American Olympic medal winners were a provocative nod to the ongoing fight for civil rights. Apollo 8's successful orbit of the moon struck the only uplifting chord in an otherwise deeply polarized, traumatic year.

Amid the tumult of 1968, Mark Meyer, Cord and Mary's youngest son, entered Yale as a member of the class of 1972. That summer, Mark received a form letter from William Sloane Coffin, the chaplain at Yale. Coffin had served in World War II and gone to work for the CIA for three years in the early 1950s because, he said, he felt that "Stalin made Hitler look like a boy scout." Later, he reexamined that outlook and choice, abandoned the CIA, and entered Yale Divinity School. By 1967, Coffin was an established antiwar icon and a prominent civil rights "freedom fighter." The U.S. government had indicted him during the Benjamin Spock conspiracy trial for his role in counseling students to resist the military draft.

Coffin's letter to incoming Yale freshmen introduced the many options of religious faith available at the university, but it also made a political case for ending the war in Vietnam. "College students more than any other group have perceived the war in Vietnam to be politically inept and morally a catastrophe," Coffin wrote. "More than any other group they have resisted the tribalistic chauvinism that passes for patriotism and have recognized that the hopes so long and cruelly deferred of the poor and colored must be realized in our time and the world around." The good chaplain was opening the door for students "to resist the temptation to 'cop out,'" as he wrote, "by failing to connect thoughtful inquiry with effective action; by matching courageous deeds with only shallow ideas; or by believing you can drug yourself to self and to God."

Coffin's letter further enraged an already apoplectic Cord Meyer. Once a world-renowned peace advocate, the man who had declared all war to be "international anarchy" now likened Coffin's letter to brainwashing. Indignant, Cord wrote letters to former Yale classmates, including Bishop Paul Moore, Cyrus Vance, Dean Acheson, and William Bundy. He urged Coffin's reprimand. While Bishop Moore found Coffin's letter somewhat "inappropriate," he did not think it was grounds for dismissal. Dean Acheson, however, did. Telling Cord that his language was far too moderate, Acheson thought Coffin's letter lacked "taste, judgment, knowledge, and maturity. He shows himself to be far less mature than the incoming freshmen, of whom my grandson is one." Acheson's letter to Cord concluded: "Bill is a gay and charming fool; but he is a fool."[69]

But William Sloane Coffin had done what Cord Meyer had never dared to do, and perhaps that was the true source of Cord's outrage—the reminder of all that he had once stood for, but that he had not had the courage to uphold. Three years into his career at the CIA, Coffin had left the Agency, disillusioned by many of the unsuccessful covert activities in which he had taken part. "It didn't work," Coffin later recalled. "Soviet intelligence detected nearly all of our efforts. Our operations ended in disaster. It was fundamentally a bad idea. We were quite naive about the use of American power."[70]

Instead, Coffin had forged a calling in the ministry, becoming a passionate advocate for human and civil rights. He won international recognition as a peace activist. He was a prolific writer and public speaker, and he published six highly acclaimed books and many articles. He became a champion for sanity in an insane world. Had Cord Meyer for one moment caught a glimpse of someone he once knew—a sight no doubt too painful to bear—he would have seen the apparition of his former self, walking hand in hand with Mary Pinchot Meyer at his side.

An even darker disclosure of CIA skulduggery came in 1972 when it was revealed that Cord Meyer had prevailed upon New York publisher Harper & Row to give the Agency the right to examine the galleys of a forthcoming book, *The Politics of Heroin in Southeast Asia*. The author was a Yale graduate student named Alfred McCoy. The book relied on McCoy's harrowing tours through the war zones of Vietnam and Laos, as well as visits to Europe's well-armed drug lords, documenting astonishing accounts of CIA dealings within the drug trade. The book's findings were as dangerous as McCoy's travels: Key figures in the heroin trade told McCoy on the record that American intelligence had collaborated with the drug trade dating back as far as World War II, and that CIA advisers were financing weapons to support the Hmong Highlanders by using CIA helicopters to transport Laotian opium to Vietnam markets. McCoy also revealed that, beginning in Guatemala in 1954, the CIA had been involved in widespread terrorism throughout Central America, including the training of death squads. The Agency had needed untraceable money to finance its clandestine operations. They had found what they desired with narco-traffickers such as Panamanian resident Manuel Noriega, who would eventually be outed as having long been on the CIA payroll.

Cass Canfield, the head of Harper & Row, found himself caving in to CIA pressure. He forced the young author McCoy to acquiesce to the Agency's demand for prior review, but the book was published largely intact, in part because the major news media had exposed the CIA's attempt to influence its content. But the fact remained that McCoy's research was particularly unwelcome in Washington in 1972. President Nixon was leading his "war on drugs" crusade. The U.S. military was still trying to recover from publicity around the massacre at My Lai and other atrocities in Vietnam. Revelations about the CIA-led assassination campaign throughout Southeast Asia, Operation Phoenix, made matters even worse.

Most astounding of all had been the news that the "golden boy" of the post–World War II peace movement—Cord Meyer himself—was leading an assault on the First Amendment at the New York office of publishing giant Harper & Row. The man whose debut short story "Waves of Darkness" had decried the futility and horror of war was now a complicit architect of secret wars and violations of democracy the world over, as well as within the United States. As one observer told journalist Merle Miller in 1972, "the man who wrote 'Waves of Darkness' must have died a little the day he walked into Harper & Row, assuming there was any of *that* man still left in Cord."[71]

There wasn't. He had been gone for more than twenty years. Mary had left just in time.

8

Personal Evolution

Happiness is beneficial for the body, but it is grief that develops the powers of the mind.

—Marcel Proust

Love, the strongest and deepest element in all life, the harbinger of hope, of joy, of ecstasy; love, the definer of all laws, of all conventions; love, the freest, the most powerful molder of human destiny.
How can such an all-compelling force be synonymous with that poor little State and Church-begotten weed, marriage?

—Emma Goldman

B EFORE THE END of her life, Mary Pinchot Meyer would be the muse and lover of two of the most influential and important men of her generation: Cord Meyer and Jack Kennedy—ironically, the top two postwar public figures highlighted in *Glamour*'s 1947 feature "Young Men Who Care." The two would cross paths in their career orbits repeatedly. At the center was Mary. At first, Cord had seemed the more promising. Poised for a meteoric rise with a stellar political future, he had access to those who would further stimulate his vision and position him for national recognition. His ascent and fall, however, would become Faustian, despite Mary's steadfast love and support,

As their marriage unraveled in 1955, so did that of their next-door neighbors at Hickory Hill. Jack and Jackie Kennedy had moved into the six-acre compound that had once been the headquarters of Civil War Army general George McClellan. The view from the Meyer terrace drew the eye straight across two

197

small ridges to the new Kennedy compound where "Lord and Lady" Kennedy reigned, but their life together was becoming strained. Early miscarriages and a stillborn birth, further complicated by Jack's compulsive philandering, would have been overwhelming to any young marriage. Author Truman Capote, a frequent guest at the Kennedys' New York dinner parties early on, recalled of Jackie, "She was sweet, eager, intelligent, not quite sure of herself, and hurt— hurt because she knew Jack was banging all those other broads."[1] In fact, Jackie would eventually follow her husband's lead where infidelity was concerned. During a trip to California in January 1956, where Jack was working on a short film about the history of the Democratic Party for the August opening of the national convention in Chicago later that year, Jackie and actor William Holden had a tryst. According to Jackie's stepbrother and sometime confidante Gore Vidal, "She had had her share of affairs with the famous, among them the actor William Holden. But I always suspected that some of these couplings were motivated by revenge on Jack, not to mention just plain stamp collecting."[2]

Or was Jackie trying to be the woman she thought her husband would find more exciting? She told Jack about the fling with Holden, claimed author Peter Evans, just a few days after it happened. Her hope was to stimulate his affection, because women who slept with powerful men were a turn-on for Jack. The plan backfired. When Jackie discovered not long after that she was pregnant, Jack became resentful, allegedly not believing the child was his. Eight months into the pregnancy in August 1956, Jackie accompanied Jack to Chicago for the Democratic National Convention, where he vied, unsuccessfully, for the vice presidential nomination.[3]

After the convention, still seething over his wife's infidelity, Jack dumped Jackie at her family's estate in Newport, Rhode Island, and flew to Europe with Senator George Smathers of Florida. The two men chartered a yacht and cruised the Mediterranean. Indulging their shared predilection for promiscuity—the yacht became a floating senatorial bordello—word reached Jack by the ship's radio that Jackie had delivered a near-full-term stillborn girl who she had already named Arabella. Jack was said to be indifferent to the news. Newspapers had picked up the story that he was "traveling" in Europe and was unable to be reached. It reportedly took Smathers another three days—and an ultimatum—to convince the Massachusetts senator to return. "If you want to run for President, you better get your ass back to your wife's bedside, or else every wife in the country will be against you." In fact, Smathers flew back with Jack, but only after the patriarch, Joseph P. Kennedy Sr., "convinced" his son to make the trip.[4]

It was, by that point, no secret Jackie wanted out of the marriage. After recovering from the stillbirth, she took off for London to play with her sister, Lee Radziwill, who had several affairs going at once with British royalty. When *Washington Post* columnist Drew Pearson got wind of all the "fun" Jackie was having sans Jack, the patriarch again took matters into his own hands. Upon Jackie's return, the elder Kennedy took her to lunch in New York at the swank Le Pavillon. He knew the marriage was on the skids, but there were more important things on the horizon: like the presidency for his son.

Jackie and Joe Sr., had always gotten along, and so rather than intimidate his daughter-in-law, the elder Kennedy struck a deal. Jackie had laid out her demands: She wanted out of the Hickory Hill estate in McLean; she didn't want to have dinner every night with the entire family when she came to Hyannis Port or Palm Beach; she didn't want to play the role of political wife, campaigning endlessly for her husband. In a word, she wanted freedom. In exchange, she agreed to keep up appearances for the sake of Jack's future political career.

That left the question of children. Without them, Jack's political future might quickly dead-end; with them, any political height was scalable. According to author Edward Klein, Kennedy put it this way: "It's up to a wife to keep a marriage together. Speaking from personal experience, I can tell you that children are the secret of any marriage. I'm going to set up a trust for your children. You will have control of it when you have children."

"And what if I can't have children?" Jackie asked.

"If you don't have any children within the next ten years," said the patriarch, "the trust fund will revert to you. The money will be yours to do with as you wish."[5]

That fall, the Kennedys left Hickory Hill for Georgetown.

By 1957, Mary Meyer had also made Georgetown her home, just a few blocks away from the new Kennedy home. In spite of his failed bid for the vice presidential nomination the year before, Jack still had his sights set on 1600 Pennsylvania Avenue. The fact that his marriage was widely understood to be window dressing didn't deter him. Mary, for her part, was adjusting to life without Cord, and without her son Michael. While her path and the future president's surely crossed, her more pressing concerns took precedence. One of her priorities was finalizing her divorce as quickly as possible. She went to Nevada, a state that expedited the process, and waited out the six-week residency requirement at a no-frills "divorce ranch" run by artist and nature photographer Gus Bundy and his wife, Jeanne.[6] There were many such places in Nevada, some offering luxury living with fine food and other perks. The Bundy divorce ranch, however, was far from luxurious and offered only four residential apartments. For Mary, it would serve her purpose splendidly, allowing her to come and go as she pleased.

Before Mary left on one of her trips to Nevada in 1958, her neighbor Jack had asked for a favor. Would she allow "a friend" to stay at her Georgetown house while she was away? The sylphlike, elegant dark-haired Pamela Turnure had been a receptionist in Kennedy's Senate office. She would eventually join his presidential campaign and become Jackie's press secretary, all while maintaining an intermittent sexual relationship with Jack. Pam had been renting an apartment in the Georgetown home of Leonard and Florence Kater. One spring night, the Katers were awakened by the sound of pebbles against their tenant's window at 1:00 A.M. They looked out their window and saw Senator Kennedy begging Pam to let him in. She did. Enraged—as "good Catholics" would be in such a situation—the Katers set out to expose Jack and destroy his chances for the presidency. They placed two tape recorders in an air vent that led to Pam's bedroom and recorded Jack and Pam's conversations, as well as their sexual activity. After that, they revoked Pam's lease.

"I was so enraged," Florence Kater told author Michael O'Brien, "that this Irish Catholic senator, who pretended to be such a good family man, might run for President that I decided to do something about it. I was very innocent and naive in those days and had no idea of the power I was up against. I knew no one would believe my story unless we had actual proof, so in addition to the tape recorders, we decided to get a photograph."[7]

Mary had to have known that Jack was involved with Pam Turnure, although it is unlikely she knew what the Katers were up to when she allowed Pam to house-sit for several weeks. One evening in July 1958, while Mary was in Nevada, the Katers staked out Mary's house and caught the senator leaving in the wee hours of the morning. "Hey, Senator!" Leonard Kater yelled. As Jack turned toward him, Kater snapped a picture. "How dare you take my picture!" Jack shouted indignantly. Florence Kater reportedly jumped out of the car and loudly proclaimed, "How dare you run for President under the guise of a good Christian!" She added, "I have a recording of your whoring. You are unfit to be the Catholic standard bearer for the presidency of this country!"[8]

Unaware of the Kater stakeout, her divorce finalized in August,[9] Mary returned from Nevada in September to find her house under the couple's surveillance. "Mary found herself drawn into a web of intrigue," an anonymous friend of hers told Leo Damore in 1990. "Pam was living with her and seeing JFK on the sly. Mary knew about the relationship. She thought Jack stupid and reckless if he seriously had his sights set on the presidency. Half-amused though, the episode left a bit of a bad taste, not only for the violation of her house—and her trust—but to be identified in gossip with one of his better-known sexual peccadilloes offended her sensibility."[10] As Mary's long-term former boyfriend Bob Schwartz had made clear, "Mary wasn't flamboyant. She was a private person in terms of protecting who she was. Her privacy was a way of being herself."[11]

Florence Kater, however, was undeterred. She took her obsession with Kennedy's philandering to the streets, attending political rallies with signs that displayed the image of Jack taken outside Mary's house. She picketed former president Harry Truman's house in Missouri while Kennedy was visiting, and she marched in front of the White House. Kater allegedly contacted more than thirty newspapers and magazines with her proof of the presidential aspirant's wayward habits. As late as April 1963, she contacted FBI director J. Edgar Hoover, but he refused to meet with her, though he likely seized on her revelations to add to Kennedy's already growing file. For a time, the *Washington Star* pursued the Kater story before abruptly dropping it, threatened by a Kennedy family lawsuit. After five years, Florence Kater finally gave up her crusade. "I had told the truth but no one would listen to me," she said. "The press wanted Kennedy to be President and that was that."[12]

In spite of the travails of divorcing Cord, Mary set her sights on the future. She longed to move forward in her new life; and brooding would play no part. She adjusted gracefully to life without Cord, who saw his sons on weekends and part of school vacations. As agreed in the divorce settlement, he would assume full charge of their education.

Still mired in grief over Michael's death, she embarked on a period of deep exploration. Artist Ken Noland became Mary's lover during this time; for the next two years, he was a significant presence. Noland later recalled that Michael's death had been a "deep, dramatic event for her," one that had "affected her balance—I think this one [her son Michael] was her favorite."[13] Her introspection during this time was as much artistic as it was personal. "Every real artist has to further themselves," said her former lover Bob Schwartz, recalling Mary's sense of commitment to herself. "She wasn't interested in trivia, at any level or any sort. She never did anything that didn't have a sense of totality about it."[14]

Even in grief, that disposition seemed to pervade her entire being. During her time in Nevada, Mary visited with Anne and Jim Truitt at their home in San Francisco, where they had moved for Jim's *Newsweek* posting. (The Truitts also visited Mary at Gus Bundy's Divorce Ranch.)[15] In 1958, Jim and Anne Truitt would name their second daughter Mary, in honor of their beloved friend. According to Jim Truitt, who had a keen interest in psychedelics and Eastern mystical traditions that embraced altered states of consciousness, it was during a visit in California that Mary had her first psychedelic experience. (It wasn't known which hallucinogen she had been introduced to, but it was likely either LSD or psilocybin). "The depths of the colors would intrigue Mary," Truitt later recalled, "because of her interest in that as an artist."[16] Just south of San Francisco, the Palo Alto Mental Research Institute was exploring the therapeutic potential of hallucinogens such as LSD and the peyote derivative psilocybin. The Beat Generation, an emerging cultural phenomenon in California's Bay Area that counted Jack Kerouac, Neal Cassidy, and Allen Ginsberg among its members, was at the vanguard of this mind-altering wonder.

LSD and other hallucinogens had been in use as psychiatric aids among the fashionable in Hollywood since the mid- to late 1950s. A number of actors, writers, musicians, and directors—people like André Previn, Aldous Huxley, Anaïs Nin, Esther Williams, Betsy Drake, Sidney Lumet, and playwright Clare Booth Luce, among them—explored the regions of their consciousness, encouraging others to partake. Luce, for her part, convinced her husband, *Time* publisher Henry Luce, to experiment with her, as well as very possibly one other notable who will be discussed later. Actor Cary Grant was so convinced of the positive impact of LSD in his life that *Look* magazine published an article about it in 1959.[17]

If Jim Truitt was correct that Mary first experimented with psychedelics in California in 1958, then it very well could have been the legendary captain Alfred M. Hubbard who first introduced her to such exploration. A former World War II OSS agent who later built a fortune as a uranium entrepreneur, Hubbard was often referred to as the "Johnny Appleseed of LSD." Hubbard himself first used the drug in 1951. He would later claim to have witnessed his own conception, saying, "It was the deepest mystical experience I've ever seen."

Hubbard befriended people like psychedelic pioneer Aldous Huxley long before Timothy Leary came upon the scene. It was Hubbard who first asserted that LSD could be enormously therapeutic, given its propensity for the inducement of transcendental mystical experiences. On his own, Hubbard administered the drug to a number of alcoholics, many of whom reportedly emerged from the experience to successfully claim a life of sobriety, at least for a while. Hubbard's early success with LSD's therapeutic possibilities moved him to set up three treatment centers in Canada in 1958, one of which reportedly attempted to treat Ethel Kennedy, wife of Robert F. Kennedy, for incipient alcoholism. She was allegedly a patient of Dr. Ross MacLean, a close associate of Hubbard's.[18]

Hubbard's vast network of business contacts, as well as his personal wealth, enabled him to procure a huge supply of LSD and to distribute it at his own expense. (He would find out years later that the CIA was monitoring him.) Hubbard wanted nothing in return; his motivation appears to have been to give humanity a new point of view. Throughout the 1950s and early 1960s, Hubbard traveled across Europe and the United States dispensing LSD to anyone who wanted to try it. According to one account, he "turned on thousands of people from all walks of life—policemen, statesmen, captains of industry, church figures, scientists."[19]

Mary might also have associated with Dr. Oscar Janiger, a Los Angeles psychiatrist who began conducting psychedelic sessions with prominent literary and artistic avant-garde figures in the mid-1950s. Janiger, also a devotee of Captain Hubbard's, had experienced his own personal transformation with psychedelics, which had, in turn, fueled his professional interest in using them in his clinical practice. Of Hubbard's visits, Janiger once memorably remarked, "We waited for him like the little old lady on the prairie waiting for a copy of the Sears Roebuck catalogue."[20]

Allen Dulles and his CIA coterie had tried, unsuccessfully, to recruit Captain Al Hubbard in the early 1950s. Hubbard wanted no part. "They [the CIA] lied so much, cheated so much. I don't like 'em," Hubbard told Janiger in 1978. He was furious about how the CIA had exploited LSD. He told Janiger, "The CIA work stinks. They were misusing it. I tried to tell them how to use it, but even when they were killing people, you couldn't tell them a goddamn thing."[21] In addition to the CIA, the U.S Army, and Britain's MI6 all had a keen interest in using LSD and other hallucinogens for chemical warfare, in what they hoped would be "mind control."

In point of fact, the CIA's top secret Special Operations Division at the Army's Fort Detrick, Maryland, facility had, in one experiment, used a crop-duster airplane in 1951 to douse the entire town of Pont-Saint-Esprit in southern France with an aerosol of highly potent LSD. That event had caused mass hysteria, affecting close to seven hundred people for several days. With hundreds of people gripped by terror in acute psychosis, wildly hallucinating, the town became a veritable insane asylum. Four people committed suicide before the trauma subsided.[22]

One CIA chemical warfare expert who was responsible, Frank Olson, realized he had made "a terrible mistake." He was so disturbed by the project, he blundered further by sharing his consternation with several colleagues. Olson soon realized that the Agency had surreptitiously dosed him with LSD as well, ostensibly to see how much greater a security risk he might become. Days later, Olson started to unravel. Agency personnel attempted to move him out of his hotel room at the Statler Hotel in New York late one night so they could secretly, under the cover of darkness, transport him for commitment to the CIA-affiliated sanitarium Chestnut Lodge in Rockville, Maryland. Frank Olson became unruly and uncooperative, and was finally thrown out of his tenth-floor hotel window, in what would for years be disguised as a suicide.[23]

According to one source, Captain Al Hubbard was immediately convinced the CIA had used LSD to destabilize Olson in 1953. He also suspected there had been a murder, not a suicide. Fifty-six years later, in his 2009 book *A Terrible Mistake*, journalist Hank Albarelli confirmed Hubbard's suspicions about this event, masterfully exposing the CIA's murder of Frank Olson—along with a myriad of details about the CIA's vast, illegal drug experiments.[24]

When the CIA found that they couldn't recruit Hubbard, they started keeping tabs on him. Hubbard's legendary purchases of LSD from Sandoz, a global pharmaceutical company in Switzerland, were being monitored. The CIA had "an agreement" whereby Sandoz would keep the Food and Drug Administration (FDA) apprised of all purchases.[25]

On his own, and long before Timothy Leary's ascent at Harvard in the early 1960s, Captain Al Hubbard was instrumental in paving the "psychedelic highway" for those who sought out the experience. Exactly what impact he may have had on Mary Meyer isn't known. Anne Chamberlin, who had been in a position to shed light on Mary's exploration with psychedelics up until the end of 2011 when she [Chamberlin] died, vehemently declined to be interviewed.

Robert Budd, another painter who was part of the Washington Color School to which Mary belonged, recalled seeing her in the company of artist Ken Noland between 1958 and 1959. "She was a beautiful, *beautiful* [Budd's emphasis] woman," Budd remembered. "We were all part of a group that used to hang out at Charlie Byrd's Showboat Lounge on Eighteenth Street and

Columbia Road. We'd meet upstairs and talk about art and music. The jazz musicians would join us between sets. Marijuana had also arrived on the scene."[26] Budd recalled that a number of artists in the Washington Color School were intensely committed to self-exploration. In the late 1950s, a group of them—including Budd himself, Mary Meyer, and Ken Noland—took weekly train trips to Philadelphia to have therapeutic bodywork sessions with Dr. Charles I. Oller, a highly respected practitioner of orgonomy—a therapeutic technique developed in the 1940s by Viennese psychoanalyst Wilhelm Reich, a former protégé of Sigmund Freud. In the 1920s, Reich had been part of Freud's inner circle—some called him "Freud's pet"—but he eventually broke with Freud. Like any paradigm challenger, Reich was both acclaimed and ostracized.

Orgonomy, sometimes referred to as "orgone therapy," attempted to break down what Reich termed "character armor," those unique configurations in the human psychic structure and body that blocked the free-flowing movement of what he termed "orgone energy," what Chinese Oriental medicine called "chi." Charged with living energy, the sexual orgasm was the mechanism for the release of this "orgonotic charge," which, after discharge, built up again in an ongoing cycle of "charge-tension-discharge-release." If life's traumatic events precipitated the development of character armor, there would be, Reich believed, an inadequate release in the orgasm function, thereby leading to rigidities in character and muscular tensions in the body, which eventually created maladaptive character states, such as becoming masochistic, sadistic, reactionary, submissive, or hateful. Orgonomic therapy sought to restore the free flow of orgone energy, not only resulting in a more complete, deeply satisfying sexual orgasm, but also yielding a more fully integrated, healthy, and happy individual.

Orgonomy represented a radical departure from conventional psychoanalysis and psychoanalytic therapy. Patients started a session by lying face up on a platform-like bed in their underwear. There, they were encouraged to deepen and to slow their breath and to allow whatever emotional expression was in their awareness to come into their being without talking about it. In the safety of the therapist's office, patients gradually surrendered to the experience of *feeling* their bodily and emotional awareness. Those with traumatic memories might be eventually encouraged to express themselves with fits of kicking and pounding, giving voice to screaming rage, as well as intense terror and deep sadness. The result was often not only catharsis, but, also, over a period of time, the diminution of the *fear of feeling* itself, thereby restoring the capacity for living more deeply. Mary Meyer's foray into orgonomy lasted only a few months, but it demonstrated once again her pioneering spirit and commitment to self-examination and personal evolution. It also evidenced the deep pain she continued to experience at the death of her son.

In the opinion of Dr. Morton Herskowitz, a close colleague of Dr. Charles Oller's, if Mary had gone to Oller for help with her grief over Michael's death, Oller "could have helped her a great deal in three months of work, because she was amenable to it." Upon viewing a picture of Mary Meyer taken in 1963, Dr. Herskowitz was impressed by "the energy and light in her eyes." He knew his colleague Oller to be an exceptional, intuitive clinician. "Oller would have validated her feelings immediately," continued Herskowitz. "With a woman of that caliber, I can imagine he would have accomplished a lot, even in a short period. Even though she was a free spirit already, to have gotten to the depths of her grief could have made a significant change in her. He would have worked on her breathing and softening of the eyes, it would have precipitated the deepest crying and expression of her grief. She would have felt very safe to feel almost anything with his guidance."[27]

Ken Noland championed Reichian therapy and believed it "profoundly affected his art during the late 1950s."[28] However, Reichian therapists in general, and orgonomists in particular, were strongly opposed to the use of *any* recreational drugs. According to Robert Budd, Dr. Oller abruptly terminated working with Noland as a patient. Budd suspected that it was "because Noland was using LSD and recommending others do it as well. I always had a feeling that Noland had crossed the line, but I have no proof."[29] Noland himself initially denied that LSD had been a part of his life at that time, then several months later mentioned to Nina Burleigh that he had used LSD with Mary. Noland also vaguely recalled something about Mary visiting Timothy Leary at Harvard in the early 1960s.[30] Eventually, Mary did undertake a more conventional course of psychotherapy during which, according to one friend, she "really started to work on herself," though her experience with orgonomy had left an indelible impression.[31]

While Mary's post-divorce activities focused on deepening self-exploration and healing, Jack Kennedy's attention was on getting to the White House, albeit while mired in marital infidelity and personal unhappiness. Jack had long been attracted to Mary, but she wasn't interested. "Mary had been aware of Jack's womanizing since college," a confidential source familiar with both of them told author Leo Damore in 1991. "She wasn't interested in becoming another notch on Jack's gun. She was a serious person of quality, not frivolity. He had always been enamored by her, but she saw through his superficiality with women, and he knew it, though she always admitted to some remote attraction to him."[32] According to author Sally Bedell Smith, Cicely Angleton once witnessed a conversation between them.

"What does Kenneth Noland have that I don't have?" Jack had asked Mary.

"Mystery," she retorted.

"The President was duly taken aback," Cicely remembered.[33] The response may have made Mary all the more alluring.

Before Jack arrived at the White House, Mary had rebuffed all his pleas for her attention, save one. Sometime during the spring of 1959, Kenneth Noland recalled attending a cocktail party with Mary at the Bradlee house in Georgetown. Jack was there, apparently letting it be known that he would formally announce his candidacy for the presidency at the beginning of 1960.[34] Noland remembered "a stirring" between the two at the party. "She was coming alive in a way Noland remembered from the early days of their own affair," wrote Nina Burleigh. That summer, Mary rented a small cabin for two weeks in Provincetown, Massachusetts, before joining Noland and his children on Long Island. Noland always suspected that she and Jack got together during that time, since the Hyannis Kennedy compound was less than an hour away.[35] According to a confidential source who spoke to author Leo Damore, they did.

"Jack was distraught over his marriage to Jackie," that source told Damore. "He was miserable. He wanted out in the worst way but he knew it would be political suicide. He visited with Mary because he knew he could talk with her. He trusted her. She was one of the few women he really respected, maybe the only one. Her independence always impressed him—she didn't need or want anything from him."[36]

"Mary didn't mince words with him that day," the source continued. "She told him he was crazy to be womanizing, that it would wreck his run for the presidency unless he got control. Jack admitted his problem but felt powerless to do anything about it. His physical health, medical difficulties were complicating things, too. At one point, Mary said he was almost in tears. He was so unhappy, and alone, she told me. Mary wasn't about to get involved with him then, though she told me she held him tenderly that day."[37]

Six years earlier, just after his marriage to Jackie, Jack said something revealing to his Senate staffer Priscilla McMillan: "I only got married because I was 37 years old. If I wasn't married, people would think I was queer."[38] The remark revealed more about Jack's concern for his political image than anything else. His father once remarked to Jack's sister Eunice, who confided doubts about Jack's political future, that "it's not what you are that counts. It's what people think you are."[39] Jack needed a glamorous, beautiful wife for his image. Shortly before marrying Jackie, he reportedly said to a Senate colleague who was trying to fix him up with a date, "Look, you might as well know, I talked to my dad and he told me now is the time to get married." He then added that his father considered Jackie to be the best choice "for a lot of reasons. I mean, she's the perfect hostess; she's got the background; and she's Catholic."[40]

Not long after his visit with Mary in Provincetown, Jack had another revealing exchange with Priscilla McMillan, herself an attractive and articulate woman who resisted his advances. "I was one of the few he could really talk to," McMillan told author David Horowitz. "Like Freud, he wanted to know what women really wanted, that sort of thing; but he also wanted to know the more mundane details—what gave a woman pleasure, what women hoped for in marriage, how they liked to be courted. During one of these conversations I once asked him why he was doing it—why was he acting like his father, why was he avoiding real relationships, why was he taking a chance on getting caught in a scandal at the same time he was trying to make his career take off. He took a while trying to formulate an answer. Finally he shrugged and said, 'I don't know really. I guess I just can't help it.' He had this sad expression on his face. He looked like a little boy about to cry."[41] McMillan, who went on to become a well-known author, later reflected on Jack's compulsion for skirt-chasing: "The whole thing with him was pursuit. I think he was secretly disappointed when a woman gave in. It meant that the low esteem in which he held women was once again validated. It meant also that he'd have to start chasing someone else."[42]

Indeed, "skirt-chasing" had become a Kennedy family heritage, what one perspicacious woman later referred to as "the wandering penis disease." It had passed from father to son. In fact, Joe Kennedy Sr., himself afflicted, once told J. Edgar Hoover that he should have gelded Jack when he was a small boy.[43] A number of prominent Kennedy biographers over the years have given credence to the fact that Jack led a kind of "double life," a life of dysfunctional compartmentalization when it came to his sexuality and relationships with women. "Yet with Jack, something different was at work than [just] a liking for women," noted historian Doris Kearns Goodwin. "So driven was the pace of his sex life, and so discardable his conquests, that they suggest a deep difficulty with intimacy."[44] Presidential historian Robert Dallek underscored the idea that "Jack was a narcissist whose sexual escapades combated feelings of emptiness bred by a cold, detached mother and a self-absorbed, largely absent father."[45] Even while married to Jackie, Jack's unabashed philandering never abated; indeed, being married only seemed to exacerbate his compulsion.

From the very beginning, soon after she met Jack in the spring of 1951, Jackie had been warned about what life with Jack would inevitably entail. His Choate schoolmate Lem Billings told her in no uncertain terms before their marriage what she could expect with a man twelve years her senior who was, as he put it, "set in his ways." Even more presciently, Jack's close friend Chuck Spaulding observed, "Jackie wasn't sexually attracted to men unless they were dangerous like [her father] old Black Jack [John V. Bouvier III]. It was one of those terribly obvious Freudian situations. We all talked about it—even Jack, who didn't particularly go for Freud but said that Jackie had a 'father crush.' What was surprising was that Jackie, who was so intelligent in other things, didn't seem to have a clue about this one."[46] Marital fidelity wasn't ever a part of this equation. Jackie valiantly tried to bury her head in the sand, but the toll it took undoubtedly aggravated the possibility of further miscarriages.

The antecedents of Jack's long-standing problem of intimacy with women had a more dynamic dimension than just the imprinting of his childhood. Author Nigel Hamilton's analysis of Jack's mother Rose Kennedy as "a cold, unmotherly, and distant woman whose main contribution to Jack's character was his strangely split psyche, leaving him emotionally crippled in his relations with women," was only one part of this equation.[47] Unlike Mary Meyer, he seemed to have had little interest in any sober self-examination, reflection, or understanding. No doubt his experience of abandonment as a child, sustained by little direct maternal care, aroused a projected vengeful disposition toward the opposite sex: Women were to be used, then discarded at his whim. Failing any deeper internal investigation, conquering his emptiness—and keeping it at bay—required an infusion of one sexual triumph after another, however momentary the relief. He had to have known he had a problem.

Nonetheless, the power of love beckoned him to romance during the same time that Mary Pinchot was in love with Bob Schwartz. During his stint as a Navy ensign in the Foreign Intelligence Branch of the Office of Naval Intelligence (ONI) in Washington, Jack began a serious affair with a beautiful blonde, blue-eyed Danish woman who had become a close friend of his sister Kathleen's. Still married but estranged from her second husband, Inga Arvad was a classic stunning bombshell. *New York Times* columnist Arthur Krock, who had helped procure her a job as a reporter at the *Times Herald*, once described Inga as "a perfect example of Nordic beauty." Slightly older than Jack, she exuded sexuality. The two had no illusion that their relationship would be anything but a passing affair. It also had to be kept secret, so that Jack's parents wouldn't find out. Jack and Inga camouflaged their connection, using Kathleen and her boyfriend, John White, making it look like just a convenient foursome. Little did Jack know, however, that his father's spy network was aware of the relationship right after their first date.

By all accounts, Jack became smitten with Inga, as did she with him, in spite of her making it clear that she "wouldn't trust him as long term companion." During World War II, many dating relationships were imbued with an ethos of "living in the present," given the reality of an unknown, uncertain future during wartime. "Inga Binga," as Jack affectionately called her, had tremendous self-assurance; her life purpose was not about just getting married and settling down. Though there are no in-depth accounts of their relationship, this was probably the deepest emotional, intimate attachment to a woman that Jack had ever made in his life up until that time. Yet, she was not the sort of woman for Jack to take home to mother and father, and he knew it.

In addition, Inga's past soon rose to create problems from another direction. Years before, as an aspiring journalist, Inga had manipulated her way into being given access to the Nazi elite, including Adolph Hitler. Attending the 1936 Olympic games in Berlin, sitting in the same box as the Führer, Inga had had her picture taken. After the United States entered the war against Germany, the FBI, already aware of Inga, began watching her when she was a student at Columbia University's Graduate School of Journalism. It was feared she might be a spy. Because Jack was now a Navy officer with security clearances for his work at the Office of Naval Intelligence, the FBI, unbeknownst to Jack, opened a file on their relationship.

Unexpectedly, in January 1942, nationally syndicated columnist Walter Winchell revealed in the *New York Mirror* that Jack and Inga were "an item." The story was so explosive that it had the potential to relieve Jack of his commission in the Navy, given the ONI's paranoia. Instead, two days after the Winchell column, Jack found himself transferred to the Charleston Naval Shipyard. He told one reporter, "They shagged my ass down to South Carolina because I was going around with a Scandinavian blonde and they thought she was a spy!"[48]

Jack and Inga spent several months exchanging love letters and talking on the phone constantly, with Inga visiting Charleston on weekends. The relationship, however, grew stormy. Among other things, Inga feared she might be pregnant. Jack knew he would never be allowed to marry her. His "fight for love" could not withstand the Kennedy family pressure, nor what would undoubtedly have been an epic confrontation with his father. He was still shackled by the expectations of paternal authority, unwilling to assert his full separation and independence. The epitaph of Jack and Inga, and the love they had shared, was being written.

For his part, patriarch Joe Sr. knew exactly what a toll his son's struggles were taking. There were FBI wiretaps on Jack's phone calls with Inga, as well as wiretaps in her hotel room when she came to visit him in Charleston. No doubt the elder Kennedy's connections arranged them. Not wanting to incur any ill will from a tempestuous Jack, or spur any rebellion, the cunning father never indicated the slightest disapproval of his son's relationship with Inga. But, according to several biographers, Winchell's column was probably engineered by Joe Kennedy himself. When Jack, with Inga's acceptance, finally ended the relationship several months later, according to these same biographers, Inga had been paid off by his father to finally leave.[49] Heartbroken, Jack now turned his attention to preventing his unpredictable, precarious health issues from sidelining him to a desk for the duration of the war. More than ever, he wanted to break away from his father and the chains of the Kennedy family that enslaved him.

Jack's closest platonic friendship with a woman was with his sister Kathleen, affectionately known as "Kick." She was perhaps the only woman contemporary in his early adult life with whom he was able to sustain an ongoing emotional connection. Just three years younger than Jack, Kick had been born fourth in the family—after Joe Jr., Jack, and Rose Marie ("Rosemary"). Because Rosemary's mental retardation relegated her to an institution, Kick was the eldest daughter in the Kennedy clan, and she and Jack forged an important bond. Both were rebellious, having contested the shackles of the Catholic Church and a mother chained to its religious dogma. Jack admired his sister's spunk, her ability to speak her mind and create a life of her own choosing. He defended her when she courageously broke with her parents' wishes by marrying non-Catholic Billy Cavendish, the young Marquess of Hartington. Unfortunately, young Cavendish was killed in the war in 1944, less than a month after their brother, Joe Jr. Devastated by these deaths, Kick and Jack, understanding more completely the frailty of life, shared an even deeper bond.

As a Massachusetts congressman in the summer of 1947, Jack visited Kick in Ireland. He was overjoyed to find her now in love with wealthy English aristocrat Peter Fitzwilliam. Fitzwilliam, however, was not only Protestant, but also still married, although the plan was that he would soon be divorced and marry Kick. Despite both Joe Sr. and mother Rose's eventual warning that they would disown her if she went ahead with this plan, Kick was undeterred. Seeing how happy she was, Jack again admired and supported his sister's boldness and independence. Moved by and envious of Kathleen's joy at being in love, he told his friend Lem Billings that in all of his relationships with women, except possibly for a short while with Inga, he had never lost himself, or fallen in love as his sister Kathleen had.[50]

Less than a year later, in May 1948, Kick and her husband-to-be died in a plane crash en route to the south of France. Her death threw Jack into deep despair, provoking a spiritual crisis about the meaning of life itself. Losing his brother Joe to the war effort could be understood and eventually accepted, but Kick's death utterly confounded Jack in a way nothing in his entire life ever had. Unwilling to tolerate his mother's glib explanation that this had been God's way of saving her daughter Kathleen from a "sacrilegious marriage," Jack had no one within his family to turn to for comfort. Not only had Kick been his best friend, she was also the only woman at the time who had provided a bridge to his confused and broken emotional life. Kick had been "the one in the family with whom he could confide his deepest thoughts," said his close friend Lem Billings.[51]

Kathleen's death left Jack emotionally barren. Resignation gripped him. "Kathleen's death depressed Jack and made him even more conscious than ever of his own mortality," noted presidential historian Robert Dallek. "He told the columnist Joe Alsop that he didn't expect to live more than another ten years, or beyond the age of forty-five."[52] Scaling the White House didn't eradicate his emptiness, nor did it ameliorate any of his physical infirmities, which sometimes intermittently became acute. Jack's rampant promiscuity grew into a bona fide sexual addiction. His reckless daring was the kind of obsessive pursuit that was not only dangerous from a national security perspective, but ultimately personally destructive. Recurrent bouts of venereal disease, originally contracted when he was a student at Harvard from sex with prostitutes, plagued him during his years in the White House.

The other ingredient in this equation was drugs, to which Jack was introduced by Max Jacobson, MD, a New York physician known as "Dr. Feel Good," who had a colorful reputation in the early 1960s for assisting fast-lane, high-society New Yorkers with their "moods." He had been introduced to Jack by his close friend Chuck Spaulding during the 1960 presidential campaign. Spaulding himself was a patient of Jacobson's, whose elixirs by injection contained any number of amphetamine derivatives. "Miracle Max," as he was also sometimes called, made more than thirty visits to the White House during the Kennedy presidency, not counting his trips to Palm Beach and Hyannis Port. So indispensable had Dr. Feel Good become that he even accompanied the president to Paris and Vienna in 1961. He also supplied Jack with vials of specially prepared concoctions, as well as the hypodermic needles to inject them on his own.[53]

One former patient of Jacobson's, who spoke on condition of anonymity, worked in the doctor's lab at night as a way to defray the costs of his services. "I would mix up some of the cocktails given to JFK," said this source. "They were labeled 'Beaker A, B, and C.' Nobody knew what was in them except Jacobson. He [Jacobson] would code label the directions as to how to mix the cocktails. There were things in those cocktails that exacerbated his [JFK's] sex drive, I'll tell you that right now!"[54] Jack became so dependent on these drugs, he had no intention of stopping them. "I don't care if it's horse piss," he told his brother Bobby, who thought he should have Jacobson's elixirs analyzed by the FDA. "It's the only thing that works."[55]

Yet whatever infirmities Jack battled—including a rampant sexual addiction—however fragmented and impaired his capacity for genuine intimacy, something kept driving him toward Mary Meyer. Had it been the memory of some young, pristine romantic force that was first awakened that Saturday evening at Choate in February 1936? Had the intensity of his wartime romance with Inga Arvad engendered some distant hope of absolution in love? Or was it the possibility of redemption, one last chance to bridge the gulf between himself and another—in love—so as to heal himself in such a way that he might become more whole?

With all his charm, good looks, wealth, and presidential aura, Jack could have attracted almost any woman, and often did. Certainly, there were many documented contenders—Helen Chavchavadze, Diana de Vegh, Mimi Beardsley (Alford), Judith Exner, and Marilyn Monroe among them—but none who became important to him in the way that Mary Meyer did. Her allure for Jack wasn't that of an imagined, superficial sexual escapade—though her eroticism, firmly imbedded in her femininity, was known to have brought many a man to his knees.

Mary's primary attraction for Jack may have ultimately been trust—in the end, love's most powerful aphrodisiac. She was independent and self-contained, free of any need for any kind of entrapment or manipulation. Jack

respected her as an equal. With Mary, the spark of redemption was likely ignited in the wounded darkness of his shadow. After all, real love was the foundation for the approach of healing, the process of which for Jack would have
required a lifelong "work-in-progress" commitment to self-examination and
recovery. Yet even in the midst of an uncontrollable, compulsive sexual addiction, the question remained. Had a shared bridge of hope with Mary helped
him further define the unique track of his presidency—a trajectory that finally
during the last six months of his life would embrace the pursuit of world peace
initiatives, away from the Cold War?

9

Mary's Mission

He's lost in the wilderness. He's lost in the bitterness.
This is a man's world, this is a man's world . . .
But it wouldn't be nothing, nothing without a woman or a girl.

—James Brown
"It's a Man's Man's Man's World"

It is true that my discovery of LSD was a chance discovery, but it was the outcome of planned experiments and these experiments took place in the framework of systematic pharmaceutical, chemical research. It could be better described as serendipity.

—Dr. Albert Hofmann

The so-called sixties "drug culture" was not a campus fad. It was a world-wide renaissance of the oldest religions.

—Timothy Leary

S ITTING AT HIS desk in a cramped office at 5 Divinity Avenue in the Center for Research in Personality at Harvard, Dr. Timothy Leary looked up and saw "a woman leaning against the door post, hip tilted provocatively," studying him intently. "She appeared to be in her late thirties. Good looking. Flamboyant eyebrows, piercing green-blue eyes, fine-boned face. Amused, arrogant, aristocratic."[1] It was April 1962, and the Harvard lecturer had for months been immersed in the onslaught of problems and crises that his Harvard Psilocybin Project had been attracting. Mounting publicity had resulted in increasing scrutiny, not all of it by any means good. Both Leary and his colleague, Professor Richard Alpert, had been recently "vigorously criticized" at a faculty meeting for ethical and empirical violations that involved giving the hallucinogen psilocybin to undergraduates. Ordered to surrender their supply, they were forbidden to continue their research.

Overwhelmed by literally hundreds of outside inquiries received each week, the affable, bubbly forty-one-year-old Irish Harvard tweed Leary was looking forward to a trip to Zihuatanejo, Mexico, in search of a more isolated retreat for his psychedelic research. As he was preparing to leave, the curious, unexpected visitor from Washington, D.C. arrived. She was someone he would encounter seven times over the next year and half. Twenty years later, in 1983, Timothy Leary recalled his initial impressions of their first meeting.

"Dr. Leary," he remembered her saying "coolly," "I've got to talk to you." She had offered her hand for a formal greeting and, Leary recalled, introduced herself as "Mary Pinchot," not Mary Meyer. "I've come from Washington," she had said, "to discuss something very important. I want to learn how to run an LSD session."[2]

Always partial to beautiful women, Timothy Leary was receptive. "That's our specialty here," he said. "Would you like to tell me what you have in mind?"

"I have this friend who's a very important man," Mary had told him. "He's impressed by what I've told him about my own LSD experiences and what other people have told him. He wants to try it himself. So I'm here to learn how to do it. I mean, I don't want to goof up or something."[3]

Timothy Leary hadn't understood at that moment that Mary was alluding to the president of the United States. Whether he was aware then that the president's sister-in-law Ethel Kennedy had reportedly undergone LSD sessions in the late 1950s wasn't known, but the president's brother-in-law Stephen Smith, husband of Jean Kennedy, had already contacted Leary about his own desire to explore LSD. Tim had referred him to another early LSD proselytizer, his close friend Van Wolfe in New York, who subsequently acted as a psychedelic guide for the Kennedy family member in the early 1960s.[4]

"Why don't you have your important friend come here with you to look over our project for a couple of days?" Leary responded. "Then if it makes sense to all concerned, we'll run a session for him."

"Out of the question. My friend is a public figure. It's just not possible."

"People involved in power usually don't make the best subjects," Leary cautioned.

"Look," she said, according to Leary. "I've heard Allen Ginsberg on radio and TV shows saying that if Khrushchev and Kennedy would take LSD together they'd end world conflict. Isn't that the idea—to get powerful men to turn on?"

"Allen says that, but I've never agreed. Premier Khrushchev should turn on with his wife in the comfort and security of his Kremlin bedroom. Same for Kennedy."

"Don't you think that if a powerful person were to turn on with his wife or girlfriend it would be good for the world?"

Nothing was certain, Leary explained. "But in general we believe that for anyone who's reasonably healthy and happy, the intelligent thing to do is take advantage of the multiple realities available to the human brain."

"Do you think that the world would be a better place if men in power had LSD experiences?" Mary asked.

"Look at the world," Leary responded. "Nuclear bombs proliferating. More and more countries run by military dictators. No political creativity. It's time to try something, anything new and promising."[5]

The two continued talking and went out for a drink. Leary invited Mary back to his house for dinner. Michael Hollingshead, a burned-out eccentric who had been a Cambridge University philosophy instructor, now living in Leary's attic, mixed more drinks as they discussed the changes that took place during the psychedelic experience. After dinner, they decided to take a low dose of magic mushrooms. While Hollingshead explained to Mary how to guide people in the throes of panic, Leary became aware of Mary's frowning and recalled the following exchange.

"You poor things," Mary said. "You have no idea what you've gotten into. You don't really understand what's happening in Washington with drugs, do you?"

"We've heard some rumors about the military," Leary said.

"It's time you learned more. The guys who run things—I mean the guys who *really* run things in Washington—are very interested in psychology, and drugs in particular. These people play hardball, Timothy. They want to use drugs for warfare, for espionage, for brainwashing, for control."

"Yes," Leary said. "We've heard about that."

"But there are people like me who want to use drugs for peace, not for war, to make people's lives better. Will you help us?"

"How?"

"I told you. Teach us how to run sessions, use drugs to do good."

Leary recalled feeling a bit uneasy. Mary seemed calculating, a bit tough, perhaps as a result of living "in the hard political world," as he put it. He asked her again who her friends were that wanted "to use drugs for peace."

"Women," she said laughing. "Washington, like every other capital city in the world, is run by men. These men conspiring for power can only be changed by women."

The next day Leary drove Mary to the airport, having "loaded her with books and papers" about the Harvard Psilocybin Project in preparation for her training as a psychedelic guide. He told Mary he didn't think she was ready to start running sessions yet. She agreed. She would come back soon, she told him, for more practice.

"And don't forget," she said. "The only hope for the world is intelligent women."[6]

Timothy Leary's 1983 book *Flashbacks* portrayed Mary Meyer during the period of 1962 to 1963 in such a way that has aroused as much fascination as it has skepticism. The biggest, most unsettled question was left unanswered: Had Mary and the president actually wandered into the psychedelic Garden of Eden together during his presidency, and if so, when, and with what result? Leary's account of his relationship with Mary also underscored Mary's ongoing antipathy toward the nefarious nature of the CIA, specifically the Agency's MKULTRA program, which was experimenting with all kinds of drugs for chemical warfare and mind control, including hallucinogens such as LSD. In addition, by April 1962, when Mary allegedly first appeared at Leary's office at Harvard, her influence in Jack Kennedy's life was already well established. Not simply a visitor to the White House residence when Jackie was away, Mary was seen in the Oval Office regularly. She attended any number of policy meetings at which the president discussed sensitive national security business and sought out her counsel.[7] Mary's close friend Anne Truitt described the importance of their relationship: "He saw she was trustworthy. He could talk to her with pleasure, without having to watch his words."[8]

Appearances to the contrary, Mary's decision to become involved with Jack wasn't motivated by a selfish, manipulative desire to turn him on to drugs. If they did share a psychedelic experience, Jack would have undoubtedly been a willing participant. Several accounts attest to the fact that Mary and Jack's love relationship was serious, not a passing fling of intermittent one-night stands. Author Leo Damore had become convinced that by the time Kennedy reached the presidency, "Jack was a broken man. He had lived a life as an instrument of his father's ambition, not his own." It was Mary, said Damore, who took Jack by the hand. "She could see the brokenness in him, and didn't need anything from him. In this relationship the power resided with Mary, and it was she, through her love, who bestowed the great gift of healing."[9] Yet Mary, too, appeared to have surrendered. "She told me she had fallen in love with Jack Kennedy and was sleeping with him," said Anne Truitt. "I was surprised but not too. Mary did what she pleased. She was having a lovely time."[10]

Just as fascinatingly, Timothy Leary's account of the mysterious "Mary Pinchot from Washington," depicted Mary as a kind of missionary for the ascension of world peace through the sagacious use of hallucinogens. Could an opportune mind-altering experience in the lives of powerful political figures, specifically the leader of the free world, awaken the kind of awareness, and leadership, that would take mankind away from war and strife toward the province of peaceful coexistence? Mary's latent intention, Leary finally realized, had not only been to invite her lover the president to take a psychedelic excursion with her, but to train a small group of eight women in Washington, all of whom who were intimately involved with powerful public figures. Could the inducement of a psychedelically induced religious mystical experience in the politically powerful support a movement away from militaristic war and domination, toward harmonious peaceful coexistence throughout the world? It appeared that Mary had hatched a plan. Her pacifism and abhorrence of all violent armed conflict motivated a curiosity she thought worthy of exploration.

In the early 1960s, the world was fighting a war, albeit a Cold War, fraught with tensions that were constantly on the verge of escalating. Watching this unfold, Mary had a "catbird seat" as Cord's wife. Perhaps through her own experience, psychedelic exploration had predisposed her to Allen Ginsberg's vision. In any case, Timothy Leary portrayed Mary as a woman in possession of considerable feminine power, someone who had undergone her own personal transformation who now wanted to become an acolyte for world peace, intent on laying the groundwork for such a mission. Yet no one else has ever gone public to substantiate Leary's claims about Mary's mission, nor publicly verified the existence of any "LSD cell group" that she was supposedly working with. There is, however, one caveat to this dilemma that will be discussed shortly.

In addition, some of Leary's critics (and there are many) even doubt that he actually had any contact with Mary Meyer at all. The majority of these critics believe he shamelessly exploited the story of Mary Pinchot Meyer, and engineered it for publicity for *Flashbacks*. In particular, the thrust of this criticism has been that if Leary had a relationship with Mary that began in 1962, why did he wait until 1983, some twenty years after the fact, to write about it? After all, Timothy Leary was a prolific author. Two of his major books from mainstream publishers, *High Priest* and *The Politics of Ecstasy*, both published in 1968—four years after Mary Meyer had been murdered—contain no mention of her.

However, it appeared that Leary did make an initial attempt to investigate Mary's murder in late May of 1965 when he returned from his around-the-world honeymoon with his new wife. He told Leo Damore, and stated in *Flashbacks*, that he had finally called Vassar College in 1965 to find out Mary's current whereabouts, only to discover she'd been murdered the previous fall. It was only at this juncture that Leary learned Mary had been married to Cord Meyer. In *Flashbacks*, Leary recorded that he broke down and sobbed at the time; he recounted the event to Damore in 1990.[11] Enlisting the support of his friends Van Wolfe and Michael Hollingshead, Leary planned to do his own investigation and write a book about it. According to Van Wolfe, someone in "police intelligence in Washington" had told him Mary's murder had been an assassination. The Leary-Wolfe plan was to "dig up the facts," but Wolfe's attorney warned him "nobody wanted this incident investigated," that it was too dangerous to pursue.[12]

Another unanswered question still lingered: If Timothy Leary had returned from his around-the-world travels to Millbrook, New York, in the early summer of 1965, why hadn't he followed Mary's murder trial, particularly after having been so shocked and upset over her murder?

In an in-depth, nearly two-hour recorded interview in 1990, never before published, Leary told Damore that he did, in fact, know the trial was about to begin that summer, but that he had been blindsided by the emotional intensity of the breakup of his new marriage, as well as the crumbling of his Millbrook community, which included an onslaught of intimidation by local police. The campaign of police surveillance and interference had started just after Leary's return, right before Ray Crump's trial for the murder of Mary Meyer. After nearly a full year of harassment, the final hammer came down in March 1966, when G. Gordon Liddy, who had been attached to J. Edgar Hoover's elite personal staff at FBI headquarters (and who would eventually become notorious as one of the Watergate break-in artists in 1972), raided Leary's Millbrook compound.

"Had this been planned deliberately to keep you away from Mary's murder trial?" Leo Damore asked Leary in 1990.

Prompted by Damore's query, Leary entertained the possibility that the harassment might well have been deliberately timed to coincide with Mary's murder trial. There had been an uptick in harassment and surveillance activity at Millbrook, said Leary, all through that summer and fall. Not wanting to stay for the winter, Tim and his new lady friend, Rosemary Woodruff, took off for the Yucatán in Mexico, only to be arrested in December 1965 at the Laredo, Texas, border crossing for "smuggling marijuana." Rosemary Woodruff would famously remark: "Have you ever been in the situation where you feel all the gears shift, when everything changes? Poignant doesn't begin to express it. I think Tim knew as well. Something like this had been waiting in the wings for a long time."[13]

Media headlines all across the country would herald the Leary arrest. The backlash against him, and all recreational drugs, had begun. In spite of doing all he could to publicize and garner support for his trial, he was convicted on March 11, 1966, and sentenced to thirty years in jail and a $20,000 fine. The judge would eventually dismiss all the charges because of a failure to advise Leary and his family of their Miranda rights. But Leary was jailed again in 1969 on other drug charges, and then fled the country in 1970 and lived in exile for nearly three years. Finally captured in Afghanistan and extradited back to the United States, Timothy Leary would remain in the California prison system until April 1976.[14] For more than ten years, Timothy Leary would be under siege, fighting for his life.

Upon his release from prison in 1976, having read the *National Enquirer* exposé about Mary's affair with Jack published earlier that year, Leary would attempt a second investigation of Mary's murder after coming across a copy of Deborah Davis's book *Katharine the Great* at the home of his friends Jon and Carolyn Bradshaw.[15] The Davis book revealed more details about who Mary Meyer had been, including her marriage to the CIA's Cord Meyer, as well as her affair with the president. So incensed had Ben Bradlee and Katharine Graham become over the book's publication—purportedly because it accused Bradlee of having CIA connections—the two pressured publisher William Jovanovich of publishing giant Harcourt Brace Jovanovich to recall and shred the book.[16]

Leary would eventually oversee a further effort by *Rebel* magazine in the early 1980s to investigate Mary's murder. He produced for Leo Damore several lengthy letters/reports from a private investigator by the name of William Triplett, whom he and *Rebel* had hired to do investigative work. Damore further confirmed the authenticity of Triplett's investigation and association with Leary in early 1991.[17]

While Timothy Leary's biographer, Robert Greenfield, lamented that Leary's book *Flashbacks* wasn't entirely accurate, he persisted in quoting many of the events in the book to support his portrait of Leary as a narcissistic miscreant. Greenfield did, however, verify in an interview for this book that Tim Leary knew Mary Meyer, and "probably did supply her with psychedelics." Moreover, Mary was using her maiden name when she began their association. He wasn't aware, perhaps intentionally so on Mary's part, that she had been married to CIA operative Cord Meyer, with whom Leary himself had had a number of combative encounters when he was part of the American Veterans Committee (AVC) during his graduate student days at the University of California at Berkeley.[18]

"Tim didn't like Cord Meyer," said Greenfield. "His secretary in Berkeley confirmed that for me, as well as his relationship with Mary. My sense was that this [Leary's relationship with Mary Meyer] did happen. If she came to him at Harvard, that's the period where he was out to turn on the world and the aristocracy—people like Robert Lowell, Barney Rosset, Charles Mingus, Theolonius Monk, and Maynard and Flo Ferguson. At Millbrook, Tim still had the patina of respectability. He looked straight. He was an ex Harvard professor. It was the early sixties, pre-psychedelic. Based on all the research I did, it seems entirely likely to me Tim would have met with somebody like this, only Tim would have not made the association, given that Mary was only identifying herself as Mary Pinchot."[19]

As authoritative and well-researched as Robert Greenfield's 2006 biography of Timothy Leary had been, Greenfield didn't have access to the important two-hour tape-recorded interview of Leary with the late author Leo Damore in November 1990. The Leary-Damore interview focused almost entirely on Leary's relationship with Mary and the events surrounding her death, in addition to what was taking place in Leary's own life at the time. During this interview, Leary offered many fascinating new details and insights about Mary and what he had learned about her activities. Damore and Leary also had a number of follow-up telephone conversations for nearly three years after the initial 1990 interview.[20]

"I knew Cord quite well in 1946 during my involvement with the American Veterans Committee," Leary told Damore. "He was an absolute fanatic who fought with everyone, a real monster-machine!"[21] Again, this may have indicated Mary's knowledge that confrontations between Cord and Leary had taken place years earlier; Mary's deception was likely deliberate. She clearly understood some of the risks involved in being identified, Leary told Damore, and she had wanted to keep a low profile from the very beginning. Throughout the interview, Leary reiterated several times that Mary never mentioned names.

"Mary first wanted to turn on the wives and girlfriends of important powerful men," Leary explained. "That's what she said. She never gave me any indication who these men were, or the women for that matter."

"Weren't you at least curious?" asked Damore.

"Mary was like a crusader," responded Leary. "The early ones were almost always crusaders for a higher consciousness, like ministers of the gospel. And a lot of them were women. Peggy Mellon Hitchcock was another." Indeed, so enthralled by the potential of hallucinogenic consciousness expansion was Ms. Hitchcock that when Leary was fired from Harvard in 1963, she and her brothers offered their family's Millbrook, New York, estate as a base for psychedelic research. The legendary en masse exodus from Cambridge to Millbrook had taken place almost immediately.[22]

"What about details? How was she putting this together?" Damore wanted to know.

"When we met, it was clear Mary was unwilling to talk about specifics," Leary recalled. "I really didn't pay that much attention to her. I helped her when I could, when she called or came up to Boston, but I never gave much thought about it until after I found out she'd been murdered. Both at Harvard and Millbrook, we were being besieged from people all over the country and all over the world. It was overwhelming and never-ending."[23]

One person still alive today, Mary's close friend Anne Chamberlin, might well be able to authoritatively comment on Mary's mission, because she was, according to Damore, part of Mary's LSD cell group in Washington. But Anne Chamberlin has repeatedly refused to be interviewed for this book, although she did apparently talk with Damore on several occasions, starting in the late 1980s. During his interview of Leary, Damore revealed that he had been in contact with Chamberlin on more than one occasion:

One of the women who was involved with Mary in the LSD group is now living in Maine. And I've talked to her at great length. Anne Chamberlin. Anne Chamberlin is a writer, an essayist, extremely wealthy, out of San Francisco, *out* of Washington—out of, out of fear, actually. And Anne is more and more forthcoming because I think enough time has passed and those people in power who felt threatened by Mary

Pinchot Meyer as a person who held an awful lot of information and a lot of secrets who could make certain politicians in this town very uncomfortable.[24]

In a follow-up request to Anne Chamberlin in early 2009, I alerted her to my ownership of the Damore material and the fact that I had become privy to some of what she had told him. I offered her every confidentiality if she would be willing to talk with me about it.[25] A week later she replied by letter: "It saddens me that you continue to pursue the long-gone phantom prey. I have nothing to say about Mary Meyer, or anything connected with Mary Meyer. I have told you this before. I am telling you now. Don't make me tell you again."[26] For whatever reason, Ms. Chamberlin never wanted to make known her relationship with Mary Meyer, nor reveal why she apparently abruptly left Washington shortly after Mary's murder.

Leo Damore was curious about other sources of information regarding Mary's possible use of psychedelics, though he wanted primarily to hear from the LSD guru himself where Mary had gone for assistance. Purportedly, there had been one other account. In 1989, C. David Heymann published the book *A Woman Named Jackie*. There, Heymann quotes from an alleged interview with former CIA counterintelligence chief Jim Angleton. Angleton was said to have told Heymann—referring to Mary's affair with Kennedy—that "Mary kept an art diary in which she began making notations concerning their meetings, of which there were between thirty and forty during their affair—in the White House, at her studio, in the homes of friends." Angleton then, according to Heymann, said that Mary and Jack "took a mild acid [LSD] trip together, during which they made love."[27]

But no record of Heymann's Angleton interview has ever been produced, nor have records of Heymann's other alleged interviews with Timothy Leary and Tony Bradlee, which he told Damore he had conducted.[28] Moreover, to my knowledge, Angleton never confirmed the statements he made to Heymann with anyone else before his death in 1987.[29] Yet Angleton's alleged statements might have been the sort of details Mary would have noted in her real diary—the one that Angleton stole on the night of her murder, not the artist's sketchbook that the Bradlees and others designated as the diary, which was only a decoy.

During his 1990 interview of Leary, Damore asked him point-blank: "Do you believe there's any doubt he [Jack] was using acid [LSD] in the White House with her [Mary]?" Leary's response was adamant: "I can't say that," he told Damore emphatically. "That was only my assumption. . . . There's no question in my mind now that she had proposed to use LSD with Jack. I had heard that Bobby had also been interested."[30]

"But from all of the hints she was giving you," Damore further pressed, "wasn't it almost a given?" Again, Leary conceded he thought it was very possible, even likely, but would go no further.[31] Six years later, in 1996, the year he died, Leary reiterated this same unwavering position to author Nina Burleigh. "Mary Meyer might have dropped acid [ingested LSD] with Kennedy," he told Burleigh, but again made it clear that "he had no proof."[32]

At the time of the 1990 Damore-Leary interview, the only other account of any drug use by Mary and Jack came indirectly from James Truitt for the breakout story he gave to the *National Enquirer* in 1976. Despite the subsequent smear campaign engineered to discredit Truitt, he was an established journalist and a former vice president of the *Washington Post,* who over the years had amassed a large set of papers and files that included portions of what Mary had confided.[33]

While researching material for her book *Katharine the Great,* author Deborah Davis read the 1976 *Enquirer* exposé and found it more than just credible. "Truitt's story in the *National Enquirer* was strangely well documented," Davis later recalled in 2009. "So much so, I actually went to Florida and talked to both the editor and writer about the story. It was after that I went to visit Jim Truitt in Mexico." Davis interviewed Truitt for more than ten hours over a three-day period during 1976. The two then corresponded further by mail.[34]

Perhaps as a prelude, Mary may have wanted to see Jack's reaction to something far less potent than a hallucinogen like LSD or psilocybin. Based on the information Mary shared with Truitt, there was at least one encounter when Mary and Jack smoked marijuana together in the White House residence. On Monday evening, July 16, 1962, according to Truitt's notes, Mary produced "a snuff box with six marijuana cigarettes" in Jack's bedroom. "Let's try it," Jack reportedly said to Mary.[35]

"She and the President sat at opposite ends of the bed and Mary tried to tell him how to smoke pot," Truitt was quoted saying in the 1976 *National Enquirer* article. "He wouldn't listen to me," Mary told Truitt. "He wouldn't control his breathing while he smoked, and he flicked the ashes like it was a regular cigarette and tried to put it out a couple of times."

"Mary said that at first JFK didn't seem to feel anything, but then began to laugh and told her: 'We're having a White House conference on narcotics here in two weeks!'"

"She said that after they smoked the second joint, Jack leaned back and closed his eyes. He lay there for a long time, and Mary said she thought to herself, 'We've killed the President.' But then he opened his eyes and said he was hungry.

"He went to get something to eat and returned with soup and chocolate mousse. They smoked three of the joints and then JFK told her: 'No more. Suppose the Russians did something now!'

"She said he also told her, 'This isn't like cocaine. I'll get you some of that.' She said JFK wanted to smoke pot again a month later, but never got around to it.

"When Mary got home that night she realized with horror that she'd left her slip in the President's bedroom. It wasn't until 8:30 the next morning that she was able to reach him by phone. 'Don't worry,' she said he told her. 'It's in the Presidential safe in an envelope with your name and the Presidential seal on it.'"[36]

While folklore maintained that the actual affair between Mary and Jack didn't begin until January 1962, it likely started much earlier.[37] According to the account Kenny O'Donnell gave to Leo Damore shortly before his death in 1977, Mary was in the White House in Jack's company shortly after he took office as president in early 1961. She often came into the White House, said O'Donnell, under the guise of "Dave Powers plus one" entries in the Secret Service logs before she was listed by her own name in the logs. The "Dave Powers plus one" entries were numerous all through 1961 and beyond. Her first documented solo private entrance into the White House residence (as noted in the White House Secret Service logs) occurred on October 3, 1961,[38] followed by some thirteen other documented private visits during the Kennedy presidency. Mary also attended all six of the White House dinner dances, as well as any number of luncheons and smaller dinner parties given by Jack and Jackie.[39] The secret lovers also met a number of times alone at the Georgetown home of Joseph Alsop, who had offered his house when he was away.[40] Finally, there were a number of instances during his presidency when Jack met with Mary at her house in Georgetown.[41]

Mary's privacy about the affair, however, no matter when it began, was of paramount concern. It appeared that she established an early ground rule in her relationship with Jack. A private person whose solitude was sacred, she didn't want to be a topic of conversation in scandal-mongering Washington, nor of yesterday's gossip, like so many of Jack's dalliances. Jack appeared to have agreed to this condition, but couldn't always restrain his bravado.

"If only we could run wild, Benjy," he said to Ben Bradlee, looking over all the women at one of the White House dinner dances.[42] Aware of Mary's beauty and allure from across the room at the third White House dinner dance in February 1962, Jack had leaned in and commented to Bradlee, "Mary would be rough to live with." According to Bradlee, it wasn't the first time Jack had made the comment. "And I agreed, not for the first time," recalled Bradlee.[43] Had Jack's remark revealed something about the nature of his relationship with Mary?

Look correspondent Laura Bergquist, married to Fletcher Knebel, a Harvard classmate of Jack's, had had access to Jack ever since his 1952 senatorial campaign. Many years later, she insightfully characterized Jack as deeply vulnerable. "I think he always felt an insecurity about himself," she told social historian Ralph Martin in an interview for his 1995 book *Seeds of Destruction*. "Not simply because he was part of the upward-mobile Irish, but because I think he recognized himself as an image that had been manufactured. And the questions came up: 'Who loves me and wants me for myself, and who loves me for what they think I am, and what I can do?'" Martin's next sentence read: "One of the women who loved him for himself was Mary Pinchot Meyer. . . ."[44]

And Mary would have demanded Jack's self-examination, demanded that he open his eyes, his heart, his soul, the core of his being to both the artifice and the reality of his existence, including his sexual promiscuity. She would have refused to allow him to hide behind his physical incapacity, his sense of obligation to his father or the Kennedy family, his fear of public ridicule or recrimination, or any indifference to such issues as civil rights or the dangers of the Cold War. She would have taken him to task in a way that some part of him deeply longed for, knowing the emotional pain he would have to confront. In order to reclaim himself, Jack would have had to brave a kind of grief and emotional intensity similar to what Mary herself had faced with the loss of her son Michael. Mary knew the drill—the crashing surf of unbearable sorrow, and what was required to survive it. The "prima female assoluta" would have been at once tender and firm with him, yet demanding that he show up, engage, and stop running.

For Jack, Mary may have represented the hope of a lost love, a magnetic, romantic passion, the kind of erotic chemistry he had once experienced with Inga Arvad, tempered by the same kind of no-bullshit, heartfelt bond he had shared with his departed sister Kathleen. Indeed, there were undoubtedly moments when Mary was "rough to live with," but something in Jack had been awakened by Mary's entrance into his life—something that kept him engaged, and apparently wanting more. Such was the fire and hope not only of love's redemption, but a more clearly defined reclamation of himself and the kind of president he wanted to become.

Kenny O'Donnell confided to Leo Damore that Mary had been quite outspoken and confrontational with the president when he was about to resume nuclear testing in April 1962. "She openly challenged him to do something different, not fall into the trap of getting into a pissing contest with the Russians," said Damore in 1992, based on O'Donnell's statements to him. O'Donnell sometimes, according to Damore, even feared Mary because of the power she had over Jack, saying the president would "feverishly" pace around the Oval Office when he wasn't able to get in touch with her by phone.[45] Vulnerability isn't necessarily a sign of weakness; very often it's the emerging strength of a healing heart crying out for connection. "Mary had a serenity about her," reflected Ben Bradlee pensively about a quality in her that he found unusual. "She was a serious person. If she fell in love with somebody, I suspect that person was really loved."[46]

For a period of time the Bradlees, particularly Tony, may well have been kept in the dark about what was taking place. Mary would have insisted that Jack keep any knowledge of their affair from them, but that presented a problem, for the Kennedys were close friends with the Bradlees, before and during Jack's presidency. Part of Mary's ground rule was to keep her sister and brother-in-law off the scent of the trail. The two lovers hatched a scheme: Jack would dote on Tony and give the impression that she, not Mary, was the Pinchot sister who caught his eye. Tony Bradlee had always lived in Mary's shadow. Four years younger, she was said to have been the "more reserved and shy of the two sisters."[47] And while they were not overtly competitive, Tony harbored a quiet jealousy toward her sister, who was always regarded as the more beautiful, more attractive, more enchanting of the two.

It was surely no accident that at the very first White House dinner dance on March 15, 1961, just two months into the Kennedy presidency, Mary was seated next to Jack at the president's table; but the price of that admission was that Tony would be seated on Jack's other side, "making the Beautiful People from New York seethe with disbelief," according to Ben Bradlee.[48] Some thought Mary's affair with Jack had not yet begun, but according to the information Kenny O'Donnell shared with Leo Damore, it surely had.

Even Jackie, it appeared, fell for the trick for a period of time. As late as April 1963, when the Bradlees were dining alone with the Kennedys at the White House, Jackie had intriguingly remarked, "Oh Jack, you know you always say that Tony is your ideal [woman]."[49] It appeared the remark already had a history. With Mary in attendance during Jack's raucous forty-sixth birthday bash on May 29 on the presidential yacht *Sequoia*, the celebration had cruised up and down the Potomac River until "1:23 A.M." It was a particularly "wild party" on a hot, humid Washington evening, complete with thunderstorms and periods of torrential rain, people drinking heavily while getting soaking wet, and Teddy Kennedy ripping half his pants off at the crotch. "But it was Jack himself," noted author Sally Bedell Smith, "who misbehaved in an especially reckless fashion."[50]

That observation was based in part on Smith's interview with Tony Bradlee. According to Tony, she played up the fact that Jack had been "following her" around that birthday evening. "He chased me all around the boat," Tony told Smith. "A couple of members of the crew were laughing. I was running and laughing as he chased me. He caught up with me in the ladies room and made a pass. It was a pretty strenuous attack, not as if he pushed me down, but his hands wandered."[51]

Yet Tony's most telling insight, expressed during her 2001 interview with Smith, was that Jack's behavior "struck me as odd." She added, "[I]t seems odder knowing what we now know about Mary [and her relationship with Jack]." The significance of her momentary discernment eluded her. Given that she was already smitten, Tony's infatuation was as much wishful thinking as Jack's behavior was a strategic ploy. "I guess I was pretty surprised," continued Tony, "but I was kind of flattered," quickly adding, "and appalled too."[52] But once again, the game had snookered Tony. It appeared she had been left in the dark right up until Mary's murder. "Jack had been attracted to her," she maintained. "He had made several unsuccessful passes. Jack was always so complimentary to me, putting his hands around my waist."[53] Years later, in 2007, Ben Bradlee still emphatically recalled how "*shocked* [Bradlee's emphasis]" she had been when she found out Mary had been having an affair with Jack.[54]

One person who wasn't fooled the evening of Jack's forty-sixth birthday in May 1963, or anytime earlier, was journalist Charlie Bartlett, a close, dear friend of Jack's who, with his wife, Martha, had first introduced him to Jackie. Bartlett, a distinguished journalist and Washington insider who spearheaded the Washington bureau of the *Chattanooga Times*, had also been a Yale classmate of Cord Meyer's. He was well acquainted with everyone in the Kennedy inner circle, and he and Martha often socialized with Jack and Jackie.

Emotionally closer to Jack than Ben Bradlee would ever become, Charlie Bartlett was perhaps one of Kennedy's primary confidantes. Jack mostly compartmentalized his close friendships, yet he confided in Bartlett what he rarely shared with anyone else. "I really liked Jack Kennedy," recalled Bartlett in late 2008 in an interview for this book. "We had great fun together and a lot of things in common. We had a very personal, close relationship." Apparently that awareness didn't go unnoticed. When Jack began his presidency, Bartlett thought it a bit odd that his Yale classmate Cord Meyer, then a chief operative in the CIA's covert action directorate, wanted to begin having a more social relationship with him. "Cord and I saw a lot of each other after Jack Kennedy became president because I think someone at CIA told Cord to keep an eye on me."[55]

Regarding Jack's relationship with Mary, Bartlett bluntly admitted, "I didn't particularly like Mary Meyer." He had known both Mary and Cord when they were married. When asked by Nina Burleigh why he never considered investigating the story of Mary Meyer, he reportedly exclaimed nervously, "Oh, I can't. Too many of my friends are a part of that one."[56] But what he didn't mention to authors Burleigh or Sally Bedell Smith was what he had come to know about Jack's affection for Mary.

"That was a dangerous relationship," Bartlett recalled. "Jack was in love with Mary Meyer. He was certainly smitten by her, he was heavily smitten. He was very frank with me about it, that he thought she was absolutely great." That there were moments when Jack couldn't contain his affection didn't go unnoticed, either. Recalling a number of excursions on the presidential yacht *Sequoia* and the Kennedy family boat *Honey Fitz*, Bartlett further added: "We had these boat parties and we could see it [Jack's affection for Mary]. I even got a little mad with him on one of the boat parties, because it was more than obvious. He took it [his relationship with Mary] pretty seriously."[57]

Charlie Bartlett's observations further dovetailed with Kenny O'Donnell statements to Leo Damore. O'Donnell, who was as close to Jack as anyone could be on a daily basis during his presidency, knew firsthand Jack's affection for Mary. "Kenny had always admired Jack as a cool champion, the man of political celebration," Damore revealed in 1992. "He saw it start to collapse because of Mary. Jack was losing interest in politics. The fun for Jack was winning the job [being elected president]."[58] Sometime in October 1963, said Damore, just a little more than a month before his death, "Jack confided to Kenny he was deeply in love with Mary, that after he left the White House he envisioned a future with her and would divorce Jackie."[59]

Mary was in the White House residence on Monday evening, August 6, 1962, just thirty-six hours after the apparent suicide of famed Hollywood sex symbol Marilyn Monroe. Her sultry "Happy Birthday, Mr. President" appearance just over two months earlier at a combined fund-raiser and birthday party for Jack in New York had already become an iconic Americana moment. Surely Mary knew that Jack had been involved with Marilyn. But had she known how the relationship had disintegrated, or how his brother Bobby had recently "taken his turn" with the world's most famous sex goddess—who had been unwilling "to go away quietly"? That Bobby Kennedy and Peter Lawford were at Marilyn's house the day she died was suspicious enough; that Bobby returned a second time that evening, according to two witnesses, immediately prior to her "suicide" was a bit more unsavory.[60] The situation, according to people who knew Marilyn closely, had become critical. Should she have proceeded with her intention to publicly reveal the affairs, the Kennedy political machine might have been dealt a severe blow. The events immediately following her death created more questions than answers.[61] Marilyn's alleged crusade "to expose the Kennedys for what they are" has had enormous reverberations, including the close guarding of fifty-four crates of Robert Kennedy's records at the John F. Kennedy Presidential Library and Museum that are so confidential even the library's director is prohibited from knowing what's in them.[62] Such have been the extensive efforts of the Kennedy image machine to keep the full disclosure of truth from the American people.

Toward the end of 1962, inside the White House Mary Meyer had become "almost part of the furniture," in the words of White House counsel Myer Feldman, according to author Nina Burleigh. "Unlike with some of the other women—and men—in the White House, the president did not ask her to leave the room when he discussed business," wrote Burleigh. "So frequent was her proximity to the president, and so obvious Kennedy's admiration for her, that Feldman felt Mary might make a good conduit to the president's ear if and when Kennedy was unavailable to discuss matters of state with him."[63] Mary's emerging presence in the White House was more than just what was documented in the entry logs.

"I'd walk in and out of the office all the time," Feldman told Burleigh, "and I would see her in the Oval Office or over in the residence. Around eight-thirty, when the day was over, often I'd walk over to the residence and she'd be sitting there. There wasn't any attempt to hide her the way there was with some of the other women."[64]

In addition, Mary's evolving position within the Kennedy White House senior staff was never second tier. Mention of her name could even be considered advantageous for employment, in the opinion of Kennedy aide and historian Arthur Schlesinger Jr. In a two-page December 1962 memo in support of fellow historian Trumbull Higgins's proposal to write the official White House account of the Bay of Pigs debacle, Schlesinger stated, "I know Higgins slightly. He is an old friend of Mary Meyer's, who knows him better."[65] Higgins eventually published a book on the Bay of Pigs fiasco entitled *The Perfect Failure* (1987), in which he concluded that President Kennedy had inherited a catastrophe in the making that had been prepared by the CIA under Kennedy's predecessor President Eisenhower.

Allen Dulles was finally granted his wish by President Dwight Eisenhower to be director of the CIA (DCI) in 1953. But Eisenhower, even before leaving office, had regretted the Dulles appointment. With the CIA's 1954 overthrow of President Jacobo Arbenz in Guatemala, Eisenhower finally realized the Agency was dangerously out of control. He was advised to get rid of Dulles, but didn't. It proved to be a huge mistake. Several years later, right before Eisenhower's May 16, 1960, peace summit with Premier Nikita Khrushchev, the CIA engineered the May 1 downing of its own U-2 reconnaissance spy flight over Russian territory as a way to undermine any possibility of rapprochement with the Soviet Union. Eisenhower had planned to orchestrate a Soviet détente before he left office, so that he could cut the defense budget and redirect resources toward America's domestic needs. That dream was quickly vanquished as tensions between the two emerging superpowers resumed unabated. Through fear-mongering, the CIA had achieved its goal, urging upon Congress the strategic necessity for further increases in its budget. As he left office, President Eisenhower would finally explode at Dulles. "The structure of our intelligence organization is faulty," he told the director. "I have suffered an eight-year defeat on this. Nothing has changed since Pearl Harbor. I leave a 'legacy of ashes' to my successor." By 1964, the Agency's clandestine service and operations would consume nearly two-thirds of its entire (classified) budget and, according to author Tim Weiner, 90 percent of the director's time.[66]

In his farewell speech, President Eisenhower warned the public to "guard against the acquisition of unwarranted influence, whether sought or unsought," by what he called "the military-industrial complex." Warning that "the potential for the disastrous rise of misplaced power exists and will persist," Eisenhower pointed to "an alert and knowledgeable citizenry" as the antidote. But the military-industrial complex of which Eisenhower spoke had a third, unnamed component: intelligence.

Established in 1947, the CIA was, from its inception, virtually unaccountable to any authority. It was subject to little, if any, congressional oversight, a fact that would increasingly haunt both President Harry Truman and his successor, President Eisenhower. As a career military general, Eisenhower was skeptical about the role of civilians in clandestine paramilitary operations. In addition, he was troubled by the fact that the Agency had a carte blanche "get out of jail free card" for anything it attempted. President Truman's 1948 National Security Council (NSC) had so imbued the Agency with unchecked, absolute power, it threatened the entire foundation of America's constitutional premise.

That year the NSC approved what became known as "Top Secret Directive NSC 10/2," a virtual bottomless pit of nefarious, illegal quicksand. The directive defined covert operations as actions conducted by the United States against foreign states "which are so planned and executed that any U.S. Government responsibility for them is not evident to unauthorized persons and that if uncovered the U.S. Government can *plausibly disclaim* any responsibility for them." Creating what came to be known as "plausible deniability," the directive sanctioned and authorized U.S. intelligence, principally the CIA, to carry out a broad range of clandestine activities and paramilitary operations that included preventive direct action, propaganda, economic warfare, sabotage, demolition, subversion against "hostile states," assassinations, and "support of indigenous anti-communist elements in threatened countries of the free world." Years later, George Kennan, the directive's original sponsor and architect, bluntly told Yale historian John Lukacs: "That was the greatest mistake I ever made in my life, because you know what the Central Intelligence Agency has devolved or evolved into."[67] In the mid-1970s, Kennan again reiterated before a U.S. Senate committee that it was "the greatest mistake I ever made."[68]

During the 1950s, in the interests of promoting American economic growth and hegemony, the emerging Dulles calling card was an uncanny expertise in overthrowing foreign governments, many of them democratically elected. Eisenhower's predecessor, President Harry Truman, had had his own confrontations with covert operations run by the Dulles cadre. Iran, in 1951, had decided to nationalize its oil industry, which before had been controlled exclusively by Britain. Winston Churchill had implored Truman before he left office in 1952 to order the CIA to join with British forces in MI6 and arrange for a coup against the newly democratically elected Mosaddeq government in Iran. Truman, without equivocation, said no. A year later, Eisenhower, seduced by Dulles, caved in. In August 1953, Operation Ajax overthrew Mohammad Mosaddeq and installed the Shah, leaving the Iranian people to suffer unimaginable horrors under the reign of SAVAK, the shah's heinous praetorian guard, trained in surveillance, interrogation, and torture by the CIA.[69]

A year after the overthrow of Mosaddeq, the CIA (again under Dulles's tutelage) would take down the government in Guatemala. President Arbenz, who had been democratically elected by his country in 1950 with 65 percent of the vote, was deemed "leftist" by the mainstream American media—no doubt reflecting the influence of the CIA's Operation Mockingbird in the press—and vulnerable to the approach of a "Soviet beachhead in the Western hemisphere." The Arbenz government's "mortal sin" was land reform in its own country; it wanted to put a stop to private corporations like the United Fruit Company taking land away from the Guatemalan peasant population. Although few knew it then, both Allen Dulles and his brother, Secretary of State John Foster Dulles, owned sizable stock in United Fruit, with Allen Dulles himself serving as a member of the company's board of trustees. The company lobbied hard for Washington to remove the Arbenz government, and in 1954, the CIA did so.[70] Under Dulles-CIA auspices, similar coups would occur in Hungary, North Vietnam, and Laos before the 1960 election.

Jack Kennedy entered his presidency as an avowed Cold Warrior. Allen Dulles wanted to take advantage of the new president's CIA sympathies as quickly as possible. Initially dazzled, then seduced, by Dulles and the aura of CIA covert operations, both Jack and his brother Bobby agreed to keep Allen Dulles in place—which included supporting, at least initially, the upcoming Bay of Pigs invasion of Cuba run by Dulles protégé Richard Bissell. The CIA had been startled by Kennedy's election; they weren't prepared for it. "When Kennedy got elected, people at CIA were alarmed," said former CIA covert operative Donald Deneselya. "Nixon was a team player, a known quantity. No one knew what was going to happen with Kennedy."[71] President Kennedy would soon boldly demonstrate why.

Early into his presidency in 1961, before the Bay of Pigs debacle, Jack had pushed hard against the CIA and the Joint Chiefs for the goal of a neutral and independent Laos in Southeast Asia. He wanted to end U.S. support of the country's anti-Communist ruler, General Phoumi Nosavan, whose puppet government had been installed by a joint CIA-Pentagon military force during the Eisenhower administration. The insistence of the new president wasn't well received; it also foreshadowed a bigger event to come. That April, the CIA launched the Cuban Bay of Pigs invasion, hoping to get rid of Fidel Castro and install (or restore) a government more sympathetic to American business interests and the interests of the Mafia, who wanted to regain possession of the lucrative casinos in Havana. The Bay of Pigs invasion was a complete, utter fiasco. It would, however, become a defining event in the Kennedy presidency and in Cold War history.

A CIA-trained, equipped, and commanded Cuban-exile brigade was used to attempt the overthrow of Castro's government. Almost laughably, Fidel Castro, along with the rest of the world's leaders, including the Russians, knew the invasion was being launched, and who was really behind it. The invasion had originally been conceived during the Eisenhower administration. Its success would inevitably depend on American air support, although that detail had not been revealed to the president before the operation began. When the moment came, Jack realized he had been tricked by the Dulles inner circle, which had attempted to possibly play upon the president's fear of appearing politically weak and inexperienced. Dulles believed Kennedy would cave in to political pressure, and thereby fall into line to make the operation a success. Awakened, Jack's rectitude intervened; realizing he had been intentionally deceived, he called the operation to a halt, willing to suffer whatever political consequences might ensue.

Years later, according to Cold War historian L. Fletcher Prouty, Supreme Court justice William O. Douglas recalled a discussion he and the president had about the debacle. "This episode seared him," said Justice Douglas. "He had experienced the extreme power that these groups had, these various insidious influences of the CIA and the Pentagon on civilian policy, and I think it raised in his own mind the specter: Can Jack Kennedy, President of the United States, ever be strong enough to really rule these two powerful agencies? I think it had a profound effect . . . it shook him up!"[72]

"We were at war with the national security people," historian Arthur Schlesinger Jr. would quietly confide to a friend many years later.[73] The enormity of the disaster wasn't lost on Jack, who told one of his highest administration officials that he wanted "to splinter the CIA in a thousand pieces and scatter it to the winds." Inside the White House, the president was seething. "How could I have been so stupid? I've got to do something about those CIA bastards."[74]

That was followed by the realization that Allen Dulles—the man who had convinced him the CIA was indispensable, as he had done with Eisenhower—was too much of a legendary figure, and that it was hard "to operate with legendary figures." He needed someone within the Agency he could trust. "I made a mistake in putting Bobby in the Justice Department. Bobby should be in CIA," he had said.[75] The Bay of Pigs fiasco would turn out to be a harbinger of worse things to come. The Kennedy administration's maiden voyage in foreign affairs, its shakedown cruise, was a rude awakening, and it would begin to reveal the kind of ruthless treachery at work.

Attending a conference on the Bay of Pigs in Cuba some forty years later in March 2001, longtime political journalist Daniel Schorr, speaking on the NPR radio program *All Things Considered*, said he had gained an entirely new perception of the fiasco:

> It was that the CIA overlords of the invasion, director Allen Dulles and deputy Richard Bissell, had their own plan of how to bring the United States into the conflict. It appears that they never really expected an uprising against Castro when the liberators landed as described in their memos to the White House. What they did expect was that the invaders would establish and secure a beachhead, announce the creation of a counterrevolutionary government and appeal for aid from the United States and the Organization of American States. The assumption was that President Kennedy, who had emphatically banned direct American involvement, would be forced by public opinion to come to the aid of the returning patriots.

"In effect," said Schorr, "President Kennedy was the target of a CIA covert operation that collapsed when the invasion collapsed."[76] Unlike any president before him, President Kennedy took responsibility for what had occurred. The American public forgave him, upsetting the well-established CIA protocol of manipulating presidents and political leaders. The president would then do what his predecessor should have done years earlier: He fired Allen Dulles and his chief lieutenant, Richard Bissell.

But getting rid of Allen Dulles didn't mean Dulles was gone. The entire upper echelon of the Agency, most of which had been recruited by Dulles, were loyal to him and would remain so. While Kennedy replaced Dulles with John McCone, a wealthy Catholic businessman, McCone was largely just a figurehead, intentionally left out of the loop, not aware of the more egregious

CIA covert operations being run by people like Richard Helms, who now occupied Richard Bissell's position at the head of the Directorate of Plans, and chief of counterintelligence Jim Angleton, both of whom would remain staunch, loyal Dulles followers. Allen Dulles would always be their boss, and they would consult him regularly after his formal departure.

The Bay of Pigs fiasco was a demarcation in the sand, an event that ultimately identified and determined the real forces that would work to undermine President Kennedy's objectives. These forces were not the Soviets, or their puppet Fidel Castro, or the so-called falling dominoes of alleged Communist takeovers. They were internal. Global American hegemony was predicated on financial and political control, even if Communism was one way underdeveloped nations sometimes developed themselves. Eventually, financial and economic control became paramount, once political control had been established. The Empire always struck back.

In addition to firing Allen Dulles, Richard Bissell, and Charles Cabell, the president made an attempt to immediately deal with the CIA and redefine its mandate by issuing two new National Security Action Memoranda (55 and 57) on June 28, 1961, whereby he stripped the CIA of its covert military operational capacity and put it back into the hands of the Pentagon and the Joint Chiefs of Staff—at least on paper.[77] Ultimately, the memoranda may not have changed anything, other than to incur the further wrath of CIA higher-ups. Kennedy then moved "quietly," according to historian Arthur Schlesinger Jr., "to cut the CIA budget in 1962 and again in 1963, aiming at a 20 percent reduction by 1966."[78]

So bold were these moves, according to L. Fletcher Prouty, they shocked the entire national security apparatus. It was the beginning of a "dead man walking" in the White House. Indeed, Allen Dulles, the man who extracted the final revenge—the man who Mary Meyer once compared to "Machiavelli, only worse"—inadvertently let it slip to a young editor many years later what he really thought: "That little Kennedy . . . he thought he was a god."[79] Little did Dulles understand his statement was just his own psychological projection. It was Dulles himself who, for nearly twenty years, "thought he was a god," as he and his CIA imperium pillaged the integrity of American democracy.

On July 20, 1961, during heightened tensions over Berlin, President Kennedy attended a National Security Council meeting. He listened attentively as the Joint Chiefs of Staff, including General Lyman Lemnitzer and Allen Dulles, who was still in charge at the CIA,[80] presented a plan for a first-strike, preemptive nuclear attack on the Soviet Union that would take place in late 1963, preceded by a well-orchestrated series of events designed to produce "heightened tensions" between the two superpowers. The scheme for "heightened tensions" was eventually codenamed "Operation Northwoods," and it had the written approval of all the Joint Chiefs of Staff in the Pentagon. According to author James Bamford, who first reported it in his bestselling book *Body of Secrets* (2002), "the plan called for innocent people to be shot on American streets; for boats carrying refugees fleeing Cuba to be sunk on the high seas; for a wave of violent terrorism to be launched in Washington, D.C., Miami, and elsewhere. People would be framed for bombings they did not commit; planes would be hijacked. Using phony evidence, all of it would be blamed on Castro, thus giving [General] Lemnitzer and his cabal [at the Pentagon] the excuse, as well as the public and international backing, they needed to launch their war."[81] Sound familiar? We need only to remember how President George W. Bush—under the direction of Dick Cheney and Donald Rumsfeld—took us into a war with Iraq under false pretenses.

Aghast at the above referenced NSC meeting in 1961, President Kennedy nonetheless respectfully asked, "Had there ever been an assessment of damage results to the U.S.S.R. which would be incurred by a preemptive attack?" and what would be "the period of time necessary for citizens to remain in shelters following an attack?" The president became so agitated that such a plan was even being considered that he directed "that no member in attendance at the meeting ever disclose even the subject of the meeting." Disgusted, he finally got up and walked out. As he made his way back from the cabinet room to the Oval Office with Secretary of State Dean Rusk at his side, he was said to have muttered, "And we call ourselves the human race."[82]

How much Jack shared with Mary about what he was up against in the early days of his presidency will probably never be known—unless perhaps Mary's real diary during the last few years of her life becomes available. Jack regarded Mary as completely trustworthy; increasingly, he sought out her counsel. Having had a life with Cord, Mary was already well acquainted with CIA skulduggery. Likely, she even knew a few things Jack didn't. Throughout his most critical moments during his presidency, Mary invariably found her way to his side, and always by invitation. No moment, however, was more critical than what occurred during the month of October 1962. Thirteen days would change everything, eventually inviting the highest of hopes, but not before a confrontation that portended nuclear annihilation.

Knowing Jack's penchant for sailing, Mary might have even mentioned her father Amos's warning to his brother Gifford in 1933: "Keep an anchor to windward in case of revolution," Amos had told his brother in a letter, referring to the Depression era that was taking a toll on American economic stability. Whether it was the fog of economic uncertainty, the fog of shady covert operations, or the fog of war itself, only a true nautical seafarer understood how quickly conditions at sea could change. A ready, unentangled anchor might well save the day, or at least until it looked as if the fog might be lifting—the appearance of which sometimes turned out to be a mirage.

10

Peace Song

An honorable human relationship, that is, one in which two people have the right to use the word "love"—is a process, delicate, violent, often terrifying to both persons involved, a process of redefining the truths they can tell each other.

It is important to do this because it breaks down human self-delusion and isolation.

It is important to do this because in so doing we do justice to our own complexity.

It is important to do this because we can count on so few people to go that hard way with us.

—Adrienne Rich

All wars are civil wars, because all men are brothers.
There is no "they." There is no "other." It is all one.

—Ram Dass
(formerly Harvard professor Richard Alpert)

You believe in redemption, don't you?

—President John F. Kennedy
May 1, 1962

SOMETIME ON MONDAY, October 22, 1962, Mary Meyer was invited to the White House for a small, impromptu dinner party that had been hastily organized by Jackie. The guest list included Jackie's sister, Lee Radziwill, friends

Benno and Nicole Graziani, and Jackie's dress designer, Oleg Cassini. Mary's escort for the evening was to be her friend and fellow artist William Walton, a longtime friend of both Jack and Bobby Kennedy who had already functioned as Mary's partner at previous White House social gatherings. For some unknown reason, however, Mary wasn't able to attend; Helen Chavchavadze took her place instead.[1] Why Mary had inexplicably canceled the engagement remained a mystery, but the fact that Jack had wanted her to be in close proximity that night was noteworthy.

Earlier that evening, before the dinner, Jack had addressed the nation on national television. Six days earlier, on October 16, he had seen detailed photographs from a clandestine U-2 reconnaissance flight that showed a secret offensive buildup of Soviet missile sites under construction on the island of Cuba. The escalating crisis had catapulted the National Security Council into days and nights of secret meetings; it would become known as the Cuban Missile Crisis. With no resolution in sight after six days, the president informed the public of the emerging crisis. "To halt this offensive buildup," President Kennedy said, "a strict quarantine on all offensive military equipment under shipment to Cuba is being initiated. All ships of any kind bound for Cuba from whatever nation or port will, if found to contain cargoes of offensive weapons, be turned back."[2]

Behind closed doors, the president and his most senior advisers sought peaceful ways to resolve the impasse, but the Joint Chiefs of Staff resisted them. So did the CIA. Both wanted to exploit the crisis to invade Cuba to get rid of Fidel Castro, even going so far as to plan a preemptive nuclear strike on the Soviet Union. Secretly, against the president's orders, the American military and the CIA would engage in a number of activities to undermine and sabotage the possibility of a negotiated settlement. President Kennedy and his advisers ordered a U.S. naval blockade of the entire island of Cuba. Its purpose was to deter any further weapons and supplies from reaching the missile sites under construction. The Cold War hard-liners, however, dismissed it as another "appeasement at Munich," wanting still to ignite a major conflagration. Finally, after nearly two weeks, masterful diplomatic pressure prevailed. The eventual removal of the Soviet missiles took place without having to bomb or invade Cuba.

In one sense, the Cuban Missile Crisis was a misnomer. It wasn't just another international political turf war between competing superpowers vying for control. The entire future of humanity itself was hanging in the balance for thirteen days; nuclear holocaust was on the horizon. It was, as author James

Douglass rightly tagged it, "the most dangerous moment in human history,"[3] as well as possibly the most dramatic event of the entire Cold War. Had it not been for some ingenious, secret back-channel communications and negotiations, the entire planet might well have become uninhabitable.

Crises, however dangerous, sometimes germinate opportunities. In spite of the horror it foreboded, the Cuban Missile Crisis and its ultimate resolution would initiate a major political shift for Kennedy's presidency. That Jack had wanted Mary in his presence on the evening he alerted the nation to the accelerating calamity suggests a reliance on her counsel. It wasn't the first time, nor would it be the last. Mary's longtime commitment to world peace, coupled with Jack's broadening insight that peace, not armed conflict, was the right path forward, inevitably made her an important asset. After the Cuban Missile Crisis, the president's evolving political trajectory would increasingly isolate him from his own National Security apparatus.

The crisis had caught Jack off guard. While the Joint Chiefs and CIA pursued a more bellicose strategy vis-à-vis Cuba and the Soviet Union, Kennedy and his Soviet counterpart, Nikita Khrushchev, had been engaged in a secret correspondence that had begun several months after their June 1961 Vienna summit. Khrushchev had initiated the letter exchange.[4] Georgi Bolshakov, a trusted Khrushchev aide and KGB agent who often posed as a magazine editor for cover purposes, delivered the first letter—a twenty-six-page missive hidden in a newspaper—to Kennedy's press secretary, Pierre Salinger, in a New York City hotel room in September 1961. The letter invited a deeper understanding between the two leaders and their countries. At Vienna, Khrushchev had sounded a decidedly different note, touting nuclear war as an option to which he would turn if necessary. In reality, the Soviet leader was exploiting Kennedy's embarrassment and weakened position since the failed Bay of Pigs invasion. Khrushchev later admitted that in the run-up to the Vienna summit, Soviet hard-liners had pushed him to grandstand. But in his first secret letter to Kennedy, Khrushchev struck a tone of conciliation: "I have given much thought of late to the development of international events since our meeting in Vienna, and I have decided to approach you with this letter. The whole world hopefully expected that our meeting and a frank exchange of views would have a soothing effect, would turn relations between our countries into the correct channel and promote the adoption of decisions which could give the peoples confidence that at last peace on earth will be secured. To my regret—and, I believe, to yours—this did not happen."

The Soviet premier compared the state of Cold War tensions with "Noah's Ark where both the 'clean' and the 'unclean' found sanctuary. But regardless of who lists himself with the 'clean' and who is considered to be 'unclean,' they are all equally interested in one thing and that is that the Ark should success-fully continue its cruise. And we have no other alternative: either we should live in peace and cooperation so that the Ark maintains its buoyancy, or else it sinks. Therefore we must display concern for all of mankind, not to mention our own advantages, and find every possibility leading to peaceful solutions of problems."[5]

Khrushchev's approach disarmed Jack, who responded two weeks later: "I am gratified by your letter and your decision to suggest this additional means of communication. Certainly you are correct in emphasizing that this corre-spondence must be kept wholly private, not be hinted at in public statements, much less disclosed to the press. . . . I think it is very important that these let-ters provide us with an opportunity for a personal, informal but meaningful exchange of views."[6]

Since the very beginning of the letter exchange, a full year before the Cuban Missile Crisis, Kennedy and Khrushchev had been building mutual trust. Both leaders were adamant about their commitment to peaceful coexist-ence. Whether Jack told Mary about the secret correspondence with Khrush-chev wasn't known, but it may have been why Mary had been so outspoken and confrontational with Jack when he decided to resume nuclear atmospheric testing in April 1962.[7] Why undo the progress that was being made, she would have argued. Mutual goodwill and hopeful intentions, however, proved no match for the progression of real-world events for both men. For his part, Khrushchev felt betrayed when he learned of the U.S. military's aggressive planning and lobbying throughout the spring of 1962 for a second invasion of Cuba, this time by overwhelming U.S. forces. At the Vienna summit in June 1961, Khrushchev had told the president that he was "very grieved by the fact" that an attack on Cuba at the Bay of Pigs had taken place. Jack had admitted to the Soviet premier that it had been "a mistake."

"I respected that explanation," Khrushchev wrote in another secret commu-nication to Kennedy dated October 26, 1962, toward the end of the Cuban Mis-sile Crisis. "You repeated it to me several times, pointing out that not everybody occupying a high position would acknowledge his mistakes as you had done. I value such frankness. For my part, I told you that we too possess no less courage; we also acknowledged those mistakes which had been committed during the his-tory of our state, and not only acknowledged, but sharply condemned them."[8]

The next day, October 27, 1962, Khrushchev wrote: "But how are we, the Soviet Union, our Government, to assess your actions, which are expressed in the fact that you have surrounded the Soviet Union with military bases; surrounded our allies with military bases; placed military bases literally around our country; and stationed your missile armaments there? This is no secret. Responsible American personages openly declare that it is so. Your missiles are located in Britain, are located in Italy, and are aimed against us. Your missiles are located in Turkey." In closing, Khrushchev pointed out:

> You are disturbed over Cuba. You say that this disturbs you because it is 90 miles by sea from the coast of the United States of America. But Turkey adjoins us; our sentries patrol back and forth and see each other. Do you consider, then, that you have the right to demand security for your own country and the removal of the weapons you call offensive, but do not accord the same right to us? You have placed destructive missile weapons, which you call offensive, in Turkey, literally next to us. How then can recognition of our equal military capacities be reconciled with such unequal relations between our great states? This is irreconcilable.[9]

President Kennedy didn't want to start a war over Cuba, but as Bobby Kennedy told Soviet ambassador Anatoly Dobrynin in a private meeting toward the end of the crisis, "If the situation continues much longer, the President is not sure that the military will not overthrow him and seize power."[10] The Pentagon, led by the bellicose U.S. Air Force Chief of Staff, General Curtis "Bombs Away" LeMay, had pushed aggressively during the first days of the crisis for an immediate surprise-bombing campaign against the Soviet missile sites in Cuba, during the period when the CIA estimated the medium-range nuclear-tipped missiles were not yet operational. This was later followed, within a matter of days, by Pentagon recommendations that a full-scale U.S. invasion follow the air strikes.

What their intelligence had not revealed, however, was that the Russians had more than forty thousand troops in Cuba who were prepared to fight an American invasion. They were armed not only with strategic missiles (the medium ICBM range missiles and their mobile launchers) discovered by the American U-2 photography, but in addition—and completely unknown to the American military and CIA at the time—ninety-eight (98) tactical, or low-yield, nuclear warheads (along with the appropriate short-range missiles and jet bombers to deliver them), which had been placed in Cuba with the specific intent of being actively used to oppose any U.S. invasion of the island.[11] Said former Defense Secretary Robert McNamara in an interview in 1998: "We didn't learn until nearly 30 years later, that the Soviets had roughly 162 nuclear warheads on this isle of Cuba, at a time when our CIA said they believed there were none. And included in the 162 were some 90 tactical warheads to be used against a US invasion force. Had we . . . attacked Cuba and invaded Cuba at the time, we almost surely would have been involved in nuclear war. And when I say "we," I mean you—it would not have been the U.S. alone. It would have endangered the security of the West, without any question."[12]

During the crisis, both the U.S. military and the CIA were secretly operating unilaterally, doing whatever they could to intensify tensions that would ignite a war. On October 28, the Air Force launched an unarmed intercontinental ballistic missile from Vandenberg Air Force Base in California, destined for the Marshall Islands in the Pacific. The ICBM test further exacerbated tensions with the Soviet Union. That the president had not ordered the test further aggravated tensions with his own military. At the same time, Strategic Air Command bombers were flying toward the Soviet Union and going past their established "turn around points," giving the impression that the United States was commencing a preemptive strike.[13] In addition, General Thomas Power, head of the Strategic Air Command (and LeMay's handpicked successor in that role), placed America's nuclear bomber force at DEFCON-2, one step away from nuclear war, by transmitting two such orders, one a voice command and one a telegram, *in the clear, unencrypted*, without President Kennedy's knowledge or permission.[14] This open-threat display was intended to provoke the USSR into responses that would justify a preemptive nuclear first strike by the United States. Also in the midst of this, the CIA was operating independently, in contravention of the president's order. Under the command of the CIA's William K. Harvey, three commando teams of sixty men each were sent into Cuba to destabilize the country in preparation for an invasion. The Agency continued these operations in spite of Kennedy's order that such destabilization efforts immediately cease and desist.

Eventually, the cooler heads of the two leaders prevailed: Khrushchev agreed to remove the missiles from Cuba, and Kennedy agreed that the United States would not invade the island. Secretly, Kennedy also promised the removal of U.S. missiles in Turkey. The American military establishment was furious with the negotiated compromise, while Kennedy's opinion of the American military establishment hit an all-time low.

The day after the Cuban Missile Crisis ended on October 28, 1962, Kennedy told senior White House adviser Arthur Schlesinger Jr., "The military are mad. They wanted to do this."[15] Two weeks later, the president told Schlesinger, "The first advice I'm going to give my successor is to watch the generals and to avoid feeling that just because they were military men their opinions on military matters were worth a damn."[16] There were no winners or losers in this crisis. "The only victory was avoiding war. For that reason alone," noted author James Douglass, "Kennedy believed, there must never be another missile crisis, for it would only repeat pressures for terrible choices that had very nearly resulted in total war."[17]

In the aftermath of the missile crisis, Mary was officially invited to two White House dinner parties on successive evenings (November 8 and 9). She and Jack may also have spent some time alone, though it's not known whether they would have done so at Joe Alsop's house or Mary's. However, "the most dangerous moment in human history" had taken a huge toll on Jack's health. With increased infusions of cortisone to combat his stress during the crisis, many of his gastrointestinal symptoms reappeared and became more acute, as did his recurrent back pains. He also became noticeably depressed. Carrying the weight of the world and future of humanity for thirteen days would have easily crushed anyone. Yet, terrible as it had been, an opportunity was lurking on the horizon, something that both he and his counterpart, Nikita Khrushchev, would soon realize.

But in the shadows, evil was very much alive, stalking not only the republic, but the president. Not only were the Joint Chiefs of Staff enraged that Cuba had not been attacked, they were also indignant that Kennedy had made concessions to Khrushchev. The Bay of Pigs fiasco in 1961 had already humiliated the military-intelligence establishment. The resolution of the Cuban Missile Crisis in October 1962 was yet another cold shower of shame, devoid of American machismo.

Before its end, 1963 would become a defining year for America, and would be forever remembered for one earthshaking moment whose repercussions would be felt throughout the world. The year began with an unobtrusive tiny earthquake of sorts, not even noticeable except to a handful of insider journalists who at the time honored a "gentlemen's agreement" not to reveal presidential indiscretions. And so, in January of that year, what seemed at first an insignificant event turned out to foreshadow an invisible tsunami, slowly making its way toward destruction. The augury would involve *Washington Post* publisher and owner Philip L. Graham.

During World War II, Philip L. Graham had trained as an Army intelligence officer. His acumen quickly elevated him to a position close to General Douglas MacArthur in the Pacific theater. There, Phil Graham made connections that would assist him for the rest of his life, including entrée with all of the CIA's seminal, well-to-do operatives—people like Allen Dulles, Frank Wisner, Richard Helms, Cord Meyer, and Desmond FitzGerald. Being of the same social class, Philip and his wife, Katharine, were accustomed to mingling with CIA heavyweights in Washington, often gathering on Sunday afternoons for an extended cocktail hour before a legendary potluck supper salon. With his marriage to Katharine Meyer in 1940, Philip L. Graham had become a member of the wealthy Agnes and Eugene Meyer family (no relation to Cord Meyer). The family's crown jewel was the *Washington Post*. Eugene Meyer had nursed the floundering newspaper ever since he bought it at auction in 1933. In 1946, he made his thirty-year-old son-in-law, Philip, its editor in chief and owner. Having earned some of the highest grades ever given at Harvard, Phil was certifiably brilliant, but also certifiably manic-depressive. Beginning in 1952, the editor in chief of the *Washington Post* was in and out of psychiatric institutions and intermittently mentally unstable.[18]

During the 1950s, the CIA initiated Operation Mockingbird, a project designed, the reader will recall, to influence the American media to slant news stories favoring the CIA's agenda or point of view, particularly those having to do with international events and foreign policy. The program had been started by Allen Dulles's top lieutenant Frank Wisner, a friend of Phil Graham's and at one time Cord Meyer's boss.[19] Wisner successfully "recruited" a number of prominent journalists to the CIA, including his friend Phil Graham, who soon helped run Mockingbird within mainstream media outlets. Using newspapers, magazines, radio and television, even Hollywood, the CIA's disinformation spin machine went to work shaping public opinion and perceptions, undermining the integrity and independence of an indispensable pillar of the democratic process.[20]

In addition, by late 1962, President Kennedy had appointed Phil Graham head of COMSAT, the new organization that operated America's communication satellites. The position allowed Graham to access certain classified operations, including the CIA's secret satellite surveillance system—the CORONA program—which provided aerial reconnaissance of the Soviet Union, China, most of Southeast Asia, and the Middle East.

By 1962, Philip and Katharine Graham's marriage had come apart and was in freefall. Estranged from Katharine, drinking heavily amid manic-depressive episodes, Phil and his new mistress, *Newsweek* reporter Robin Webb, were living together and hosting dinner parties for Washington's social elite. Phil Graham and President Kennedy were also friends. According to some accounts, they had been known to philander together as a team. "The pair of them were sleeping around with the same people," said Jean Friendly, wife of *Post* editor Al Friendly. Eventually, both Phil and Katharine Graham became aware of President Kennedy's affair with Mary Meyer.[21]

In mid-January 1963, Phil and Robin Webb flew to Phoenix on the *Post*'s chartered jet. During one intoxicated evening, Graham intruded on dinner at the midwinter meeting of the Associated Press board of directors at the Arizona Biltmore Hotel. Phil proceeded to ask if he could address the audience, at which point he became unhinged. According to David Halberstam's 1975 account, Graham addressed his audience as "fat bastards" who were "afraid of the truth," that he "wouldn't wipe his ass with any of their papers."[22] *Newsweek* foreign correspondent Arnaud de Borchgrave, a witness, said the crowd became "thunderstruck" with disbelief as Graham "singled out various publishers and began to revile them." Mr. de Borchgrave told author Carol Felsenthal that Graham's "around the bend" but "brilliant" performance consisted of caricaturing all of the important media people present—including Otis Chandler of the *Los Angeles Times*, Ben McKelway of the *Washington Star*, and others, finally accusing them all of "having no balls."[23]

But it was author Deborah Davis who, in 1979, based on her interviews with James Truitt, first claimed that Graham had told the crowd, many of whom knew him, that he was going to reveal exactly who was sleeping with whom in Washington, beginning with President Kennedy. It was at this moment that Graham revealed that the president's "favorite was now Mary Meyer, who had been married to CIA official Cord Meyer and was the sister of Ben Bradlee's wife, Tony."[24] Davis then claimed that someone at the dinner who witnessed Graham's outburst called President Kennedy at the White House to alert him. This information allegedly came from James Truitt, who was at Katharine Graham's house when a call came in for her, allegedly from President Kennedy himself. Katharine at that very moment was meeting with *Post* executives at her home. They began strategizing how to bring Phil back "forcibly" and commit him to a psychiatric hospital. According to Truitt's statements to Davis, he himself apparently got on the phone with Kennedy and asked him to send Phil's doctor, Dr. Leslie Farber, to Phoenix on a military jet.[25]

Over the years, there has been some controversy as to whether Phil Graham's "meltdown" that January had actually included his blurting out the fact of Mary and Jack's affair. Neither Bernard Ridder of the *St. Paul Pioneer Press* nor *Los Angeles Times* publisher Otis Chandler, both of whom were present that evening, remembered any such utterances about Mary Meyer by Graham.[26] William Shover, a young reporter at the time for the *Arizona Republic-Phoenix Gazette*, who was also present that evening, did confirm years later that Phil was present at the event, and that he was drunk. "Phil was in the audience and asked if he could speak," recalled Shover. "He walked up and took the microphone." Though Shover didn't remember any specific details, he did recall that "Phil became very emotional, overwhelmed with what he was saying, broke down, and started crying." Shover also remembered Phil had been on a tirade against many members of the press that evening, but could not recall him talking about President Kennedy or Mary Meyer. He reiterated that position in an interview for this book in 2009.[27]

Ben Bradlee, who was not present at the Phoenix episode, has always maintained he never heard anything about Phil Graham mentioning the affair between Mary and Jack during the incident, and was adamant that if it had occurred, he and Tony would have come to know about it.[28] Anne Truitt also went on record, saying, "James [Truitt] would have told me if Phil had mentioned Mary. It would have worried him terribly."[29] Anne assumed, of course, that Jim was confiding to her all that he knew, and that may not have been the case. The exact story of the event has remained unclear. Unfortunately, Katharine Graham's own secondhand account of the event in her 1998 book *Personal History* was superficial and misleading. "No one present that night has ever told me exactly what happened or what Phil said," Katharine insisted.[30]

The most intriguing investigation of this event, however, came from Carol Felsenthal in 1993 with the publication of her unauthorized biography of Katharine Graham, entitled *Power, Privilege and the Post*. Again, the Washington "grand duchess" attempted for a second time what she had done to the Deborah Davis book: She and her "pit bull entourage" tried to stop the Felsenthal publication. Felsenthal recalled "receiving pages of complaints from Kay's lawyers," hoping their intimidation might thwart her efforts to publish. It didn't. They knew she was going to fight it, and so they eventually just disappeared.[31]

Not wanting to fall into the same pit as Deborah Davis, Carol Felsenthal made sure that her book was not only thoroughly and meticulously researched, but completely scrutinized as well. "Because of what happened with the Deborah Davis book," said Felsenthal, "this book was vetted and re-vetted. I would have never been able to get away with something that wasn't thoroughly checked."[32] In 1993, her book was also serialized in *Vanity Fair*, known for its rigorous fact checking.

Included in the book was Phil Graham's reference to Mary Meyer and President Kennedy that evening: "Phil announced that he was going to tell them who in Washington was sleeping with whom, and that he might as well start at the top with John Kennedy, who was sleeping in the White House with Mary Meyer. While his audience waited for the next name to drop, he declared, 'I don't know what you other sons of bitches are going to do, but I'm going home now and screw my girl.'"[33] Based on in-depth interviews with both Jean Friendly (who was not only one of Kay Graham's closest friends, but also the wife of the *Post*'s managing editor, Al Friendly) and insider Elizabeth Frank, Felsenthal never received any request for a retraction of this statement, nor was she ever told that her account was inaccurate. In addition, according to Felsenthal, Ben Bradlee read her book and told a journalism class at USC that "he had read every entry [in the book] and he thought it was fair."[34]

What was never disputed, however, was the fact that Phil Graham had been forcibly sedated, taken by ambulance to the airport, and flown back to Washington from Phoenix on the day following his outburst. Why was this so necessary? Equally mysterious, the following day, January 18, Phil's mistress, Robin Webb, called the White House at 6:18 P.M. EST from Phoenix and asked to speak with the president.[35] Whether she spoke to him wasn't clear, but what was the purpose of her call?

Upon his return to Washington, Phil Graham wanted to be placed, according to the Deborah Davis account, at the George Washington University Hospital.[36] Perhaps lucid enough to realize he might have been able to leave a university hospital more easily than a private psychiatric hospital, Phil may have become aware that Katharine had obtained a court order committing him to Chestnut Lodge. As early as 1952, Chestnut Lodge, a private psychiatric sanitarium, along with Sheppard Pratt in Baltimore, were regularly used undercover by the CIA. The Agency needed psychiatric facilities to deal with "indiscreet" employees—operatives who possessed or had access to high-level classified information, who were either "cracking up" or otherwise not conforming to established security protocols. According to one former CIA official, "Throughout the 1950s, Agency employees in need of psychiatric care, that I was aware of, either went to Chestnut Lodge or Sheppard Pratt Hospital in Baltimore."[37]

Phil remained at Chestnut Lodge for approximately two weeks under the care of Dr. Leslie Farber and Dr. John Cameron. He finally convinced them to release him, whereupon he visited Katharine for one day, then flew to New York with his lawyer, Edward Bennett Williams. There, he plotted to wrest complete control of the *Washington Post* away from Katharine, changing his will at least twice over a period of several months, giving Robin Webb a controlling interest in his estate.[38] All through the winter and spring of 1963, Katharine was both devastated and humiliated by the entire course of events, but determined to prevent the *Post* from falling into Phil's control and ownership, even if it meant she had to have Phil declared insane.[39]

Phil Graham's Phoenix outburst in January was further destabilizing. Contemplation of such a diabolical deed as the overthrow of an American president would need the kind of trustworthy tentacles that could stretch deep into the grinding wheels of media establishments. Around town, word had gone out: Phil Graham could no longer be trusted.[40]

Eleven days after the incident in Phoenix on January 28, Mary Meyer signed into the White House residence using her own name. Jackie, who was away at her rented hideaway, Glen Ora, decorating the family's new Wexford estate, had become aware of the affair. According to Kennedy aide Godfrey McHugh, "Jackie knew about his [Jack's] women." She had, in fact, asked McHugh, a man she had once dated, to tell her about her husband's women.[41] Bill Walton, the closest to Jack, Bobby, and Jackie, uncharacteristically let it slip to author Ralph Martin: "You know, in the end, Jackie knew everything. Every girl. She knew her rating, her accomplishments."[42] But Mary wasn't just another dalliance for Jack, and Jackie knew it. By 1963, Mary had become a fixture in the president's life, as close a confidante as he was capable of having.

On March 8, 1963, the Kennedys hosted their sixth and, as fate would have it, last White House dinner dance. Mary attended on the arm of Blair Clark, an old friend of Jack's from Harvard. "I brought Mary to one of the White House parties," Clark recalled in 1983, and "she simply disappeared for a half hour. Finally I went looking for her. She had been upstairs with Jack and then had gone walking out in the snow. So there I was, 'the beard' for Mary Meyer."[43] The bottom of Mary's dress was muddy and wet, indicating that she had been walking outside. She later told her friend Anne Truitt that she had become "unhappy" and taken a walk. Upon returning, she couldn't find Blair Clark, and so, according to Sally Bedell Smith, "Bobby Kennedy called a White House limousine, put her in the back and sent her home."[44]

During the evening of the final dinner dance, Jackie told her dinner partner, Adlai Stevenson, "I don't care how many girls [Jack sleeps with] as long as I know he knows it's wrong, and I think he does now. Anyway that's all over for the present."[45] A beleaguered, increasingly desperate Jackie, trying to save face, told Stevenson she and her sister had "always talked about divorce as practically something to look forward to." Then she told him, "I first loved you" when she had met Stevenson in Illinois shortly after she and Jack were married.[46]

By March, Jackie had not yet announced publicly she was pregnant, but it appeared she had given Jack an ultimatum, just prior to that evening. Had Jack attempted to end the affair with Mary that evening, or had the two staged the contretemps to appear that way? Whether their split that night was real or not, the separation didn't last long, at least officially. On May 29, Mary would attend the president's forty-sixth birthday party on the presidential yacht *Sequoia*.

In April 1963, President Kennedy's future trip to Dallas, Texas, was discussed privately between himself, Vice President Johnson, and his chief aide, Kenny O'Donnell. On April 23, Johnson announced plans for Kennedy's trip to Dallas during a luncheon speech to Texas newspaper and radio station executives. The next day, the *Dallas Times Herald* wrote about the announcement.[47]

During the Easter weekend of April 13–14, special White House aide Joseph W. Shimon enjoyed the company of his daughter, Toni, who lived on Long Island with her mother. Shimon had worked in the White House at the highest levels. In 1963, he was assigned officially as a "Washington Police Inspector," though he was also secretly working for the Justice Department and was a liaison to the CIA, having risen up through the ranks through the Metropolitan Police Department beginning in the early 1930s. Shimon had established a reputation for discretion in service to various presidents. He had won the confidence not only of President Franklin Roosevelt, but his successors as well. President Kennedy consulted Shimon regularly. The two were known to have taken numerous walks together on the White House grounds.[48]

Shimon had one child, a college-age daughter named Toni, with whom he was extremely close in spite of being divorced from her mother. During the 1963 Easter weekend, Shimon and his daughter Toni were walking near Shimon's North Stafford Street home in Arlington, Virginia, when he revealed something to his daughter that would come back to haunt her. As they strolled together, Toni began to feel a sense of foreboding, suspecting she would soon be missing her father's company once again. Something else was coming, however, something she couldn't foresee.

"You're on the outside and I'm going to hit you with something," Shimon told his daughter. "Tell me right off the top of your head what you think."

"Okay," she said, not expecting to hear what followed.

"The vice president [Lyndon Johnson] has asked me to give him more security than the president," said Shimon. As they continued walking, Toni's mood began to darken. There was something ominous in her father's voice, she remembered feeling.

"What's he afraid of, Dad?" she asked her father.

"What do you think?" Her father responded, wanting to see if she understood and connected the dots. There was an awkward silence. She knew she was being tested. Toni would remember that moment and the darkness that had come over her that day.

"Something's coming down, Dad," she said. "Does President Kennedy know about this?"

"I haven't mentioned it," she remembered her father telling her.

"What do you think?" her father asked again.

"Something's going to happen and Johnson knows about it," Toni immediately responded.

"Good girl!" said Shimon, proud of his tutelage of his only child.[49]

Later that spring, Mary returned to Boston for her third visit with Timothy Leary. Without mentioning any names, she reportedly alluded to Phil Graham's outburst in Arizona earlier that year. "Oh God, where to begin," Leary recalled her saying. "There's a tremendous power struggle going in Washington. A friend of mine was losing the battle, a really bloody one. He got drunk and told a room of reporters about me and my boyfriend.[50]

"It's really scary," Mary continued. "You wouldn't believe how well-connected some of these people are, and nobody picked it up."[51] Mary was alluding to the fact that Graham's Phoenix outburst had not appeared in any newspaper or media outlet. She urged Leary to keep a lower profile with his psychedelic research. They also discussed the state of world affairs, with Mary telling him, "America doesn't have to be run by these cold-war guys. They're crazy, they are. They don't listen. They don't learn. They're completely caught up in planning World War III. They can't enjoy anything but power and control."[52] Her comments to Leary suggested that Jack might have told her about the July 1961 National Security Council (NSC) meeting in which the Pentagon and the CIA seriously considered a preemptive nuclear attack on the Soviets in late 1963.

Leary invited Mary to Mexico for further training in leading psychedelic sessions. She declined and offered a warning: "If you stir up too many waves, they'll shut you down. Or worse." She no longer trusted the phones or the mail, she told him, but said she would find a way to stay in touch. "And do be careful," she underscored.[53]

On the sixth of May, 1963, the Harvard Corporation voted to fire Timothy Leary, not for giving hallucinogens to students, but for failing to show up and teach some of his classes that spring. Leary received the news while in Mexico. He appeared to be relieved. His former Harvard boss, Professor David McClelland, the man who originally brought Leary to the university in 1959, thought he had become psychotic; his biographer thought he'd never been happier.[54] Five years later, Leary reflected on his firing from Harvard:

> I was never able to commit myself to the game of Harvard or even to the game of rehabilitation. Not even to the game of proselytizing for LSD itself. Nothing that doesn't ring true to my ancient cell wisdom and to that central vibration beam within can hold my attention for very long. From the date of this session it was inevitable that we would leave Harvard, that we would leave American society, and that we would spend the rest of our lives as mutants, faithfully following the instructions of our internal blueprints, and tenderly, gently disregarding the parochial social insanities.[55]

While in residence that May just north of Acapulco, Leary lamented: "One thing that didn't happen was a visit from Mary Pinchot. I received a short cryptic note, postmarked Washington, D.C., typed and unsigned." The note read:

> PROGRAM GOING VERY WELL HERE. EXTREMELY WELL!!!
> HOWEVER, I WON'T BE JOINING YOU. TOO MUCH PUBLICITY.
> YOUR SUMMER CAMP IS IN SERIOUS JEOPARDY.
> I'LL CONTACT YOU AFTER YOU RETURN TO USA.[56]

The note, in all probability, was from Mary, but what did it mean? According to author Leo Damore, it was corroborating evidence of a "mild LSD trip" that Mary and Jack had shared at Joe Alsop's home in Georgetown in May 1963. Sometime after Damore's November 1990 interview with Timothy Leary, it appeared that Damore learned of this event. When I met with Damore in April 1993, he confided that the same confidential source who had told him about Mary and Jack's rendezvous in Provincetown, Massachusetts, during the summer of 1959 had later also confided that Mary and Jack had, in fact, taken a "mild LSD trip" together several weeks before Jack's commencement address at American University, and before his forty-sixth birthday party on May 29. Despite my repeated inquiry about the identity of the source, however, Damore would never reveal it.[57]

As to the note's authenticity, it appeared to be legitimate: Timothy Leary was well known to be an obsessive pack rat who never threw away anything. According to his biographer, Robert Greenfield, Leary's hoarding of his papers, letters, any kind of communication whatsoever, was legendary. "Throughout his life, Tim saved every scrap of paper that had ever crossed his desk," said Greenfield. "The archive he had assembled was second to none. The sheer volume of the 465 boxes holding his papers was so overwhelming that at his death, they entirely filled a large two-bedroom apartment in the San Fernando Valley."[58]

During what would turn out to be the last five months of his life, President Kennedy would further define himself and his presidency. His newfound political trajectory would eventually distance him from Cold War ideology and move him closer to setting the stage for world peace. For years, Kennedy had been quietly nurturing the notion of disarmament. The Cuba debacles had awakened and emboldened the president. Twice burned by both the military and the CIA, Kennedy's independence became clear. After the Cuban Missile Crisis and for the remainder of his presidency, he sought not only to avoid military and intelligence oversight, but also to evade their scrutiny as well. He was determined to forge a path toward setting the world stage for peace.

Yet despite ongoing secret negotiations with Prime Minister Harold Macmillan of Great Britain and Khrushchev in the early part of 1963, President Kennedy seemed pessimistic about the possibility of a nuclear arms treaty. At his news conference on March 21, when asked about the possibility of a test-ban agreement, he replied, "Well, my hopes are dimmed, but nevertheless I still hope." On May 20, just three weeks before his historic, unprecedented commencement address at American University on June 10, he was quoted as saying, "No, I'm not hopeful, I'm not hopeful. . . . We have tried to get an agreement [with the Soviets] on all the rest of it and then to the question of the number of inspections, but we were unable to get that. So I would say, I'm not hopeful at all."[59]

Whatever transpired during the latter half of May remains unknown, but something somewhere seems to have made a significant impact. No other presidential address in history would provoke such a remarkable impact on world opinion—or stir the latent hope of mankind—as did President Kennedy's American University commencement address on June 10, 1963. Kennedy wanted the entire world to *believe* in the possibility of peace. As Secretary of State Dean Rusk noted after the speech, "The speech was remarkable, I feel, because it had so much of President Kennedy personally in it. . . And because it reflected his total commitment to peace."

If some part of his transformation was catalyzed by a horizon-altering psychedelic excursion with Mary Meyer, then so be it. He wouldn't have been the first iconic figure in human history to partake, nor would he be the last. Stepping out of the proverbial box of normal perception— surrendering to what Timothy Leary once referred to as the "niagara of sensory input"—has, in fact, changed the course of events and perspectives for many respected notables. Dr. Francis Crick, the Nobel laureate and progenitor of modern genetics, reportedly was under the influence of LSD when he first deciphered the double-helix structure of DNA sixty years ago. Before his death in 2004, he told a colleague that he had often used small doses of LSD to boost his powers of thought. It was reported that "it was LSD, not Eagle's warm beer, that helped him to unravel the structure of DNA, the discovery that won him the Nobel Prize."[60]

Bill Wilson, founder of Alcoholics Anonymous, was first introduced to LSD in 1956 by psychedelic pioneer Aldous Huxley, author of *Brave New World* and *The Doors of Perception*. He emerged completely enthusiastic about the experience, believing that the drug was a kind of "miracle substance" that had the potential to facilitate a deeper spiritual connection with life—something he was convinced was missing for people who struggled with alcohol addiction. Enthralled by his own realizations, Wilson continued his own exploration of LSD well into the 1960s, at one point considering "a plan to have LSD distributed at all A. A. meetings nationwide."[61]

The late Steve Jobs, a Reed College dropout and the founder of Apple Computer (now Apple, Inc.), became a veritable New Age Thomas Edison— possibly one of the greatest technological inventors and entrepreneurs the world has ever witnessed. He once told author John Markoff that he "believed that taking LSD was one of the two or three most important things he had ever done in his life," and that people who had never taken psychedelics would never be able to fully understand him.[62]

In a televised interview with political commentator and comedian Bill Maher in 2009, acclaimed film director Oliver Stone said of psychedelics: "I wouldn't be here if it hadn't been for it. I grew a lot. It opened my mind." Stone later added, "Those people who stayed human in the platoons [in Vietnam], in the combat platoons I saw, were doing grass [smoking marijuana]. It kept them human throughout a very deadening process."[63]

No longer regarded as just a passing fad of the 1960s counterculture, the long-awaited resurgence in psychedelic research has finally resumed. Since 2008, at Johns Hopkins, Harvard, and UCLA, U.S.-government-sponsored studies with the hallucinogen psilocybin have repeatedly demonstrated that subjects who volunteered for this opportunity came to regard their experience as one of the most meaningful, spiritually significant events in their lives. The experience of ordinary people in this kind of research has resembled those recorded in the annals of mystical traditions. Dr. Roland Griffiths at Johns Hopkins now entertains the idea that the human brain may, in fact, be "hardwired" to undergo these kinds of "unitive" experiences.[64]

Whatever curiosity might have propelled Jack Kennedy to partake of a "mild" psychedelic excursion, beyond Mary Meyer's example, will probably never be revealed, unless Mary's diary turns up. In any case, even a minimal dose of a psychedelic like LSD or psilocybin could have chemically catalyzed the opening of Jack's "hard-wired" capacity for a "unitive" state of consciousness. It would have further set into motion the insights already taking hold in the president for an entirely new political trajectory, away from the Cold War.

The president wrote his American University address with a small cadre of trusted aides who worked hard to keep its contents from the Cold War national security establishment.[65] The powerful speech marked an abrupt departure from Cold War bluster and announced a new era of global cooperation and coexistence. Ascending the dais at 10:30 that morning, the president said, "I have, therefore, chosen this time and place to discuss a topic on which ignorance too often abounds and the truth is too rarely perceived—yet it is the most important topic on earth: world peace."[66]

The press immediately dubbed it Kennedy's "peace speech," and two days later, the *New York Times* gave it only a tepid response: "Generally there was not much optimism in official Washington that the President's conciliation address at American University would produce agreement on a test ban treaty or anything else," wrote reporter Max Frankel.[67] This, despite the fact that the speech was perhaps the most visionary, spiritual clarion call of awakening ever put forth across the divide of all nation-states, and mankind.

First, as Kennedy outlined the new direction his administration would undertake, he invited all Americans to examine what the advent of a genuine peace would mean for them: "What kind of peace do I mean? What kind of peace do we seek? Not a Pax Americana enforced on the world by American weapons of war. Not the peace of the grave or the security of the slave. I am talking about genuine peace, the kind of peace that makes life on earth worth living, the kind that enables men and nations to grow and to hope and to build a better life for their children—not merely peace for Americans but peace for all men and women—not merely peace in our time but peace for all time."[68] An American president was holding the entire world in his arms. His emerging vision of peace for the planet was no less important than his vision of peace for his country, for in the "unitive" state of consciousness, we are all one.

Unwilling to let his own countrymen off the hook, the president then challenged the notion that if only the Soviets would "adopt a more enlightened attitude," there would be peace. World peace, Kennedy exhorted, was everyone's responsibility: "I also believe we must examine our own attitude—as individuals and as a nation—for our attitude is as essential as theirs." Historian Arthur Schlesinger Jr. would later assess the remark as "a sentence capable of revolutionizing the whole American view of the Cold War."[69] Kennedy's first invitation urged all Americans to reframe their thinking:

> First: Let us examine our attitude toward peace itself. Too many of us think it is impossible. Too many think it unreal. But that is a dangerous, defeatist belief. It leads to the conclusion that war is inevitable—that mankind is doomed—that we are gripped by forces we cannot control. We need not accept that view. Our problems are manmade—therefore, they can be solved by man. And man can be as big as he wants. No problem of human destiny is beyond human beings. Man's reason and spirit have often solved the seemingly unsolvable—and we believe they can do it again.[70]

The evolution of humanity toward world peace would require, the president underscored, a "gradual evolution in human institutions." He would go on to say:

Genuine peace must be the product of many nations, the sum of many acts. It must be dynamic, not static, changing to meet the challenge of each new generation. For peace is a process—a way of solving problems. . . . Peace need not be impracticable, and war need not be inevitable. By defining our goal more clearly, by making it seem more manageable and less remote, we can help all peoples to see it, to draw hope from it, and to move irresistibly toward it.[71]

Encouraging all Americans to "reexamine our attitude towards the Soviet Union," this dramatic oration was as much for the Russian people as it was for America. Kennedy accepted his share of responsibility (much of it manufactured by the CIA) for the destructive Cold War mentality that had so far prevailed, saying, "We are both caught up in a vicious cycle in which suspicion on one side breeds suspicion on the other, and new weapons beget counter-weapons."

Today, should total war ever break out again—no matter how—our two countries would become the primary targets. It is an ironic but accurate fact that the two strongest powers are the two in the most danger of devastation. All we have built, all we have worked for, would be destroyed in the first 24 hours.[72]

President Kennedy then reminded his audience of the following:

Among the many traits the peoples of our two countries have in common, none is stronger than our mutual abhorrence of war. Almost unique, among the major world powers, we have never been at war with each other. And no nation in the history of battle ever suffered more than the Soviet Union suffered in the course of the Second World War. At least 20 million lost their lives. Countless millions of homes and farms were burned or sacked. A third of the nation's territory, including nearly two thirds of its industrial base, was turned into a wasteland—a loss equivalent to the devastation of this country east of Chicago.[73]

He then called for a strengthening of the United Nations, highlighting the need for the UN to become the final arbiter for world peace crisis and conflict, "capable of resolving disputes on the basis of law, of insuring the security of the large and the small, and of creating conditions under which arms can finally be abolished." That had been, in 1945, the sanguine vision of Cord Meyer in a postwar world struggling for peace. But it would be his archrival Jack Kennedy who would finally articulate the inspiration that would echo into eternity. "For in the final analysis," said the president, "our most basic common link is that we all inhabit this small planet. We all breathe the same air. We all cherish our children's future. And we are all mortal."[74]

The president also announced his intention to establish a telephone hotline between the Soviet premier's office and the White House. Such a phone line, the president told his audience, could help deter "dangerous delays, misunderstandings, and misreadings of other's actions which might occur at a time of crisis." Yet the most important, groundbreaking announcement in this address was Kennedy's declaration that he would not only cease nuclear atmospheric testing immediately, but soon join Prime Minister Macmillan and Premier Khrushchev in Moscow for talks that he hoped would yield the first nuclear test ban treaty: "[T]o make clear our good faith and solemn convictions on the matter, I now declare that the United States does not propose to conduct nuclear tests in the atmosphere so long as other states do not do so. We will not be the first to resume. Such a declaration is no substitute for a formal binding treaty, but I hope it will help us achieve one. Nor would such a treaty be a substitute for disarmament, but I hope it will help us achieve it."[75]

President Kennedy's conclusion was no less dramatic, or unclear:

All this is not unrelated to world peace. "When a man's ways please the Lord," the Scriptures tell us, "he maketh even his enemies to be at peace with him." And is not peace, in the last analysis, basically a matter of human rights: the right to live out our lives without fear of devastation; the right to breathe air as nature provided it; the right of future generations to a healthy existence?

While we proceed to safeguard our national interests, let us also safeguard human interests. And the elimination of war and arms is clearly in the interest of both.[76]

So stunned was Soviet Premier Nikita Khrushchev by the magnificence of the Kennedy address, he called it "the greatest of any American President since Roosevelt." Khrushchev immediately ordered that it be rebroadcast throughout every city in the Soviet Union, an unprecedented event. Three weeks later, on July 4, both Nikita Khrushchev and his colleague Leonid Brezhnev sent President Kennedy a telegram:

DEAR MR. PRESIDENT, On the occasion of the national holiday of the United States of America—Independence Day—we send to you and the American people our warm congratulations and best wishes for peace and prosperity. In our times—the age of harnessing atomic energy and penetration into the depths of the universe—the preservation of peace has become in truth a vital necessity for all mankind. We are convinced that if the governments of our two countries, together with the governments of other states, displaying a realistic approach, firmly choose the road of elimination of points of international tension and of broadening commercial cooperation, then peoples everywhere will welcome this as a great contribution to the strengthening of universal peace.[77]

In spite of Kennedy's earlier pessimism for a nuclear test ban treaty with the Soviets, in the wake of his American University address, "John Kennedy and Nikita Khrushchev began to act like competitors in peace. They were both turning," wrote author James Douglass.[78] Equally groundbreaking was the speed with which the treaty would be drafted and ratified. The moment had to be seized quickly. Kennedy had asked W. Averell Harriman to lead the American team, but it was the president himself who prepared them, making sure they understood the critical importance of what was about to occur. They were all sworn to confidentiality. Once Harriman arrived in Moscow on July 14, Kennedy would be in contact with him three and four times a day. "Spending hours in the cramped White House Situation Room, Kennedy personally edited the U.S. position, as if he were at the table himself," said historian Richard Reeves. "The Soviets were astonished when they realized the American President had the power to make decisions on a matter like this without consulting any bureaucracy."[79] That was only because Kennedy had taken matters into his own hands. He well knew such a treaty would never occur had he worked through the national security channels of the CIA and the Pentagon. On July 25, just six weeks after the American University address, Averell Harriman put his initials on the Limited Test Ban Treaty in Moscow. It began with the following commitment: "Each of the Parties to this treaty undertakes to prohibit, to prevent, and not carry out any nuclear weapon test explosion, or any other nuclear explosion . . . in the atmosphere, beyond its limits, including outer space, or under water, including territorial waters or high seas."[80]

The following evening, President Kennedy delivered yet another historic address, announcing on American television his delegation's success in Moscow. "I speak to you tonight in a spirit of hope," he began. "Yesterday a shaft of light cut into the darkness. Negotiations were concluded in Moscow on a treaty to ban all nuclear tests in the atmosphere, in outer space, and under water. . . . But the achievement of this goal is not a victory for one side—it is a victory for mankind. A journey of a thousand miles," the president concluded, "must begin with a single step."[81]

June 10, 1963, had also brought with it a small, private celebration. Just before 8:00 P.M., "at the next to last minute," with Jackie away at Camp David, Jack decided to stop by Joe Alsop's house in Georgetown. Opting to just "come for a drink," the president would stay for more than an hour, as guests for the Alsop's dinner party began to arrive.[82] Mary Meyer was already there. If, as Joe Alsop described it, Jack was "in a gay mood" that early June evening, Mary herself must have been ablaze, and not just because flowers everywhere were coaxing her smile. Jack had now ventured where Cord could never have gone. Her mission had become illuminated into her mosaic—a subliminal "peace song" whose emerging, though still faint, melody had just premiered for all mankind earlier that day.

During cocktails in the Alsop garden, Mary sat with Jack on one side and Ambassador William Attwood, her former prep school and college beau, on the other. Attwood would recall four years later that on that evening the three of them had turned to the enjoyable recollection of past events, "reminiscing about our school days," with Mary as his date at Choate, and how Jack "happily recalled having cut in on her on the dance floor. . . . it was impossible to imagine that, inside of a year," wrote Attwood, "both of them would be murdered, he in Dallas and she in Georgetown."[83]

However historic and unparalleled, Kennedy's American University speech became not only a turning point away from Cold War mayhem toward peace, but a watershed moment for the newfound trajectory of his presidency. The very next day, June 11, the president delivered his groundbreaking civil rights address in response to his successful challenge of Alabama governor George

Wallace, who had tried, and failed, to prevent two black students from registering at the University of Alabama. In this address, Kennedy revealed the same compassion, warmth, and sensitivity that had been on display a day earlier. He underscored and illuminated that there was a direct link between political equality and freedom and the attainment of world peace. Without the former, there could not be the latter. "This nation," said the president, "was founded by men of many nations and backgrounds. It was founded on the principle that all men are created equal, and that the rights of every man are diminished when the rights of one man are threatened." He continued: "The Negro baby born in America today, regardless of the section of the State in which he is born, has about one-half as much chance of completing high school as a white baby born in the same place on the same day, one-third as much chance of completing college, one-third as much chance of becoming a professional man, twice as much chance of becoming unemployed, about one-seventh as much chance of earning $10,000 a year, a life expectancy which is seven years shorter, and the prospects of earning only half as much."[84]

Kennedy called on "every American, regardless of where he lives, [to] stop and examine his conscience about this and other related incidents." Regarding race relations, America was in "a moral crisis as a country and a people," and he promised to deliver landmark legislation "giving all Americans the right to be served in facilities which are open to the public—hotels, restaurants, theaters, retail stores, and similar establishments." He would instruct the Justice Department "to participate more fully in lawsuits designed to end segregation in public education." Equality and civil rights, the president said, had to begin "in the homes of every American in every community across our country." But just after midnight on the night of the president's televised address, Medgar Evers, a prominent leader of the National Association for the Advancement of Colored People (NAACP), was shot and killed in his driveway in front of his family by white supremacist Byron De La Beckwith.

During the afternoon of June 12, Mary Meyer called Evelyn Lincoln, the president's personal secretary, at the White House and was transferred to Jack. They talked for nearly twenty minutes.[85] That night, Mary was escorted by her fellow artist Bill Walton to a small dinner party at the White House, hosted by the president and the First Lady. Two nights later, with Jackie at Camp David, Mary returned unescorted to the White House residence.

On June 26, in the midst of Kennedy's ten-day trip across Europe, more than a million and a half people in West Berlin's Rudolph Wilde Platz, adjacent to the Brandenburg Gate, turned out to welcome the American president. It would be the largest crowd that Kennedy would ever address, and he would famously declare, *"Ich bin ein Berliner!"* ("I am a Berliner!") Kennedy spoke directly to what the people of a divided Germany wanted to hear. He addressed "the right to be free . . . the right to unite their families and their nation in lasting peace, with good will to all people." Five months later, the city of West Berlin would honor the slain American president by renaming the square in which he had spoken "John F. Kennedy Platz." He returned from Europe just after two o'clock the morning of July 3. That evening, Mary joined him in the White House residence.[86] Seven months pregnant, Jackie had retreated to Hyannis Port for the summer with her two children.

Sometime in late June, Mary had reportedly returned to Boston and met Timothy Leary at a downtown seafood restaurant. According to Leary's account, she chided him in a playful manner for having attracted too much publicity in Mexico. "They're not going to let CBS film you drugging people on a lovely Mexican beach," she told him. "You could destroy capitalism and socialism in one month with that sort of thing." Mary was unusually giddy and happy that day, Leary recalled. She talked as if her "program" in Washington had achieved some major goal, and Leary was keen to know more.[87]

"Never mind all that," Mary said, unwilling to disclose details. "While you've been goofing around, I've been working hard. My friends and I have been turning on some of the most important people in Washington."[88] Again, Mary wouldn't reveal who these "important people" were; she was always tight-lipped and discreet. Given the timeline, however, it appeared to be another reference to the fact that she and Jack had recently shared a psychedelic experience together. In addition, there was an allusion to someone else, someone other than Jack, and part of the group of "important people," which will be discussed shortly. Years later, during their 1990 interview, both Leo Damore and Timothy Leary reached a similar conclusion about the identity of this person.[89]

August augured an ominous event that might have foreshadowed worse things to come. At the end of June, *Washington Post* owner-editor Philip Graham had finally broken off his affair with Robin Webb and returned to Chestnut Lodge sanitarium. By all accounts, he had been making solid progress when he left Chestnut Lodge on a weekend pass the morning of August 3 to visit Katharine at their Glen Welby estate in Warrenton, Virginia. Within hours, Phil Graham was dead, a small-bore shotgun wound to the head, an apparent suicide.

There were conflicting accounts of Graham's death, just as there had been about his alleged behavior in Phoenix. According to author David Halberstam, everyone he talked to said Phil had been "getting better; everyone thought he was getting better," and that was why he had been permitted to leave on the weekend. Regarding the circumstances of his death, Halberstam said only that "Kay was in a different room of the house at the time."[90] In Deborah Davis's 1979 account, Phil and Katharine "spent some time together, and then Katharine took a nap. Phil went downstairs and sat on the edge of the bathtub and shot himself in the head."[91] In Carol Felsenthal's "thoroughly" vetted book, based on a number of interviews with people close to Katharine, she and Phil "had a happy morning together." They played tennis and had lunch. In the early afternoon, Phil said he was going bird hunting. Their estate was well stocked with shotguns used for hunting. At about 1:00 P.M., "Kay went to her second-floor bedroom for a nap." Phil apparently went downstairs to a first-floor bathroom, "sat on the side of the bathtub, propped a .28 gauge shotgun against his head, and pulled the trigger."[92]

According to Katharine Graham's own 1998 account, the two had lunch on the back porch and then went upstairs together for a nap. There was no mention of Phil talking about going hunting. "After a short while," wrote Katharine, "Phil got up, saying he wanted to lie down in a separate bedroom he sometimes used. Only a few minutes later, there was the ear-splitting noise of a gun going off indoors. I bolted out of the room and ran around in a frenzy looking for him. When I opened the door to a downstairs bathroom, I found him."[93]

Whatever inconsistencies in these accounts, the question arose: Had Phil once again shown his brilliance by having fooled the staff of Chestnut Lodge as to how much he was improving while he supposedly masterminded the plan of his own suicide? Yet suicide would nullify the revisions to his will that he had made throughout 1963, cutting out Katharine. Katharine, after Phil's death, walked away with complete control of the *Washington Post* and everything else.

In the three different editions of Deborah Davis's *Katharine the Great,* the author never wavered from the view that Phil's death was a suicide. But in 1992, after the third edition had been published, Davis gave an interview in which she made public the fact that she "got a call from a woman who claimed that she knew for a fact that it [Phil's death] was murder."[94] To my knowledge, she never followed up on the call. But it coincided with another previously undisclosed piece of this puzzle.

When Leo Damore talked with Dovey Roundtree in 1991 about Katharine Graham, Roundtree told him that a young black woman attorney by the name of Barbara L. Smith had been working in her office in 1963. Barbara was the granddaughter of William Wadsworth Smith, the caretaker of the Graham's Glen Welby estate at the time of Phil's death.[95] Dovey and her young colleague Barbara had become quite close, she told Damore; when Barbara's grandfather died, she asked Dovey to speak at his funeral.

"I went with Barbara to her grandfather's funeral, who was buried on a mountain side that Mrs. Graham gave to him when he was a younger person," recounted Roundtree to Damore. Katharine Graham and one of her sons had attended William's funeral, and Katharine had also spoken. "She stood in that pulpit, and talked about her love for this man. And the church was *quiet* [Dovey's emphasis]. I mean *quiet*. Not from grief, but *quiet*." Not one to confuse important details, Dovey Roundtree confided to Damore that, according to Barbara, Mrs. Graham had called on Barbara's grandfather "to go upstairs and bring this man [Phil Graham] downstairs. She called to him and he went up and put him in . . . Barbara tells it . . . he took him in his arms and brought him down" after he had allegedly shot himself.[96] Although there was never a shred of physical evidence that anyone other than Phil had pulled the trigger, questions lingered. Had he been—in some way—"encouraged" to do so? And if so, by whom and for what reason?

"Anybody can commit a murder, but it takes an expert to commit a suicide," said legendary CIA asset William ("Bill") R. Corson, mentor to Roger Charles, an investigative journalist and a former Marine lieutenant colonel, both of whom will figure prominently in a future chapter.[97] Corson was never "officially" employed by the CIA, but he often worked closely with Jim Angleton and Robert Crowley, both of whom were deeply ensconced in the Agency's covert action directorate. The three were also the closest of friends.

By the early 1960s, the Technical Services Staff (TSS) within the CIA, headed by the infamous Dr. Sidney Gottlieb, had a huge arsenal of drugs and other substances that could be clandestinely administered to unwitting victims to create such states as suicidal depression, brain tumors, cancer, or death from natural causes, leaving no trace of any foreign toxin in the body. Under congressional scrutiny in 1975, CIA director William Colby openly exhibited to Senator Frank Church and his committee a CIA-manufactured pistol equipped with undetectable poison darts that would, when silently fired "without perception" at its intended human target, induce a fatal heart attack, leaving no trace of any toxin. Colby's sham exhibition was just the tip of the iceberg of the CIA arsenal.[98]

Since the 1950s, highly classified CIA programs—with code names such as MKULTRA, Artichoke, Paperclip, MKNAOMI—often utilized psychiatric facilities, including nearby Chestnut Lodge and Sheppard Pratt. The Agency spent untold millions to find and develop drugs and other methods, both conventional and esoteric, to bring people under various states of control. It's no secret the CIA was interested in all the ramifications of "mind control"—altering, or erasing, or even remaking a subject's mind in whatever direction the Agency wanted. Mind "erasure" was of paramount importance for CIA personnel who were no longer mentally stable, and at risk of revealing classified information. Another long-standing CIA obsession was to create a "Manchurian candidate"—a project involving the use of hypnosis, drugs, deprivation, or other means as a way to turn an individual into a programmable assassin, even to take his own life.

If Phil Graham's death was something other than a suicide, what had been the motive to get rid of him, and who would have benefited? While Phil's overall prognosis and recovery seemed to have improved by the summer of 1963, his long-term stability remained uncertain. Did that mean there might be more embarrassing episodes of public disclosures about people in high places? Would he still, at some point, attempt to wrest control of the *Post* away from Katharine? And who would be in charge of the *Post's* editorial disposition if Phil was no longer running the paper?

Sometime after the 1961 Bay of Pigs fiasco, Phil had reportedly had an "acute manic-depressive incident"—prior to his Phoenix, Arizona, outburst in January 1963—during which he had talked openly of "the CIA's manipulation of journalists" and how they were being used to promote whatever slant the Agency wanted promoted. This finally disturbed him, he reportedly admitted to his friends in the CIA. Increasingly, Graham turned against newsmen and politicians whose code was one of "mutual trust" and silence in order to protect those whose reputations might be compromised by revealing association with the CIA.

"He had begun to talk, after his second breakdown, about the CIA's manipulation of journalists," said author Deborah Davis. "He said it disturbed him. He said it to the CIA." Word had started to go out that Phil could no longer be trusted.[99]

If Phil Graham made revisions to his will during the last two years of his life, none of them were upheld after his death. His widow immediately assumed the role of publisher of the *Post*. Katharine reverted to the policies Phil had set in place before his 1961 disenchantment. That included, according to journalist Michael Hasty, "the supporting of efforts of the intelligence community in advancing the foreign policies and economic agenda of the nation's ruling elites."[100] FAIR news analyst Norman Solomon was even more blunt in 2001 when he wrote: "Her [Katharine Graham's] newspaper mainly functioned as a helpmate to the war-makers in the White House, State Department and Pentagon."[101] For years after Phil's death, the *Washington Post* continued its tack of employing all kinds of well-known propaganda techniques, as Michael Hasty had pointed out: ". . . evasion, confusion, misdirection, targeted emphasis, disinformation, secrecy, omission of important facts, and selective leaks." It was therefore no surprise that Katharine Graham, in a speech at the CIA's Langley headquarters in 1988, said the following: "We live in a dirty and dangerous world. There are some things the general public does not need to know and shouldn't. I believe democracy flourishes when the government can take legitimate steps to keep its secrets and when the press can decide whether to print what it knows."[102]

Why would Phil Graham have committed suicide at a time when, by all accounts, his condition was improving? In June, with Katharine's support, he had voluntarily returned to Chestnut Lodge. Well into July, those who visited Phil all spoke of his increasingly stable disposition, of his coming to terms with his illness and making a recovery. Might he have succeeded in returning to his former life and continuing his reign at the *Post*? Whether he recovered or not, the risk may well have been that the wealthy, powerful media mogul Phil Graham was no longer willing to toe the party line, that he could no longer be counted on to turn a blind eye if needed.

The silent, invisible tsunami was approaching. An excruciating, earth-shattering moment in American history was about to explode in three months' time. As little as possible could be left to chance. Not only would there be a well-planned, well-executed conspiracy to take out a sitting American president, but an even more critical and insidious conspiracy—a cover-up—had to be successfully, and immediately, orchestrated in the aftermath. That, of course, meant all the major sources of news—newspapers—had to be securely on board, willing to turn a blind eye to the government's contrived, fictitious post-assassination narrative, as well as Allen Dulles's appointment to the Warren Commission. In the approaching moments of a horrific calamity, Phil Graham, owner and editor of the *Washington Post*, had become a problem. Increasingly regarded as a loose cannon, he could no longer be trusted; he had criticized the CIA's infiltration of the media and its manipulation of news, as well as having ceremoniously told off some of the CIA's own collaborators—publishers and senior editors of the mainstream media—in person, in Phoenix, in January 1963.

O n August 9, Jack and Jackie lost their second child at birth, a boy they had named Patrick Bouvier. Jackie had gone into premature labor two days earlier, and the infant succumbed to complications. Jack reportedly wept inconsolably.[103] For Jackie, the loss had to have been compounded by her realization that, in the wake of her son's death and on the eve of her tenth wedding anniversary, Jack and Mary Meyer were still very much involved.

A month later, Jack and Jackie would celebrate their anniversary in Newport, Rhode Island. Jack would reportedly get down "on one knee, begging Jackie not to go" on a private cruise with Aristotle Onassis.[104] She was apparently unmoved by his display; she would spend the first two weeks of October cruising the Aegean with Onassis on his yacht *Christina*, her sister, Lee, brother-in-law Stas Radziwill, and friends Sue and Franklin Roosevelt Jr. in tow. For Jackie, it was now payback time. The White House would spin the trip as a getaway for Jackie's convalescence, but Bobby Kennedy was furious; he vehemently detested Onassis. Franklin Roosevelt Jr., no stranger to the rogue Onassis, asked Bobby how he should position himself during the trip. Bobby grimly replied, "Sink the fucking yacht!"[105]

Peter Evans, author of *Ari*, the only authorized biography of Aristotle Onassis, later documented in his subsequent book *Nemesis* that it was on this October cruise that Jackie and Onassis first became lovers. "According to Onassis," wrote Evans, "Jackie's susceptibility at that moment was considerable, especially in the context of her hurt at Jack's continuing unfaithfulness." Evans's research had led him to Mary Meyer: "It was this affair, believed one White House insider, that was the final straw that persuaded Jackie to continue with the cruise despite her husband's objections and pleas to cut it short."[106]

S ometime before September 24, Timothy Leary said, he received a late-afternoon telephone call from Mary Pinchot. Leary described her as sounding on the verge of "hysteria." She had rented a car at New York's LaGuardia Airport and had driven up to Millbrook, wanting to meet with Leary privately, but not at the estate. They agreed on a more remote location where, as he wrote, the "trees were turning technicolor" with fall's foliage, the "sky glaring indigo—with the bluest girl in the world next to me."[107]

According to Leary, Mary told him: "It was all going so well. We had eight intelligent women turning on the most powerful men in Washington. And then we got found out. I was such a fool. I made a mistake in recruitment. A wife snitched on us. I'm scared." She burst into tears. Initially, Leary thought her state might have been the result of a bad drug experience; he attempted to console her. She corrected him. Her state of mind wasn't drug-related at all. "That's all been perfect," she told him. "That's why it's so sad. I may be in real trouble. I really shouldn't be here." Leary asked a second time if she was, at that moment, on drugs.

"It's not me. It's the situation that's fucked up. You must be very careful now, Timothy. Don't make any waves. No publicity. I'm afraid for you. I'm afraid for all of us." The gravity of Mary's concern was still lost on Leary. He suggested that they go back to the house and have some wine, "maybe a hot bath and figure out what you should do." Mary persisted.

"I know what you're thinking," she said. "This is not paranoia. I've gotten mixed up in some dangerous matters. It's real. You've got to believe me. Do you?"

"Yes, I do," he finally replied.

"Look, if I ever showed up here suddenly, could you hide me out for a while?"

"Sure."

"Good." Mary then pulled a pill bottle out of her handbag.

"This is supposed to be the best LSD in the world. From the National Institute of Mental Health. Isn't it funny that I end up giving it to you?"[108]

Timothy Leary watched Mary drive away. It would be the last time he would see her alive.

Mary wasn't one to be spooked easily by anything. Leary had no idea what other woman in Washington could be causing her such alarm. During the 1990 Leary-Damore interview, however, the Millbrook incident was discussed at some length.[109] Both Leary and Damore had come to believe that the woman in question—the woman Mary believed had betrayed her ("A wife snitched on us")—was, in fact, Katharine Graham. Damore's theory was that in her desperation to bring her husband under control, Katharine was frantic enough to try anything, including supporting Phil in undertaking a psychedelic exploration. That meant, according to Damore, that Katharine Graham might have been one of the eight women in Mary's group. His conversation with Anne Chamberlin, a close friend of Katharine Graham's, may have led him to this conclusion.

Katharine Graham's biggest influence in this direction, however, likely came from her close friends Henry and Clare Booth Luce, who were, like Katharine and Phil Graham, media moguls. The Luces owned Time Inc. Over the years, Katharine Graham and Clare Booth Luce would become very dear friends.

In the late 1950s, her marriage unraveling because Henry wanted to leave her for a younger woman, Clare Booth Luce, like Mary Meyer, first experimented with LSD. Under the direction of Dr. Sidney Cohen, Clare, at loose ends, further continued her exploration during a time of personal turmoil. In spite of her extraordinarily successful careers, which included writing four critically acclaimed Broadway plays in the 1930s, serving as managing editor of *Vanity Fair* from 1933 to 1934, becoming a two-term congresswoman in the 1940s, serving as American ambassador to Italy from 1953 to 1956, and finding herself regarded as one of the world's ten most admired women— Clare described herself as "deeply unhappy."[110] Again, like Mary Meyer and Peggy Mellon Hitchcock, Clare's psychedelic voyages would turn her into an LSD proselytizer. Starting in 1954 and through 1968, both *Time* and *Life* would publish a number of enthusiastic articles about hallucinogens. According to Columbia University historian Alan Brinkley, Clare also believed that her use of hallucinogens had "saved our marriage."[111]

Katharine Graham first caught sight of Henry and Clare Booth Luce in 1948. She marveled at "how important they looked—and indeed they were."[112] The two couples fast became friends in 1954. Clare became aware of Phil Graham's deterioration sometime in 1962,[113] the same year that Mary Meyer first introduced herself to Timothy Leary and told him she wanted to bring together a group of women who were involved with politically powerful men in Washington. Following Phil Graham's death in 1963, Katharine turned to Clare as a role model: "Clare gave me interesting and useful guidance on how to handle myself at work . . . much of it being about a woman in a man's world. I took to heart what she said."[114] Years after the *Washington Post*'s Watergate crisis, Katharine would recall how she had, during critical moments, "engaged in a behind-the-scenes back-and-forth with Clare Booth Luce."[115]

With her husband unraveling, it was not only possible, but very likely, that the increasingly desperate Katharine turned to Clare Booth Luce for guidance and advice, her marriage having survived a similar crisis. If Clare believed LSD had "saved" her marriage, she might well have counseled Katharine in that direction. And given Clare's endorsement of LSD as a cutting-edge therapeutic tool, Katharine may have sought out Mary Meyer for assistance—not only to help Phil, but herself as well.

By 1963, however, it appeared Phil was beyond Katharine's reach, that he would continue to wrest control of the *Post* away from her. According to Deborah Davis, "Katharine had pretty much given up on the marriage," yet was desperate to retain control of her family's newspaper. In an interview Davis gave in 1992, she told *Steamshovel Press* editor Kenn Thomas that "there's some speculation that either she arranged for him [Phil] to be killed or somebody said to her, 'don't worry, we'll take care of it.'"[116] While Leo Damore, Timothy Leary, and Deborah Davis never definitively connected all the dots, the "somebody" in this equation, in this author's opinion, was the same element within the CIA that was orchestrating the assassination of President Kennedy. "Anybody can commit a murder," said legendary CIA asset Bill Corson, "but it takes an expert to commit a suicide."

Katharine Graham's Faustian deal with the devil would give her complete control and ownership of the *Washington Post*, provided she maintained the same polices and agreements her husband had arranged before his "enlightenment," post–Bay of Pigs. The deal had to have included Katharine not squealing on anything the Agency wanted kept secret, as well as her revealing any matters the CIA wanted to know about—including Mary Meyer's influence on the president. Undoubtedly, Mary was aware of the kind of power the CIA wielded, as well as its treachery, and Katharine's betrayal likely opened up an entirely new can of worms, even perhaps allowing Mary the realization that Phil's demise might well become a harbinger of hers. Danger was lurking. Only the chosen few knew they were going to go to the source to cut off the head of the snake. Mary would be spared—so long as she made no waves. For Mary, that would eventually become impossible.

On September 24, the president traveled with Mary and her sister to their family's Grey Towers estate in Milford, Pennsylvania, to dedicate a gift from the Pinchot family to the U.S. Forest Service. It consisted of a large parcel of Pinchot family land, as well as the Pinchot mansion, the former residence of Mary's uncle Gifford Pinchot. Tony still had no inkling of her sister's affair with Jack. "There was no sexual thing evident," she told author Sally Bedell Smith. "He was easy with both of us. I always felt he had liked me as much as Mary. You could say there was a little rivalry."[117]

After the dedication ceremony, Jack and the two sisters went to their mother's house to look at old family pictures. The elderly Ruth Pinchot, once a spirited champion of women's equality and liberation, was now supporting Barry Goldwater in his bid to unseat Kennedy in 1964. Jack reportedly took it in stride and was jovial throughout the visit.

Unexpectedly, that same day the U.S. Senate ratified the president's Limited Nuclear Test Ban Treaty with the Soviet Union and the United Kingdom. Much had been done to convince the American public of the treaty's importance. Under Jack's supervision, Norman Cousins and the Citizens Committee for a Nuclear Test Ban Treaty had led a successful campaign for public approval. Nikita Khrushchev would sign the treaty sixteen days later. The Soviet premier considered the treaty to be his country's and America's greatest mutual achievement. He proposed that the two leaders use it as an opening "to seek solutions of other ripe international questions." In a letter that followed, Khrushchev outlined certain tasks for immediate consideration, including ratification of a nonaggression pact between the countries of NATO and member states of the Warsaw Pact; creation of nuclear-free zones in various regions of the world; and a ban on the future spread of all nuclear weapons. He closed the letter with the following: "Their implementation would facilitate a significant strengthening of peace, improvement of international relations, would clear the road to general and complete disarmament, and, consequently, to the delivering of peoples from the threat of war."[118]

"Khrushchev's vision, as inspired by the test ban treaty," wrote James Douglass, "corresponded in a deeply hopeful way to Kennedy's American University address. In his letter, Khrushchev was signaling his readiness to work with Kennedy on a host of projects. If the two leaders should succeed as they had on the test ban treaty, in only a few of Khrushchev's suggested projects, they would end the Cold War."[119]

With the ratification of the test ban treaty and Khrushchev's imminent signing of the document, Kennedy had successfully fashioned a new path, bringing the world closer to a "genuine peace." That he had learned the good news when he was with Mary, and that she, too, had long nurtured the goal of a world moving toward peace without war, had to have been a profound, defining moment between the two. An extraordinary accomplishment had unfolded that day, finally taking place at Mary's family home. According to Kenny O'Donnell, present that day at the Pinchot estate, Mary and Jack were furtively smiling at one another, the news of the ratification having reached the presidential entourage.[120]

Also that September, President Kennedy signaled his intention to develop two additional, significant paths toward peace: a plan for a secret rapprochement with Fidel Castro that would eliminate Cuba as a campaign issue in the 1964 election; and a new road map for ending U.S. involvement in Vietnam by the start of his second term as president. With regard to the latter, that September, Kennedy sent Defense Secretary Robert McNamara and General Maxwell Taylor on a ten-day fact-finding expedition in Vietnam, the goal of which was to determine America's exit strategy from the war. Kennedy took the long view, reportedly confiding to his adviser Kenny O'Donnell, "In 1965, I'll become one of the most unpopular Presidents in history. I'll be damned everywhere as a Communist appeaser. But I don't care. If I tried to pull out completely now from Vietnam, we would have another Joe McCarthy 'red scare' on our hands, but I can do it after I'm reelected. So we had better make damned sure I *am* reelected."[121] President Kennedy's National Security Action Memorandum 263 (NSAM 263) became a testament to his intention to withdraw from Vietnam.

In his 1987 book *The Twilight Struggle*, former ambassador William ("Bill") Attwood documented that he was a special adviser on African affairs at the United Nations in September 1963. He then mentioned that he was talking to ABC news reporter Lisa Howard about Africa when she casually brought up the fact that she had recently interviewed Fidel Castro. In an interview for this book, Bill Attwood's wife, Simone, added something more. Simone was adamant that both she and Bill knew of "Mary's affair with Kennedy. I think a lot of people knew," she added. According to Simone, after Bill's return from Africa in June, Mary Meyer had had a hand in persuading Attwood, her former boyfriend, to contact Lisa Howard as a way to begin moving the sour relationship with Cuba toward rapprochement.[122] Already, as early as March 1963, President Kennedy had been instructing his staff to "start thinking along more flexible lines" vis-à-vis the island nation and its leader. According to White House aide Gordon Chase, who became Bill Attwood's White House contact that fall, Kennedy was interested in "quietly enticing Castro over to us."[123]

A secret Bill Attwood–Lisa Howard alliance with Cuba's United Nations representative Carlos Lechuga developed. Lechuga told Attwood that Kennedy's American University address had impressed Castro, and he invited

Attwood to Havana to begin a dialogue with the Cuban leader. The CIA, meanwhile, was taking it all in. The Attwood-Howard effort with Cuba on Kennedy's behalf became a target of CIA surveillance. According to David Talbot, "In one call to Havana, [Lisa] Howard was overheard excitedly describing Kennedy's enthusiasm for rapprochement. The newswoman had no sense of the shock waves she was causing within the halls of Washington power."[124]

On October 3, Jean Daniel, editor of the French weekly *L'Observateur*, told Bill Attwood that he was on his way to Havana to see Castro. Attwood arranged for Daniel to meet with Kennedy before he left for Cuba. "When I left the Oval Office of the White House," Daniel recalled, "I had the impression that I was a messenger for peace. I was convinced that Kennedy wanted rapprochement, that he wanted me to come back and tell him that Castro wished the rapprochement too."[125]

On the very day of President Kennedy's assassination, November 22, Daniel was meeting with Fidel Castro. "I was happy about the message I was delivering. These two men seemed ready to make peace. I am *certain* about this! *Certain!* Even after all these years."[126] It was during this meeting with Fidel Castro that both men first learned that President Kennedy had been assassinated. According to Daniel, after a long, shocked silence, Castro had said: "This is terrible. They are going to say we did it. . . . This is the end of your mission."[127] And it was. The Pentagon and the CIA had been working clandestinely against the president's efforts to change policies towards both Cuba and Vietnam. Noted author David Talbot: "As the only man in the room who consistently opposed military escalation in Vietnam, the president was compelled to operate in a stealthy fashion to avoid becoming completely isolated within his own government."[128]

During the fall of 1963, the Vietnam situation markedly deteriorated, with U.S. officials split over whether to back a military coup in Vietnam to oust the Diem regime. On October 2, journalist Arthur Krock's column in the *New York Times* had quoted reporter Richard Starnes, whose interview with "a high United States source" privy to CIA operations in Saigon, had been, by Krock's standards, unassailable: "The C.I.A.'s growth was 'likened to a malignancy' which the 'very high official was not sure even the White House could control any longer,'" Krock wrote. He added, "If the United States ever experiences [an attempt at a coup to overthrow the government] it will come from the C.I.A. and not the Pentagon. The agency 'represents a tremendous power and total unaccountability to anyone.'"[129]

Mary Pinchot
1942 *Vassarion* — Vassar College Yearbook

April 1939: Mary Pinchot and Bill Attwood at Princeton University's House Parties Weekend. The other woman sitting behind them is Betty Drayton.

Circa late 1942–1943. Mary Pinchot as a journalist for *United Press International* (UPI) and *Mademoiselle.*

Cord and Mary Meyer during the late 1940s when Cord was the rising star in the United World Federalist movement.

Summer of 1951 at Grey Towers in Milford, Pennsylvania. Seated left to right are Cord Meyer, Mary Meyer, and Wistar Janney.

Fall 1954: Family camping trip in Virginia's Blue Ridge Mountains. Left to right is Mary Meyer, Michael Meyer (back), Cord Meyer, and the author Peter Janney (age seven years). Michael Meyer would be hit and killed by a car two years later in December 1956.

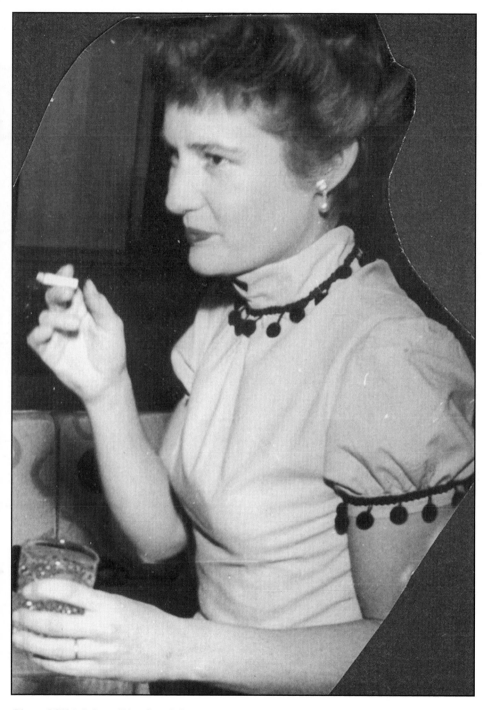

Circa 1954. Mary Pinchot Meyer at a costume party in Washington, D.C.

Mary Pinchot Meyer at President Kennedy's 46th birthday party on May 29, 1963, on the presidential yacht *Sequoia*.

September 24, 1963: Dedication of the Pinchot Institute in Milford, Pennsylvania. Possibly the only picture of Mary Meyer and President Kennedy together, taken with Mary's mother, Ruth Pinchot. The U.S. Senate ratified President Kennedy's Limited Nuclear Test Ban Treaty that same day.

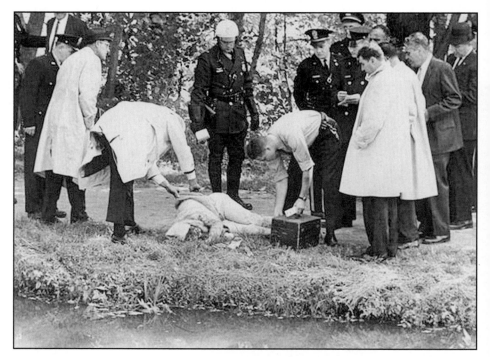

The crime scene on the C & O towpath within ninety minutes after the murder of Mary Pinchot Meyer on October 12, 1964.

The murder scene on the day after Mary Meyer's murder (October 13, 1964). Note the scuba diver in the canal looking for the murder weapon, which was never found.

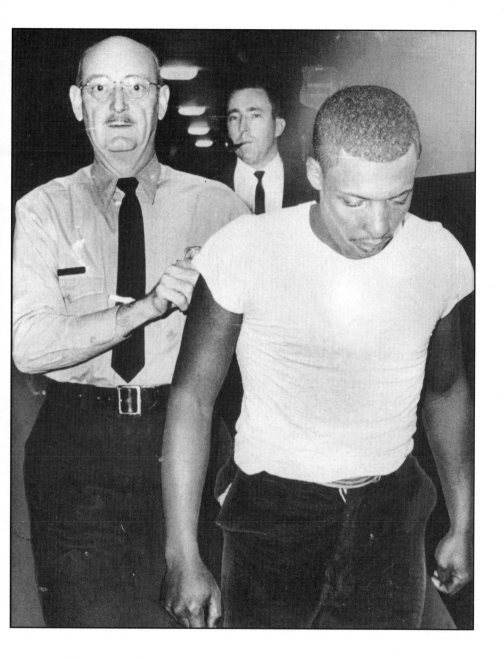

Raymond Crump Jr. being processed at D.C. Police Headquarters after his arrest during the afternoon of October 12, 1964.

Dovey J. Roundtree, Esq. at the time of the 1965 trial for the murder of Mary Pinchot Meyer. She would successfully defend her client Raymond Crump Jr. who was acquitted of all charges.

Author Leo Damore in 1982 when he was forty-three years old, seven years before he began his investigation of the murder of Mary Meyer. In 1995, he committed suicide under suspicious circumstances.

1971. Katharine Graham and Ben Bradlee emerging victorious from a Pentagon Papers legal hearing in Washington, D.C.

Circa 1962. Wistar Janney at his home in Washington, D.C.

James Jesus Angleton, Chief of Counterintelligence at CIA, answering questions on September 25, 1975, before the Senate Intelligence Committee in Washington. Angleton was answering questions concerning the CIA's cover-up of reading the mail of many prominent Americans, including the mail of Richard M. Nixon. (Photo credit: George Times / *The New York Times.*)

Mary Pinchot Meyer's gravestone at the Pinchot family plot in the Milford, Pennsylvania, cemetary. She lies next to her son Michael Pinchot Meyer.

A month later, the Catholic president of Vietnam, Ngo Dinh Diem, and his brother were assassinated by a CIA-funded coup. The event devastated Kennedy. Secretary of Defense Robert McNamara had been present when Kennedy received the news; he would later say he had never seen the president so upset.[130] That afternoon, Jack asked Mary to be with him. It appears this was Mary's last documented trip to the White House, though it remains unknown whether it was the last time they saw one another.

Mary's whereabouts when she first heard the fatal news from Dallas are also unknown. At 5:14 that afternoon, only hours after Jack's death, she attempted to call his personal secretary Evelyn Lincoln, but had to leave her number with the White House switchboard.[131] Later, Mary asked Anne Truitt to spend the night with her at her house in Georgetown. "She was so sad," recalled Truitt. "I tried to comfort her. We cried, but we didn't talk that much."[132]

As Jack lay in the Capitol Rotunda on Sunday, Mary visited his casket. On Monday, November 25, she attended the funeral and sat with Tony, who would years later recall that her sister "didn't seem very upset. It puzzled me."[133] At the burial at Arlington Cemetery later that day, Mary was seen by one of her former art students, Ariel Dougherty, who had been in Mary's painting classes at Georgetown Day School in the late 1950s. Alone, solemn, dressed in a long, gold-colored suede coat that belted around her waist, a scarf loosely wrapped around her neck, Mary stood adjacent to the gravesite throughout the entire ceremony.[134] As far as their vision for world peace had come, it had been—in one instant on November 22, 1963—completely obliterated.

In October 1963, Cuban UN ambassador Carlos Lechuga had delivered an official message to President Kennedy that Fidel Castro desired a lasting peace with the United States. But the province of a global peace would never be a goal for Lyndon Johnson. Four days after Kennedy's assassination, President Lyndon Johnson signed National Security Action Memorandum 273 (NSAM 273), which set the tone for increased U.S. involvement in Vietnam by transferring the burden of increased covert operations against North Vietnam from South Vietnam to the United States. The following March, Johnson penned NSAM 288, initiating the full escalation of the Vietnam War. Before its end, in undoubtedly the worst and most costly blunder of American foreign policy, approximately 3.8 million people would lose their lives, including more than 58,000 American combat soldiers.

A little more than a week after Dallas, Timothy Leary received a disturbing phone call from Mary Meyer. "Ever since the Kennedy assassination I had been expecting a call from Mary," wrote Leary in *Flashbacks*. "It came around December 1. I could hardly understand her. She was either drunk or drugged or overwhelmed with grief. Or all three."[135]

"They couldn't control him any more," said Mary between her sobbing and crying. "He was changing too fast. They've covered everything up. I gotta come see you. I'm afraid. Be careful."[136] Leary later recalled this exchange in 1990. He told Leo Damore, "She was very upset, distraught. Her call spooked me. And I never imagined she'd be killed less than a year later."[137]

PART THREE

"ON ONE SMALL condition," said Claudius, having been asked to promise his feared grandmother the Lady Livia Augustus that he would implore the new Roman Emperor Caligula to make her a goddess after her death.

"You see, there's so much I want to know," continued Claudius. "I'm a historian and I want to know the truth. When people die, so much dies with them, and all that's left are pieces of paper that tell lies."

"He wants to know the truth and he calls it a small condition!" exclaimed the Lady Livia Augustus.

"Grandmother, who killed Marcellus?" asked Claudius.

"I did!" said the Lady Livia Augustus.[1]

---

1   From the 1976 BBC Masterpiece Theatre production of *I, Claudius.* (Based on: *I, Claudius: from the autobiography of Tiberius Claudius born 10 B.C. murdered and deified A.D. 54.* and *Claudius the God,* both authored by Robert Graves. New York: Vintage International Edition, 1989, originally published by Random House, 1935.

11

After Dallas

Do not forget your dying king. Show this world that this is still a government of the people, for the people, and by the people. Nothing, as long as you live, will ever be more important. It's up to you.

—Attorney Jim Garrison
(during his summation
to the jury in the film *JFK*)

There's something so mysterious about an orchid. They look as though they had been grown in damp underground caves by demons. They're evil sickly flowers with no life of their own, living on borrowed strength.

—Mary Pinchot (Meyer)
(from her short story "Futility,"
Vassar Review and Little Magazine, 1941)

A SHOCKED AND traumatized nation attempted to fathom the death of its president. The eye of the storm was centered in Washington, encased within a hurricane of concealed controversy. In Dallas, an hour and fifteen minutes after the president's death, a man by the name of Lee Harvey Oswald, who worked in the Texas School Book Depository—the place where shots had allegedly been fired at the president—was arrested in a Dallas movie theater. Oswald had, according to one eyewitness, entered the theater "shortly after 1:00 P.M."[1] Charged first with the murder of police officer J. D. Tippit, which had taken place at approximately 1:15 P.M. several blocks away, Oswald was eventually charged with the assassination of the president several hours later.

281

Two days later, in one of the most bizarre, phantasmagorical events ever witnessed on national television, Oswald was fatally shot by a man identified as Jack Ruby, adding to the bewilderment of an already stunned audience of viewers. So unprecedented had been the spectacle of horror, Agnes Meyer, mother of *Washington Post* publisher Katharine Graham, reportedly seethed, "What is this, some kind of goddamn banana republic?"[2] The American media struggled to sustain a semblance of calm and order, still insistent Lee Harvey Oswald had been the lone crackpot assassin and had acted unilaterally. But observers and journalists in other countries had already started speculating Oswald had been killed to keep him from talking.

Public distraction, supported by an obsequious, manipulative media, has long obscured what diligent researchers over the years have uncovered: that before Dallas, there were at least two other plots to assassinate President Kennedy. One assassination attempt against the president was planned to take place in Chicago on November 2, 1963. It would have involved multiple gunmen, as well as a designated "patsy," a mentally handicapped ex-Marine named Thomas Arthur Vallee. Curiously, like Lee Harvey Oswald, Thomas Vallee had also served at a U-2 base in Japan under the Joint Technical Advisory Group (JTAG), the CIA's code name for its U-2 spy plane surveillance unit. Vallee then "found work" in the fall of November 1963 in a building overlooking a Chicago street immediately adjacent to an L-shaped turn that would be on the route for the upcoming presidential motorcade. The plot finally had been foiled only because certain members of the Secret Service had acted quickly. President Kennedy had also canceled the trip as a result of President Diem's assassination in South Vietnam. Having uncovered evidence in Chicago of a four-man assassination hit team with high-powered rifles, the Secret Service arrested two members of the team, although two others escaped.[3]

A second plot was set to unfold during President Kennedy's trip to Miami on November 18, but the presidential motorcade was canceled. Word of the plot had been forwarded to the Secret Service from police intelligence in Miami. A secretly tape-recorded meeting between Miami police informant Willie Somerset and right-wing extremist Joseph Milteer on November 9 had revealed that an assassination attempt might be made in Miami "from an office building with a high-powered rifle."[4] Consequently, the president flew by helicopter from the Miami airport to the Americana Hotel, where he delivered his scheduled speech.

While the magnitude of such threats would have been communicated to the president, it wasn't clear how much detail was given to him. However, according to one Washington insider with ties to the Kennedy family, quoted in a 1996 article by Bennett Bolton and David Duffy, "Jack told Mary before his death that he believed there was a conspiracy in the works to assassinate him, and that the people behind the plot were close to him."[5] In an interview for this book, Bennett Bolton verified the research he and his partner undertook for the article, though he wouldn't divulge the source of the quote.[6] What was certain was that weeks before Dallas, it appeared the president had been marked for a well-organized assassination.[7]

Though Mary has been previously portrayed as not believing in any conspiracy to assassinate her lover the president, her biographer claiming that she "accepted the idea that Oswald was the lone assassin,"[8] the deeper evidence beneath the surface reveals a far different story. Throughout the last year of her life, Mary Pinchot Meyer was deeply engaged in exploration; her suspicion had been aroused, and it grew stronger. She wanted to know the real truth of what had taken place. Understandably preoccupied with Jack's assassination, she maintained a collection of "clippings of the JFK assassination" in the bookcase in her bedroom, next to the place where she kept her diary.[9] The lingering question was how far Mary had gone in her investigation, and what impact it might have had. She wasn't the kind of person to stand idly aside in the face of an event of this magnitude. She was well aware of her ex-husband Cord's work and his connection to Operation Mockingbird, the CIA's infiltration of the media. Her vigilance would have caused an awareness of whatever narrative the media was peddling, particularly if Jack had shared with her any information about what the Secret Service had uncovered earlier in November.

Mary was a "Washington insider" with many relationships and connections inside the Kennedy coterie and beyond. As such, she was privy to information and individuals that few people could access. Given the president's regard for her, her presence within the intimate confines of the White House for two years had accorded her an unique status. Kenny O'Donnell certainly respected Mary as a special, trusted person in the president's life. There were even times, he told Leo Damore, where he "feared the hold she had on Jack."[10]

In fact, Mary had sought out O'Donnell several weeks after the assassination, inquiring about his recollection of events that horrific day in Dallas.

According to O'Donnell's statements to author Leo Damore, he (O'Donnell) confided to Mary what both he and Dave Powers had witnessed from their vantage point in the car directly behind the president's. The smell of gunpowder, the sound of rifle shots, as well as other features of gunfire were well known to the two close Kennedy advisers, both seasoned World War II combat veterans. Both remained adamant for the rest of their lives that at least *two shots* had come "from behind the fence [on the grassy knoll]," in *front* of the motorcade. What O'Donnell had told Mary, he reiterated to author Leo Damore, although O'Donnell never spoke about it publicly. His account was further confirmed twenty-five years later by Speaker of the House Tip O'Neill in his 1987 memoir *Man of the House*. At a private dinner five years after the Kennedy assassination, O'Neill recalled a conversation with Kenny O'Donnell and Dave Powers, during which they had told him that at least "two shots" had come from in front of the motorcade "behind the fence."[11]

"That's not what you told the Warren Commission," the astonished Tip O'Neill had said to O'Donnell.

"You're right," O'Donnell replied. "I told the FBI what I had heard, but they said it couldn't have happened that way and that I must have been imagining things. So I testified the way they wanted me to. I just didn't want to stir up any more pain and trouble for the family."

"I can't believe it," the Speaker said. "I wouldn't have done that in a million years. I would have told the truth."

"Tip, you have to understand," continued O'Donnell. "The family—everybody wanted this behind them." Before O'Neill published his memoir, he checked with Dave Powers to make sure his memory was not failing him, since O'Donnell had already died. "As they say in the news business," wrote O'Neill, referring to Powers, "he stands by his story."[12]

Not only did Dave Powers stand by his story, he went several steps further a few years later. WCAP radio producer Woody Woodland in Lowell, Massachusetts, interviewed Dave Powers in late 1991, shortly after the release of Oliver Stone's film *JFK*. At the time, Powers was still the museum curator of the John F. Kennedy Presidential Library and Museum at the University of Massachusetts in Boston. After the interview, Powers walked with Woody Woodland to his car.

"I know this is a painful subject matter for you, Mr. Powers," said Woodland as they walked into the parking lot. "But have you seen that movie [Oliver Stone's film *JFK*]?" Powers confirmed he had indeed already seen the film.

"What did you think of it?" inquired Woodland.

"I think they got it right," said Powers.

"Really?" said Woodland, somewhat taken aback.

"Yes," continued Powers. "We were driving into an ambush. They were shooting from the front, from behind that fence [on the grassy knoll]."

"But you didn't say that to the Warren Commission," Woodland pressed.

"No [I didn't], we were told not to by the FBI," Powers replied.[13]

Whatever conversation Mary had with O'Donnell, her worst suspicions would have likely been confirmed. Over the years, scores of other eyewitness accounts from people who were in Dealey Plaza at the time of the assassination have been gathered, analyzed, and published that corroborate the O'Donnell-Powers account. Specifically, over fifty people, including Senator Ralph Yarborough, who was riding in the third car of the motorcade with Lyndon Johnson, immediately behind O'Donnell and Powers, would recount that the motorcade had actually come to a near-complete stop—immediately before the fatal head shot to the president.[14]

But the real clincher was what the FBI was doing to the most important witnesses in Dallas: pressuring them by whatever means necessary to conform to a deliberately contrived narrative—that there were just three shots, all from *behind* the motorcade, and all from the Texas School Book Depository. The second conspiracy—to manipulate and cover up the real evidence of the first—was under way posthaste, and neither Kenny O'Donnell nor Dave Powers, in the aftermath of the dastardly deed of Dallas, was willing publicly "to take a bullet for the truth." Had they done so, they could have altered the course of history as we know it today. Instead, they succumbed to the intimidation of J. Edgar Hoover and the FBI; and the cancerous malignancy rapidly spread.

Immediately after Dallas, there were a number of suspicions swirling around Washington that Mary, given her position, would unquestionably have accessed. According to some accounts, there were direct accusations leveled at the CIA almost immediately, and from within the Kennedy family itself. In his 2007 book *Brothers*, David Talbot recounts the fact that Bobby Kennedy, upon learning that his brother had been killed, placed a telephone call to a ranking official at CIA headquarters in Langley—reportedly less than an hour after the shooting—demanding to know, "Did your outfit have anything to do with this horror?"[15] Bobby's question was confounding and staggering. What would have led the attorney general of the United States to suspect that the nation's premier intelligence apparatus—the Central Intelligence Agency—might be involved in assassinating the president?

Whether it was at the prompting of Bobby's phone call, or on his own initiative, CIA director John McCone arrived at the Kennedy compound in McLean a short time later that afternoon. For three hours on that November 22 day, the two walked together on the grounds of the Hickory Hill estate. According to historian Arthur Schlesinger Jr., Bobby directly confronted McCone about whether the Agency had assassinated his brother. Schlesinger claims that Bobby later reported: "You know, at the time I asked McCone . . . if they [the CIA] had killed my brother, and I asked him in a way he couldn't lie to me, and they hadn't."[16] That may have been Bobby's feeling at the time, but it would very quickly change.

While Bobby's fears and concerns may have initially been assuaged that afternoon, he knew that McCone, "a wealthy Republican businessman from California with no intelligence background, was not in control of his own agency."[17] Bobby Kennedy's own monitoring of the Agency right after the Bay of Pigs had acquainted him with many of the CIA's operational plans and methods; in fact, Bobby himself knew more about many of these things than McCone. John McCone had replaced Allen Dulles, the infamous father of American intelligence whom Jack had fired. But the elite of the Agency—people like Dick Helms, Jim Angleton, Cord Meyer, Tracy Barnes, Bill Harvey, even Bob Crowley—still "carried the flag" for Allen Dulles behind the scenes. Their loyalty to Dulles kept McCone in the dark, ostensibly because his strict Catholic religious principles might have been offended by many of the CIA's covert operations. "Bobby would realize that while he had taken his question to the very top of the CIA," Talbot concluded, "he had asked the wrong man."[18]

There would be more whispers—above and beyond the O'Donnell-Powers eyewitness account—from those accompanying the presidential entourage in Dallas that day, some of whom Mary Meyer knew well. They were either too scared or too shocked, but several knew from contacts within the Secret Service that there had been more than one shooter, that there had, in fact, been a conspiracy to assassinate the president.[19]

Four days after Dallas, *Life* magazine published its November 29 issue, which featured thirty-one selected poor-quality black-and-white frames from Abraham Zapruder's famous home movie, the film that would become legendary for revealing to the world the "kill shot" that exploded President Kennedy's head. Carefully scripted, *Life*'s presentation would reinforce the manufactured narrative of disinformation that only three shots had been fired, all from *behind* the motorcade, and all from the Texas School Book Depository. *Life*'s publisher, C. D. Jackson, was a former CIA asset and a friend of Allen Dulles's. It wasn't an accident that the "carefully edited" photos showed up so quickly. Likely, Mary would have seen the issue of *Life*, though it's not known whether it became part of her collection of "clippings of the JFK assassination" that she kept in "the bookcase in her bedroom" next to her diary. For the first time, however, the public became aware that something called "the Zapruder film" was in existence, though it would be barred from the public until 1975.

But though many, including Mary, were suspicious, only a few people were directly aware that immediately following the events in Dallas, an elite group within the National Security apparatus were moving quickly to contain anything that might reveal a conspiracy. Nowhere was this chicanery more evident than what took place with Abraham Zapruder's infamous 8-millimeter home movie during the weekend following the assassination. For years, controversy has surrounded the alleged chain of custody of the original Zapruder film, and the three copies that were processed later in the afternoon of November 22. What remained unknown until 2009—not just to Mary, but to the rest of us—was that the original (not a copy) 8-millimeter home movie taken by Abraham Zapruder was, in fact, delivered to the CIA's most secretive facility, the National Photographic Interpretation Center (NPIC) in Washington. The film was delivered by two Secret Service agents at approximately ten o'clock on Saturday evening, November 23, the day after the assassination.

CIA director John McCone had called NPIC director Arthur Lundahl several hours earlier and told him to prepare for the delivery of a film—not yet known publicly as "the Zapruder film"—that had captured the assassination. McCone told Lundahl he wanted a full briefing on the film's contents early the following morning—Sunday, November 24. Lundahl immediately called his chief assistant, Dino Brugioni, to make preparations for the film's Saturday evening arrival.

"I was the duty officer at NPIC that weekend," Brugioni recalled in early 2009 in an interview for this book. "Lundahl called me and told me to assemble a crew and get into work. He told me it was going to involve pictures and that the Secret Service wanted support. I called Ralph Pearce, our best photogrammatist, and then Bill Banfield. We were there when the film arrived. It was 10 or 11 [P.M.] in the evening."[20]

In placing the Zapruder film in the hands of the NPIC, McCone was enlisting the help of the man who was arguably the world's foremost photo analyst. Known as the father of modern imagery analysis and imagery intelligence, Arthur C. Lundahl had been recruited by the CIA in 1953 to head the agency's Photographic Intelligence Division (PID); he would be designated the first director of NPIC when it was formally created in 1961. Lundahl, in his capacity as NPIC's first director, expanded the center into a national, multidepartmental component of the intelligence community, hiring over a thousand employees drawn from the CIA and the Department of Defense. NPIC was, indeed, as one former employee referred to it, "Lundahl's Palace." Starting with President Eisenhower, Art Lundahl's presidential briefings became legendary during an era when aircraft such as the U-2, the SR-71 Blackbird, and satellite imagery reconnaissance programs were made operational. A "Lundahl briefing" was considered the gold standard by which all other intelligence briefings to presidents were judged. Serving Presidents Eisenhower, Kennedy, Johnson, and Nixon, all of whom had nothing but the highest praise for his knowledge and expertise, Art Lundahl retired in 1973, having received a personal letter and a silver memento of the Cuban Missile Crisis from President Kennedy, as well as the CIA's Distinguished Intelligence Medal. Her Majesty Queen Elizabeth II eventually named Lundahl a Knight of the British Empire.

Equally impressive was Art Lundahl's chief assistant and "right-hand man," Dino Brugioni, who later established himself, subsequent to his career at NPIC, as a highly acclaimed author in the field of photo intelligence and analysis (*Eyeball to Eyeball, Photo Fakery,* and recently (2010) *Eyes in the Sky: Eisenhower, the CIA and Cold War Aerial Espionage*). Prior to entering the intelligence world, Dino Brugioni had distinguished himself as part of a World War II bomber crew that flew sixty-six successful missions. Highly trained and thoroughly competent in all aspects of photographic imagery and analysis, Brugioni regularly accompanied his boss to the White House and all "seventh-floor" classified briefings at NPIC and CIA headquarters.

That Saturday, however, the day after the assassination, Dino Brugioni and his crew were caught off guard by what arrived late that evening: an already-developed 8-millimeter home movie film that was, according to Brugioni, the *original* film that Abraham Zapruder had taken of the Kennedy assassination the day before. The film had been developed the day before on Friday afternoon in Dallas right after the assassination.[1] The world's foremost photographic intelligence center, however, didn't have an in-house, 8-millimeter film projector. Despite the late hour, crew member Bill Banfield called the manager of Fuller & d'Albert, a local photo supply store in downtown Washington at his home, and arranged to pick up a brand-new 8-millimeter projector that night. While Banfield was procuring the projector, Dino Brugioni and Ralph Pearce examined the film with a microstereoscope.

"The film arrived in a reel which was inside a box," Brugioni recalled. "We went 'white glove'[2] all the way. I'm sure it was the original. Everything pointed [that] we were working with the original. We viewed the film at least three or four times. We ran it first at the regular speed, then ran it at various different speeds. The Secret Service pointed out what they wanted."

Brugioni and his crew weren't prepared for what they were about to see. The assembled team in the NPIC briefing room gasped in horror. "What grabbed us all were his [JFK's] brains flying through the air," Dino told me solemnly. "We counted all the frames in the briefing room and told the two Secret Service agents what we could do, and what we couldn't."[21] One of the major concerns Brugioni remembered was whether the president had been hit by gunfire while he passed the Stemmons Freeway sign, which blocked the view in the film. "Do you remember seeing the motorcade slowing down or stopping before the fatal head shot?" I asked him. "How many different shots, and from what directions, do you remember discussing or analyzing?" Brugioni said he didn't remember.

Under the vigilant eyes of the two Secret Service agents, the NPIC crew worked through the night, printing various frames on two identical sets of briefing boards. When Director Lundahl arrived at NPIC early next morning, he reviewed the notes that Brugioni had prepared, and took the two sets of identical briefing boards to his meeting with Director John McCone at CIA headquarters in Langley. The Secret Service also left early the next morning, taking with them the film, and a list of all the people who had been present for the night's work, which included "at least seven support staff" in addition to Dino Brugioni, Ralph Pearce, and Bill Banfield.

---

1   When first developed by Kodak in Dallas the day of the assassination, the film was still in its unslit, 16-mm wide "double 8" home movie film format, as received from the factory and as loaded into the camera. After three contact prints (copies) were struck at another lab in Dallas, the Kodak lab then slit (or split) the original and all three copies, as was normal practice, and joined the two halves of each of them together, thereby marrying the A and B sides, with a splice so that each film could then be played on a home 8-mm projector.

2   According to Dino Brugioni, the term 'white glove' denoted NPIC's highest sensitivity level used while working on all original film.

Sometime between November 24 and December 9, McCone told Bobby Kennedy that he thought "there were two people involved in the shooting [of President Kennedy]," despite the FBI's and the media's attempt to maintain Lee Harvey Oswald as the only assassin. McCone's remark to Bobby Kennedy likely had been engendered by Lundahl's NPIC early morning briefing on Sunday, November 24. McCone's disclosure was subsequently noted by Arthur Schlesinger Jr. in his diary on December 9, after he had spent the previous evening with Bobby Kennedy.[22]

In the days ahead, Bobby Kennedy turned to a close group of trusted friends and advisers as he attempted to make sense of what had happened in Dallas. If the head of the CIA had privately shared with him the fact that there were at least two shooters (by definition, a conspiracy), that detail was likely shared by Bobby with people in his inner circle, as it had been with Arthur Schlesinger. Certainly, it underscored an undeniable reality: the director of Central Intelligence, John McCone, had let it slip that there had, in fact, been, a conspiracy to assassinate President Kennedy. How close Mary Meyer was to anyone in Bobby's entourage wasn't definitively known, but she was very likely acquainted with some of them. Given her relationship with Jack, she had to have known some of what was being revealed.

Meanwhile, unknown to anyone—even to Dino Brugioni, who was the weekend duty officer at NPIC—on Sunday night, November 24, hours after Brugioni and his crew had concluded their work for Lundahl's briefing Sunday morning, a second, ultra-classified Zapruder film event took place at NPIC. That Sunday night, a lone Secret Service agent showed up at the NPIC with a *different* Zapruder film. Identifying himself as "Bill Smith," he was met by the NPIC's deputy director, Captain Pierre Sands, USN. Sands escorted "Smith" into a room with two NPIC employees: Morgan Bennett ("Ben") Hunter and Homer McMahon. McMahon years later said that the session that night was so sensitive and classified, even his own supervisor was not informed of the event. The two employees—Hunter and McMahon—were sworn to secrecy. "There was no record of this event," McMahon stated in a lengthy interview to the Assassination Records Review Board (ARRB) in July 1997. "There was no codename attached to this operation. I was sworn to secrecy and it could not be divulged."[23]

Secret Service agent "Bill Smith" told Homer McMahon that he had just come from Rochester, New York, where the 16-millimeter film now in his possession had been "processed" earlier that day at the CIA's "Hawkeye" facility (sometimes referred to as "Hawkeyeworks").[3] Classified and designated top secret, known for its state-of-the-art "clean facility," the CIA Hawkeye facility in Rochester required all technicians to wear full body suits of special fabric to avoid contamination.

"Hawkeye had the capability to do almost anything with any film product," recalled Brugioni. While there is still debate among Kennedy assassination researchers as to whether the Zapruder film has been altered, the recent revelations by Dino Brugioni, along with Homer McMahon's 1997 interview at the ARRB, clearly underscore the likelihood of alteration. That alteration plausibly could have taken place sometime after early Sunday morning, when the original 8-millimeter film left NPIC, and before Sunday night, when some *version* of the film returned to NPIC in a 16-millimeter format. The CIA's Hawkeye facility in Rochester was the ideal place, technically superior and capable of such an alteration. "They could do anything," Brugioni repeated emphatically.

Interviewed once on the telephone and twice in person by the staff of the Assassination Records Review Board in 1997, Homer McMahon was blunt, his statements staggering. After reviewing the 16-millimeter film at NPIC that Sunday evening, November 24, with his assistant Morgan Bennett Hunter, he was sure, he told the ARRB, that "about eight (8) shots" had been fired at the president's limousine.

"[As to how many shots were fired] what was it that you observed on the film's examination, in your opinion?" asked Jeremy Gunn, the chief counsel to the ARRB.

"About eight shots," said the former NPIC employee Homer McMahon in 1997.

"And where did they come from?" Gunn further inquired.

"Three different directions, at least," replied McMahon. "I expressed my opinion that night, but it was already preconceived. I did not agree with the analysis at the time. I didn't have to. I was [just] doing the work. That's the way

---

3   The 16-mm Zapruder film delivered to Homer McMahon by "Bill Smith" was an *unslit* double 8 home movie which McMahon believed to be the original film. He vividly and independently recalled during his first (telephonic) ARRB interview that this 16-mm wide film (from which he made enlargements of individual frames for briefing boards) contained *opposing 8-mm wide image strips going in opposite directions*, the precise characteristics of an original film right out of the camera before the A and B sides had been slit to 8-mm width and spliced together. That is, what had been a slit, 8-mm wide original film on Saturday night (November 23) when it had been delivered to Dino Brugioni, had been magically transformed back into an *unslit, 16-mm wide* double 8 "original" film 24 hours later, when it was delivered to Homer McMahon. The clear implication here is that the courier from the Hawkeye facility delivered to McMahon an altered film, masquerading as a camera original. Since the film had been altered, it had to be handled by a different group of NPIC employees; therefore at the second NPIC event on Sunday night (November 24), Dino Brugioni, who was the NPIC duty officer in charge that weekend, and his crew were never notified of this event. Instead, Homer McMahon and his assistant Ben Hunter were brought in to handle the altered film, and help create a second set of (sanitized) briefing boards.

I felt about it. It was preconceived. You don't fight city hall. I wasn't there to fight them. I was there to do the work."

"Do you remember what [Secret Service agent] Smith's analysis was?" asked Douglas P. Horne, chief analyst for military records at the ARRB.

"He thought there were three (3) shots," recalled McMahon. "He went with the standard concept, that Oswald was the shooter."[24]

When I interviewed Dino Brugioni in 2009, he was both shocked and mystified when he heard about the subsequent Zapruder film event that had taken place at the NPIC Sunday evening (November 24). As the NPIC on-call duty officer during the assassination weekend, Brugioni should have been notified. He wasn't, and for good reason. Why? Homer McMahon and Ben Hunter had assisted in the preparation of a set of briefing boards that were significantly different in size and composition (as well as, presumably, in image content) from those made on Saturday night by Brugioni and his colleagues. When shown photos of the one surviving set of Homer McMahon's briefing boards made on November 24, Brugioni categorically told me that they were *not* the briefing boards he had made on Saturday night.[25] It appeared that the skulduggery that had taken place was known only at the highest levels, part of a well-organized cover-up, to which even mid-to-upper level CIA officers like Brugioni weren't privy.

In the spring of 2011, I visited Dino Brugioni at his home in Virginia to further discuss the Zapruder film. I showed him a high-resolution image of the one and only frame in the extant Zapruder film that graphically depicts the fatal head shot, frame 313. Dino was incredulous there was *only* one frame of the head explosion—then repeatedly rejected the possibility, based upon what he had personally witnessed when he had viewed the camera-original Zapruder film on Saturday evening, November 23, 1963. I asked him several times, "Was there more than one frame?" Dino responded unequivocally there was indeed:

"Oh yeah! Oh yeah . . . I remember all of us being shocked. . . . it was *straight up* [gesturing high above his own head] . . . *in the sky*. . . . There should have been more than one frame. . . . I thought the spray was, say, three or four feet from his head. . . . what I saw was more than that [in the image of frame 313 being shown to him] . . . it wasn't low [as in frame 313], it was high . . . *there was more than that in the original*. . . . It was way high off of his head . . . and I can't imagine that there would only be one frame. What I saw was more than you have there [in frame 313]."[26]

Why was it necessary to alter the film and produce a different version of what had occurred? According to AARB staff member Douglas P. Horne, author of the 2009 five-volume *Inside the Assassination Records Review Board,* "they had to remove whatever was objectionable in the film—most likely, the car [the president's limousine] stop, seen by over fifty witnesses in Dealey Plaza, and the exit debris which would inevitably have been seen in the film leaving the *rear* of President Kennedy's head. They would also have had to add to the film whatever was desired—such as a large, painted-on exit wound generally consistent with the enlarged, altered head wound depicted in the autopsy photos, which were developed the day before on Saturday, November 23, by Robert Knudsen at NPC [Naval Photographic Center] Anacostia."[27] Horne was adamant in his book about the falsity of the photographic record:

> The brain photographs in the National Archives today *cannot be,* **and are not** [Horne's emphasis]**,** photographs of President Kennedy's brain. This we now know beyond any reasonable doubt. The purpose for creating this false photographic record was to suppress evidence that President Kennedy was killed by a shot or shots from the front, and to insert into the record false "evidence" consistent with the official story that he was shot only from behind. This discovery is the single most significant "smoking gun" indicating a government cover-up within the medical evidence surrounding President Kennedy's assassination, and is a direct result of the JFK Records Act, which in turn was fathered by the film *JFK.*[28]

Simply put, the conspiracy to murder the president, if it were to succeed, had to be matched by an equal, and perhaps more elaborate, conspiracy to manipulate the evidence to support the contrived narrative of only three shots, all fired from *behind* the president's motorcade from the sixth floor of the Texas School Book Depository, from one rifle, by one man. While eyewitness accounts in general are often vulnerable to misinterpretation, physical forensic evidence is much less so, and therefore poses a far greater challenge.

The most significant efforts were applied to the manipulation of physical evidence with respect to the gunshot wounds inflicted on President Kennedy's body. As documented by David Lifton in *Best Evidence* (1980), President Kennedy's body did not make an uninterrupted journey from Parkland Memorial Hospital in Dallas to Bethesda Naval Hospital near Washington, D.C. As Lifton explained in his bestselling and carefully documented forensic thriller,

President Kennedy's body left Dallas in an ornamental, bronze ceremonial casket, wrapped in cloth bedsheets—and yet it arrived at Bethesda Naval Hospital in a cheap, gray shipping casket, encased in a zippered, rubberized body bag.

As Lifton pointed out, there was a *possibility* that some—or all—of the president's wounds had been tampered with prior to the arrival of his body at Bethesda. Indeed, the entry wound in the throat had been enlarged—obliterated, actually—by the time the Bethesda autopsy began at 8:15 P.M., and the posterior head wound had been dramatically enlarged to five times its original size, so that it encompassed not just the rear of the skull, as it had when first seen in Dallas, but the top and the right side as well, when examined at Bethesda. Lifton also presented persuasive evidence that Kennedy's shipping casket arrived at Bethesda close to fifteen minutes *prior* to the official motorcade from Andrews Air Force Base carrying the bronze Dallas casket. This meant that the bronze Dallas casket seen by millions on television was empty when it was off-loaded from Air Force One at Andrews. In 1997, the ARRB obtained an official military report that verified, *beyond all reasonable doubt*, the earlier arrival of President Kennedy's body at Bethesda, thus proving there had been a break in the chain of custody of the body, prior to the autopsy. ARRB staff member Douglas Horne, in his 2009 book *Inside the Assassination Records Review Board*, using new evidence gleaned from the ARRB's ten autopsy witnesses, provided confirmation of Lifton's 1980 hypothesis that President Kennedy's wounds had, in fact, been altered prior to the commencement of the 8:15 P.M. Bethesda autopsy.[29]

Both Douglas Horne and David Lifton agree today that the entry wound in President Kennedy's throat was crudely tampered with in transit, prior to the body's arrival at Bethesda. But whereas Lifton speculated in his book that Kennedy's head wounds were surgically altered prior to arrival at Bethesda, Horne has presented a compelling case that postmortem surgery—forensic tampering—was actually performed at Bethesda Naval Hospital *prior* to the start of the official autopsy. All the facts point to the conclusion that evidence tampering of the most serious nature—the clandestine expansion of JFK's head wound and the removal of evidence (bullet fragments and brain tissue)—was performed by Dr. James J. Humes, the lead Navy pathologist, as part of a Navy cover-up of the medical evidence, *after* President Kennedy's body arrived at 6:35 P.M., and *before* the start of the official autopsy at 8:15. The autopsy photos and x-rays in the National Archives collection today, Horne has concluded, actually demonstrate the results of clandestine surgery performed by the Naval pathologist, *not* the damage caused by bullets in Dallas. This was, and remains, an intentional misrepresentation by the U.S. government.[30]

Horne and Lifton are also in agreement that the "best evidence"—the body of the deceased president—was surgically altered to (1) remove evidence prior to the autopsy, and (2) to radically change the appearance and size of both the head wound and the entry wound in the throat, so that they were much more compatible with the myth of one lone shooter firing from behind the motorcade. All evidence of frontal entry on President Kennedy's body was surgically removed prior to the commencement of his autopsy.[31] As of 2012, Douglas Horne and David Lifton have together established the clear-cut obstruction of justice that took place in the forensic alteration of President Kennedy's wounds. No longer speculation, it is now an undeniable fact.

And that is why one problem in the immediate aftermath of President Kennedy's assassination wouldn't go away—a piece of conspiracy evidence available to Mary Meyer and anyone else observing events unfolding in "real time" in the media. After the president had been declared dead, the two attending physicians in Dallas, Dr. Malcolm Perry and Dr. Kemp Clark, gave a short press conference. According to Tom Wicker of the *New York Times*, the two physicians described the president's throat wound on the afternoon of the assassination: "Mr. Kennedy was hit by a bullet in the throat, just below the Adam's apple," they said. "This would have had the appearance of a bullet's entry."[32] In fact, when Dr. Perry was asked by a reporter at the press conference immediately following the announcement of President Kennedy's death, he confirmed this opinion—that President Kennedy's throat wound was an entrance wound. If the government was about to declare that all shots came from behind the president, Dr. Perry was unknowingly, and indirectly, asserting there had been more than one shooter, again making the president's assassination by definition a conspiracy.

Reporter:	Where was the entrance wound?
Dr. Perry:	There was an entrance wound in the neck. As regards the one on the head, I cannot say.
Reporter:	Which way was the bullet coming on the neck wound? At him?
Dr. Perry:	It appeared to be coming at him.

Reporter: Doctor, describe the entrance wound. You think from the front in the throat?

Dr. Perry: The wound appeared to be an entrance wound in the front of the throat; yes, that is correct.[33]

That evening after the press conference, according to Audrey Bell, the nurse who had been the supervisor of the operating and recovery rooms at Parkland Memorial Hospital, Dr. Perry was harassed by a barrage of telephone calls all through the night "from people at Bethesda Naval Hospital who were trying to get him to change his mind about the opinion he had expressed at the Parkland Memorial Hospital press conference the day before; namely, that President Kennedy had an entry wound in the front of his neck." In an interview by ARRB members Douglas P. Horne and Jeremy Gunn on March 20, 1997, Audrey Bell confirmed her conversation with Dr. Perry when, on the morning of November 23, she had learned about the pressure he was being subjected to.[34] The second conspiracy—the cover-up—had been under way immediately after the assassination.

During the months that followed, however, Dr. Perry did alter his conclusion, finally testifying before the Warren Commission that the throat wound "could be consistent with an exit wound."[35] The relentless pressure applied to Dr. Perry amounts to another "alteration" of evidence in an attempt to prove that the shooting came from behind the motorcade—that is, from Oswald— and not from sharpshooters positioned somewhere in front of the motorcade, likely behind the fence on the grassy knoll.

Nonetheless, long before the Warren Commission proceedings began, the theory of "throat wound as entrance wound" was gaining traction, as were some other anomalies. Mary Meyer's access to Kenny O'Donnell shortly after the events in Dallas likely provoked her suspicion as well as horror, and his perspective had to have aroused her curiosity. O'Donnell had been a *witness* to the fact that the shots were fired from in front of the limousine, not from where Oswald was alleged to have been.

Before the end of the first month after the assassination, two articles appeared in national media outlets raising considerable doubt that there had been only one shooter. The first article, by attorney Mark Lane, was entitled "Oswald Innocent? A Lawyer's Brief;" the second, by history professor Staughton Lynd and Jack Minnis, was called "Seeds of Doubt: Some Questions about the Assassination."[36] Whether either of these articles were included among Mary's "clippings of the JFK assassination" or not, it is quite likely that she would have come across them, as she would have been on the lookout for further validation of her growing suspicion concerning the treachery taking place in the cover-up.

Attorney Mark Lane's article, "Oswald Innocent? A Lawyer's Brief," was published in the left-leaning *National Guardian* on December 19. Lane had offered his feature gratis to any number of periodicals, including the *New Republic*, *Look*, *Life*, the *Saturday Evening Post*, and the *Progressive*. No one would touch it. The *New York Times*, unwilling to muster any journalistic courage or integrity of its own, yet not wanting to be outdone, knowing what was coming, published a story about Lane's *National Guardian* article the very same day it appeared, suggesting they had gone to the trouble of obtaining an advance copy.[37] Lane's article immediately ignited a firestorm of controversy, and its publication would become a defining moment in his career, setting the stage for an unrelenting pursuit that ultimately took him to a showdown at the doorsteps of the CIA in 1985. So many additional press runs of Lane's article were needed to keep newsstands supplied, the *Guardian* editors eventually reprinted it as a special pamphlet. It was inconceivable that such an article—published within a month of events in Dallas—would have escaped Mary's attention.

The then thirty-seven-year-old Mark Lane took no prisoners with his "Oswald Innocent? A Lawyer's Brief." Already, the *New York Times* on November 26 had published the text of Dallas district attorney Henry Wade's press conference, given shortly after Oswald's murder. Wade had presented fifteen assertions concerning the sole guilt of Lee Harvey Oswald. Lane scrutinized not only Wade's assertions, but also the contrived narrative that was emerging. He challenged the government's narrative and exposed its many inconsistencies and half-truths. Point by point, Lane rebutted every allegation that Wade had made about Oswald's guilt, particularly those reprinted uncritically by the *New York Times* itself. Indeed, Wade's remarks about Oswald were nothing but distorted half-truths that would not have stood up in any court proceeding. Charging, for example, that Oswald had murdered police officer J. D. Tippit before being arrested, Wade never reconciled the original statement of Dallas authorities that Tippit was shot in a movie theater, and their subsequent assertion that "he had been shot on a street," only to then change it again by moving the murder to a different street.

Most notable was Lane's forceful argument that President Kennedy's throat wound was one of entrance, not exit:

A motion picture taken of the President just before, during and after the shooting, and demonstrated on television showed that the President was looking directly ahead when the first shot, which entered his throat, was fired. A series of still pictures taken from the motion picture and published in *Life* magazine on Nov. 29 show exactly the same situation. The *Life* pictures also reveal that the car carrying the President was well past the turn from Houston St. and a considerable distance past the [Texas School book] depository building. The *Life* estimate in an accompanying caption states that the car with the President was 75 yards past the sixth-floor window when the first shot was fired.[38]

Lane then reviewed five separate newspaper accounts, including the *New York Times*, that quoted the Parkland Memorial Hospital doctors who had examined Kennedy's body—Dr. Kemp Clark, Dr. Malcolm Perry, and Dr. Robert McClelland—all of whom had described the throat wound as "an entrance wound." In particular, Lane pointed out that Dr. McClelland, too, had been quoted as saying that he saw bullet wounds every day, "sometimes several a day. This [President Kennedy's throat wound] did appear to be an entrance wound."[39]

Finally, lambasting the media for the uncritical reporting that had convicted Oswald before any defense could be assembled and before the evidence had been properly examined, the outspoken young attorney was unequivocal about the implications of the falsehoods that were being concocted to prove Oswald's guilt. "Let those who would deny a fair consideration of the evidence to Oswald because of a rage inspired, they say, by their devotion to the late President, ponder this thought," Lane wrote. "If Oswald is innocent, then the assassin of President Kennedy is still at large."[40]

Two days later, on December 21, the *New Republic* published an article entitled "Seeds of Doubt: Some Questions about the Assassination." It was authored by Spelman College history professor Staughton Lynd, who would move to a position at Yale in 1964, and Jack Minnis, a graduate student in political science at Tulane University and the research director for the Student Nonviolent Coordinating Committee (SNCC). Like Mark Lane's article, this article in the liberal *New Republic* would articulate some of the bedrock questions about the assassination that would never be satisfactorily reconciled by the Warren Report and that persist to this day. This article, too, had likely captured Mary's attention, coming immediately on the heels of the Lane exposé.

Citing *New York Times* reporter Tom Wicker's November 23 interview of the two Dallas attending physicians, the authors arrived at the same conclusion as Mark Lane regarding President Kennedy's throat wound: It was an entrance wound, indicating that at least one shot had been fired from in front of the motorcade. Taken together, both articles articulated issues that ruled out the possibility that Oswald, or any one person alone, could have pulled off a feat of the magnitude that had occurred that day in Dallas.

Throughout his life, Mark Lane would valiantly continue to lead a crusade to obtain the truth about President Kennedy's assassination. Immediately after Dallas, he founded the Citizens' Committee of Inquiry. Speaking almost daily to the fact that there had been a conspiracy that was now being covered up, Lane even volunteered to defend the deceased Lee Harvey Oswald in front of the Warren Commission; however, the offer was rejected. Oswald's mother, Marguerite Oswald, would retain Lane to defend her son's reputation anyway. Lane's books would eventually become international bestsellers—after Mary had been murdered. She would not live to finally witness attorney Mark Lane (*Hunt v. Liberty Lobby*) expose E. Howard Hunt on the witness stand in January 1985 for the pathological liar he was: Hunt *had*, in fact, been in Dallas on the day of the assassination, acting as one of the paymasters for the conspiracy. Leslie Armstrong, the jury's forewoman, would state to the media in attendance immediately following the trial's conclusion: "The evidence was clear. The CIA had killed President Kennedy, Hunt had been part of it, and that evidence so painstakingly presented, should now be examined by the relevant institutions of the United States government so that those responsible for the assassination might be brought to justice."[41]

In Washington, the *Post*, as well as the rest of the national media, avoided the story about the jury's verdict—a case in which the unanimous jury, on the basis of the evidence presented during the trial, had found the CIA's role in the president's assassination to be conclusive.

On December 22, an unusually newsworthy editorial appeared in the *Washington Post*, followed by a somewhat ominous event. President Harry Truman was the author of the editorial, "U.S. Should Hold CIA to Intelligence," published in the morning edition of the *Post*, one month, to the day, after the assassination. Mary Meyer, who had a delivered-daily subscription to the *Post*, would have to have seen the Truman editorial that morning. It contained an eerie warning, even a kind of coded message for the most discerning. "There is something about the way the CIA has been functioning that is casting a shadow over our historic position and I feel we need to correct it," concluded Truman at the end of his editorial. Suggesting something sinister, the former president regretted what he had given birth to in 1947:

> For some time I have been disturbed by the way CIA has been diverted from its original assignment. It has become an operational and at times a policy-making arm of the Government. This has led to trouble and may have compounded our difficulties in several explosive areas.

That Truman was making such a statement exactly one month to the day after Dallas was astounding in and of itself. His warning was ominous. "But there are now some searching questions that need to be answered," wrote the former president. "I, therefore, would like to see the CIA be restored to its original assignment as the intelligence arm of the President, and whatever else it can properly perform in that special field—and that its operational duties be terminated or properly used elsewhere." Like the slain president, who had intended to neuter the operational arm of the CIA after his reelection in 1964, President Truman had come to a similar conclusion about the Agency—and with good reason.[42]

According to veteran researcher and author Ray Marcus, the editorial appeared only in the first edition of the *Post* that morning. It was omitted from all subsequent editions that day. Who would have made the decision to limit its publication? Moreover, the editorial was never picked up by any other media outlet, nor discussed by any other journalist, columnist, or broadcast commentator. It simply evaporated from the public landscape.

"I can't read it any other way but [as] a warning by him [President Truman] that the CIA was involved in the [JFK] assassination," said Marcus. "If that wasn't what he meant, then I can't imagine he would have written and/or released it then for fear of having it read that way."[43] Was Truman trying to alert the nation to the CIA's involvement? Marcus came into possession of a draft of the editorial from the Harry S. Truman Library and Museum that was dated December 11, 1963. "To me, this further strengthens the already high probability that in warning of the Agency's excesses he had the assassination in mind."[44] Marcus reiterated that same position in an interview for this book.[45]

Unknown to Mary, however, or anyone else at the time, was the fact that Allen Dulles, the former CIA director defrocked by President Kennedy after the Bay of Pigs failure, undertook a personal covert operation of his own after the short-lived Truman editorial appeared. At the very first executive session of the Warren Commission on December 5, 1964, Allen Dulles had wasted no time, not only in establishing himself as the so-called intelligence expert, but also in immediately attempting to control and narrow the parameters of the entire inquiry. At that meeting, according to author Peter Dale Scott, the disgraced spymaster took it upon himself to give each member of the commission a copy of a book that argued that all American assassinations, unlike European ones, were the work of solitary, deranged, and disaffected gunmen, thereby using his influence to immediately discourage any real investigation into the possibility of conspiracy.[46]

Whatever the ordinary reader's interpretation of Truman's *Washington Post* editorial, Allen Dulles would clearly have understood the former president's implicit message. Again, according to Ray Marcus and based on his research of documents at the Truman Library, Dulles traveled to President Truman's home in Independence, Missouri, on April 17, 1964, using as a pretext for his visit a scheduled talk he was to give in Kansas City, Missouri, that evening. His real mission, however, was almost certainly to document that his meeting with Truman took place that day so that he could then fabricate a story that Truman had come to disavow his December 22 editorial in the *Washington Post*.[47]

Four days later, on April 21, 1964, Dulles wrote a four-page memorandum to a former colleague, CIA general counsel Lawrence Houston, documenting his meeting with President Truman on April 17. It was in this memorandum that Dulles fabricated Truman's retraction of his December 22 *Washington Post* editorial; the memorandum would be placed in CIA files. It first documented all the extraneous topics of Dulles's conversation with Truman, as well as all the adulation he had bestowed upon his former boss during their meeting. The Dulles memorandum then documented their discussion of Truman's editorial in the *Post*. Allegedly, Dulles had produced a copy of the editorial that he proceeded to review with Truman in person. Dulles claimed in his memorandum to Houston that Truman had "studied attentively the *Post* story and seemed quite astounded by it. In fact, he said that this was all wrong. He then said he felt it had made a very unfortunate impression."[48]

But President Truman never wavered from the position he had stated in his December 22 *Washington Post* editorial, in which he had completely opposed the CIA's covert operations arm. In fact, and ironically, one year exactly after Kennedy's historic American University address, Truman repeated his warning in a June 10, 1964, letter to *Look* magazine managing editor William

Arthur, underscoring his position that the CIA "was not intended to operate as an international agency engaged in strange activities."[49]

Why would Allen Dulles—the man whom Mary Meyer once compared to "Machiavelli, only worse"—go to such extremes to discredit a former president's written opinions? While the Truman editorial had been cut off at the pass, Dulles had to be worried about the possibility the editorial might be resuscitated at some point, adding weight to suspicions of CIA involvement in the death of the president and its subsequent cover-up.

"Dulles would have wanted to be in position to flash the Truman 'retraction,' with the hope that this would nip any serious questioning in the bud," said disaffected former CIA analyst Ray McGovern, who in 2003 co-founded the organization Veteran Intelligence Professionals for Sanity (VIPS). "As the *de facto* head of the Warren Commission, Dulles was perfectly positioned to exculpate himself and any of his associates, were any commissioners or investigators—or journalists—tempted to question whether the killing in Dallas might have been a CIA covert action."[50] The Dulles-Truman incident in April 1964 was yet another example of chicanery that illustrated the actions Allen Dulles and his loyal cadre were prepared to undertake in order to protect themselves and the secrets of the Agency they served.

One person Mary was almost sure to have sought out after Dallas was her friend and fellow artist William ("Bill") Walton, the man who had been her escort to many of the White House social events she had attended. According to Leo Damore, Mary had engaged Walton's counsel sometime in 1964. Walton had been aware, Damore said, of how distraught she was. According to Damore, he discreetly divulged to Mary the fact that Bobby long suspected the worst of foul play in his brother's demise, but that he had to keep a low profile for the time being. It was too dangerous to do anything else. Bobby did have a plan, Walton told her. Bobby would position himself to take back the presidency, but it would be years before he could do anything. "Throw yourself back into your work" had been his advice, as he, too, despaired over what had occurred. That's what he was doing, he told her.[51] It is not known whether Walton ever revealed to Mary the secret, historic mission he had undertaken at Bobby's request during a trip to the Soviet Union shortly after Jack's burial.

Bill Walton had met Jack Kennedy in Georgetown after World War II, and their friendship developed into something extraordinarily special. "I think he was deeply fond of me," Walton recalled in 1975. "I was of him. I haven't had many male friends as close as he became finally."[52] Fondly calling him "Billy Boy," Jack allowed Walton a level of access to the White House that few enjoyed. And so did Jackie, who thoroughly enjoyed his company and came to rely upon him. She also took a keen interest in Walton's two children, Matthew and Frances, whom Bill was raising alone since his divorce.

"I got to know Jackie Kennedy a good deal," recalled Bill Walton's son, Matthew, in an interview for this book. "She came around to our house a lot. She was very kind to me, and paid attention to me. I wrote a diary in those days, and she's the only one of my father's friends I mentioned. She listened to me and remembered our conversations later."[53]

But the other variable that made Walton "safe" was his sexual orientation. Though Walton was not openly gay (which in that era and social strata would have been social suicide), it was clear where his proclivities lay. Even so, he was "a man's man," yet "safe" to women like Jackie who came to revere his confidence.

Over the years, Walton had become the supreme Kennedy confidant and loyalist, not only to Jack and Jackie, but to Bobby as well. Both Jack and Jackie shared intimate secrets with him, often using him to communicate with one another. A bit older than both Jack and Bobby, Walton brought to the table an urbane sense of tasteful style and elegance that had its foundation in sincerity coupled with integrity. The president appointed him chairman of the Fine Arts Commission in 1963. Jackie and Bill Walton collaborated to safeguard various historic sections of the city, including the period architecture around Lafayette Square in downtown Washington. Yet, unlike the other political animals who surrounded the Kennedys, Walton had no need to play favorites; he had no expectation or desire of any reward. No doubt privy to any number of intimate secrets regarding Jack and Jackie, as well as Bobby, Walton never betrayed their confidences—not even to his children—or revealed the full extent of his access during his lifetime.

Having escorted Mary Meyer to the White House on many occasions, he obviously was aware of her romantic liaison with Jack, as were a number of other people—even if Ben and Tony Bradlee wanted to maintain they weren't. How much Jack actually confided in Billy Boy about his feelings for Mary (as he had done with Charlie Bartlett), no one knows, not even Walton's own children. The Walton trademark was always zipped lips. "He didn't talk much about what he really knew," recalled Matthew, "either about the Kennedy assassination or Mary Meyer's murder."[54] Surprisingly, not even Walton's children were aware of their father's secret mission after Dallas, ostensibly for the support of the arts in Russia.

In fact, it was not until 1997, some thirty-four years after Dallas, and three years after Walton's own death, that Yale historian Timothy Naftali and Russian historian Aleksandr Fursenko revealed the staggering account of the mission Bobby Kennedy had asked Walton to undertake immediately following President Kennedy's burial. Before Dallas, Walton had been scheduled to leave for Russia on November 22 on a goodwill mission to open a dialogue with Russian artists. The idea was part of President Kennedy's many-tiered peace initiative with the Soviet Union that had begun with his American University commencement address in June, followed by the historic nuclear test ban treaty in August. Walton was to be the president's emissary to Leningrad and Moscow, where he would preside over the opening of an American graphic arts exhibit for the U.S. Information Agency. But as he was preparing to leave for Russia that day, he received word of the president's death and immediately canceled his trip.

A few days after the president's burial at Arlington Cemetery, Bill Walton and his children, Matthew and Frances, visited Bobby Kennedy's Hickory Hill estate. Jackie and Bobby were both present. Years later, in an interview for this book, Walton's daughter, Frances Buehler, still vividly remembered Bobby taking her father into another room with Jackie and "closing the door." She also recalled seeing her father walking with Bobby alone outside later that afternoon. "We had no idea what was being said," recalled Frances. In fact, the pieces of that puzzle would not be fully revealed to her until 2007, when her brother showed her David Talbot's book *Brothers*.[55]

As author Talbot details in his book, Bobby Kennedy, like his brother, trusted Bill Walton unconditionally. The loyal Kennedy ally had proven his integrity on innumerable occasions and to a degree rarely seen in the political snake pit of Washington. That day, during the Waltons' visit to Hickory Hill, within days of the assassination, Bobby and Jackie asked their close friend to quickly reschedule his artistic mission to Russia. They wanted him to deliver a special, secret message to Georgi Bolshakov, formerly a KGB agent under journalistic cover in Washington, who the Kennedys had come to rely upon when they needed to communicate with Khrushchev directly during critical moments. Indeed, Bolshakov had once been referred to by *Newsweek* as the "Russian New Frontiersman" because he had become so close to Bobby. Official Washington was, of course, averse to using a known KGB agent for diplomatic missions, but that didn't stop Bobby from developing a substantial relationship that had proven its reliability over time.[56]

Bobby and Jackie knew that through Bolshakov their message to the Soviets would be directly communicated to Nikita Khrushchev. They wanted "the Russian who they felt best understood John Kennedy to know their personal opinions of the changes in the U.S. government since the assassination." On November 29, Walton resuscitated his trip to Russia. He had explicit instructions from Bobby to bypass the American Embassy upon arrival in Moscow and to meet with Bolshakov at some unofficial location, so Walton sat down with Bolshakov at the Sovietskaya restaurant. Walton's message was crystal clear: "Dallas was the ideal location for such a crime," he told the Soviet intelligence officer. "Perhaps there was only one assassin, but he did not act alone." Bolshakov, who had been deeply upset by the assassination, listened intently as Walton explained that the Kennedys now believed there had been a large domestic political conspiracy at work. While Oswald appeared to have ostensible connections to the Communist world, the Kennedys believed that the president had been murdered by "domestic opponents."[57]

Walton also communicated an even bigger bombshell: that the Kennedys considered the selection of Lyndon Johnson for the vice presidency to have been "a dreadful mistake." Lyndon Johnson's ties to big Texas oil and military defense companies would, in their own way, sabotage John Kennedy's unfinished plans for world peace and détente with the Soviet Union. "Robert McNamara, in his position of secretary of defense, was the only one to be trusted now," he said. He described McNamara as "completely sharing the views of President Kennedy on matters of war and peace." Bobby did have a plan, Walton told Bolshakov, to eventually retake the White House where he would then continue his brother's vision for world peace, but that wasn't going to be possible before 1968.[58] Yet this historic mission further demonstrated how the Kennedys, from the very beginning, never believed in the Warren Commission or the final Warren Report, released in September 1964. If, as Bobby Kennedy believed, his brother "had been killed by a powerful plot that grew out of one of the government's secret anti-Castro operations," they were sadly powerless to do anything about it, "since they were facing a formidable enemy and they no longer controlled the government."[59]

Bill Walton appeared never to have never talked about his secret mission to Moscow with anyone. Even his own children weren't aware of it until years after his death. "My father never really said much about the Kennedy assassination, even though he had the entire-volume set of the Warren Commission," recalled Matthew. He did recall a strange outburst from his father one evening at dinner shortly after his Moscow return. Had Oswald really done it?

a friend asked him at dinner. Bill Walton, the usually calm, even-tempered, urbane gentleman, exploded. "It doesn't fucking matter!" he yelled, startling everyone at the table. "Who gives a shit!"[60]

Ten months later—the day Mary Pinchot Meyer was murdered—Bill Walton received the upsetting telephone call. "My father answered the phone and then told me she [Mary Meyer] had been shot, shot on the towpath," Matthew said. Further recalling that his father was never given to emotional outbursts, Matthew said the elder Walton did something very uncharacteristic. "I was so struck at how upset he was," Matthew continued. His father had become enraged. "What's happening to everybody?" Walton screamed. "Everybody I know is killed, murdered, assassinated. Killed by strangers!" Whereupon he rushed outside and burst into tears. "He wasn't the kind of person who usually did this," his son recalled. "It was so unusual for him to burst out in the way he did."[61]

Had the murder of Mary Meyer signaled a reminder—don't talk, your life, possibly that of your children, might well be in danger? Walton was never given to gossiping anyway, even whispering. Nonetheless, as Bobby's presidential bid started to take form in 1968, Bill Walton once again embraced the Kennedy dream, excitedly planning to do whatever he could for Bobby's campaign. And once again—this time forever—the Kennedy dream would die with Bobby's assassination. Bill Walton retreated into seclusion, even stopped painting for an extended period. According to Matthew, his father could occasionally be heard yelling, "Fuck life!"[62]

The Kennedy antipathy toward Lyndon Johnson was well known. "A dreadful mistake" had indeed taken place when Johnson manipulated himself into the position of vice president. Mary had to have known of both Jack's and Bobby's animosity toward him, and she likely knew they intended to dump him prior to the 1964 election. Lyndon Johnson had long since become a political liability. His involvement in scandals with his aide Bobby Baker and business tycoon Billie Sol Estes were about to make headlines. By 1963, Billie Sol Estes had been convicted on more than fifty counts of fraud. Leaks from prison suggested he had paid off the vice president on any number of occasions. Evelyn Lincoln, President Kennedy's personal secretary, noting the implications, asked the president three days before Dallas (November 19) who his choice for a running mate might be. "He looked straight ahead, and without hesitating he replied, 'At this time, I am thinking about Governor Terry Sanford of North Carolina. But it will not be Lyndon.'"[63]

During the summer of 1963, *Life* magazine had been developing a major feature story concerning Vice President Lyndon Johnson and his scandalous dealings with Bobby Baker. The in-depth story was scheduled for publication in late November, right after the president's trip to Dallas. The story, according to James Wagenvoord, at the time the chief assistant to *Life*'s Publishing Projects Director, Phil Wootton, had been researched and written by members of the senior staff at *Life* who had a direct line to Bobby Kennedy. The article would be published without bylines.

"It was all coming from Bobby," recalled Wagenvoord. "It was going to blow Johnson right out of the water. We had him. He was done. Bobby Baker had taken the fall for Johnson. Johnson would have been finished and off the 1964 ticket, and would have probably been facing prison time."[64]

In fact, on the very day of Kennedy's assassination in Dallas, the Senate Rules Committee on Capitol Hill was meeting, presided over by Senator B. Everett Jordan of North Carolina. During the proceedings, Senator John Williams of Delaware—who in October had already begun investigating the activities of Lyndon Johnson's close aide Bobby Baker—was being given documented testimony from a panicked Don Reynolds, a close associate of Bobby Baker's, who had been asked by Baker to arrange Lyndon Johnson's life insurance policy. The Reynolds bombshell was that he had seen Bobby Baker with a suitcase containing what Baker alleged was a $100,000 payoff to Lyndon Johnson for his role in securing the Tactical Fighter Experimental (TFX) contract for General Dynamics in Fort Worth, Texas. Reynolds also stated that he had refused several attempts by Johnson to buy his silence. However, Reynolds's testimony abruptly ended when news reached the committee that President Kennedy had been assassinated. What was clear was Reynolds's information would not only have ended Lyndon Johnson's political career, it also would have resulted in a criminal indictment.

In November 2009, former *Life* magazine assistant to the executive editor James Wagenvoord revealed to John Simkin, the founder of the U.K. Spartacus Educational website, the logistics of what took place at *Life* immediately subsequent to the Kennedy assassination: "The LBJ/Baker piece was in the final editing stages and was scheduled to break in the edition of November 29 or December 6 (on the newsstand four to five days earlier than the date). It had been prepared in relative secrecy by a small special editorial team. On Kennedy's death, research files and all numbered copies of the nearly print-ready draft were gathered up by my boss (he had been the top editor on the team) and shredded. The issue that was to expose LBJ instead featured the Zapruder film."[65]

Wagenvoord further substantiated in an interview for this book how the CIA's Operation Mockingbird was controlling *Life* magazine at the time. "All of our people would always go down to Washington to be debriefed by the CIA after they did big world trips before they came home," recalled Wagenvoord. "That was our news source. A lot of the high-level executives in publishing companies had been involved with the OSS during the war. The whole publishing thing was hooked into the government so tightly, in the same way the Internet companies are now."[66]

Edward K. Thompson, editor at *Life* during 1963, was, according to Wagenvoord, a close friend of Allen Dulles's. Wagenvoord remembered being introduced to Dulles in Thompson's office, having been called to the office to deliver a $10,000 check made out to the former CIA director. "We paid Allen Dulles $10,000 for a nothing story," recalled Wagenvoord. But that event paled alongside what Wagenvoord witnessed at *Life*'s offices on Sunday morning, November 24—*before* Oswald was gunned down on national television.

As James Wagenvoord stood outside his boss's office, a man in a gray suit pushed through the glass door that opened from the elevator bank. He handed Wagenvoord a lumpy manila envelope. "This is Oswald material," the man said, giving Wagenvoord the package as he flashed his FBI credentials, and then quickly left.[67] Wagenvoord remembered opening the envelope and taking out a small, blue plastic reel that appeared to be a short 16-millimeter film, which he viewed later that day. The unsolicited footage, which had been shot months earlier by a New Orleans television news cameraman, was of Oswald handing out pro-Castro flyers on Canal Street near the World Trade Center in New Orleans, an event that had been staged to falsely portray Oswald as a Communist sympathizer, which, of course, he wasn't. "An hour later [after the film arrived at *Life*] the Fat Lady sang an encore. Jack Ruby shot Oswald," said Wagenvoord. The government's second conspiracy, the cover-up, had already penetrated the major media outlets, including *Life*.[68]

Within seventy-two hours after the events in Dallas (and one day after the president's funeral), President Lyndon Johnson signed a new National Security Action Memorandum (NSAM 273) that initiated the escalation of America's involvement in Vietnam. The reader will recall from the previous chapter that President Kennedy had created a strategy for America's extrication from Southeast Asia, which was formalized by the then top secret policy document National Security Action Memorandum 263 (NSAM 263), issued on October 11, 1963, ordering the removal of a thousand troops before the end of 1963, and the rest by the end of 1965.[69] On the afternoon of Kennedy's funeral, however, Johnson met in a closed-door session with Secretary of Defense McNamara, Secretary of State Dean Rusk, CIA director John McCone, and Vietnam ambassador Henry Cabot Lodge (whom President Kennedy had already planned to fire). "I am not going to lose Vietnam," Johnson declared. "I am not going to be the president who saw Southeast Asia go the way China went."[70] A month later at a White House Christmas Eve reception, meeting with the Joint Chiefs of Staff, Johnson told them, "Just let me get elected [in 1964], and then you can have your war."[71]

As 1964 unfolded, Mary, along with the rest of the country, would witness a horrific sea change taking shape. In January, the Joint Chiefs sent their new president a memo urging him to formally increase the U.S. commitment to Southeast Asia, as well as to consider a bombing campaign against North Vietnam, ostensibly as a strategy to win the war more quickly. Johnson willingly complied. By year's end, there would be more than twenty-three thousand troops in the region, well more than the sixteen thousand advisers present when Kennedy was assassinated. To get the bombing campaign against North Vietnam started, something else was needed: the perception by congressional leaders that it was warranted.

The so-called Gulf of Tonkin Incident became the pretext to do just that—a contrived event during a stormy night in August in the Gulf of Tonkin off the coast of North Vietnam. On August 2, the destroyer USS *Maddox*, then operating within the framework of a program of joint U.S.–South Vietnamese covert operations against North Vietnam—the kind of covert actions encouraged and justified by NSAM 273—was attacked by North Vietnamese PT boats that were reacting to these covert operations by defending the territorial integrity of North Vietnam. This first of two reported events in the Gulf of Tonkin off the coast of North Vietnam was a light and inconclusive skirmish that inflicted no serious damage on the USS *Maddox*.

Two days later, the USS *Maddox* and USS *Turner Joy* reported a second so-called torpedo boat attack in the Gulf of Tonkin. Following initial confusion on board the two ships, as well as in Washington, D.C., it was later ascertained that the event reported on August 4 was a "phantom attack," a nonevent in which the reporting vessels had mistaken low-lying clouds on their radar scopes during bad weather for enemy warships, and in which jumpy U.S. Navy sonarmen had imagined that they heard as many as nine torpedoes being launched against them by the "enemy." President Lyndon

Johnson and Secretary of Defense Robert McNamara exaggerated the nature of the second "attack," and falsely claimed U.S. Navy vessels, innocently operating on the high seas, had been attacked by Communist forces. This nefarious plan worked like a charm, to their everlasting discredit, and ultimately to America's misfortune. A manipulated Congress, once again led to view the reported incident as an escalation in the global Cold War between East and West, responded with the Gulf of Tonkin Resolution—a blank check for President Johnson's unlimited proliferation of a hot war in Vietnam. Sadly, a nonevent had been used as a casus belli to justify the escalation of U.S. involvement in Vietnam from a so-called technical advisory effort into a U.S.-led shooting war. With the Tonkin Gulf Resolution, President Kennedy's 1963 policy of disengagement and withdrawal from Vietnam had irrevocably been overturned, just eight months after his assassination. Until its repeal in May 1970, the Tonkin Gulf Resolution provided the "legal" basis for all subsequent escalation and continuation of the Vietnam War by both President Johnson and his successor, Richard Nixon.

Where was Secretary of Defense Robert Strange McNamara—the ally who had so steadfastly stood with Jack Kennedy the previous October to formulate the end of such a senseless military debacle? What had happened to the brilliant, loyal tactician of Kennedy's dream of peace in Southeast Asia? And why was he, McNamara, now walking obsequiously behind Johnson in his macho warmongering? McNamara, even in later life, when he realized it had all been so very wrong, would never answer that question. In an 2006 interview, author David Talbot confronted McNamara with the most singularly important question ever articulated regarding the escalation of the Vietnam War in 1964 and thereafter: "Why did he [McNamara] allow himself to become the brains of the war under LBJ after plotting with JFK to disengage from it?"

Despite a superficial public "mea culpa," Robert McNamara would forever avoid any real accountability or responsibility. His answer to Talbot—"Oh, I don't want to talk about that"[72]—revealed once again his patronizing chief executive arrogance, as if the deaths of 3.8 million Vietnamese,[73] as well as the deaths of more than 58,000 American combat soldiers (and an estimated 200,000 subsequent suicides of Vietnam veterans[4]) had no meaning in his equation. Such were "the best and the brightest" during the Cold War era.

---

4   A retired Veterans Administration doctor recently estimated that the number of Vietnam Veteran suicides was 200,000. The reason the official suicide statistics were so much lower was that in many cases the suicides were documented as accidents, primarily single-car drunk driving accidents and self-inflicted gunshot wounds that were not accompanied by a suicide note or statement. According to this doctor, the underreporting of suicides was primarily an act of kindness to the surviving relatives.

That year, Mary could not have helped but witness McNamara's betrayal of Kennedy's peace agenda—a betrayal that permitted Lyndon Johnson's reckless, destructive escalation to occur. It must have left her utterly demoralized to observe the White House, now inhabited by a ruthless, criminal cowboy, who, after a few years of being hammered by journalists—"Why were we in Vietnam?"—finally gave them his answer. At a private meeting with reporters, according to presidential historian Robert Dallek, President Lyndon Johnson offered his rejoinder: He casually "unzipped his fly, drew out his substantial organ and declared, 'This is why!' "[74] It must have been so deeply reassuring for all those who would at some point meet their death in Vietnam, as well as for the ones who had already made "the ultimate sacrifice," to finally comprehend the glorious, principled cause for which they were fighting and dying.

Whatever her suspicions before the release of the Warren Report, Mary's views had apparently made her a person of interest to someone. Author Nina Burleigh documented the fact that Mary's "maid found the doors to the garden open on a January [1964] morning while Mary and her sons were upstairs asleep" in their house on Thirty-Fourth Street in Georgetown. Reportedly, Mary filed a report with the police. When she returned from being away the following summer, wrote Burleigh, Mary was sure someone had been in her house. There was also an incident in which Mary found a very heavy door ajar in her basement, "a door neither she nor her sons could open without help." According to one Burleigh source, who remained anonymous, on more than one occasion Mary had wondered aloud, "What are they looking for in my house?" The incidents escalated throughout 1964. "She [Mary] did say to me she was scared about seeing somebody in her house," said Mary's friend Elizabeth Eisenstein in her interview with Burleigh. "She thought she had seen somebody leaving as she walked in. She was frightened."[75]

Even more revealing was Burleigh's interview with CIA wife Joanne ("Joan") Bross. Her husband, John, had been a longtime CIA covert action specialist, coming out of the OSS, another of Allen Dulles's "dream boys." With a Harvard blue-blooded pedigree, John Bross eventually rose to become deputy director of the Agency in 1963, a position he would hold until his retirement in 1971. The Brosses were close to all the upper-level CIA honchos, including the Angletons and the Meyers. Joan Bross and Mary were close enough that Mary, who dreaded CIA social functions and parties, would call Joan for information. "She always asked me how many people were going to be there," recalled Joan. "She was thinking about serious things and hated small talk, I think. She was asking big questions such as, 'Why are we here?'" Joan Bross also indicated that Jim Angleton had boasted to her that he had bugged not only Mary Meyer's telephone, but her bedroom as well. How long this had been going on, or when it had started, was never revealed, perhaps never known. According to Bross, the wiretaps could have begun as early as 1961 when Kennedy first took office, implying that Angleton may have known of Kennedy's interest in Mary for some time.[76] Without question, Angleton, and every other high-level CIA official, had been aware of Mary's undisguised contempt for the Agency. From the very beginning of Cord's CIA tenure, she had increasingly made no secret of her loathing of Allen Dulles; after her divorce, she would have been regarded as even more dangerous.

That spymaster Jim Angleton had the means to accomplish whatever he wanted was never in question. "Angleton ran everything, controlled everything in the CIA," said Joe Shimon, who served in the White House officially as a "Washington Police Inspector," but revealed to his daughter he was also working undercover for the CIA, and was their principal liaison to Mafia boss Johnny Roselli.[77] If Mary was using her telephone to discuss any of her suspicions or research into Jack's downfall, as well as what she had come to discover and was recording in her diary, Jim Angleton knew about it.

According to Leo Damore, Angleton's "Mary spying" escalated into a full-blown surveillance operation at the time the Warren Report was released in late September 1964. She had bought the paperback version, said Damore, and read it carefully, becoming further enraged at the cover-up taking place. According to Damore, her copy had notes in the margins, with a great many page corners turned over for future reference.[78]

Someone else—a man who never knew Leo Damore or his research—independently came to a nearly identical conclusion just before Christmas of 1992: former CIA contract operative Robert D. Morrow, whose 1992 book *First Hand Knowledge* largely went unnoticed when it first appeared. Damore, in fact, never mentioned Morrow, nor was there any reference to him in Damore's notes. Several well-regarded assassination researchers had already documented Morrow's long-standing role as an undercover Agency employee in the cesspool of the CIA-funded anti-Castro Cuban community that was determined to destabilize Castro's government. Morrow also claimed he became part of the plot to assassinate Kennedy, though some of Morrow's claims have also been questioned, even discredited. Nonetheless, Morrow remained, until the time of his death, a widely cited source in the assassination controversy, often consulted as an authority on various CIA operations. One of the best books ever written about the Kennedy assassination, Dick Russell's *The Man Who Knew Too Much*, relied on several of Morrow's accounts, which were corroborated by other books, one of which was author Noel Twyman's book *Bloody Treason* (1997).

In *First Hand Knowledge*, Robert Morrow provides a chilling account of an event that took place prior to Mary Meyer's murder. Shortly after the Warren Report was released, Morrow claimed, he was urgently called to Washington by his CIA boss, Marshall Diggs, who told Morrow, "There is a very prominent lady here in Washington who knows too much about the Company [the CIA], its Cuban operations, and more specifically about the President's assassination." Diggs went on to say the woman's talking might open up a lot of trouble for the CIA's anti-Cuban counterfeit money operation, an effort that Morrow himself had been running, and which Bobby Kennedy had shut down before his brother's assassination. Not understanding the significance of Diggs's comment, Morrow reminded his boss that the Warren Commission hadn't found out about the counterfeiting operation, and he therefore thought himself safe.

"I wish his brother thought that," Diggs reportedly said.

"You mean RFK?"

"Yes, RFK," exclaimed Diggs. "Now damn it, listen. As I said, there's a certain lady in town who has an inside track to Langley, and most importantly, to Bobby. Fortunately, an intimate friend of mine is one of her best friends." It was at that point Robert Morrow learned the identity of the woman that Diggs was referring to: Mary Meyer.[79]

Morrow's counterfeit money operation had been run by an anti-Castro Cuban by the name of Mario Kohly, the son of the former Cuban ambassador to Spain under the Batista regime before Castro took power in 1959. At that time, Kohly came to the United States to set up an organization known as the Cuban Liberators. He was introduced to Marshall Diggs, who eventually recruited Morrow in 1960 as a CIA contract agent. Shortly after his recruitment, Morrow met with high-level CIA covert operative Tracy Barnes, who asked Morrow to become Mario Kohly's CIA contact. According to one account, if the Bay of Pigs operation had been successful, the CIA was going to replace Fidel Castro as the president of Cuba with Mario Kohly.

"To get to the point," Diggs told Morrow in 1964, "[Mary] Meyer claimed to my friend that she positively knew that [CIA] Agency-affiliated Cuban exiles and the Mafia were responsible for killing John Kennedy. Knowing of my association with [Mario] Kohly, my friend immediately called me." Diggs urged Morrow to contact Kohly and tell him what was happening.

"So, what do I tell Kohly?" Morrow asked Diggs.

"Tell him what I told you—that as soon as the Meyer woman has the whole story, Robert Kennedy is going to be told that CIA-affiliated Cuban exiles and the Mafia killed his brother. Tell him, for God's sake, to make sure he has us covered, or Miami and New Orleans will be down the drain, and maybe us with them." Readers will recall, however, that Bobby Kennedy had already suspected the involvement of a CIA anti-Castro element in his brother's demise, but he had shared that observation with just a few of his closest, trusted advisers and with members of his family.[80]

"My God, Marshall, you're serious?" Morrow exclaimed to Diggs, realizing that his old boss was intimating that Mary Meyer should be eliminated immediately.

"Believe it. Even Tracy [Barnes] is concerned. Even though he could sanction it, he wouldn't dare put a hit on her [Mary Meyer]. At least not now."

Several days later, Robert Morrow met with Mario Kohly in New York and, as Diggs had instructed, relayed to Kohly the emerging problem of Mary Meyer's knowledge.

"Just tell Diggs I'll take care of the matter," said Kohly to Morrow.[81]

A week later, Mary Meyer was dead. Robert Morrow immediately came to suspect his meeting with Kohly had triggered Mary Meyer's death, and that Mario Kohly had set it all up. The entire incident sent Morrow into despair.

While author Nina Burleigh chose to dismiss Morrow's account as "rife with holes"—never identifying what exactly those "holes" were[82]—further inquiry suggests his account of Mary Meyer's death may well have been reliable. Author John Williams, professor emeritus of human development and family studies at the University of Wisconsin, befriended Robert Morrow in 1993, and remained close to him right up until his death in 1998. Since 2009, he has been at work on a book about Morrow, based on the four years he spent with him.[83]

According to John Williams, in an interview for this book, he was with Morrow at his house when Nina Burleigh called to interview him for her *A Very Private Woman*. Williams recalled his impressions of the conversation. He didn't think Morrow and Burleigh hit it off particularly well, largely because Morrow was still protective of what he knew, and "he found Burleigh's attitude devious."[84] Morrow had already shared with Williams his distress over Mary Meyer's death. His visit with Mario Kohly right before Mary's death had become the catalyst for her murder. "Bob was feeling deep shame around having told Kohly what he did about Mary Meyer," said Williams in 2004. At one point, Williams told Morrow's wife, Jeanne, that he thought Bob was more upset over

Mary Meyer's death than he was with the entire conspiracy to assassinate the president; his wife concurred.[85]

"Few people understand the kind of pressure Morrow felt during the Warren Commission," Williams maintained. "He told me he thought about committing suicide on more than one occasion. If the Warren Commission ever got beyond Oswald, it would only be a short time before Morrow himself would be implicated, even though he wasn't in Dallas that day. But what really impressed me was the intensity of guilt he was feeling about Mary Meyer's death."

John Williams had spent four years interviewing Morrow, combing everything Morrow had written and researched. The two talked intimately about all of Morrow's undercover assignments. Morrow was not only a CIA contract agent, but for more than two years he had also been the right-hand man of Tracy Barnes, one of the CIA's most senior covert action specialists. They had started working together early in 1961, right after Marshall Diggs had recruited Morrow into the Agency.

"After Dallas, Bob wanted to know what had exactly happened," said Williams. "He got a lot of information from Tracy Barnes, and others in the Agency, but couldn't get beyond Tracy to see who was involved in Mary Meyer's murder, and why it had occurred. For years, Morrow had been riddled with guilt over what he told Kohly and the fact that Mario Kohly had said, 'Don't worry, I'll take care of it.'"[86] Whether it was his guilt or just an obsessive need to know, Morrow continued to investigate Mary Meyer's death. According to Williams, he "was constantly sifting through volumes of information."

Shortly before his death, Bob Morrow's ongoing research, as well as what Williams called "Morrow's wonderful, intuitive sense" had changed his (Morrow's) mind about who had murdered Mary Meyer. "Toward the end," said Williams, "Bob told me more and more, 'I don't think Kohly did it, I think Angleton did it.'"[87]

12

How It Went Down:
The Anatomy of a CIA
Assassination – Part I

Be sure you put your feet in the right place, then stand firm.

—Abraham Lincoln

He who passively accepts evil is as much involved in it as he who helps
to perpetuate it.
He who accepts evil without protesting against it is really cooperating
with it.

—Martin Luther King Jr.

WITH NEW ENGLAND blanketed by a winter blizzard in early 2004, I found
myself stranded in Santa Monica, California, when my return flight to
Boston was canceled. Rescheduling at a local travel agency, I ran into Hollywood actor Peter Graves. Graves, readers may recall, was one of the stars of the
1966 television series *Mission Impossible*. The show was a fictionalized chronicle
of an ultrasecret team of American government agents known as the Impossible Missions Force. Peter Graves played the part of Jim Phelps, the team
leader who began each episode selecting a cadre of skilled contract agents
to accomplish the assigned clandestine mission. Each week a new episode
followed the exploits of the elite Impossible Missions Force as it employed
the latest technological gadgets and state-of-the-art disguises in an effort to

sabotage unfriendly governments, dictators, crime syndicates—any enemy of American hegemony. The organization that masterminded these covert operations was never revealed, yet a little imagination led to the doorstep of the CIA. So successful was *Mission Impossible*, it has currently (as of 2011) spawned four blockbuster Hollywood action films starring Tom Cruise.

As Peter Graves and I waited in line, I introduced myself, then started regaling him with how I had watched the show with my father, who had been instantly enamored, never wanting to miss an episode. Mentioning my father's CIA career, and how he'd been such a fan of Graves's character, Jim Phelps, I shared with him the memory of one particularly exciting episode, filled with intricate disguises, duplicity, and intrigue. At the end of the episode, my father had abruptly chortled, intriguingly smiling, finally blurting out, "We do it better."

"I'm not at all surprised," Peter Graves shot back. "We had several ex-CIA people who worked with the writers for the show. We could never have thought a lot of that stuff up on our own."

The serendipity of this encounter eluded me for months. For years during my research, the "Rubik's Cube" of the murder of Mary Meyer had remained impenetrable—until a mysterious linchpin was uncovered and further corroborated. It was only then that I began to understand the ingenious design that had been employed—one that created the illusion of something very different from what had actually occurred.

Throughout the three years Leo Damore spent interviewing attorney Dovey Roundtree, the two were unequivocally convinced that Ray Crump Jr. could never have murdered Mary Pinchot Meyer. The seasoned defense attorney, imbued with an instinctive, gut-level feeling for who people really were—saints and murderers alike—never forgot her impressions upon first meeting Crump. "He was," Roundtree said in her 2009 autobiography, "incapable of clear communication, incapable of complex thought, incapable of grasping the full weight of his predicament, incapable most of all, of a murder executed with the stealth and precision and forethought of Mary Meyer's [murder]."[1]

Yet tow truck driver Henry Wiggins Jr. had, in fact, seen *somebody* standing over Mary's corpse within fifteen seconds or so right after the second, final shot rang out. Whoever it was, he might well have been approximately "5 feet 8 inches" in height and weighed "185 pounds." But it couldn't have been Ray Crump. Indeed, the most intriguing aspect of Wiggins's testimony during the trial concerned the appearance, clothes, and demeanor of the man he saw standing over the body. Wiggins had described the color and style of the clothes in some detail—dark trousers, black shoes, a beige-colored, waist-length, zippered jacket, and a dark-plaid brimmed golf cap—all of which matched what Crump had been wearing that day. Prosecutor Alfred Hantman had explicitly asked Wiggins about the appearance of the man he saw standing over the body:

Hantman:	Could you tell the court and the jury the state of the jacket at the time you saw it on the individual who stood over the body of Mary Meyer?
Wiggins:	The jacket appeared to be zipped.
Hantman:	Did you see the jacket torn in any manner at the time?
Wiggins:	I didn't notice any tear.[2]

Nor had Wiggins mentioned seeing any stains—blood or anything else—on the zipped-up, light-colored beige jacket worn by the man who supposedly, just seconds before, had been engaged for more than one minute in a violent, bloody struggle during which the first gunshot, according to the coroner, had produced "a considerable amount of external bleeding."[3] In fact, Wiggins never indicated anything about the man's appearance being in any way disheveled, given the murder that had just taken place. Neither his demeanor nor his clothes had ever, according to Wiggins's testimony, indicated the man had been in any struggle just seconds before. His golf cap was perfectly in place; his jacket, clean and zipped.

Also intriguing was the demeanor of the man. Upon looking up and seeing Wiggins staring at him, he was composed and unconcerned—certainly not at all agitated or anxious that Wiggins had spotted him.

Hantman:	Now, what, if anything did you see this man do who you say was standing over a woman on the towpath at that time?
Wiggins:	Well, at that time, when I saw him standing over her, he looked up.
Hantman:	Looked up where?
Wiggins:	Looked up towards the wall of the canal where I was standing.
Hantman:	Were you looking directly at him at that point?
Wiggins:	I was looking at him.
Hantman:	Then what happened?

Wiggins: I ducked down behind the wall at that time, not too long, and I come back up from behind the wall to see him turning around and shoving something in his pocket.[4]

The man then, Wiggins added, "turned around and *walked* [author's emphasis] over straight away from the body, down over the hill [embankment]."[5] It was as if he *wanted* Wiggins to see him before he, according to Wiggins, calmly walked away over the embankment. His unflustered demeanor appeared to contrast sharply with that of a trembling, petrified Ray Crump, only because they weren't the same person.

Nearly thirty years later, in 1992, Leo Damore interviewed Henry Wiggins. The government's star witness still vividly remembered, Damore said, the man standing over the woman's body. "He wasn't afraid," Wiggins recalled to Damore. "He didn't appear to be worried that he'd been caught in the act. He looked straight at me." Ray Crump's acquittal, however, had come as a surprise to Wiggins. He confided to Damore that he felt "strung along" by the prosecution and had been "used" to present their case. After Wiggins testified, Hantman told him that he "hadn't done well as a witness." Wiggins told Damore, "I just told the truth as I saw it. That's all. The police didn't do a damn thing to support it."[6]

As the interview came to an end, Henry Wiggins proffered one last reflection about what had happened that day. "You know, sometimes I've had the feeling I was kinda set up there that morning to see what I saw."[7] It was the kind of remark that wouldn't have been lost on a crime sleuth—someone like Sherlock Holmes, or Leo Damore.

Almost from the moment Lieutenant William L. Mitchell, USA, had appeared at D.C Metropolitan Police headquarters the day after Mary's murder, attorney Dovey Roundtree's suspicions had been aroused. Mitchell told police he not only believed he had passed the murder victim as he ran eastward toward Key Bridge from Fletcher's Boat House that day, but also that he was sure he had passed a "Negro male" following her. His description of the man and his clothes closely matched Wiggins's.

In an effort to convict Crump, neither the police nor the prosecution team had bothered to investigate William L. Mitchell's story. Carefully and methodically during the trial, Mitchell additionally described how he had passed "a couple walking together twice," as well as another runner, also passed twice, someone that he thought "was a young student . . . about twenty, wearing bermuda [*sic*] shorts."[8] Mitchell said he first came upon the couple "on the road leading down to the canal [towpath] near Key Bridge." Having run out to Fletcher's Boat House, Mitchell claimed to have passed the couple a second time "half way between Key Bridge and Fletcher's. . . . And this time I was running back from Fletcher's and they were walking West at the time." Mitchell said he twice passed the other runner "wearing bermuda shorts," both times "close to Fletcher's Boat House." All of this took place, he testified, before he stopped at the westward end of the narrow footbridge to allow the westward-headed Mary Meyer to cross.[9] Nobody, however, had corroborated Mitchell's story, or ever testified to seeing Mitchell on the canal towpath the day Mary Meyer was murdered.

The reader will recall that police officer Roderick Sylvis, having raced to Fletcher's Boat House to close off the exit within minutes after the murder, had himself encountered a white couple, "a young man and woman . . . in their thirties" walking westward about "fifty feet" from Fletcher's Boat House approximately ten to fifteen minutes after he and his partner, Frank Bignotti, arrived. However, the officers, in a peculiar lapse of procedure, had neglected to get the couple's names. Moreover, no matter in which direction the "bermuda shorts" runner was headed, at some point he, too, would have run into the murder scene, either before or after the police had arrived. But his identity, like that of the young white couple, would remain unknown. With such an intense, all-encompassing, citywide—even national—media blitz taking place, why hadn't the "bermuda shorts" runner and the young white couple come forward to police, as William L. Mitchell had? Why hadn't the police broadcast a request for them to do so?

Throughout their many hours of tape-recorded discussions that began in 1990, both Dovey Roundtree and Leo Damore independently reached the same inevitable conclusion: the personage of William L. Mitchell was highly suspicious. Roundtree had tried in vain to speak with Mitchell before the trial, she told Damore, but he would never return her phone calls. During several years of intense research, Leo Damore did what he did best: doggedly and exhaustively chased down any lead in order to get what he wanted. His signature tenacity took him on a journey that began with Mitchell's listing in the *Department of Defense Telephone Directory* [DoD Directory] in the fall of 1964. Upon giving his account to police the day after the murder, William Mitchell said he was stationed at the Pentagon. His listing in the DoD Directory read: "Mitchell Wm L 2nd Lt USA DATCOM BE1035 Pnt." It included a telephone extension of 79918.[10] Mitchell also gave his address as 1500 Arlington Boulevard, Arlington, Virginia—a building known as the Virginian. According to the Arlington telephone directory in 1964, Mitchell lived in apartment 1022, and his telephone number was (703) 522-2872. His name would remain listed until 1968, and then vanish.

During Damore's extensive search, William L. Mitchell was nowhere to be found. He had left no forwarding address. Neither the directories of the U.S. Military Academy at West Point nor of the Army itself produced any identification or record of any William Mitchell stationed at the Pentagon in 1964. No record was ever located. At the time of Mitchell's trial appearance, *Washington Star* reporter Roberta Hornig identified Mitchell as "a Georgetown University mathematics teacher."[11] But no one at Georgetown University could ever locate any record of any "William L. Mitchell" having ever taught there. If Mitchell had been employed by Georgetown University, Damore reasoned, he might have been using a different name, or the record had been intentionally removed.

Sometime in 1992, Damore interviewed former CIA contract analyst David MacMichael, who still lived in the Washington area. The two soon became friends. "Leo wanted to know who this guy [William L. Mitchell] really was," said MacMichael in 2004 during an interview for this book. He was sure he [Mitchell] had misrepresented himself as to his real identity." On one occasion, MacMichael recalled, he and Damore drove out to Mitchell's former address, the apartment building at 1500 Arlington Boulevard in Arlington, Virginia. There, MacMichael confirmed to Damore that the address had been a known "CIA safe house."[12] That observation was further corroborated by another former CIA operative, Donald Deneselya, who added that during his employment at the Agency in the early 1960s, the CIA regularly used faculty positions at Georgetown University as covers for many of its covert operations personnel. That fact was further substantiated by former disaffected Agency veteran Victor Marchetti, whose books—*The CIA and the Cult of Intelligence* and *The Rope Dancer*—the CIA had tried to suppress from publication.[13] Any trail of Mitchell's identity or subsequent whereabouts, however, appeared to have vaporized.

Still searching for Mitchell in early 2005, I was introduced to military researcher and investigative journalist Roger Charles. A former lieutenant colonel in the Marine Corps, Charles was a Naval Academy graduate who had been a platoon leader in Vietnam before serving under the late colonel David Hackworth as part of the organization Soldiers for the Truth (now called

Stand for the Troops). Early in his journalism career, Roger Charles had fired his first salvo with a *Newsweek* cover story entitled "Sea of Lies." The story exposed the Pentagon's attempted cover-up of the USS *Vincennes*'s downing of an Iranian civilian airliner in 1988. In 2004, Charles had been part of a *60 Minutes II* team headed by Dan Rather that aired the first photographs to reveal some of the most unconscionable American military behavior since the My Lai Massacre during the Vietnam War: the prisoner abuse in Iraq at Abu Ghraib. Charles had been an associate producer for the *60 Minutes II* segment, "Abuse at Abu Ghraib." He and his colleagues provided the viewing public with a picture of the horrors inflicted by American soldiers on Iraqi prisoners. That year, the segment would win the prestigious Peabody Award.[14]

Roger Charles had learned his craft under the tutelage of former marine colonel William R. Corson, author of the controversial book *The Betrayal.* Courageously exposing President Lyndon Johnson's corrupt, deliberate deception during the Vietnam War in 1968, Corson created a huge crisis that nearly brought him a court-martial. However, had Corson not done what he did, the Vietnam War would undoubtedly have been even further prolonged. Corson went on to write several more books, including *The Armies of Ignorance, Widows,* and *The New KGB: Engine of Soviet Power,* which he coauthored with Robert T. Crowley, an elite operative in the CIA's covert action directorate and a close colleague and friend of Jim Angleton's. (All three individuals will be discussed further in the next chapter.) Not only did Roger Charles become Corson's protégé and chief research assistant, but a trusted confidant, and eventually the executor of the Corson estate.

With regard to William Mitchell, Roger Charles was asked to review Mitchell's office listing in the 1964 DoD telephone directory. Through his own channels, he sent an inquiry to the U.S. Army military database in St. Louis for any "William Mitchell" who was stationed at the Pentagon in 1964. There was none. Further examining other Pentagon directories, Charles discovered that Mitchell's name no longer appeared after the fall 1964 edition. He next investigated the military personnel who were located physically adjacent to Mitchell's alleged office (BE 1035), creating a list of approximately twenty individuals. Fifteen of those individuals could be verified through their military records, but none of the other five servicemen—Mitchell and four others in adjacent offices—had any military record in any service database. The phantom William L. Mitchell had indeed evaporated into thin air.

"This is a typical pattern of people involved in covert intelligence work," Charles later reported to me. "I've come across this kind of thing many times.

People like this don't want to be found. They're taught how to evade all the conventional bureaucracies and channels. They don't leave any traces. These people work undercover in places like the Pentagon all the time. Given what I see here—the fact that he's got no matching military record I can locate—it's almost a certainty this guy Mitchell, whoever he was or is, had some kind of covert intelligence connection. It's very strong in my opinion."[15]

Sometimes serendipity entwines with providence. In December 2009, I read H. P. Albarelli's recently published book, *A Terrible Mistake: The Murder of Frank Olson and the CIA's Secret Cold War Experiments.* Albarelli's magnum opus took me by the hand and held me hostage for several days. Extensively researched, the book not only provided the most convincing account of how the CIA "terminated" one of its own, but possibly the best history ever written of the Agency's infamous MKULTRA program. Albarelli and I soon began talking, and he inquired about my progress. I mumbled something about the trail having ended at "1500 Arlington Boulevard" in Arlington, Virginia. After a moment of silence, Albarelli told me he had lived at that same address when he was a student at George Washington University many years ago. I then mentioned my phantom—William L. Mitchell—and some of the dead-end information I had amassed. "William Mitchell?" Albarelli repeated. He said he would get back to me later; he thought he had come across the name before. Indeed, he had.

An important Albarelli source—someone whom the author had known for many years and whose information had been corroborated by other sources— had revealed in September 2001 something more about the identity of William Mitchell. The source, whose name Albarelli did not want to reveal, specifically identified a man by the name of "William Mitchell" as a member of "Army Special Forces kill teams" that operated domestically for the CIA and the National Security Agency (NSA). The source said he and Mitchell had become friends over the years. When Albarelli had further pressed his source in 2001 as to Mitchell's identity, he said Mitchell was often connected with the Air Force, and that he sometimes used the aliases "Allen Crawford" and "Walter Morse." At this juncture in his 2001 interview, Albarelli had written in his notes that Mitchell had been "involved" in the "Mary Cord Meyer case." "Meyer murdered on towpath," Albarelli's notes read. Mitchell "did it," the source had told him, "at the request of the Agency's [CIA's] Domestic K [contracts] Office in D.C."[16]

Stunned by this sudden revelation, I asked Albarelli if he would telephone the source and confirm several of the statements he'd made during his 2001 interview. In his first attempt at this follow-up, the source wasn't home, but his wife, whom Albarelli also knew well, was. He asked her about Mitchell. She clearly remembered him, but wasn't at all fond of him. Mitchell and her husband, she told Albarelli, always drank too much when they were together; "they were drunk and crazy for days," she said. She found herself "nervous" when Mitchell was around because "he had guns, all kinds of guns, all the time." She told Albarelli that during one of Mitchell's visits, things had gotten so out of control, she had asked him to leave.[17]

When Albarelli called back later that day, he reported he did finally reach the source, but he wasn't amenable to talking about Mitchell, or even acknowledging whether Mitchell was still alive. Did Mitchell have kids? Albarelli asked. "Yeah, he had a few kids but I never met them or his wife," the source replied. (The reader will come to know why this question was important.) Bluntly, Albarelli then asked whether he remembered telling him in 2001 that Mitchell had killed Mary Meyer. "Heard he killed a lot of people," replied the now tight-lipped source. "What difference does it make now?"[18]

By the end of 1992, "playing his cards close to his vest," Leo Damore had learned something else. In the course of his interview with Timothy Leary in 1990, Damore told Leary that Mary's real diary still existed and that he believed he had discovered its whereabouts. "Angleton offered the diary in 1980 to a person who I know. . . . I know where it is," Damore told Leary. Then he added, "The man who I believe has it is maddeningly this week in Hawaii."[19] Leo had sometimes cryptically referred to Mary's diary as "the Hope Diamond" of the Kennedy assassination, and perhaps for this reason, he faithfully guarded not only the fact that he had eventually come into possession of it, but its contents as well. He finally revealed both to his attorney Jimmy Smith on March 31, 1993, in a conversation that will shortly be discussed in more detail.

The person to whom Angleton had shown Mary's diary in 1980 was a man named Bernie Yoh. In 1980, Yoh ran an organization in Washington called Accuracy in Media (AIM). Founded in 1969, AIM described its purpose as the pursuit of "fairness, balance, and accuracy in news reporting." It claimed to do for print media what the Fox News Network now purports to do for TV news—providing "fair and balanced" reporting. A simple survey of AIM's intimate connection with many conservative causes, however, left little doubt as to its real purpose: AIM was a mouthpiece for extreme right-wing views. In addition, early in the Vietnam era, Bernie Yoh had his own affiliations with CIA undercover work, although he denied ever having worked for the Agency.[20]

When David Martin's *Wilderness of Mirrors* was published in 1980, *Newsweek* carried a positive review of the book that had infuriated former CIA counterintelligence chief Jim Angleton, only because of Martin's unflattering portrayal of him. The book details the cause of Angleton's termination in disgrace from the Agency in late 1974. His paranoia had, for years, paralyzed crucial intelligence gathering by the Agency. He had also violated innumerable laws, as had the Agency as a whole, through mail tampering and privacy invasions of hundreds of individual citizens. Finally, CIA director William Colby fired him. Angleton was devastated. He sought out Bernie Yoh at AIM, asking him to "counter-spin" the recent *Newsweek* story in a way that was favorable to him. Yoh willingly obliged by publishing "An AIM Report" in defense of Angleton.

In his 1990 interview with Leo Damore, Bernie Yoh revealed more about Angleton's astonishing behavior in 1980—a time when the battered, bruised reputation of the CIA's most elite Cold Warrior had taken a huge tumble. The grateful Angleton started hanging out at AIM's offices. One day, according to Yoh, Angleton had "flashed his credentials," mentioning JFK and the towpath murder of his mistress Mary Pinchot Meyer, also mentioning her tell-all diary.

"Angleton had said, and not without a bit of pride showing," Yoh told Damore, "'*I have the diary*,' almost wanting me to ask him to produce it, eager to share the special secrets he had tended with such skill during his glory days at CIA." That conversation, Yoh remembered, had taken place in light of some prior discussion about the Kennedy administration and related matters. At the time, Yoh himself had not fully grasped what Angleton was actually referring to.

"What diary?" Yoh asked Angleton at the time.

"That woman that was killed in Georgetown. I took care of everything," Angleton had said. According to Yoh, Angleton then produced the diary which he still had intact in his possession, and handed it to Yoh—to show him "the real Kennedy."

"It's her diary," Angleton said, as he gave what was presumably a copy to Yoh.[21] At some point, Yoh shared with Damore what Angleton had given him. This was how Leo Damore had finally come into possession of Mary's *true* diary.

In his conclusive attempt to finally understand how the murder of Mary Meyer had been orchestrated, Leo Damore consulted former Air Force colonel and CIA liaison L. Fletcher Prouty in 1992.[22] Prouty, the reader will recall, knew all about the inner workings of America's intelligence apparatus, having been summoned to countless classified briefings with Allen Dulles and his brother, Secretary of State John Foster Dulles, even at their homes when necessary. Prouty had also attended many of the CIA's MKULTRA meetings and was considered part of "the nerve center" of the "military–industrial complex" during its establishment in the late 1950s. As one of the architects of America's secret government, Fletcher Prouty had created a network of clandestine agents throughout the military and other government agencies, including the FBI. But after facilitating many CIA coups d'état around the globe, including military support for these operations, he became deeply disturbed when he discovered the CIA's involvement in the assassination of President Kennedy. He resigned his Air Force commission in 1964 and began writing the secret history of the Cold War.[23] Prouty's two books, *The Secret Team* (1973) and *JFK: The CIA, Vietnam, and the Plot to Assassinate John F. Kennedy* (1996), have remained two of the most authoritative works of that era. It wasn't an accident that film director Oliver Stone used Fletcher Prouty as the template for the character of X, played by Donald Sutherland, in the film *JFK*.

At the end of 1992, unable to locate Mitchell or any forwarding address, Leo Damore had reached an impasse. His last resort was sending a letter to Mitchell to his last known address—the CIA "safe house" at 1500 Arlington Boulevard in Arlington, Virginia. While the actual contents of Damore's letter were never known, it had to have contained something that would motivate Mitchell to reply; and that could have only been what Damore had learned from Fletcher Prouty. Had Prouty, in fact, revealed Mitchell's true identity? It was never known. But sometime between the evening of March 30, 1993, and early morning of March 31, Leo Damore's telephone rang. The caller identified himself as "William Mitchell." He had received Leo's letter, he said, and had also read Leo's book *Senatorial Privilege*. He agreed to talk with Damore, but made it clear he didn't want to be labeled the fall guy in history. The two reportedly talked for four hours.

At approximately 8:30 on the morning of March 31, 1993, the telephone of James ("Jimmy") H. Smith, Esq., in Falmouth, Massachusetts, began to ring. Jimmy Smith and Leo Damore were the closet of friends. Their camaraderie deep, they genuinely enjoyed each other's company. Often, as they parted, either in person or on the phone, Leo would invariably give his friend, a stalwart Boston College alumnus, his favorite parting shot, ". . . and *fuck* Holy Cross [college]!" Jimmy was also Damore's attorney, and Leo had dedicated his 1988 book *Senatorial Privilege* to him, for it had been Jimmy who years earlier introduced Leo to Senator Ted Kennedy's cousin Joe Gargan—the man who ultimately would reveal to Damore what had been taking place behind the scenes while Mary Joe Kopechne's drowned body lay trapped underwater in Ted Kennedy's car at Chappaquiddick.

Jimmy Smith had returned to his private law practice after a stint as a U.S. magistrate and federal trial judge. A longtime Kennedy insider, and a member of the elite Kennedy "Irish Mafia," Smith had been one of Robert Kennedy's chief advance men for his presidential campaign in 1968. As an honorary pallbearer at Bobby's St. Patrick's Cathedral funeral in New York, Jimmy had stood by the casket "at the last hour," along with Kenny O'Donnell, George Plimpton, Jimmy Breslin, and others. Having endured Jack's assassination five years earlier, Smith was so traumatized by Bobby's death, he momentarily lost his struggle with alcoholism. Scarred again by the second Kennedy assassination, Kenny O'Donnell lost his own battle and died in 1977. Determined to save himself, Smith had returned to his law practice on Cape Cod and recommitted to a life of sobriety.

"I've solved the case!" were Leo's first excited words when Smith answered the phone. Reaching for the yellow legal pad he unfailingly kept on his desk next to his phone, attorney James H. Smith began writing what would turn out to be six pages of notes, all of which he meticulously saved. The following account is reconstructed from Smith's original notes (see appendix 3), interpreted and explained by Smith over many hours of reviewing their meaning and context.

"I cracked it!" Smith remembered Leo shouting on the phone. "I got the guy—and the [JFK] assassination link, too!" Smith quickly began writing, trying to keep up with Leo's exhilaration. Damore mentioned a name, and Jimmy asked him to repeat it: "William L. Mitchell," said Damore. "He was an ex-FBI man!" Damore then revealed that he had Mary's real diary in his possession ("The diary found!") and that in the diary, Mary had made a connection between the Kennedy assassination and the CIA that involved "James Angleton." Mitchell, said Damore, had confessed to him a few hours earlier that morning: The murder of Mary Meyer had been "a CIA operation" in which Mitchell had been the assassin.[24]

"Mitchell" confirmed that his name, "William L. Mitchell," was an alias and that he now lived under another alias in Virginia. He said his position at the Pentagon in 1964 had been just "a light bulb job," a cover for covert intelligence work. He had done stints in the Air Force, the Army, and the Navy, he told Damore, all of which were also part of his cover, and he had also been "an FBI man" when circumstances required it. His listed residence at 1500

Arlington Boulevard in Arlington, Virginia, Mitchell told Damore, was in fact a CIA safe house. He was now seventy-four years old and had five children.

It had been "an operation," Mitchell disclosed. He had been "assigned" in September 1964 to be part of a "surveillance team" that was monitoring Mary Meyer. Mitchell appeared to suggest that the trigger for the surveillance had been the release of the Warren Report: "24 Sept Warren Report. She hit [the] roof." Damore reiterated that Mary had bought a copy of the paperback version of the Warren Report when it first came out.[25] She was outraged by the cover-up taking place. According to Smith's notes, "She went to husb [ex-husband, Cord Meyer] + [and] husb [Cord] to Angleton . . ." This particular detail came from Mary's diary. Damore was emphatic: It was the "Angleton connection w/CIA [with the CIA]" and the CIA's orchestration of the events in Dallas that put her in harm's way. "Mary – stepped in shit! She would not back down. Her [something] too strong + [and] too powerful."[26]

Throughout 1993, Leo Damore had always been emphatic, as he was that morning with Jimmy Smith, that it wasn't Mary's affair with Jack that had put her in jeopardy; it was what she had been able to put together, as Smith's notes revealed, about "the murder of JFK." Her indignation at the cover-up in the Warren Report pushed her to confront her ex-husband, Cord, and possibly Jim Angleton as well. Smith's notes, however, indicated that it had to have been Cord who conveyed to Jim Angleton how infuriated Mary had become. Whether Mary subsequently had a separate confrontation with Jim Angleton alone, or with Cord present, wasn't clear. But it was almost certain both men realized—knowing Mary as well as they did—that she wasn't the kind of person who was going to keep quiet.[27]

Regarding Mitchell, Damore told Smith: "I got [the] word [about him]— he's a killer— + [and] he [also] has 5 kids!"[28] It appeared "William L. Mitchell" had been a trained assassin. Fletcher Prouty's former network of agents had included FBI personnel as well as CIA operatives.[29] It also gave further credence to what author H. P. Albarelli had been told by his longtime source in 2001: that "Mitchell" had been "involved" in the Mary Meyer murder, and that he, in fact, "did it at the request of the Agency's [CIA's] Domestic K [contracts] Office in D.C."[30] Mitchell, it appears, told Damore something almost identical: "On the murder . . . A CIA K [contract]. . . . A CIA individual."[31]

On page 5 of his notes, Smith wrote: "Leo had talked to Prouty (Oliver Stone guy.)" It then appeared that Fletcher Prouty had assisted Damore in understanding more clearly how Mary Meyer's murder had itself been a microcosmic copy of what had taken place in Dallas. Like Lee Harvey Oswald, Ray

Crump Jr. had been used as the patsy. And, as in Dallas, Mary's murder had all been planned in advance, designed to take place in an open setting, away from home territory—creating the illusion of an arbitrary, indiscriminate randomness to explain the event. The murder, Smith's notes read, had been "set up away from [Mary's] home in [a] public place." It was followed by the speedy apprehension of a plausible suspect, a patsy who happened to have been in the wrong place, at the wrong time. The police would also unknowingly feed the details to the media that would, in turn, be used to publicly imply the suspect's guilt, complete with mug shots of suspect Ray Crump in handcuffs at the murder scene and the police station. It had all been "standard CIA procedure," Mitchell said to Damore, as recorded in Smith's notes. The couple on the towpath that morning—and seen by police officer Roderick Sylvis—had been spotters for the operation, Mitchell disclosed, as was "the bermuda [sic] shorts" runner that no one had seen except Mitchell.[32]

Scribbled at the bottom of page 3 of Jimmy's notes were the words "New Agent Richard Pine."[33] Richard Pine had recently become Leo Damore's new literary agent. "Did Leo ever tell you that he thought he had solved the murder of Mary Meyer?" I asked Pine in the fall of 2004.

"Yeah, I believe he did," recalled Pine. "I remember he had lots of tape. I think I remember he kept them in some kind of private place where no one could get at it. . . . He felt he had such dynamite material on such powerful people."[34] Yet despite the Mitchell bombshell revelations Damore possessed, all of which he recorded, he never turned in a manuscript for "Burden of Guilt" to his new agent. Two and half years later, Leo Damore, on October 2, 1995, would take his life one day after William Safire reviewed Ben Bradlee's memoir *A Good Life* in the *New York Times*.

Damore's former wife, June Davison, kindly gave me as much assistance as she could in my attempt to locate Damore's tapes. At my request in 2004, she made searches of their home in Old Saybrook, Connecticut, but could find nothing. I even went to Damore's last residence in Centerbrook, Connecticut, where he had received the phone call from Mitchell and then placed the call to Jimmy Smith on the morning of March 31, 1993. Fruitlessly, I scoured the area around the building, thinking he might have buried the tapes somewhere near, but to no avail.

In April 1993, shortly after the Mitchell call, Leo Damore returned to Washington and met with his research assistant, Mark O'Blazney, for lunch at the Henley Park Hotel. In 2008, in an interview for this book, Mark O'Blazney and his wife, Tanya, a Georgetown University Russian language instructor, talked about the luncheon. O'Blazney had worked for Damore for more than two years. He, too, had come to the conclusion that whoever William Mitchell was, he had to have been involved in Mary's murder.

O'Blazney still vividly recalled the April 1993 meeting with Damore. "Leo was very excited that day," he said. "He told me he'd taped the call with Mitchell. That day at lunch he had the transcription already completed and kept referring to it." O'Blazney's wife, though not present at the luncheon, corroborated what Mark had told her later on that after his meeting with Damore.

"Part of Mitchell's plan," O'Blazney remembered Damore saying, "was maybe taking Mary down when a low-flying commercial airplane was flying over on its way into National [airport] . . . something about muffling the sound of gunshots. But I also remember Leo saying Mitchell told him that witnesses were placed at the murder scene. The whole thing was a set-up."[35]

"An operation . . . standard CIA procedure" was what Mitchell, according to Smith's notes, called the murder of Mary Meyer.[36] Mitchell had been assigned sometime in September 1964 to a surveillance team that was monitoring Mary Meyer. At some point—the precise date is unknown—the order was given to "terminate" her. It was to be done in a public place, then made to look like something it wasn't. From their surveillance, the team knew Mary's routine of taking walks around noon on the C & O Canal towpath, that she would typically walk out to Fletcher's Boat House and then return, a distance of about four miles in total. Within that venue, a designated kill zone had to be selected where Mary would be accessible. By choosing an outside location, rather than her home, the planners wanted to create the impression of a wanton, random act of violence, unrelated to Mary's identity or political connections. It had to be skillfully executed with *Mission Impossible* precision beyond the intersection of where Canal Road intersected the busier Foxhall Road. The ideal time for such an operation was determined to be a weekday, when the towpath was less frequented. The operation's planners very likely were prepared to carry out their mission on any number of days, depending on certain variables—including the availability of an appropriate patsy. These were the kind of painstaking calculations and details that were involved in the extensive planning of professional assassinations.

There were any number of challenging factors to control and overcome; any significant mistake or oversight could be disastrous. As little as possible could be left to chance—including the whereabouts that day of Mary's ex-husband, Cord Meyer. Was it just coincidence Cord would conveniently be out of town in New York on CIA business on the day of his ex-wife's murder?

The team put into place to conduct this operation likely consisted of at least six to eight operatives, not including the actual architects of the plan itself, or the ancillary adjacent personnel dispatched to monitor and control other important operational details. In addition, in order to execute an operation of this nature, there had to be some kind of command center in the C & O Canal area to coordinate logistics; it would have to include radio communication to and from Mitchell, and his team, on the towpath itself.

The operational plan of "standard CIA procedure," similar in design to what had taken place in Dallas, albeit on a much smaller scale and within a shorter time sequence, called for a patsy—someone who could be unknowingly and immediately easily framed. Such an operation required the use of disguises and/or costumes, an absolute necessity. No other entity on earth had resources like the CIA's Technical Services Division (TSD) under the direction of Dr. Sidney Gottlieb. They could do almost anything, and quickly—from preparing lethal poisons that left no trace, to procuring articles of clothing and undetectable disguises on short notice.[37]

Ray Crump Jr. had been picked up by his girlfriend, Vivian, in her car "very early that morning," shortly after eight.[38] Crump was playing hooky from work. That morning, Crump and Vivian didn't have enough money for a motel room. Crump had likely been spotted by the CIA team early that morning, as he and Vivian began walking out from the Georgetown entry point of the towpath to some predetermined area he was familiar with from earlier fishing trips to the area. It was still probably two to three hours before the murder would take place. There may have been more than one candidate for patsy the team was monitoring that morning before a decision was made. Eventually, someone was assigned—with a radio—to keep tabs on Crump and his whereabouts. Whoever the designated patsy, the operation would have immediately had to procure clothing similar to what he was wearing. In Crump's case, that meant generic dark shoes, dark pants, a light-beige-colored Windbreaker and a dark-plaid golf cap—easily and quickly obtainable from the CIA's TSD personnel, who were likely standing by as support personnel.

A specialized team from the CIA's TSD had the capability of transforming almost anyone into whatever was called for, including changing someone's race from white to black if necessary. But there was a problem not even the elite TSD could overcome on such short notice: immediately finding someone on the operational team that day who had a build and stature as slight as

Ray Crump's. So they had to make do with what was available—the man they used for the stand-in, the Ray Crump look-alike, was larger than Crump. That discrepancy would, in the end, create enough reasonable doubt to enable a masterful attorney, Dovey Roundtree, to thwart one of the key elements of the mission: railroading Ray Crump into being convicted for Mary Meyer's murder, thereby enabling the cover-up.[39] And so the man Henry Wiggins witnessed—the Ray Crump look-alike standing over Mary's body after the second fatal gunshot—was significantly taller and heavier than Ray Crump.

Until Mary exited her studio that morning and started walking toward the canal, Mitchell's team would not have been green-lighted and alerted to begin positioning themselves. Another member of the surveillance team—again, someone with a radio—had to be assigned to monitor her whereabouts from the moment she left her house and arrived at her studio earlier that morning. When it was clear shortly after noon that she was headed for her daily walk on the canal towpath, all operational parameters would have been initiated.

The mysterious, stalled Nash Rambler had likely already been placed adjacent to the designated kill zone on the canal. The Rambler could have been set up earlier that morning—or several mornings in a row—before the operation was finally given green-lighted-to-go status. At some point the key(s) to the stalled vehicle would be delivered to the Key Bridge Esso station with a request for someone to fix the vehicle. Henry Wiggins was operating the station's tow truck that morning. "I was sent from the station where I normally work," testified Henry Wiggins, "to the other Esso station [at Key Bridge] owned by my employer to pick up a man there and go start a disabled vehicle on Canal Road, approximately seven blocks" away.[40]

Mary's surveillance likely began three weeks before her death, maybe even longer. The team already would have had a good idea how fast she walked, and approximately how long it would take her to reach the wooden footbridge, a place where the vegetation around the towpath area became denser. Her assassination would eventually take place exactly 637.5 feet west of the footbridge. There were two sets of spotters, Mitchell admitted to Damore, "a couple walking together" and another runner wearing Bermuda shorts, who were clearly tracking Mary's whereabouts on the towpath and likely communicating by radio to some unknown command center in the area. Mitchell had indicated to Damore in 1993 that there had been more than one spotter during the operation.[*]

Immediately prior to the murder, Mitchell could not have been running on the towpath; he and the dressed-up Ray Crump look-alike were positioning

333

themselves on standby status. The entire operational was crystallizing—waiting for whoever was going to be servicing the stalled Nash Rambler to show up (and unknowingly play the role of "witnesses"), and waiting for Mary Meyer to approach the designated kill zone.

Meanwhile, another member of the operational team had to be monitoring the whereabouts of the real Ray Crump and reporting his activity to the command center. The team had to know where Crump was situated and when he and Vivian reached the spot on the Potomac where their tryst would take place. Even if Crump and Vivian had arrived at the towpath entrance in Georgetown as late as 10:30 A.M., that still gave the team close to two hours to set up, orchestrate, and carry out the assassination of Mary Meyer. It had likely been rehearsed many times.

The story Ray Crump told attorney Dovey Roundtree was that he and Vivian had gone to a particular spot on the bank of the Potomac that he was familiar with, having fished there before. They did some drinking, he said, then "fooled around a little," at which point Ray passed out on some rocks at the water's edge.[41] Disoriented, perhaps a bit intoxicated, Ray slipped into the river, quickly coming to his senses as the cold water engulfed him. He couldn't swim; he panicked and struggled to climb out, likely tearing his trousers and cutting his hand in the process.

Vivian had disappeared, however, while Ray was passed out from intoxication. Why she had just abandoned Ray was mysterious. Had she been deliberately lured away after Ray had passed out? If Ray was being monitored and set up as a patsy, then Vivian's mere presence—an alibi for Ray—was an obstacle the operation had to surmount. Was it just serendipity that Vivian decided on her own to walk away when she did? Or had she, in some way, been forced to move out of the area shortly before, or immediately after, the murder—before Ray awoke from his stupor? The terrified Vivian would never testify, even with Ray's life hanging in the balance. She told Roundtree she feared "being killed by her husband," should he discover her affair.[42] Whether Vivian was more forcibly threatened by something else will probably never be known.

As soon as Henry Wiggins and Bill Branch arrived at approximately 12:20 P.M., the operation to terminate Mary Meyer would have been fully greenlighted by radio communication. Mitchell would have been signaled by radio that the "witnesses"—Wiggins and Branch—were in place. According to Wiggins's trial testimony, "less than a minute" after his arrival, he heard what "sounded like a woman screaming." Mary's screams from the canal lasted "about twenty seconds," Wiggins said, before the first gunshot rang out.

As Mary walked westward into the predetermined "kill zone," coordinated with the location of the stalled Nash Rambler, Mitchell would emerge from the embankment area and approach Mary from behind. In a full embrace, pinning Mary's arms at her side, Mitchell now *needed Mary to scream* in order to attract the attention of whoever was servicing the Rambler. As a highly trained, skilled assassin, he could have easily, quickly shot Mary before she was even aware of what was occurring. Or he could have picked her off with a high-powered rifle from behind an adjacent tree as she walked by. Why didn't he? Because Mary's screaming, her cries for help, were essential to drawing in the *witnesses* to the ostensibly random, senseless murder taking place—to motivate whoever was attending the stalled vehicle to run across Canal Road and witness the Ray Crump look-alike standing over her body.

Whether Mitchell underestimated Mary's strength and lost his grip, or whether he let go of her because he expected she would fall to the ground, fatally wounded, after his first shot, isn't known. But Mary appeared to have broken away and tried to escape over the embankment, finally grabbing a birch tree limb with her saturated, blood-soaked glove in order to steady herself.

That wouldn't do for Mitchell, or the operational intent of the mission. Mary had to be positioned close, or right next to, the canal itself where the murder scene would be clearly visible to someone looking across from the Canal Road wall. So Mitchell quickly grabbed Mary again and dragged her some twenty-five feet from the embankment to the canal's edge, where, with a perfectly placed shot under her right shoulder blade angled slightly to the left, he killed her instantly. Also executed with extreme precision was Mitchell's escape, quickly accomplished by slipping into the woods, as the Ray Crump look-alike rapidly assumed his position, standing over the now slain body of Mary Pinchot Meyer.

Almost immediately after hearing the first gunshot, Wiggins started moving toward the wall of the canal across the street from the stalled vehicle that he and his partner had come to fix. While he was running "diagonally [to the right] across the [Canal] road," he then recounted, "I heard another shot just as I was reaching the wall of the canal."[43] Peering over the wall and looking to his right on an angle,[44] he witnessed the Ray Crump look-alike standing over Mary's body, dressed as Crump himself had been dressed that day—dark shoes, dark pants, a light-colored windbreaker, and a dark-plaid brimmed golf cap—someone Wiggins would repeatedly describe as having a "medium build" who was about "5 feet 8 inches" and weighed "185 pounds."

After Mitchell twice shot and killed Mary, the upper part of his body and/ or clothes would have almost certainly been spattered in Mary's blood. Asked by Dovey Roundtree during his trial testimony the color of the clothing he was wearing that day, Mitchell responded, "I had on a sweat suit. . . . The sweat shirt, I believe, was red, the sweat pants were blue, and the track shoes were red and white."[45] He may well have been dressed in that manner. The red sweatshirt would have to some degree camouflaged the bloodstains. His likely escape was through the Foundry Underpass, the nearest exit out of the area. As a highly trained assassin from the "Army Special Forces kill teams," according to Albarelli's longtime source, Mitchell would have had little difficulty evading detection by police.

While Mitchell had no trouble eluding police, the reader will recall that a man thought to be a "Negro male," very possibly the Ray Crump look-alike, had been momentarily spotted by officer Roderick Sylvis *west* of the murder scene more than an hour after the murder had occurred. This "Negro male," as Sylvis described him during the trial, would also elude capture, disappearing and staying hidden, as he had no doubt been trained to do.

By all accounts, Ray Crump was arrested sometime between 1:15 and 1:30 P.M.[46] Yet when he was first spotted by Detective Warner at least ten to fifteen minutes—approximately 1:00 P.M.—before his actual arrest by Detective Crooke, Crump wasn't wearing a light-colored beige jacket or any cap. Only *after* Crump was under arrest—now approaching 1:30 P.M.—did Wiggins remark to Detective Crooke that Crump looked like the man he saw standing over the body, but he wasn't wearing any hat or jacket.[47]

Indeed, if Crump wasn't in possession of his jacket or cap when first spotted by Detective Warner, nor at the time of his arrest sometime around 1:15 P.M. or a few minutes later, how could Harbor Precinct policeman Frederick Byers have received a radio call at "about one o'clock" to look for a "light colored beige jacket?"[48] Who made the call to Harbor Precinct to initiate the jacket search? How did they know that Crump wasn't wearing a jacket or a golf cap at the time? How did they know he'd had one on before then? Why was it so important?*

The answer, of course, was that the CIA operation was in control of everything. Once Crump had become the designated patsy, the team knew where he was and what he was doing at all times, and especially what he was wearing. They had gone to great lengths to duplicate his clothing for the man standing over the body, who was to be seen by Wiggins. They also knew, from their surveillance of Crump, that he had jettisoned his jacket and cap, or perhaps lost them when he had inadvertently slipped into the Potomac. It had taken Byers less than forty-five minutes to locate Crump's jacket. How did he know where to look along the Potomac River shoreline? Likely because he was given enough direction by the CIA's operating team. Ultimately, without these two critical pieces of Crump's clothing—the jacket and the cap—there would be no circumstantial evidence against Ray Crump. But with their recovery, there was enough to begin framing Crump for the murder.

By 2:00 that afternoon, Deputy Coroner Linwood Rayford had arrived at the murder scene, and he pronounced Mary Meyer dead at 2:05 P.M. Meanwhile, Crump was in handcuffs and still at the murder scene. He didn't leave the scene immediately after he was arrested because too many police cars were blocking the exit at the Foundry Underpass. Crump was finally escorted away from the area sometime between 2:00 and 2:15 P.M. and taken to police head-quarters.[49] His jacket would be delivered to Detective Crooke "around 3:00 P.M." In handcuffs, wearing a white T-shirt, Ray would be photographed and paraded around police headquarters. Before the end of the day, the media would begin drilling Crump's guilt into the public psyche. The "trial by news-paper" had begun.

The only thing left to do was to establish Mary's identity for police, but in a controlled manner. A detail such as this was critically important and would be carefully managed; it was part of the CIA's "operation."

Here, I must interject an episode that took place in the course of my own exploration of this mystery. By 2006, after several years of painstaking re-search, I had not yet fully grasped how comprehensive an "operation" Mary's murder had been. There were still too many unanswered questions, too many lingering details I wasn't able to resolve, and I had nowhere to go for answers. Early one morning, hours before dawn in February 2006, I awoke disoriented, soaking wet as if sick with a fever in a night sweat. With darkness all around, I struggled to make sense of my current disposition. Had I been dreaming? No, not exactly. I felt as if I'd been talking to someone in another dimen-sion, almost sensing some lingering presence in my bedroom with me. But I could see no one. Increasingly anxious, I closed my eyes and focused on my breathing. Like a waterfall, rainbows of cascading images and thoughts from months of intensive study and research tumbled through my awareness. And then it happened. A horrid insight suddenly gripped me, though not yet fully comprehended or understood.

A veiled form of the clue had actually been in public view for years, since 1980 in fact, but I hadn't noticed it then, or even when it appeared more dramatically in 1995. That February morning, I realized the "master key" was in Ben Bradlee's 1995 memoir, *A Good Life: Newspapering and Other Adventures.* There, having waited more than thirty years, Bradlee revealed that the person who had first alerted him to his sister-in-law's demise on the day of her murder had been none other than my father, Wistar Janney: "My friend Wistar Janney called to ask if I had been listening to the radio. It was just after lunch, and of course I had not. Next he asked if I knew where Mary was, and of course I didn't. Someone had been murdered on the towpath, he said, and from the radio description it sounded like Mary."[50]

The reader may recall in an earlier chapter the mention of the telephone call that Ben Bradlee received "just after lunch" from his CIA friend. The truth was, Bradlee never revealed that his "friend" Wistar Janney was a high-level career CIA officer in this passage.[51] This had been the very first moment, Bradlee claimed, when he had learned that something might have happened to his sister-in-law, Mary Meyer. His next sentence reads: "I raced home."

My father, the reader will also recall, had been a career officer of the CIA since 1949, almost from the Agency's inception. While not officially titled in clandestine services or the agency's covert Directorate of Plans, his responsibilities had moved him through any number of different directorates in the Agency during the 1950s and 1960s, including the Office of Current Intelligence (OCI), as it was named at the time, and then the newer directorate Science and Technology (S&T).

What time of day did "just after lunch" actually represent? "Probably sometime after two o'clock, two-thirty, somewhere in that region or so," Bradlee said, in an interview for this book in 2007.[52] That, of course, was the time frame when the coroner had arrived (2:00 P.M.) at the murder scene and had pronounced the victim dead (2:05 P.M.). Her identity was still unknown. Ray Crump, it will be remembered, was just leaving the murder scene in handcuffs on his way to police homicide headquarters.[53] The only thing left to do for the "operation" was to establish the victim's identity. The terrible, lingering question, its stench still as foul today as it was on the afternoon of Mary's murder, was how much did Ben Bradlee really know about what was actually taking place? And when did he first know it?

How uncannily convenient that Wistar Janney just happened to be "listening to the radio" in his CIA office, where he allegedly heard a "radio description" about a murder that had just taken place on the canal. And of course the very first thought that popped into his mind was that it had to be Mary Meyer. For what possible reason would Wistar Janney think that an unidentified murder victim was Mary Meyer? Furthermore, Mary's outspoken, disapproving comments against the CIA not only drew resentment and outright hostility from other CIA wives, it also infuriated men like my father, whose blood boiled at the slightest criticism of his beloved CIA from anyone. Why would Wistar Janney, a trusted friend of Cord Meyer's, have been thinking about Mary Meyer that day (or any other day)? Was it possible that his call to Ben Bradlee "just after lunch" was designed not only to notify him of the event, but begin the final piece of the "operation"—establish the identity of the murder victim?

Everything else had been completed. Mary Meyer had been successfully assassinated. The patsy, Ray Crump, had been arrested and was in custody. A conveniently placed eyewitness had identified Crump, standing over the victim just seconds after the fatal second gunshot. The media would soon proclaim him guilty in the public mind. "William L. Mitchell" would show up at police headquarters the next day to reinforce the Wiggins eyewitness account. Crump was about to be convicted in the media in a matter of hours. Game, set, and match.

At the Janney family home during the evening of Mary's murder, a bit of veiled intrigue was occurring. Away at boarding school that fall, I was unaware of what took place. However, my younger brother, Christopher, fourteen at the time, was living at home. During the course of my research, I asked him to recollect what happened that evening. Christopher recalled that during dinner there had been absolutely no mention of Mary Meyer's murder. But sometime after dinner, "it had to be quarter to eight, if not eight, Dad was sitting at his desk in the den paying bills," he said, "listening to music, when the phone rang on his desk." Christopher was in his bedroom nearby with his door open doing homework. Our mother, he remembered, was in the master bedroom, most likely either reading or working at her desk.

"Dad picked up the phone in the den," said Christopher. The next thing he remembered was hearing our mother, hysterically crying out, "Oh no! Oh no!" He rushed into the den, wanting to know what happened.

"Mary Meyer has been shot," he remembered our father saying. Christopher further recollected it had been "the police" who had called our father "because they couldn't reach Cord, so Dad was next on the list, something like that." Both parents were upset, Christopher recalled. "Dad was more calm. Mom was more hysterical, but that was the first they'd heard about it."[54]

During the seven-year period I worked on this book, my mother volunteered on two separate occasions—and with no prompting from me—her own recollections of that evening. I made a point of not leading her in any direction; I just listened and let her talk. On both occasions, she distinctly remembered the phone call that evening. "That was the first we'd heard about it," she said repeatedly.

Shortly after "the police" phone call that evening, my father and Steuart Pittman (who had been married to Mary's sister, Tony, before Ben Bradlee, and who remained close to Mary's ex-husband, Cord Meyer), drove to National Airport to pick up Cord upon his return from New York.

Had the telephone call to Wistar Janney that evening come from "the police," or from someone from CIA coordinating the operation? Since Wistar answered the call, it was his assertion alone. What was clear was that it was time to create another illusion: the grieving ex-husband, Cord Meyer, needed the appearance of being comforted.

Recall another extremely critical detail: Sometime during the afternoon of Mary's murder, after calling Ben Bradlee, Wistar Janney had called Cord Meyer in New York, informing him of what had occurred. Feigning surprise and incredulity in his 1980 book, *Facing Reality*, Cord acknowledged it had indeed been his friend Wistar who had called him that afternoon: "In October of 1964, I was in New York City attending a meeting when I received a call from an old friend, Wistar Janney. As gently as he could, he broke the news that Mary had been found dead on the tow path along the canal that borders the Potomac, apparently murdered that afternoon by an unknown assailant. To my incredulous questions, he assured me that there could be no mistake. I flew back to Washington immediately to learn all that there was to know . . . Mary's friends had identified her body."[55]

Once again, "the cat was out of the bag"—as early as 1980: Wistar Janney had known, *during the afternoon of the murder*, the identity of the 'unidentified' murder victim. Yet he had played ignorant when he arrived home to his family, and said nothing until the mystery phone call took place. Cord Meyer, like Bradlee fifteen years later, would conveniently omit the fact in the previous description that his "old friend, Wistar Janney," was, like himself, a high-level CIA official.

How could my father have known anything whatsoever about Mary Meyer's death that day, unless, of course, he had been involved? How had he been able to inform both Ben Bradlee and Cord Meyer about it hours before the police had identified the victim? Recall that Mary's identity hadn't been established officially until Ben Bradlee identified her in the D.C. morgue, "sometime after six o'clock in the evening," in the company of Sergeant Sam Wallace of the Metropolitan Police Department. Given the facts established, the only logical explanation was that Wistar Janney was part of the CIA operation to "terminate" Mary Pinchot Meyer, as was Cord Meyer himself, although peripherally and indirectly.

But why would Cord Meyer risk identifying Wistar Janney in 1980 as the "old friend" who had called him on the day of the murder? The same question might be asked of Ben Bradlee, especially considering the incriminating time frame of the Janney phone call ("just after lunch") in Bradlee's account. There are several possible reasons for their statements. First, neither Cord Meyer nor Ben Bradlee wanted to be accused of withholding critical information in their respective memoirs as to how they had first learned of Mary's death. Since Cord had, it seemed, safely revealed this fact in 1980 with no repercussions, Bradlee may have thought in 1995 that it was safe for him to do so, given the longer span of time that had elapsed.

Yet Bradlee's 1995 revelation of the phone call from Wistar Janney was, and still is, potentially more damaging because his entire memoir account contradicts his 1965 trial testimony. Furthermore, had it been revealed at the trial that CIA official Wistar Janney had called Bradlee to inform him of Mary's death "just after lunch"—in other words, less than two hours after the murder took place, with Mary's identity still unknown to police—attorney Dovey Roundtree might have nailed Bradlee as a possible accessory to murder. The trial would have been over as soon as it had begun.

Still another lingering question was whether the prosecution at any time knew about either of Wistar Janney's calls—to Cord Meyer or to Ben Bradlee. If prosecuting attorney Alfred Hantman knew and withheld that information, he could have been disbarred for suborning perjury. The courtroom proceedings would have been exposed as nothing but a sham (as some believed they had been all along), engineered to convict Ray Crump as part of a greater cover-up, not only of Mary Meyer's assassination, but of President Kennedy's as well.

Finally, a more obvious reason that both Cord Meyer and Ben Bradlee felt it safe to reveal their respective calls from Wistar Janney was simply this: By 1980, Wistar Janney was dead; he died suddenly in January 1979 of a heart attack while playing squash with his friend Jack Oliver, just after lunch at the Metropolitan Club in Washington.

And so, on the evening of Mary's murder, Wistar Janney feigned his entire reaction to his wife and youngest son. Six weeks later, home from boarding school for Thanksgiving, I would sit at our family dinner table and listen to my mother reveal the murder of Mary Meyer earlier that fall. During her explanation, some part of me would also observe my father vacantly staring off into space. It would take more than forty years to finally realize that it had been his ghostly, eerie silence that evening that had so deeply haunted my psyche.

In the post-Watergate era of the late 1970s, the CIA had experienced a slow walk through hell. The Agency was in tatters, its reputation in shambles. As it was, the CIA feared annihilation in the Church Committee hearings, though ultimately, thanks to the machinations of Richard Helms, it had managed to fend off the ultimate, well-deserved verdict for having instigated America's first and only coup d'état: President Kennedy's assassination and its subsequent cover-up.

To make matters worse for Wistar Janney, investigative reporting was fast becoming a career choice for talented young journalists. Bob Woodward and Carl Bernstein, under the ironic tutelage of Ben Bradlee and *Washington Post* owner Katharine Graham, had raised the bar. The *Post*'s Watergate exposés had made the prospect of journalism glamorous again. Revealing "deep politics" and "secret history" was becoming a national obsession. Cord Meyer's 1980 memoir, *Facing Reality*, would reveal Wistar's knowledge of Mary's identity long before the police knew. How long would it take before some hotshot journalist would actually read and study the Crump trial transcript, only to then connect the dots buried in Ben Bradlee's testimony, and possibly persuade Bradlee to reveal Wistar's call to him that day before Mary's body was even cold? Or would it be Seymour Hersh himself—already having sacked the venerable CIA sacred cow James Jesus Angleton in 1975—who would finally bring down the hammer on Wistar's head? Perhaps Wistar thought a graceful, grand exit from the play of life would spare everyone—never realizing that eventually, one way or another, the sins of the father would be visited upon the son.

During the last two years of his life, Wistar Janney was living his own private version of hell. His beloved Agency had fallen into disrepute, and with it the reputation of many of those who had been there at the beginning. Retirement at age sixty loomed ominously on the horizon, and he wasn't at all happy about it, nor did he have any substantive plans as to how he might occupy himself. Even a doctoral graduate student in clinical psychology such as myself could see he was intermittently agitated, still drinking heavily, sneaking cigarettes whenever he could. His depression, coupled with an ongoing heart condition and no regular exercise, created an ideal prescription for an acute, made-to-order coronary event.

What, indeed, had Wistar Janney been thinking that dreary winter day in January 1979 at the Metropolitan Club? After eating his typical high-caloric, saturated-fat lunch, accompanied by a generous side order of martinis, Wistar went upstairs and played his predictably aggressive game of squash. It was, as the Beatles song lyric echoed, "a ticket to ride," but one with no return.

13

How It Went Down:
The Anatomy of a CIA
Assassination – Part II

He was a brilliant tactician who had the patience to cultivate orchids as a hobby. He was the master of manipulation who cultivated evidence. Opening people's mail—that was his program, collecting their pictures and diaries—this is what James Jesus Angleton did.

When I put on my conspiracy cap and muse about who were the powerful men that are ultimately responsible for JFK's assassination, be they Mafia bosses or corporate bosses or whoever they were, I cannot envision a plan that did not have designed into its very fabric a failsafe mechanism to neutralize the intelligence and security apparatus and insure that there would be no real investigation. Whoever they were, their reach extended into this apparatus to someone who knew its workings so well that he could design a plot that could do this.

My pick is James Jesus Angleton for who he was, who he knew, and because [Lee Harvey] Oswald was his creature from cradle to grave.

—Professor John M. Newman
Historian and author of *Oswald and the CIA*[1]

COMFORTED BY HIS CIA colleague Richard Helms and his close friend Jim Angleton, Cord Meyer had wept openly at Mary's funeral. His former wife, the love of his life and the mother of his three children, had again departed,

345

this time forever. The finality had to have evoked a myriad of emotions for Cord. Sixteen years later, in his book *Facing Reality*, Cord starkly concluded the following: "I was satisfied by the conclusions of the police investigation that Mary had been the victim of a sexually motivated assault by a single individual and that she had been killed in her struggle to escape." Cord then proceeded to insist that in spite of unspecified "journalistic speculation that Mary's death was the result of some complicated Communist plot," he was absolutely sure there "was no truth whatever to these stories" and "never suspected the tragedy of having any other explanation than the one the metropolitan police reached after careful investigation of all the evidence."[2]

Cord's defense of the official story was nothing less than a ploy—a deflection away from the stubborn facts that have forever haunted this case and remained unexplained until now. It was no coincidence he was out of town on the day of Mary's murder. His absence had to have been part of the operation, designed to create an appearance of innocence for Cord. Removing him physically from Washington had diverted any suspicion of his involvement. If Mary confronted Cord with her accusations of CIA involvement in Kennedy's assassination after she had read through the Warren Report—as Leo Damore maintained from having read her diary—Cord's complicity would have been inevitable. How could one of the highest-ranking CIA covert operatives *not* know about such an undertaking? Indeed, E. Howard Hunt's deathbed confession—that Cord was part of the 'mastermind' behind Dallas—might have contained some kernel of truth. Yet there would never be proof, at best only scant evidence—except possibly for the contents of Mary's diary.

Cord Meyer died in the spring of 2001. To my knowledge, after the release of his book *Facing Reality* in 1980, he never said anything further publicly regarding the death of his former wife. Two years later, however, Cord's former research assistant and Meyer family friend Carol Delaney was quoted in C. David Heymann's book *The Georgetown Ladies' Social Club* as saying the following: "Mr. Meyer didn't for a minute think that Ray Crump had murdered his wife or that it had been an attempted rape. But being an Agency man, he couldn't very well accuse the CIA of the crime, although the murder had all the markings of an in-house rubout."[3] The statement was breathtaking, particularly coming from someone so close to Cord. The only question was, had Ms. Delaney actually said it?

Provocative as it was, the statement was never confirmed by Carol Delaney on the record. Yet in the last seven years, I've seen nothing indicating that she ever repudiated it. When I first questioned Ms. Delaney in 2004, she wouldn't give me an answer. Instead, she immediately called Cord's widow, Starke Meyer, informing her of the book project I was undertaking. Starke then took it upon herself to "sound the alarm," calling Mary Meyer's sons, Quentin and Mark, as well as other members of the Pinchot-Meyer clan, even calling my mother, not only to complain ("What does he think he's doing?"), but to urge everyone to remain silent. The attempted stonewalling replicated author Nina Burleigh's experience when she first began her own research for *A Very Private Woman* in the mid-1990s. The CIA's community of former operatives, their wives and families, secretaries and research assistants, adhered to a Mafia-like code of silence. To challenge their version of events was to call into question the entire edifice of the secretive house of cards within which they lived.

Six years after my first attempt to interview Ms. Delaney, I called her again in 2010, asking her a second time to confirm or deny her account of Cord Meyer's statements, attributed in Heymann's book. Hostile, Ms. Delaney wanted to know, "Are you a friend of the Meyer family?" "Yes," I said, "I've known the family for more than fifty-five years." But she still wouldn't answer the question. "Why don't you send me an email, and I'll think about it," she finally said, then abruptly hung up. Her statement was just code for cowardice; she never said anything further, at least not to me.[4]

The other Cord Meyer tidbit in Heymann's undocumented book was what the author alleged Cord himself had said to him shortly before his death. Heymann claims he managed to sneak into Cord's nursing home to ask him about Mary's murder—specifically, who Cord thought had committed "such a heinous crime"? According to Heymann, Cord "hissed . . . the same sons of bitches that killed John F. Kennedy."[5] However titillating the statement, Heymann's credibility has been seriously called into question over the years.[6] Visiting his New York residence, I gently inquired whether he had taped his interview with Cord. He hadn't.[7] When I finally confronted him, he became defensive and insulting. Several days later he left me a voice mail, saying, "I'm beginning to think you're working for the CIA . . ."[8]

It is perhaps inevitable, given Jim Angleton's ubiquitous CIA presence, that my journey should reach some finality with him. So overpowering was his influence that after his unceremonious dismissal by CIA director William Colby in 1974, two of Angleton's closest comrades conspired to preserve his reputation and reign by gathering up his files and cultivating sympathetic writers to rehabilitate his tattered legacy. In so doing, they set in motion a complex chain of events that shone the bright light in unexpected ways upon some of the most significant questions surrounding Mary Meyer's murder. That chain of events bears the most careful scrutiny, not because it is conclusive in and of itself, but because, in the aggregate, and viewed in context of other statements and documented facts, it moves us ever closer to the horrifying truth.

The chief architect of the mission to burnish Angleton's controversial career was one of the Agency's most formidable covert action specialists, Robert T. Crowley. A Chicago-born West Pointer who'd served in Army intelligence during World War II in the Pacific, Crowley joined the Agency at its inception and rose quickly through the ranks despite the fact that he lacked the Ivy League pedigree of most of his associates. As assistant deputy director for operations, he was second in command in the clandestine services directorate until his retirement in the mid-1980s. Nicknamed "the Crow," he was one of the tallest men to ever to work at the Agency, and his career was legendary. Crowley was the chief go-to guy in the CIA's liaison with multinational corporations—the largest of which was International Telephone and Telegraph (ITT)—which the Agency often used as fronts for moving large amounts of money to fund international covert operations. Intimately involved with the CIA's overthrow of the democratically elected Allende government in Chile in 1973, Crowley had earned the highest regard from his colleagues.

In *Molehunt: The Secret Search for Traitors That Shattered the CIA* (1992), author David Wise referred to Crowley as "an iconoclast, and a man of great wisdom with a gift for metaphor."[9] Within the Agency, and particularly within covert operations and counterintelligence activities, mutual loyalty and trust among operatives were always the gold standard of conduct. In evaluating personnel for any covert operation, Crowley's quintessential question, a reference to the intricate teamwork required in deep-sea diving, inevitably came down to this: "Would I want this guy on my air hose at two hundred feet?"[10]

Two Crowley colleagues who most definitely wanted "the Crow" on their "air hose" were William R. Corson and the already well-known, mercurial James Jesus ("Jim") Angleton, the CIA's notorious counterintelligence chief. Bob Crowley and Bill Corson were "bosom buddies," the closest of friends and colleagues, and together coauthored a book in 1985 entitled *The New KGB: Engine of Soviet Power*. While Bill Corson was never officially titled in the Agency, his close ties to both Crowley and Angleton, as well as his many covert operations for U.S. intelligence, were well known. Corson was a brilliant strategist, an intellectual powerhouse in his own right, and a man who didn't want to be ultimately tied to anybody or anything. On the verge of being promoted to brigadier general in 1968, Corson had literally walked away in disgust from his Marine Corps career by doing the unthinkable: exposing in his book *The Betrayal* President Lyndon Johnson's White House lunacy and the venality of America's entire Vietnam War effort.[11] As Cold War intelligence historian Fletcher Prouty once quipped to author Joseph Trento, "For Bill Corson, the CIA was support staff. He needed to know; they didn't."[12]

"The Three Musketeers"—Corson, Crowley, and Angleton—thus formed a unique phalanx of "intelligence intelligentsia," and while it might not have been exactly "all for one" or "one for all," their commitment and loyalty to each other and, of course, the Agency were legendary, as was their alcohol consumption. When William Colby finally sacked Angleton in 1974, it was Corson and Crowley who devised a plan to secretly squirrel away Angleton's most highly classified, top secret files out of Langley. The cache allegedly included Mary Meyer's real diary.

Toward the end of their careers, the Three Musketeers appeared to have decided it was time for the world to know their true history, or at least some of it. It was Bill Corson who initially started to court newspaper reporter Joseph Trento in 1976.[1] Forcing Trento to jump through any number of hoops to prove his trust, Corson one day told him it was time he met Jim Angleton. "You've got to know him before he drinks and smokes himself to death," announced Corson, who was far along the same path himself. A few days later, Trento met Angleton for the first time. Sometime after Bob Crowley's CIA retirement, it would be Angleton who closed the circle and introduced Trento to Crowley. Once a lone pyramid protecting America's most dastardly deeds, the Musketeers had chosen a scribe, or so it appeared. They were going to reveal to Joe Trento some of "the secret history" of the CIA.

Somewhat reluctantly, Bob Crowley went along with the plan, at least for a while. Crowley, it turns out, may not have trusted Trento in the end. After Angleton died in the spring of 1987, Corson and Crowley began volunteering to Trento some of Angleton's most cherished secrets, files they had kept "in trust for their old friend." The deal was that nothing could be published until 1997, ten years after Angleton's death. When Bill Corson died in 2000, Joe Trento managed to come "into possession of all of his files, tapes, and writings." When Bob Crowley passed away several months later that same year, "his extensive files—and those of James Angleton—were also turned over to me," wrote Trento in the preface of his 2001 book, *The Secret History of the CIA*.[13]

---

1   Author Joseph Trento refused to be interviewed for this book.

But very possibly not everything was turned over. At least six years before his death and well before the onset of his final health crisis, Crowley had become a bit disenchanted with Trento. According to this account, Crowley had decided he wanted the truth to come out about the CIA's role in the Kennedy assassination. Whether this had Angleton's and Corson's blessing wasn't entirely known. For years, Corson had met regularly and held court with a group of his former students from the Naval Academy. The group enjoyed long lunch discussions together, coupled with a generous intake of alcohol. One favorite topic was the Kennedy assassination, and the flap that Oliver Stone's film *JFK* had been creating since its release in 1991. J. Michael Kelly, a former student of Corson's at Annapolis, gave two interviews for this book in which he stated definitively that Corson had told him in 1998 that he had in his possession, in his safe-deposit box, *the* critical Crowley document that outlined the CIA's engineering of the Kennedy assassination "from soup to nuts."[14]

Michael Kelly clearly recalled he had asked Corson in 1998, "Bill, don't you think Oliver Stone did a disservice to America by implicating the Armed Forces and the Joint Chiefs of Staff?" Corson was already into his second lunch martini. At that moment, Corson reached over, said Kelly, and slapped him on the arm, saying, "Michael, I'll tell you, you've got my permission when I die to take my attorney, who is Plato Cacheris, go to my safe-deposit box with Plato—he'll let you in there—and you'll find out who *really* killed John Kennedy."[15]

Two other former students of Corson's were aware of this exchange and vouched for it: Roger Charles, who had assisted me in the identification of William L. Mitchell, and who became the executor of Corson's estate; and a senior FBI agent named Tom Kimmel, the grandson of four-star Admiral Husband E. Kimmel, who served as commander in chief of the U.S. Pacific Fleet at the time of the Japanese attack on Pearl Harbor.[16]

J. Michael Kelly never forgot what Corson had told him. Within two months after Corson's death, Kelly contacted Corson's executor, Roger Charles, whom he knew well from their days together at Annapolis. They discussed the matter and agreed the next step was to approach Corson's attorney, Plato Cacheris, whose office was in the same building as Joseph Trento. Cacheris had been a well-known figure in Washington power circles for years, first defending Nixon attorney general John Mitchell of Watergate fame, then representing Fawn Hall, who worked with Oliver North during the Iran-Contra scandal. His clients included the infamous CIA spy Aldrich Ames, as well as the FBI's Robert Hanssen, both of whom were able to avoid the death penalty, thanks to Cacheris's legal prowess. Of course, in exchange, both had to reveal every-thing they had given the Soviets, before Cacheris brokered the deal.

So Kelly got together with Cacheris over lunch at a restaurant called Mor-ton's on a Thursday. He told Cacheris what Corson had said to him, and that he had Corson's permission to open his safe-deposit box, all of which was sup-ported by Corson's executor, Roger Charles. Cacheris seemed to play along with the request at the time, said Kelly, and was actually enthusiastic about it. He told Kelly he would get back to him on the Monday of the following week. But when Cacheris called, he abruptly stepped back, saying something to the effect that he didn't have "written authorization" to allow Kelly to open Cor-son's safe-deposit box. It would never happen. Kelly has since always suspected that after his lunch with Cacheris, the lawyer had contacted Joe Trento. No doubt Trento regarded whatever was in Corson's safe-deposit box as a part of Corson's papers that had been legally bequeathed to him. Thus Trento was able to secure the contents of Corson's safe-deposit box. According to Kelly, Trento knew the contents were highly incriminating of the CIA.

Though Plato Cacheris would admit he knew Bill Corson, in an inter-view for this book he said he didn't think he had ever "represented him." He wouldn't say for sure whether he remembered having lunch with J. Michael Kelly, but he affirmed unequivocally that he and Joe Trento never went into Bill Corson's safe-deposit box. Despite writing a blurb for the back of Tren-to's book *Secret History*, Cacheris said he only knew Trento "very superficially," though he admitted they did work in the same building at one time.[17] How-ever, Roger Charles, Corson's executor, was adamant that "Plato was Bill's at-torney during the *The Betrayal* flap. It was definitely a good move on Bill's part to use Plato, who beat the military brass and LBJ down when they were after Bill's scalp." Furthermore, Bill Corson's son, Chris, was sure "he [Plato Cach-eris] was dad's attorney" during his parents' divorce. Chris then conferred with his mother and asked her what she recalled about Plato Cacheris. "Plato Cacheris *was* dad's attorney," said Chris to Roger Charles after talking with his mother. "He settled the divorce in 1966 in Washington, D.C. and [it] was stated in court that he [Cacheris] was also dad's retained attorney for matters above and beyond that."[18]

For whatever reason, it seems that Cacheris wanted to distance himself not only from Bill Corson *and* Joe Trento, but also from having facilitated Trento's procurement of the contents of Corson's safe-deposit box. The importance of this event will soon become clear.

In the end, it was not Joe Trento who precipitated Bob Crowley's most critical revelations of Agency secrets, but a relatively obscure, unknown writer calling himself Gregory Douglas. "Douglas"—whose real name is Peter Stahl and whose email alias is sometimes "Walter Storch"—captured the attention of both Corson and Crowley in 1995, at which point the Crowley saga took a critical turn. It was Corson's former student, senior FBI agent Tom Kimmel, who brought to his mentor's attention Douglas's recently published *Gestapo Chief: The 1948 Interrogation of Heinrich Müller* (volume 1, 1995). Gregory Douglas, it appeared, had a vast knowledge of Nazi Germany, including the Gestapo, an abbreviation of the German word for "Secret State Police," of which Heinrich Müller had been director during World War II. In the first volume of *Gestapo Chief,* Douglas documented the fact that Heinrich Müller and a number of other high-level Nazi officials, scientists, and the like had all become covert CIA assets at the end of World War II. They were smuggled into the United States under new identities to join America's Cold War against the Soviets. The undertaking was finally revealed as the CIA's Operation Paperclip and has been well documented since, although there is still debate as to whether Heinrich Müller was part of it. Douglas claims that he met Müller in California and the two became instant friends, with Müller eventually giving Douglas some of his personal diaries.

For some reason, both Corson and Crowley were immediately smitten with the Douglas book; they believed the Douglas account was accurate, and they thought the author had been courageous for stepping forward to write such an account. In fact, they were so enamored that they contacted him and began a collegial relationship. Two years later, in 1997, Corson and Crowley, the two biggest intelligence titans of the Cold War, each contributed a short, highly favorable foreword to Douglas's second volume of what would become a trilogy about Müller and his life in the United States. Crowley in particular, it seemed, gave Douglas an unqualified stamp of approval: "Where possible, each revelation has been challenged and examined using all available resources to include: individual military records, released US communication intercepts and captured documents. To date, the Müller documents have met every challenge."[19]

In early 1996, Bob Crowley and Gregory Douglas began an intense telephone relationship that lasted nearly three years.[20] Often speaking with Douglas in substantial detail as frequently as twice a week, Crowley allegedly started to reveal intimate details about people and operations he had been involved with during his CIA career, including the Kennedy assassination.

Intrigued by what he was hearing, Douglas allegedly began, apparently unbeknownst to Crowley, tape-recording and transcribing many of the calls.

By the end of 1996 Crowley and Douglas, who had still not met face-to-face, finally scheduled a luncheon for Monday, December 9, 1996, at the University Club of Washington. Tom Kimmel and Bill Corson were also invited to the lunch. Crowley's plan, according to Douglas, was that he and Douglas were first going to meet alone before noon. Crowley wanted to personally deliver to Douglas a collection of CIA documents relating to the Kennedy assassination, in particular a lengthy document that Crowley himself had written and typed, entitled "Operation Zipper." This document, reprinted in Douglas's 2002 book, *Regicide*, was Crowley's "personal insurance policy, should someone start to point the finger at him," said Gregory Douglas in 2007 in an interview for this book. "He would take down everyone if this should happen. He considered the Zipper document to be his most important paper."[21] Douglas was also aware that Crowley had made a copy of the document for Bill Corson, and that Corson was keeping it in his safe-deposit box.

Unfortunately, the day before the University Club luncheon, Crowley was hospitalized with an acute case of pneumonia. Crowley's wife Emily recalled, "Bob was so looking forward to meeting this guy, but he never did. He felt very bad about it."[22] Douglas showed up in Washington anyway and had lunch with Bill Corson and Tom Kimmel, a fact Kimmel subsequently confirmed.[23]

The Crowley-Douglas telephone relationship resumed in earnest shortly thereafter, and Douglas allegedly continued to record their conversations, transcribing each of them. But Douglas has never produced any of the actual recordings on which Crowley's voice might be confirmed. This, among other things—including Douglas's history of shady dealings and trouble with the law—has led to skepticism regarding the journalistic credibility of "Gregory Douglas," now considered a pariah within the JFK assassination research community. But it turns out that Gregory Douglas's material, which precisely matches the sworn testimony of principals in the diary caper, may in fact hold several "master keys."

Throughout the mid- to late 1990s, Crowley's evolving admiration of Douglas continued to baffle Tom Kimmel, the senior FBI man. "The guy [Gregory Douglas, a.k.a. Peter Stahl] was obviously enormously bright," Kimmel recalled in 2007. "But I could never understand why Corson and Crowley embraced Stahl so unequivocally. I just couldn't understand it because Corson and Crowley were introspective, very accomplished intelligence officers, especially Crowley—not one to go off half-cocked at all. They didn't raise any objections or doubts, and that was not the way they approached anything. I mean, these guys doubted everything and everybody, but not Stahl. I could never figure that out."[24]

Pressured by his family in late 1997, Bob Crowley would again be admitted to the hospital for exploratory surgery for lung cancer. Again, as legend had it, fearing he wouldn't come out alive, he packed up two footlockers of documents and sent it all by mail to Gregory Douglas before going to the hospital. The deal was that they were not to be opened until after Crowley's death. Crowley, unfortunately, came back from the hospital with severe dementia, remained mostly bedridden, and died in October 2000.

Shortly after receiving the cache of Crowley documents, Douglas mentioned the transaction to Tom Kimmel. Increasingly concerned by the national security implications, and knowing something of the enormity of Crowley's involvement in CIA covert operations, Kimmel started pressuring Douglas to reveal what Crowley had given him. But Douglas wouldn't break his agreement with Crowley.

"Crowley knew Stahl [Gregory Douglas] was crazy enough to publish whatever he gave him," Kimmel revealed in an interview for this book. Did he, Kimmel, believe Crowley wanted the real story of the Kennedy assassination to be revealed? I asked

"That's why he gave it all to Stahl as opposed to Trento or someone else," replied Kimmel. At the time, so alarmed had Kimmel finally become, he ordered an FBI team to investigate the matter, even dispatching a female agent to Crowley's house. "It was Bob's relationship with him [Gregory Douglas] she was investigating," recalled Crowley's wife, Emily, in 2007. "The FBI lady was very down on him. I'm not sure why, but she was."[25]

It's not clear whether anyone has ever seen, or verified, the documents Crowley allegedly sent to Douglas, other than what Douglas included in his 2002 book *Regicide,* which highlighted Crowley's Operation Zipper record. Nor has anyone ever been able to listen to any of the Crowley-Douglas conversations that Douglas allegedly recorded. When I asked Douglas to produce the tapes, he said he had destroyed them, but later contradicted himself. However, the transcriptions of these alleged calls were available. I reviewed many of them in detail, traveling to Chicago to meet with Douglas on several occasions. Some of the transcripts remain not only intriguing, but also fascinating in terms of certain pieces of information—including specific details about Mary and Cord Meyer that Douglas, in my opinion, could never have fabricated.

In January 1996, Douglas began asking Crowley for specifics about the Kennedy assassination. Point-blank, he asked Crowley: "Was Oswald a patsy?" Crowley's answer was simple and complete: "Sure. He worked for us once in Japan at Atsugi and also for ONI [Office of Naval Intelligence]. Not high level, but he was a soldier after all." Crowley then mentioned what a "first class bitch" Oswald's wife, Marina, had been to deal with when she finally realized the impasse she was in. "No wonder she did what we told her," he said.

The two men then chauvinistically ruminated about "the mystery of women," with Crowley finally blurting out, "Most company [CIA] wives are a pack of nuts. Did I mention Cord's wife?" Douglas vaguely remembered the name Cord Meyer from somewhere, but he wasn't sure. He appeared to know nothing in 1996 about Mary Meyer.

Crowley then described Cord's wife as a "very attractive woman but her sister [Tony] was even better. She married Bradlee who is one of the company's [CIA's] men. He's on the *Post* now. Cord's wife was what they call a free spirit, liked modern art, ran around naked in people's gardens and so on. Pretty, but strange and unstable. She and Cord got along for a time but time changes everything. They do say that, don't they? They broke up and Cord was so angry at being dumped, he hated her from then on. She took up with Kennedy. Did you know that?"

"No," replied Douglas.

"Oh yes. After Mary—that was her name, Mary. You haven't heard about her?"

"No," Douglas said again.

"After Kennedy bought the farm," Crowley continued, "ex-Mrs. Meyer was annoyed. She had become the steady girlfriend and he was very serious about her. Jackie was brittle, uptight and very greedy. Poor people usually are. Mary had money and far more class and she knew how to get along with Jack. Trouble was, she got along too well. She didn't approve of the mass orgies and introduced him to pot and other things. Not a good idea. Increased chances for blackmail or some erratic public behavior. But after Dallas, she began to brood and then started to talk. Of course she had no proof but when people like that start to run their mouths, there can be real trouble."

"What was the outcome?" asked Douglas.

"We terminated her, of course," Crowley told him.

"That I didn't know. How?"

"Had one of our cleaning men nail her down by the towpath while she was out for her daily jog."

"Wasn't that a bit drastic?"

"Why? If you knew the damage she could cause us."

"Were you the man?" Douglas wanted to know.

"No, Jim Angleton was. And [Ben] Bradlee, her brother-in-law, was in the know. After she assumed room temperature, he and Jim [Angleton] went over to Mary's art studio to see if she had any compromising papers, and ran off with her diary. I have a copy of it."

"Could I see it?" asked Douglas.

"Now, Gregory, don't ask too many questions. Maybe later."

Later on, during the same conversation, Crowley referred to his colleague Cord Meyer as a "nasty, opinionated, loud, general asshole." Douglas was curious to know how Cord felt about the CIA "terminating" his wife. Crowley replied matter-of-factly: "Ex-wife. Let's be accurate now. Ex-wife. When Jim [Angleton] talked to Cord about this, Cord didn't let him finish his fishing expedition. He was in complete agreement about shutting her up. Gregory, you can't reason with people like her. She [Mary] hated Cord, loved Kennedy, and saw things in the Dallas business that were obvious to insiders or former insiders, but she made the mistake of running her mouth. One of the wives had a talk with her about being quiet, but Mary was on a tear and that was that." Crowley then added, "It wasn't my decision [to "terminate" Mary Meyer]. I was there, but Jim [Angleton] and the others made the final decision. You know how it goes."[26]

The two continued their conversations throughout 1996 about various aspects of the Kennedy assassination, but in early April of that year the subject of Mary Meyer came up again. In this instance, Crowley talked about how the sale of *Newsweek* to the *Washington Post* had been engineered by the CIA's Richard Helms.

"In the early 1960s," Crowley said, "Helms told Bradlee that one of his relatives wanted to sell *Newsweek*, and Bradlee brokered the deal with the *Post* people. We [the CIA] had a firm 'in' with the *Post* [already] and now with *Newsweek*, a powerful opinion molder and a high-circulation national magazine." Crowley continued: "Then there was the towpath murder. Cord's ex-wife was one of Kennedy's women and everyone felt she had too much influence with him, not to mention her hippifying him with LSD and marijuana. We can discuss the Kennedy business some other time, but Mary was threatening to talk and you know about the rest."[27]

Without access to Douglas's tape-recorded phone calls with Bob Crowley, it is impossible to confirm whether the voice speaking was Crowley's, and therefore impossible to verify the authenticity of the statements. Moreover, the unsavory character of "Gregory Douglas" (a.k.a. Peter Stahl and/or Walter Storch) leaves a great deal to be desired. And yet there remain details included here that are confirmed by other, more credible sources already presented.

First of all, Crowley's allegation that Cord Meyer was devastated after Mary left their marriage was true. It was well known to Cord's CIA colleagues and closest friends that he had been furious. "Cord was so angry at being dumped, he hated her from then on," said Crowley. Indeed, Mary's departure from the marriage had turned Cord upside down. He became increasingly hostile, and increasingly alcoholic. Cord, the reader will recall, had once lunged for Ben Bradlee's throat during a Washington dinner party conversation subsequent to his divorce from Mary. Cord's Yale classmate, U.S. attorney David Acheson, recalled Cord physically threatening to fight another guest "at a dinner party at my house. We had to tell him to calm down. Cord could be downright mean."[28] Crowley's account also dovetailed with what journalist Charlie Bartlett, Cord's close friend and Yale classmate, told me: "Cord was shaken after his divorce. He played on the wild side. He was drinking too much and making an ass out of himself."[29]

Second, Crowley mentions *twice* the fact that both Angleton and Bradlee *together* were in Mary's studio sometime after her murder that evening. According to Crowley's account, it appears that Jim Angleton had, in fact, accompanied Ben Bradlee to Mary's studio on the night of the murder, and that this was when Mary's real diary had been stolen. How could Crowley—or Gregory Douglas—have fabricated the content of Bradlee's obscure 1965 trial testimony, if it weren't true? Bradlee himself appeared to have lost track of his various versions of the story, as he completely contradicted his own sworn testimony thirty years later in his memoir.

Leo Damore told his attorney Jimmy Smith that he had recovered Mary's diary ("The diary found!"), and that it, or a copy of it, had apparently come from Bernie Yoh in 1990, to whom Jim Angleton himself had given it in 1980. That likely meant that Angleton had made at least one copy of the diary, before giving what he had to Yoh.

Damore, the reader will recall, had been very specific about what was in the diary: "Mary made connection w/ it [the Kennedy assassination] . . . CIA involved . . . James Angleton." Her murder, said Damore, had been "an operation. . . . standard CIA procedure." "It wasn't the affair," he said, "but the murder of JFK" that had done Mary in. "Mary – stepped in shit! She would not back down . . . "[30]

As Crowley allegedly told Douglas, "she [Mary] made the mistake of running her mouth . . . she was threatening to talk." He also said: "Good old Ben and his friend Jim went to Mary's little converted garage studio which Ben just happened to own, and finally found her diary. They took it away and just as well they did. She had it all down in there, every bit of the drug use, all kinds of bad things JFK told her as pillow talk, and her inside knowledge of the hit [Kennedy's assassination]. Not good."[31] Crowley's account of what Mary's diary actually contained further dovetailed with what Damore had told his attorney, Jimmy Smith, was in the copy of the diary that he (Damore) now possessed. Mary's mosaic had been completed. She had finally put the pieces together and was getting ready to talk. Alas, it was Mary's "inside knowledge of the hit" that made it necessary for her to be "terminated."

Intriguing also, was Crowley's statement about how they had used another CIA wife to try to persuade Mary to keep quiet: "One of the wives had a talk with her about being quiet but Mary was on a tear and that was that." The reader will also recall from a previous chapter CIA contract agent Robert Morrow's account of a conversation with his CIA boss, Marshall Diggs, in which Diggs told him the following: ". . . there's a certain lady [Mary Meyer] in town who has an inside track to Langley, and most importantly, to Bobby [Kennedy]. Fortunately, an intimate friend of mine is one of her best friends. . . . [Mary] Meyer claimed to my friend that she positively knew that Agency-affiliated Cuban exiles and the Mafia were responsible for killing John Kennedy. Knowing of my association with [Mario] Kohly, my friend immediately called me."[32] Was Diggs's "intimate friend" the CIA wife that Crowley said "had a talk with her [Mary] about being quiet"? Additionally, recall that right before his death, Robert Morrow told his biographer-to-be, John Williams, that he was more sure than ever that "Angleton did it."[33]

If the Crowley account approximates some level of truth, it also increases the likelihood that Mary and Jack did have some involvement with psychedelics, that Mary had been "hippifying him with LSD and marijuana." Crowley also mentions that "everyone [within the CIA] felt she had too much influence with him." Kenny O'Donnell had expressed a similar fear regarding Mary's influence. Mary did, in fact, have significant influence with Jack, particularly in matters that involved the pursuit of world peace after the Cuban Missile Crisis. Was it any surprise then that Jack, according to O'Donnell, wanted to divorce Jackie so that he could be with Mary after he left the White House?[34]

There is one last linchpin to the Crowley-Douglas caper that gives it further credibility. After the publication of Joseph Trento's *The Secret History of the CIA* in 2001, Gregory Douglas sent Trento a congratulatory email in November 2001. It read, in part, as follows:

From: G Douglas [email address withheld]
Sent: Monday, November 19, 200 11:17 P.M.
To: Joe Trento [email address withheld][2]
Subject:

Dear Mr. Trento:

I got your address from Walter Storch.

I enjoyed reading your book on the CIA and was gratified to see your comments on the CIA's employment of Heinrich Müller on page 29. Also gratified to note your citation of Crowley's CIA files as a source.

Bob sent me two large boxes of his files in 1996 in which his connections with Müller were documented therein. I have written six books on the subject of Müller and his CIA connections and authoritative support is certainly helpful.[35]

Here, Douglas noted Trento had verified, through Crowley's bequeathed papers and files, that Heinrich Müller had, in fact, been employed by the CIA. Douglas then mentioned the fact that Crowley had sent him "two large boxes of his files in 1996." Trento appeared to be oblivious to the Douglas bombshell statement. In a subsequent email communication later that same day, Douglas also mentioned "there is a new book coming out around Christmas [2001] on the Kennedy assassination with great emphasis on papers from Crowley." Unbeknownst to Joe Trento, Douglas was referring to his own book, *Regicide*.

It would be another year—November 2002—before Trento read *Regicide*, and when he did, he began to see red. He threatened Douglas immediately:

---

2   Both Joe Trento's and Gregory Douglas's email address have been purposely withheld. Having received email from both in previous years, I can verify that the email addresses above were valid and still in use.

From: Joe Trento [email address deleted]
To: G Douglas [email address deleted]
Subject: RE:
Sent: Sunday, November 03, 2002 7:14 P.M.

Just read a copy of the Kennedy book. I want you to know, as I told Walter earlier, that I am the literary executor of Bob Crowley and that I have the legal right to all of his documents. I notice that you are using documents from him in your book and this has to be stopped right now. This is a gross slander on the reputation of a fine American and, I want you to know, these papers are all classified documents under Federal law and you may not keep or use them. I intend to write to your publisher and inform him that if he does not cease and desist selling this book, I will sue him and you. Also, I have strongly suggested to both Emily and Greg [Bob Crowley's son] that they sue you for defaming Bob's good name. Now you can stop all of this legal action by sending me a full list of all the papers you got from Bob and then sending me the actual papers. Apparently you got an original file that Bob made a copy of and gave to Bill Corson. This copy was retrieved by myself after Bill's death and returned to the proper agency but apparently, Bob had sent out the original to you. As you know, Bob was badly failing in his last years and I and others, including Tom Kimmel, think it was a low blow for you to trick a trusting Bob into giving you sensitive papers. If you want to avoid future problems, I suggest you do as I say, make a list of all your documents you got from Bob, send it to me and then return all of these documents to me immediately. Tom Kimmel has told me all about you and I want you to know I won't hold still for any monkey business from you and if you don't want the FBI knocking your door down, do as I say.

Joe[36]

Joe Trento had just inadvertently confirmed that the Crowley documents Douglas had in his possession were, indeed, legitimate. That included the Crowley "Master Plan"—the file entitled "Operation Zipper," which was a time line and a logistical account of telephone calls, meetings, people, and places, all indicating how the CIA had orchestrated the plan to assassinate the president of the United States.[37] Nowhere in Trento's book *The Secret History of the CIA* does he even mention or allude to Crowley's "Operation Zipper" document (although Trento was well aware it existed); nor had Trento discussed the CIA's involvement in the Kennedy assassination. Instead, Joe Trento had done what Bob Crowley feared he would do: He pimped Angleton's ridiculous, longtime public assertion that the Kennedy assassination was the work of the Soviet KGB using Lee Harvey Oswald as a tool.[38] Trento appeared to be unaware (or possibly colluding to obfuscate the truth) that Angleton himself had designed the demonic, viral master plan that would paralyze the entire national security apparatus, including the CIA, except for a "gifted few," from discovering the real conspiracy that had actually taken place under Angleton's direction. Trento's shoddy journalism was both underhanded and deceitful.[39]

Likely, it was attorney Plato Cacheris who alerted Trento to the importance of Corson's safe-deposit box. In any case, Trento noted the contents were "returned to the proper agency," undoubtedly referring to the CIA. But he also finally realized it had only been a *copy*—"apparently, Bob [Crowley] had sent out the original to you." The cat, indeed, was out of the bag!

Two hours after receiving the Trento threat, Gregory Douglas responded in kind:

From: G Douglas [email address deleted]
Sent: Sunday, November 03, 2002 9:15 P.M.
To: Joe Trento [email address deleted]
Subject: RE:

Mr. Trento:

The documents I received from Bob Crowley, mailed by his son Greg, in 1996, were freely given to me as an author. Bob had been assisting me with important material for several years previously.

His only caveat was that I not make use of these before he died and I have not done so.

I know from Bob that he gave a copy of the Kennedy file to Corson and that it vanished after his death.

What I have are the originals and also the originals of many other fascinating subjects.

361

Please be advised that Bob sent these to me *prior* to his death and that they therefore do not fall under any literary property over which you now claim to have rights.

In answer to your specific demands, be advised that I have no intention of sending you any list of this material in question and neither do I have any intention of sending you anything else.

In the event that you dare to address me again, I will personally post some of the more sensitive documents on the Internet and personally thank you for having sent me these from your own holdings of Crowley's papers.

Bob told me you were a light weight hack and it is also obvious that you have no knowledge of the law.

GD[40]

It would seem the elusive, infamous Gregory Douglas (a.k.a. Peter Stahl/ Walter Storch) may have been somewhat truthful regarding what had transpired between himself and Bob Crowley. But it will never be known *how* truthful, unless Douglas produces both the Crowley cache of documents and the recordings he allegedly made of their conversations. Yet despite the remaining ambiguity surrounding the Crowley-Douglas affair, the details purportedly revealed by Crowley—about Mary Meyer, her diary, and her murder—are solidly supported and substantiated by other events and accounts covered in this book.

Ben Bradlee never took kindly to anyone who accused him of having CIA connections. Bob Crowley not only reiterated Bradlee's role in bringing *Newsweek* to the *Post* through the gracious hands of the CIA's Richard Helms, but he also referred to Bradlee as "one of the company's [CIA's] men," who was "on the *Post* now." Had the sale of *Newsweek* to the *Post* started opening doors for "good old Ben"? During the 1950s and 1960s, working for, or with, the CIA, directly or indirectly, didn't necessarily mean being on the CIA payroll as an employee. In the Cold War era, many journalists considered cooperation with the CIA a kind of patriotic duty. After Watergate, however, it was considered deeply suspicious, if not downright duplicitous, because so much CIA chicanery had been exposed.

Deborah Davis and her book *Katharine the Great* paid the ultimate price in 1980 when, under great pressure from both Ben Bradlee and Katharine Graham, her publisher, William Jovanovich, recalled and shredded her book—some twenty thousand copies—just two months after the book's release. (It appears that "Freedom of the press," as A. J. Liebling once famously put it, "is guaranteed only to those who own one"). It was Davis's assertion in her book that Bradlee's job as press attaché at the American Embassy in Paris in 1952–1953 functioned as a CIA front at the time. Bradlee was writing propaganda aimed at "persuading" Europeans that Julius and Ethel Rosenberg were spies and deserved to be executed. Of course, Bradlee was purposely not on any CIA payroll as an employee; that would have made it too obvious. Yet his assertion that he "never worked for the CIA" was just semantics.[41]

In later editions of *Katharine the Great*, Davis included documents that corroborated Bradlee's CIA connections. One such document was a United States Government Office Memorandum, dated December 13, 1952, which a Rosenberg case assistant prosecutor named Mr. Maran wrote to Assistant U.S. Attorney Myles Lane describing Bradlee's request to examine the Rosenberg file, which Maran was safeguarding (see appendix 4). Bradlee stated to Maran that he (Bradlee) had been sent to review the Rosenberg case file "by Robert Thayer, who is the head of the C.I.A. in Paris." Bradlee also disclosed, again according to Maran, that he was to have been met "by a representative of the CIA at the airport, but missed connections," and was therefore "trying to get in touch with Allen Dulles but . . . [had] been unable to do so."[42] Despite the first edition of the Davis book being recalled in early 1980, damage to Bradlee's reputation had already been done. It upset Bradlee profoundly—and shook the pedestal onto which the *Washington Post* had been elevated since Watergate.

"He [Bradlee] went totally crazy after the book came out," said Davis in an interview in 1992. "One person who knew him told me then that he was going all up and down the East Coast, having lunch with every editor he could think of saying that it wasn't true, he did not produce any propaganda. And he attacked me viciously and he said that I had falsely accused him of being a CIA agent. And the reaction was totally out of proportion to what I had said."[43]

It would seem Ben Bradlee's penchant for impenetrable deception, his playing fast and loose with pivotal facts and events that he hoped had long escaped public scrutiny, has all along been part of the Bradlee persona, karmically following like a shadow. How could Bradlee in 1965 testify under oath during the Crump murder trial that he had entered Mary's studio with no trouble on *the night of the murder*, and then thirty years later spin a cock-and-bull story that he only first entered the studio the *next day* with his wife? "We had no key," said Bradlee, "but I got a few tools to remove the simple padlock, and we walked toward the studio, only to run into Jim Angleton again, this time actually in process of picking the lock."[44] Part of the Bradlee story may have been designed to convince the public that he and Angleton, and the CIA, had always been adversaries, when they had been nothing of the sort. In this particular case—breaking into Mary Meyer's studio to find her diary—they were collaborating. Bradlee never once publicly mentioned he had been inside Mary's studio on the night of the murder. The only revelation of that fact was contained in the 1965 Crump murder trial transcript; it was never again mentioned by Bradlee himself, or anyone else (until now), including journalist-author Ron Rosenbaum or Nina Burleigh.

And who, if anybody, had accompanied Bradlee when he went to the studio on the night of Mary's murder? According to CIA covert operative Bob Crowley, it was Jim Angleton. It was at this time, said Crowley—who mentioned it twice—that the real diary (not Mary's artist sketchbook—the decoy) was discovered and given to Angleton for safekeeping. Ultimately, the exact account of what actually took place may never be fully known. But more than likely, as Crowley maintained, the diary was taken on the night of her murder—either from Mary's studio, or from the bookcase in her bedroom. Mary's bedroom, according to the statements Jim Truitt made to Ron Rosenbaum in 1976, was where she usually kept it.[45]

Finally, one last bit of commentary on the 1995 Bradlee memoir. On the one hand, concerning Mary's murder, the memoir was so rife with factual errors, omissions, and contradictions that it cried out for careful scrutiny. (There was a reason why Ben Bradlee turned down Leo Damore's request for an interview in 1991).[46] On the other, Bradlee had further divulged *the most critical and revealing event* of the entire Mary Meyer murder conspiracy: CIA man Wistar Janney's telephone call "just after lunch" informing Bradlee that "someone had been murdered on the towpath . . . and from the radio description it sounded like Mary."[47]

Ben Bradlee was even more circumspect in 2010 when being interviewed for David Baldacci's *Hardcover Mysteries* television documentary about Mary Meyer's murder. Asked off-camera by director Gabe Torres how he first learned that Mary had been killed that day, Bradlee responded cryptically, "A friend called me," carefully choosing not to reveal the identity of the "friend."[48]

Forty-five years earlier, Bradlee had been equally tight-lipped. "Mr. Bradlee, I have just one question," said defense attorney Dovey Roundtree during the Crump murder trial in 1965. "Do you have any personal, independent knowledge regarding the causes of the death of your sister-in-law? Do you know how she met her death? Do you know who caused it?"

"Well, I saw a bullet hole in her head," Bradlee replied, dodging her inquiry.

"Do you know who caused this to be?" persisted Roundtree.

"No, I don't," Bradlee maintained.[49]

It had to have been a defining, life-changing moment in the life of forty-three-year-old Benjamin Crowninshield Bradlee. Nine months earlier, he and others had conspired to erase his sister-in-law's private life. Privy to the "master key event" of Wistar Janney's telephone call, Bradlee, once again, lied through omission, withholding not only the critical evidence of Mary's diary (the motive), but also the Janney telephone call (evidence of conspiracy). Was it just a case in which the ends justified the means?

At the time of the trial in July 1965, Bradlee's career was already being transformed. Several months earlier, in March, he had been wooed back to the *Washington Post* after a fourteen-year hiatus by none other than Katharine Graham herself. That August, a month after the trial ended, Bradlee returned to the *Post*, where he had once worked as a "crime reporter," with a new title: "Deputy Managing Editor." Less than three months later, in October that same year, he would be promoted to "Managing Editor."[50]

In 1976, after the first revelation of Mary's relationship with President Kennedy appeared in the *National Enquirer*, Bradlee told journalist Ron Rosenbaum in an interview that there had been no "CIA angle," no Agency "shadow" in Mary's demise. "If there was anything there," boasted Bradlee, "I would have done it [written the story] myself."[51] The statement was as ludicrous as it was egregious. But it pales against the statement in his 1995 memoir in which he mischaracterizes and thereby minimizes the last moments of Mary Meyer's life: "She [Mary] was walking along the towpath by the canal along the Potomac River in Georgetown, when she was grabbed from behind, wrestled to the ground, and shot just once under her cheek bone as she struggled to get free. She died instantly."[52]

No. Mary hardly "died instantly." By all police, witness, and forensic accounts, she struggled mightily, screaming for twenty seconds or more, before the first gunshot ripped through her skull. Death be not proud, nor even swift. Whatever Mary's thoughts or feelings during the final conscious seconds of her life, she had to be aware her death was fast approaching, yet she would not succumb without a fight, before the second fatal shot ended her life. Perhaps Ben Bradlee wanted to assuage his guilt by publicly spinning yet another yarn that his sister-in-law hadn't really suffered, or that she hadn't faced head-on the terrifying realization that her life was about to end violently. Whatever his motivation, Ben Bradlee played as fast and loose with the facts in this instance as he had with nearly every other aspect of Mary's death.

Tony Bradlee, subsequent to the death of her sister and the "shock" of discovering Mary's affair with Jack, retreated to studying sculpture at the Corcoran School of Art, as well as exploring the mystical and spiritual traditions of George Gurdjieff and his disciple P. D. Ouspensky. During the next few years, her marriage to Ben slowly disintegrated. For the Bradlees, "Jack Kennedy and Mary Meyer had been murdered out of our lives," noted Ben during his meteoric rise on the *Post,* "out of our reservoir of shared experience, and we both had changed in coping with their loss."[53]

Mary's death took a severe toll, not only on her children, but also on other members of her extended family. "Mary believed the world could change . . . she was such a fascinating figure in the family," said Nancy Pittman Pinchot, daughter of Tony Bradlee by her first marriage to Steuart Pittman. "She had a quality of aliveness. We watched the full flowering of Mary as the kind of woman that Mom [Tony Bradlee] might have become. Instead, Mom lived off the idea that JFK had a crush on her for years—before she disappeared up the asshole of spirituality. It was such a blow to her to find out Mary and Jack had been together."[54]

Asked in a letter by Leo Damore in 1991 whether she would be willing to be interviewed about the events surrounding her sister's death, Tony avoided any possibility of an encounter, replying, "I feel as I have always felt—that the case is closed, that Crump was indeed guilty. Also, I am loathe to get involved in going over that event again, with all its unhappy memories."[55] Tony Bradlee died in Washington on November 9, 2011.

Up until the very end of 2011 (December 31st to be exact) when she died just shy of her ninety-first birthday, Anne Chamberlin, a former Vassar classmate and close friend of Mary Meyer's, had remained the only person left who could have perhaps unraveled some of the impenetrable, unanswered questions surrounding the last years of Mary Meyer's life, and death. A known friend to Katharine Graham, regarded as an intrepid, charmingly sharp-witted commentator, who had a "distinguished and eclectic career" as a freelance journalist, Anne also maintained throughout her life an extraordinary level of physical health and vitality through a daily, grueling exercise regime.[56] And yet, as adventurous and fearless as she appeared, she refused—even ran—from wanting to be associated with anything to do with Mary Meyer after her death. Her phone interviews with Leo Damore in the early 1990's indicated she'd been a part of Mary's Washington "LSD group" that took shape in 1962, yet she became indignant when I asked to talk with her about this. According to Damore, Chamberlin fled Washington for Maine out of fear, shortly after Mary's murder, side-stepping being named in any of the accounts surrounding Mary's death. Had Anne Chamberlin been privy to something so dangerous that she feared for her life, should she reveal what she knew?

James Jesus Angleton had what might be called a "second career" sending newspaper reporters and journalists on never-ending wild-goose chases. Sailing on the edge, always well-oiled and three sheets to the wind, Angleton relished seeing how far he could push their limits of gullibility; and, like a Shakespearean actor, he did so convincingly, often leaving many of them awe-struck, as if they had just been given the actual location of Noah's Ark or the whereabouts of Jimmy Hoffa's body. There was a reason why former military intelligence officer and historian John Newman, author of *Oswald and the CIA*, a person with more than twenty years of experience as an analyst for U.S. military intelligence, told me during an interview for this book that he considered Angleton as "one of the most diabolical figures in all of human history."[57] What took place in 1976 after the *National Enquirer* exposé involving Mary's relationship with Kennedy supported historian Newman's point of view.

The 1976 *Enquirer* story had opened a huge can of worms. It would take a masterful performance from the master Angler himself, along with supporting actors like Ben Bradlee, to neutralize its implications. The elite circle of Mary's acquaintances—the people who had taken an "omertà oath" of allegiance never to reveal the facts surrounding either her diary or her murder—had to figure out how to hoodwink journalists Rosenbaum and Nobile, who were intent on writing the whole story. The two most high-profile players among them—Jim Angleton and Ben Bradlee—were forced to make a showing. For whatever reason, Cord Meyer and Anne Chamberlin would remain hidden, as would Anne Truitt, and to a large extent Tony Bradlee. Like his misleading trial testimony in 1965, Bradlee's 1976 selective recollections carefully excluded the most critical events. Dare it be said that had Rosenbaum and Nobile become aware of these linchpin events, the Angleton-CIA house of cards would have collapsed immediately.

But it didn't collapse, and for several reasons. Within the hallowed halls of the Agency, the ruling leaders of America's premier intelligence establishment had learned how to manage almost any crisis, particularly when it came to accountability to the public, or even to Congress. In CIA parlance, it's called "a limited hang-out." With their backs to the wall, the Agency gives up a few classified, titillating tidbits, making everyone feel as though they've actually come clean, when in fact they've done nothing of the sort, continuing to withhold what is most critical. No greater master ever demonstrated this technique more skillfully than James Jesus Angleton, the "Delphic Oracle" of counterintelligence, the chief himself. Angleton was the consummate actor and seducer. He completely dazzled Ron Rosenbaum and coauthor Phillip Nobile into thinking that they had closed the door on the case, solving everything. Alas, the authors declared, Mary's murder, like Jack's before her, was a random, indiscriminate, violent murder committed by a deranged, lone gunman.

So powerfully beguiling and enchanting was Angleton's influence on Rosenbaum in 1976, it likely ignited his fascination with Angleton's mentor, Soviet double agent Kim Philby. Philby and Angleton had met during Angleton's stint in the OSS during World War II, while Philby was ostensibly working for the British Secret Intelligence Service. Under the masterful Philby tutelage, Angleton learned all the fundamentals of the craft of intelligence, including masterminding the world of counterintelligence. Angleton came to revere his mentor just the way Philby wanted him to; it was part of Philby's strategy. After the war, Philby would come to Washington as the chief British intelligence liaison to the fledgling CIA. The eager-beaver Angleton consulted Philby on almost everything, sharing with him all that was going on at the highest levels of American intelligence. Therein lay Angleton's tragic fatal flaw—trusting anybody, and particularly Kim Philby. That mistake would eventually eviscerate Angleton, and he would never recover, only deteriorate. Kim Philby, as it was finally revealed in 1963, was a Russian spy, an agent allied with the KGB. So deeply had the entire arena of American intelligence been penetrated that Angleton sank even deeper into paranoia, his daily alcohol-nicotine intake dismembering his overall capacity and grasp on reality, cell by cell. Everything, and everybody, viewed through the Angleton prism, was vermin—moles, to be exact—digging relentlessly and eternally, no matter how circuitous the route, toward Langley, Virginia, their final destination CIA headquarters. That was the footprint that "Mother" Angleton would create and leave behind.

To his great credit, in an attempt to further describe what the life of Kim Philby must have been like, journalist Ron Rosenbaum delivered a riveting, quintessential vision of the character of Kim Philby—unaware he was also describing someone he had encountered years earlier:

> The mole, the penetration agent in particular, does not merely betray; he *stays*. He doesn't just commit a single treacherous act and run; his entire being, every smile, every word he exchanges, is an ultimate violation (an almost sexual penetration) of all those around him. All his friendships, his relationships, his marriages become elaborate lies requiring unceasing vigilance to maintain, lies in a play-within-a-play only he can follow. He is not merely the supreme spy; he is above all the supreme *actor*. If, as [John] le Carré once wrote, "Espionage is the secret theater of our society," Kim Philby is its Olivier.[58]

Indeed, for a time, Kim Philby had been "the secret theater's" Olivier; and inevitably, that meant James Jesus Angleton had been his understudy. Angleton had successfully modeled his entire being on how Philby had shaped his own. Eventually, karma delivered fate. It was no accident that the obsessive mission of "Angleton the mole hunter," forever protecting his beloved Agency no matter what the cost, resulted in paralyzing entire sections of the CIA's operational directorates, and eventually gave rise to the biggest crisis the American intelligence establishment ever faced.

By the 1960s, it was well known within the highest levels that the CIA had been penetrated. During that time, Edward Clare Petty, a protégé of Angleton's and a member of the Special Investigations Group within Counterintelligence (CI/SIG), was ordered to begin an extended study to identify who the mole was, and how he was able to operate. Angleton, of course, thought his clout would allow him to contain the study, and slant it in any direction he wanted. Such turned out not to be the case. Before his retirement in 1975, Petty turned in his report, revealing to his superiors, including CIA director William Colby, that the mole Angleton had been hunting for twenty-five years was, in fact, Angleton himself. One source confirmed that the so-called Petty Report was so explosive that it had been kept under armed guard when it was first completed. Jim Angleton had been officially fired by Colby in December 1974, ostensibly because he had violated the Agency's charter, infringing upon the privacy rights of certain citizens, as disclosed by investigative journalist

Seymour Hersh in the *New York Times*. While all true, Angleton's real reign of terror had been far more nefarious.

So in 1976, when authors Rosenbaum and Nobile relied on Jim Angleton as a primary source for their seminal article "The Curious Aftermath of JFK's Best and Brightest Affair," their efforts to solve the mystery were immediately contaminated—they allowed themselves to be seduced by one of the greatest tricksters of the twentieth century. In addition, Rosenbaum's own certainty about his rightness further precluded any real penetration and exposure of the evil that had been perpetrated.

In 1964, Angleton's reputation was legendary, in and out of the Agency. Covert operative David Atlee Philips once made the comment that "Angleton was CIA's answer to the Delphic Oracle: seldom seen but with an awesome reputation nurtured over the years by word of mouth and intermediaries padding out of his office with pronouncements which we seldom professed to understand fully but accepted on faith anyway."[59] Together with Allen Dulles, with the completion of the Warren Report in 1964, Angleton had not only just masterminded the greatest cover-up in all of American history, but had duped the entire national security apparatus, including the CIA, into believing that Oswald had been collaborating with both Cubans and the Soviet KGB during his trip to Mexico in the fall of 1963, setting up his plan to assassinate President Kennedy later that fall. President Lyndon Johnson then used "the Mexico City trump card" of a World War III nuclear confrontation that would kill 40 million Americans in the first hour to persuade people like Supreme Court justice Earl Warren to make sure the Warren Commission would establish Oswald as a lone nut assassin acting on his own.[60] William Colby would say of Angleton in 1973: "Mr. A is an institution." In 1980, Clare Booth Luce, wife of Time-Life publisher Henry Luce, told Angleton in private communication, "There's no doubt you are easily the most interesting and fascinating figure the intelligence world has produced, and a living legend."[61]

Every detail, however minute, had to be taken into account in an "operation" of such magnitude as Mary's "termination," so as to arouse as little suspicion as possible. Jim Angleton was Cord Meyer's closest and dearest friend, and the godfather to his children. (Angleton was supposedly also a "dear friend" of Mary's, though with friends like Angleton, who needs enemies?) And so the question still remains: Why hadn't Jim Angleton called Ben Bradlee "just after lunch" on the day of Mary's murder, as well as his dear friend and colleague Cord Meyer later that afternoon—particularly after his wife Cicely's alleged panicked call to him at CIA headquarters who believed the murdered woman might be Mary? Why not Angleton instead of Wistar Janney? The answer: Any overt involvement by "Mother" Angleton would have forever raised dangerous suspicion.

Wistar Janney, on the other hand, wasn't officially titled in the CIA's covert action directorate, although Victor Marchetti had made it clear: "Your father was a company man." A respected friend to both Cord Meyer and Ben Bradlee, Wistar Janney was the ideal go-between, someone who could contact, signal, or coordinate, among all three men: Angleton, Bradlee, and Cord Meyer. The infamous Angleton had given himself another role to play—that of procuring Mary's diary and any other artifacts, personal papers, letters, and the like that might incriminate the CIA in her murder, or President Kennedy's assassination.

And Jim Angleton succeeded in his mission. The "Lady Livia Augustus in drag" got everything he wanted. With aplomb, he had completely erased the most important phase of Mary's life. With the information that Jim Truitt provided to the *National Enquirer*, the master fly-fisherman Angler himself, known for designing his own special fishing lures, cast his bait into just the right pool, then hooked one of his biggest catches of all time, journalist Ron Rosenbaum, intricately steering and anchoring him to the lone gunman/Ray Crump theory. Unaware, Rosenbaum had been delicately reeled into Angleton's nexus of deception, while the master himself then drove away in his signature black Mercedes. Darth Vader couldn't have done it any better.

Finally invaded by the mole of cancer, the "Delphic Oracle" Angleton at last confronted the final curtain on the stage of life. Even the mercurial spymaster, stricken with lung cancer and facing imminent death, earnestly, and finally, acknowledged to his scribe, Joe Trento, that Jack Kennedy and Mary Meyer "were in love. They had something very important."[62] In another end-of-life "epiphany," he told his faithful penman: "I realize how I have wasted my existence, my professional life," adding "I was always the skunk at the garden party, and even your friends tire of that."

His marriage to Cicely ruptured, and his two children estranged from him, Jim Angleton's last paternal effort was to seek out his daughter, Truffy, who had joined Yogi Bhajan's effort to bring Kundalini yoga to the West. Truffy had years before converted to the Sikh religion. Eventually her mother, Cicely, before her death in 2011, and her sister Lucy would find a second home there, too. According to one source who knew the family well, Jim Angleton regularly consulted with Yogi Bhajan as his "spiritual adviser" in the final years of his life. Whether it was because he wanted to understand what had driven his daughters to renounce their former existence, or whether he wanted "spiritual absolution" as death drew near, his family had mostly abandoned him.

During one of Angleton's final meetings with author Joseph Trento, the frail, emaciated, cancer-ridden "Ichabod Crane" surrendered more secrets. The man whose all-encompassing power "had struck fear into most of his colleagues, the man who had been able to end a CIA career with a nod or a phone call," Trento wrote, was finally crumbling. Jim Angleton would tell his scribe, "You know, the CIA got tens of thousands of brave people killed. . . . We played with lives as if we owned them. We gave false hope. We—I—so misjudged what happened."[63]

"You know how I got to be in charge of counterintelligence?" Angleton blurted out to Trento. "I agreed not to polygraph or require detailed background checks on Allen Dulles and 60 of his closest friends. They were afraid that their own business dealings with Hitler's pals would come out. They were too arrogant to believe that the Russians would discover it all." Later in the same conversation, Angleton added, "There was no accountability. And without real accountability everything turned to shit."[64]

How had it all gone so wrong, Trento wanted to know? Weak and trembling, a cup of one of his beloved exotic teas now his most treasured companion, James Jesus Angleton gave the author his final parting reflection:

Fundamentally, the founding fathers of U.S. intelligence were liars. The better you lied and the more you betrayed, the more likely you would be promoted. These people attracted and promoted each other. Outside of their duplicity, the only thing they had in common was a desire for absolute power. I did things that, in looking back on my life, I regret. But I was part of it and loved being in it. . . . Allen Dulles, Richard Helms, Carmel Offie, and Frank Wisner were the grand masters. If you were in a room with them, you were in a room full of people that you had to believe would deservedly end up in hell.

Then, as he slowly sipped his tea, he added, "I guess I will see them there soon."[65]

Ron Rosenbaum's final observation about the murder of Mary Meyer was a "Postscript" to his original 1976 article that was included in his 2000 anthology *The Secret Parts of Fortune*. There, he described an encounter one night in the late 1980s in the Hollywood Hills of California with "a well-known West

Coast figure," an obvious attempt for some reason to camouflage the identity of Timothy Leary.

Lampooning Leary's assertions that Mary Meyer had been killed "because of what she knew about the CIA plot to kill JFK," then ridiculing Leary's view that "Nixon had planned to expose the CIA's role in JFK's death—which was really what was erased from the eighteen minute gap on the Watergate tape"— Rosenbaum continued to brag of how thoroughly he had read the Crump trial transcript, how meticulously he had "reinvestigated the whole case," how he had "interviewed most of the principals," and that "no evidence was ever adduced that gives the slightest hint there was a conspiracy behind Mary Meyer's murder—or that her death had any relation to her secret liaison with JFK."[66]

Just as egregious, Rosenbaum's parting reflection to his readers was that Nina Burleigh's *A Very Private Woman* was what he termed "a recent careful reinvestigation" that further supported his overall opinion that Mary's death had been "a random assault by a stranger."[67] And yet in the fall of 1995, three years before Nina Burleigh published her book, five years before Ron Rosenbaum's final statement on the matter would appear in his 2000 anthology, Ben Bradlee had dramatically coughed up what Cord Meyer had only cryptically mentioned in 1980: the phone call "just after lunch" from Wistar Janney. Nina Burleigh, in particular, knew exactly who Wistar Janney was, having spent many hours interviewing me, starting in 1996, two years before her book was published. Simply put, both Cord Meyer and Ben Bradlee had, however inadvertently, revealed "the master key" that proved conspiracy—a fact that neither Rosenbaum nor Burleigh had even bothered, or possibly dared, to consider.

"No lie can live forever," Martin Luther King Jr. once remarked. In the sacrosanct halls of the CIA, where such kingpins as Jim Angleton, Richard Helms, Cord Meyer, Wistar Janney, and others lied professionally and with impunity, a decision had been made. They may have agonized a bit—after all, Mary Pinchot Meyer was well bred, beautiful, and of the same class, one of 'their own.' But the stakes were too high. If she talked and told what she had come to understand about what really had taken place in Dallas, what had been done to her beloved ally, the president, and the country, and by whom, people with influence would have listened to her, people such as Philip L. Graham of the *Washington Post*, had he still been alive. That made Mary Meyer very dangerous.

These imperious CIA men lived in a world that answered to no authority; they knew exactly what they were doing, and how it had to be done. Engraved in the floor of the lobby at the CIA's Langley headquarters is the Agency's motto: "Ye shall know the truth and it shall set you free." But it was nothing more than window-dressing, camouflage for "the ends justify the means"—the CIA's true, unwritten code for dealing with anything, or anyone, that happened to inconveniently get in its way. And so it would be with Mary Pinchot Meyer.

And yet their fatal flaw, no matter how much water would pass under the proverbial bridge, was to underestimate something much more forceful and compelling than their corrupted, villainous power. It was, in its purest form, the supreme force of truth itself, and the human need to pursue and know it, no matter what the cost.

PART FOUR

"**N**ERO IS MAD," said Claudius. "He will destroy the empire. His excesses will demand the return of the republic and you, my son, will return to restore it. The republic will live again!"

"I don't believe in the republic," said Britannicus, son of Claudius. "No one believes in the republic anymore! No one does, except you. You're old, father, and out of touch. I want my chance to rule. And rule Rome as it should be ruled. If you love me, give me that chance."

"Let all the poisons that lurk in the mud hatch out," mumbled Claudius alone to himself. "Write no more Claudius, write no more. I have told it all, as I said I would. And as the Sybil prophesized, I have told the truth. I have set the record straight. It is all here for remote posterity. Come death, and draw the final curtain. I am tired, oh so tired."[1]

---

1   From the 1976 BBC Masterpiece Theatre production of *I, Claudius*. (Based on: *I, Claudius: from the autobiography of Tiberius Claudius born 10 B.C. murdered and deified A.D. 54.* and *Claudius The God,* both authored by Robert Graves. New York: Vintage International Edition, 1989, originally published by Random House, 1935.

14

EPILOGUE

There are only two mistakes one can make along the road to truth:
Not going all the way, and not starting.

—The Buddha

The American people live in a country where they can have almost
anything they want.
And my regret is that it seems that they don't want much of anything
at all.

—Eugene Debs

D URING THE JOURNEY of writing this book, many people asked me whether
Leo Damore really committed suicide. Of course he did, I told them.
He shot himself in the presence of a nurse and a police officer in October
1995. There was no conspiracy here, I maintained; the facts spoke for them-
selves. But I soon reckoned those weren't the only "facts" that surrounded
Leo's demise.

For two years, Leo's former wife, June Davison, graciously allowed me to
read all of Leo's private diaries. I wanted to know anything that might further
offer clues, particularly about the last few years of his life. While Leo purposely
never mentioned any of his most secretive research in his journals, he did
recount some of his battles with panic attacks, anxiety, and depression—all
of which started to emerge several months after his telephone conversation
with William L. Mitchell at the end of March 1993. Yet in my own dealings
with Leo during 1993, he appeared to be generally optimistic after our visit

in April of that year and the subsequent phone contact we shared during that summer. Leo made no secret of the fact that he had met with the person who, he believed, was Mary's assassin, the same man who had testified at the trial, but I didn't press him for further details, as I was preoccupied with grief over a broken marital engagement. That fall, however, he was still working on the manuscript for "Burden of Guilt," though he was increasingly agitated and upset.

Another of Leo's closest friends, who asked to remain anonymous, agreed to be interviewed for this book. She and Leo had talked many times after his 1993 telephone interview with Mitchell, as well as after Leo's subsequent in-person interview with Mitchell. That meeting, the friend said, was even more definitive because Leo had learned, she said, about some of the other people who had assisted in the operation. Some weeks later, however, Leo told his friend he was sure he was being followed, "watched," and he was growing increasingly alarmed. In early 1994, he believed he'd been "poisoned," she said. He wasn't sure how, or when it happened, but he knew something was wrong. He had also taken a number of precautions with his tapes and transcriptions, his manuscript, and what she remembered as "some other material." It was all well-hidden, the friend said, and couldn't be found. Leo was becoming more frantic, more anxious, agitated, and unable to focus. Increasingly paranoid, under financial pressure, he apparently consulted not one but two different psychiatrists, both of whom were giving him different psychotropic medications.

About a month before he shot himself in October 1995, Leo called me, desperately pleading for a place to live, and threatening suicide. Not having heard from him for months, I realized at that point how serious his deterioration had become. I pleaded with him to immediately check into a hospital, even offered to accompany him, should he need assistance. Later on, I would discover his friend Jimmy Smith had received a similar plea, again shortly before Leo took his life. Following his death, Leo's former wife told me his autopsy had revealed an undiagnosed brain tumor. Had Leo Damore, I wondered, been poisoned in such a way that he was driven to suicide?

Starting in the 1950s, under the direction of the CIA's Dr. Sidney Gottlieb, the Agency's MKULTRA program had developed an arsenal of undetectable elixirs for getting rid of people when it became necessary. For the CIA, murder became 'standard operating procedure,' as demonstrated by CIA Director William Colby in his testimony before the Church Committee in 1975.[1] In April 1953, James Speyer Kronthal, a brilliant, young Allen Dulles protégé and deputy, who was in line for a high-level job at the Agency, was found dead in his Georgetown home in what police said was a suicide. The night before, Kronthal had been confronted by his boss Dulles for his sexual orientation. His "crime" was that he was gay. Years later, it was revealed that Soviet intelligence had identified Kronthal as a homosexual through its review of captured Nazi files from World War II. Then, while working for the CIA in Switzerland, Kronthal had been secretly filmed with young boys by the Soviets before blackmailing him into becoming a spy.

"Allen [Dulles] probably had a special potion prepared that he gave Kronthal should the pressure become too much," the CIA's Robert Crowley told author Joseph Trento. "Dr. Sidney Gottlieb and the medical people produced all kinds of poisons that a normal postmortem could not detect. Kronthal, from a powerful family in New York, could not bear having his secret homosexuality become a new case for Senator Joseph McCarthy."[2] Nor could Allen Dulles allow anyone, or anything, to threaten his intelligence empire.

Leo Damore's "suicide" had become all the more disturbing, not only to me, but to his dear friend Jimmy Smith as well. Smith became convinced that Leo had been driven to take his own life. "Leo didn't know anything about guns," said Smith. "Where in hell did he get a gun?" For years, Smith had warned his friend to "take precautions." He was sure Leo was becoming involved in dangerous matters. "For Christ's sake, Leo, be careful," said Jimmy at the end of almost every phone call. And so, in the wake of Leo's death, trailing my own journey's conclusion, Bill Corson's echo kept dogging me at every turn: "Anybody can commit a murder, but it takes an expert to commit a suicide."

There comes a time when every journey approaches a conclusion. It took me by surprise, when I met a kindred soul whose father, too, had been a CIA officer. There's a kind of unwritten, sometimes unacknowledged, bond among those of us whose fathers were involved with the fledgling CIA during the Cold War era. Author Nina Burleigh's interview with Jane Barnes, daughter of the elite CIA covert operative Tracy Barnes—who Robert Morrow believed was part of Jim Angleton's inner circle that decided Mary's fate—underscored not only the experience of living within the "shadowy" world of never really knowing what our fathers were doing, but the fantasy life we as children invented to compensate for this emptiness.

"We thought of Daddy as James Bond," Jane Barnes recalled to Burleigh. Apparently a Barnes family neighbor, acquainted with all the gadgetry, murder, and intrigue described in Ian Fleming's and John le Carré's books, had once said to Tracy, "These books must be nonsense."

"On the contrary," Tracy Barnes had replied. "They're understated."[3] Like Jane's father, my own had also revered Ian Fleming's mythic character. He took great delight in family outings to the latest James Bond films that so glamorously dramatized and glorified the swashbuckling world of "secret agents." But we as children, the Cold War's "CIA brats," were not allowed to know the real life our fathers had chosen. "Most people," said the character of Noah Cross (played by John Huston) in the film *Chinatown*, "never have to face the fact that at the right time, at the right place, they're capable of anything." Such was the double life our fathers led; and eventually, one way or another, it exacted a karmic retribution on us children.

Quentin Meyer, Mary and Cord Meyer's oldest son, would no longer talk to me after he became aware of this book project, nor would his brother, Mark. Intermittently, and over time since the early 1970s, Quentin's mental illness had overtaken him with one debilitating episode after another. It was painful to accept, even more so to watch. In the fall of 2009, author Katie McCabe shared with me her experience after a book-signing event for her Dovey Roundtree biography, *Justice Older Than the Law*, at a Georgetown senior center. There, in the circle of attendees, sat a slumped-over, seemingly elderly man who listened quietly, his head down on his chest. When the talk was over, he approached McCabe and asked her to sign the book, "To Quentin." The sponsor of the event later told McCabe that the man was Quentin Meyer, son of Cord and Mary Meyer. His mere presence at the event spoke volumes; somewhere within, a part of Quenty still yearned to know the elusive, essential truth that had robbed him of his selfhood, the demons too horrifying to confront. Would it be Dovey Roundtree's heroic defense of Ray Crump that might ignite a smoldering spark to light? No words were exchanged that day, no more of Quenty pleading, "What happened to my mother?" as he had on the telephone late one night with Timothy Leary so many years before.

And so, it was by serendipity again, that someone I had contacted asked Toni Shimon, the daughter of the late Joseph W. Shimon, whether she would be willing to talk with me. When I met Toni in 2005, our chemistry was almost instantaneous, only because we shared a certain bond of somewhat similar circumstances growing up in Washington. Indeed, Toni Shimon and I had much in common. Like most of us, Toni, during her formative years, hadn't known the true nature of her father's work. As a young adult, however, she persuaded her father, little by little, to confide pieces of information he probably shouldn't have. Joe Shimon deeply loved his only daughter, and he didn't want to lose her—or himself.[4]

Shimon was a unique individual. He was determined to remain a faithful, honest father to his only daughter while being called to duty to "take care of" some of the most "sensitive" problems in the hidden cesspools of Washington. Born in 1907, Shimon first worked as a uniformed policeman in the D.C. Metropolitan Police Department, starting in the early 1930s. He quickly distinguished himself, rising through the ranks to become a detective. By the time of President Franklin D. Roosevelt's inauguration in 1933, Shimon had already established a reputation for being able "to get the job done" with the utmost discretion. He would gain the confidence not only of President Roosevelt, but each of his successors—Truman, Eisenhower, Kennedy, Johnson, and Nixon—all of whom revered his many talents.

While officially assigned to the White House as a "Washington Police Inspector," Shimon was also secretly working for the Justice Department through the U.S. Attorney's Office. In the late 1940s, though still stationed at the White House, he was part of a secret, organized crime task force. The work was dangerous—so dangerous, in fact, that his wife, Elizabeth, feared for her safety and that of their only child, Toni. The couple finally divorced in the late 1940s, when Toni was just two years old. Elizabeth had pleaded for years for Joe to find a different line of work. She was terrified her husband would be killed, their only child orphaned. Moreover, she abhorred the work hours he kept, the secrecy, people showing up at all hours of the day and night, and the impromptu meetings that took place in her kitchen, when she would have to leave.

It became no secret to Toni that her father carried a gun wherever he went. She had thought her dad was part of the Metropolitan Police Department in Washington, D.C., though not a uniformed officer. Told her father was stationed at the White House during the Roosevelt administration, then a chief inspector for the U.S. Attorney's Office, all the while maintaining police department status, she began to wonder. Who is he? What does my father do?

Toni Shimon was the apple of her father's eye. He adored her; she adored him, and the way he always looked after her, even after the divorce. The two missed each other terribly when Toni went back to her mother's home on Long Island after periodic visits. The divorce had been a huge adjustment for everyone, but Joe Shimon, a true patriot who believed he was working for the betterment of his country, had made his choice.

During one of her visits to Washington in the late 1950s, Toni found herself sitting in the kitchen with her father before he left for work. Her father's work habits and dress code didn't escape his growing daughter's inquisitiveness.

"Dad, you say you're a policeman, but you're always at the White House," inquired the curious young girl. "Why do you need a gun inside the White House?"

Her father looked at her quizzically, she remembered, as though he was wondering if now might be the time he might dare to answer. Isolation, secrecy, deception—all of the required masks—had exacted a toll. Unbearable loneliness and disconnection were often the initial symptoms. With the dissolution of his marriage and family, Joe Shimon had lost the opportunity to share each day of his daughter's life and childhood.

"My father always believed that he was working for the betterment of the country," recalled Toni. "It cost him dearly, but his work was everything to him. In spite of the divorce and my living on Long Island with my mother, I would visit him often. We were very close." Though Shimon did eventually remarry, he never told his new wife the truth about what he really did in the world, fearing it might endanger her life as well.

Perhaps the prospect of a deepening father-daughter relationship with his thirteen-year-old daughter that morning overpowered his usual, sometimes necessary reticence. At that moment, without any further deliberation, father Joe took a calculated risk. Reaching into his coat pocket, Joe Shimon pulled out five or six different identification badges, said Toni, and dropped them all on the kitchen table for inspection. Eager, Toni looked closely at each badge: D.C. Police Department, U.S. Secret Service, U.S. Department of Justice, White House identification badge, and finally, Central Intelligence Agency. After examining each one, she glanced at her father with confusion.

"Dad, you're in everything," she said, now more confused than ever. "Is that why every president gives you gifts?"

"Does that bother you?" said Joe, hoping he hadn't made a mistake by revealing what he had.[5]

Shimon's gamble paid off. The father and daughter would continue to deepen their newfound relationship, despite the divorce and the dissolution of the family. Joe began to share even more. As Toni grew and matured, she considered a career in law enforcement. Joe Shimon made no bones about the fact that he hated J. Edgar Hoover. He had already confided to Toni how corrupt and evil he thought Hoover was; he then told her the truth about Hoover's sexual orientation, his secret affair with his colleague Clyde Tolson, and how he, Shimon, was always inevitably called in to clean up any number of messes that easily could have embarrassed all of Washington, especially J. Edgar himself.[6]

Recall in chapter 10 the mention of the Easter weekend in April 1963, when during their final stroll along North Stafford Street in Arlington before Toni went back to New York, Joe Shimon engaged his daughter, alerting her to how Vice President Lyndon Johnson had been intent on getting more security than President Kennedy, just six months before Dallas. Shimon had tested his daughter as to what she thought it meant.

"What's he [Johnson] afraid of?" Toni wondered out loud, only to then conclude moments later: "Something's going to happen and Johnson knows about it," she blurted out.

The uneasy memory of "the Easter good-bye walk" would be eclipsed soon enough by her telephone call to her father's White House office on November 22, 1963.

"Dad!" she cried out, having heard the news of the president's assassination.

"These things happen, honey," Shimon said calmly while his daughter wept. A moment later he told her, "I don't want to talk about it now."

Toni was in college in North Carolina in the fall of 1964 when Mary Meyer was murdered. The news of her death came to Toni's attention the following spring, as the trial of Ray Crump began to take center stage in the Washington media. After the Kennedy assassination, Toni was already witnessing a seismic shift in her father's disposition. Their relationship had grown exceptionally close, but by 1964 Joe Shimon had become withdrawn, more cautious.

"The only time in my entire life I ever saw fear in my father was when I would ask him about who really killed Kennedy," recalled Toni. "He would look at me. I could see his fear. 'Don't push me' he would say, adding, 'It would be dangerous for you to know the truth.' And then he would just change the subject."

During her spring vacation in 1965, Toni and her father began talking one day. She was eager to ask her father's opinion about what had actually happened to Mary Meyer.

"Dad, who was she?" asked the inquisitive Toni. "All these people keep dropping dead." She was already aware of several suspicious deaths that appeared to have some link to the Kennedy assassination.

"I know," Shimon responded quietly. Toni remained silent, knowing at some point he would continue.

"She was one of Kennedy's paramours," Shimon revealed. "He was very close to her."

"But what did she know?" asked Toni.

"She knew a lot because Kennedy was fond of her, very fond of her. She was part of his inner circle."

"But who would kill her, Dad?"

"Who killed the president?" Shimon shot back immediately, almost angrily. It was a rhetorical question, followed by more silence. Toni had learned how to probe her father as much as she could, but there were limits. This time he was more blunt about it. Turning to face his daughter, he looked her in the eyes.

"There are certain things I will never tell you because if anyone finds out you know, or they think you know, your life could be in danger," he said solemnly. "Honey, I don't ever want you to be in that position."

Lost in thought, continuing to comprehend the sea of change she had witnessed in her father since Dallas, Toni started retreating, emotionally withdrawing. Her withdrawal wasn't lost on the father. Just as he had in the late 1950s morning breakfast encounter, the father again risked something further.

"She [Mary Meyer] was eliminated because she knew too much," her father blurted out, unwilling this time to look at her when he spoke, though then calmly adding: "People are eliminated. Honey, you don't know how many people are just eliminated, just on the operating table alone. They just need to be disposed of. And don't ever believe what you read in the papers. It's all made up."[7]

That day and its memory wasn't lost on Toni Shimon, nor on me when she revealed it. Author Jim Marrs, in his 1989 book *Crossfire*, had established a chronological list, based on the dates of their death, of more than a hundred individuals—all of whom were shown to have possessed some important detail of the conspiracy to assassinate President Kennedy. Their deaths during the twenty years following the events in Dallas were suspicious. More than thirty people on this list had been killed in violent gun-related circumstances. Mary Meyer's murder was number fifteen on this list.[8] It wasn't just Mary's murder anymore, but *all* the suspicious "suicides," "heart attacks," "cancers," or "accidents"—Phil Graham, Frank Wisner, Jim Truitt, Leo Damore. Even author John H. Davis, who refused to complete Leo Damore's research about what had really happened to Mary ("I decided I wanted to live"), could be included.

During the 1970s, America's Bicentennial came and went, its underbelly not lost on Toni Shimon or her father. Chipping away little by little, Toni continued her attempts to bore into her father's mysterious treasure trove of knowledge. "I wanted to know everything about who my father was, and what he did," mused Toni. "The problem was, the more I knew, the more complicated—and scarier—it got."

In 1973, the film *Executive Action* was released into movie theaters across the country. Directed by David Miller, the screenplay was co-written by Dalton Trumbo, Donald Freed, and attorney Mark Lane. Starring Burt Lancaster, the film depicts the assassination of President Kennedy as engendered by a cabal of wealthy industrialists and powerful rulers who had been angered by Kennedy's policies—everything from his reduction of the oil depletion allowance, to his approach to the Russians with overtures of world peace and, of course, the possibility of a pullout from Vietnam. For these power brokers, the most frightening prospect of all, however, was the specter of an unbeatable "Kennedy dynasty" lasting decades. The cabal therefore enlisted a group of CIA-backed Cubans embittered over the Bay of Pigs fiasco, along with several high-level, disgruntled American intelligence agents whose best efforts to destroy Castro's Cuba had been needlessly sacrificed and betrayed. While the film itself was only marginally successful at the box office, it was the first attempt to present a clear alternative to the Warren Report, nearly twenty years before Oliver Stone's film *JFK*. Some would later credit the film with reopening the entire debate about Kennedy's assassination.

"Watch this film very carefully," Joe Shimon implored his daughter after its release. "That was how it [the JFK assassination] was exactly planned. Think about the state of Texas. What would happen if Kennedy ended the war [in Vietnam]?"

"The economy would suffer," Toni remembered replying.

"Right!" exclaimed Shimon. "Our country runs on a war economy." Time and time again, the film kept coming up in their discussions, and the inquisitive daughter would want to delve more deeply into the assassination. Eventually, when things were getting too close for comfort, Shimon would fall back on what would become a familiar refrain: "Honey, I have loyalties. People are eliminated. I will go to my grave with what I know."[9]

But that didn't stop Toni from continuing to pry. Like many of his generation, Joe Shimon was a drinker, but a careful drinker, not given to excess. As the years wore on, he would talk a little more openly while having drinks with his daughter. In early 1975, in the wake of Watergate, alarmed by allegations of CIA misdeeds, the U.S. Senate—through its investigative body known as the Church Committee—attempted to tread on the CIA's sacred ground. Joe

Shimon would be called to testify, but he told his daughter he considered the committee's inquest a joke and treated it as such; they weren't really serious enough to get to the bottom of anything, he told her. What Joe Shimon didn't tell the Church Committee, he would tell his daughter in 1976, and also disclose to *Washington Post* columnist Jack Anderson in 1988.[10]

Those disclosures started, recalled Toni, when she brought up the fact that there had seemed to be a lot of strange people coming to her father's house when she would be visiting during the early 1960s. They would meet in the kitchen in the evening. They would talk; they would drink; eventually, they would leave. Shimon confided he was the principal liaison to the Mafia, a connection that was part of his CIA credentials. When they had started working on Castro's assassination, the meetings were held at Shimon's house. People like Johnny Roselli, Sam Giancana, Santo Trafficante, and the CIA's William ("Bill") K. Harvey were regulars at these meetings, along with some sporadic attendance by Jim Angleton. "My father loved Bill Harvey," said Toni, recalling this time period in her life. "He was also close friends with Jim Angleton, and of course Sam [Giancana] and Johnny [Roselli]."[11]

William ("Bill") K. Harvey, a pear-shaped, bulging-eyed alcoholic endomorph who had once been paraded before President Kennedy as the CIA's exemplar of Ian Fleming's James Bond, had the career track of a bona fide sociopath. He had originally joined the FBI in 1940, only to then challenge one of Hoover's protocols. The squabble that ensued led Harvey to resign; he joined the CIA instead. Harvey was eventually assigned by Richard Helms to head the Agency's "Executive Action" program created to develop assassination operations on foreign leaders. The reader may recall that during the Cuban Missile Crisis, contravening all orders from the White House, Bill Harvey had organized and dispatched three commando teams consisting of more than sixty individuals to Cuba to wage any destabilization possible as preparation for what he believed would be an inevitable invasion of the island. When Bobby Kennedy finally found out about what Harvey had done, he was furious. After the Cuban Missile Crisis had ended, Harvey found himself "moved" to the CIA station in Rome, but he quickly returned.

The plot to kill Fidel Castro, code-named Operation Mongoose, began to take shape in November 1961. Shimon's revelations to *Washington Post* columnist Jack Anderson included the fact that the covert operation had the blessings of America's most notorious underworld figures. Santo Trafficante, who had controlled much of Cuba's underworld before Castro took power in 1959—particularly the lucrative Cuban casinos—had told Shimon explicitly,

"I'll get you the contacts [assassins], give you lots of names. But keep me out of it." Harvey and Johnny Roselli then recruited the hit men recommended by Trafficante. In all, a total of six teams were sent to Havana, but none succeeded; they never returned nor were they heard from again.[12]

Joe Shimon realized, as did Bill Harvey and Johnny Roselli, that Castro must have found out he was being targeted. The hired assassins were true professionals—experienced and tested. They would not have all have failed repeatedly unless Castro had been waiting for them. "You don't have *that* many misses, with these fellows not coming back," Shimon told Anderson. Furthermore, during this time, there were only six individuals who were involved in the CIA's plot to use organized crime to eliminate Castro. According to Shimon, there had been no paper trail of the effort; nothing had been written down.

Shimon's suspicion pointed toward Trafficante. He suspected that Trafficante had tipped off Castro about the CIA's plans to assassinate him. *Post* columnist Jack Anderson noted correctly that although Trafficante had been initially jailed by Castro when he first took power, losing all his assets including the casinos, he somehow, "for some inexplicable reason," escaped from jail and Cuba unscathed, then returned to the U.S. with all his treasure intact. "Suddenly Trafficante is released. . . . He comes back here with all his assets, with the yacht. . . . Others eventually got out, but they left Cuba broke." Trafficante quickly expanded his hegemony in the crime underworld in the South, almost overnight. Shimon eventually asked his friend Sam Giancana about Trafficante's reliability, and Giancana confirmed for Shimon that he didn't regard him as reliable, because "he was a rat." The CIA had come to the same conclusion, eventually calling off their friends in organized crime, and looked for other ways to dispose of Cuba's leader.

Playing to Jack Anderson's well-known appetite for a more conspiratorial spin on the role of Castro and Cuba in the Kennedy assassination, Shimon tried to paint a picture for Anderson in which Castro had conspired with Trafficante to assassinate President Kennedy as payback for the attempts on Castro's life, telling Anderson that his conclusion was "confirmed by Harvey who had other information from the CIA." Anderson naively took the bait. Shimon would continue to tell him that "they [the CIA] had other sources, too. They were satisfied that this had to be retaliation by Castro."[13]

What Joe Shimon hadn't told Anderson, he did eventually share with his daughter: Trafficante was furious with Shimon for having questioned his allegiances. So furious, in fact, that in 1964, he took out a contract on Shimon's life as well on his daughter and on his wife.

"I was so upset when he sat me down to talk about this in 1976," recalled Toni. "I was visiting Dad in Washington when he told me about this. He was still very afraid to talk about the Kennedy assassination. I vividly remember him telling me, 'Look, honey, if anything happens to me, watch the movie *Executive Action*. You'll understand then why I couldn't talk.'"

For Toni, additional pieces of the puzzle about her father began to take shape. During her college years, as she considered a career in law enforcement, her father asked her to seriously think of joining the FBI. She told him she would consider it, only later telling her mother about her father's request. Her mother became furious at her former husband, knowing full well the danger her daughter might fall into. Years later, Shimon confided to Toni, "We wanted you to work for the FBI so you could spy on Hoover for us."

"Dad, who is 'we'?" she asked him. She would finally learn that even as late as 1989, after the Reagan administration, her father was maintaining regular contact with a group of people who had inside knowledge at all times.

"He always knew what was going on in the White House," Toni recalled, "long after he left there. I finally learned that he was a part of what might be called 'the shadow government.' My father did a lot for President George H. W. Bush. He was a die-hard Republican, yet so conflicted about Bush, he voted for Bill Clinton in 1992, only to regret it later."

In the early 1990s, Toni had the kind of conversation with her father that she never would have anticipated. It was a bad dream come true. The former "Washington Police Inspector" would finally spill to his daughter what he had never revealed to anyone else, other than the people he was working for. It happened unexpectedly.

"I remember him telling me how much he disliked the Kennedys, that after their assassinations, he knew it was the best thing ever to happen in our country," said Toni, thinking back. Probed even further, father Joe continued talking, perhaps knowing that the end of his life was approaching.

"Bobby Kennedy was a mean son of bitch," said Shimon, obviously remembering how the former attorney general had tried to implicate him in a wiretapping scandal. "No one I knew liked him. He was mean and nasty and thought it was him who should be president. We all told him and the president that Texas wasn't a friendly place."

"The Kennedys had mob ties," he continued, "but the biggest crooks in this country are the Bushes. The Bush family is big on control, they control a lot of the government." The conversation progressed, Toni recalled, with her father stating that his former Washington-based company, Allied Investigators, whose offices were located on Dupont Circle in Washington, was just a CIA front that had been used for most of his undercover work.

She wasn't prepared for the next round of her father's fireworks, however. It was the kind of dreaded moment that one hopes is only a nightmare, a bad dream from which to finally awaken unscathed.

"Our government has murdered a lot of people when they get in the way," he told his daughter.

"How do you know this, Dad?" She wasn't expecting a definitive response, but just curious as to what she might come to know or understand. After a few moments of silence, Joe Shimon continued.

"Among my many jobs, I used to kill people," he told his daughter matter-of-factly. "Our government hired me and others to do this sort of work." It wasn't a bad dream, or a nightmare. It was real. Truth is an equal opportunity employer that never discriminates. When it arrives, the MasterCard statement from the Bank of Truth doesn't offer an option of "partial payment." Instead, it dictates its own terms of "pay me now, or pay me later." But, invariably, all of us eventually have to reckon. I had confronted this dilemma myself, just as Toni Shimon had. She had wanted to know her father, never imagining what this might actually reveal.

"You did?" Toni exclaimed softly, as the echo of her father's last words penetrated like nails, one after another, into her heart.

"The government hired me to kill people," continued Shimon. "It's a job, and usually the people who get killed deserve it. You have to [kill people], if that's what you're told to do."[14]

The story had now come full circle. Perhaps Toni hoped, like any number of us during the Cold War, that the truth about what our fathers were actually doing in the world might finally offer some consolation. If it did, it came with a huge price tag. As to her father's admission, "it really turned me off," Toni said during our final interview. "I loved my father very much."

"I wish you could have spent some time with Dad," she said, as our talk that day was coming to an end. "I think he knew about the whole plan to take out Mary Meyer, probably through Bill Harvey. They were very close."

"What makes you say that?" I asked.

"Just the way he spoke about it," she replied. "I just knew he knew. Whatever Bill Harvey was up to, it always came out of Jim Angleton's office. Dad once remarked Angleton ran everything, controlled *everything* in the CIA."[15]

I thanked Toni once again and gathered my materials, making my way to the car. The trip back to Massachusetts, across Long Island Sound on the New

London ferry, would be a relief, I kept telling myself. But it wasn't. Toni had further confirmed all my suspicions, authenticating an even darker shadow.

I stood on the bow of the New London ferry as it made its way across Long Island Sound. It was the middle of February 2007, still bitterly cold and dark. The boat rocked through the oncoming swells, inching toward the Connecticut shoreline. My thoughts inevitably returned to Mary and all that she must have endured during the year after Jack's death: the anguish, the loneliness, the fear of what she faced that final year, before deciding to finally go public with what she had discovered. If Paul Revere had been the "midnight messenger" to warn his fellow countrymen in Lexington and Concord of the British military approach, Mary Pinchot Meyer had planned to make her own "midnight bareback ride" to warn the citizens of a country that its government had been demonically stolen from each and every one of them.

They had killed Jack because he and his ally-in-peace Nikita Khrushchev were steering the world away from the Cold War toward peace, thereby eliminating the military-industrial-intelligence complex's most treasured weapons—the fear of war, the fear of "Communist takeover," and the manipulative use of Fear itself. The Cold War was about to end, and with it the covert action arm of the Central Intelligence Agency. The Agency would have been all but neutered, its funding and resources cut, its menacing grip on public opinion exposed and eliminated. It also meant the eventual curtailment of many of the defense industries, including the proliferation of nuclear arms. There would have been no war in Southeast Asia or Vietnam; that, too, was about to end. A rapprochement with Fidel Castro and Cuba was on the horizon. Both Jack and Fidel wanted "a lasting peace."

Little attention had been paid to the parting words of a previous president. President Eisenhower had warned the American public in early 1961 of the evil that had spawned since World War II: "In the councils of government, we must guard against the acquisition of unwarranted influence, whether sought or unsought, by the military-industrial complex. The potential for the disastrous rise of misplaced power exists and will persist." Indeed, it had; so much so that in less than three years, anyone who tried to stop it—including the elected president of the United States—would be eliminated.

Simply put, peace—particularly world peace—wasn't good for business, nor for American military and economic hegemony. Whatever enlightenment Mary and Jack may have finally engendered together, it had evolved into a part of Jack's newfound trajectory of where he wanted to take not only his presidency in 1963, but the entire world. It was the pursuit of peace that was about to take center stage; and that voyage would no longer include any obsequious bow to the insanity of America's war machine driven by the legacy of Allen Dulles and his ass-kissing cronies.

After Dallas, amid utter horror and shock, Mary had taken it upon herself to discover and make sense of the truth of the conspiracy that had taken place—only to realize the magnitude of the second conspiracy, a cover-up taking place right before her eyes. There, in her diary, she had reached an understanding. It was her own mosaic of people, events, circumstances, and exploration that informed her understanding—not only of the evil that had taken place in Dallas, but of the villainous darkness that was now enveloping all of America. She had furiously confronted her ex-husband, Cord Meyer, possibly Jim Angleton as well, with what she had discovered, not fully realizing the extent of their own diabolical ruthlessness. The Warren Report was ultimately nothing more than a house of cards; once ignited with the right matchstick, it would be engulfed in flames. If Mary courageously went public with who she was, and what she knew, making clear her position in the final years of Jack's life, people with influence would take notice; the fire of suspicion around Dallas would erupt into a conflagration.

She had to be eliminated.

"Forget her, Jake. It's Chinatown." The concluding line of Roman Polanski's film wafted through my mind, tempting me away from the task that now clearly lay ahead. Nausea was overtaking me, but it wasn't the ferry pitching through the oncoming swells, veteran ocean sailor that I was. It was Mary's revulsion for the CIA, now mine as well, that gripped me in its vise. Alone on the deck, hands outstretched toward the last bit of light on a short winter's day, I unleashed my screams toward the sky, only to then collapse at the rail, sobbing one more time. In a certain way, my torment had come to an end, yet behind it there was an unbearable sadness, and not just my own. The shining beacon of America—a promise unlike any other for humanity—was being extinguished, as it had been in Rome. But unlike Rome, America would not be engulfed by flames. It would instead succumb to something far more sinister, invisible, and corrosive: ignorance. Ignorance dipped in fear-mongering and dazzled by fabricated myths had become the breeding ground for official stupidity, darkness, and senseless wars. Ignorance had once again become evil's greatest handyman. As Benjamin Franklin wisely noted, "It is in the region of ignorance that tyranny begins."

Mary Pinchot Meyer had been struck down before she could speak publicly. Leo Damore had fallen, very likely poisoned into uncontrollable despair. John Davis, having picked up Leo's mantle, finally opted out, his life threatened. He "wanted to live," he said, shortly before a crippling stroke.

The familiar taste of salt water on my lips called me back inside my body. The wind and ocean spray danced all around, the cold of winter now an accustomed companion. I headed back inside the ferry's cabin for warmth. Somber, yet still resolute, I knew right then and there I would do whatever it took, pay whatever price was required, to allow this story—this small but essential piece of history—to see the light of day.

15

Post Script

I believe, too, that in winning acquittal for Ray Crump, I made it impossible for the matter of Mary Pinchot Meyer's murder to be sealed off and forgotten, as the government so clearly wanted to do. There is much about the crime that bears the most serious and sustained investigation, and to the extent that my efforts in defending Raymond opened the path for researchers seeking to know more about the troubling circumstances surrounding her death, I am gratified.[1]

—Dovey J. Roundtree, Esq.
Justice Older than the Law

We seek a free flow of information. . . . We are not afraid to entrust the American people with unpleasant facts. . . . For a nation that is afraid to let its people judge the truth and falsehood in an open market is a nation that is afraid of its people.

—President John F. Kennedy
February 26, 1962

WITH THE PUBLICATION and release of the first edition of *Mary's Mosaic* in April 2012, I looked forward to a new chapter in my life, and perhaps a bit of a rest. The completion of the book, after all, was a major life event, and something that I had only faintly pondered back in 1976. Thirty-five years is a long time. Looking ahead after the book was released, I found myself contemplating the arrival of spring in New England—memories of smelling lilacs in bloom, running Crane Beach in Ipswich at low tide, even possibly falling in love again, though no one had yet appeared. I had no idea what life was about to position on the path before me, or that it would take me by complete surprise.

While most of the reviews on the *Mary's Mosaic* Amazon page were favorable, there were two that attempted to discredit my efforts. The first, written by JFK researcher Lisa Pease, was easily disposed of, given her well known worship of the late President Kennedy, and her rejection of any evidence that might tarnish his character. In July, I posted a lengthy response to Pease and her partner James DiEugenio (who would later follow with his own diatribe) on LewRockwell.com. My response was widely disseminated.[1]

The second negative review, however, was more difficult to deal with, at least initially. Posted on Amazon in early August, the review was, I later learned, written by a DiEugenio protégé whose name, I discovered, was Tom Scully, but he would identify himself on Amazon only as "Rational Voice." Discussing his critical post of *Mary's Mosaic* in an email to a University of Georgia law professor, Scully identified himself as "a moderator at the Internet forum, JFK Debate, created by John Simkin."[2]

Mr. Scully focused his attack on the conclusions I had presented about the prosecution witness William L. Mitchell, who testified at the 1965 Meyer murder trial (*U.S. v. Ray Crump, Jr.*), and who had identified himself to police on the day after the murder. Scully took issue with my assertion that Mitchell had either possibly been Mary Meyer's assassin or part of the assassination team that took her life. He listed in his Amazon review seven citations that he had located in various academic articles/journals, in which William L. Mitchell had identified himself as a mathematician and subsequently a professor at California State University, Hayward. In one citation, Mitchell had listed his address between 1963–65—the period of the Meyer murder and the trial—as 1500 Arlington Blvd, Arlington, Virginia. This address, the reader will recall, is the one that three former CIA personnel had identified to me as a designated "CIA safe house."

Ironically, in his effort to discredit me and *Mary's Mosaic*, Tom Scully opened up an unforeseen opportunity. I renewed my contact with the Peabody Award-winning investigative journalist and author Roger Charles, who had been instrumental in discovering Mitchell's suspicious 1964 Pentagon affiliation while he was allegedly an Army lieutenant. Charles contacted his twice-nominated Pulitzer Prize colleague Don Devereux, who had been essential in

---

1   See the following: "The Autodafé of Lisa Pease and James DiEugenio," posted on July 6, 2012 at the following link: http://lewrockwell.com/orig13/janney3.1.1.html

assisting Charles with research for his 2012 book *Oklahoma City: What the Investigation Missed—and Why It Still Matters*. Although we were unable to duplicate Scully's Google search, the three of us closely examined the citations he had brought to light. In several of the citations, William L. Mitchell listed references to his education—Cornell University (B.M.E. degree in 1962), Harvard University (M.S. Degree in 1963), and the University of California, Berkeley (Ph.D. in Mathematics 1970). We subsequently corroborated all three degrees with the registrars at each of these institutions.

Gaining access to the Cornell University Alumni Directory through a friend, I learned that Mitchell had listed his current residential address and phone number in northern California. Then, through another friend, I acquired access to the Harvard Alumni Directory, where I discovered that William Mitchell's middle name was "Lockwood," thereby giving us another needed piece of the puzzle to further penetrate his true identity.

Having already scheduled a trip to Los Angeles, I decided that I would make additional time to travel to the northern California city where Mitchell was supposedly now living. Fearing this odyssey could be gravely dangerous, some of my friends implored me to desist, or at least to arm myself or hire an armed bodyguard. I contemplated the situation for days, but in the end decided that I would go alone, without a weapon, and with only a copy of *Mary's Mosaic* and a notebook in my hand. I had come too far to pass up this opportunity, and I would never have forgiven myself had I turned away out of fear. Indeed, there was a certain amount of risk involved; such is the nature of important matters that attempt to uncover a truth that has been heretofore hidden.

On the morning of August 27, I knocked on the front door of Mitchell's house. An older woman, still dressed in her nightgown, opened the door and I introduced myself. When I asked for William Mitchell, she told me that he wasn't home at the moment. In response to her inquiry about my business with him, I merely stated that I was an author and I wanted to talk with him about the trial testimony that he had given in Washington, D.C., during the summer of 1965. The woman said she didn't believe "Bill" had ever lived in Washington, and that perhaps I was mistaken. I politely played along with her inquiry, finally stating that perhaps I would try again later in the day.

That afternoon, I returned to Mitchell's house with a small digital recorder concealed inside my notebook; again, I knocked on his front door. After a few moments, the door opened. A lean, fit older man, less than six feet in height and with a short beard, opened the door. The following is the verbatim exchange that ensued.

"Mr. Mitchell?" I asked.

"Who are you?" demanded Mitchell, a bit hostile and clearly paranoid.

"My name is Peter Janney. I'm an author." With a copy of my book in my hand, I continued. "I wrote this book called *Mary's Mosaic . . .*"

"I'm not interested," said Mitchell angrily, annoyed that he had been found. "See you later!"

"Could I just talk to you . . ." I pleaded.

"No!" said an increasingly enraged Mitchell.

"I came from Boston . . ."

"I don't care! I'm not interested! See you later!" he said, slamming the door shut in my face.

Turning to walk away, I breathed a sigh of relief. I was still alive and unharmed, though wobbling a bit from the encounter. I drove immediately to the local post office to mail Mitchell a copy of my book, along with a cover letter I had already prepared, having anticipated the possibility of this outcome. In the letter, I merely asked him, for the sake of the truth, to please reconsider talking with me. He has yet to respond.

That August evening, I realized that my short encounter with William L. Mitchell had changed everything. However unsettling my confrontation was, the path before me became illuminated. There was clearly more work to do—and something more to finish in what I had begun over thirty-five years ago. And so, as the beginning of the 50th anniversary of the JFK assassination approached in the fall of 2012, a new horizon of possibility was emerging with William Mitchell's reappearance.

Would it be possible to finally learn exactly what had taken place on the morning of October 12, 1964, on the C & O Canal towpath in Washington, D.C.? Who *really* was William Lockwood Mitchell, and who was he working for in the fall of 1964? Was Mitchell the "trigger-man" who terminated Mary Meyer's life, or not? Was he part of the team that had been ordered to assassinate her, or not? Moreover, was the man I had just confronted the same person who phoned Leo Damore in 1993 to reveal his involvement in the Meyer murder? Would Mitchell, if he talked, shed further light on the cover-up of the JFK assassination that had taken place in the fall of 1964? These questions, and a host of others, had been reignited. Returning to Massachusetts, I conferred with Roger Charles and his colleague Don Devereux, who quickly decided to come out of retirement for this effort, bringing with him noted private investigator

Robert Arthur of Global Investigations and Security Consulting in Scottsdale, Arizona. Everything was about to change. Working together, the four of us would uncover a hidden history of a man who was attempting to camouflage his true identity and whereabouts during critical periods in his life.

WILLIAM LOCKWOOD MITCHELL, we learned, was born on July 25, 1939, in New York City. His father was Victor Irving Mitchell, and his mother's maiden name was Doris Sheehan. Mitchell's middle name "Lockwood" came from his paternal grandmother, Kathryn "Kitty" B. Lockwood. The Mitchells moved to Mamaroneck, New York, from Norwalk, Connecticut, in 1940. When one tracks the Mitchell name at Ancestry.com, the family tree lists William Mitchell's father and mother, and his younger brother James, but the caption "Private" appears where the birthplace of their first born son William should be listed.[3] The family then moved to Chappaqua, a moderately wealthy New York suburb in Westchester County, where both William Mitchell and his brother James, who was born two years later in 1941, grew up. Sometimes referred to as "Bill" or "Mitch," Mitchell attended Horace Greely High School in Chappaqua, and graduated in the class of 1957. Pictured repeatedly in his high school yearbook, *The Quaker*, Mitchell was a four-year member of the Science Club; a stand-out athlete in basketball, track, and tennis; and elected to the National Honor Society for his final two years.[4]

In the spring of 1957, Cornell University accepted William Mitchell into the five-year Bachelor of Mechanical Engineering (B.M.E. degree) program in the Sibley School of Mechanical and Aerospace Engineering. Mitchell would receive the B.M.E. degree in the spring of 1962. Yet curiously, the *only* picture of William Mitchell at Cornell during his entire five-year residence was his engineering class section photo published in April 1962 in *The Cornell Engineer*, an obscure engineering school periodical. The caption under the class section snapshot identifies each student in the section, including "Mitchell, William."[5] Even during his senior year, no picture of Mitchell was published in the undergraduate yearbook, *The Cornellian*. This was baffling, since many, if not all, of Cornell's five-year undergraduate engineering students had their photos, particularly senior photos, in the main Cornell yearbook, which featured some of their biographical information, i.e., home town, high school, honor society memberships, etc. But not William Mitchell, whose middle name "Lockwood" was never once mentioned in any general Cornell undergraduate yearbook or periodical during his years there.[6] Was this, and the picture anomaly, intentional? Despite having been easily visible during the last two years of high school (as evidenced in his high school yearbooks), had Mitchell been "advised" during his undergraduate years to keep the lowest profile possible?

Very possibly, yes. However, my research colleagues and I were able to finally document that in the fall of 1960 William Mitchell was part of the U.S. Army Reserve Officer Training Corps (ROTC) at Cornell. In fact, that fall he was designated, and listed, as a "Distinguished Military Student." His name was listed in one Army ROTC document as: "Mitchell, William Lockwood." This document was not an inter-departmental Cornell record, but part of the "U.S. Army ROTC Instructor Group," dated "23 September 1960" and addressed only to "Personnel Concerned."[7]

Once Mitchell graduated from Cornell in 1962, having completed the Army ROTC program, it wasn't clear whether he had been slated for a two or three-year term as a commissioned officer. What was clear, however, was that immediately following Cornell, Mitchell entered the Graduate School of Arts and Sciences at Harvard University for a one-year Master of Science (M.S.) degree in "Applied Sciences." Harvard University Registrar's office in Cambridge, Massachusetts, confirmed that Mitchell was granted his M.S. degree in June 1963. Yet the question that remained was whether his matriculation at Harvard in 1962 had been part of his military service, or whether he'd been granted a one-year deferment?

The "pea-soup" fog of Mitchell's trail continued to thicken. In 2004, I had asked Roger Charles to procure William L. Mitchell's military service record from the National Personnel Records Center (NPRC) in St. Louis. He was told then that there was no record for Army lieutenant "William L. Mitchell" working in the Pentagon between 1963 and 1965, despite Mitchell's listing in the Department of Defense telephone directory. Armed now with Mitchell's date of birth, his middle name, and the first five digits of his Social Security number, obtained through the indefatigable efforts of private investigator Bob Arthur, we went back to the NPRC in the early fall of 2012 and again requested his record, only to be told once again that even with this identifying data, there was still no record for any William L. Mitchell with those characteristics.[8] In early November, I talked via telephone to a "Mr. Jones" at the NPRC, who told me that there were exactly 5,411 William Mitchell's in his database, 300 of which were "William L. Mitchell," but none with a Social Security number beginning with the three digit prefix that we had identified as belonging to Mitchell.[9] The Office of Veterans Affairs index, also penetrated through Roger Charles's efforts, had a number of William L. Mitchells, but none beginning with the Mitchell prefix. While government databases are not always 100% reliable, it is highly improbable in this day and age that anyone could be listed in any military database with just a military identification number, and no Social Security number.

The murkiness of the "Mitchell mirage" then deepened. In June of 2012, I made contact with Senior Homicide Detective Daniel D. Whalen of the Washington, D.C., Police Homicide Squad. I had written to him, telling him of my recently published book and the additional evidence that I had uncovered after its publication regarding Mary Meyer's murder. Detective Whalen had read *Mary's Mosaic*. Keenly aware of his department colleagues who had worked on the case in 1964, he was quite willing to sit down with Roger Charles and me in October 2012 to discuss it. When we introduced him to the saga of William L. Mitchell, he was clearly intrigued.[2]

Whalen began his own probe with the NPRC in St. Louis. With access to law enforcement's classified database, Detective Whalen ascertained Mitchell's full Social Security number and submitted it to the NPRC, along with his full name and date of birth. Typically, when law enforcement makes an inquiry to the NPRC, they receive a response within days. And indeed, Whalen received a telephone call from St. Louis, less than a week after his inquiry, telling him that they could not locate any 'William Lockwood Mitchell,' or any 'William L. Mitchell' in their database with the Social Security number and date of birth he had given them. The NPRC response to Detective Whalen was then followed with a letter reaffirming this finding.[10]

Where is William Mitchell's service record? Has the record been "flagged," "classified," or removed from the database for some reason? Or had Mitchell's record perished in the 1973 fire that took place at the NPRC, which, according to the NPRC's own estimate, destroyed approximately 16–18 million "Official Military Personnel Files"? Not likely. According to the NPRC itself, the only Army records that were affected by the fire pertained to "Army personnel discharged [from] November 1, 1912 to January 1, 1960."[11] William Mitchell did not begin his alleged Army commission until sometime after June 1962.

Was the NPRC's ostensible inability to locate Mitchell's record a case of what is known in FOIA circles as a "Glomar Response" or "Glomarization" on the part of the government? These terms entered the lexicon in 1975, when the CIA refused to release to journalists records of the CIA's salvaging vessel, the *Glomar Explorer*, and its covert attempts to recover nuclear weapons from a sunken Soviet submarine. The CIA chose to "neither confirm nor deny" the existence of the project—clearly indicating that information was, in fact, being

---

2   To date, Roger Charles and I have met with Detective Whalen on four separate occasions (as of May 15, 2013).

withheld—as well as its ongoing attempts to prevent any media coverage of the *Glomar Explorer's* mission. A "Glomar Response," however, is significantly different than a standard FOIA denial when a federal agency acknowledges that it has the requested records but will not release them. The government's invocation of the Glomar Response has been upheld by the courts, but in 1986 a devious amendment was passed as part of the Anti-Drug Abuse Act that gave federal agencies the legal right to lie to FOIA requesters if the material being sought touches on "national security interests."[3]

This leads to the following conclusion: Given the fact that the Office of Veterans Affairs had no record of any William Lockwood Mitchell, nor did any of the Army Registers from 1962 to 1967, the NPRC response to the FOIA request for Mitchell's service record—declaring that no such record exists or can be located—is therefore very likely just plain deceit. Mitchell completed the Army ROTC program at Cornell, then stated on his twenty-fifth high school reunion questionnaire in 1982 that he had been in the U.S. Army and stationed at Ft. Eustis in Virginia.[12] Add to that resume his listing in the Pentagon's Department of Defense telephone directory starting in the fall of 1964 and extending through the summer of 1967.[13]

During interviews with a number of classmates who knew Mitchell at Cornell, some of whom were also in the various Cornell-administered ROTC programs, a story began to emerge of how Mitchell had come to be stationed at Ft. Eustis in Newport News, Virginia. Mitchell was described by many who knew him (though no one knew him well) as "very private," "serious," "bright," "disciplined," "a whiz at math," and "a physical fitness buff." Several classmates, one of whom was Mitchell's roommate at one point, recalled an incident that allegedly occurred very early in Mitchell's military career. The story circulated that the normally reticent Mitchell was in a class one day while on active duty and did something distinctly out of character. The class was being taught by a superior officer who apparently wasn't particularly competent with the subject matter he was presenting. At one point, the superior officer made an egregious factual error. Mitchell then openly confronted the instructor and corrected the mistake in front of the class. Embarrassed, the senior officer began to take steps to reprimand the recalcitrant Mitchell and had him transferred to "water transport duty at some obscure post in Virginia."[14] Another

---

3   In an April 27, 2011, ruling, Judge Cormac J. Carney of the Central District of California did not challenge the right of U.S. government agencies to lie to a FOIA requester, but he did rule emphatically against their right to lie to a U.S. Court in the process. However limited this hollow victory, the Obama Justice Department is currently attempting something much more sinister in its proposed revision of FOIA rules: giving any governmental agency the legal right to lie and deceive in its response to any FOIA request.

classmate speculated that Mitchell had been court-martialed for insubordination because he had refused a direct order. In either event, Mitchell was quickly transferred. During the 1960s, Ft. Eustis in Newport News, Va. was, in fact, the Army's main transportation facility, a place where Mitchell himself stated in 1982 he had been stationed.[15]

The "Mitchell conflict-with-authority incident," however, had all the markings of a contrived "set-up" aimed at camouflaging what was really taking place: a "sheep-dip" operation aimed at creating the cover for Mitchell's entrance into the world of covert intelligence. Ft. Eustis, it turns out, is less than thirty minutes by car from the CIA's main training facility—Camp Peary in Williamsburg, Virginia, sometimes referred to as "The Farm." Another Cornell classmate, a New Jersey attorney who had also been at one time one of Mitchell's roommates and a ROTC buddy, and who had graduated in 1961, recalled this same incident, saying "then they found better uses for him, and he ended up in intelligence," though he wasn't sure whether it was Army intelligence or CIA.[16]

Had William Mitchell's route into the world of intelligence resembled that of Robert M. Gates (the only Director of Central Intelligence (DCI) to rise from the entry level of the CIA to the very top job)? Gates, who was awarded the Agency's highest distinction, the Distinguished Intelligence Medal, on three separate occasions, also served as Secretary of Defense for two consecutive presidents. In his 1996 book *From the Shadows*, Robert Gates revealed how the CIA had recruited him in the fall of 1965 when he was a graduate student at Indiana University.[4] Less than a year later, in August 1966, he would join what he termed "the mystical brotherhood of CIA." Yet he was given no draft deferment by the Agency and would enter the U.S. Air Force "under CIA sponsorship" by way of the U.S. Air Force Officer Training School (OTS) just a few weeks after entering the Agency. Gates was commissioned as a Second Lieutenant in 1967 and would remain at that rank until 1969, when his service ended.[17]

The most important question, however, still remained unanswered: After Mitchell's graduation from Harvard in the spring of 1963, and soon to be followed by his alleged "reprimand" and "banishment" to Ft. Eustis in Virginia, had he spent the better part of a year at the CIA's Camp Peary before ostensibly landing at the Pentagon in the fall of 1964 with a listing in the Department of Defense telephone directory? A part of the answer to this question (and others) lay in the information Roger Charles was able to unearth about

---

4   According to one trusted source, Robert Gates was recruited by the CIA's legendary Howard "Rocky" Stone.

the man who was technically Lt. William Mitchell's Pentagon commanding officer—Lt. Colonel Ralph Heller Cruikshank. Ironically, this information was as easy to obtain as William Mitchell's was difficult.

SIX WEEKS BEFORE the murder of Mary Meyer took place in the fall of 1964, Lt. Colonel Ralph Heller Cruikshank[5] was appointed Chief of the Army War Room Support Division on September 1, 1964 in the Pentagon's Army Data Support Command (DATCOM) office—the same office (BE1035) where Lt. William L. Mitchell was supposedly stationed with a listing in the Department of Defense telephone directory.[18]

When Cruikshank first came to Washington in 1960, he had just finished a year at The Defense Language Institute Foreign Language Center (DLIFLC) in Monterey, California, studying the Russian language. Often referred to as just "Monterey," the DLIFLC is the military's primary foreign language school, where military service members study foreign languages at an accelerated pace in courses ranging from 24 to 64 weeks in length.

Cruikshank's military record, however, was littered with intelligence assignments.[19] Before reporting to the Pentagon, Lt. Col. Cruikshank had spent the great majority of fourteen years (1946–60) in a variety of intelligence assignments, including some that were highly sensitive. His duties stateside included the 82nd Airborne Division at Ft. Bragg, which at the time was the world-wide "rapid response" contingency force for the Army. The intelligence component for the 82nd Airborne Division unit would have required the maximum, top secret security clearance given for any Army tactical unit. Upon arriving in Washington in 1960, Cruikshank was immediately sent to the Army's Strategic Intelligence School for a five-week, elite training course that involved the Army's most "sensitive topics," the content of which would have never been identified in any course catalogue description. Indeed, according to Roger Charles, the Army's "strategic intelligence course" was a euphemism for some of the military's most highly classified intelligence matters. Was it just coincidence that upon the completion of this course, Lt. Col. Cruikshank created an entirely new career track in computers and data processing, while he still maintained a position within the Pentagon in "Military Intelligence"? From 1960 to 1961, Cruikshank's resume lists several short-term courses in "9400

---

5   Starting in the fall of 2012 and through April 2013, Roger Charles interviewed thirteen (13) people, who had
     either known or had contact with Ralph Heller Cruikshank between 1963 and 1975.

Programming," "Systems Analyst Course," etc. By July 1961, he was given his first assignment as an automated data processing (ADP) officer.[20]

How did Cruikshank, who didn't even have a college degree, end up as a computer geek, ostensibly performing jobs that would have only been given to someone with advanced management and technical skills to supervise the introduction of this entirely new capability into the Army's operation center? And why was he quickly promoted to "Chief, Army Operations Spt [Support] Division"[21] in the fall of 1964 with Lt. William Mitchell allegedly under his command in Pentagon office BE1035? Unless Cruikshank's new career path was just an elaborate cover for further work in covert intelligence, the change in career trajectory made no sense at all.

Four people stationed in the Pentagon in either BE1035 or one of its adjacent offices in the fall of 1964 recalled Cruikshank, but the general consensus was no one really knew what he was actually doing. He seemed to float around the fringes and was always in a hurry, vaguely attached to something that never fit into any larger focus. "Cruikshank's organization, whatever it was, had to be put somewhere," recalled retired Capt. Rome Smyth. "It was down in some shit-hole in the basement of the Pentagon. His [Cruikshank's] crowd was down there building something, but no one ever knew what it was." In spite of the fact that Cruikshank was purported to be in command of the office, another individual in the same office said he "didn't recall any contribution from Cruikshank or his subordinates. They certainly had no involvement in our project." When the four were asked if they had any recollection of a Lt. William Mitchell, no one remembered him.[22]

Lt. Col. Ralph Heller Cruikshank was, according to Roger Charles, "a lock" to make full colonel with all the retirement benefits of a significantly higher rank, yet he retired at the end of April 1966 without promotion and immediately went to work in the State Department. Why would the Army have let him retire, particularly as it ramped up for the Vietnam War? And yet by 1968 Cruikshank was, in fact, *in* Vietnam, not technically in the Army, but working under the auspices of the Civil Operations and Revolutionary Development Support (CORDS)—the integrated group that consisted of the CIA, the U.S. Agency for International Development (USAID), and the State Department, along with U.S. Army personnel who provided the necessary manpower. Among its many nefarious operations, CORDS was responsible for the CIA's controversial Operation Phoenix—the most brutal, targeted assassination program of the Viet Cong infrastructure ever undertaken. In 1968, Phoenix was run by none other than the CIA's William Colby, who, five years later, would become the head of the Agency in 1973.

Cruikshank's job performance "has been outstanding," wrote the legendary John Paul Vann, a chief CORDS deputy, in a work-related performance review dated September 27, 1968.[23] But none of the people who knew Cruikshank in CORDS had anything good to say about him, and certainly couldn't recall any "outstanding" job performance. "He wasn't well thought of, or well-liked," remembered CORDS staffer Joe Langlois, who knew Cruikshank at that time, in addition to having conferred with two of his former colleagues about him. Mr. Langlois had worked in most of the provinces assigned to the III Corp division of CORDS.[24] Meanwhile, the controversial John Paul Vann would become the subject of Neil Sheehan's scathing 1988 Pulitzer Prize-winning book, *A Bright Shining Lie: John Paul Vann and America in Vietnam.*[25] Like the legendary William R. Corson before him, Sheehan's blistering analysis of America's "betrayal" (the title of Corson's book) and egregious blunder in Vietnam was hailed as one of the best books ever written on the subject.

Having officially retired from the Army in 1966, Cruikshank should have been listed in the Army Retired Officer Register starting in 1967, but his name doesn't appear there, nor in the subsequent 1968 or 1969 registers.[26] In June 1973, Ralph Heller Cruikshank again allegedly "retired" from USAID, though he told the personnel department at that time that "it is my intention to remain in country" [Vietnam]. For two more years, he did so.[27] Once more, why would a "computer geek" elect to stay in Vietnam after terminating his employment with the "State Department" and/or USAID?

With the evacuation and fall of Saigon in April 1975, Cruikshank—according to one of his sons—was on the second-to-last helicopter out of Vietnam,[28] yet in Cruikshank's own account a very different scenario had occurred, raising further questions about what had actually taken place.

THE DAY AFTER Mary Meyer's murder, October 13, 1964, the reader will recall that Lt. William L. Mitchell went to D.C. Police and said that he had been running on the C & O Canal towpath the day before and believed that he may have passed the about-to-be victim shortly before her murder. According to Homicide Squad Captain George R. Donahue, Mitchell reported that he had likely passed the victim and "described in detail the clothes worn by Mrs. Meyer." Even more intriguing, Mitchell stated that about two hundred yards behind her was a "Negro male" following her, wearing a dark cap and a light-colored windbreaker jacket with dark trousers and dark shoes—clothes that were similar to those eyewitness Henry Wiggins had described as the attire of the man standing over Mary Meyer's dead body.[29]

The appearance of an upstanding white Army lieutenant working dutifully at the Pentagon had given police the kind of ultimate credibility that in their minds would seal Ray Crump's conviction for the murder of Mary Pinchot Meyer. No further investigation would be needed, and none was ever attempted—in spite of the fact that at the bloody crime scene, there was no forensic evidence linking Crump, or any of his clothes, to the murder, or to the body of Mary Meyer.

But nine months later in July 1965, the Meyer murder trial had had an unexpected outcome. The government hadn't counted on a defense attorney who would expose their case for the sham that it was. So comprehensive was her preparation, so poised and thorough her understanding and knowledge of all the case particulars, as well as the law itself, that attorney Dovey J. Roundtree had, in the end, made a mockery of the prosecution's attempt to frame an innocent man for a murder he couldn't have possibly committed. That summer, justice itself had become the fundamental defendant in Washington's corridors of power. But on Day One of the trial, then increasingly prevalent throughout, Roundtree's genie of 'reasonable doubt' had been let out of the bottle, and then finally triumphant as jury foreman Edward O. Savwoir gave Judge Howard Corcoran, and the courtroom, a verdict of "not guilty" on July 30.

Despite the scramble of Washington's media gargoyles, including the *Washington Post's* newly appointed deputy managing editor Ben Bradlee, to insist that Ray Crump had literally gotten away with murder, the stunning verdict would have undoubtedly sent shock waves to William Mitchell's superiors in the clandestine echelons of covert intelligence operations. Mitchell had testified at the trial, cleverly (but clearly) supporting the prosecution's attempt to frame Crump. Allegedly no longer in the Army at the time of the trial, yet still maintaining a listing in the Department of Defense telephone directory that would remain intact through the summer of 1967, Mitchell somehow let it be known to one newspaper reporter that he was teaching mathematics at Georgetown University, though no record of his employment there was ever located.[30]

Was it coincidence that Mitchell quickly vanished after the trial ended? Had a decision been made to move him out of the country? Given Ray Crump's acquittal, any enterprising journalist, or citizen who became "unsettled" about the Meyer murder might easily have become suspicious of Lt. William L. Mitchell's entry into the fray based solely on a cursory study of the trial transcript. What better way for the government to avoid further scrutiny than to remove Mitchell—give him "the golden parachute" and get him out of the country for a while. Obviously, Mitchell couldn't tell anyone he'd been given a "CIA stipend." Cornell University acquaintances remembered Mitchell boasting about some kind of "Fulbright" or "Eisenhower Fellowship" that took him to the University of London. Mitchell even listed himself in one academic citation as a "Fulbright Fellow University of London, 1965–66;"[31] yet no documentation was ever located for Mitchell's assertion of a connection with a Fulbright or Eisenhower Fellowship.[32] What did finally emerge, however, was that Mitchell had spent a year at the London School of Economics (LSE), where he was awarded the LSE's "M.Phil. degree" in 1966 in "Operational Research."[33]

On his way to California, upon his return stateside sometime during the summer of 1966, Mitchell was, according to a former Cornell roommate he visited, affectedly "smoking a pipe and calling everyone 'bloody blokes.'" One former fraternity brother recalled, "Before the Army, Mitchell was 'Mr. Ivy League' with button-down shirts, crew-neck sweaters, and khaki slacks. After the Army, he was a 'hippy.' " Others also reported that Mitchell became something of a "cultural hippy" in his post-Army years as well as a "serious academic."[34] Had this new persona been an intentional invention, part of Mitchell's post Army–covert intelligence instruction, in an attempt to begin to erase his past and lay down a false trail? Or, had the newfound '1960s counterculture hippie' been truly transformed—'radicalized' by some life experience? It wasn't clear; the fog surrounding Mitchell still hadn't lifted. Nevertheless, using just the name "William Mitchell," he entered the Ph.D. Mathematics program at the University of California (Berkeley) in the fall of 1966, and received his degree in 1970.

D URING THE 1969 academic year, Mitchell began teaching as an instructor at California State University's College of Business and Economics in Hayward (known today as Cal State, East Bay). Using the name "William L. Mitchell," he was then hired as an assistant professor, starting in the 1972–73 academic year. Two years later, however, something very odd took place. Beginning with the 1974–75 catalog, William L. Mitchell changed his name. He would, henceforth from then on in 1974, *only* be listed as "Bill Mitchell," further obscuring his real identity and location. He rose to the rank of associate professor, and his last listing was for the 1989–90 academic year at which point he became emeritus.[35] His current emeritus listing at Cal State, East Bay reads as follows:

MITCHELL, BILL (1969), *Associate Professor of Business Administration:* B.M.E., 1962, Cornell University; M.S., 1963, Harvard University; Ph.D., 1970, University of California, Berkeley. Emeritus, 1989.[36]

The mysterious William Mitchell transformation to "Bill Mitchell" was further substantiated in September 1978 when he purchased the property in California where he now resides. In early 1992, Mitchell transferred this property, by way of a Quitclaim Deed, to the "Bill Mitchell Trust." Perhaps in a further effort to lay down a false trail, was also the intriguing fact that in 1983 "Bill Mitchell" used a second, presumably bogus Social Security number on at least one occasion, and did so in a manner that connected to his current residence.[37]

What might have prompted Mitchell's deliberate, and subsequently pervasive, name change in 1974? A possible explanation was that with the resignation of President Richard Nixon in 1974, an aggressive media and a heretofore negligent Congress began uncovering shocking abuses by the CIA, FBI, and other intelligence related government bureaucracies—abuses that had led to covert action programs involving assassinations. The CIA in particular had been monitoring the Watergate situation from the very beginning, starting with, and even before, E. Howard Hunt and his White House plumbers' break-in at the Democratic National Headquarters in the Watergate apartment complex. The CIA knew what was coming. Given the subsequent public outcry, the Agency's era of little or no Congressional oversight was about to come to an abrupt end, putting the world of espionage and "dirty tricks" under an intolerable microscope. Starting with the Church Committee in 1975, followed by the 1976 House Select Committee on Assassinations (HSCA), the pervasive public investigation of the CIA's "family jewels," particularly with regard to the political assassinations of the 1960s, nearly destroyed it. Very likely in 1974, William L. Mitchell, who had been listed as a faculty member at a well-known educational institution since 1972, was still being "advised" as to how to take precautions, how to create false trails to obscure his location and true identity. His transition in 1974 to just "Bill Mitchell" created a new layer of anonymity, further minimizing the chances of his being discovered, as well as being able to hide in plain sight.

Yet by 1982, had Mitchell possibly believed the worst was over? After all, there had been no Congressional probe about Mary Meyer's demise. Unscathed—and more importantly undiscovered—had Mitchell succumbed to the guilt of having lived with a secret for nearly twenty years? The perils of a "double life" involving deep secrecy for anyone—the loneliness and isolation—often take a terrible toll, as the hunger for deeper, more meaningful human connection becomes overwhelming. Had the halcyon care-free days of Horace Greely High School in the sleepy little village of Chappaqua, New York been Bill Mitchell's last semblance of normalcy, something he possibly may have deeply longed for?

For whatever reason, with the approach of his twenty-fifth high school reunion, "Bill Mitchell" gave some rather forthcoming answers to his high school class questionnaire. Here, he listed his current residential address in northern California, along with his telephone number, identifying himself as "university teacher/scientist" and "single." Asked what had happened in his life since graduation, he wrote the following: "study: Cornell, Harvard, Univ. Calif., Berkeley, London School of Economics. Military service: US Army-Ft Eustis, Va & Washington, DC. Lived and worked in London, Oslo, Stockholm, and Berkeley." To the question of what cities he had lived in for the past twenty-five years, he wrote: "Ithaca, N.Y., Cambridge, Mass., Washington, D.C., Williamsburg, Pa.; London, Helsinki, Oslo, Stockholm, Zurich; Berkeley, Ca."

The oddity of Mitchell's listing "Williamsburg, Pa."[6] was indeed peculiar. Was this an error on his part, had he meant instead to say "Williamsburg, Va." —the location of the CIA's training facility Camp Peary? Or, had he intentionally used "Pa." instead of "Va." so as not to give any indication of his association with Williamsburg, Virginia? Yet why mention "Williamsburg" at all?

When asked about his most interesting experiences since his 1957 high school graduation, Mitchell revealed that just that spring (1982) he had returned from a "visit to the Jung Institute in Zurich." This was followed by his answers to the inquiry regarding "hobbies, interests, sport activities," where he listed "classical music (particularly Medieval, Renaissance & Baroque), playing the recorder, harpsichord and piano, watercolor painting, Jungian psychology, hiking and backpacking, folk dancing, travel, oriental cultures, mythology, LSD running/jogging (long, slow distance!), literature, science, dreams, meditation, films . . ."[38]

---

6   In 1963-64, Williamsburg, Pa. had a population of less than 1000 people. There was no industry there; no media outlets. The town is located more than 170 miles from Washington, D.C. and 350 miles from Ft. Eustis in Virginia.

It's not at all clear what took place during Mitchell's visit to the Jung Institute in Zurich in the spring of 1982, or how he pursued his stated interest in "Jungian psychology." Had he participated in some course or workshop there? Had he explored the therapeutic process of Jungian analysis in an attempt to reckon with his past? In 1982, Bill Mitchell was about to become forty-three years old, and something was likely "rattling his cage."

The approach of mid-life often precipitates a kind of turning point for each of us. Long known as the "mid-life crisis," it is a period that is frequently fraught with deeper introspection and self-examination, in addition to being intermittently emotional and upsetting. Were Bill Mitchell's disclosures in his twenty-fifth high school reunion questionnaire a part of his emergence from isolation in an attempt to reclaim his earlier childhood innocence and be fondly remembered by his former high school classmates?

The caption next to William Mitchell's 1957 senior high school photo was from William Shakespeare's play *King Richard II*. It read: "Mine honour is my life; both grow in one: Take honour from me, and my life is done." Was it possible that William Lockwood Mitchell in 1964 had allowed himself to become "Cold War cannon fodder"? Was he then in the spring of 1982 attempting to lance that pus-filled boil upon his soul in an attempt to reclaim his "honour"? The brutal killing of another human being eventually (if not immediately) takes an ineradicable toll on the perpetrator(s). Whatever contact Mitchell attempted in 1982 with the people in his past, it very quickly faded; according to his high school webmaster, he has not been heard from since, despite a number of attempts to contact him.[39]

Throughout the numerous interviews[7] starting in the fall of 2012 conducted by investigative journalist Don Devereux with Mitchell's Cornell classmates and roommates, some of whom were in Army ROTC with Mitchell, in addition to his colleagues at Cal State, East Bay, the picture that emerged was that of a person who rarely shared any information about his past—never allowing people to get close, to know him in any substantial manner. As they thought about it, all of the people interviewed were astonished at how little they actually knew about Mitchell, his parents, his past, where he came from, etc. Only one person recalled, for instance, Mitchell ever mentioning Chappaqua, New York, after having visited Mitchell there; and only one interviewee mentioned that Bill had once recalled how his father "had taken him to Army football games at West Point." So reclusive had Mitchell's life been that a woman who had been

---

7   Don Devereux of Tempe, Arizona, conducted interviews with sixteen (16) different people, some of whom were
     interviewed on multiple occasions, all of whom at one time had known William L. Mitchell.

involved with him, and who had lived in London for two years, never knew he had gone to school there—until Don Devereux mentioned it to her.

All through late 2012 into 2013, word among those interviewed was spreading about William Mitchell's role in *Mary's Mosaic*. People who had once been acquainted with the secluded Mitchell were starting to talk to one another. Several interviewees told Don Devereux to talk with Bill Mitchell's brother, James Mitchell, who was two years behind Bill at Cornell. Devereux did, in fact, make several attempts to contact James via telephone and email, even visiting a restaurant he owned in his hometown of Phoenix where he lived, hoping to run into him, but to no avail. Finally writing James a letter in early February (2013), Devereux made it clear that "the elephant in the room" was President Kennedy's assassination, that the same people who had orchestrated it had likely also terminated Mary Meyer the following year, making his brother Bill's suspicious entrance into the Meyer murder case highly suspect. "Bill really needs to know what looks to be heading his way," wrote Devereux. Several days later, Devereux's phone rang.

"This is Jim Mitchell. Don't contact me again. I have nothing to talk to you about," said the caller in a hostile voice.

"Okay," said Devereux. "That's all I needed to hear, and thanks for calling me." The conversation abruptly ended.[40]

In early March, Roger Charles, Don Devereux, and I huddled to discuss our next step. It was decided that Devereux would make an attempt to contact Bill Mitchell directly by telephone, using his listed phone number. Devereux made the call but there was no answer, only the mechanical default message, "Please leave a message," which he did. Later that day, William Lockwood Mitchell (aka Bill Mitchell) called back.

"Don't bother me any more. Don't send me anything in the mail. Thank you," said Mitchell anxiously, but politely, then hanging up on Devereux.[41]

The curtain had fallen on our research effort. Had Mitchell's "little dark secret" about the 1964 demise of Mary Pinchot Meyer become a family secret? The Mitchell brothers, for whatever reason, had decided not to talk or comment. That, perhaps, was the most far-reaching admission so far. Should the murder case of Mary Meyer now be reopened, would America's national security apparatus ever allow William Lockwood Mitchell to be subpoenaed to testify? Or would he just disappear into new ethers of obscurity, perhaps by accidental death or suicide? Once again, my mind echoed William Corson's aphorism to his disciple Roger Charles: "Anyone can commit a murder, but it takes an expert to commit a suicide."

Post Script

WITH THE LITERARY success of his 1988 book *Senatorial Privilege: The Chappaquiddick Coverup*, author Leo Damore soon began to use his emerging visibility to launch his next book project. Word quickly spread that his focus would be on the life and death of Mary Pinchot Meyer. Yet coincidentally in 1990, just as Damore had begun a most thorough research effort, the D.C. Police Department, allegedly under the rules of its twenty-five year "retention schedule" and "storage procedures" destroyed its existing Meyer murder case files and exhibits. In spite of the fact that there was no statute of limitations for murder, the case was considered "administratively closed."[42] Increasingly frustrated, and unable to learn the whereabouts of William Mitchell, Damore wrote him a letter in late 1992 at his last known address (a CIA "safe house" as documented by three former CIA personnel), reportedly after conferring with former Air Force colonel and CIA liaison L. Fletcher Prouty, who had been instrumental in forming a network of clandestine agents throughout the military and other government agencies, including the FBI.[8]

The purported confessional telephone call to author Leo Damore at the end of March 1993 by someone claiming to be Mitchell now invites some new consideration. First, attorney James Smith's notes about the call, taken when Damore called Smith within hours after his conversation with the person claiming to be Mitchell, reflected Damore's statements that William Mitchell had been married with five children and was now living under another name in Virginia. None of this appears to be true. In addition, the real William L. Mitchell was not seventy-four years old in 1993, but fifty-four. There has also been, so far, no indication that Mitchell ever had any liaison with the FBI.

Secondly, given what is now known about William Lockwood Mitchell, the 1993 Damore phone call also raises several new questions: Most importantly of course, was Damore actually talking to the real William Mitchell, or someone impersonating him? Or, was the real William Mitchell calling, and purposely not being entirely truthful about certain details of his life, so as to keep Damore from locating him and further delving into his past, while giving Damore disinformation mixed in with some fact as a way to eventually discredit him, should he publish anything about Mitchell? Absence of evidence doesn't always establish evidence of absence; William Mitchell's military service record likely remains intentionally hidden for good reason—to conceal his real affiliations and assignments after his 1962 Cornell graduation.

---

8   The reader may find it helpful to review pages 326–28. After facilitating a number of CIA coups d'état around the globe, including military support for these operations, Fletcher Prouty became deeply disturbed when he discovered the CIA's involvement in the assassination of President Kennedy. He retired from the Air Force in 1964 and began writing about the secret history of the Cold War.

What is clear is that *something* in Damore's letter to Mitchell had driven *somebody* to make this telephone call. Attorney Smith's notes clearly indicated that Mitchell (or whoever) didn't want to become "the fall guy in history" for the murder of Mary Meyer. Why would Mitchell, assuming that he was the one making the call, have even bothered to respond to Damore's inquiry? Was it possible that Mitchell was frightened or worried that Damore, in his capacity as an established crime-sleuth,[9] was already well on his way to "outing" him as someone involved in her murder? This also may explain why Mitchell and his brother James declined to make any statement in response to our 2013 inquiries.

Finally, if in fact Damore subsequently met with Mitchell some time after the call (as he told me and at least one other friend), had it been the real William Lockwood Mitchell who showed up, or someone impersonating him? That remains unknown. Very possibly, Mitchell—or the people advising him—had become aware that Damore was closing in on the explosive truth of what had really taken place in the fall of 1964 as Mary Meyer walked toward her death. Had a decision also been reached by someone to eliminate Leo Damore?

Sometime in April 1993, after the supposed personal meeting with Mitchell (or whoever pretended to be him), Leo Damore's agitation was spawned; his paranoia grew, and became more acute. He was sure he was being watched—even followed—and eventually believed he had been poisoned. In fact, Damore became so incapacitated that he was unable to finish his book about Mary Meyer. His life would continue to spiral downward, finally reaching a suicidal depression that drove him to take his own life in the fall of 1995.[10]

O NE YEAR LATER, since the 2012 publication of *Mary's Mosaic*, spring has come late to New England. The past winter had been cold and interminable. My agitation around an unresolved responsibility had become unsettling, my peace unmoored, despite the arrival of light-filled longer days with a brightening sun that beckons toward summer's solstice and beyond. And yet, with the discovery of a still living, still mysterious William Lockwood Mitchell, I could not—I will not—just let this go. Were I to be on my deathbed today, taking my last few breaths, confronting the final, most important question—"Did I love well?"—a primordial despair of a life unfulfilled would become my final companion. And that would not suffice, nor be acceptable. There was

9 The Smith notes mention that the caller had read Damore's book *Senatorial Privilege* and was impressed with how Damore had handled Joe Gargon, Senator Edward Kennedy's cousin. See Appendix 3.
10 See pp. 377–79.

then, in my final deliberation this spring, one more door to open, one more journey to take for the sake of learning the truth about the murder of Mary Pinchot Meyer, and all its implications.

I N THE JANUARY 1967 edition of *Ramparts Magazine,* an article appeared entitled "The Children of Vietnam." It was written by a thirty-year-old political science instructor at Mercy College in Dobbs Ferry, New York. On leave of absence from teaching, he had spent six weeks in the spring of 1966 traveling and living in the Sancta Maria Orphanage in the Vietnamese Gia Dinh Province as a freelance correspondent. Having been sanctioned by the Military Assistance Command of the U.S. government and by the government of Vietnam, he visited a number of orphanages and hospitals. By his estimate in 1966, already over a million children had been either wounded, maimed, burned, or killed by the atrocity of America's war in Vietnam. The *Ramparts* article "The Children of Vietnam" had a preface written by the late Dr. Benjamin Spock, who underscored the enormity of the inhumane, unspeakable barbarism America was perpetrating there. The author of the article was William F. Pepper, who was at the time the Executive Director of the Commission on Human Rights in New Rochelle, New York.[43]

When the Rev. Martin Luther King, Jr. read the article shortly after its publication, he invited William Pepper to speak to his congregation. For Pepper, the 1967 meeting would precipitate the deepest of bonds with the Nobel Prize winner and civil rights leader, as well as the King family. Publicly labeling the U.S. government the "greatest purveyor of violence in the world," Martin Luther King would be assassinated one year after his initial meeting with Pepper. While a nation had lost one its most eloquent, influential advocates of peace and civil rights, James Earl Ray—another poor, disenfranchised loner like Ray Crump—was framed for the King murder by authorities in the U.S. government. Predictably, a craven, shameless media conspired to dupe the public with yet another false narrative.

Having become an attorney in 1977, William F. Pepper struggled for ten years (1988–98) to get James Earl Ray a full trial. Ray, who entered a guilty plea on March 10, 1969, on advice of his attorney to forego a jury trial where he might have been subject to the death penalty if convicted, recanted his confession three days later. Ray would die in prison in 1998 of liver failure, but that didn't stop the undaunted attorney William Pepper. Representing the King family in a final effort to establish the truth about the assassination of Martin Luther King, Jr., Pepper filed a wrongful death civil lawsuit (*King v.*

Jowers and Other Unknown Co-Conspirators) in Memphis, Tennessee, in 1999. All of the evidence related to the King assassination was brought forth in a court of law and under oath. The trial lasted thirty days with over seventy witnesses, all of whom put evidence into the legal record. In less than an hour of deliberation, a jury of six white and six black jurors found former Memphis police officer Loyd Jowers and local, state, and federal government agencies guilty of conspiring to assassinate Martin Luther King. Contained in the court record was evidence that the FBI, CIA, and the U.S. military had been involved in the conspiracy.

Once again, betraying the fundamental ethic and principles of journalism, America's corporate-driven media avoided both the story and the landmark verdict, just as they had done in 1985 in attorney Mark Lane's trial against the CIA's E. Howard Hunt. "The evidence was clear," said jury forewoman Leslie Armstrong at the end of the Hunt trial to the few media representatives present. "The CIA had killed President Kennedy, Hunt had been a part of it and that evidence so painstakingly presented, should now be examined by the relevant institutions of the United States government so that those responsible for the assassination might be brought to justice."[11]

William Pepper's tenacity, his gallantry, and commitment to use the rule of law to expose the truth, is presently being tested in the case of the 1968 assassination of Robert F. Kennedy. Pepper has gathered evidence of a second shooter in Robert Kennedy's assassination and is currently submitting it. If the matter is allowed to be heard in a judicial proceeding, it will likely open a door for the exoneration of alleged assassin Sirhan Sirhan, thereby proving that a conspiracy was at work to assassinate Robert Kennedy.

The Ides of March became a turning point in Roman history, as it did for me in 2013. Dovey Roundtree's legacy and spirit had visited me. Embracing a new journey, I am now focused on the task of reopening the legal investigation of the 1964 murder of Mary Pinchot Meyer, thereby hopefully subpoenaing William Lockwood Mitchell under oath to testify. With all that we have ascertained during the last year, it is entirely worthy of consideration. And to my great delight, Dr. William F. Pepper, Esq. has agreed to take the case and spearhead the effort. It is possibly the last door to open.

Posterity may one day have the fortitude and commitment to embrace the difficult truths and realities that our government and its confederate media have gone to such great lengths to conceal from its citizens. But that day is still

---

11   See pp. 298–99.

far away. As citizens of this country, each of us must find our unique role and position in keeping the torch and cause of real democracy and truth alive, and available to all. Without doing so, we will surely descend into further moral and physical decay, the evidence of which is already upon us. Do not give up hope. Stay positive; and take action with those who will amplify your voice. Our strength lies in the numbers of people who are no longer willing to tolerate our government's denial and injustice—and the atrocities it continues to perpetuate domestically, and around the world.

Mary Pinchot Meyer was assassinated because she wanted to impart a critically important truth to the American public at a very crucial moment in history. Her torch and flame belongs to each of us, and should be honored as such.

APPENDICES

Appendix #1: FBI Crime Lab Report for the Murder of Mary Pinchot Meyer

Appendix #2: Confidential U.S. Justice Memorandum, February 24, 1965

Appendix #3: Notes Taken by Attorney James ("Jimmy") H. Smith on His Telephone Call with Leo Damore, March 31, 1993, at Approximately 8:30 A.M.

Appendix #4: Ben Bradlee's 1952 Rosenberg Case Press Liaison with the CIA

Appendix 1:
FBI Crime Lab Report for the Murder of Mary Pinchot Meyer

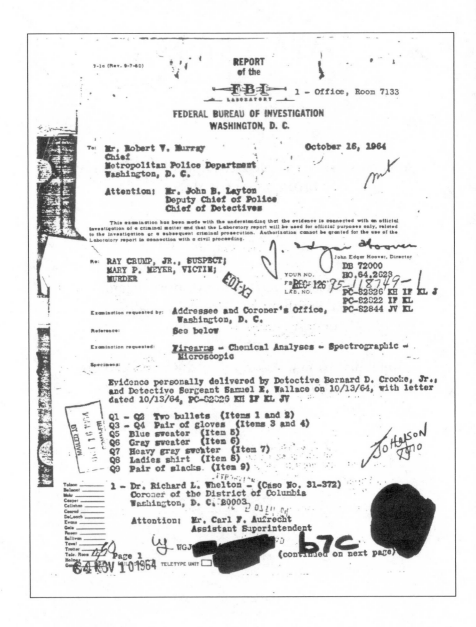

Q10 - Q11 Pair of shoes (Items 10 and 11)
Q12 Jacket (Item 12)
Q13 Sweat shirt (Item 13)
Q14 Sport shirt (Item 14)
Q15 Button (Item 15)
Q16 Piece of tree trunk (Item 16)

Evidence personally delivered by Technician ▓▓▓▓▓▓ b7C
on 10/13/64, with letter dated 10/13/64, PC-82622 JF KL

K1 Blood sample from victim
K2 Lipstick smears from victim

Evidence personally delivered by Detective Sergeant Samuel E.
Wallace and Detective Bernard D. Crooke, on 10/14/64, with
letter dated 10/14/64, PC-82344 JV KL

Q17 Dark-colored plaid cap (Item #18)
K3 Tube of lipstick, "Cherries in the Snow" (Item #17)

Results of examination:

The two bullets, specimens Q1 and Q2, are .38
S & W lead bullets of Remington-Peters manufacture which
were fired from a barrel rifled with five lands and grooves,
right twist. Rifling impressions such as those found on
these specimens are produced by some models of revolvers
chambered for the .38 S & W cartridge which carry the brand
names of Smith and Wesson, National Arms, Hopkins and Allen,
Harrington and Richardson, Empire State Arms Company, Iver
Johnson, Mervin Hulbert and Company, and possibly others.

The marks remaining on specimens Q1 and Q2 are
suitable for comparison with test bullets obtained from
suspect weapons recovered.

The hole which appears in the right shoulder area (back)
of each of the three sweaters and the white shirt, specimens
Q5 through Q8, is like that which would be produced by firing
a weapon with the muzzle of that weapon in contact with the
outer garment, specimen Q5.

Nothing was found during a microscopic examination
of the interior of the pockets of the Q12 jacket which would
allow a determination as to whether or not a recently discharged
firearm had been placed into one of these pockets.

Page 2
PC-82826 KH

(continued on next page)

It was ascertained by grouping tests conducted on the K1 blood sample that the victim belonged to blood group "O." Group "O" human blood was identified on the Q16 piece of tree trunk and on the Q3 through Q11 items of clothing of the victim.

The results of preliminary chemical tests for blood conducted on very small diluted appearing stains on present on the upper front portion and left sleeve of the Q12 jacket were positive, thereby indicating the possible presence of blood in these stains. However, there was an insufficient amount of material in the stains on the jacket to permit confirmatory blood tests or origin tests to be conducted. The examination of specimens Q13 and Q14 disclosed no indication of the presence of blood on these specimens.

No semen was identified on the clothing of the victim and suspect.

Numerous light blue woolen fibers that match in microscopic characteristics the light blue woolen fibers composing the Q5 blue sweater were found adhering to the Q16 piece of tree trunk. These fibers could have originated from this sweater.

It is pointed out that textile fibers do not exhibit enough individual microscopic characteristics to be positively identified as originating from a particular source to the exclusion of all other similar sources.

No fibers were found on the suspect's clothing, specimens Q13 and Q14, that could be associated with the victim's clothing, specimens Q5 through Q9.

No fibers were found on the Q12 jacket that could be associated with the victim's clothing.

No Negroid hairs were found in the debris removed from specimens Q5 through Q9. No Caucasian hairs were found in the debris removed from specimens Q12, Q13 and Q14.

Black head hairs of Negroid origin were found in the pockets and in the debris removed from the Q12 jacket. These

Page 3
PC-82826 KH

(continued on next page)

hairs have been mounted on glass slides for possible future comparisons with a head hair sample of the suspect.

No identifying, or dry cleaners, markings were found on the Q12 jacket.

The Q15 button is similar to the remaining buttons on the Q5 sweater in color, design, construction and size. This button could be one of those missing from the Q5 sweater.

The Q17 cap is badly worn and contains no markings that would aid in identifying its owner. Two black head hair fragments of Negroid origin were found in this cap. These fragments have been mounted on a glass slide for possible future comparisons. Specimen Q17 is approximately a size 6 3/4.

Faint red smears are present on the back of the jacket, specimen Q12. These smears have a wax like appearance when viewed microscopically; hence, it is possible these are lipstick smears.

The Q12 red smears and the lipsticks of specimens K2 and K3 were examined by means of a spectrophotometer with respect to the type of dye. The results revealed that the dye on each of the specimens was different; therefore, it was not possible to associate any of the specimens with each other.

The items of evidence listed above will be retained in the Laboratory until called for by a representative of your Department.

Page 4
PC-02026 XII

Appendix 2:
Confidential U.S. Justice Memorandum, February 24, 1965

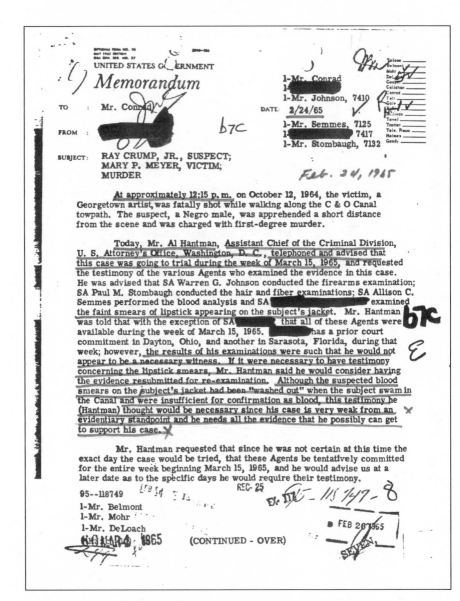

UNITED STATES GOVERNMENT

Memorandum

TO : Mr. Conrad

FROM :

SUBJECT: RAY CRUMP, JR., SUSPECT;
MARY P. MEYER, VICTIM;
MURDER

1-Mr. Conrad
1-
1-Mr. Johnson, 7410
1-Mr. Semmes, 7125
1- 7417
1-Mr. Stombaugh, 7132

DATE: 2/24/65

Feb. 24, 1965

At approximately 12:15 p.m. on October 12, 1964, the victim, a Georgetown artist, was fatally shot while walking along the C & O Canal towpath. The suspect, a Negro male, was apprehended a short distance from the scene and was charged with first-degree murder.

Today, Mr. Al Hantman, Assistant Chief of the Criminal Division, U. S. Attorney's Office, Washington, D. C., telephoned and advised that this case was going to trial during the week of March 15, 1965, and requested the testimony of the various Agents who examined the evidence in this case. He was advised that SA Warren G. Johnson conducted the firearms examination; SA Paul M. Stombaugh conducted the hair and fiber examinations; SA Allison C. Semmes performed the blood analysis and SA examined the faint smears of lipstick appearing on the subject's jacket. Mr. Hantman was told that with the exception of SA that all of these Agents were available during the week of March 15, 1965. has a prior court commitment in Dayton, Ohio, and another in Sarasota, Florida, during that week; however, the results of his examinations were such that he would not appear to be a necessary witness. If it were necessary to have testimony concerning the lipstick smears, Mr. Hantman said he would consider having the evidence resubmitted for re-examination. Although the suspected blood smears on the subject's jacket had been "washed out" when the subject swam in the Canal and were insufficient for confirmation as blood, this testimony he (Hantman) thought would be necessary since his case is very weak from an evidentiary standpoint and he needs all the evidence that he possibly can get to support his case.

Mr. Hantman requested that since he was not certain at this time the exact day the case would be tried, that these Agents be tentatively committed for the entire week beginning March 15, 1965, and he would advise us at a later date as to the specific days he would require their testimony.

95--118749

REC-25

1-Mr. Belmont
1-Mr. Mohr
1-Mr. DeLoach

1965 (CONTINUED - OVER)

FEB 26 1965

Memorandum to Mr. Conrad
Re: RAY CRUMP, JR., SUSPECT;
MARY P. MEYER, VICTIM;
MURDER
95-118749

      Mr. Hantman advised that in the event it was necessary to contact him regarding other commitments that might come up during this period, that his telephone number is Government Code 1204, extension 536.

ACTION:

      For information.

2

Appendix 3:

Notes Taken by Attorney James ("Jimmy") H. Smith on His Telephone Call
with Leo Damore, March 31, 1993, at Approximately 8:30 A.M.

The following pages are copies of the notes attorney James Smith took on
the morning of March 31, 1993, when author Leo Damore called him. The six
(6) pages of notes document the telephone call and what was said during the
course of the conversation. After Smith shared these notes with me in 2004,
we spent hours together over a three-year period going over each line, thereby
further stimulating Smith's recall and accuracy. As of 2011, Smith has reviewed
this appendix and fully endorses it to be true and accurate.[1]

Each page of the notes has been transcribed so that the reader can make
sense of what took place during their conversation. There is also a discussion
of the information that is given on each page for better understanding.

---

1   Author interview with James H. Smith, Esq. April 2, 2011.

Page 1: Notes of attorney James Smith's telephone call with Leo Damore on March 31, 1993.

Page 1: Transcription

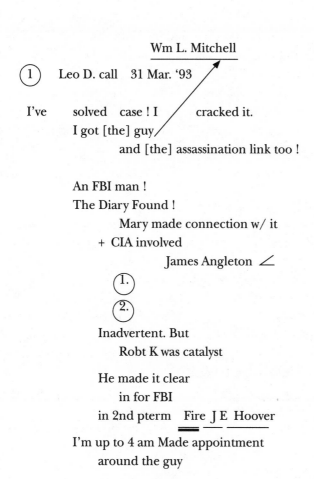

Wm L. Mitchell

(1) Leo D. call   31 Mar. '93

I've   solved   case ! I   cracked it.
I got [the] guy
          and [the] assassination link too !

An FBI man !
The Diary Found !
          Mary made connection w/ it
          + CIA involved
                    James Angleton ∠
                    (1.)
                    (2.)

Inadvertent. But
          Robt K was catalyst

He made it clear
          in for FBI
          in 2nd pterm   Fire J E Hoover

I'm up to 4 am Made appointment
          around the guy

Introduction

These notes were taken by attorney James H. Smith on a telephone call with his client and dear friend Leo Damore on the morning of March 31, 1993. Damore's tapes of his phone conversation with "William L. Mitchell" were not found among Damore's belongings after his death, nor was a transcript of the call ever located. However, Jimmy Smith has aided the author in the reconstruction and interpretation of his notes from Damore's account of his conversation with Mitchell.

The time of Damore's call, according to Smith, was between 8:00 and 8:30. There are two pieces of this mosaic that Damore reveals on page 1: that he finally had telephone contact with "William L. Mitchell" the night before; and that he, Damore, had come into possession of Mary's diary—a fact that he had not revealed before.

Page 1 Discussion

Excitedly, Damore announces that he believes he has finally solved the murder of Mary Meyer. He tells Smith that "Mitchell" was a former FBI liaison, and that he, Damore, has been up most of the night ("up to 4 am") talking to him. The two apparently made an appointment to meet in person.

Damore also indicates that he has examined Mary's diary—in which Mary made a connection with "it"—JFK's assassination and the CIA's involvement, where "James Angleton" figures prominently. Also in Mary's diary, according to Damore, was Mary's knowledge that Bobby Kennedy ("Robt K was catalyst") was going to "fire" FBI director J. Edgar Hoover after President Kennedy was reelected in 1964. The inference here is that Hoover may have also wanted Mary Meyer dead for fear of what she knew, perhaps about Hoover himself or about the FBI's involvement in the assassination and its cover-up, or both.

Page 2: Notes of attorney James Smith's telephone call with Leo Damore on March 31, 1993

Page 2: Transcription

(2) He lives under another
name in Va.
* The Real Estate ∠ [angle] did it +
New clip
Wash Star: math teacher
* at Georgetown

" A light bulb Job"
at Pentagon
(74 yr old) as an Air F. – A. – + N

We had hard leg work
A CIA safe house at 1500
Arling. Blvd. ⬆ A CIA K
(On murder / CIA inv.
He appeared at Trial !
Leo got his record : /
* + Made contact with him (
Last time . Wrote him letter +
On phone 4 hours + he's talking +
I taped it all !
The
Angleton connection w/ CIA

Page 2 Discussion

According to Smith, Damore revealed that "William L. Mitchell" currently lived under a different alias in Virginia. "The Real Estate" angle referred to Damore's letter having been sent to 1500 Arlington Boulevard in Arlington, Virginia, which was "Mitchell's" previous address. "Mitchell" revealed to Damore during the call that his job listing in the Pentagon directory was just "a light bulb Job," and that at certain times he was active in the Air Force, the Army, and the Navy. His age at the time of the call was seventy-four.

At the time of Crump's trial in 1965, "Mitchell" was, according to a *Washington Star* "news clip" by reporter Roberta Hornig, no longer serving in the military but allegedly "a Georgetown University mathematics teacher."*

"We had hard leg work" referred to the fact that Damore had finally learned from another former CIA operative that Mitchell's building at 1500 Arlington Boulevard was a known "CIA safe house," but Damore was never able to locate any record of any "William L. Mitchell" as a mathematics teacher at Georgetown (nor was this author).

According to Jimmy Smith, Damore explicitly told him that "Mitchell" confessed ("he's talking") to Damore: that the murder of Mary Meyer was a CIA contract ("A CIA K"), that the CIA was involved ("CIA inv"), and that "Mitchell" himself was the CIA individual who had been the assassin. "Mitchell" appeared at the trial with a fabricated account in order to corroborate the frame-up of Ray Crump Jr. Damore then told Smith that he had "taped" the entire call with "Mitchell." Damore then referenced the subject "The" "Angleton connection w/ CIA," which continues on the next page.

Page 3: Notes of attorney James Smith's telephone call with Leo Damore on March 31, 1993

Page 3: Transcription

(3.)

Mary – stepped in shit !
She would not back down Her [she was]
too strong + too powerful

1.　　　J. E. H. lived next door to LBJ
Breakfast together Sun AM
Gave LBJ kids dog "Edgar"

J. E. H. hated CIA

But James Angleton close Pal

" Drinkers "

COLBY ⟶ says

How come guys talking ?

(1) Does not want to be Fall
guy in history. Plus
(*Senatorial Privilege* respect) - Joe G.)

(2) I Got word – he's a killer - - -
+ he has 5 kids !

Checking to do

(3.) Wash / Post ↓

"Knew" + Fear Mary !
" A Good of country . . . ."

For

Spectacular
Ending

New Agent (Richard Pine) .

Page 3 Discussion

Referring to a passage in Mary's Diary, Damore emphatically tells Smith that Mary had made up her mind to find some way to go public with what she knew. She was "too strong, too powerful," and wasn't about to "back down." But, said Damore, "Mary – stepped in shit !"

It's not clear whether Damore, in talking about Hoover ("J.E.H."), is taking the following revelation from Mary's diary. Hoover and LBJ were close pals; for years they had Sunday morning breakfasts together, and Hoover gave LBJ's "kids" a dog named "Edgar." Hoover did, however, hate the CIA, but he was friendly and a sometime drinking pal with "James Angleton," probably because Angleton held the ultimate "dirt" on Hoover: compromising pictures of Hoover's sexual relationship with his colleague Clyde Tolson.

Damore makes reference to William Colby at the time of the Watergate hearings and the House Select Committee on Intelligence, in which the CIA was under intense scrutiny. "How come guys [are] talking?" may be a reference to disclosures at that time. Damore then says that "William L. Mitchell" does "not want to become the fall guy in history" for the murder of Mary Meyer. It appears that before "Mitchell" called Damore, he had read Damore's book, *Senatorial Privilege*, about Ted Kennedy's saga at Chappaquiddick. "Mitchell," said Damore to Smith, respected how Damore had handled Kennedy's cousin Joe Gargon's disclosures to Damore in the book.

Damore specifically states that he already knows who "Mitchell" really is, which was likely revealed to him by L. Fletcher Prouty. "I got [the] word— he's a killer [assassin]—[and] he has 5 kids." Damore then makes the comment that the *Washington Post* "knew" and "Fear Mary" because she intended to speak out, so her murder was done for the "good of the country."

Damore's new literary agent was Richard Pine in New York, who confirmed his representation of Damore, and thought he remembered Damore talking about certain aspects of this call.[2]

---

2   Richard Pine, interview by the author, October 21, 2004.

Page 4: Notes of attorney James Smith's telephone call with Leo Damore on March 31, 1993

Page 4: Transcription

(4.)   ON MARY

Who pulled Trigger - - - ?

" An Operation "

He was assigned (Sept)

Part of Surveil. Team

24 Sept Warren Report . She hit
     roof.

She went to husb +

husb to Angleton + he

    ⟨ protect his ass + FBI

It was _NOT_ the love affair

      * _But_ The murder of JFK

Ben Bradlee w/ Newsweek Bureau then

    then ⟍ Mgr. Ed of Wash Post

      6 mo ⟍ Exec. Editor ! ! cut the
                 shit

plus Phil Graham suicide

    suspicious also

Servant brought body etc.

Kennedys stepping on lots of Toes !

Page 4 Discussion

"On Mary" and the question, "Who pulled trigger . . . ?" Damore tells Smith that the murder of Mary Meyer was "an operation," where "Mitchell" and others had first been assigned to a surveillance team in September 1964 around the time the Warren Report was released. This may have occurred before the Warren Report was released, in anticipation of it. It's not clear.

When the Warren Report was released to the public on September 24, Mary had purchased a paperback copy. Realizing the immensity of the cover-up taking place, "she hit [the] roof." Her Diary makes clear that she first confronted Cord, Damore told Smith, and then Cord informed his close friend Jim Angleton ("husb to Angleton") about how upset Mary was. The inference was that Mary confronted Cord that she wasn't going to stand-by and let the cover-up proceed without speaking out. She may have also confronted Angleton as well. "It was not the love affair [with JFK], but the murder of JFK," and how Mary had finally put certain things together, that pushed Jim Angleton, Cord Meyer, and others to terminate the life of Mary Meyer.

Damore then expressed his suspicions about Ben Bradlee's meteoric rise at *The Washington Post,* telling Smith that Bradlee had become Executive Editor within six months after he had become the Managing Editor. That was incorrect; Damore had his facts wrong. After meeting with Katharine Graham in March 1965, Bradlee moved from *Newsweek* to the *Post* in August as the "Deputy Managing Editor;" but he was promoted in less than three months in October to the job of "Managing Editor." Three years later in 1968, he became Executive Editor.[3]

Damore also told Smith that he believed Philip Graham's death was suspicious; he didn't believe it was a suicide. He mentioned to Smith what Dovey Roundtree had told him about what the Graham caretaker had done immediately after the death ("Servant brought body etc."). Lastly on this page, Damore's comment about "Kennedys stepping on lots of toes!" refers to the fact that Jack and Bobby had been operating very independently during the Kennedy presidency.

---

3   Bradlee, Ben. *A Good Life - Newspapering and Other Adventures.* New York: Simon & Schuster, 1995. pp. 274-283.

Page 5: Notes of attorney James Smith's telephone call with Leo Damore on March 31, 1993

(5.)

Mary Pinchot Meyer

Leo has talked to
Prouty (Oliver Stone sey.)
in New Zealand JFK Nov 63
+ Stiggers info a
Lee H. Oswald in Press
Already there!
[When] there only
accused that very
afternoon!!
in: prepared in relevance
something a number of
May P. M. 1. Murder
2. Carport △
3. Lone Gun
4. Case closed
5. Rene!

Same mod →

w/ Post - Picked by newspaper!
news shots... G. G.. G.

this any offense!
there A
witness! - It was
in two patch Wm Mitchell A Fokker!
So Contrived!
* A set up: ready to... frame
in public place ..

Page 5: Transcription

⑤.

Mary Pinchot Meyer

Leo had talked to
Prouty   (Oliver Stone guy.)
   in New Zealand JFK Nov '63
*   + staggering info on
      Lee H. Osw in Press
Already there !
   How when why
         accused that very
         afternoon ! !

         prepared in advance
Same   *   Same thing w murder of
Mod ⟶   Mary P. M.   1. murder
                  2. Caught △
                  3. Lone Gun
                  4. Case solved
                  5. Home !

   W/ Post -   Trial by newspaper !
            Mug shots . . . G. – G . . G .

         His only offense !
   Then a   It was
*   Witness ! – Wm Mitchell   A Faker !
      on Tow path   So contrived !
            *   **A set up** away from home
         in public place . .

443

Page 5 Discussion

Damore reveals to Smith that he had talked at some length to L. Fletcher Prouty, who had created a network of clandestine agents throughout the military and other government agencies including the FBI. However, after facilitating for the CIA many coups d'état around the globe, he was deeply disturbed by the revelation of what he quickly came to discover: the CIA's involvement in the assassination of President Kennedy. Prouty resigned his Air Force commission in 1964 and began to study and prepare for publication his account of the secret history of the Cold War. His two books, *The Secret Team* and *JFK: The CIA, Vietnam, and the Plot to Assassinate John F. Kennedy*, have since become classics in understanding America's Cold War era. So thorough and compelling had Prouty's analysis been that film director Oliver Stone used his personage for the character of "Mr. X" in his film *JFK*.

Damore recounts to Jimmy Smith that Prouty had been in New Zealand at the time of Kennedy's assassination. Prouty told Damore that there was a "staggering" amount of information on Lee Harvey Oswald "already there" in the news, detailing the "how where why" of the assassination when, in fact, Oswald had only been "accused that very afternoon!!" Damore says that Prouty concluded, "[Therefore] prepared in advance," meaning the assassination.

It was Prouty who finally assisted Damore in putting certain pieces of the murder of Mary Meyer into focus, as well as identifying "William L. Mitchell" as an assassin. A similar ("Same Mod[el]") CIA template was used for Mary's murder whereby (1) the murder first takes place; (2) a patsy is "Caught" (arrested); (3) a "Lone Gun" (no conspiracy); (4) "case solved" via a "trial" in the media; and (5) "Home!," perhaps meaning "home free."

The notes indicate a powerful role played by the *Washington Post*—"Trial by newspaper!" Ray Crump's "mug shots" were everywhere. Damore regarded the murder trial as "so contrived," with fabricated evidence that included "William L. Mitchell" as a witness, "A Faker!" Finally, Mitchell confesses to Damore that the murder of Mary Meyer had been "a set up away from home in [a] public place." That had been the Kennedy assassination model referred to.

Page 6: Notes of attorney James Smith's telephone call with Leo Damore on March 31, 1993

Page 6: Transcription

(6.)   31 Mar '93

Standard CIA Procedure
   guy + woman on Path . . . .
" X "
         └ spotter etc . etc . . . etc. "
Leo thinks this guy had 1 or 2 [spotters]
My moment of Truth –   – .

Page 6 Discussion

Smith again records the date of the telephone call as "31 Mar 93."

The setup for the murder, Mitchell told Damore, was "standard CIA procedure"—implicitly confirming that there were a number of people involved in the operation. This very likely meant that the operation was radio-controlled with a command center somewhere in the vicinity of the murder.

"Mitchell" then revealed that the young couple walking on the towpath that morning, who police officer Roderick Sylvis had briefly questioned but neglected to ask for identification, were "spotters" ("guy + woman on path . . .") for the operation. They were keeping tabs on where Mary Meyer was in the course of her walk along the towpath. Leo told Smith that he "thinks this guy had 1 or 2" spotters working directly with him.

The call ends with Damore telling Smith that he believes he has finally come to "my moment of truth" after finally locating "Mitchell" and having this conversation.

"The guy [William L. Mitchell] opened up and confessed to Leo," Smith told me in 2004. "He knew Leo had the capacity to be fair and accurate, and this guy "Mitchell" didn't want to be another patsy like Oswald. I can remember Leo telling me that. He [Mitchell] didn't want to be the fall guy in history."[4]

---

4   Author interview with James H. Smith, Esq. April 7, 2004.

Appendix 4:
Ben Bradlee's 1952 Rosenberg Case Press Liaison with the CIA

Office Memorandum • UNITED STATES GOVERNMENT

TO   MR. LANE   DATE: 12/13/52

FROM   MR. MARAN

SUBJECT: Rosenberg case —

Press

On December 13, 1952 a Mr. Benjamin Bradley called and informed me that he was an Attache with the American Embassy in Paris, that he had left Paris last night and arrived here this morning. He advised me that he was a former Federal Court Reporter for the Washington Post and that he was sent here to look at the Rosenberg file in order to answer the Communist propoganda about the Rosenberg case in the Paris newspapers.

He advised me that it was an urgent matter and that he had to return to Paris Monday night. He further advised that he was sent here by Robert Thayer, who is the head of the C.I.A. in Paris. His 'phone number here was Rhinelander 4-2595.

After conferring with you I advised Mr. Bradley that before we could allow him to examine the file in the Rosenberg case, we would have to get clearance from the Department of Justice in Washington.

He stated that he was supposed to have been met by a representative of the C.I.A. at the airport but missed connections.

He has been trying to get in touch with Allen Dulles but has been unable to do so. I advised him to call the State Department in Washington, and to have them get the Department of Justice in Washington to get clearance for us to allow him to look at the Rosenberg file.

Mr. Bradley advised me that he would probably call you first to find out if he could look at the matters in the file which were public record, and if not would follow my suggestion about calling the C.I.A. or the State Department in Washington.

12/13/52

Mr. Bradlee displayed his credentials and desired to look thru the original public record of the trial. Mr. Maran brought it up. Sam Bradlee worked on the record from 2:30 — 6:30 night.

450

Appendix 4:
Ben Bradlee's 1952 Rosenberg Case Press Liaison with the CIA

(Transcribed)

[Mr. Maran, an assistant prosecutor on the Rosenberg case, informs assistant U.S. attorney Myles Lane that Benjamin Bradlee says he is on a CIA assignment to answer Communist propaganda.]

Office Memorandum . United States Government

Date: 12/13/52

To: MR. LANE

From: MR. MARAN

Subject: Rosenberg case

On December 13, 1952 a Mr. Benjamin Bradlee called and informed me that he was Press Attache with the American embassy in Paris, that he had left Paris last night and arrived here this morning. He advised me that he was a former Federal Court Reporter for the Washington Post and that he was sent here to look at the Rosenberg file in order to answer the Communist propaganda about the Rosenberg case in the Paris newspapers.

He advised me that it was an urgent matter and that he had to return to Paris Monday night. He further advised that he was sent here by Robert Thayer, who is the head of the C.I.A. in Paris. His phone number here was Rhinelander 4-2595.

After conferring with you I advised Mr. Bradlee that before we could allow him to examine the file in the Rosenberg case, we would have to get clearance from the Department of Justice in Washington.

He stated that he was supposed to have been met by a representative of the C.I.A. at the airport but missed connections.

He has been trying to get in touch with Allen Dulles but has been unable to do so. I advised him to call the State Department in Washington, and to have them get the Department of Justice in Washington to get clearance for us to allow him to look at the Rosenberg file.

Mr. Bradley advised me that he would probably call you first to find out if he could look at the matters in the file which were public record, and if not would follow my suggestion about calling the C.I.A. or the State Department in Washington.

[Handwritten addendum:]
12/13/52
Mr. Bradlee displayed his credentials and desired to look thru the official public record of the trial. Mr. Maran brought it up. Mr. Bradlee worked on the record from 2:30 - 6:30.

NOTES

Prologue

1. Erik Hedegaard, "The Last Confessions of E. Howard Hunt," *Rolling Stone*, April 5, 2007.

2. This entire section was based on a collection of notes over a period of nearly twenty years that I began writing in the early 1970s. As a training clinical psychologist, it was part of my orientation to begin an intensive period of personal psychotherapy that lasted a number of years. All of the vivid recollections in this chapter were based on memories that had been elicited, and noted, in various psychotherapeutic encounters.

3. In the fall of 1966, New Orleans district attorney Jim Garrison reopened his investigation into the Kennedy assassination, after having made the mistake of turning over his earlier investigation to the FBI, which did nothing. Within days after Dallas, Garrison had arrested David Ferrie as a possible associate of Lee Harvey Oswald's. Further convinced that Oswald could never have acted alone, Garrison soon widened his net to include Guy Banister and Clay Shaw.

    In March 1967, Garrison arrested Clay Shaw for conspiring to assassinate President Kennedy. Shaw's trial would not begin until January 1969, but in the spring of 1968, after having been undermined by *Life* magazine, Garrison visited with *Look* magazine's managing editor, William ("Bill") Attwood, who had been a Princeton classmate of my father's. Garrison, according to author Joan Mellen, "outlined his investigation through lunch, dinner, and into the night." Attwood became so impressed with what Garrison had discovered that he called his friend Bobby Kennedy "at one in the morning." *Look* was prepared to do a major feature story on the Garrison investigation, but Attwood unexpectedly suffered a significant heart attack, and the article never materialized. See Joan Mellen, *A Farewell to Justice* (Dulles, Va.: Potomac Books, 2005), p. 259.

Introduction

1. David S. Lifton, *Best Evidence: Disguise and Deception in the Assassination of John F. Kennedy* (New York: Dell, 1982). See also Douglas P. Horne, *Inside the Assassination Records Review Board: The U.S. Government's Final Attempt to Reconcile the Conflicting Medical Evidence in the Assassination of JFK.*, 5 vols. (printed by author, 2009).

2. Joan Mellen, *A Farewell to Justice* (Dulles, Va.: Potomac Books, 2005), pp. 383–384. Mellen further discussed and confirmed this event in an interview by this author on November 19, 2006.

3. Gaeton Fonzi, *The Last Investigation* (New York: Thunder's Mouth Press, 1993), p. 31; Gaeton Fonzi, interview by the author, February 24, 2010.

4. David Talbot, *Brothers: The Hidden History of the Kennedy Years* (New York: Free Press, 2007), p. 381. See also, Anthony Summers, *Conspiracy* (New York: Paragon House, 1989), pp. 143–149. That Lee Harvey Oswald was part of a 1959 false defection program administered through the Office of Naval Intelligence (ONI) in Nags Head, North Carolina, was first discussed in an interview that Summers conducted with former CIA officer Victor Marchetti, who later confirmed this account in an interview by this author on October 4, 2007. According to author Joan Mellen, the ONI program was overseen by the CIA's counterintelligence chief, James Jesus Angleton. Upon Oswald's return to the U.S. in 1962, he was, in fact, "debriefed" by a CIA officer named Aldrin ("Andy") Anderson. The debriefing report was read by CIA officer Donald Deneselya, who confirmed this in an interview for this book on May 25, 2007, as well as in the 1993 PBS *Frontline* program, "Who Was Lee Harvey Oswald?"

5. Ibid. David Talbot, *Brothers: The Hidden History of the Kennedy Years* (New York: Free Press, 2007), p. 381.

6. L. Fletcher Prouty, *JFK: The CIA, Vietnam, and the Plot to Assassinate John F. Kennedy* (New York: Citadel, 1996), p. 81.

7. Ibid., p. xxii.

8. Martin Duberman, *Waiting to Land: A (Mostly) Political Memoir, 1985–2008* (New York: New Press, 2009), p. 288.

9. David Brooks, "Bookshorts: Kennedy's Big Mess; Savitch's Sad Life," *Wall Street Journal*, August 16, 1988, p. 26.

10. Gale Reference Team, "Biography: Damore, Leo J. (1929–1995)," *Contemporary Authors* (Farmington Hills, Mich.: Thompson Gale, 2004).

11. Francis I. Broadhurst, "A Refreshing View of Kennedy," *Cape Cod Times*, November 18, 1993.

12. Letter from Seymour Hersh to Mark O'Blazney, November 1, 1995.

13. Ibid.

14. James H. Smith, Esq. interview by the author, April 6, 2004. Smith recounted verbatim the conversation with his friend John H. Davis.

Chapter 1. *Fate's Engagement*

1. Mary Pinchot, "Requiem," *New York Times*, January 25, 1940, p. 16. The poem was a tribute to her half-sister Rosamond Pinchot, who committed suicide in 1938.

2. The nature of Mary Meyer's involvement with President Kennedy and their mutual concern with world peace initiatives, away from the Cold War, is the focus of this book and will be demonstrated throughout. Significant support for this perspective came from former presidential adviser Kenneth P. O'Donnell's extensive interviews with the late author Leo Damore, shortly before O'Donnell's death, as well as other sources and interviews with Damore. The most recent account of Mary Meyer's influence in the Kennedy White House was provided by David Talbot in his book *Brothers: The Hidden History of the Kennedy Years* (New York: Free Press, 2007).

3. James McConnell Truitt, letter to author Deborah Davis, dated May 11, 1979. The letter was part of the files of the late author Leo Damore, and was confirmed by author Deborah Davis in 2005.

4. Mary Meyer's intention to go public with her revelations about the CIA's involvement in the Kennedy assassination has been documented in a number of sources. It was revealed, according to author Leo Damore, in Mary's real diary, which Damore finally obtained and described in detail to his attorney, James H. Smith, Esq., on March 31, 1993 (see Appendix 3). Mary Meyer's awareness of CIA involvement in the Kennedy assassination is also alluded to by Robert Morrow in his book *First Hand*

Knowledge: How I Participated in the CIA-Mafia Murder of President Kennedy (New York: S.P.I. Books, 1992), 275–280, and in two transcripts of alleged conversations between CIA covert action specialist Robert T. Crowley and author Gregory Douglas on January 27, 1996, and April 2, 1996. The mutually reinforcing effect of these sources, and the way in which they aggregate, establish Mary Meyer's intention to go public (after the Warren Report's release in September) with all that she had discovered throughout the year of 1964, are discussed in greater detail in chapters 11, 12, and 13 and the Epilogue.

5. Leslie Judd Ahlander, "Frederick Drawings Exhibited," *Washington Post*, November 24, 1963, p. G10.

6. Leo Damore, interview by the author, Centerbrook, Conn., February 1992. Between 1992 and 1994, there were at least five face-to-face meetings between Damore and this author, in addition to numerous follow-up telephone conversations regarding the life of Mary Meyer, her death, and Damore's research. Damore stated that Mary Meyer had sought out Bill Walton's counsel in early 1964.

7. See note 4 above. Leo Damore, who had acquired a copy of Mary Meyer's real diary, told his attorney, James E. Smith, on March 31, 1993, that Mary had made a decision to go public with what she had discovered, sometime after the Warren Report had been released. See Appendix 3. Chapters 11, 12, and 13 also cover this arena thoroughly.

8. Ron Rosenbaum and Phillip Nobile, "The Curious Aftermath of JFK's Best and Brightest Affair," *New Times*, July 9, 1976, p. 29. "Mary Meyer was accustomed to leaving her diary in the bookcase in her bedroom where, incidentally, she kept clippings of the JFK assassination." In 1976, the authors interviewed some of the people closest to Mary Meyer who had intimate knowledge of her habits during the last year of her life. In addition, according to Leo Damore, Mary also talked with presidential adviser Kenneth P. O'Donnell shortly after the Kennedy assassination. See note 2 above.

9. Nina Burleigh, *A Very Private Woman: The Life and Unsolved Murder of Presidential Mistress Mary Meyer* (New York: Bantam, 1998), p. 304.

10. Anne and James Truitt had moved to Tokyo shortly after Anne's sculpture exhibit *Black, White, and Grey* opened in January 1964 at the Wadsworth

Atheneum in Hartford, Connecticut. Her husband, James, was Japan's bureau chief for *Newsweek*.

11. Morrow, *First Hand Knowledge*, p. 277. As noted in note 4 above, this event was also mentioned by former CIA official Robert T. Crowley in a conversation to author Gregory Douglas in January 1996. See Chapter 13 for further discussion of the way in which these sources are mutually corroborating.

12. Leo Damore revealed Mary Meyer's altercation with Cord Meyer to his attorney, James H. Smith, Esq., during the above-referenced telephone call of March 31, 1993. Smith took six pages of notes on this call, which are reproduced in Appendix 3.

13. Confidential source who asked to remain anonymous, interview with the author, Washington, D.C., March 10, 2006.

14. Rosenbaum and Nobile, "Curious Aftermath," p. 22.

15. I am indebted to award-winning Boston fine artist Shelah Horvitz for her insightful analysis of some of the last paintings of Mary Pinchot Meyer, as well as Horvitz's overall knowledge of the Washington Color School artists.

16. Rosenbaum and Nobile, "Curious Aftermath," p. 22. Part of this description was based on the authors' interviews with principals in 1976, as well as the clothing Mary Meyer wore that day, which was documented in the trial transcript, United States of America v. Ray Crump, Jr., Defendant, Criminal Case No. 930-64, United States District Court for the District of Columbia, Washington, D.C., July 20, 1965. Volume 1: pp. 4-7.

17. Burton Hersh, *The American Elite and the Origins of the CIA* (New York: Scribner, 1992), p. 439.

18. Burleigh, A *Very Private Woman*, p. 11.

19. Damore, interview.

20. Ibid. According to Damore, Kenny O'Donnell had shared with him that Mary Meyer had pushed hard for President Kennedy to protect the Chesapeake and Ohio Canal towpath area.

21. Herbert S. Parmet, *JFK: The Presidency of John F. Kennedy* (New York: Dial, 1983), p. 306. In addition, Leo Damore said he had interviewed

Mr. Parmet, who gave him a number of other details about what he had learned about Jack's relationship with Mary Meyer.

22. Bernie Ward and Granville Toogood, "Former Vice President of Washington Post Reveals JFK 2-Year White House Romance," *National Enquirer*, March 2, 1976, p. 4. In addition, Leo Damore had interviewed an anonymous source who was a close friend of Mary Meyer's who gave him more details about this encounter, which he discussed with me in 1992.

23. Ibid. Ward and Toogood, *National Enquirer*, March 2, 1976, p. 4. Damore interview with anonymous source, as with me in 1992.

24. The extent of John F. Kennedy's difficulty with emotional intimacy, particularly with women, has been well documented in the following: Nigel Hamilton, *JFK: Reckless Youth* (New York: Random House, 1992), and two books by Ralph G. Martin: *A Hero for Our Time: An Intimate Story of the Kennedy Years* (New York: Macmillan, 1983) and *Seeds of Destruction: Joe Kennedy and His Sons* (New York: G. P. Putnam's Sons, 1995). In addition, presidential historian Robert Dallek's *An Unfinished Life: John F. Kennedy, 1917–1963* (Boston: Little, Brown, 2003) further documents this arena thoroughly, as does Doris Kearns Goodwin's *The Fitzgeralds and the Kennedys* (New York: St. Martin's, 1987). All five volumes address John Kennedy's emotional maternal deprivation and the toll it took on him. President Kennedy's sexual addiction and reckless philandering is further documented by Seymour Hersh's *The Dark Side of Camelot* (New York: Back Bay Books, 1997). See also chapter 6 for further discussion.

25. Anne Truitt, *Daybook: The Journal of an Artist* (New York: Pantheon, 1982), p. 165.

26. Parmet, *JFK*, p. 306.

27. Burleigh, *A Very Private Woman*, p. 226.

28. See Chapter 8. Mary Meyer's initial foray into psychedelics, according to James Truitt, appears to have taken place in the San Francisco Bay area during a late-1950s visit with Jim Truitt and his wife, Anne. Deborah Davis, interview by Leo Damore, February 23, 1991; Deborah Davis, interview by the author, March 17, 2009. During Davis's research for her book *Katharine the Great* in 1976, she traveled to Mexico to interview Jim Truitt for more than ten hours over a three-day period. The two then corresponded further by mail. Nina Burleigh also references the likelihood

of Jim Truitt's influence for "Mary's initiation into drug experimentation." See Burleigh, *A Very Private Woman*, pp. 171–172).

29. During his never-before-published two-hour interview by Leo Damore on November 7, 1990, Timothy Leary commented extensively on Mary Meyer's experience with psychedelics and the impact it had on her worldview and in her life. Timothy Leary, interview by Leo Damore, Washington, D.C., November 7, 1990. See also Chapters 8 and 9.

30. Timothy Leary, *Flashbacks: An Autobiography* (Los Angeles: J. P. Tarcher, 1983), p. 129. Also, during his 1990 interview with Leo Damore, Leary spoke at some length about how Mary Meyer defined her mission with psychedelics. See chapter 9.

31. Leary, interview. See also Leary, *Flashbacks*, p. 156.

32. Ward and Toogood, "White House Romance," p. 4; Damore, interview. Damore repeatedly stressed that Mary Meyer had been in large measure "a healer" in Kennedy's tortured emotional life. Some of Damore's insight had been based on his talks with Kenny O'Donnell regarding Mary Meyer's influence on the president.

33. Leary, *Flashbacks*, p. 191.

34. Ibid., p. 162. In addition, since the first edition (1979) of Deborah Davis's *Katharine the Great* (which was recalled and shredded due to pressure from Ben Bradlee and Katharine Graham), there has been controversy over whether Phil Graham actually mentioned during his infamous "meltdown" in Phoenix at a newspaper convention in January 1963 the fact that Mary Meyer was having an affair with President Kennedy. Carol Felsenthal, whose 1993 book *Power, Privilege and the Post* was thoroughly checked and vetted, maintains that Phil Graham did, in fact, reveal the affair during his drunken tirade. In an interview for this book, Ms. Felsenthal stated the following: "Because of what happened to the Deborah Davis book, my book was vetted and re-vetted. I would never have been able to get away with something that wasn't thoroughly checked." In addition, Felsenthal also revealed that Ben Bradlee "told a journalism class at USC that he had read every entry [in the Felsenthal book] and he thought it was fair." Carol Felsenthal, interview by the author, August 10, 2010.

35. In an interview Nina Burleigh conducted with CIA wife Joanne ("Joan") Bross, Ms. Bross stated that James Angleton bragged on more than one

occasion that he had wiretapped Mary Meyer's telephone and bugged her bedroom. See Burleigh, *A Very Private Woman* 18, pp. 124–125. In addition, during Leo Damore's above-mentioned telephone call to his attorney, James H. Smith, Esq., on March 31, 1993, Damore said that he had just talked for several hours with "William L. Mitchell," who confessed to being part of a surveillance team assigned to Mary Meyer around the time of the Warren Report's release to the public in September 1964.

36. Rosenbaum and Nobile, "Curious Aftermath," p. 29.

37. The description of the final seconds of Mary Meyer's life and what occurred at the scene of her death was outlined in detail in prosecuting attorney Alfred Hantman's fifteen-page opening statement at the trial of Ray Crump, Jr. in July 1965. See trial transcript, United States of America v. Ray Crump, Jr., Defendant, Criminal Case No. 930-64, United States District Court for the District of Columbia, Washington, D.C., July 20, 1965, Vol. l: pp. 2–17.

38. According to the 1965 trial testimony of Dr. Linwood Rayford, the deputy coroner, the second shot was placed over Mary Meyer's right shoulder blade, "angling from right to left and slightly downward," where its trajectory would traverse the chest cavity, "perforating the right lung and the aorta . . ." Trial transcript, pp. 71–72. In 1991, Dr. Rayford told Leo Damore that "whoever assaulted this woman intended to kill her." Dr. Linwood L. Rayford, interview by Leo Damore, Washington, D.C., February 19, 1991.

Chapter 2. *Murder on the Towpath*

1. Henry Wiggins Jr., interview by Leo Damore, Washington, D.C., April 2, 1992.

2. Trial transcript, United States of America v. Ray Crump, Jr., Defendant, Criminal Case No. 930-64, United States District Court for the District of Columbia, Washington, D.C., July 20. 1965, pp. 132–133, 293.

3. Ibid., p. 240–241.

4. Ibid., p. 240–241, p. 246.

5. Ibid., pp. 133–137; Henry Wiggins Jr., interview by Leo Damore, Washington, D.C., April 2, 1992.

6. Trial transcript, pp. 262, p. 264.

7. Ibid., p. 218.

8. Ibid., p. 240, p. 248.

9. Ibid., p. 343; p. 345.

10. Ibid., p. 352; Roderick Sylvis, interview by the author, Wake Forest, North Carolina, July 23, 2008.

11. Trial transcript, p. 354.

12. Ibid., pp. 348–349.

13. Wiggins interview.

14. Trial transcript, p. 452.

15. Rosenbaum, Ron and Phillip Nobile, "The Curious Aftermath of JFK's Best and Brightest Affair," *New Times,* July 9, 1976, p. 24.

16. Trial transcript, pp. 232–265. Henry Wiggins reiterated his account several times throughout the trial.

17. Ibid., p. 359.

18. Ibid., p. 361.

19. Ibid., p. 381.

20. Ibid., p. 370.

21. Ibid., p. 407, p. 413. Byers told prosecuting attorney Alfred Hantman that it had been "[a]bout 1:00 o'clock or a little after" when he got the radio request to look for the jacket and cap (407). Under cross-examination by defense attorney Dovey Roundtree, he reiterated that it was "approximately 1:00 o'clock" when he received his instructions to look for the jacket (p. 413).

22. Ibid., p. 419.

23. Ibid., p. 67.

24. Ibid., p. 710.

25. Ibid., p. 254.

26. Unnamed colleague of Detective Bernard Crooke, interview by Leo Damore, Washington, D.C., October 28, 1990.

27. Ibid.

28. Rosenbaum and Nobile., "Curious Aftermath," p. 24.

29. Wiggins, interview.

30. Ibid.

31. Ibid.

32. Ibid.

33. Ibid.

34. Ibid.

35. Trial transcript, pp. 455–456.

36. Ibid., p. 634.

37. George Peter Lamb, interview by Leo Damore, Washington, D.C., December 20, 1990.

38. Ibid.

39. Ibid.

40. Ibid.

41. Ibid.

42. "Laborer Is Charged in Slaying of Artist; Mrs. Meyer Shot to Death on Towpath," *Evening Star*, October 13, 1964, p. B-1.

43. Ibid.

44. Ibid.

45. Dr. Linwood L. Rayford, interview by Leo Damore, Washington, D.C., February 19, 1991.

46. Ibid.

47. Trial transcript, pp. 71–75.

48. Ibid., pp. 71–72.

49. Ibid., pp. 71–75.

50. Rayford, interview.

51. Although Detective Edwin Coppage testified at the trial that the gloves were removed at the murder scene by Detective Bernie Crooke, Dr. Rayford testified that he remembered the victim had been wearing the gloves at the murder scene. Trial transcript, p. 67, p. 79, p. 81, p. 90, p. 669. Crooke had already left the murder scene with Ray Crump

before Rayford arrived at approximately 2:00 P.M. Rayford, interview. Rayford specifically remembered that the gloves were removed at the autopsy and given to Crooke after 3:45 P.M on the day of the murder.

52. Dovey Roundtree, interviews by Leo Damore, 1990–1993. During these interviews, Dovey Roundtree shared numerous documents relating to her defense of Ray Crump, including the account given to her by Robert Woolright the morning he came to pick up Crump for work.

53. Ibid. In a discussion with Leo Damore regarding the testimony of Elsie Perkins, Dovey Roundtree mentioned that Crump's jacket had been a Father's Day present given to him by his wife, Helena, and their children the preceding June. See also the testimony of Elsie Perkins, trial transcript, pp. 485–507.

54. Trial transcript, p. 468, pp. 485–507.

55. Ibid., p. 486.

56. Ibid., pp. 467–505. Also, Dovey Roundtree told Leo Damore during several interviews that no one in Ray Crump's family, church community, or anyone she interviewed ever recalled Ray Crump with a firearm of any kind. Ray's brother, Jimmy Crump, had at one time years earlier owned a .22-caliber rifle, but that was the extent of any firearm noted in Crump's immediate and extended family.

57. Trial transcript, pp. 43–47.

58. "Woman Shot Dead on Tow Path," *Evening Star*, Washington, D.C., October 12, 1964, p. A-1.

59. Alfred E. Lewis and Richard Corrigan, "Suspect Seized in Canal Slaying; Woman Dies in Robbery on Towpath," *Washington Post*, October 13, 1964, p. A-1.

60. "Laborer Is Charged," p. A-1.

61. Ben A. Franklin, "Woman Painter Shot and Killed on Canal Towpath in Capital," *New York Times*, October 14, 1964.

62. Trial transcript, pp. 438–449.

63. Report of the FBI Laboratory, Federal Bureau of Investigation, Washington, D.C., October 16, 1964, addressed to Mr. Robert V. Murray, Chief, Metropolitan Police Department, Washington, D.C., DB 72000, HO.64.2623, pp. 1–4. See Appendix 1.

64. "Rape Weighed as Motive in Death of Mrs. Meyer," *Evening Star*, October 14, 1964, Metro sec., p. B-1.

65. "Meyer Slaying—Police Have 'Mystery' Witness," *Washington Daily News*, October 14, 1964.

Chapter 3. *Conspiracy to Conceal*

1. Leo Damore, interview by the author, Centerbrook, Conn., February 1992. During this interview, Damore revealed many of the details that Kenneth O'Donnell had shared with him about what had taken place between Mary Meyer and President Kennedy during the dedication of the Pinchot Institute for Conservation at Grey Towers on September 24, 1963.

2. Nina Burleigh, *A Very Private Woman: The Life and Unsolved Murder of Presidential Mistress Mary Meyer* (New York: Bantam, 1998), pp. 16–25.

3. Alfred E. Lewis and Richard Corrigan, "Suspect Seized in Canal Slaying; Woman Dies in Robbery on Towpath," *Washington Post*, October 13, 1964, p. A-1.

4. Susan Fletcher Witzell, "Gardeners and Caretakers of Woods Hole," *Spritsail: A Journal of the History of Falmouth and Vicinity* (Woods Hole, Mass.: Woods Hole Historical Collection) 19, no. 2 (Summer 2005): p. 31.

5. Bishop Paul Moore, interview by Leo Damore, February 5, 1991.

6. Ibid.

7. "Bishop at Meyer Rites Asks Prayer for Killer," *Evening Star*, October 15, 1964, p. B2.

8. Ibid.

9. Moore, interview.

10. Joseph J. Trento, *The Secret History of the CIA* (Roseville, Calif.: Prima, 2001), p. 282.

11. Moore, interview.

12. Bernie Ward and Granville Toogood, "Former Vice President of Washington Post Reveals JFK 2-Year White House Romance," *National Enquirer*, March 2, 1976, p. 4.

13. Ron Rosenbaum and Phillip Nobile, "The Curious Aftermath of JFK's Best and Brightest Affair," *New Times*, July 9, 1976, p. 33.

14. Ibid., p. 22.

15. Burleigh, *A Very Private Woman*, p. 244.

16. Ben Bradlee, *A Good Life: Newspapering and Other Adventures* (New York: Simon & Schuster, 1995), 266.

17. Trial transcript, United States of America v. Ray Crump, Jr., Defendant, Criminal Case No. 930-64, United States District Court for the District of Columbia, Washington, D.C., July 20. 1965, p. 43.

18. Rosenbaum and Nobile, "Curious Aftermath," p. 32.

19. Bradlee, *Good Life*, 266; Ben Bradlee, interview by the author, Washington, D.C., January 31, 2007.

20. Testimony of Ben Bradlee, trial transcript, p. 43.

21. Bradlee, *Good Life*, pp. 266–267.

22. Rosenbaum and Nobile, "Curious Aftermath," p. 33.

23. Ibid., p. 32.

24. Ibid., p. 29.

25. Ibid.

26. James DiEugenio, "The Posthumous Assassination of John F. Kennedy," in *The Assassinations: Probe Magazine on JFK, MLK, RFK, and Malcolm X*, ed. James DiEugenio and Lisa Pease (Los Angeles: Feral House, 2003), pp. 339–345.

27. Rosenbaum and Nobile, "Curious Aftermath," p. 29.

28. Ward and Toogood, "White House Romance," p. 4.

29. Bradlee, *Good Life*, p. 267.

30. Rosenbaum and Nobile, "Curious Aftermath," p. 32.

31. Trial transcript, pp. 46–47.

32. Cicely D'Autremont Angleton and Anne Truitt, "In Angleton's Custody," letter to the editor, *New York Times Book Review*, November 5, 1995.

33. Ibid. This was further confirmed by the account that Tony Bradlee gave to author Sally Bedell Smith. See: Sally Bedell Smith, *Grace and Power: The Private World of the Kennedy White House* (New York: Random House, 2004), p. 286.

34. William Safire, "Editor's Notes," *New York Times*, October 1, 1995.

35. Tom Mangold, *Cold Warrior: James Jesus Angleton; The CIA's Master Spy Hunter* (New York: Simon & Schuster, 1991), pp. 327–330; Trento, *Secret History*, pp. 410–411; Newton "Scotty" Miler, interview by the author, February 15, 2005. All three of these sources attest to the fact that Angleton kept a voluminous set of files in a number of different safes at CIA headquarters in Langley, Virginia. Scotty Miler became Angleton's chief of operations and was part of Angleton's elite unit known as the Special Investigations Group (CI/SIG). He mentioned several times that Angleton never destroyed any file or document. "He kept everything," said Miler.

36. Adam Bernstein, "Antoinette Pinchot Bradlee, Former Wife of Prominent Washington Post Executive Editor Benjamin C. Bradlee, Dies at 87," *Washington Post*, November 14, 2011.

37. Letter to the editor, "The Angleton Children Tell Their Side," *Washington Post*, December 2, 2011.

38. Rosenbaum and Nobile, "Curious Aftermath," p. 33.

39. Sally Bedell Smith, *Grace and Power: The Private World of the Kennedy White House* (New York: Random House, 2004), p. 286. Also, in an email to this author on July 27, 2010, author Sally Bedell Smith said she had conducted an extensive interview with Tony Bradlee in January 2001 and a follow-up in September 2001.

40. Ibid. According to author Sally Bedell Smith, "After James Truitt's interviews with the *National Enquirer*, Tony decided to destroy the diary. She called Anne Truitt (by then divorced from James), who lived across the street in Washington, and they watched the notebook burn in Tony's fireplace." p. 286.

41. Bradlee, interview.

42. Bradlee, *Good Life*, pp. 269-270.

43. Ibid., p. 268.

44. Bradlee, interview.

45. Sally Bedell Smith, *Grace and Power: The Private World of the Kennedy White House* (New York: Random House, 2004), p. 286.

46. Ibid.

47. Rosenbaum and Nobile, "Curious Aftermath," p. 33.

48. Smith, *Grace and Power*, p. 286.

49. Timothy Leary, *Flashbacks: An Autobiography* (Los Angeles: J. P. Tarcher, 1983), p. 194.

50. Nancy Pittman Pinchot, interview by the author, November 18, 2009. According to Ms. Pinchot, a niece of Mary Meyer's, this diary still exists somewhere in Milford, Pennsylvania. It contained an account of Mary's struggle with her father Amos's deteriorating mental condition, subsequent to his daughter Rosamund's suicide, as well as at least one other relationship with a man Mary Meyer was involved with at the time, in addition to William Attwood. This particular diary was also read and referenced by Bibi Gaston in *The Loveliest Woman in America* (New York: William Morrow, 2008). Because of the nature of my book, the Meyer-Pinchot family denied me access to this earlier diary of Mary Meyer's.

51. Rosenbaum and Nobile, "Curious Aftermath," p. 29.

52. Evelyn Patterson Truitt, letter to Anthony Summers, March 10, 1983. The letter was shared with this author by Anthony Summers.

53. Jefferson Morley, *Our Man in Mexico: Winston Scott and the Hidden History of the CIA* (Lawrence: University Press of Kansas, 2008). pp. 277-283. In addition, U.S. Ambassador to Mexico Thomas Mann told author Dick Russell that he "always suspected that he [Win Scott] might have been murdered . . . When you get involved in that sort of thing [the CIA and the world of intelligence], one is not surprised, if you know that world, when people drop dead real quick." Russell also interviewed Winston Scott's son, Michael, who told Russell that an ex-CIA colleague of his father's had confided that "certain people" had come by to see Win when he was bedridden after his backyard fall, which everyone believed had precipitated his death. This CIA source, according to Michael Scott, "had expressed strong doubt that his [Win Scott's] death was an accident." Michael Scott then added, "I was told that James Angleton was on a plane to Mexico within an hour of my dad's death, so quickly that he carried no visa or passport and was held for a while at customs. He finally arrived pretending to be there for my father's funeral. But he had really come to get his files." (Dick Russell, *The Man Who Knew Too Much* (New York: Carroll & Graf Publishers, 2003. pp. 295-297).

54. Leary, *Flashbacks*, p. 194.

55. Rosenbaum and Nobile, "Curious Aftermath," p. 22.

56. Ibid. p. 29.

57. Alexandra Truitt, interview by the author, October 11, 2005.

58. Timothy Leary, interview by Leo Damore, Washington, D.C., November 7, 1990.

59. Carol Felsenthal, *Power, Privilege and the Post: The Katharine Graham Story* (New York: Seven Stories Press, 1993), p. 198n.

60. Cord Meyer Jr., *Facing Reality: From World Federalism to the CIA* (New York: Harper & Row, 1980), p. 143.

Chapter 4. *Deus Ex Machina*

1. "History, Hume, and the Press," Letter to John Norvell Washington, dated June 14, 1807, *The Letters of Thomas Jefferson: 1743–1826.* (Located at the University of Virginia Electronic Text Center). See the following: http://etext.virginia.edu/toc/modeng/public/JefLett.html

2. George Peter Lamb, interview by Leo Damore, May 23, 1991.

3. Katie McCabe, "She Had a Dream," *Washingtonian*, March 2002, pp. 52–60, pp. 124–130.

4. Ibid., p. 55.

5. Ibid., p. 56.

6. Ibid., p. 55.

7. Ibid., p. 56.

8. Ibid., p. 60.

9. Ibid., pp. 57–58.

10. Katie McCabe and Dovey Johnson Roundtree, *Justice Older Than the Law: The Life of Dovey Johnson Roundtree* (Jackson: University Press of Mississippi, 2009), p. 90.

11. McCabe, "She Had a Dream." p. 60.

12. Dovey Roundtree, interview by Leo Damore, Washington, D.C., November 4, 1990.

13. Ibid.

14. The fact that Ray Crump had been with a girlfriend named Vivian on the towpath at the time of Mary Meyer's murder was revealed to attorney Dovey Roundtree by both Ray Crump himself and by his mother,

Martha Crump. Dovey Roundtree, interview by Leo Damore, Washington, D.C., April 4, 1992. See also McCabe and Roundtree, *Justice Older Than the Law*, pp. 195.

15. Dovey Roundtree, interview by Leo Damore, Washington, D.C., April 4, 1992.

16. Ibid.

17. Ibid.

18. Ibid.

19. Ibid.; Dovey Roundtree, interviews by Leo Damore, Washington, D.C., February 23, 1991, and April 4, 1992. Roundtree's conversations with the woman named Vivian are also covered in some detail in *Justice Older Than the Law*, pp. 195–196.

20. Roundtree, interview, February 23, 1991.

21. Roundtree, interview, November 4, 1990.

22. Ibid.

23. The distances mentioned were taken from the trial transcript, United States of America v. Ray Crump, Jr., Defendant, Criminal Case No. 930-64, United States District Court for the District of Columbia, Washington, D.C., July 20, 1965, p. 119, pp. 710–711. The distances were measured again by the author on February 6, 2008, using GPS portable technology and found to be accurate within ten feet.

24. U.S. Park Police officer Ray Pollan, interview by Leo Damore, Washington, D.C., December 19, 1990.

25. Lamb, interview, May 23, 1991.

26. Ibid.

27. Crump v. Anderson, June 15, 1965, 122 U.S. App. D.C., 352 F.2d 649 (D.C. Cir. 1965). Circuit Judge George Thomas Washington pointed this out in his dissent during Crump's appeal for a writ of habeas corpus, which was denied.

28. Trial transcript., p. 710.

29. Blue v. United States of America, 342 F.2d 894 (D.C. Cir. 1964), p. 900. The case was argued on May 18, 1964, and decided on October 29, 1964.

30. Lamb, interview, May 23, 1991.

31. George Peter Lamb, interview by the author, May 12, 2010.

32. U.S. v. Ray Crump, Jr., U.S. District Court for the District of Columbia, Criminal No. 930- 64. CJ# 1317-64. "The Clerk of said Court will please enter the appearance of Dovey J. Roundtree and George F. Knox, Sr. as attorneys for defendant in the above entitled cause." George Peter Lamb and the Legal Aid Association withdrew from the Crump case on November 3, 1964.

33. Lamb, interview, May 23, 1991.

34. Roundtree, interview, November 4, 1990.

35. Ibid.; Dovey Roundtree, interviews by Leo Damore, Washington, D.C., September 26, 1990, May 25, 1991, and April 4, 1992. In each of the interviews, Roundtree made it clear that her client, Ray Crump, was deteriorating mentally soon after entering his plea. She continued to believe that he was being abused by prison guards, in spite of daily visits from her and his family.

36. McCabe and Roundtree, *Justice Older Than the Law*, p. 193.

37. Ibid.

38. *U.S. v. Ray Crump, Jr.*, United States District Court For The District of Columbia. Criminal No. 930-64. *Motion for Mental Examination*. Filed November 12, 1964. Harry M. Hull, Clerk. The motion also supports Detective Bernie Crooke's statement to Dovey Roundtree that he had smelled beer when he arrested Crump at approximately 1:15 p.m. on October 12, 1964.

39. Superintendent Dale C. Cameron, MD, Department of Health, Education, and Welfare, St. Elizabeth's Hospital, Washington, D.C., to Clerk of the Criminal Division for the United States District Court for the District of Columbia, January 13, 1965.

40. *Crump v. Anderson*, pp. 42–59. The transcript of the coroner's inquest on October 19, 1964, is no longer available.

41. Jerry Hunter, Esq., interview by Leo Damore, Washington, D.C., November 6, 1990.

42. Roundtree, interview, February 23, 1991.

43. McCabe and Roundtree, *Justice Older Than the Law*, p. 197.

44. Roundtree, interview, February 23, 1991.

45. River Patrolman police officer Frederick Q. Byers of the Harbor Patrol testified on three different occasions that he retrieved a jacket alleged to have belonged to Crump at 1:46 P.M on the afternoon of the murder. Trial transcript, p. 408, p. 409, p. 413. The distance computed to Three Sisters Island was from a GPS navigation instrument and Google Earth maps.

46. Both Wiggins and Branch would testify at the murder trial that they had no knowledge of the ownership, the work ticket, or the ultimate disposition of the stalled Nash Rambler sedan or who owned the vehicle. Trial transcript, p. 254, pp. 312–313.

47. David Acheson, interview by the author, Washington, D.C., December 10, 2008.

Chapter 5. *Trial by Fire*

1. Dovey Roundtree, interview by Leo Damore, Washington, D.C., May 25, 1991.

2. Charles Duncan, Esq., interview by Leo Damore, Washington, D.C., December 20, 1990.

3. Roundtree, interview, May 25, 1991.

4. Ibid.

5. United States Department of Justice, confidential memo addressed to "Mr. Conrad," February 24, 1965.

6. Roundtree, interview, May 25, 1991.

7. Ibid.

8. Dovey Roundtree, interview by Leo Damore, Washington, D.C., February 23, 1991.

9. Ibid.

10. Trial transcript, United States of America v. Ray Crump, Jr., Defendant, Criminal Case No. 930-64, United States District Court for the District of Columbia: Washington, D.C., July 20, 1965, p. 3.

11. Ibid., p. 4.

12. Ibid., p. 6.

13. Ibid., pp. 6–7.

14. Ibid., pp. 12–15.

15. Ibid., p. 16.

16. Dovey Roundtree, interview by Leo Damore, Washington, D.C., April 4, 1992.

17. Trial transcript, pp. 46–47.

18. Ibid.

19. Alfred Hantman, Esq., interview by Leo Damore, Washington, D.C., May 21, 1991.

20. Trial transcript, p. 47.

21. Cord Meyer Jr., *Facing Reality: From World Federalism to the CIA* (New York: Harper & Row, 1980), p. 143. Upon his return to Washington on the evening of Mary Meyer's murder, Cord Meyer was met at the airport by his former brother-in-law and Washington attorney Steuart Pittman and career CIA official Wistar Janney.

22. Trial transcript, pp. 75–76.

23. Ibid., p. 70.

24. Ibid., p. 96.

25. Ibid., p. 383.

26. Ibid., p. 575.

27. Ibid., pp. 110–112.

28. Ibid., p. 122.

29. Ibid., p. 122.

30. Ibid., p. 124.

31. Ibid., p. 140.

32. Ibid., p. 130.

33. Ibid., pp. 131–132.

34. Ibid., p. 134.

35. Ibid., p. 136.

36. Ibid., p. 710.

37. Ibid., p. 137.

38. Ibid.

39. Ibid., p. 142.

40. Ibid., p. 207.

41. Ibid., p. 208.

42. Robert S. Bennett, Esq., interview by the author, Washington, D.C., November 11, 2009.

43. Trial transcript, p. 210.

44. Ibid., pp. 237–238.

45. Ibid., p. 241.

46. Ibid., p. 306.

47. Ibid., pp. 306–307.

48. Hantman, interview.

49. The distance from the 4300 block of Canal Road at the point that was directly across from the murder scene on the towpath to Fletcher's Boat House was measured by both an automobile odometer and a GPS instrument and was found to be exactly 1.63 miles.

50. Trial transcript, p. 343.

51. Ibid., pp. 342–343.

52. Ibid., p. 352.

53. Roderick Sylvis, interview by the author, Wake Forest, N.C., July 23, 2008.

54. Ibid.

55. Trial transcript, pp. 345–347.

56. Sylvis, interview, July 23, 2008.

57. Trial transcript, p. 349.

58. Ibid., pp. 349–350.

59. Ibid., p. 350.

60. Ibid., p. 351.

61. Ibid.

62. Ibid., p. 342.

63. Sylvis, interview, July 23, 2008; Roderick Sylvis, telephone interview by the author, July 30, 2008.

64. Trial transcript, p. 359.

65. Ibid., p. 379.

66. Ibid., p. 381.

67. Ibid., p. 370.

68. Ibid., pp. 372–373.

69. Ibid., p. 378.

70. Ibid., pp. 407–413.

71. Ibid., p. 395, p. 424, p. 564.

72. Ibid., pp. 451–452.

73. Roberta Hornig, "Teacher Says He Passed by Mrs. Meyer," *Washington Evening Star*, July 27, 1965.

74. Trial transcript, p. 657.

75. Ibid., p. 634.

76. Ibid., p. 658.

77. Ibid., pp. 658-659.

78. Ibid., pp. 766–767.

79. Ibid., p. 803.

80. Katie McCabe, interview by the author, September 22, 2008. The event was also mentioned by Nina Burleigh in *A Very Private Woman: The Life and Unsolved Murder of Presidential Mistress Mary Meyer* (New York: Bantam, 1998), p. 269.

81. Trial transcript, pp. 943–944.

82. Hantman, interview.

83. Ibid.

84. Edward Savwoir, telephone interview by Leo Damore. From Damore's notes, this appears to have occurred during the winter of 1989, though it is not completely clear. Savwoir died in Washington, D.C., on June 19, 1989.

85. George Peter Lamb, interview by the author, April 28, 2010.

86. Roundtree, interview, May 25, 1991.

87. Katie McCabe and Dovey Roundtree, *Justice Older Than the Law: The Life of Dovey Johnson Roundtree* (Jackson: University Press of Mississippi,

2009), p. 218. Also, in two of author Leo Damore's interviews with Dovey Roundtree (February 23, 1991 and May 25, 1991), she expressed her belief that Ray had been repeatedly beaten, abused, and "probably raped" during his eight months in jail before trial.

88. Robert S. Bennett, *In the Ring: The Trials of a Washington Lawyer* (New York: Crown, 2008), p. 36; Bennett, interview.

89. Burleigh, *A Very Private Woman*, p. 336.

90. Ibid., p. 281.

91. Ibid., p. 275.

92. McCabe and Roundtree, *Justice Older Than the Law*, pp. 190–192.

93. Ibid., p. 218.

94. Ibid., p. 189.

95. Roundtree, interview, April 4, 1992; Dovey Roundtree, interview by Leo Damore, Washington, D.C., March 4, 1993; McCabe and Roundtree, *Justice Older Than the Law*, pp. 205–206.

Chapter 6. *"Prima Female Assoluta"*

1. Ron Rosenbaum and Phillip Nobile, "The Curious Aftermath of JFK's Best and Brightest Affair," *New Times*, July 9, 1976, p. 25.

2. Ibid., p. 33.

3. Gifford Pinchot, *Breaking New Ground* (Washington, D.C.: Island Press, 1998), p.10. In this account, Gifford noted that his grandfather Cyrille was forced to leave France for participating in a plan to free Napoléon from the island of St. Helena. Cyrille Pinchot's actions in France are also discussed in "Edgar Pinchot," in *Commemorative Biographical Record of Northeastern Pennsylvania* (Chicago: T. H. Beers, 1900), p. 277; and Alfred Mathews, *A History of Wayne, Pike and Monroe Counties, Pennsylvania* (Philadelphia: R. T. Peek, 1886), pp. 862–863.

4. Nancy P. Pittman, "James Wallace Pinchot (1831–1908): One Man's Evolution Toward Conservation in the Nineteenth Century," *Yale F&ES Centennial News* (Fall 1999): 4.

5. Char Miller, "All in the Family: The Pinchots of Milford," *Pennsylvania History* (Spring 1999): p. 126.

6. Ibid., p. 130.

7. Elaine Showalter, ed., *These Modern Women: Autobiographical Essays from the Twenties* (New York: Feminist Press, 1989), p. 126.

8. Ibid., pp. 3-27.

9. Ibid.

10. Ibid.

11. Ruth Pinchot to Amos Pinchot, July 2, 1923, Amos Pinchot Papers, 1863–1943, Family Correspondence, container 3, Library of Congress.

12. William Attwood, diary entries, December 21, 1935–January 30, 1936. The Attwood family graciously allowed me access to Bill Attwood's private diaries, which were extensive, right up until his death in 1989.

13. Robert Dallek, *An Unfinished Life: John F. Kennedy, 1917–1963* (Boston: Little, Brown, 2003), p. 79.

14. Ralph G. Martin, *Seeds of Destruction: Joe Kennedy and His Sons* (New York: G. P. Putnam's Sons, 1995), p. xxi.

15. Choate School letter to Leo Damore, October 5, 1992. The letter documents William Attwood's date for Winter Festivities Weekend, February 1936, and the fact that John F. Kennedy (Class of 1935) was in attendance.

16. Nina Burleigh, *A Very Private Woman: The Life and Unsolved Murder of Presidential Mistress Mary Meyer* (New York: Bantam, 1998), p. 57.

17. William Attwood, diary entry, February 21, 1936.

18. Ibid.

19. William Attwood, *The Reds and the Blacks: A Personal Adventure* (New York: Harper & Row, 1967), pp. 133–134.

20. William Attwood, diary entry, March 24, 1936.

21. Ibid., May 11, 1939.

22. Ibid., June 14, 1939.

23. Ibid.

24. Ibid, June 15, 1939.

25. Bibi Gaston, *The Loveliest Woman in America* (New York: William Morrow, 2008), p. 32.

26. Burleigh, *A Very Private Woman*, p. 61.

27. Mary Pinchot, "Requiem," *New York Times*, January 25, 1940, p. 16.

28. Gaston, *Loveliest Woman*, p.18, p. 253.

29. Rosenbaum and Nobile, "Curious Aftermath," p. 25.

30. A former 1942 Vassar classmate of Mary Meyer's who asked to remain anonymous, interview by the author, November 27, 2009.

31. Cord Meyer Jr., *Facing Reality: From World Federalism to the CIA* (New York: Harper & Row, 1980), p. 34.

32. Croswell Bowen, "Young Man in Quest of Peace," *PM Sunday* 3, no. 237 (March 21, 1948): p. 8.

33. Rosenbaum and Nobile, "Curious Aftermath," p. 29.

34. Anonymous Meyer classmate, interview.

35. Burleigh, *A Very Private Woman*, pp. 72–73.

36. Robert L. Schwartz, interview by the author, New York, N.Y., October 16, 2008.

37. Ibid.

38. Burleigh, *A Very Private Woman*, p. 76.

39. Schwartz, interview.

40. James McConnell Truitt to Deborah Davis, January 30, 1979.

41. Schwartz, interview.

42. Ibid.

43. Ibid.

Chapter 7. *Cyclops*

1. Croswell Bowen, "Young Man in Quest of Peace," *PM Sunday* 3, no. 237 (March 21, 1948): p. m6.

2. Cord Meyer Jr., "Waves of Darkness," *Atlantic Monthly,* January 1946, p. 77.

3. Ibid, p. 80.

4. Bowen, "Young Man," p. m 7.

5. Ibid.

6. Ibid.

7. Charles Bartlett, interview by the author, Washington, D.C., December 10, 2008.

8. Bowen, "Young Man," p. m7.

9. Cord Meyer Jr., *Facing Reality: From World Federalism to the CIA* (New York: Harper & Row, 1980), pp. 4–5.

10. Merle Miller, "One Man's Long Journey: From a One World Crusade to the 'Department of Dirty Tricks,,'" *New York Times Magazine*, January 7, 1973.

11. Bowen, "Young Man," p. m8.

12. Cord Meyer Jr., Journal, 1945–1967, September 1944, box 5, Papers of Cord Meyer, Manuscript Division, Library of Congress.

13. Bowen, "Young Man," p. m8.

14. Ibid., p. m6.

15. John H. Crider, "Veterans Caution on Parley Hopes," *New York Times*, May 3, 1945.

16. Nigel Hamilton, *JFK: Reckless Youth* (New York: Random House, 1992), p. 702.

17. Ibid., p. 700.

18. Robert Dallek, *An Unfinished Life: John F. Kennedy, 1917–1963* (Boston: Little, Brown, 2003), pp. 114–116.

19. Benjamin C. Bradlee, *Conversations with Kennedy* (New York: W. W. Norton, 1975), pp. 34–35. See also Nina Burleigh, *A Very Private Woman: The Life and Unsolved Murder of Presidential Mistress Mary Meyer* (New York: Bantam, 1998), p. 315–20.

20. U.S. Senate Select Committee on Intelligence (SSCI), Restricted, top secret testimony given by Joseph W. Shimon, September 12, 1975. The document was provided to the author from Joseph Shimon's daughter, Toni Shimon.

21. Bowen, "Young Man," p. m7.

22. Bartlett, interview.

23. Cord Meyer Jr., Journal, 1945–1967, entry dated November 2, 1945, box 5, Papers of Cord Meyer, Manuscript Division, Library of Congress.

24. Hamilton, *JFK*, p. 703.

25. Ibid., pp. 690–691.

26. Anne Truitt, *Daybook: The Journal of an Artist* (New York: Pantheon, 1982), pp. 200–201.

27. Bowen, "Young Man," p. m9.

28. Cord Meyer Jr., "A Serviceman Looks at the Peace," *Atlantic Monthly*, September 1945.

29. Bowen, "Young Man," p. m 9.

30. Ibid.

31. Ibid.

32. Hubert H. Humphrey to Cord Meyer Jr., October 21, 1949, box 1, Papers of Cord Meyer, Manuscript Division, Library of Congress..

33. Wesley T. Wooley, "Finding a Usable Past: The Success of the American World Federalism in the 1940s," *Peace & Change* 24, no. 3 (July 1999).

34. "Young Men Who Care," *Glamour*, July, 1947, pp. 27–29.

35. Meyer, *Facing Reality*, p. 55.

36. Meyer Journal, January 3, 1950.

37. Ibid., March 18, 1950.

38. Ibid., May 24, 1951.

39. Ibid., June 8, 1951.

40. Ibid., March 31, 1951.

41. Allen Dulles to Cord Meyer Jr., February 23, 1951, and March 31, 1951, box 1, Papers of Cord Meyer; Cord Meyer Jr. to Allen Dulles, March 14, 1951, and May 23, 1951, box 1, Papers of Cord Meyer; Cord Meyer Jr. to Gerald E. Miller, May 23, 1951, box 1, Papers of Cord Meyer; Dean Acheson to Cord Meyer Jr., February 8, 1951, box 1, Papers of Cord Meyer. There were also letters between journalist Walter Lippman and Cord during 1951 that might have suggested Lippman's assistance to Cord in procuring some kind of job as a journalist, but nothing specific.

42. Meyer, Journal, December 10, 1945.

43. Ibid.

44. Victor Marchetti, interview by the author, Ashburn, Va., October 4, 2007.

45. Meyer, Journal, January 3, 1950.

46. Anonymous source, interview by the author, February 3, 2004.

47. Meyer, Journal, February 26, 1953.

48. Ibid., September 7, 1953. Here, Cord wrote several pages on what had occurred on the afternoon of August 31.

49. Meyer, *Facing Reality*, pp. 70–71.

50. Meyer, Journal, February 1, 1954. Cord recorded here the outcome of his trip to New York.

51. Ibid., November 8, 1954.

52. Benjamin C. Bradlee, *A Good Life: Newspapering and Other Adventures* (New York: Simon & Schuster, 1995), p. 159.

53. James McConnell Truitt letter to Deborah Davis, May 11, 1979. The letter was part of the files of the late author Leo Damore and was subsequently verified by author Deborah Davis.

54. Meyer., Journal, October 18, 1955.

55. Ibid.

56. James McConnell Truitt letter to Deborah Davis, January 30, 1979. This event was also reported in Deborah Davis's *Katharine the Great* (p. 230) and Nina Burleigh's *A Very Private Woman* (p. 204).

57. David, Acheson, interview by the author, Washington, D.C., December 10, 2008.

58. Meyer, Journal, December 30, 1956.

59. Ibid., January 15, 1957.

60. Cord Meyer Jr., "Notes" 1957, box 5, Papers of Cord Meyer.

61. Truitt, *Daybook*, p. 165.

62. Meyer, "Notes."

63. Ibid.

64. Meyer, "Waves of Darkness," p. 80.

65. Miller, "One Man's Long Journey," p. 9.

66. Victor, Marchetti, interviews by the author, Ashburn, Va., November 18, 2005, and October 4, 2007. See also Carl Bernstein, "The CIA and the Media," *Rolling Stone*, October 20, 1977.

67. Evan Thomas, *The Very Best Men* (New York: Simon & Schuster, 1995), p. 330.

68. Scottie Lanahan, "Are You Playing the Games by the Rules in Washington?," NEWS to Me . . . , *Washington Post*, April 2, 1967, p. H2.

69. Letter from the office of William Sloane Coffin Jr. at Yale University to the entering class of 1972, August 8, 1968, box 1, Papers of Cord Meyer; Cord Meyer, Jr. to Bishop Paul Moore, September 13, 1968, box 1, Papers of Cord Meyer; Cord Meyer Jr. to Cyrus R. Vance, September 26, 1968, box 1, Papers of Cord Meyer; Cord Meyer Jr. to Dean Acheson, September 26, 1968, box 1, Papers of Cord Meyer; Cord Meyer Jr. to William P. Bundy, September 26, 1968, box 1, Papers of Cord Meyer; Bishop Paul Moore to Cord Meyer Jr., September 13, 1968, box 1, Papers of Cord Meyer; Dean Acheson to Cord Meyer Jr., October 1, 1968, box 1, Papers of Cord Meyer.

70. Marc D. Charney, "Rev. William Sloane Coffin Dies at 81; Fought for Civil Rights and Against a War," *New York Times*, April 13, 2006.

71. Miller, "One Man's Long Journey," p. 53.

Chapter 8. *Personal Evolution*

1. Gerald Clarke, *Capote: A Biography* (London: Cardinal, 1989), p. 271.

2. Gore Vidal, *Palimpsest: A Memoir* (New York: Penguin, 1995), p. 311.

3. Peter Evans, *Nemesis* (New York: HarperCollins, 2004), pp. 29–33.

4. Peter Collier and David Horowitz, *The Kennedys: An American Drama* (New York: Summit, 1984), p. 209. Another source confirmed this account as early as 1978; see Kitty Kelley, *Jackie Oh!* (Secaucus, N.J.: Lyle Stuart, 1978), pp. 57–58.

5. Edward Klein, *All Too Human: The Love Story of Jack and Jackie Kennedy* (New York: Pocket Books, 1996), pp. 220–221.

6. In 1931, the state of Nevada reduced the residency requirement for divorces to six weeks using the catch-all grounds of "mental cruelty." This made Nevada the go-to place for a divorce. Because a woman who wished to avoid the embarrassment of getting a divorce in her hometown could be incognito in sparsely populated Nevada, this choice was popular with many women from prominent families.

7. Michael O'Brien, *John F. Kennedy: A Biography* (New York: St. Martin's, 2005), p. 441.

8. Ibid., pp. 441–442.

9. Mary P. Meyer v. Cord Meyer, Jr., Case No. 175609, Findings of Fact, Conclusions of Law and Decree, Second Judicial District Court of the State of Nevada, August 19, 1958.

10. Confidential source, interview by Leo Damore, Washington, D.C., 1991.

11. Robert Schwartz, interview by the author, New York, N.Y., October 16, 2008.

12. O'Brien, *John F. Kennedy*, p. 442.

13. Kenneth Noland, telephone interview by Nina Burleigh, September 13, 1996.

14. Schwartz interview.

15. James McConnell Truitt letter to Deborah Davis, May 11, 1979.

16. Deborah Davis, interview by Leo Damore, February 23, 1991; Deborah Davis, interview by the author, March 17, 2009. During Deborah Davis's research for her book *Katharine the Great* in 1976, she traveled to Mexico and interviewed Jim Truitt for more than ten hours over a three-day period. The two then corresponded further by mail. Nina Burleigh also references the likelihood of Jim Truitt's influence on "Mary's initiation into drug experimentation." See Nina Burleigh, *A Very Private Woman: The Life and Unresolved Murder of Presidential Mistress Mary Meyer* (New York: Bantam, 1998), pp. 171–172.

17. Laura Bergquist, "The Curious Story Behind the New Cary Grant," *Look*, September 1, 1959.

18. Martin A. Lee and Bruce Shlain, *Acid Dreams: The CIA, LSD, and the Sixties Rebellion* (New York: Grove, 1985), p. 93.

19. Ibid., p. 51.

20. Ibid.

21. Alfred Hubbard, interview by Dr. Oscar Janiger, October 13, 1978. A number of sources have referenced this interview, including the best history of the entire era ever written: Lee and Shlain's *Acid Dreams*, cited in note 18 above.

22. H. P. Albarelli Jr., *A Terrible Mistake: The Murder of Frank Olson and the CIA's Secret Cold War Experiments* (Walterville, Ore.: Trine Day, 2009). pp. 350-352. See also: H. P. Albarelli Jr. and Jeffrey Kaye, "Cries From the Past: Torture's Ugly Echoes," *Truthout*, Sunday, May 23, 2010. www.truthout.org.

23. Albarelli, *A Terrible Mistake*. This is, by far, the most thorough account of Frank Olson's death and the history of the CIA's MKULTRA program.

24. Ibid.

25. Lee and Shlain, *Acid Dreams*, pp. 52–53.

26. Robert Budd, interview by the author, January 21, 2004.

27. Morton Herskowitz, D.O., interview by the author, May 17, 2004.

28. Burleigh, *A Very Private Woman*, p. 165.

29. Budd, interview.

30. Noland, interview, September 13, 1996; Kenneth Noland, interview by Nina Burleigh, Carlyle Hotel, New York, N.Y., December 1996. In a follow-up email to me on July 6, 2005, author Burleigh shared the fact that Ken Noland and Mary frequented jazz clubs in Washington, D.C., and that Noland had talked with Burleigh "abt [*sic*] their LSD use." Despite my own association with Kenneth Noland when he and Mary Meyer taught art at Georgetown Day School in the 1950s, he declined to speak with me. I am indebted to Nina Burleigh, who graciously shared a copy of her notes taken during these interviews.

31. Burleigh, *A Very Private Woman*, p. 175.

32. Confidential source, interview.

33. Sally Bedell Smith, *Grace and Power: The Private World of the Kennedy White House* (New York: Random House, 2004), p. 235.

34. Ben Bradlee, interview by the author, Washington, D.C., January 31, 2007.

35. Burleigh, *A Very Private Woman*, p. 180.

36. Confidential source, interview.

37. Ibid.

38. Lee and Shlain, *Acid Dreams*, p. 192.

39. Ibid., p. 133.

40. Ibid., p. 189.

41. Collier and Horowitz, *Kennedys*, p. 176.

42. Robert Dallek, *An Unfinished Life: John F. Kennedy, 1917-1963* (Boston: Little, Brown, 2003), p. 152. See also Collier and Horowitz, *Kennedys*, p. 176; Doris Kearns Goodwin, *The Fitzgeralds and the Kennedys* (New York: St.

Martin's, 1987), p. 838; Ralph G. Martin, *A Hero for Our Time: An Intimate Story of the Kennedy Years* (New York: Macmillan, 1983), p. 240. During an interview with this author in Cambridge, Massachusetts, on July 8, 2009, Priscilla J. McMillan claimed to have no recollection of making the quoted statements, or of the interviews she had given to David Horowitz and Robert Dallek. Both authors, however, confirmed with me that they had, in fact, interviewed Priscilla J. McMillan, and that she gave the statements as quoted in their respective books. David Horowitz confirmed this with me by telephone on July 13, 2009, and Robert Dallek confirmed it via email on July 14, 2009.

43. Martin, *Hero for Our Time*, p. 240.

44. Goodwin, *Fitzgeralds and the Kennedys*, pp. 837–838.

45. Dallek, *Unfinished Life*, p. 152.

46. Collier and Horowitz, *Kennedys*, p. 194.

47. Nigel Hamilton, *JFK: Reckless Youth* (New York: Random House, 1992), pp. 690–691.

48. Dallek, *Unfinished Life*, p. 84.

49. Ibid., p. 85.

50. Goodwin., *Fitzgeralds and the Kennedys*, p. 848.

51. Ibid., p. 858.

52. Dallek, *Unfinished Life*, p. 154.

53. Seymour M. Hersh, *The Dark Side of Camelot* (New York: Back Bay Books, 1997), pp. 234–236.

54. Anonymous source, interview by the author, November 14, 2009.

55. Hersh, *Dark Side of Camelot*, p. 237.

Chapter 9. *Mary's Mission*

1. Timothy Leary, *Flashbacks: An Autobiography* (Los Angeles: J. P. Tarcher, 1983), p. 128.

2. Ibid.

3. Ibid., p. 129.

4. Timothy Leary, interview by Leo Damore, Washington, D.C., November 7, 1990.

5. Leary, *Flashbacks*, p. 129.

6. Ibid., pp. 128–130.

7. Nina Burleigh, *A Very Private Woman: The Life and Unsolved Murder of Presidential Mistress Mary Meyer* (New York: Bantam, 1998), p. 194. Burleigh's interview with White House counsel Myer Feldman provides the most specific, thorough documentation of how closely President Kennedy relied on the counsel of Mary Meyer.

8. Sally Bedell Smith, *Grace and Power: The Private World of the Kennedy White House* (New York: Random House, 2004), p. 255.

9. Leo Damore, interview by the author, Centerbrook, Conn., February 1992.

10. Smith, *Grace and Power*, p. 254.

11. Leary, *Flashbacks*, pp. 227–231.

12. Leary, interview.

13. Robert Greenfield, *Timothy Leary: A Biography* (New York: Harcourt, 2006), p. 245.

14. Ibid., pp. 423–427.

15. Carolyn Pfeiffer Bradshaw, interview by the author, March 20, 2009. Ms. Bradshaw confirmed that she and her late husband, Jon, were very close friends of Timothy and Barbara Leary and that they spent a great deal of time together.

16. Leary, interview. See also Timothy Leary, "The Murder of Mary Pinchot Meyer," premier issue, *Rebel: A Newsweekly with A Cause*, no. 1 (January 1984): pp. 44–49. In addition, author Carol Felsenthal covers this topic thoroughly in her book *Power, Privilege, and the Post: The Katharine Graham Story* (New York: Seven Stories Press, 1993.)

17. In Leo Damore's possession were two letters/reports from investigator William Triplett. The first was dated "14 December 1983" and was eight single-spaced typewritten pages in length. It was addressed to "Timothy Leary P.O. Box 69886, Los Angeles, CA. 90069." The second letter/report was dated "5 January 1984" and was six pages in length. Sometime in early 1991, Damore communicated with Triplett, who responded to Damore in a letter dated March 7, 1991, in which he verified his previous work with Timothy Leary. Copies of all three letters are currently in my possession.

18. Robert Greenfield, interview by the author, January 23, 2009.

19. Ibid.

20. Leary, interview. Damore followed up with Leary in several telephone calls over the next two-plus years into March 1993, as his notes indicate, with regard to specific questions that arose from the initial interview in 1990.

21. Timothy Leary's relationship with Cord Meyer was also documented by Leary biographer Robert Greenfield, who told me that Leary's secretary in Berkeley verified this when he interviewed her. Greenfield, interview.

22. Peggy Mellon Hitchcock, interview by the author, March 16, 2009.

23. Leary, interview.

24. Ibid.

25. Peter Janney letter to Anne Chamberlin, January 27, 2009.

26. Anne Chamberlin letter to Peter Janney, February 5, 2009.

27. C. David Heymann, *A Woman Named Jackie* (New York: Carol Communications, 1989), p. 375. In a letter to Leo Damore dated July 3, 1990, Heymann wrote, "I also interviewed people like Mary's sister, Tim Leary and others who knew her [Mary Meyer]."

28. I could locate no interview with Timothy Leary, Tony Bradlee, or James Angleton in any of the material that C. David Heymann had provided to the Special Collections and University Archives at SUNY–Stony Brook's Memorial Library.

29. Heymann, *Woman Named Jackie*, p. 651. In his notes for Chapter 22, Heymann stated that he had interviewed "James Angleton," but provided no citation as to the date or location of such interview. Recently, much of Heymann's so-called research has met with increasing criticism, questioning its veracity. See, for instance, Lisa Pease's review of Heymann's book *Bobby and Jackie: A Love Story* (2009) at Citizens for Truth about the Kennedy Assassination, www.ctka.net/reviews/heymann.html.

30. Leary, interview.

31. Ibid.

32. Burleigh, *A Very Private Woman*, p. 341–38.

33. In a letter dated March 10, 1983, Jim Truitt's second wife, Evelyn Patterson Truitt, told author Anthony Summers the following: "My husband's files

[James McConnell Truitt] were all stolen by an ex-CIA agent, Herbert Barrows. I called the F.B.I. but don't know what happened to his 30 years of carefully kept records."

34. Deborah Davis, interview by the author, Washington, D.C., March 17, 2009. I also had a number of subsequent phone conversations with Ms. Davis about Timothy Leary, whom she came to know well, in addition to Jim Truitt.

35. Bernie Ward and Granville Toogood, "Former Vice President of Washington Post Reveals JFK 2-Year White House Romance," *National Enquirer*, March 2, 1976, p. 4.

36. Ibid.

37. January 1962 was the date first disclosed by James Truitt in the March 1976 issue of the *National Enquirer*. Ibid.

38. White House Secret Service logs at John F. Kennedy Presidential Library and Museum, Boston, Mass. This date was also substantiated by Sally Bedell Smith and Nina Burleigh in their respective books, *Grace and Power* and *A Very Private Woman*, pp. 329-330.

39. Smith, *Grace and Power*, pp. 233–234. This is the latest and most thoroughly researched book documenting these facts.

40. Herbert S. Parmet, *JFK: The Presidency of John F. Kennedy* (New York: Dial, 1983), pp. 306–307.

41. Dino Brugioni, interview by the author, January 30, 2009. During the Kennedy presidency, Brugioni was the top deputy for Arthur C. Lundahl, director of the CIA's most secretive facility: the National Photographic Interpretation Center (NPIC). Brugioni knew personally some of the agents in Kennedy's Secret Service detail; they told him that they took the president on a number of occasions to Mary Meyer's house in Georgetown. Brugioni is also the author of the best-selling book *Eyeball to Eyeball: The Inside Story of the Cuban Missile Crisis* (New York: Random House, 1990).

42. Benjamin C. Bradlee, *A Good Life: Newspapering and Other Adventures* (New York: Simon & Schuster, 1995), p. 268.

43. Benjamin C. Bradlee, *Conversations with Kennedy* (New York: W. W. Norton, 1975), p. 54.

44. Ralph G. Martin, *Seeds of Destruction: Joe Kennedy and His Sons* (New York: G. P. Putnam's Sons, 1995), p. 371.

45. Damore, interview. Damore mentioned this incident the very first time we met in February 1992 and repeated it several times subsequent to that.

46. Ben Bradlee, interview by the author, Washington, D.C., January 31, 2007.

47. Burleigh, *A Very Private Woman*, p. 43.

48. Bradlee, *A Good Life*, p. 232.

49. Bradlee, *Conversations with Kennedy*, p. 187. Bradlee said the remark was made on April 29, 1963.

50. Smith, *Grace and Power*, p. 364.

51. Ibid., p. 365.

52. Ibid.

53. Ibid., pp. 144–145.

54. Bradlee, interview.

55. Charles Bartlett, interview by the author, Washington, D.C., December 10, 2008.

56. Burleigh, *A Very Private Woman*, p. 298.

57. Bartlett, interview.

58. Damore, interview. Damore also shared O'Donnell's comments with his close friend and attorney Jimmy Smith, as well as with Timothy Leary during their interview in November 1990.

59. Ibid.

60. Donald H. Wolfe, *The Last Days of Marilyn Monroe*. (New York: William Morrow, 1998), pp. 461–462; Donald H. Wolfe, interview by the author, June 2, 2005. Wolfe's account was meticulously researched and substantiated by several different sources.

61. Wolfe, *Last Days of Marilyn Monroe*, p. 462.

62. Bryan Bender, "A Dark Corner of Camelot," *Boston Globe*, January 23, 2011.

63. Burleigh, *A Very Private Woman*, p. 194.

64. Ibid.

65. Arthur Schlesinger Jr., Memorandum for the President, December 29, 1962, JFKPOF-065-019, Papers of John F. Kennedy, Presidential Papers, President's Office Files, John F. Kennedy Presidential Library and Museum, Boston, Mass. See also Burleigh, *A Very Private Woman*, p. 194.

66. Tim Weiner, *Legacy of Ashes* (New York: Doubleday, 2007), p. 167. See also Tim Weiner, "The True and Shocking History of the CIA," July 30, 2007, RINF News, www.rinf.com/alt-news/latest-news/the-true-and-shocking-history-of-the-cia/876/.

67. John Lukacs, *George Kennan: A Study of Character* (New Haven, Conn.: Yale University Press 2007), p. 98.

68. Peter Grose, *Gentleman Spy: The Life of Allen Dulles* (New York: Houghton Mifflin, 1994), p. 293.

69. The most recent and thorough account is Stephen Kinzer's *All the Shah's Men* (New York: John Wiley & Sons, 2003).

70. John Foster Dulles and the law firm Sullivan & Cromwell had been the legal counsel for the United Fruit Company for decades. John Foster and Allen Dulles were both major shareholders in the company, with Allen serving as a member of United Fruit's board of trustees. See Stephen Kinzer, *Overthrow: America's Century of Regime Change from Hawaii to Iraq* (New York: Times Books, 2006), pp. 129–130; Walter La Feber, *Inevitable Revolutions: The United States in Central America* (New York: W. W. Norton, 1993), pp. 120–121.

71. Donald E. Deneselya, interview by the author, Washington, D.C., April 10, 2007.

72. L. Fletcher Prouty, *JFK: The CIA, Vietnam, and the Plot to Assassinate John F. Kennedy* (New York: Citadel, 1996), p. 155.

73. Joan Mellen, *A Farewell to Justice* (Dulles, Va.: Potomac Books, 2005), p. 162. Author Mellen's exact reference for this quote was as follows: "Forty years later, historian Arthur Schlesinger Jr., a Kennedy adviser, would remark quietly to Jim Garrison's old classmate Wilmer Thomas that they had been at war with 'the national security people.'"

74. Richard Reeves, *President Kennedy: Profiles of Power* (New York: Touchstone, 1993), p. 103.

75. David C. Martin, *Wilderness of Mirrors* (Guilford, Conn.: Lyons Press, 1980), p. 118.

76. Daniel Schorr, commentary on Noah Adams's NPR program *All Things Considered,* March 26, 2001.

77. John M. Newman, *JFK and Vietnam: Deception, Intrigue, and the Struggle for Power* (New York: Warner , 1992), pp. 98–99.

78. Arthur M. Schlesinger Jr., *A Thousand Days: John F. Kennedy in the White House* (New York: Houghton Mifflin, 1965), p. 428.

79. Willie Morris, *New York Days* (Boston: Little Brown, 1993), p. 36.

80. According to James Srodes in his book *Allen Dulles: Master of Spies* (Washington, D.C.: Regnery, 1999), p. 547, Dulles did not learn that he would be fired from the CIA until the last week of August 1961. President Kennedy then announced on September 27 that John A. McCone would replace him.

81. James Bamford, *Body of Secrets: Anatomy of the Ultra-Secret National Security Agency* (New York: Random House, 2002), p. 82.

82. James K. Galbraith and Heather A. Purcell, "Did the U.S. Military Plan a Nuclear First Strike for 1963?," *American Prospect* 5, no. 19 (September 1994): pp. 88–96.

Chapter 10. *Peace Song*

1. Sally Bedell Smith, *Grace and Power: The Private World of the Kennedy White House* (New York: Random House, 2004), p. 315.

2. John F. Kennedy, "Cuban Missile Crisis Address to the Nation" (televised speech, October 22, 1962), American Rhetoric, www.americanrhetoric. com/speeches/jfkcubanmissilecrisis.html (authenticity certified).

3. James W. Douglass, *JFK and the Unspeakable: Why He Died and Why It Matters* (Maryknoll, N.Y.: Orbis Books, 2008), p. 20.

4. Known as the "Pen Pal Correspondence," the private letters between Kennedy and Khrushchev were published together in the State Department's *Foreign Relations of the United States [FRUS], 1961–1963,* vol. 6., *Kennedy-Khrushchev Exchanges* (Washington, D.C.: U.S. Government Printing Office, 1966). They can also be accessed online; see "Kennedy-Khrushchev Exchanges," U.S. Department of State, www.state.gov/www/ about_state/history/volume_vi/exchanges.html. All quotations from that correspondence appearing in this chapter were obtained at that web page.

5. Letter from Chairman Khrushchev to President Kennedy, September 29, 1961, "Kennedy-Khrushchev Exchanges," no. 21. See note 4 above for location.

6. Letter from President Kennedy to Chairman Khrushchev, October 16, 1961, "Kennedy-Khrushchev Exchanges," no. 22. See note 4 above for location.

7. Leo Damore, interviews by the author, February 1992 and October 1992. Damore shared a number of incidents that Kenny O'Donnell had told him about concerning Mary and Jack, specifically mentioning Mary confronting Jack on the dangers of the resumption of nuclear testing in April 1962.

8. Telegram from the Embassy in the Soviet Union to the Department of State, October 26, 1962, "Kennedy-Khrushchev Exchanges," no. 65.

9. Letter from Chairman Khrushchev to President Kennedy, October 27, 1962, "Kennedy-Khrushchev Exchanges," no. 66.

10. Nikita Khrushchev, *Khrushchev Remembers*, trans. and ed. Strobe Talbott (New York: Bantam, 1971), pp. 497–498.

11. Michael Dobbs, *One Minute to Midnight: Kennedy, Khrushchev, and Castro on the Brink of Nuclear War* (New York: Knopf, 2008), p. 4. See also Robert S. McNamara, *In Retrospect: The Tragedy and Lessons of Vietnam* (New York: Vintage, 1996), p. 341; Douglas P. Horne, *Inside the Assassination Records Review Board: The U.S. Government's Final Attempt to Reconcile the Conflicting Medical Records in the Assassination of JFK* (printed by author, 2009), pp. 1710–1711, pp. 1716–1718, p. 1774. The most thorough account is contained in John D. Gresham and Norman Polmar, *Defcon-2* (Hoboken, N.J.: John Wiley & Sons, 2006).

12. Interview with Robert S. McNamara, December 6, 1998, Episode 11, National Security Archive, George Washington University. Located at: http://www.gwu.edu/~nsarchiv/coldwar/interviews/episode-11/mcnamara1.html

13. Richard Rhodes, *Dark Sun: The Making of the Hydrogen Bomb* (New York: Simon & Schuster, 1995), p. 575. The author interviewed a retired SAC wing commander who told him, "I knew what my target was—Leningrad." The wing commander's SAC alert bombers "deliberately flew past their turn around points toward Soviet airspace, an unambiguous threat

which Soviet radar operators would certainly have recognized and reported. The bombers only turned around when Soviet freighters carrying missiles to Cuba stopped dead in the Atlantic."

14. Gresham and Polmar, *Defcon-2*, pp. 244–246.

15. Arthur M. Schlesinger Jr., *Robert Kennedy and His Times* (Boston: Houghton Mifflin, 2002), p. 524.

16. Ibid., p. 525.

17. Douglass, *JFK and the Unspeakable*, p. 44.

18. For background information on the life of Philip L. Graham, see David Halberstam, *The Powers That Be* (New York: Knopf, 1975); Deborah Davis, *Katharine the Great: Katharine Graham and the Washington Post* (New York: Harcourt Brace Jovanovich, 1979); Katharine Graham, *Personal History* (New York: Vintage, 1998); and Carol Felsenthal, *Power, Privilege and the Post: The Katharine Graham Story* (New York: Seven Stories Press,1993).

19. There is extensive documentation of the existence of the CIA's Operation Mockingbird, as noted in previous chapters. I am particularly indebted to the former CIA operative and author Victor Marchetti for the information he provided me during my interview with him on November 18, 2005, and October 4, 2007, in Ashburn, Virginia.

20. Felsenthal, *Power, Privilege and the Post*, pp. 372–373.

21. Ibid., pp. 197–198.

22. Halberstam, *Powers That Be*, pp. 381–382.

23. Ibid., pp. 215–216.

24. Davis, *Katharine the Great* (1979), p. 164.

25. Ibid.

26. Smith, *Grace and Power*, p. 349.

27. William Shover, interview by the author, March 18, 2009. Leo Damore also interviewed Shover on October 8, 1993.

28. Ben Bradlee, interview by the author, Washington, D.C., January 31, 2007.

29. Smith, *Grace and Power*, p. 349.

30. Graham, *Personal History*, p. 310.

31. Carol Felsenthal, interview by the author, August 10, 2010.

32. Ibid.

33. Felsenthal, *Power, Privilege and the Post*, p. 216.

34. Felsenthal, interview.

35. White House telephone logs, calls to Evelyn Lincoln on January 18, 1963, John F. Kennedy Presidential Library and Museum, Boston, Massachusetts.

36. Davis, *Katharine the Great* (1979), p. 165.

37. H. P. Albarelli Jr., *A Terrible Mistake: The Murder of Frank Olson and the CIA's Secret Cold War Experiments* (Walterville, Ore.: Trine Day, 2009), p. 115.

38. Davis, *Katharine the Great* (1979), p. 165. See also Felsenthal, *Power, Privilege and the Post*, p. 206, p. 210.

39. Ibid., p. 168; Deborah Davis, interview by the author, March 17, 2009. See also "An Interview with Deborah Davis," in *Popular Alienation: A Steamshovel Press Reader*, ed. Kenn Thomas (Lilburn, Ga.: IllumiNet Press, 1995), p. 83; Felsenthal, *Power, Privilege and the Post*, pp. 371–373.

40. Davis, *Katharine the Great* (1979), p. 160.

41. Ralph G. Martin, *Seeds of Destruction: Joe Kennedy and His Sons* (New York: G. P. Putnam's Sons, 1995), 322–323.

42. Ibid., p. 372.

43. Ralph G. Martin, *A Hero for Our Time: An Intimate Story of the Kennedy Years* (New York: Macmillan, 1983), p. 354.

44. Smith, *Grace and Power*, pp. 351–352.

45. Ibid., p. 352. Adlai Stevenson's letter to Marietta Tree on March 10, 1963, is in the collection Papers, 1917–1995, housed in the Arthur and Elizabeth Schlesinger Library on the History of Women in America, Radcliffe Institute for Advanced Study, Harvard University, Boston, Mass.

46. Smith, *Grace and Power*, p. 352.

47. Horne, *Assassination Records Review Board*, 5: pp. 1382–1383.

48. Toni Shimon, interviews by the author, June 17, 2004, February 15, 2007, January 7, 2008, and March 30, 2010.

49. Shimon, interview, February 15, 2007.

50. Timothy Leary, *Flashbacks: An Autobiography* (Los Angeles: J. P. Tarcher, 1983), p. 162.

51. Ibid.

52. Ibid.

53. Ibid., p. 163.

54. Robert Greenfield, *Timothy Leary: A Biography* (New York: Harcourt, 2006), p. 199.

55. Timothy Leary, *High Priest* (Oakland, Calif.: Ronin, 1968), pp. 256–257.

56. Leary, *Flashbacks*, p. 171.

57. Leo Damore, interview by the author, Centerbrook, Conn., April 1993. Damore and I discussed the postcard Mary Meyer had allegedly sent Leary (*Flashbacks*, p. 171), which, according to Damore, was further confirmation of what his confidential source had told him. I suspected that the source of this information was Mary Meyer's close friend Anne Chamberlin, whom I also knew, but who refused to be interviewed by me. Anne Chamberlin died on December 31, 2011.

58. Greenfield, *Timothy Leary*, p. 547. As of June 2011, the entire Timothy Leary archive has been purchased by the New York Public Library. The collection includes some 335 boxes of papers, videotapes, photographs, and more. See Patricia Cohen, "New York Public Library Buys Timothy Leary's Papers," *New York Times*, June 16, 2011, p. C1–2.

59. Glenn T. Seaborg, *Kennedy, Khrushchev, and the Test Ban.* (Berkeley: University of California Press, 1983), p. 199.

60. Alun Rees, "Nobel Prize Genius Crick Was High on LSD when He Discovered the Secret of Life," Associated Newspapers, 2004. This article originally appeared in the *Mail on Sunday* (London), August 8, 2004. It can be viewed at Serendipity, www.serendipity.li/dmt/crick_lsd.htm.

61. Alcoholics Anonymous, *"Pass It On": The Story of Bill Wilson and How the A.A. Message Reached the World* (New York: Alcoholics Anonymous World Services, 1995), pp. 370–371. See also Rich English, "The Dry Piper: The Strange Life and Times of Bill Wilson, Founder of A.A.," *Modern Drunkard Magazine*, www.moderndrunkardmagazine.com/issues/01-05/0105-dry-piper.htm.

62. John Markoff, *What the Dormouse Said: How the 60s Counterculture Shaped the Personal Computer Industry* (New York: Viking, 2005), pp. xviii–xix.

63. Interview with Oliver Stone on *Real Time With Bill Maher* HBO (episode #159). Original airdate: June 27, 2009.

64. R. R. Griffiths, W. A. Richards, U. McCann, and R. Jesse (2006) "Psilocybin can occasion mystical experiences having substantial and sustained personal meaning and spiritual significance." *Psychopharmacology* 187: pp. 268–283. Also, Griffiths, R. R.; Richards, W. A.; Johnson, M. W.; McCann, U. D.; Jesse, R. 2008. "Mystical-type experiences occasioned by psilocybin mediate the attribution of personal meaning and spiritual significance 14 months later." *Journal of Psychopharmacology* 22(6): pp. 621-632.

65. Theodore Sorensen, interview by the author, January 10, 2006.

66. John F. Kennedy, "American University Commencement Address" (speech, American University, Washington, D.C., June 10, 1963), American Rhetoric, www.americanrhetoric.com/speeches/jfkamericanuniversityaddress.html (authenticity certified).

67. Max Frankel, "Harriman to Lead Test-Ban Mission to Soviet in July; Kennedy Envoy Expected to Tell Khrushchev of Hope for Nuclear Breakthrough," *New York Times,* June 12, 1963, p. 1.

68. Kennedy, "American University Commencement Address."

69. Arthur M. Schlesinger Jr., *A Thousand Days: John F. Kennedy in the White House* (New York: Houghton Mifflin, 1965), p. 311.

70. Kennedy, "American University Commencement Address."

71. Ibid.

72. Ibid.

73. Ibid.

74. Ibid.

75. Ibid.

76. Ibid.

77. Message from Chairmen Khrushchev and Brezhnev to President Kennedy, July 4, 1963, Department of State, Presidential Files: Lot 66 D 204 (no classification marking). The source text is a Department of State translation of a commercial telegram from Moscow. Another copy of this message and the transliterated Russian text is in the National Security Files, Countries Series, USSR, Khrushchev Correspondence, John F. Kennedy Presidential Library and Museum, Boston, Mass.

78. Douglass, *JFK and the Unspeakable*, p. 46.

79. Richard Reeves, *President Kennedy: Profiles of Power* (New York: Touchstone, 1993), p. 545.

80. Ibid., p. 549.

81. John F. Kennedy, "Limited Nuclear Test Ban Treaty Address to the Nation," (televised speech, July 26, 1963), American Rhetoric, www.americanrhetoric.com/speeches/jfknucleartestbantreaty.htm (authenticity certified).

82. Joseph Alsop to Evangeline Bruce, June 12, 1963, Joseph Alsop and Steward Alsop Papers, Part III, Box 130, Library of Congress.

83. William Attwood, *The Reds and the Blacks: A Personal Adventure* (New York: Harper & Row, 1967), pp. 133–134.

84. John F. Kennedy, "Civil Rights Address" (televised speech, June 11, 1963), American Rhetoric, www.americanrhetoric.com/speeches/jfkcivilrights.htm (authenticity certified).

85. White House Telephone Memorandum for June 12, 1963, John F. Kennedy Presidential Library and Museum, Boston, Mass. "Mrs. Meyers [*sic*]" called at 2:14 P.M. and was transferred to the president by Evelyn Lincoln. Mrs. Lincoln recorded her phone number as "FE 7 2697."

86. White House Secret Service logs show "Mary Meyers" signed in at 7:30 P.M. on July 3, 1963, and was escorted to the White House residence. John F. Kennedy Presidential Library and Museum, Boston, Mass.

87. Leary, *Flashbacks*, p. 178.

88. Ibid., pp. 178–179.

89. Timothy Leary, interview by Leo Damore, Washington, D.C., November 7, 1990.

90. Halberstam, *Powers That Be*, pp. 382–383.

91. Davis, *Katharine the Great* (1979), p. 169.

92. Felsenthal, *Power, Privilege and the Post*, p. 218.

93. Graham, *Personal History*, p. 331.

94. "Interview with Deborah Davis," p. 83.

95. Graham, *Personal History*, p. 332. Katharine Graham documented "William Smith" as their "caretaker" at Glen Welby at the time of Phil Graham's death.

96. Dovey Roundtree, interview by Leo Damore, Washington, D.C., February 23, 1991.

97. Bill Corson made this remark to Roger Charles at the time of the Senate subcommittee hearings led by Senator Frank Church in 1977 when Charles commented on the number of alleged "suicides" that had taken place in connection with the Kennedy assassination. Roger Charles reiterated Corson's comment to me in December 2010.

98. William E. Colby, testimony, U.S. Senate, September 16, 1975, *Hearings Before the Select Committee to Study Governmental Operations with Respect to Intelligence Activities,* vol. 1, pp. 16–17.

99. Davis, *Katharine the Great* (1979), p. 160.

100. Michael Hasty, "Secret Admirers: The Bushes and the Washington Post," *Online Journal,* February 5, 2004.

101. Norman Solomon, "Katharine Graham and History: Slanting the First Draft," July 19, 2001, FAIR: Fairness and Accuracy in Reporting, www.fair.org/index.php?page=2140.

102. Speech given in 1988 by *Washington Post* editor-owner Katharine Graham at CIA headquarters in Langley, Virginia, to senior CIA employees. See the following: Stephen L. Vaughn, *Encyclopedia of American Journalism* (New York: Routledge, 2008), p. 201.

103. Smith, *Grace and Power,* p. 395.

104. Ibid., p. 398.

105. Peter Evans, *Nemesis* (New York: HarperCollins, 2004), p. 77.

106. Ibid., p. 105.

107. Leary, *Flashbacks,* pp. 190–191.

108. Ibid.

109. Timothy Leary, interview by Leo Damore, Washington, D.C., November 7, 1990.

110. Stephen Siff, "Henry Luce's Strange Trip—Coverage of LSD in *Time* and *Life,* 1954–1968," *Journalism History* 34, no. 3 (Fall 2008): pp. 126–134.

111. Alan Brinkley, *The Publisher: Henry Luce and His American Century* (New York: Knopf, 2010), p. 434.

112. Graham, *Personal History,* p. 196.

113. Ibid., p. 305.

114. Ibid., pp. 343–344.

115. Ibid., p. 492.

116. "Interview with Deborah Davis," p. 83.

117. Smith, *Grace and Power*, p. 411.

118. Telegram from the Embassy in the Soviet Union to the Department of State, October 10, 1963, "Kennedy-Khrushchev Exchanges," no. 118.

119. Douglass, *JFK and the Unspeakable*, p. 267.

120. Leo, Damore, interview by the author, Centerbrook, Conn., February 1992.

121. Kenneth P. O'Donnell and David F. Powers, *Johnny, We Hardly Knew Ye: Memories of John Fitzgerald Kennedy* (New York: Pocket Books, 1973), p. 16.

122. Simone Attwood, interview by the author, Ithaca, N.Y., November 3, 2009.

123. Gordon Chase, "Cuba—Policy," White House memorandum, April 11, 1963, access link in "Kennedy Sought Dialogue with Cuba: Initiative with Castro Aborted by Assassination, Declassified Documents Show," National Security Archive, www.gwu.edu/~nsarchiv/NSAEBB/NSAEBB103/index.htm.

124. David Talbot, *Brothers: The Hidden History of the Kennedy Years* (New York: Free Press, 2007), p. 228.

125. Interview with Jean Daniel, *Kennedy and Castro: The Secret History*, Discovery/Times, November 25, 2003.

126. Ibid.

127. Ibid.

128. Talbot, *Brothers*, p. 217.

129. Arthur Krock, "The Intra-Administration War in Vietnam," In the Nation, *New York Times*, October 3, 1963, p. 34.

130. Robert McNamara made the following comment during Errol Morris's film *The Fog of War*: "I was present with the President when together we received information of that coup. I've never seen him more upset. He totally blanched. President Kennedy and I had tremendous problems with Diem, but my God, he was the authority, he was the head of state. And he

was overthrown by a military coup. And Kennedy knew and I knew, that to some degree, the U.S. government was responsible for that."

131. Nina Burleigh, *A Very Private Woman: The Life and Unsolved Murder of Presidential Mistress Mary Meyer* (New York: Bantam, 1998), p. 220.

132. Smith, *Grace and Power*, p. 444.

133. Ibid., p. 454.

134. Ariel Dougherty, interview by the author, December 3, 2009. Ms. Dougherty was a student at Georgetown Day School in Washington, D.C., when Mary Meyer and Ken Noland taught art studio classes in the late 1950s, as was the author.

135. Leary, *Flashbacks*, p. 194.

136. Ibid. Timothy Leary also reiterated this event to Leo Damore during his interview of November 7, 1990.

137. Leary, interview.

Chapter 11. *After Dallas*

1. Jim Marrs, interview by the author, August 13, 2011. See also: John Armstrong, "Harvey, Lee and Tippit: A New Look at the Tippit Shooting," *Probe*, January-February, 1998 issue (Vol.5 No. 2). http://www.ctka.net/pr198-jfk.html

    While the 1964 Warren Report maintained that officer J.D. Tippit was shot and killed by Lee Harvey Oswald at about 1:15 P.M., many researchers continue to place Oswald in the balcony of the Texas Theater "shortly after 1:00 P.M." According to author Marrs, and assassination researcher John Armstrong, Butch Burroughs was an employee at the Texas Theater. He heard someone enter the theater shortly after 1:00 P.M. and go to the balcony. It was Lee Harvey Oswald who had apparently entered the theater and gone to the balcony without being initially seen by Burroughs. At approximately 1:15 P.M., Oswald came down from the balcony and bought popcorn from Burroughs. Burroughs then watched him walk down the aisle and take a seat on the main floor.

2. Matthew Walton, interview by the author, Woods Hole, Mass., August 28, 2007. Matthew recalled Agnes Meyer making the remark to his father, William Walton.

3. James W. Douglass, *JFK and the Unspeakable: Why He Died and Why It Matters* (Maryknoll, N.Y.: Orbis Books, 2008), pp. 202–207, pp. 213–214. See also Abraham Bolden, *The Echo from Dealey Plaza* (New York: Harmony, 2008), pp. 55–56, p. 58. Secret Service agent Bolden documented the initial evidence for this assassination attempt in Chicago.

4. Anthony Summers, *Not in Your Lifetime* (New York: Marlowe, 1998), pp. 308–309.

5. David Duffy and Bennett Bolton, "JFK's Secret Mistress Assassinated Because She Knew Too Much," *National Enquirer*, July 9, 1996, p. 17.

6. Bennett Bolton, interview by the author, November 8, 2005.

7. Douglass, *JFK and the Unspeakable*, pp. 213–217.

8. Nina Burleigh, *A Very Private Woman: The Life and Unsolved Murder of Presidential Mistress Mary Meyer* (New York: Bantam, 1998), p. 220. Interviewing only Mary Fischer on the topic of Kennedy's assassination, Burleigh never pursued any of Mary Meyer's concerns about what had really happened in Dallas, leaving the reader to believe that she ultimately was convinced that Lee Harvey Oswald was responsible for the death of the president.

9. Ron Rosenbaum and Phillip Nobile, "The Curious Aftermath of JFK's Best and Brightest Affair," *New Times*, July 9, 1976, p. 29.

10. Leo Damore, interview by the author, Centerbrook, Conn., February 1992. Damore spoke often to me about what Kenny O'Donnell had told him regarding Mary Meyer's influence on President Kennedy.

11. Tip O'Neill, *Man of the House: The Life and Political Memoirs of Speaker Tip O'Neill*, with William Novak (New York: Random House, 1987), p. 178.

12. Ibid.

13. WCAP Radio producer and talk show host Woody Woodland interviewed Douglas P. Horne, author of *Inside the Assassination Records Review Board: The U.S. Government's Final Attempt to Reconcile the Conflicting Medical Evidence in the Assassination of JFK*, 5 vols. (printed by author, 2009) on the air on November 19, 2009, from Lowell, Massachusetts. During that interview, Mr. Woodland recounted verbatim his conversation with Dave Powers in late 1991, following the release of Oliver Stone's film *JFK*.

14. Jim Marrs, *Crossfire: The Plot That Killed Kennedy*. New York: Carroll & Graf, 1989), p. 482.

15. David Talbot, *Brothers: The Hidden History of the Kennedy Years* (New York: Free Press, 2007), p. 6. See also Talbot's notes, p. 411.

16. Arthur M. Schlesinger Jr., *Robert Kennedy and His Times* (Boston: Houghton Mifflin, 2002), p. 616.

17. Talbot, *Brothers*, p. 7.

18. Ibid.

19. This was confirmed in my interview on July 15, 2009, with an individual who wanted to remain anonymous, and who knew well the person who had been in the presidential entourage in Dallas on November 22, 1963. The person in the president's entourage also knew Mary Meyer very well.

20. Dino Brugioni, interview by the author, February 13, 2009. I first contacted Mr. Brugioni by telephone on January 30, 2009. It was during that initial interview I first learned that he had worked closely with my father, Wistar Janney, on several operations. When I made a passing reference to the Zapruder film, Brugioni corrected my reference and told me that the CIA had been in possession of the film the day after the assassination. This revelation prompted a subsequent series of interviews between Brugioni and myself that took place on February 12, 13, 14, March 6, 10, and April 30, 2009. I later visited Dino Brugioni at his home in Hartwood, Virginia, on June 27, 2009, for additional clarification and input.

21. Ibid.

22. Schlesinger, *Robert Kennedy and His Times*, p. 616. See "Author's journal, December 9, 1963," p. 988n49.

23. Homer McMahon, interview by the Assassination Records Review Board (ARRB), July 14, 1997, National Archives II, College Park, Md.

24. Ibid.

25. Brugioni, interview, February 13, 2009.

26. Dino Brugioni, interview by the author, Hartwood, Va., April 28, 2011.

27. Horne, *Assassination Records Review Board*, 4: p. 1241.

28. Ibid., 3: p. 778.

29. Ibid., 1: p. 58, p. 76, p. 171; ibid., 3: pp. 727–881.

30. Ibid., 2: pp. 630–640. See also Appendix 23 and Appendix 28 in that volume.

31. David S. Lifton, *Best Evidence: Disguise and Deception in the Assassination of John F. Kennedy* (New York: Macmillan, 1980); Horne, *Assassination Records Review Board, Volume II.*

32. Tom Wicker, "Gov. Connally Shot; Mrs. Kennedy Safe," *New York Times,* November 23, 1963,. p. 1.

33. White House Transcript 1327-C. This is a verbatim record of the remarks made by Dr. Perry and Dr. Clark at the Parkland Memorial Hospital's press conference, which convened at 3:16 P.M on November 22, 1963. It is available at the Mary Ferrell Foundation's website (www.maryferrell. org). See also Horne, *Assassination Records Review Board, 2:* p. 646.

34. Horne, *Assassination Records Review Board, 2:* pp. 644–645.

35. Testimony of Dr. Malcolm Perry, March 25 and March 30, 1964, Warren Commission Proceedings. See also Horne, *Assassination Records Review Board, 2:* pp. 648–649.

36. Mark Lane, "Oswald Innocent? A Lawyer's Brief," *National Guardian,* December 19, 1963. Staunton Lynd and Jack Minnis, "Seeds of Doubt: Some Questions About the Assassination," *New Republic,* December 21, 1963, pp. 14-20.

37. Peter Kihss, "Lawyer Urges Defense for Oswald at Inquiry," *New York Times,* December 19, 1963.

38. Mark Lane, "Oswald Innocent? A Lawyer's Brief," *National Guardian,* December 19, 1963.

39. Ibid. Also, see the following: Mark Lane, *Plausible Denial: Was the CIA Involved in the Assassination of JFK?,* (New York: Thunder's Mouth Press, 1991), p. 355. Lane quoted the December 1, 1963. article found in the *St. Louis Post-Dispatch.*

40. Mark Lane, "Oswald Innocent? A Lawyer's Brief," *National Guardian,* December 19, 1963. Also in *Plausible Denial: Was the CIA Involved in the Assassination of JFK?,* by Mark Lane (New York: Thunder's Mouth Press, 1991), p. 360.

41. Lane, *Plausible Denial,* p. 322.

42. Harry S. Truman, editorial, "U.S. Should Hold CIA to Intelligence Role," *Washington Post,* December 22, 1963, A11. This was the title of the editorial as it appeared in the paper on the morning of December 22, 1963,

but for some unknown reason it has since been cited as "Limit CIA Role to Intelligence."

43. John Kelin, *Praise from a Future Generation: The Assassination of John F. Kennedy and the First Generation Critics of the Warren Report* (San Antonio, Tex.: Wings Press, 2007), p. 451.

44. Ibid., p. 553n62; John Kelin, interview by the author, September 16, 2010.

45. Ray Marcus, interview by the author, September 28, 2010.

46. Peter Dale Scott, *Deep Politics and the Death of JFK* (Berkeley: University of California Press, 1996), p. 295.

47. Marcus, interview. John Kelin also told me he discussed this incident with Ray Marcus at some length in an interview with me on September 16, 2010, as did the disaffected former CIA analyst Raymond McGovern on February 26, 2011.

48. Memorandum for Mr. Lawrence R. Houston, General Counsel, from A. W. Dulles, Subject: Visit to the Honorable Harry S. Truman Friday Afternoon, April 17, 2 p.m. Doc. 95, Miscellaneous Historical Documents Collection, Harry S. Truman Library and Museum, Independence, Mo.

49. Harry S. Truman to William B. Arthur, *Look,* June 10, 1964, in *Compromised: Clinton, Bush, and the CIA*, by Terry Reed and John Cummings (New York: S.P.I. Books, 1994), p. ii.

50. Ray McGovern, "Are Presidents Afraid of the CIA?," December 29, 2009, Common Dreams (CommonDreams.org); Ray McGovern, interview by the author, February 26, 2011.

51. Leo Damore stated that he had talked with William Walton and that Walton confirmed Mary had come to him grief-stricken after President Kennedy's assassination, though there was no tape of any recorded interview or notes in any of Damore's research. The discreet Walton may have insisted that their interview not be recorded.

52. Interview with William Walton, box 56 (folder 4) and box 96 (folder 9), Papers of Clay Blair, Jr., American Heritage Center, University of Wyoming.

53. Walton, interview.

54. Ibid.

55. Buehler, Frances, interview by the author, Woods Hole, Mass., June 5, 2006; Walton, interview.

56. Talbot., *Brothers*, pp. 25–34.

57. Aleksandr Fursenko and Timothy J. Naftali, *One Hell of a Gamble: Khrushchev, Castro, and Kennedy, 1958–1964* (New York: W. W. Norton, 1998), p. 345.

58. Ibid.

59. Talbot, *Brothers*, p. 8.

60. Walton, interview.

61. Ibid.

62. Ibid.

63. Evelyn Lincoln, *Kennedy and Johnson* (New York: Holt, Rinehart & Winston, 1968), pp. 204–205.

64. James Wagenvoord, interview by the author, January 9, 2011.

65. James Wagenvoord profile, Spartacus Educational, November 3, 2009. www.spartacus.schoolnet.co.uk/JFKwagenvoord.htm. In addition, James Wagenvoord, interview by the author, January 9, 2011.

66. James Wagenvoord, interview by the author, January 9, 2011.

67. Ibid.

68. Ibid.

69. John M. Newman, *JFK and Vietnam: Deception, Intrigue, and the Struggle for Power* (New York: Warner, 1992), pp. 446–447.

70. Tom Wicker, *JFK and LBJ: The Influence of Personality Upon Politics* (New York: William Morrow, 1968), p. 185.

71. Stanley Karnow, *Vietnam: A History* (New York: Viking, 1983), p. 326. Karnow has always been convinced of this quote's accuracy, having heard it from General Harold K. Johnson, then the Army chief of staff, who was in attendance at the White House Christmas Eve meeting with President Johnson.

72. Talbot, Brothers, p. 219.

73. Ziad Obermeyer, Christopher J. L. Murray, and Emmanuela Gakidou, "Fifty Years of Violent War Deaths from Vietnam to Bosnia: Analysis of Data from World Health Survey Programme," *British Medical Journal* 336,

no. 28 (June 2008). The method used by the authors indicated that 3.8 million Vietnamese died in the protracted fighting in Vietnam, mostly from 1955 to 1975, compared to previous estimates cited by the researchers of 2.1 million.

74. Robert Dallek, *Lyndon B. Johnson: Portrait of a President* (Oxford, U.K.: Oxford University Press, 2005), p. 315.

75. Burleigh, *A Very Private Woman*, p. 226.

76. Ibid., pp. 124–125, p. 204.

77. Toni Shimon, interview by the author, Long Island, N.Y., February 15, 2007.

78. Leo Damore, interviews by the author, Centerbrook, Conn., February 1992 and April 1993.

79. Robert D. Morrow, *First Hand Knowledge: How I Participated in the CIA-Mafia Murder of President Kennedy* (New York: S.P.I. Books, 1992), pp. 274–280.

80. Talbot, *Brothers*, p. 18.

81. Morrow. *First Hand Knowledge*, pp. 279–280.

82. Burleigh, *A Very Private Woman*, p. 292.

83. John Williams, interview by the author, February 2, 2004.

84. Ibid.; In addition, John Williams, interviews by the author, May 18, 2007, and November 16, 2009; Jeanne ("Hap") Morrow, interview by the author, January 28, 2004.

85. Williams, interview, May 18, 2007. Jeanne ("Hap") Morrow, interview by the author, January 28, 2004.

86. Williams, interviews, May 18, 2007.

87. Ibid.

Chapter 12. *How it went down: The Anatomy of a CIA Assassination – Part I*

1. Katie McCabe and Dovey Johnson Roundtree, *Justice Older Than the Law: The Life of Dovey Johnson Roundtree* (Jackson: University Press of Mississippi, 2009). p. 191.

2. Trial transcript, United States of America v. Ray Crump, Jr., Defendant, Criminal Case No. 930-64, United States District Court for the District of Columbia, Washington, D.C., July 20, 1965, p. 211.

3. Ibid., p. 178.

4. Ibid., pp. 136–137.

5. Ibid., p. 137.

6. Henry Wiggins, interview by Leo Damore, Washington, D.C., April 2, 1992.

7. Ibid.

8. Trial transcript, pp. 658–659.

9. Ibid., pp. 657–659.

10. *Department of Defense Telephone Directory*, Fall 1964, Area Code 202 Dial Oxford Plus Extension Number or Liberty 5-6700 • Interdepartmental Code II, p. 91. This particular directory was part of Leo Damore's material and research. All past Defense Department directories can located at the Library of Congress.

11. Roberta Hornig, "Teacher Says He Passed by Mrs. Meyer," *Washington Star*, July 27, 1965.

12. David MacMichael, interview by the author, June 22, 2004. Leo Damore interviewed Mr. MacMichael repeatedly during 1992.

13. Donald E. Deneselya, interview by the author, Washington, D.C., May 29, 2007; Victor Marchetti, interview by the author, Leesburg, Va., October 4, 2007.

14. As of 2011, Roger Charles is coauthoring a book with Andrew Gumbel about Timothy McVeigh and the Oklahoma City bombing in 1995, entitled *Oaklahoma City: What the Investigation Missed and Why It Still Matters* (William Morrow, 2012).

15. Roger Charles, interview by the author, June 10, 2005.

16. Confidential written interview notes from author H. P. Albarelli Jr. dated September 2001 and faxed to the author on February 11, 2010.

17. H. P. Albarelli Jr., communications by email and telephone with the author, February 12, 2010.

18. Ibid.; personal communications between H. P. Albarelli Jr. and his confidential source on February 12 and 13, 2010, as reported to the author via Albarelli's emails and follow-up telephone conversations.

19. Timothy Leary, interview by Leo Damore, Washington, D.C., November 7, 1990.

20. Hilaire du Berrier, *Background to Betrayal: The Tragedy of Vietnam* (Appleton, Wis.: Western Islands, 1965), p. 143. Du Berrier documents that Bernie Yoh did "public relations" work for the president of South Vietnam, writing that "Bernie Yoh was the stooge to fly back and forth between Washington and Saigon; to Saigon so he could say he had been there, then back to America to tell editors, women's clubs and congressmen, 'Don't believe what you hear. I have just come from Vietnam. I have been in the jungles with the guerillas, killing Communists, and we are winning. You are not going to desert Vietnam as you did my country, are you?" Author David Martin said, however, that "Yoh denied to me that he had ever worked for the CIA, saying that he thought they were too stupid for him to have anything to do with them, but he had lectured to the U.S. Air War College on a subject in which he claimed world-class expertise, psychological warfare." See David Martin, "Spook Journalist Goulden," August 11, 1998, *DC Dave's*, www.dcdave.com/article1/081198.html.

21. Bernie Yoh, telephone interview by Leo Damore, Washington, D.C., October 30, 1990. Damore wrote two pages of typewritten notes on the call. It's not known whether Damore taped the telephone interview.

22. Leo Damore, to his attorney, James H. Smith, on the morning of March 31, 1993. The exact date of Damore's communication with Prouty is not known. See Appendix 3.

23. L. Fletcher. Prouty, *The Secret Team: The CIA and Its Allies in Control of the United States and the World* (Costa Mesa, Calif.: Institute for Historical Review, 1973), Passim. Prouty's duties at the Pentagon were to provide the CIA with the military resources needed to carry out its clandestine operations. He created a secret, well-trained network of agents throughout the military service sectors and U.S. government agencies, including the FBI and the FAA, and inside various foreign governments.

24. James H. Smith, Esq., interview by the author, April 7, 2004.

25. Leo Damore stated to this author on several occasions starting in 1992 that Mary Meyer had bought a paperback copy of the Warren Commission's report when it first went on sale in September 1964.

26. Ibid. See also Appendix 3.

27. Leo Damore interview by the author, Centerbrook, Conn., April 1993.

28. See Appendix 3.

29. Prouty, *Secret Team*, p. 141, p. 268, pp. 335–336, p. 418.

30. Albarelli, confidential written interview notes.

31. Smith, interview. See also page 2 of Appendix 3.

32. Ibid. See also page 6 of Appendix 3.

33. 33 See page 3 of Appendix 3.

34. Richard Pine, interview by the author, October 21, 2004.

35. Mark O'Blazney, interview by the author, Washington, D.C., November 27, 2008.

36. Smith, interview. See also pages 4–6 in Appendix 3.

37. Joseph J. Trento, *The Secret History of the CIA* (Roseville, Calif.: Prima, 2001), p. 89. Nowhere is the capacity of the CIA's Technical Services Division better explained than in H. P. Albarelli Jr.'s book *A Terrible Mistake: The Murder of Frank Olson and the CIA's Secret Cold War Experiments* (Walterville, Ore.: Trine Day, 2009).

38. McCabe and Roundtree, *Justice Older Than the Law*, p. 195. See also trial transcript, p. 493. Crump's neighbor, Elsie Perkins, testified that she saw Crump leave his house that morning "between five minutes of eight and eight o'clock."

39. Trial transcript, p. 140.

40. Ibid., pp. 129–130.

41. McCabe and Roundtree., *Justice Older Than the Law*, p. 195.

42. Ibid., pp. 195–196.

43. Trial transcript, p. 134.

44. Ibid., p. 259.

45. Ibid., p. 661.

46. Ibid., p. 425.

47. Ibid., p. 569.

48. Ibid., pp. 407–408.

49. Ibid., p. 608, p. 649.

50. Benjamin C. Bradlee, *A Good Life: Newspapering and Other Adventures* (New York: Simon & Schuster, 1995), p. 266.

51. In passing, Bradlee did reference Wistar Janney earlier in his memoir (p. 118), but the page reference was not part of Wistar Janney's heading in the index of the Bradlee memoir. The passage read as follows: "Socially our crowd consisted of young couples, around thirty years old, with young kids, being raised without help by their mothers, and without many financial resources. The Janneys—Mary and Wistar, who worked for the CIA; the Winships—Leibe and Tom who worked for Senator Lev Saltonstall of Massachusetts . . ."

52. Ben Bradlee, interview by the author, Washington, D.C. January 31, 2007.

53. Trial transcript, p. 608, p. 649.

54. Christopher Janney, interview by the author, February 20, 2010.

55. Bradlee, *Good Life*, p. 143.

Chapter 13. *How it went down: The Anatomy of a CIA Assassination – Part II*

1. John M. Newman, "James Jesus Angleton and the Assassination of John F. Kennedy" (lecture, "Cracking the JFK Case," symposium sponsored by the Assassination Archives and Research Center, Washington, D.C., November 19, 2005).

2. Cord Meyer Jr., *Facing Reality: From World Federalism to the CIA* (New York: Harper & Row, 1980), pp.143-144.

3. C. David Heymann, *The Georgetown Ladies' Social Club* (New York: Atria Books, 2003), p. 167.

4. Carol Delaney, telephone communication with the author. February 22, 2010.

5. Heymann, *Georgetown Ladies' Social Club*, p. 168.

6. The most recent criticism of author C. David Heymann's journalistic credibility has come from researcher Lisa Pease. See her review of Heymann's

book *Bobby and Jackie: A Love Story* (2009) at Citizens for Truth about the Kennedy Assassination, www.ctka.net/reviews/heymann.html.

7. C. David Heymann, interview by the author, New York, N.Y., March 18, 2005.

8. C. David Heymann, voice mail left on the author's home telephone, March 9, 2007.

9. David Wise, *Molehunt: The Secret Search for Traitors That Shattered the CIA* (New York: Random House, 1992), p. 38.

10. Ibid., p. 293.

11. Zack Corson (son of Bill Corson), interview by the author. New York, N.Y., October 25, 2007.

12. Joseph J. Trento, *The Secret History of the CIA* (Roseville, Calif.: Prima, 2001), p. xiii.

13. Ibid.

14. J. Michael Kelly, interviews by the author, March 9, 2004, and April 12, 2007. Mike Kelly and Tom Kimmel were classmates at Annapolis. Roger Charles, who became the executor of Bill Corson's estate, was in the class behind them. All three were mentored by Bill Corson when he taught at the U.S. Naval Academy.

15. J. Michael Kelly, interview by the author, March 9, 2004.

16. Both Roger Charles and Tom Kimmel recalled and confirmed the accuracy of this event. Roger Charles, interview by the author, April 13, 2007; Thomas K. Kimmel, interview by the author, May 14, 2007.

17. Plato Cacheris, Esq., interview by the author, Washington, D.C., April 27, 2007.

18. Roger Charles, email communication with the author, December 5, 2007.

19. Gregory Douglas, *Gestapo Chief: The 1948 Interrogation of Heinrich Müller,* vol. 2 (San Jose, Calif.: R. James Bender Publishing, 1997), p. 5.

20. Emily Crowley, interview by the author, March 24, 2007; Thomas K. Kimmel, interview by the author, March 13, 2007. In a telephone conversation in early 2011, Philip Kushner, a lecturer in the Department of Mathematics at the University of Texas, also told the author that he had talked with Bob Crowley's wife, Emily, and she had verified her late husband's telephone relationship with Gregory Douglas.

21. "Gregory Douglas" (Peter Stahl), interview by the author, Aurora, Ill., April 10, 2007.

22. Emily Crowley, interview.

23. Kimmel, interview, March 13, 2007.

24. Ibid.; Thomas K. Kimmel, interview by the author, November 20, 2008.

25. Emily Crowley, interview.

26. Transcription of alleged tape-recorded telephone conversation between Robert Crowley and Gregory Douglas, January 27, 1996.

27. Transcription of alleged Crowley-Douglas conversation, April 2, 1996.

28. David Acheson, interview by the author, Washington, D.C., December 10, 2008.

29. Charles Bartlett, interview by the author, Washington, D.C., December 10, 2008.

30. James H. Smith, Esq., interview by the author, April 7, 2004, quoting from pages 1, 3, 4, 5, and 6 of his notes on his March 31, 1993, conversation with Leo Damore. See Appendix 3.

31. Crowley-Douglas conversation, January 27, 1996.

32. Robert L. Morrow, *First Hand Knowledge: How I Participated in the CIA-Mafia Murder of President Kennedy* (New York: S.P.I. Books, 1992), p. 277.

33. John Williams, interviews by the author, May 18, 2007, and November 16, 2009; Jeanne Morrow, personal communication with the author, January 28, 2004.

34. During the author's three-year association with Leo Damore starting in 1992, Damore mentioned O'Donnell's comments on this matter repeatedly. Damore's former wife, June Davison, also remembered Leo discussing O'Donnell's statement with her, as did Damore's attorney, James H. Smith, Esq.

35. Email communication from Gregory Douglas to Joseph Trento, , November 19, 2001, given to the author by Gregory Douglas.

36. Email communication from Joseph Trento to Gregory Douglas, November 3, 2002, given to the author by Gregory Douglas.

37. The Operation Zipper file appears prominently in Gregory Douglas's *Regicide: The Official Assassination of John F. Kennedy* (Huntsville, Ala.: Monte Sano Media, 2002.

38. There are two excellent sources for how the CIA, and particularly James Jesus Angleton, controlled Lee Harvey Oswald, starting with his fake defection to Russia in 1959: John Newman, *Oswald and the CIA* (1995; repr., New York: Skyhorse, 2008), pp. 613–637; James W. Douglass, *JFK and the Unspeakable: Why He Died and Why It Matters* (Maryknoll, N.Y.: Orbis Books, 2008), pp. 75–84.

39. In John Newman's latest edition of *Oswald and the CIA* (pp. 613–637), the author included a new chapter entitled "Epilogue, 2008:—The Plot to Murder President Kennedy; A New Interpretation." Here, as a result of records made available through of the passage of the 1993 JFK Records Act, historian Newman sheds light "on the nature and design of the plot and the national security cover-up that followed." He continues:

> In my view, whoever Oswald's direct handler or handlers were, we must now seriously consider the possibility that [James Jesus] Angleton was probably their general manager. No one else in the Agency had the access, the authority, and the diabolically ingenious mind to manage this sophisticated plot. No one had the means necessary to plant the WWIII virus in Oswald's files and keep it dormant for six weeks until the president's assassination. Whoever those who were ultimately responsible for the decision to kill Kennedy were, their reach extended into the national intelligence apparatus to such a degree that they could call upon a person who knew its inner secrets and workings so well that he could design a failsafe mechanism into the fabric of the plot. The only person who could ensure that a national security cover-up of an apparent counterintelligence nightmare was the head of counterintelligence (p. 637).

40. Email communication from Gregory Douglas to Joseph Trento, November 3, 2002, given to the author by Gregory Douglas.

41. Deborah Davis, *Katharine the Great: Katharine Graham and Her Washington Post Empire* (New York: Sheridan Square Press, 1991), p. 304. See also Appendix 4.

42. Davis, *Katharine the Great* (1991), p. 286. See also Appendix 4.

43. "An Interview with Deborah Davis," in *Popular Alienation: A Steamshovel Press Reader*, ed. Kenn Thomas (Lilburn, Ga.: IllumiNet Press, 1995), pp. 79–81.

44. Benjamin C. Bradlee, *A Good Life: Newspapering and Other Adventures* (New York: Simon & Schuster, 1995), 267.

45. Ron Rosenbaum and Phillip Nobile, "The Curious Aftermath of JFK's Best and Brightest Affair," *New Times*, July 9, 1976, p. 29.

46. Ben Bradlee, interview by the author, Washington, D.C., January 31, 2007.

47. Bradlee, *Good Life*, p. 266.

48. Gabe Torres, interview by the author, Washington, D.C., April 22, 2010. As a chief consultant for this production, I had purposely not been present during the filming of Bradlee's segment, but conferred with Torres afterward. Torres had been made aware of the Wistar Janney phone call, however.

49. Trial transcript, United States of America v. Ray Crump, Jr., Defendant, Criminal Case No. 930-64, United States District Court for the District of Columbia, Washington, D.C., July 20, 1965, p. 47.

50. Bradlee, *Good Life*, pp. 274–283.

51. Rosenbaum and Nobile, "Curious Aftermath," p. 32.

52. Bradlee, *Good Life*, p. 266.

53. Ibid.

54. Nancy Pittman Pinchot, interview by the author, December 2, 2008.

55. Antoinette Bradlee letter to Leo Damore, dated July 29, 1991.

56. Betsy Karasik, "Anne Chamberlin: A life to emulate," *Washington Post*, January 6, 2012.

57. John Newman, personal communication with the author, Harrisonburg, Va., April 29, 2004.

58. Ron Rosenbaum, *The Secret Parts of Fortune: Three Decades of Intense Investigations and Edgy Enthusiasms* (New York: Random House, 2000), pp. 503–504.

59. David Philips, *The Night Watch* (New York: Atheneum, 1977), p. 189.

60. Nowhere is this thesis more carefully and thoroughly researched than in the most recent edition of John Newman's *Oswald and the CIA* (1995; repr., New York: Skyhorse, 2008). See "Epilogue, 2008: The Plot to Murder President Kennedy; A New Interpretation," pp. 613–637.

61. Tom Mangold, *Cold Warrior: James Jesus Angleton; The CIA's Master Spy Hunter* (New York: Simon & Schuster, 1991), p. 30, p. 358n1.

62. Trento, *Secret History*, p. 280.

63. Ibid., p. 479.

64. Ibid., pp. 478–479.

65. Ibid.

66. Rosenbaum, *Secret Parts of Fortune*, p. 143.

67. Ibid., pp. 141–143.

Chapter 14. Epilogue

1. William E. Colby, testimony, U.S. Senate, September 16, 1975, *Hearings Before the Select Committee to Study Governmental Operations with Respect to Intelligence Activities*, vol. 1, pp. 16–17.

    During the Church Committee's Senate investigations in 1975, CIA director William Colby presented to committee chairman Frank Church a pistol resembling a .45-caliber automatic equipped with a telescopic sight. *Time* magazine reported that "the gun fires a toxin-tipped dart, almost silently and accurately up to 250 ft. Moreover, the dart is so tiny— the width of a human hair and a quarter of an inch long—as to be almost undetectable, and the poison leaves no trace in a victim's body."

    Senator Church referred to the pistol as follows: "As a murder instrument, that's about as efficient as you can get, is it not?" To which Colby's response was, "It's a weapon, a very serious weapon." *Time* further revealed "the agency has also developed two other dart-launching pistols, as well as a fountain pen that can fire deadly darts and an automobile engine-head bolt that releases a toxic substance when heated."

2. Joseph Trento, *The Secret History of The CIA* (Roseville, Ca: Prima Publishing, 2001), p. 89.

3. Nina Burleigh, *A Very Private Woman: The Life and Unsolved Murder of Presidential Mistress Mary Meyer* (New York: Bantam, 1998), p. 133.

4. Toni Shimon, interviews by the author, June 17, 2004, February 15, 2007, and January 7, 2008.

5. Ibid., February 15, 2007.

6. Anthony Summers, *The Secret Life of J. Edgar Hoover* (London: Victor Gollancz, 1993), pp. 81–84. Joseph Shimon's professional life is well documented in this book.

7. Shimon, interview, February 15, 2007.

8. Jim Marrs, *Crossfire: The Plot That Killed Kennedy* (New York: Carroll & Graf, 1989), pp. 558–566.

9. Shimon, interviews, February 15, 2007, and January 7, 2008.

10. Jack Anderson and Joseph Spear, "Witness Tells of CIA Plot to Kill Castro," *Washington Post*, November 1, 1988.

11. Shimon, interview, January 7, 2008.

12. Anderson and Spear, "Witness Tells of CIA Plot," C19.

13. Ibid.

14. Shimon, interview, February 15, 2007.

15. Ibid.

Chapter 15. Post Script

1. Katie McCabe and Dovey Roundtree, *Justice Older than the Law: The Life of Dovey J. Roundtree* (Jackson: University Press of Mississippi, 2009), p. 218.

2. Email communication between T. James Scully and University of Georgia law professor Donald Wilkes dated August 10, 2012. Professor Wilkes kindly forwarded this email to me on September 13, 2012.

3. The Mitchell entry in Ancestry.com in early 2013 listed William Mitchell's father and mother, and his brother James, but only the caption "Private" in place of their first born.

4. Next to his senior picture, the 1957 yearbook of the Horace Greely High School (*The Quaker*) in Chappaqua, New York, lists "William Mitchell" with the aforementioned extracurricular activities.

5. *The Cornell Engineer*, April 1962, p. 37.

6. Starting in the fall of 2012, and with the assistance of a current Cornell undergraduate, I painstakingly reviewed the main Cornell yearbook (*The Cornellian*) for every one of the years that William Mitchell was in attendance at Cornell (1958–1962). While Mitchell's name was listed as only "William Mitchell" in the 1962 Cornell yearbook as a member of the general engineering honor society known as Tau Beta Phi, as well as the mechanical engineering honor society known as Pi Tau Sigma, there was no picture of Mitchell anywhere. In the 1962 graduating senior section of the year book (*The Cornellian*), where each senior is pictured, the

following successive alphabetical entries are listed. There is no senior listing for **WILLIAM LOCKWOOD MITCHELL** on page 400 where it should be, right after **PETER HARLON MITCHELL**, or anywhere else in the 1962 yearbook:

DONALD CHARLES MITCHELL Phoenix, Ariz. Electrical Engineering. BEE. West High School. Eta Kappa Nu, Sec.; IVCF, Pres.; John McMullen Regional Scholarship; Dean's List.

PETER HARLON MITCHELL Westfield, N. J. Electrical Engineering. BEE. Cheltenham High School. ex. Eta Kappa Nu; Mu Sigma Tau; AIEE·IRE ; John McMullen Regional Scholarship; Dean's List.

WILLIAM MOBBS Ithaca. Civil Engineering. BCE. Ithaca High School. Big Red Band; Concert Band; New York State Engineering and Science Scholarship; Dean's List.

7.   This document was procured through the Army ROTC offices at Cornell University. Dated "23 September 1960," it lists the "Distinguished Military Students for the School year 1960-61." The list is comprised of thirty-two (32) Army ROTC students, and addressed as follows: "To: Personnel Concerned." It is signed by "C.H. Blumenfeld, Colonel, Artillery PMS".

8.   Dated November 12, 2012, Roger Charles received a letter from the NPRC stating the following: "Thank you for contacting the National Personnel Records Center. We have been attempting to verify the veteran's military service from the information that has been provided. We have conducted extensive searches of every records source and alternate records source at this Center; however, we have been unable to locate any information that would help us verify the veteran's military service." On August 29, 2012, in a separate request to the NPRC, I asked for Mitchell's service record using his full name, date of birth, and the first five digits of his social security number. I received an identical letter back from the NPRC, again dated November 12, 2012.

9.   Author telephone call with someone identifying himself as "Mr. Jones" at the NPRC on November 8, 2012.

10.   Detective Whalen conveyed this information to Roger Charles and myself on January 10, 2013, during one of our meetings with him at police headquarters in Washington, D.C.

11. A complete history of the NPRC fire on July 12, 1973, can be viewed online at the following link: http://www.archives.gov/st-louis/military-personnel/fire-1973.html

12. Using the name "Bill Mitchell," he submitted a written questionnaire for his 25th reunion for the class of 1957 at Horace Greely High School in Chappaqua, New York, in 1982. He stated that he had been in the U.S. Army and was assigned to Ft. Eustis, which is located in Newport News, Virginia.

13. William L. Mitchell first appears in the Pentagon's Department of Defense (DoD) quarterly telephone directory in the fall of 1964 (p. 91). During this time (1964–67), the directory was published four times a year: fall, winter, spring, and summer. Mitchell's listing continues for winter 1965 (p. 100); spring 1965 (p. 102); summer 1965 (p. 102); fall 1965 (p. 104); winter 1966 (p. 106); spring 1966 (p. 108); summer 1966 (p. 112); fall 1966 (p. 113); winter 1967 (p. 111); spring 1967 (p. 115); summer 1967 (p. 131). The summer 1967 listing was the last time Mitchell was listed in the DoD directory. He is not listed in the fall 1967 directory, nor beyond.

14. This interview was conducted by Don Devereux on December 14, 2012. The names of all the interviewees are intentionally being withheld. Mr. Devereux is a long-term member of Investigative Reporters and Editors (IRE). He participated in IRE's "Arizona Project" in 1976–77 during the aftermath of the car-bomb murder of Phoenix journalist Don Bolles, which won a number of national news media awards for public service. Individually, Don has also received a press award from New Mexico environmentalists in 1977. Questioning the official response to the Bolles homicide, he continued work on the case from 1979 to 1988 for the *Scottsdale Progress,* winning an Arizona Press Club 1981 nomination for state newsperson of the year and placing as a finalist. His investigative work for the print media also earned him two Pulitzer nominations. In addition, Devereux has published many articles, commentaries, and reviews since the mid-1960s, including the *New Mexico Review, Voice of the Southwest, New Times, Washington Times,* and the *San Francisco Examiner.*

15. See note #14 above.

16. Interview conducted via telephone by Don Devereux on January 9, 2013. The name of the interviewee is intentionally being withheld.

17. Robert M. Gates, *From the Shadows: The Ultimate Insider's Story of Five Presidents and How They Won the Cold War* (New York: Simon & Schuster Paperbacks, 1996), pp. 19–20.

18. On October 1, 1964, The Adjutant Generals' Office (TAGO) listed Lt. Col. R. Cruikshank as "Army War Room SPT Branch" located in Pentagon office BE1035.

19. Included in what investigative journalist Roger Charles was able to obtain was Lt. Col. Ralph Heller Cruikshank's application for federal employment, consisting of a ten-page resume of many of his military and intelligence assignments.

20. Ibid.

21. Ibid. On his application for federal employment, Ralph Heller Cruikshank listed his exact position title from "1 September 1964 to 1 May 1966" as "Chief, Army Ops Cen Spt Div" [Chief, Army Operations Center Support Division].

22. During the winter of 2013, Roger Charles interviewed the following individuals: Col. Leon M. Miller; the son of Major James H. Fette; Capt. Rome Smyth; and Maj. J. G. Peura. Also, author follow-up interview with Capt. Rome Smyth on May 6, 2013.

23. Dated October 20, 1968, the Agency for International Development Supervisor's Certification for Step Increase for "CRUIKSHANK, Ralph H.," in connection with AID Mission: Vietnam, is signed by "T. S. Jones" on September 20, 1968, and John P. Vann (with the title "Dep CORDS, III CT2") on "9-27-68."

24. A fifty-year trusted associate of Roger Charles has known Joe Langlois for many years and considers him to be highly credible. During Charles's conversation in early 2013 with Langlois, he also recalled that Cruikshank was rumored to have "program problems," meaning security problems, which meant that this could have enabled Cruikshank to have "carte blanche" to carry out his "other mission," the covert one. While this was never fully substantiated, the possibility of a covert mission would help explain Cruikshank's mysterious mission in Vietnam.

25. See the following: Neil Sheehan, *A Bright Shining Lie: John Paul Vann and America in Vietnam.* (New York: Vintage Books, September 1989).

26. Lt. Col. Ralph Heller Cruikshank's absence from any of the 1967–69 Army Retired Officer's Registries is highly suspicious and unusual, according to Roger Charles.

27. *United States Government Memorandum* dated May 29, 1973 from "Ralph H. Cruikshank" to "Mr. Floyd Spears, Personnel, USAID." "Subject: Retirement." The memorandum read as follows: "This is to advise you that upon my retirement, effective June 30, 1973, it is my intention to remain in country. Attached is a copy of a letter which has been forwarded to the Army Finance Center at Indianapolis, Indiana, regarding my Army retirement."

28. Interview conducted via telephone by Roger Charles with Frank Peter Cruikshank III, son of Ralph Heller Cruikshank on January 10, 2013.

29. See pp. 61–62 of *Mary's Mosaic*. As noted, Captain Donahue's comments were contained in the following articles: "Rape Weighed as Motive in Death of Mrs. Meyer." *The Evening Star,* October 14, 1964, Metro section, p. B-1; and "Meyer Slaying—Police have 'Mystery' Witness." *The Washington Daily News,* October 14, 1964.

30. According to the official trial transcript, the person identifying himself as "Mr. William L. Mitchell" testified on Monday, July 26, 1965. Prosecutor Alfred Hantman makes reference during the trial to the fact that Mitchell is no longer in the Army. The day after Mitchell testified, July 27, *Washington Star* reporter Roberta Hornig mentioned Mitchell in an article headlined "Teacher Says He Passed by Mrs. Meyer." *The Washington Evening Star,* July 27, 1965. Ms. Hornig identified Mitchell in this article as "a Georgetown University mathematics teacher," then added the following: "Mitchell, who was then [on the day of the Meyer murder] an Army lieutenant . . ." During the early 1990s, author Leo Damore queried officials at Georgetown University about Mitchell's employment there, but he was unable to locate any documentation of that employment. In 2004, I again contacted Georgetown and asked for verification of Mitchell's employment, but was told there was none.

31. See the following: T. C. Hsiao (Editor), *Who's Who in Computer Education and Research: Vol.3. Faculty and Research Staff of the Directory of Computer Education and Research.* Canadian Science and Technology Press, 1975. p. 192.

32. The U.S. Grantee Directory (Students, Teachers, Research Scholars, Lectures & Specialists) published by the Department of State's Bureau of Educational and Cultural Affairs for years 1964–1967 has no listing for any William Mitchell. Fulbright Papers Research Assistant Vera Ekechukwu, M.A., at the University of Arkansas in an email dated September 19, 2012, also further stated that there was no listing for any William L. Mitchell or William Lockwood Mitchell in any of the "Fulbright Grantee Directories" housed in the Special Collections there. In addition, Peter Vandewater of the Institute of International Education in Washington, D.C. told Roger Charles in an email dated September 13, 2012, that "We checked the Fulbright directories from 1964-1967 and were not able to find a record for William Lockwood Mitchell listed. I hope this information is helpful to you." Similarly, on December 12, 2012, Roger Charles contacted the Eisenhower Foundation and was told that there was no William L. Mitchell listed in their database or alumni directory, or any indication that Mitchell had been awarded an Eisenhower Fellowship.

33. In an email dated May 1, 2013, Jessica Winterstein, Deputy Head of the London School of Economics (LSE) Press Office, confirmed to Roger Charles that "William Lockwood Mitchell was registered as being awarded an MPhil in 1966 in Operational Research."

34. From September 2012 to April 2013, investigative journalist Don Devereux interviewed more than sixteen (16) different people who either knew Mitchell at Cornell or when he was teaching at Cal State, East Bay. See also note #14 above.

35. Interview by Don Devereux with Cal State, East Bay Reference Librarian Paul MacLennan on September 18, 2012. In a follow-up interview on October 2, 2012, MacLennan stated that William L. Mitchell made the transition to "Bill Mitchell" effective with the 1974–75 academic year class catalog and faculty listing.

36. See the following: *Directory of Emeritus Faculty*, California State University, East Bay. (http://www20.csueastbay.edu/oaa/files/docs/DirectoryEmeriti.pdf)

37. Private investigator Robert Arthur of *Global Investigations and Security Consulting* in Scottsdale, Arizona, was an indispensable asset in all of the research involving William L. Mitchell and related individuals.

38. See the following link: http://www.hghs57.org/mitchell.htm

39. Interview with Bill Miller, webmaster for the Class of 1957 of Horace Greely High School, conducted by Don Devereux on April 23, 2013. On April 24, 2013, Mr. Miller emailed Devereux a copy of the questionnaire that Mitchell had filled out for their 25th reunion in 1982.

40. Telephone call made from James Mitchell to Don Devereux on February 13, 2013.

41. Telephone call made from William L. Mitchell (aka Bill Mitchell) to Don Devereux during the evening of March 7, 2013.

42. During a meeting that took place on January 10, 2013, with Roger Charles and myself, senior Homicide Detective Daniel Whalen of the D.C. Police Department disclosed that the Meyer murder case files were destroyed in 1990 under the department's twenty-five year retention schedule for "administratively closed cases."

43. William F. Pepper, "The Children of Vietnam." *Ramparts Magazine,* January, 1967, pp. 45–68.

SELECTED BIBLIOGRAPHY

Albarelli, H. P., Jr. *A Terrible Mistake: The Murder of Frank Olson and the CIA's Secret Cold War Experiments.* Walterville, Ore.: Trine Day, 2009.

Attwood, William. *The Reds and the Blacks: A Personal Adventure.* New York: Harper & Row, 1967.

———. *The Twilight Struggle: Tales of the Cold War.* New York: Harper & Row, 1987.

Ayton, Mel. *Questions of Controversy: The Kennedy Brothers.* Sunderland, U.K.: University of Sunderland Press, 2001.

Bamford, James. *Body of Secrets: Anatomy of the Ultra-Secret National Security Agency.* New York: Anchor, 2002.

Bennett, Robert S., *In the Ring: The Trials of a Washington Lawyer.* New York: Crown, 2008.

Benson, Michael. *Who's Who in the JFK Assassination.* New York: Citadel, 1993.

Blakey, Robert G., and Richard N. Billings. *Fatal Hour.* New York: Berkley, 1981.

Blum, William. *Killing Hope: The U.S. Military and CIA Interventions Since World War II.* Monroe, Maine: Common Courage, 1995.

Bolden, Abraham. *The Echo from Dealey Plaza.* New York: Harmony, 2008.

Bradlee, Benjamin C., *Conversations with Kennedy.* New York: W. W. Norton, 1975.

———. *A Good Life: Newspapering and Other Adventures.* New York: Simon & Schuster, 1995.

———. "He Had That Special Grace." *Newsweek,* December 2, 1963.

Brinkley, Alan. *The Publisher: Henry Luce and His American Century.* New York: Knopf, 2010.

Brown, Walt. *The Warren Omission: A Micro-Study of the Methods and Failures of the Warren Commission.* Wilmington, Del.: Delmax, 1996.

Brugioni, Dino A., *Eyeball to Eyeball: The Inside Story of the Cuban Missile Crisis.* New York: Random House, 1990.

———. *Eyes in the Sky: Eisenhower, the CIA and Cold War Aerial Espionage.* Annapolis, Md.: Naval Institute Press, 2010.

Burleigh, Nina. *A Very Private Woman: The Life and Unsolved Murder of Presidential Mistress Mary Meyer.* New York: Bantam, 1998.

Casey, Constance. "Memoirs of a Congressman's Daughter." *Washington Post Magazine,* April 19, 1992.

Clarke, Gerald. *Capote: A Biography.* London: Cardinal, 1989.

Collier, Peter, and David Horowitz. *The Kennedys: An American Drama.* New York: Summit, 1984.

Corson, William R. *The Betrayal.* New York: W. W. Norton, 1968.

Dallek, Robert. *Lyndon B. Johnson: Portrait of a President.* Oxford, U.K.: Oxford University Press, 2005.

———. *An Unfinished Life: John F. Kennedy, 1917–1963.* Boston: Little, Brown, 2003.

Damore, Leo. *The Cape Cod Years of John Fitzgerald Kennedy.* 1967. Reprint, New York: Four Walls Eight Windows, 1993.

———. *Senatorial Privilege: The Chappaquiddick Cover-Up.* Washington, D.C.: Regnery Gateway, 1988.

Davis, Deborah. *Katharine the Great: Katharine Graham and Her Washington Post Empire.* New York: Sheridan Square Press, 1991.

———. *Katharine the Great: Katharine Graham and the Washington Post.* New York: Harcourt Brace Jovanovich, 1979.

DiEugenio, James, and Lisa Pease, eds. *The Assassinations: Probe Magazine on JFK, MLK, RFK, and Malcolm X.* Los Angeles: Feral House, 2003.

Dobbs, Michael. *One Minute to Midnight: Kennedy, Khrushchev, and Castro on the Brink of Nuclear War.* New York: Knopf, 2008.

Douglas, Gregory. *Gestapo Chief: The 1948 Interrogation of Heinrich Müller.* Vol. 1. San Jose, Calif.: R. James Bender, 1995.

———. *Gestapo Chief: The 1948 Interrogation of Heinrich Müller.* Vol. 2. San Jose, Calif.: R. James Bender, 1997.

———. *Gestapo Chief: The 1948 Interrogation of Heinrich Müller.* Vol. 3. San Jose, Calif.: R. James Bender, 1998.

———. *Regicide: The Official Assassination of John F. Kennedy.* Huntsville, Ala.: Monte Sano Media, 2002.

Douglass, James W., *JFK and the Unspeakable: Why He Died* and *Why It Matters.* Maryknoll, N.Y.: Orbis Books, 2008.

du Berrier, Hilaire. *Background to Betrayal: The Tragedy of Vietnam.* Appleton, Wis.: Western Islands, 1965.

Duberman, Martin. *The Uncompleted Past.* New York: Random House, 1969.

———. *Waiting to Land: A (Mostly) Political Memoir, 1985–2008.* New York: New Press, 2009.

Epstein, Edward Jay. *Deception: The Invisible War between the KGB and the CIA.* New York: Simon & Schuster, 1989.

Escalante, Fabian. *JFK: The Cuba Files.* New York: Ocean Press, 2006.

Evans, Peter. *Nemesis.* New York: HarperCollins, 2004.

Felsenthal, Carol. *Power, Privilege and the Post: The Katharine Graham Story.* New York: Seven Stories Press, 1993.

Fetzer, James H., ed. *Assassination Science: Experts Speak Out on the Death of JFK.* Peru, Ill.: Catfeet Press, 1998.

———. *The Great Zapruder Film Hoax: Deceit and Deception in the Death of JFK.* Chicago: Catfeet Press, 2003.

Murder in Dealey Plaza: What We Know Now That We Didn't Know Then about the Death of JFK. Peru, Ill.: Catfeet Press, 2000.

Fonzi, Gaeton. *The Last Investigation.* New York: Thunder's Mouth Press, 1993.

Fursenko, Aleksandr, and Timothy J. Naftali. *One Hell of a Gamble: Khrushchev, Castro, and Kennedy, 1958–1964.* New York: W. W. Norton, 1998.

Galbraith, James K. and Heather A. Purcell. "Did the U.S. Military Plan a Nuclear First Strike for 1963?" *American Prospect* 5, no. 19 (September 1994).

Gaston, Bibi. *The Loveliest Woman in America.* New York: William Morrow, 2008.

Goodwin, Doris Kearns. *The Fitzgeralds and the Kennedys.* New York: St. Martin's, 1987.

Graham, Katharine. *Personal History.* New York: Vintage, 1998.

Greenfield, Robert. *Timothy Leary: A Biography.* New York: Harcourt, 2006.

Gresham, John D., and Norman Polmar. *Defcon-2.* Hoboken, N.J.: John Wiley & Sons, 2006.

Groden, Robert J., *The Killing of a President.* New York: Viking Studio, 1993.

Grose, Peter. *Gentleman Spy: The Life of Allen Dulles.* New York: Houghton Mifflin, 1994.

Halberstam, David. *The Powers That Be.* Chicago: University of Illinois Press, 2000.

Hamilton, Nigel. *JFK: Reckless Youth.* New York: Random House, 1992.

Hersh, Burton. *The American Elite and the Origins of the CIA.* New York: Scribner, 1992.

———. *Bobby and J. Edgar.* New York: Carroll & Graf, 2007.

Hersh, Seymour M. *The Dark Side of Camelot.* New York: Back Bay Books, 1997.

Heymann, C. David. *The Georgetown Ladies' Social Club.* New York: Atria Books, 2003.

———. *A Woman Named Jackie.* New York: Carol Communications, 1989.

Hillsman, Roger. *To Move a Nation.* New York: Doubleday, 1967.

Holland, Max. *The Kennedy Assassination Tapes.* New York: Knopf, 2004.

Hollingshead, Michael. *The Man Who Turned On the World.* New York: Abelard-Schuman, 1974.

Horne, Douglas P. *Inside the Assassination Records Review Board: The U.S. Government's Final Attempt to Reconcile the Conflicting Medical Evidence in the Assassination of JFK.* 5 vols. Printed by author, 2009.

Hougan, Jim. *Secret Agenda: Watergate, Deep Throat and the CIA.* New York: Random House, 1984.

Hunt, E. Howard. *American Spy: My Secret History in the CIA, Watergate, and Beyond.* Hoboken, N.J.: John Wiley & Sons, 2007.

Karnow, Stanley. *Vietnam: A History.* New York: Viking, 1983.

Kelin, John. *Praise from a Future Generation: The Assassination of John F. Kennedy and the First Generation Critics of the Warren Report.* San Antonio, Tex.: Wings Press, 2007.

Kelly, Tom. *The Imperial Post: The Meyers, the Grahams, and the Paper That Rules Washington.* New York: William Morrow, 1983.

Kessler, Ronald. *Inside the CIA.* New York: Pocket Books, 1992.

Khrushchev, Nikita. *Khrushchev Remembers.* Translated and edited by Strobe Talbott. New York: Bantam, 1971.

Lane, Mark. *A Citizen's Dissent: Mark Lane Replies.* New York: Holt, Rinehart & Winston, 1968.

———. *Last Word: My Indictment of the CIA in the Murder of JFK.* New York: Skyhorse, 2011.

———. *Plausible Denial: Was the CIA Involved in the Assassination of JFK?* New York: Thunder's Mouth Press, 1991.

———. *Rush to Judgment.* Greenwich, Conn.: Fawcett Crest, 1967.

Lattin, Don. *The Harvard Psychedelic Club.* New York: Harper One, 2010.

Leary, Timothy. *Flashbacks: An Autobiography.* Los Angeles: J. P. Tarcher, 1983.

———. *High Priest.* Oakland, Calif.: Ronin, 1968.

———. "The Murder of Mary Pinchot Meyer." *The Rebel: A Newsweekly with a Cause,* January 1984.

Lee, Martin A., and Bruce Shlain. *Acid Dreams: The CIA, LSD, and the Sixties Rebellion.* New York: Grove, 1985.

Lifton, David S. *Best Evidence: Disguise and Deception in the Assassination of John F. Kennedy.* New York: Macmillan, 1980.

Lincoln, Evelyn. *Kennedy and Johnson.* New York: Holt, Rinehart & Winston, 1968.

Livingstone, Harrison Edward. *The Radical Right and the Murder of John F. Kennedy.* Victoria, B.C.: Trafford, 2004.

Loftus, John. *America's Nazi Secrets.* Walterville, Ore.: Trine Day, 2010.

Lukacs, John. *George Kennan: A Study of Character.* New Haven, Conn.: Yale University Press, 2007.

Mangold, Tom. *Cold Warrior: James Jesus Angleton; The CIA's Master Spy Hunter.* New York: Simon & Schuster, 1991.

Marchetti, Victor, and John D. Marks. *The CIA and the Cult of Intelligence.* New York: Dell, 1980.

Markoff, John. *What the Dormouse Said: How the 60s Counterculture Shaped the Personal Computer Industry.* New York: Viking, 2005.

Marks, John D. *The Search for the "Manchurian Candidate": The CIA and Mind Control.* New York: W. W. Norton, 1979.

Marrs, Jim. *Crossfire: The Plot That Killed Kennedy.* New York: Carroll & Graf, 1989.

Martin, David C. *Wilderness of Mirrors.* Guilford, Conn.: Lyons Press, 1980.

Martin, Ralph G. *A Hero for Our Time: An Intimate Story of the Kennedy Years.* New York: Macmillan, 1983.

———. *Seeds of Destruction: Joe Kennedy and His Sons.* New York: G. P. Putnam's Sons, 1995.

McCabe, Katie. "She Had a Dream." *Washingtonian* (March 2002).

McCabe, Katie, and Dovey Johnson Roundtree. *Justice Older Than the Law: The Life of Dovey Johnson Roundtree.* Jackson: University Press of Mississippi, 2009.

McClellan, Barr. *Blood, Money and Power.* New York: Hanover House, 2003.

McKean, David. *Tommy the Cork: Washington's Ultimate Insider from Roosevelt to Reagan.* South Royalton, Vt.: Steerforth Press, 2004.

McKnight, Gerald D. *Breach of Trust: How the Warren Commission Failed the Nation and Why.* Lawrence: University Press of Kansas, 2005.

McNamara, Robert S. *In Retrospect: The Tragedy and Lessons from Vietnam.* New York: Vintage, 1996.

Meager, Sylvia. *Accessories after the Fact: The Warren Commission, the Authorities, and the Report.* New York: Vintage, 1976.

Mellen, Joan. *A Farewell to Justice.* Dulles, Va.: Potomac Books, 2005.

Menand, Louis. "Acid Redux: The Life and High Times of Timothy Leary." *New Yorker*, June 26, 2006.

Meyer, Cord, Jr. *Facing Reality: From World Federalism to the CIA*. New York: Harper & Row, 1980.

———. "On the Beaches." *Atlantic Monthly*, October 1944.

———. "Peace Is Still Possible." *Atlantic Monthly*, October 1947.

———. *Peace or Anarchy*. Boston: Little Brown, 1947.

———. "A Serviceman Looks at The Peace." *Atlantic Monthly*, September 1945.

———. "Waves of Darkness." *Atlantic Monthly*, January 1946.

———. "What Are the Chances." *Atlantic Monthly*, July 1946.

Miller, Merle. "One Man's Long Journey: From a One World Crusade to the Department of Dirty Tricks." *New York Times Magazine*, January 7, 1973.

Morley, Jefferson. *Our Man in Mexico: Winston Scott and the Hidden History of the CIA*. Lawrence: University Press of Kansas, 2008.

Morris, Willie. *New York Days*. Boston: Little Brown, 1993.

Morrow, Robert D. *First Hand Knowledge: How I Participated in the CIA-Mafia Murder of President Kennedy*. New York: S.P.I. Books, 1992.

Newman, John M. *JFK and Vietnam: Deception, Intrigue, and the Struggle for Power*. New York: Warner, 1992.

———. *Oswald and the CIA*. 1995. Reprint, New York: Skyhorse, 2008.

O'Brien, Michael. *John F. Kennedy - A Biography*. New York: St. Martin's, 2005.

O'Donnell, Kenneth P., and David F. Powers. *Johnny, We Hardly Knew Ye: Memories of John Fitzgerald Kennedy*. New York: Pocket Books, 1973.

O'Neill, Tip. *Man of the House: The Life and Political Memoirs of Speaker Tip O'Neill*. With William Novak. New York: Random House, 1987.

Ordway, Samuel H. *Dedication of the Pinchot Institute for Conservation Studies*. Milford, Pa.: Conservation Foundation, 1963.

Parmet, Herbert S. *Jack: The Struggles of John F. Kennedy*. New York: Dial, 1980.

———. *JFK: The Presidency of John F. Kennedy*. New York: Dial, 1983.

Philips, David. *The Night Watch*. New York: Atheneum, 1977.

Pinchot, Mary. "Futility." *Vassar Review and Little Magazine*. Poughkeepsie, N.Y.: Lansing-Broas, 1941.

———. "Requiem." *New York Times*, January 25, 1940.

Posner, Gerald. *Case Closed*. New York: Anchor, 2003.

Prouty, L. Fletcher. *JFK: The CIA, Vietnam, and the Plot to Assassinate John F. Kennedy*. New York: Citadel, 1996.

———. *The Secret Team: The CIA and Its Allies in Control of the United States and the World*. Costa Mesa, Calif.: Institute for Historical Review, 1973.

Reed, Terry, and John Cummings. *Compromised: Clinton, Bush, and the CIA*. New York: S.P.I. Books, 1994.

Reeves, Richard. *President Kennedy: Profiles of Power*. New York: Touchstone, 1993.

Reeves, Thomas C. *A Question of Character*. New York: Free Press, 1991.

Rhodes, Richard. *Dark Sun: The Making of the Hydrogen Bomb*. New York: Simon & Schuster, 1995.

Rosenbaum, Ron, and Phillip Nobile. "The Curious Aftermath of JFK's Best and Brightest Affair." *New Times*, July 9, 1976.

———. *The Secret Parts of Fortune: Three Decades of Intense Investigations and Edgy Enthusiasms*. New York: Random House, 2000.

Russell, Dick. *The Man Who Knew Too Much*. Rev. ed. New York: Carroll & Graf, 2003.

———. *On the Trail of the JFK Assassins: A Groundbreaking Look at America's Most Infamous Conspiracy*. New York: Skyhorse, 2008.

Russo, Gus. *Live by the Sword: The Secret War against Castro and the Death of JFK*. Baltimore: Bancroft Press, 1998.

Schlesinger, Arthur M., Jr. *Journals: 1952–2000*. New York: Penguin, 2007.

———. *Robert Kennedy and His Times*. Boston: Houghton Mifflin, 2002.

———. *A Thousand Days: John F. Kennedy in the White House*. New York: Houghton Mifflin, 1965.

Scott, Peter Dale. *Deep Politics and the Death of JFK*. Berkeley: University of California Press, 1996.

Seaborg, Glenn T. *Kennedy, Khrushchev, and the Test Ban*. Los Angeles: University of California Press, 1983.

Shackley, Ted. *Spymaster*. Dulles, Va.: Potomac Books, 2005.

Showalter, Elaine, ed. *These Modern Women: Autobiographical Essays from the Twenties*. New York: Feminist Press, 1989.

Smith, Matthew. *JFK: The Second Plot*. Edinburgh: Mainstream, 1992.

Smith, Sally Bedell. *Grace and Power: The Private World of the Kennedy White House*. New York: Random House, 2004.

Sorensen, Theodore C. *Kennedy*. Old Saybrook, Conn.: Kopeck & Kopeck, 1965.

Stevens, Jay. *Storming Heaven: LSD and the American Dream*. New York: Grove, 1987.

Stockton, David. *Flawed Patriot: The Rise and Fall of CIA Legend Bill Harvey*. Washington, D.C.: Potomac Books, 2006.

Summers, Anthony. *Conspiracy: The Definitive Book on the JFK Assassination.* New York: Paragon House, 1989.

———. *The Secret Life of J. Edgar Hoover.* London: Victor Gollancz, 1993.

———. *Not in Your Lifetime.* New York: Marlowe, 1998.

———. *The Kennedy Conspiracy.* London: Time Warner Paperbacks, 2002.

Talbot, David. *Brothers: The Hidden History of the Kennedy Years.* New York: Free Press, 2007.

Thomas, Evan. *The Very Best Men.* New York: Simon & Schuster, 1995.

Thomas, Kenn, ed. *Popular Alienation: A Steamshovel Press Reader.* Lilburn, Ga.: IllumiNet Press, 1995.

Trento, Joseph J. *Prelude to Terror.* New York: Carroll & Graf, 2005.

———. *The Secret History of the CIA.* Roseville, Calif.: Prima, 2001.

Truitt, Anne. *Daybook: The Journal of an Artist.* New York: Pantheon, 1982.

———. *Turn: The Journal of an Artist.* New York: Viking, 1986.

Twyman, Noel H. *Bloody Treason: The Assassination of John F. Kennedy.* Rancho Santa Fe, Calif.: Laurel, 1997.

United States of America v. Ray Crump, Jr., Defendant. Criminal Case No. 930-64, United States District Court for the District of Columbia, Washington, D.C., July 20, 1965.

Vidal, Gore. *Palimpsest: A Memoir.* New York: Penguin, 1995.

Waldron, Lamar. *Ultimate Sacrifice: John and Robert Kennedy, the Plan for a Coup in Cuba, and the Murder of JFK.* With Thom Hartmann. New York: Carroll & Graf, 2005.

Ward, Bernie, and Granville Toogood. "Former Vice President of Washington Post Reveals JFK 2-Year White House Romance." *National Enquirer,* March 2, 1976.

Whitcomb, Christopher. *Black.* Boston: Little, Brown, 2004.

Wilford, Hugh. *The Mighty Wurlitzer: How the CIA Played America.* Cambridge, Mass.: Harvard University Press, 2008.

Wise, David. *Molehunt: The Secret Search for Traitors That Shattered the CIA.* New York: Random House, 1992.

Wolfe, Donald H. *The Last Days of Marilyn Monroe.* New York: William Morrow, 1998.

Wrone, David R. *The Zapruder Film: Reframing JFK's Assassination.* Lawrence: University Press of Kansas, 2003.

Zepezauer, Mark. *The CIA's Greatest Hits.* Chicago: Odonian Press, 1994.

ACKNOWLEDGMENTS

THE COMPLETION OF this project represents the culmination of more than thirty-five years of contemplation and inquiry that began in 1976. Nearly fifty years after the mysterious murder of Mary Pinchot Meyer on the Chesapeake and Ohio Canal towpath in Washington, D.C., there is still a dearth of information and evidence as to exactly what occurred. We may never discover all the answers, but we now know nearly all of the questions.

When I first considered this project in 2003, my initial endeavor was to collaborate with Christopher Keane, a Hollywood screenwriter. During this collaboration, along with Garby Leon's guidance, and additional support from Linda Lichter, Esq., the film script *Lost Light* was conceived. But I soon realized that much of the story still remained unresolved and unknown. Further exploration and research were needed.

In 1992, I had the good fortune to meet and befriend the late author Leo Damore. Our friendship progressed rapidly before his untimely "suicide" in October 1995. Leo shared many of his insights into not only what he believed had occurred between Mary Meyer and Jack Kennedy, but how and why her murder had been orchestrated, as he had also done with his dear friend and attorney James ("Jimmy") H. Smith.

In 2004, I was able to locate Damore's chief research assistant, Mark O'Blazney, in suburban Washington, D.C. To his credit, Mark had guarded most of the Damore "treasure trove" in hopes that someday, someone might come along and pick up where Leo had left off. Author John H. Davis had, in fact, attempted such a feat in 1996, but he, too, had faltered.

It was the Damore family who finally made it possible for me to undertake in depth this project, allowing me to access additional material in their possession. I am particularly indebted to Leo's former wife, June Davison, who graciously shared with me a number of the insights Leo had previously shared with her. As well, Leo's children—Chuck, Leslie, and Nicholas—all put their faith in me.

Were it not, however, for Leo's attorney, Jimmy Smith, it's doubtful I would ever been able to unravel the crucial pieces of Leo's most important discoveries. Having saved a set of historically important notes from a telephone conversation with Leo in 1993, Jimmy will always be one of the unsung heroes in the quest for the truth regarding the murder of Mary Pinchot Meyer.

During my five years of intensive writing, a number of new people—many of whom were women—found their way into my life and offered their insights and guidance. Barbra Dillenger, who I had known many years before, went way beyond the call of duty to keep me focused. Katie McCabe, coauthor with Dovey Roundtree, Esq., of Roundtree's biography, *Justice Older Than the Law*, never allowed me to lose sight of some of the most important revelations in this book. Her steadfast support throughout this experience was an inspiration to be remembered.

During the Cold War, it might have been "a man's world," but the power of women and their emerging sisterhood was demanding to be heard and taken seriously. Sanity in an insane world needs guardians. As many of my women friends pointed out, an acolyte for world peace had been engendered in Mary Pinchot Meyer. Antonia Kabakov never allowed me to lose sight of this, and very patiently lent me her support and love, amidst a number of my challenges. Renowned author and astrologer Tracy Marks wouldn't allow me to forsake certain principles. Amid "bumps in the road," my dear friend Janet Clark always showed up at critical moments. Former childhood Georgetown Day School chum Ariel Dougherty, who had been an art student of Mary Meyer's in the 1950s, reminded me of small but important details. And during some of my most difficult moments, Joanna Duda took me by the hand and walked with me to the edge—only then to suggest that I just jump into the abyss. I did.

I am indebted to author James W. Douglass for his valuable and indispensable work *JFK and the Unspeakable.* Mr. Douglass's journey into the real vortex of the presidency and assassination of President John F. Kennedy is unparalleled. His willingness to take the time to explain certain minutiae has been invaluable. In addition, author Douglas P. Horne's five-volume set, *Inside the Assassination Records Review Board* (2009), is unprecedented—not only does it further clarify the conspiracy that took place in Dallas on November 22, 1963, but also the conniving subterfuge that took place in its aftermath. As a researcher, author, and friend, Doug Horne is a true patriot and a great American.

Acknowledgments

There is a special collection of people who provided me with additional, invaluable assistance. My Princeton classmate Robert R. Cullinane freely gave me his time and some of his invaluable search resources via the Princeton University Library. I wish especially to thank Dick Russell for his stellar work *The Man Who Knew Too Much*. Dick's seventeen-year odyssey writing his book, as well as the personal insights he shared, have been a guiding light. Toni Shimon, daughter of the late Joseph W. Shimon, took a huge risk in opening up to me about what had transpired between her and her father. Her disclosures in the Epilogue are historically important. Author Anthony Summers gave me a number of critical insights, as did others, including: Victor Marchetti, Hank Albarelli, Donald Deneselya, Tom Kimmel, J. Michael Kelly, Deborah Davis, Carol Felsenthal, Dino Brugioni, John Williams, Shelah Horvitz, Donald H. Wolfe, Bob Schwartz, Joan Mellon, Garby Leon, Joel Kabakov, Tiffany Graham, Shannon Mow, Sandy Forman, Esq., Adina Gewirtz, William Pepper, and journalist Charles Bartlett. Timothy Leary's biographer, Robert Greenfield, shared many observations from his years of research, as did Tim Leary's wife, Barbara, and his former colleagues Ralph Metzner and Peggy Mellon Hitchcock. In addition, my gratitude to the family of the late William ("Bill") Attwood cannot go unmentioned. Attwood's wife, Simone, and his daughter, Susan, graciously allowed me to examine and reference Bill's extensive diaries.

Maintaining the discipline of writing often required a small army of ancillary health professionals to regularly step into my life (as did a certain, undisclosed quantity of Peet's coffee). Bill Mueller of Cambridge Health Associates has intuitively known for more than twenty-five years where the acupuncture needles belong on my sometimes exhausted body. My chiropractor, Dr. Ian Boehm, always made himself available to me, sometimes on a moment's notice. Physical therapist Connie Sardelis kept my back and shoulders from becoming frozen. When nothing else seemed to work, homeopath Begabati Lennihan found me a remedy that forged a will of steel. I will always remain eternally grateful to my dear friend and ally George Dillinger, M.D.

Last, I wish to prostrate myself before several editors, Kelly Horan and Margot White among them. Tony Lyons, the head of Skyhorse Publishing in New York, courageously stepped forward to give *Mary's Mosaic* a home, and the entire Skyhorse team followed in an outstanding collaboration.

To all of you, and all my "ethereal friends," I bow in gratitude and give you my deepest, heartfelt thanks.

533

About the Author

P ETER JANNEY GREW up in Washington, D.C. during the Cold War era of the 1950s and 1960s. His father Wistar Janney was a senior career CIA official. The Janney family was intimately involved with many of Washington's social and political elite that included the family of Mary and Cord Meyer as well as other high-ranking CIA officials and dignitaries such as Richard Helms, Jim Angleton, Tracy Barnes, Desmond FitzGerald, Bill Colby, and John Bross.

A graduate of Princeton, Peter completed a doctoral degree in psychology at Boston University in 1981 and has been a licensed psychologist for over 30 years. In 2002, he earned an MBA degree at Duke University's Fuqua School of Business. *Mary's Mosaic* is his first book. He currently resides by the sea in Beverly, Massachusetts.

INDEX

Index

Index

Index

Index

Index

Index

Index

Index

Index

Index

Index

Index

transformation to "Bill Mitchell": as
measure to create anonymity, 407;
and Quitclaim Deed, 407; second
Social Security number, 407; while
instructor at Cal State, East Bay,
406–407, 520
vanishing of, after Crump trial, 405–406
and Williamsburg Pa, and Va, 408
and young white couple, 132, 320–321,
448
Monroe, Marilyn
alleged suicide of, 231
and Bobby Kennedy, 231
JFK's affair with, 231
Moore, Bishop Paul, Jr.
Ben Bradlee, 68
officiating at Mary Meyer's funeral,
68–69
"paranoia surrounding Mary's murder,"
69
and Pinchot family, 68–69
relationship with Cord Meyer, 68, 194
Moore, Purcell (private investigator for
Dovey Roundtree)
pursuit of repair ticket for stalled Nash
Rambler, 104
and Ray Crump's girlfriend Vivian, 95
Murray, Robert V. (D.C. Police Chief), FBI
Crime Lab Report delivered to, 60, 98
Museum of Modern Art (Buenos Aires)
(*See* Pan American Union)
NAACP
legal team: Dovey Roundtree, 93;
Supreme Court Justice Thurgood
Marshall, 93
Medgar Evers, 105, 264
Naftali, Timothy (author): on William
Walton's trip to Russia, 34
National Archives
alteration of JFK autopsy photos, 293,
295
and author Joan Mellen, 20–21
and CIA threats, 21
classified assassination documents at, 21,
293, 295
JFK's brain photographs, 293, 295
Oswald's phony defection to Russia, 21
National Enquirer (newspaper)

1976 exposé "Former Vice President of
Washington Post Reveals JFK 2-Year
White House Romance," 1–3, 18,
70, 72–73, 75, 78, 80, 82, 139, 221,
225, 365, 367, 371
and Deborah Davis, 221, 225
and James Truitt, 1, 70, 80, 225, 371
National Personnel Records Center
(NPRC)
1976 fire at and destruction of files, 399
and Detective Daniel D. Whalen, 399
inability to locate William Mitchell's
military service records, 398–400,
516; and Glomar response,
399–400
"Mr. Jones" on "William Mitchells" in
database, 398
response to FOIA requests, 399–400
National Photographic Interpretation
Center (NPIC)
Arthur C. Lundahl, 287–290
"Bill Smith," 290–291
and CIA, 287–292
Dino Brugioni, 287–292
Homer McMahon, 290–292
Morgan Bennett Hunter, 290–292
Secret Service, 289–292
Zapruder Film, 287–292
National Security Action Memoranda
(NSAM), 55
NSAM 57, 237
NSAM 263, 275, 309
NSAM 273, 277, 309
NSAM 288, 277
National Security Council (NSC) and "Top
Secret Directive 10/2" (June 18, 1948)
CIA's unchecked power, 233
Cuban Missile Crisis, 242–243
meeting of July 20, 1961, 237–238
"plausible deniability," 233
Newman, John M. (author-historian)
Angleton's handling of Oswald, 345, 512
author interview with, 367
on James Angleton, 345
Oswald and the CIA, 345, 367, 512
Nixon, Richard M.
and Arthur Lundahl briefing, 288
Gulf of Tonkin Resolution, 310

Index

Index

Index